# Rethinking Music

# Rethinking Music

Edited by

NICHOLAS COOK

&

MARK EVERIST

OXFORD

UNIVERSITY PRESS

# OXFORD

UNIVERSITY PRESS

Great Clarendon Street, Oxford OX2 6DP

Oxford University Press is a department of the University of Oxford.
It furthers the University's objective of excellence in research, scholarship,
and education by publishing worldwide in

Oxford New York

Athens Auckland Bangkok Bogotá Buenos Aires Cape Town
Chennai Dar es Salaam Delhi Florence Hong Kong Istanbul Karachi
Kolkata Kuala Lumpur Madrid Melbourne Mexico City Mumbai
Nairobi Paris São Paulo Shanghai Singapore Taipei Tokyo Toronto Warsaw

with associated companies in Berlin Ibadan

Oxford is a registered trade mark of Oxford University Press
in the UK and in certain other countries

Published in the United States
by Oxford University Press Inc., New York

British Library Cataloguing in Publication Data

Data available

Library of Congress Cataloging in Publication Data
Rethinking music / edited by Nicholas Cook and Mark Everist.
p. cm.
Includes bibliographical references and index.
1. Musicology. 2. Music—Theory—20th century. I. Cook,
Nicholas, 1950– . II. Everist, Mark, 1956– .
ML3791.1.R48 1999 780—dc21 97-7579
ISBN 0-19-879003-1 (hbk)
ISBN 0-19-879004-X (pbk)

7 9 10 8

Typeset by Best-set Typesetter Ltd., Hong Kong
Printed in Great Britain
on acid-free paper by
Biddles Ltd.,
Guildford & Kings Lynn

# *Preface*

'Music may be what we think it is', Philip Bohlman writes at the beginning of
the first chapter; 'it may not be'. That catches the tone of this book very well.
The history of musicology and music theory in our generation is one of loss of
confidence; we no longer know what we know. And this immediately throws into
doubt the comfortable distinction between the objective description of fact and
the subjective judgement of value—an assumption whose power can hardly be
underestimated. It underlies many of the day-to-day activities with which the
discipline of musicology is concerned, from the choice of concert programmes
to the marking of student assignments, from the selection of research topics to
the refereeing of journal articles. It is only to be expected, then, that musicologists will recoil at the implications of Bohlman's statement: they may feel that
they know what music is, that they can recognize a worthwhile research proposal when they see one, and that they do not need someone else to expose their
own ideological positions. Indeed, they may not consider that they occupy any
ideological positions at all.

And yet a widespread loss of confidence remains, visible most obviously in the
uneasy tension between a self-aware critical stance and the day-to-day practice
of musicology. However finely tuned he or she may be to the pitfalls of music
history constructed around a series of 'master-works', what musicologist
working on an archival or institutional project is likely to ignore (and not
publish) material that relates to a major named composer? Imagine that he or
she is engaged in the study of an eighteenth-century English aristocrat who was
interested in the music of the Indian subcontinent, but who turns out to have
left records of hearing Mozart in London: however well aware the musicologist
may be of the inadequacy of predicating the history of eighteenth-century
music on a Bach–Haydn–Mozart paradigm, the temptation to report on the
Mozart connection would be simply too great to ignore.[1] In such cases the institutional pressures to gain a position, tenure, promotion, and grants are likely to
override the intellectual priorities of the discipline.

Not surprisingly, then, many musicologists have sought to resolve—or at least
to evade—such uneasy tensions through an unquestioning adherence at
all costs to some fixed theoretical point; not just Schenker or Marx, but Adorno,
Benjamin, and even Dahlhaus have acquired the status of authorities who do
not require (and maybe do not admit) question or challenge. The tendency is
widespread: the ways in which more recent writers such as Nattiez, Kerman, or
McClary are 'used' betray a similar pattern of respect for—or it might be more
accurate to say dependence on—authority. Of these authors, perhaps only

[1] Ian Woodfield, 'New Light on the Mozarts' London Visit: A Private Concert with Manzuoli', *Music & Letters*, 76
(1995), 187–208.

Kerman has been subjected to the challenge he deserved, in the form of the many reviews of and commentaries on *Contemplating Music* (to give the book's American title; the no-contemplation-please-we're-British title was simply *Musicology*).[2] And it is the notion of authority that is central both to Kerman's critique of musicology and to the objections that have been raised against it.

In his chapter Jim Samson notes that Kerman 'unhelpfully' associated positivism in historical musicology with formalism in analysis, and in terms of Bohlman's axiom it is true that the two stand for diametrically opposed positions. The kind of formalist music theory that Kerman was talking about (the neo-serial approaches emanating from Princeton and the set-theoretical approaches emanating from Yale[3]) represented an assertion that music is what we make it. Like the compositions of the Darmstadt avant-garde, such theory took history by the scruff of the neck, and made an existential statement that music shall be precisely what we think it is, no more and no less. (The heady atmosphere of that world, which somehow managed to combine hard-edged scientific values with those of late 1960s alternative culture, is best captured in Benjamin Boretz's monumental dissertation 'Metavariations', published over a period of four years in successive issues of the then Princeton house journal, *Perspectives of New Music*;[4] its muted echoes may be detected in Joseph Dubiel's contribution to the present work.) By contrast, what Kerman characterized as musicological positivism—the steady accumulation of source studies and monumental editions—assumes a total separation of the researcher from what is researched. For the musicological positivist (as indeed for some of Kerman's earlier 'formalists', like Schenker), the music is *there*, regardless of what we think it is, and it will coincide with what we think it is only to the extent that we happen to be right. Formalism and positivism, then, are similar, in that each embodies a stance of unproblematical authority; the difference is that in the one case authority is invested in the musical thinker, while in the other it is invested in the music that is thought of. And while responses from theorists to Kerman's work were thin on the ground, reactions from musicologists were damagingly predictable: Kerman's view of source studies was rightly seen as narrow, and was criticized for failing to take account of the complexity of textual study. But this was the extent of the response; there seemed to be a general perception that the musi-

---

[2]  Joseph Kerman, *Contemplating Music* (Cambridge, Mass., 1985); *Musicology* (London, 1985).

[3]  The reference is to the work of Milton Babbitt and Allen Forte respectively. The remaining member of the dominant triumvirate of 'formalist' music theory is David Lewin, formerly Forte's colleague at Yale, but now at Harvard. Some key references: Babbitt, 'Past and Present Concepts of the Nature and Limits of Music' and 'The Structure and Function of Music Theory', both in Benjamin Boretz and Edward T. Cone (eds.), *Perspectives on Contemporary Music Theory* (New York, 1972), 3–9, 10–21; Stephen Dembski and Joseph N. Straus (eds.), *Words about Music* (Madison, 1987); Forte, *The Structure of Atonal Music* (New Haven, 1973); Lewin, *Generalized Musical Intervals and Transformations* (New Haven, 1987) and *Musical Form and Transformation: 4 Analytic Essays* (New Haven, 1993).

[4]  Benjamin Boretz, 'Meta-Variations: Studies in the Foundations of Musical Thought (I)', *Perspectives of New Music*, 8/1 (1969), 1–74; 'Sketch of a Musical System (Meta-Variations, Part II)', *PNM* 8/2 (1970), 49–111; 'The Construction of Musical Syntax', *PNM* 9/1 (1970), 23–42; 'Musical Syntax (II)', *PNM* 9/2–10/1 (1971), 232–69; 'Meta-Variations, Part IV: Analytical Fallout (I)', *PNM* 11/1 (1972), 146–223; 'Metavariations, Part IV: Analytical Fallout (II)', *PNM* 11/2 (1973), 156–203.

cologist had done his or her job by pointing out Kerman's shortcomings. In this way, Kerman's more fundamental objections to received notions of musicological authority remained unaddressed.

Of course, Kerman's characterizations were really caricatures; few except exhibitionists openly admitted to being formalists or positivists in the aftermath of the publication of Kerman's book. But his critique would not have created the furore it did if the cap hadn't fitted. And what Kerman's formalism and positivism have in common is more than anything else an attitude: the sense of an established discipline, the sense that there is work to be done, and that there are known ways of doing it.[5] That attitude has largely collapsed in the ten years since Kerman's book came out. Fissures between the different strands of professional activity have become increasingly apparent: you can easily find yourself expounding the values of compositional unity in Haydn and Mozart to a class of undergraduates in the morning, and drafting an academic paper that deconstructs the concept of unity or challenges the construction of a history of Viennese eighteenth-century chamber music around just two composers in the evening. (Ellen Koskoff puts such pedagogical double binds in a cross-cultural context in her contribution to this book.) Other aspects of professional work, too, have developed new and often troublesome dimensions of meaning: in her chapter, Kay Shelemay describes the problems that arise for ethnomusicologists when their subjects 'talk back', and several contributors grapple with the ethical consequences of their actions as teachers, researchers, and (as Ralph Locke puts it) 'informed citizens and members of the human race'. But such problems begin at home, and none is more pressing than that of the participation of women in the discipline. Anyone who has had the opportunity to compare meetings of the American Musicological Society (approximately equal numbers of males and females, with the latter perhaps in the majority) with those of the Royal Musical Association (besuited fifty-somethings) will be aware of the speed with which change can take place, and Suzanne Cusick's contribution is a sympathetic attempt to put the matter in perspective.

In the aftermath of the near collapse of classical music as a form of public entertainment in North America and its recent rebirth in Britain in the form of play-list-oriented commercial radio stations and news-stand magazines, it is not just the disciplinary integrity of musicology that has become problematic; it is, to put it bluntly, the relationship between musicology and the rest of the universe. (Where does musicology come on anybody's list of global priorities? When we look back on our lives, will we be able to justify our career choice to ourselves?) Seen from this discomfiting perspective, Kerman's formalism and positivism begin to acquire the same kind of nostalgic aura as the tail-fins of American cars in the Fifties: they are a reminder that things were so much

---

[5] Of course, Kerman's uncritical view of the subdivisions within the discipline—seeing them as unchanging or given—could itself be seen as reflecting a positivistic bias (we are grateful to Giorgio Biancorosso, formerly a master's degree student at King's College, London, now a doctoral candidate at Princeton, for this observation).

simpler in those days, when people knew what they believed, and believed what they knew. Or was it ever really like that? We seem to be well on the way to creating a disciplinary myth that divides musicological history into two discrete ages, the old and the new, separated by Kerman's opening of Pandora's box (or rather his public announcement that it was being opened). There is good reason to be suspicious of any myth whose motivation is too transparent, and the before Kerman/after Kerman paradigm serves equally the interests of those who see musicology as having come of age in the last decade and those who see today's post-formalist, post-positivist, post-everything agenda as a betrayal of the discipline.

Yet, as myths go, this is quite a helpful one, because the current configuration of the discipline (if, that is, it still makes sense to think of it as a discipline) can be usefully summarized in terms of the different impact that Kerman's critique had on different musicologists—which is to say, at the least, music historians, theorists, and ethnomusicologists. For ethnomusicologists, Kerman's book reinforced an existing sense of difference *vis-à-vis* the rest of the musicological establishment; Kerman confessed to a lack of interest in non-Western music, and made no serious effort to incorporate the complexities of ethnomusicological thought into his vision of musicology. (The present book, by contrast, is intended to convey the inseparability of ethnomusicology from a musicology more generously conceived.) Historical musicologists, on the other hand, had their centrality within the academic musical firmament confirmed, but were directed to elevate their gaze from the positivist purview of dusty texts to a humane, critically informed musicology. Under the slogan of 'criticism', Kerman created the vacuum that was filled by what came to be called the 'New Musicology'; this resulted in a dramatic expansion of the musicological agenda in the decade after 1985.

Opinions vary as to how the term 'New Musicology' came about.[6] An impor-

---

[6] Canonic texts underpinning the New Musicology are Rose Rosengard Subotnik, *Developing Variations: Style and Ideology in Western Music* (Minneapolis, 1991); Susan McClary, *Feminine Endings: Music, Gender, and Sexuality* (Minneapolis, 1991); Ruth Solie (ed.), *Musicology and Difference: Gender and Sexuality in Music Scholarship* (Berkeley, 1993); Carolyn Abbate, *Unsung Voices: Opera and Musical Narrative in the Nineteenth Century* (Princeton, 1991); Lawrence Kramer, *Music as Cultural Practice, 1800–1900* (Berkeley, 1990). A special issue of *Current Musicology* entitled 'Approaches to the Discipline' reveals something of the range of positions encompassed within the New Musicology (*Current Musicology*, 53 (1993); see in particular the exchange between Lawrence Kramer and Gary Tomlinson). As many of these names illustrate, the empowerment of the female voice in musicology played a major role in this expansion of the musicological agenda; the gender imbalance between the two parts of the present volume reflects the fact that, despite the efforts of scholars such as Marion Guck and Marianne Kielian-Gilbert, music theory remains a distinctly male-dominated discipline. (There are some strong hints as to why this might be the case in Suzanne Cusick's chapter.) There is as yet no authoritative conservative response to the New Musicology. The best known rebuttal, directed specifically at gender-oriented musicology, is Pieter van den Toorn's 'Politics, Feminism, and Contemporary Music Theory', *Journal of Musicology*, 9 (1991), 275–99, incorporated in his more comprehensive book-length critique, *Music, Politics, and the Academy* (Berkeley, 1995); see also Ruth Solie's 'What do Feminists Want? A Reply to Pieter van den Toorn', *Journal of Musicology*, 9 (1991), 399–410. At least one other musicologist, to our knowledge, is working on a comparable book. See also Charles Rosen, 'Music à la Mode', *New York Review of Books*, 61/12 (23 June 1994), 55–62, and the subsequent exchange of letters between Rosen and Lawrence Kramer, *New York Review of Books*, 61/15 (22 Sept. 1994), 74–6.

tant early usage was in a paper presented to the American Musicological Society's annual meeting in Oakland in 1990: Lawrence Kramer's abstract for 'Carnaval, Cross-Dressing, and Women in the Mirror' claimed a place for the paper in 'the new musicology that tries to situate musical structures within their larger cultural context'.[7] But this aim is shared by a much larger musicological constituency than Kramer suggested. Few music 'historians' would claim that they were doing much else, while some would claim that Kramer's view of a 'larger cultural context' is actually a rather narrow one. The range of musical repertories encompassed by Kramer and those who endorse his scholarly programme is similarly narrow; so too is the range of theoretical engagements with that repertory. Finally, the orientation of this kind of 'new musicology' towards the musical work rather than the culture that constructs it means that there is something deeply unhistorical—if not, indeed, anti-historical—about it. In a paradoxical way, then, Kramer's brand of 'new musicology' lays itself open to the same charge as formalism: that it constructs musical works as timeless, and in this sense autonomous, entities.

Despite such contradictions, the effect of these developments, together with the prolonged and sometimes acrimonious debates to which they gave rise, was (to borrow Ralph Locke's term) to massively 'reinvigorate' the field of musicology, or some of its furrows at least. It is hardly surprising, however, that the enlarged outlook that Kerman adumbrated in the name of criticism took the form of a largely *un*critical admixture and dissemination of new or borrowed methodologies, ideologies, and buzz-words. It was also characterized by a reluctance to encompass any *rapprochement* between theoretical approaches, the result of which was a curiously serial process in which theoretical positions were taken up and cast aside: Geertzian thick description, narratology, *Annalisme*, and the Bloomian 'anxiety of influence' were all explored and then discarded in turn.[8] Multivalency—the acknowledgement of the possibly equal validity of multiple interpretations, adumbrated for the first time by Harold Powers in 1984—itself seems almost to have emerged as a passing phase, to be replaced by the next critical position.[9] But at least dealings with most of these disciplinary

---

[7] *Abstracts of Papers Read at the Joint Meetings of the American Musicological Society, Fifty-Sixth Annual Meeting; Society for Ethnomusicology, Thirty-Fifth Annual Meeting; Society for Music Theory, Thirteenth Annual Meeting, November 7–11, 1990, Oakland, California* (Urbana-Champaign, Ill., 1990), p. 8. The paper was published without reference to the 'new musicology' in Solie (ed.), *Musicology and Difference*, 305–25.

[8] For musicological applications of these approaches see Gary Tomlinson, 'The Web of Culture: A Context for Musicology', *19th-Century Music*, 7 (1984), 350–62; Philip V. Bohlman, 'On the Unremarkable in Music', *19th-Century Music*, 16 (1992), 203–16; William Weber, 'Mentalité, tradition et origines du canon musical en France et en Angleterre au xviiie siècle', *Annales: économies, sociétés, civilisations*, 44 (1989), 849–72; Jane Fulcher, 'Current Perspectives on Culture and the Meaning of Cultural History in France Today', *Stanford French Review*, 9 (1985), 91–104; Kevin Korsyn, 'Towards a New Poetics of Musical Influence', *Music Analysis*, 10 (1991), 3–72; Joseph N. Straus, 'The Anxiety of Influence in Twentieth-Century Music', *Journal of Musicology*, 9 (1991), 430–47; *idem*, *Remaking the Past: Musical Modernism and the Influence of the Tonal Tradition* (Cambridge, Mass., 1990). See also Richard Taruskin, 'Revising Revision', *Journal of the American Musicological Society*, 46 (1993), 114–38.

[9] A formal interest in questions of multivalence seems to have peaked in disagreements about the interpretation of Puccini: Allan Atlas, 'Crossed Stars and Crossed Tonal Areas in Puccini's *Madama Butterfly*', *19th-Century Music*,

models had the advantages of consistency and integrity. In retrospect they appear responsible and even cautious by contrast with, say, Kramer's opportunistic (and soon obsolete) amalgam of speech-act theory, its Derridean critique, and New Historicism. And this provides the context for the 'rethinking' to which this book bears witness, the principal characteristic of which is a conscientious and often self-conscious accommodation between established methodologies and new horizons.[10]

Whereas the New Musicologists annexed new terrain in the name of musicology, the principal concern of our contributors might be best characterized as careful cultivation. Conquest is giving way to colonization, which is perhaps also to say that controversy is giving way to compromise. Jim Samson sets the tone of this reconciliation when he suggests that 'the time is ripe to point beyond a debate that is in danger of growing wearisome'. Controversy, after all, arises out of certainty, even if it is only the certainty that nothing can be certain. If much New Musicological writing embodied what might be called a rhetoric of coercion, demanding that attention be paid to the broad range of music's meanings and condemning traditional musicology for its narrow focus, our contributors are, by comparison, slow to demand or to condemn. What is characteristic of their approach is more often an openness to the multiplicity of possible interpretations and a studied avoidance of value judgement. The source of this lies in the problematization of authority and a more generous attitude not only to endeavours in different musical fields, but also to the value of different sources of musical interpretation. What is adumbrated in this book might perhaps be described as a 'musicology of the provisional'.

It would not be entirely unreasonable to complain that the New Musicology deconstructed everything *except* the disciplinary identity of musicology, and that in the narrow (principally North American) sense which distinguishes musicology from music theory; paradoxically, the musicology/theory boundary remained generally intact, and sometimes even became more marked, as the boundaries between musicology and other humanities disciplines became increasingly fuzzy. If Kerman sought to redirect musicology, he effectively sought to abolish theory as a serious intellectual pursuit, and he did so by means of what might be described as a systematic misunderstanding of its aims and achievements.[11] For Kerman, analysis combined the worst attributes of nineteenth-

---

14 (1990), 186–96; Roger Parker, 'A Key for Chi? Tonal Areas in Puccini', *19th-Century Music*, 15 (1992), 229–34; Allan Atlas, 'Multivalence, Ambiguity and Non-Ambiguity: Puccini and the Polemicists', *Journal of the Royal Musical Association*, 118 (1993), 73–93.

[10] In this sense there is perhaps a basic difference between the idea of 'rethinking' music and that of the 'New' Musicology—terms which Treitler elides at the beginning of his chapter. Whereas a certain finality is implicit in the label 'New', the concept of rethinking is iterative; as Bohlman puts it, 'we rethink music out of the belief that we missed something first time round'. And in view of Treitler's gloss on the prefix *re-*, it is striking that the penultimate sentence of his chapter calls for 'a realignment: the re-aestheticization as well as the re-historicization of music'!

[11] In addition to *Contemplating Music/Musicology*, see Kerman's 'How We Got into Analysis, and How to Get Out', *Critical Inquiry*, 7 (1980), 311–31.

century ideology and naïve scientific positivism; it was predicated on a mono-lithic conception of organic unity (which it saw as a universal attribute of music, rather than a historical contingency) and executed by means of mechanical dis-covery procedures. It was, in short, a solution in search of a problem. There is no need here to offer a refutation of Kerman's cruel caricature of analysis; that job has frequently been undertaken (and in his chapter Nicholas Cook offers a critique of similar arguments advanced by Leo Treitler). But again, there was enough truth in the charge for at least some of the mud to stick, and much of the controversy associated with the New Musicology revolved around the kind of 'close reading' that analysis conspicuously embodies. Put in a nutshell, the issue was whether the kind of direct communion with music that has tradition-ally been seen as the goal of analysis is a viable—or indeed a reputable—aim. Analysis was seen as suspect because it attempted to provide 'purely musical' (that is to say, formalistic) explanations for what were in reality socially medi-ated meanings; it held out the false promise of an unmediated, unproblematic familiarity with the music of other times and places.[12]

Kerman's attack and the subsequent emergence of the New Musicology, then, effectively presented theorists and analysts with the same two alternatives that it presented to historical musicologists. One, obviously, was to ignore the fuss and get on with the job; that remains a professionally viable option (although how long this will continue to be the case is another matter), but it is not one that is explored here. The other was to rethink the discipline, not so much in the sense of inventing new analytical tools or historical methodologies, but in the sense of trying to decide what these tools and methodologies can tell us, or perhaps of coming to the conclusion that no final, universally applicable decision on the matter is possible or even desirable. If the writers represented in the present book have a common aim, this is it. Some focus on methods such as semiotics, whereas others focus on topics such as the musical surface or the concept of unity; some focus on the disciplinary identity of musicology or engage with more traditional questions of history, whereas others focus on the relationship of analysis to such activities as performance and composition. But in virtually every case there are the same underlying concerns: what are we doing when we analyse or contex-tualize music, and why are we doing it? What kind of truth can analysis or his-torical musicology reveal, and how might it relate to other kinds of truth about music? Should we be speaking of truth at all? Or does the act of engaging in analysis or the writing of history lock us into a predetermined epistemological stance? If so, how can we do analysis or history, yet question the premises that govern what we do?

---

[12] This position has been most uncompromisingly advanced by Gary Tomlinson, according to whom 'it is the act of close reading itself that carries with it the ideological charge of modernism' ('Musical Pasts and Postmodern Musi-cologies: A Response to Lawrence Kramer', *Current Musicology*, 53 (1993), 18–24, p. 22). The controversy over close reading resonates throughout this special issue of *Current Musicology*; see in particular Kramer's response to Tomlinson (25–35) and Stephen Blum's 'In Defense of Close Reading and Close Listening' (41–54). Leo Treitler critiques Tomlinson's arguments in his contribution to the present book.

To ask such questions, let alone to try to answer them, is to step beyond the narrow boundaries of analysis and historical musicology as characterized by Kerman. Whereas Kerman envisaged and championed a musicology that went beyond positivism, he seems to have been unable to imagine what it might mean for theory to go beyond formalism; it is as if he saw some internal contradiction in the idea of theory and analysis being 'critical', let alone self-critical. But there is no such contradiction, and the present book provides ample demonstration of this. To take a single example, many of our contributors grapple in one way or another with the issue of musical autonomy. They attempt to locate the concept of autonomy in its historical and social context (Samson, Cusick, Fink, Treitler), probing the relationship between formalism and hermeneutics (Whittall, Burnham, Rink) or between analytical representation and experience (Maus, Cook, Dubiel). They assume neither music's self-sufficiency (as early proponents of formalism did) nor its lack thereof (in the manner of much of the New Musicology). Instead, they attempt to formulate the ways in which music operates autonomously, and to establish limits beyond which the concept of musical autonomy ceases to be viable or, at any rate, useful. In a word, they problematize the issue of musical autonomy. And in so doing, they problematize their own role as analysts and historians of music—albeit without lessening their commitment to their discipline.

There are widespread rumours (not all of them emanating from historical musicologists) of the death of analysis. If analysis is understood as Kerman understood it, as a discipline predicated on the blithe assumption of music's separateness from the rest of the universe, then the rumours may well be true. But a better way of expressing it is that, after a lengthy period during which it was preponderantly absorbed with issues of method and technique (in other words, with problems of its own generation), analysis is moving outwards to embrace the issues of value, meaning, and difference that increasingly concern other musicologists. Samson envisions the possibility that under these circumstances 'analysis as a separate discipline (though not as an activity) will lose its identity in a mesh of wider critical perspectives, its tools and practices drawn into and absorbed by those wider perspectives'. Maybe, then, musicology is absorbing analysis. Or maybe, as we broaden our reading of music from text to world, it is analysis that is absorbing musicology. It is hardly worth arguing the toss; in intellectual (though not, to be sure, in institutional) terms, it doesn't make much difference which way round you put it. And that is why we offer this book under a totalizing title that conveys the connectedness of all musical thinking and, of course, rethinking.

Nicholas Cook
Mark Everist

# Contents

Contributors     xv

Introduction     1

## PART I

1 Ontologies of Music    *Philip V. Bohlman*     17

2 Analysis in Context    *Jim Samson*     35

3 Beyond Privileged Contexts: Intertextuality, Influence, and Dialogue    *Kevin Korsyn*     55

4 Autonomy/Heteronomy: The Contexts of Musicology *Arnold Whittall*     73

5 Going Flat: Post-Hierarchical Music Theory and the Musical Surface *Robert Fink*     102

6 The Challenge of Semiotics    *Kofi Agawu*     138

7 An Experimental Music Theory?    *Robert Gjerdingen*     161

8 Concepts of Musical Unity    *Fred Everett Maus*     171

9 How Music Matters: Poetic Content Revisited    *Scott Burnham*     193

10 Translating Musical Meaning: The Nineteenth-Century Performer as Narrator    *John Rink*     217

11 Analysing Performance and Performing Analysis    *Nicholas Cook*     239

12 Composer, Theorist, Composer/Theorist    *Joseph Dubiel*     262

## PART II

13 The Institutionalization of Musicology: Perspectives of a North American Ethnomusicologist    *Bruno Nettl*     287

14 Other Musicologies: Exploring Issues and Confronting Practice in India    *Regula Burckhardt Qureshi*     311

15 The History of Musical Canon    *William Weber*     336

16 The Historiography of Music: Issues of Past and Present *Leo Treitler*     356

17 Reception Theories, Canonic Discourses, and Musical Value *Mark Everist*     378

18 The Musical Text    *Stanley Boorman*     403

19 Finding the Music in Musicology: Performance History and Musical Works    *José A. Bowen*     424

20  Popular Music, Unpopular Musicology    *John Covach*                    452

21  Gender, Musicology, and Feminism    *Suzanne G. Cusick*                471

22  Musicology and/as Social Concern: Imagining the Relevant
    Musicologist    *Ralph P. Locke*                                       499

23  The Impact and Ethics of Musical Scholarship
    *Kay Kaufman Shelemay*  ←                                              531

24  What Do We Want to Teach When We Teach Music? One
    Apology, Two Short Trips, Three Ethical Dilemmas, and
    Eighty-Two Questions    *Ellen Koskoff*                                545

Index                                                                      561

# Contributors

KOFI AGAWU is Professor of Music at Yale University. He is the author of *Playing with Signs: A Semiotic Interpretation of Classic Music* and *African Rhythm: A Northern Ewe Perspective.*

PHILIP V. BOHLMAN teaches ethnomusicology at the University of Chicago, where he also holds positions in Jewish Studies and Southern Asian Studies, and serves as a member of the Center for Middle Eastern Studies. Among his recent publications are *Disciplining Music: Musicology and Its Canons,* which he co-edited with Katherine Bergeron, and *The World Centre for Jewish Music in Palestine 1936–1940: Jewish Musical Life on the Eve of World War II.*

STANLEY BOORMAN is a Professor at New York University, where he also directs the Collegium Musicum. He has worked primarily in the mid-Renaissance and in the history of music printing, has compiled the Glossary for the *New Grove Dictionary of Music Printing and Publishing,* and is completing a detailed bibliographical catalogue of the editions of Ottaviano Petrucci.

JOSÉ A. BOWEN is Director of the Centre for the History and Analysis of Recorded Music (CHARM) at the University of Southampton; he is currently working on a book entitled *The Conductor and the Score: A History of the Relationship between Interpreter and Text.* He is also an active composer with experience in jazz and film, a nomination for the Pulitzer Prize, and commissions from Hubert Laws, Jerry Garcia, and the Allegri Quartet.

SCOTT BURNHAM, Associate Professor of Music at Princeton University, is the author of *Beethoven Hero,* a study of the values and reception of Beethoven's heroic style, and *Music and Spirit: Selected Writings of A. B. Marx* (forthcoming).

NICHOLAS COOK is Professor of Music at the University of Southampton. His publications range from aesthetics to psychology, and from Beethoven to popular music; recent books include a Cambridge Music Handbook on *Beethoven's Ninth Symphony, Analysis Through Composition,* and *Analysing Musical Multimedia.*

JOHN COVACH is Associate Professor of Music at the University of North Carolina at Chapel Hill. He is co-editor of *In Theory Only* and has published widely on twelve-tone music, the philosophy of music, and rock music. He has co-edited a collection of essays entitled *Analyzing Rock Music,* forthcoming from Oxford University Press.

SUZANNE G. CUSICK teaches music history and criticism at the University of Virginia. Her recent publications include essays on Francesca Caccini, Monteverdi, the gender politics of classical music performance, and the possible relationships between sexualities and musicalities.

JOSEPH DUBIEL teaches composition and theory at Columbia University, and co-edits *Perspectives of New Music*.

MARK EVERIST is Professor of Music at the University of Southampton. He has written books on the sources of thirteenth-century polyphonic music and on the thirteenth-century motet; current projects include a book provisionally entitled *Music Drama at the Paris Odéon, 1824–28* and three volumes in the ongoing Oiseau-Lyre edition of the *Magnus Liber Organi*.

ROBERT FINK is Assistant Professor of Musicology at the Eastman School of Music, and a founding editor of the journal *repercussions*. He is currently researching a book on musical minimalism, desire, and consumer society.

ROBERT O. GJERDINGEN was trained at the University of Pennsylvania by Eugene Narmour, Leonard B. Meyer, and Eugene K. Wolf. He is the author of *A Classic Turn of Phrase: Music and the Psychology of Convention*, translator of Carl Dahlhaus's *Studies on the Origin of Harmonic Tonality*, and is working on a book on Mozart and the galant style.

KEVIN KORSYN received his Ph.D. in Music Theory from Yale University, and currently teaches at the University of Michigan, where he is Director of Graduate Studies. In 1991 he received the Young Scholar Award from the Society for Music Theory for his article 'Schenker and Kantian Epistemology'. He is currently writing a book called *Decentering Music: A Postdisciplinary Fantasy* for Oxford University Press, New York.

ELLEN KOSKOFF is Associate Professor of Ethnomusicology at the University of Rochester's Eastman School of Music, where she teaches courses in ethnomusicology and world music. She is the editor of *Women and Music in Cross-cultural Perspective* and has written extensively on the musical practices of Lubavitcher Hasidim, as well as on gender and music issues. Her recent publications include 'Where Women Play: The Role of Musical Instruments in Gender Relations', 'The Language of the Heart: Men, Women and Music in Lubavitcher Life', and 'Miriam Sings Her Song: The Self and Other in Anthropological Discourse'. In addition to her teaching and research activities, she is the Director of the Eastman School's Balinese *gamelan angklung*.

RALPH P. LOCKE is Professor of Musicology at the University of Rochester's Eastman School of Music. His publications include *Music, Musicians, and the Saint-Simonians*, articles on orientalism in Western opera, and several chapters in *Cultivating Music in America: Women Patrons and Activists since 1860*, which he co-edited with Cyrilla Barr.

FRED EVERETT MAUS teaches music at the University of Virginia. He has written on dramatic and narrative qualities of instrumental music, gender studies, aesthetics, and recent American music.

BRUNO NETTL is Emeritus Professor of Music and Anthropology at the University of Illinois. Among his several books, the best known are *Theory and Method in Ethnomusicology* and *The Study of Ethnomusicology*, and the most recent *Blackfoot Musical Thought: Comparative Perspectives*, *The Radif of Persian Music*, and *Heartland Excursions: Ethnomusicological Perspectives on Schools of Music*.

REGULA BURCKHARDT QURESHI is Professor of Music, Director of the Centre for Ethnomusicology, and Adjunct Professor of Anthropology and Religious Studies at the University of Alberta. Her recent publications include *Sufi Music of India and Pakistan: Sound, Context, and Meaning in Qawwali* as well as the co-edited *Muslim Families in North America*, and *Voices of Women: Essays in Honor of Violet Archer*. She is working on a book on Hindustani music making.

JOHN RINK is Reader in Music at Royal Holloway, University of London. He has published in the fields of theory and analysis, nineteenth-century music, and performance studies. Recent books include *Chopin: The Piano Concertos*, *The Practice of Performance: Studies in Musical Interpretation*, and *Chopin Studies 2*. He is active as a pianist.

JIM SAMSON is Professor of Music at the University of Bristol. He has published widely on the music of Chopin and on analytical and aesthetic topics in nineteenth- and twentieth-century music.

KAY KAUFMAN SHELEMAY is an ethnomusicologist who has published widely on musical traditions of Ethiopia, the Middle East, and urban America. Professor of Music and Chair of the Music Department at Harvard University, Shelemay's books include *Music, Ritual and Falasha History* and *A Song of Longing: An Ethiopian Journey*.

LEO TREITLER is Distinguished Professor of Music at the Graduate School and University Centre of the City University of New York. He is author of *Music and the Historical Imagination* and of a forthcoming collection of essays on the transmission of music in the Middle Ages (Oxford University Press), and he is general editor of the forthcoming revised version of Oliver Strunk's *Source Readings in Music History* (W. W. Norton).

WILLIAM WEBER, Professor of History at California State University, Long Beach, has written on eighteenth- and nineteenth-century musical topics addressed to both musicologists and historians.

ARNOLD WHITTALL is Emeritus Professor of Music Theory and Analysis, King's College, London. His main publications are in the field of twentieth-century music and music theory.

# Introduction

## Part I

In 'Ontologies of Music' (Chapter 1), Philip Bohlman attempts a basic ground-clearing exercise, sketching out a kind of cross-cultural calculus of musical possibility. He provides a representative taxonomy of what kind of thing (or what kind of not-thing) music may be or be seen to be; he offers a sample of the ways in which music may relate (or not relate, or be seen not to relate) to society. As he emphasizes, to speak of 'music' is already to predicate a particular kind of existence for it, as compared with 'musics', or with cultures that do not have a term for 'music', or, for that matter, with the 'hegemonic universality' implied by *die Musik*. Bohlman stresses the political aspects of such 'nominalist strategies', and indeed of all systems of representation. 'Thinking—or even rethinking—music', he says, 'is at base an attempt to claim and control music as one's own'; and a few pages later he adds that 'Claiming a music as one's own recognizes music as an object'. Ultimately, then, musicologists cannot escape the ontology of music that they constitute by thinking it, by rethinking it, by writing about it; as Bohlman puts it, 'Ideally, I should endeavour to represent non-Western ontologies of music; I should draw on "other" metaphysics no more nor less than my own. I can't. . . . I've responded to the dilemma by capitulating to it, by writing this essay at all.'

Bohlman emphasizes that 'Music's ontologies are not . . . separable from the practices of music'. In other words, without an ontology there can be not only no reflection on music, but no music to reflect on. But it is obvious that musicology's ontologies, if they may be called that, are inseparable from the attempt to formulate musical insights and experiences in verbal form, and as Bohlman says, 'The metaphysical conundrums that result from the inability to unravel the distinctions between music and language are legion.' (This is a theme that recurs throughout this first part.) In 'Analysis in Context' (Chapter 2), Jim Samson attempts to unravel, if not the distinctions between music and language (that would be too much to ask), then at least some of these musicological ontologies. He offers an interpretation that is at once historical and ideological, showing how analysis emerged as a distinct discipline in tandem with the autonomous work of art. We have, then, the paradoxical phenomenon of a discipline that is predicated on the synchronic (music analysis, you might say, is music minus history), but which turns out to be itself grounded in a particular historical moment. From this premiss, Samson draws a number of conclusions concerning the epistemology of analysis. He rejects the idea that analysis might stand 'in a similar relation to the work as science does to the natural world'; on the contrary, he argues, 'In music analysis the subject is irredeemably implicated.' Indeed, he goes so far as to claim that 'music analysis is as much a form of self-analysis (raising all the familiar problems of the "I" describing itself) as an empirical explanation of the other'.

Another way of saying this is that analysis involves interpretation, and interpretation involves the possibility (indeed the logical necessity) of other interpretations. Three things can be seen to follow from this. One is that analysis is irreducibly pluralistic. 'The formalist enterprise', says Samson, 'retains its constituency and much of its potency, but it is now just one of several options open to the wider community of analysts.' The second is that analysis is fictive, and its substance lies in metaphor; Samson points out that the very idea of 'absolute music' (epitomized by Hanslick's 'tonally moving forms'[1]) is predicated on the metaphor of space, and stresses the need 'to scrutinize the nature of the images, models, or metaphors used in analysis, since their *modus operandi* defines the gap between our experience and our description of that experience'. The final conclusion, in Samson's words, highlights 'motivations rather than methods'; analysis—any analysis—responds to 'the need to share our reactions (especially our enthusiasm and excitement), and there are no restrictions on their authentic expression'. In this way 'the old formalism, no less than the New Musicology, may take its impetus from pleasure and intensity'. In associating this final argument with Barthes's 'pleasure of the text', Samson stresses the postmodern qualities of contemporary analysis as he sees it; its summarizing trait, he observes, is 'a focus on the signifier, and a replacement of the single signified by a recursive intertextuality'.

Where Samson sees an implicit postmodernism in today's analytical practice, Kevin Korsyn argues that 'Although music research has sometimes adopted post-structural insights, we have been reluctant to face the radical consequences of such thought'. In 'Beyond Privileged Contexts: Intertextuality, Influence, and Dialogue' (Chapter 3), he offers an approach that draws explicitly on post-structuralism, and in particular the work of Mikhail Bakhtin. Analysts, Korsyn says, have traditionally looked for a quasi-grammatical unity in the compositions they study. But the unity of a sentence is not an appropriate model for music. We should be comparing music not with language but with utterances, which is to say the use of language in real-life communicative situations. And Bakhtin has shown how utterances are not unified in the same way that sentences, by definition, are; on the contrary, they are characterized by the irreducible heterogeneity, the multiple consciousness, that Bakhtin termed 'dialogic'. In the same way, Korsyn argues, 'We need new paradigms for analysis, new models that will allow both unity and heterogeneity.'

---

[1] Eduard Hanslick, *On the Musically Beautiful*, trans. Geoffrey Payzant (Indianapolis, 1986), 29.

Korsyn goes on to provide a practical example of what this might mean, showing how the first movement of Brahms's String Quartet Op. 51 No. 1, embodies 'stratified musical languages . . . [that] do not merge, do not coalesce; instead, Brahms creates a plurality of unmerged voices'. The result, says Korsyn, is to decentre the listener, denying him or her a stable, privileged position from which to experience or interpret the music. Comparing his own analysis with David Lewin's (which emphasizes Brahms's synthesis of oppositions), Korsyn concludes: 'The non-convergence, the abrasion, of discourses seems to me more essential than any dialectical resolution'. (Following Samson, we might say that Korsyn's Bakhtinian reading of the quartet represents an option, an interpretation, no more nor less valid than any other; Korsyn does not, presumably, wish to privilege heterogeneity over unity, but rather to establish an orientation within which both concepts are available to the analyst.) And he extends his Bakhtinian paradigm to cover music history as well. 'Just as music analysis has generally privileged unity over heterogeneity,' he writes, 'so music history has preferred continuity to discontinuity.' Indeed, he sees a 'complicity' in the traditional relationship between analysis and history: each, he argues, is predicated on an artificial and unsustainable distinction between text and context. If Samson traces the emergence of analysis as a distinct discipline in tandem with the autonomous musical work, Korsyn in effect writes an epitaph for both.

Arnold Whittall's 'Autonomy/Heteronomy: The Contexts of Musicology' (Chapter 4) can usefully be read side by side with Korsyn's chapter, and not only because it includes a sympathetic critique of Korsyn's reading of Brahms. Whittall is responding to the same post-structural and New Musicological currents as Korsyn, but in his case the aim to reach an accommodation between established methodologies and new horizons is more overt. For Whittall, 'A deconstructed musicology ceases to be musicology at all if it resists direct engagement with the composer and composition, and side-steps the possibility that works of art may be defences against the world as much as products of the world.' This links with Whittall's earlier remark, which he makes in relation to Elliott Carter's *Scrivo in vento*, that 'In linking work to world, it is still the work that dominates, because it represents a triumph over the world: it is a product of the world that transcends its context'. For Whittall, then, what Dahlhaus called the relative autonomy of music remains a possibility, and with it an 'interpretative musicology', a 'multivalent analysis [which] can balance the claims of poetics and formalism within a coherent discourse'. If Whittall admits that 'even the most unambiguous texts prove to contain the makings of doubt and uncertainty', his aim nevertheless seems to be to demonstrate that the converse is also true: the makings of 'an interpretative musicology that is adequately plural and adequately coherent' can be found even amidst the doubt and uncertainty of present-day musicological and analytical writing.

In a memorable phrase, Whittall refers to 'that inescapable binary stand-off between music and language'; like Charles Seeger, he locates the musicological juncture at the intersection between tone and word. In 'Going Flat: Post-Hierarchical Music Theory and the Musical Surface' (Chapter 5), Robert Fink focuses on this intersection by subjecting a key musicological metaphor to just the kind of in-depth scrutiny that Samson asked for. There are two main strands to what he says. One is to show how the metaphor of the musical 'surface' (and its implied correlate, 'depth') accomplishes cultural work. Analysts, Fink argues, seem to be possessed by a 'fear of the surface'; they see the musical surface, with all its alluring charms, as something to be explained away, its illusory status revealed. Religious parallels to this position might suggest themselves, but Fink's exploration takes a different direction: he shows how the idea of depth enables the musical construction of a sense of bourgeois interiority. And he backs up this claim by showing how Schenker associated the musical surface with superficiality in all aspects of life, ranging from what he saw as creeping Americanization to the mass uprisings that took place in Vienna between 1918 and 1923. Nothing could more clearly demonstrate the historical embeddedness of Schenker's commitment to the autonomy and transcendence of music.

The second strain of Fink's argument is more technical. He shows how, even in the master-work tradition that submits so elegantly to hierarchical analysis, it is possible to turn Schenkerian analysis on its head and discover linear ascents, continuities that leap from one salient point to another, 'rid[ing] on top of the musical surface'. He does not claim that these constructs are 'in' the music; the linear ascent, he says, 'is prolonged, if at all, in our minds; and its dynamism exists there, too—as desire'. But he claims that the resulting 'transgressive wedge between the surface and the depths' captures an essential aspect of the listening experience, and one that becomes increasingly important as the music under scrutiny approaches our present postmodern age. 'When we recognize new kinds of space in a late twentieth-century piece of music,' he asks, 'shouldn't our analytical models . . . "mutate" right along with them?' This might be read against Whittall's 'acknowledgement of the innate cultural modernism of analytical work, whatever the period of music we happen to be concerned with'; like Korsyn, Fink is explicitly concerned to develop postmodern strategies of interpretation. There remains, however, an unresolved issue of what might be termed analytical anachronism. If we need postmodern strategies of interpretation for postmodern music, does that mean we need pre-modern strategies of interpretation for pre-modern music? Or, as analysts, are we openly engaged in recasting the music of previous ages in light of present-day sensibilities? Are Korsyn's Brahms and Fink's Beethoven simply late twentieth-century constructions? Could we reasonably expect them to be anything else? Or is it possible for the composers to somehow 'talk back' to us, like Shelemay's informants, but through their music?

In 'The Challenge of Semiotics' (Chapter 6), Kofi Agawu scrutinizes an even more deeply engrained metaphor for music: the metaphor of music as language. Obviously the issue of music's language-like status does not lend itself to a yes/no resolution; Agawu carefully sets out a list of affinities and differences between music and language, which leads him to the conclusion that 'the metaphor is useful to the extent that it forces its users to confront its limitations'. On the basis of this, Agawu proceeds to an examination of some well-established procedures of semiotic analysis, which are modelled on the procedures of structural linguistics and purport to bring a hard-edged, scientific quality to the analysis of musical texts. By comparing different but equally well-formed analyses of a single musical passage, Agawu shows how the selection of a particular analytical format necessarily embodies an aesthetic judgement; despite appearances, he says, semiotic analyses 'subtend "semantic" meanings whether or not such meanings are made explicit'. Indeed, Agawu stresses the *need* for analyses to be informed by such judgements; as he puts it, 'The view that an explicit, rule-governed approach to segmenting tonal music is likely to produce counter-intuitive ("unmusical") insights is not to be dismissed lightly.' Accordingly, he goes on to offer a Schenkerian analysis of the same passage as 'a more musical approach to segmentation'.

Agawu is as aware as anybody of the dangers of essentialism that are presented by the use of terms like 'musical' and 'unmusical'. His employment of them reflects not a covert aesthetic absolutism, but rather a frank acceptance that anlysis cannot escape the hermeneutic circle. 'Analyses', he says, 'convince because they are good performances, not because they are intellectually rigorous.' But this does not mean that the explicit discovery procedures of semiotic analyses have no value for the analyst. 'By clarifying the ways in which we know musical facts,' Agawu writes, 'semiotics plays a much needed role in promoting greater self-awareness among analysts.' Moreover, it can bring something of the clarity of formalism to the study of aspects of music traditionally seen as beyond the scope of precise analysis. Agawu outlines several ways in which semiotic approaches might lead to a refinement of current discussions of musical meaning, through providing 'a rigorous mechanism for laying bare the enabling structures of any music theory'.

Robert Gjerdingen's 'An Experimental Music Theory?' (Chapter 7) springs from a similar impulse. Citing the example of medieval artists, who drew what they knew and not what they saw, he graphically demonstrates how theory can become circular and self-validating in the absence of proper empirical controls. 'Today,' he writes, 'whenever I attend a meeting of music theorists, I am struck by the conviction with which old beliefs are invoked as eternal verities'; concepts like 'tonality' and 'voice-leading' are spoken of as if they were objective phenomena or causal forces. Gjerdingen recognizes that the values of formalism are no longer uncritically accepted: 'Recent attempts to "problematize" these verities', he admits, 'have resulted in complexified dogma.' But he continues: 'The basic terms of the debate, however, remain unchanged. . . . The self-stabilizing, corroborating effect of interdependent premises precludes fundamental revisions, major discoveries, or even accidental breakthroughs.' Gjerdingen finds this sour assessment paradoxically confirmed by recent attempts on the part of music theorists to subject their own assumptions to empirical investigation (he focuses on experiments on the perception of tonal unity); the incompetence of such attempts, judged by standards of professional psychological adequacy, illustrates the gulf that separates the disciplines.[2] If such experiments were well received among the music-theoretical community, adds Gjerdingen, that is because 'the crowd . . . was more interested in the critique than the experimental method. In our rush toward fashionable criticism—and I presume no one would wish to be thought "uncritical"—we must be careful not to let knowing once again outstrip seeing.'

But the picture is not all gloom and doom. The examples of Rameau, Riemann, and Meyer, says Gjerdingen, show that fruitful interaction between music theory and experimentation is possible; and for the future, 'Theorists should, as many now do, collaborate with psychologists, acousticians, cognitive scientists, neurologists, behavioural scientists, and others who want to join in exploring the many aspects of music. The premisses of discourse within the discipline of music

---

[2] Since the principal object of Gjerdingen's critique is one of the editors, Nicholas Cook, he may perhaps claim as editor's perk the right to reply. In his critique of my article on tonal closure, Gjerdingen says that 'One does not claim that the null hypothesis is true'. And indeed I didn't; rather, in the discussion section of my article (where, as Gjerdingen puts it, 'the music psychologist is given license to speculate') I considered what it might mean *were the null hypothesis in fact to be true*. (My discussion is hedged with words like 'if, 'indicate', and 'suggest', omitted in Gjerdingen's quotations.) But in any case, my results run parallel with other empirical tests of structural features of music to which aesthetic significance has traditionaly been ascribed, and (in Vladimir Konečni's words) 'When a substantial number of studies—using different methods and domains of enquiry . . . but all asking the same basic questions—all obtain a negative answer, this cumulative evidence begins to count' ('Elusive Effects of Artists' "Messages" ', in W. R. Crozier and A. J. Chapman (eds.), *Cognitive Processes in the Perception of Art* (Amsterdam, 1984), 71–93); to discourage speculation under such circumstances would be to stifle the very openness to empirical data that Gjerdingen is advocating. Certainly my experiment was unsophisticated by the standards of experimental psychology (though in private correspondence the psychologist Rudolf Radocy called it 'excellent from a methodological standpoint'). But it opened up music-theoretical debate on the issue (see esp. Joseph Swain, 'Music Perception and Musical Communities', *Music Perception*, 11 (1994), 307–20), and subsequent experimentation has supported its general conclusions (Barbara Tillmann and Emmanuel Bigand, 'Does Formal Musical Structure Affect Perception of Musical Expressiveness?', *Psychology of Music*, 24 (1996), 3–17, and further research forthcoming). But of course I would welcome its replication and extension by music psychologists who have both the necessary skills and the equally necessary access to funding for such purposes.

Gjerdingen suggests that I misrepresent the results of Clarke and Krumhansl's experiments. When I claimed that 'What is strikingly absent from the criteria adopted in the Mozart is any sign of specifically *tonal* features', the italicized 'tonal' linked with the italicized 'tonal' on the previous page, where I referred to the 'hierarchical structure that lies at the heart of GTTM [and] shows how compositions can be coherent in a specifically *tonal* manner'; I went on to define this in terms of Lerdahl's distinction between stability and salience. The features listed by Clarke and Krumhansl, and mentioned by Gjerdingen, relate to surface disjunctions and are hence 'salient', in Lerdahl's sense, rather than tonal. (Clarke and Krumhansl themselves comment that 'It is striking . . . that with the two very different pieces used in this study, listeners cite similar features as indicators of segment boundaries. There are only two differences . . . : the greater emphasis on pauses and silences as grouping factors in the *Klavierstück* than in the *Fantasie*, which is a direct result of the more continuous nature of the music in the Mozart, and the greater importance of repetition as a boundary indicator in the Stockhausen' ('Perceiving Musical Time', *Music Perception*, 7 (1990), 429). My argument at this point revolves around Lerdahl's statement (which I quote) that 'the grammatical force of tonal pitch structures can be gauged by their ability to override surface salience'; that is why I was talking about 'grammatical' or 'ungrammatical' qualities. I entirely agree with Gjerdingen's conclusion that terms like 'grammaticality' 'simply do not constitute appropriate objects for the confident manipulations of Aristotelian logic'—indeed, that is the very point I thought I was making!

theory should be capable of meeting the challenge of translation into domains where inexactitude is never mistaken for subtlety.' The problem, of course, lies in who is to set the agenda for such collaboration; if one discipline's inexactitude is another discipline's subtlety, then, equally, one discipline's self-validation can be another's hermeneutic circle. Such, at any rate, is suggested by the juxtaposition of Gjerdingen's chapter with Fred Maus's 'Concepts of Musical Unity' (Chapter 8), which seeks to rehabilitate the nowadays unfashionable notion of musical unity. Like the experiments that Gjerdingen criticizes, Maus is concerned with the experience of music as unified; he wants to relocate the focus of analytical enquiry away from the musical patterns visible in scores and towards the experience of musical listeners. And he warns against the analytical tendency to assume a direct correlation between the two: 'Confronted with a demonstration, on the basis of a score, that some kind of musical pattern exists,' he writes, 'one may be tempted to conclude that the pattern explains features of one's experiences, even though one does not recognize the pattern as such in listening. . . . One should resist such hypothetical analytical explanations.'

This, of course, is just where experimental verification might be expected to come in; the whole point of perceptual experiments, after all, is that they can identify factors which impinge upon experience without being consciously recognized as such. But there are two problems. One is a point that Gjerdingen makes in relation to experiments concerning tonal unity: there are 'manifest difficulties', he says, 'in attempting to apply rigorous methods to poorly defined, culturally contingent phenomena'. The trouble is that the sort of experiences Maus is talking about—and indeed, the sort of experiences that analysts talk about in general—are not only hard to define; they are affected by any number of contingent factors relating to the musical or social context, the listener's background and motivation, and so on. The second problem is even more fundamental. Maus is talking about listeners' experiences, but he is not talking just about their past experiences. He points out how conducting an analysis typically results in 'a somewhat altered experience' of the music. And he observes that if he communicates his analytical interpretation to others, they 'may find that their future experiences alter in light of my description'. Analytical enquiry, then, does not simply—maybe does not primarily—aim to represent experiences as they *are*; it aims to represent experiences as they are not, but fruitfully might be. The agenda of such an enterprise simply does not coincide with that of experimental psychology, and the 'translation' that Gjerdingen calls for is consequently likely to be not so much a 'challenge' as a chimera.

In 'How Music Matters: Poetic Content Revisited' (Chapter 9), Scott Burnham focuses centrally on the issues of musical autonomy and meaning that weave in and out of most of the chapters in this book. Like Agawu, he rejects the conventional distinction—what might be called the Hanslick/Wagner line—between the intrinsic and the extrinsic meaning of music. 'The operative dichotomy', he writes, 'is not between the explicit poetic critic and the explicit formal analyst, but between surveyors of the open work and purveyors of the closed work.' Burnham is making essentially the same point as Maus: analysis that is worthy of the name contributes to the experience, and hence the aesthetic significance, of music. Its effect, then, is to keep the music open to new interpretation, and hence to sustain its capacity to engender new meaning. By contrast, analysis that purports to explain the music once and for all, to provide the 'key' to it, stops the piece 'dead in its tracks as a viable artwork'. And Burnham's point is that both the analysis that keeps the piece open and the analysis that closes it off may equally well be cast in 'formal' or 'poetic' terms.

The largest part of the chapter illustrates Burnham's argument by comparing and contrasting approaches to Beethoven's music that range from the formal to the poetic. In the case of the anomalous return of the scherzo in the finale of Beethoven's Fifth Symphony, for instance, Burnham begins by showing that is possible to explain what Beethoven does in purely technical terms. Then he counterposes his formal analysis with hermeneutic readings drawn from Kretzschmar, Bekker, Tovey, and E. M. Forster. He concludes that the novelist's reading, for all its lack of technical language, is in some ways the most sophisticated of all; it articulates the ethical—and even mythical—qualities of Beethoven's music. In the words of Burnham's title, Forster's poetic interpretation explains 'how music matters' to us, in a way that no merely technical explanation ever can. But it saying this, Burnham has no intention of relapsing into old-fashioned attitudes according to which music is seen as 'something that primarily encodes some other order of experience, and, like all codes, demands to be broken, and is not satisfactorily negotiated until it is translated'. On the contrary, he says, 'we *need* to understand music as music, as an autonomous language, if we want to grant it the power to speak of other things.' In this way, he concludes, 'we are far from abandoning the idea of music's immanence, for we reckon with it continually'.

Burnham believes in relative autonomy with a vengeance. 'Music is simply not reducible to any other circumstances,' he says, 'whether cultural, historical, biographical, or sexual, and any attempt to make it so has only a cartoonish reality.' And the considered defence of this essentially Hanslickian position (a position that accords with what Hanslick actually said, rather than with what he was long said to have said) forms an important element in the rethinking of theory prompted by the New Musicology. Agawu speaks of the 'central fact that both composer- and work-immanent prescriptions ultimately determine the work's strongest meanings'; Samson speaks of the 'considerable protection for analysis' within boundaries defined by recognition of 'the heavily mediated character of any analytical insight'. While analysis, then, can no longer plausibly claim to embody the whole truth, it can claim to be a *necessary* component of any adequate reading of musical meaning, whether aesthetic or social (as if the two could be disentangled from one another). And a specific illustration of this is provided by 'Translating Musical Meaning: The Nineteenth-Century Performer as Narrator' (Chapter 10), in which John Rink asserts the indispensability of 'close study of the score—"structural analysis"—in order to reveal its particular message or meaning'.

Like Burnham, Rink refuses to distinguish between musical and extra-musical meaning. His aim, he says, is to show 'how the performer of nineteenth-century music can bring the score to life as a *narrator* of the expressive message inherent therein'. And for Rink, this aim is equally hermeneutical, analytical, and practical—indeed, more than anything else practical, for performance, he says, 'has unique powers to communicate in the original expressive idiom rather than some foreign (verbal) language'. Rink demonstrates what he has in mind by means of a close reading of Liszt's *Vallée d'Obermann*. He considers not only the different versions of the work, but also a variety of intertextual links with Schubert's song 'Der Wanderer'; these give depth and precision to the qualities of alienation and vacillation which the music derives from its programmatic association with Senancour's novel *Obermann*. Next, he links these expressive associations with the recurrent wave-like patterns that can be found in all parameters of the music, from the smallest scale to the largest; there is, Rink claims, 'a structural homology between [the protagonist's] *vacillation* on the one hand and the music's *oscillation* on the other'. On the basis of this, he presents an analytical ' "intensity curve"—that is, a graphic presentation of the music's ebb and flow, its "contour" in time, determined by all active elements . . . working either independently, in sync, or out of phase with one another to create the changing degrees of energy and thus the overall shape'.[3] The result is a temporal framework for performance that 'mediate[s] between the poetic and the structural'.

Whereas Rink moves from the analysis of poetic content towards consequences for performance, Nicholas Cook's 'Analysing Performance, and Performing Analysis' (Chapter 11), moves from performance towards a consideration of the performative dimension of theory as a whole. He argues that the existing analysis-and-performance literature marginalizes performance by conceiving it exclusively in terms of the projection of compositional structure. (In this he agrees with Maus, who writes that the analytical emphasis on musical works 'notoriously neglects the contribution of performance, typically treating the performer's contribution as, at best, a kind of edifying commentary on the work itself'; Suzanne Cusick's chapter in Part II adds a gendered dimension to such neglect.) Drawing upon the pragmatist critique of structural linguistics, which has much in common with the Bakhtinian approach advanced by Korsyn, Cook argues that we place too much emphasis on what performance *represents*, and too little on what it *does*. Where established approaches look for a more or less smooth translation from analysis to performance, he sees an essential incommensurability between music as writing and music as performance; in this

---

[3] Rink's intuitively derived 'intensity curves' may be compared with the empirically derived tempo graphs discussed in José Bowen's chapter in Part II.

context, structurally oriented performance becomes just one option among others, in the same way that Samson sees the 'formalist enterprise' in analysis as just one option among others. But Cook's main purpose in examining the analysis-and-performance literature is to gain insight into the strategies of analytical and theoretical writing in general. Echoing views expressed by other contributors to this volume, he suggests that there is 'an evolving consensus on what might be called a performative epistemology of music theory'; in other words, analysis does not simply reflect meaning that is already in music, but participates in its construction. This, he argues, is the best defence against the Kerman/Treitler critique of analysis.

Cook's final argument for the importance of what he calls 'the performative perspective' is that it provides the only adequate epistemological basis for the methodological pluralism that is so prominent a feature of today's analytical world. In 'Composer, Theorist, Composer/Theorist' (Chapter 12), Joseph Dubiel provides a vivid picture of what might be called the performative micro-theories to which pluralism gives rise. Writing from a composer's viewpoint, Dubiel emphasizes the extent to which composers manipulate not sounds (or not just sounds), but the frames of mind in terms of which the sounds are experienced. 'What strikes and intrigues us about a piece of music', he says, 'is as much a matter of how we shape ourselves to the music as of what is presented to us as music.' Dubiel links these frames of mind, which are as diverse as the sounds to which they correspond, with Benjamin Boretz's concept of 'attributive theory'— theory, that is to say, which is inseparable from perception, and which contributes to the determination of what there is to perceive. But that doesn't mean the theory is the same as the perception; as Dubiel puts it, 'While a theory, in the sense of a shaping frame of mind, must always be there . . . it will also always, in so far as it can be reconstructed as a general *frame* of mind, fall short of the music whose perception it enables.' (We are back to the gap between experience and its representation that Samson mentions, and that Cook also discusses.) It follows that experiences can't be translated into analyses; rather, 'the value of analyses will ultimately be their value as ear-openers.'

On such an account, Dubiel admits, 'the "theories" that are ways of hearing are theories of remarkable instability and diversity'. Should we really call them theories at all, then? An answer, perhaps, is implicit in Dubiel's statement that 'the theory of *music* interests me less than the theories of *pieces* (or of *hearings* of pieces); or rather, the theory of music interests me chiefly as a body of aids to and constraints on the formation of much smaller, more idiosyncratic theories'. These experience-rich microtheories are open to verification or refutation ('Often', says Dubiel, 'you come up against something awfully like empirical resistance—and back you go to the drawing-board'), but they aspire to no scientific generality. Instead, as Dubiel points out, they resemble 'articulated ontologies for the music to which they apply—sets of possible entities, configured by possible relations, open to choice'. What Dubiel is describing, in fact, is a perfect illustration of what Bohlman calls 'the constant ontological probing that music-making engenders'. Or, to put it another way, Dubiel is saying that music may be what we think it is; it may not be—and that, of course, is just where Bohlman began.

## Part II

The essays in the second part of *Rethinking Music* point up the ambiguity of what music is: text, history, society, or institution. Treating music as all of these things alongside the idea of music as structure or system is a fair reflection of the current state of the range of musical studies at the end of the second millennium.

This part begins with the reflections of two ethnomusicologists on the nature of the discipline. Bruno Nettl's wide-ranging account of the ways in which musicology is institutionalized (Chapter 13) is a valuable point of departure and context for all the chapters that follow. Regula Qureshi (Chapter 14) goes slightly further, and looks harder at the ways in which 'other' musicologies function and how they might affect either traditional or current musicologies; this is clearly illustrated by the multi-layered frames of reference for the nineteenth-century treatise on Indian music, the *Ma'dan-ul-Mausiqi*, its relationship to classical Sanskrit treatises and the connecting traditions of Indian music from the thirteenth century to the British Raj.

Both Stanley Boorman and José Bowen consider music as a form of text. Boorman (Chapter 18) discusses music as printed or written information, and Bowen (Chapter 19) treats music as sonic information. The points of convergence consist of more than the subject-matter of their chapters. Both point to the importance of what might be seen as 'peripheral' qualities in an edition or a performance, and identify differences between features that identify a musical work (pitch and rhythm) and 'additional . . . qualities which are necessary to realize a work in sound'.[4] However, although Boorman's subject-matter—primary source materials, the mistrust that they should engender, and the necessity of historicizing the issue of consistency—is a clearly defined sub-discipline of musicology, for Bowen, 'Music in Performance' is a sub-discipline that requires inventing.

Bowen's attempts to lay down guide-lines for the scope and methods of an approach to the analysis of music in performance invoke central questions broached elsewhere in this book: his claim that 'music as work' replaces 'music as event' during the course of the nineteenth century echoes similar observations on the nature of the autonomy of the musical work elsewhere in this volume. Like Boorman, he finds it impossible to side-step the question of

---

[4] Although the quotation comes from Bowen, it could just as easily have come from Boorman.

historically informed performance, and, also like Boorman, finds it difficult to disagree with Richard Taruskin's conclusion that it is in essence a modernist phenomenon.[5] In this respect, and in his claim that his example of a Debussy *prélude* moves from performance *to* score, Bowen comes very close to Boorman's position on the relationship of musical text and performance. Both authors have a clear sense of history behind their comments, even if it is rarely articulated.

Traditional questions of history are considered by William Weber, Leo Treitler, and Mark Everist. Weber's 'The History of Musical Canon' (Chapter 15) gives a valuable overview of the subject, and substantiates the claim that, although much of what we identify as the canon today owes its existence to an origin in the early nineteenth century, canonic pressures on repertories go back at least as far as the eighteenth century and probably as far as the sixteenth.

Treitler, in 'The Historiography of Music: Issues of Past and Present' (Chapter 16), engages with a different historiographical trajectory: the question of musical autonomy. His account of the subject complements those in Part I. Returning to Panowsky's idea of a *provisional* autonomy of the work of art (Panowsky's domain was of course art history), Treitler not only points to the necessity of retaining some sense of musical autonomy, but identifies the logical inconsistency of much of the so-called New Musicology, which seeks to abandon concepts of autonomy. He writes:

[I]f postmodern theory would put aside the aestheticization of music that was a project of the early nineteenth century . . . then how can postmodern historical interpretation be based on musical analysis that claims to reveal musical *experience* which, no matter how broadly drawn, arises from those aesthetic conceptions? This contradiction is not evaded by musical analysis that is superficial and unengaged, that lacks the conviction of hammer-and-tongs analysis, as though to avoid entrapment in the aesthetic.

And, pulling fewer punches, he goes on to suggest that '[McClary's proposals of music as social discourse] seem precariously close to interpretations that are driven by little more than the need to make them'.

This wide-ranging account of a possible way forward for a historiography of music points to the presence of a provisionally autonomous work in a diachronic context: 'The kinds of hazards to such survival that the [music-historical] object confronts in transmission constitute a subject that must be high on the agenda of the study called "historiography".' This challenge is picked up in Everist's 'Reception Theories, Canonic Discourses, and Musical Value' (Chapter 17), in which Treitler's 'hazards to survival' are represented both as sites of reception and as pressures on canonic discourse. Jumping off from Weber's account of the

---

[5]  Modernist, and—as an intellectual concept, perhaps—exhausted. It was originally intended to include a chapter on historically informed performance, but it proved impossible to find an author who could feel that there was something useful that could be said beyond a summary of conclusions of arguments current in the 1980s. Significantly, the question of performance has moved in very different directions, as the chapters on performance in this book bear witness.

history of musical cannon, this chapter considers the ways in which canons might be constructed and the effects that such canons may have on the ways in which we currently construct music history.

Kay Shelemay and Ralph Locke invite us to consider the impact of musicology outside academia. Shelemay's 'The Impact and Ethics of Musical Scholarship' (Chapter 23) takes Falasha liturgical music as a case-study, and asks what happens when the subjects of musicological study 'talk back' to the scholar. In a revealing sentence, she claims that her qualifications for carrying out her research were based on an assumption that she 'call[s] into question: that music (and musical research) is removed from any practical reality, and that it holds no potential for, and poses no challenge to, our understanding of other domains of everyday life'. A different spin on the same idea is given by Locke when he suggests that the relevance of musicology to society is in doubt only if 'one works on the operating assumption that musicology and music are more or less *irrelevant* to society, are indeed not *themselves* social phenomena'. Locke's 'Musicology and/as Social Concern: Imagining the Relevant Musicologist' (Chapter 22) calls for the making explicit of implicit ideological agenda, points to the social concerns of a large number of composers and performers in an extraordinarily wide-ranging and thoughtful account, passes through a review of the implications of and for language of the existence of such a 'relevant musicologist', before considering questions of freedom and responsibility with which such an individual might find him or herself involved.

Suzanne Cusick's encyclopaedic account of feminism in musicology (Chapter 21) evolves from a story of the exclusion of Ruth Crawford from the founding meeting of the New York Musicological Society in 1930. From this point, Cusick builds up a matrix of references to this event that explain how a history of music and the discipline of musicology may be seen from a feminist perspective, and how musicology's subject and object are gendered as masculine. One of her conclusions aligns itself clearly with one of the principal threads running through this volume; for Cusick, the ultimate feminist issue is the concept of *the music itself*. Her closing remarks echo another issue. She writes:

By legitimizing multiple perspectives on, and experiences of, music, feminist musicologies promise to provide us with ways to rejoice in the wide variety of phenomena that might be called 'music'. . . . Further, they promise to liberate us from the intellectual restrictions imposed by an anachronistic, early modernist view of 'science', allowing us stunning new liberties in our interpretations of music and musical experiences.

Not only an excellent introduction to a subject whose literature is enlarging at a speed that many may find daunting, Cusick's chapter aligns many of the principal aims of feminist musicologies with those of more thoughtful musicologies whose intellectual origins lie elsewhere.

John Covach (Chapter 20) poses an opposition between popular music and unpopular musicology, and makes the not unreasonable claim that the study of popular music enriches our understanding of the history of music by opening up fresh perspectives on the field. His argument is backed up by a critical account of the work of Robert Walser and Susan McClary, John Shepherd and Richard Middleton. Whereas these scholars acknowledge the central social dimension in the study of popular music, Covach argues—in an interesting and quasi-reactionary fashion—that the understanding of popular music as embedded in society or as a social text 'is not the principal manner in which its practitioners have tended to understand most popular music'. He goes on to argue for the study of popular music not only as a social text, but additionally as an autonomous cultural artefact:

I find that many of the claims made in popular-music scholarship, interesting and reveal-ing though they sometimes are, never really capture the popular-music experience as I understand it. In short, I distrust the popular-music scholars' claims that this music is meaningful in ways that are principally socially constructed.

In developing the argument this way, Covach is coming close to an ongoing dis-trust of the *soi-disant* New Musicology found throughout *Rethinking Music*.

Ellen Koskoff (Chapter 24) asks about what happens when we try to translate some of these concerns into the practicalities of teaching programmes. Taking two very different case-studies, she reaches the conclusion that 'although it may matter a great deal what musics we as individuals or social groups love, give meaning to, and value, ultimately it will not really matter what musics we teach'. On the way, she makes a range of observations that echo those of Locke and Everist on the question of canon, society, and the academy. She agrees with Locke on the power of canonic works in society, and implicitly with Everist on the power of the academy as an agent of canon formation.

# Part I

# 1

## *Ontologies of Music*

### Philip V. Bohlman

#### I. Rethinking 'Thinking Music'

Music may be what we think it is; it may not be. Music may be feeling or sensuality, but it may also have nothing to do with emotion or physical sensation. Music may be that to which some dance or pray or make love; but it's not necessarily the case. In some cultures there are complex categories for thinking about music; in others there seems to be no need whatsoever to contemplate music. What music is remains open to question at all times and in all places. This being the case, any metaphysics of music must perforce cordon off the rest of the world from a privileged time and place, a time and place thought to be one's own. Thinking—or even rethinking—music, it follows, is at base an attempt to claim and control music as one's own.

The title of this book, *Rethinking Music*, suggests from the outset that the disciplines of Western musical study make certain ontological assumptions about the nature of music, even as they interpellate its position as an object of study. 'Thinking' and 'music' are coupled naturally, as if they were just 'out there'; indeed, their ontological juxtaposition enjoys a special status in a project that would dislodge the disciplines of music from methods that have dominated Western intellectual history during the past two centuries. Music, however, may be something other than an object about which one thinks or can think; it may be a practice extrinsic to musical thought. In this essay I examine the ways in which some ontologies of music are constructed and articulated. The plural in my title does not refer to 'ontologies of music' around the world, the ways we think about music and the ways others think about music. Instead, I maintain that multiple ontologies of music exist at both the individual and local level, as well as at the global level. My recognition of plural ontologies, therefore, maps both individual musical experiences and the landscapes of world music cultures and world-music culture.

There are conceptual difficulties with which I must reckon from the beginning. Ideally, I should endeavour to represent non-Western ontologies of music; I should draw on 'other' metaphysics no more nor less than my own. I can't. I'm confronted with a dilemma I can't resolve; nor do I want to suggest that modern ethnomusicology has come up with—or could come up with—a strategy that would empower me to resolve such a dilemma. This dilemma could not be more evident than in the fact that I take it upon myself to write about ontologies of music other than my own. Rarely does anyone care about ontologies of music other than one's own, much less write about them. I've responded to the dilemma by capitulating to it, by writing this essay at all.

My purpose, nevertheless, is not to establish a theoretical framework that would allow the reader to step into and analyse ontologies of music other than his or her own. Instead, I urge the reader to seize upon the plural and apply it to him- or herself; that is, to perceive in this essay metaphysical routes that connect self to others, but that ultimately lead back to self. Along these routes each individual encounters multifarious musics with complex metaphysical meanings, which contribute in turn to individually constructed ontologies. I attempt to represent some of these routes here. Neither this essay nor any other could represent all such routes, but it is nevertheless my intent to be as representative as possible, thereby allowing several possible metaphysical maps to reveal themselves. My choice of a cartographic metaphor, I should point out, is neither arbitrary nor rhetorical; for I hold the position, together with many modern geographers, that maps represent only the illusion of political realities, which are instead constantly being enacted and undermined through human experience. Ontologies of music possess a similar quality of enactment through experience, the attempts to pin down a hard and fast reality that constantly eludes one like the mirage to which one for ever draws closer.

Before turning to the heart of the essay, in which I examine some of the metaphysical routes along which ontologies of music reveal themselves, I should like to identify the most important conditions characteristic of music's ontologies, at least in so far as I have considered these as a Western ethnomusicologist. While I should not claim these conditions to be universal, they are intentionally inclusive. I could not know if I had achieved universality, but I can at least endeavour to be inclusive.

The metaphysical condition of music with which we in the West are most familiar is that music is an *object*. As an object, music is bounded, and names can be applied to it that affirm its objective status. As an object, moreover, music can assume specific forms, which may be inscribed on paper or magnetic tape, and language systems can assign names to music and its objective properties. By contrast, music exists in the conditions of a *process*. Because a process is always in flux, it never achieves a fully objective status; it is always becoming something else. As a process, music is unbounded and open. Whereas names may be assigned to it, they are necessarily incomplete.

The metaphysical conditions to which I have referred as objects and processes dominate Western ontologies of music, although they are found in musical thought throughout the world and at different historical moments. To these common conditions I should like to introduce two more, thereby intentionally blurring any tendency to bracket the West from the rest of the world. The first of these I shall call 'embeddedness', whereby I mean to suggest that music joins other activities, and, indeed, is inseparable from them. In many cases, embeddedness means that music has no name assigned to it; in other cases, we abstract certain of its attributes (e.g. 'melody' or 'rhythm') and assign names to them. Embeddedness may be systemic, as when we speak of language as musical or of myth as conveyed by music, or it may be arbitrary, as when ambient sounds are reimagined as musical sounds. The second of these additional ontological conditions I shall call 'adumbration'. Under such conditions, music itself is not present, but its effects or the recognition of its presence elsewhere are; it is recognized because of the shadow it has cast. Adumbration comes into play as a metaphysical condition especially when a culture's (often a religion's) ontology of music needs to negate the presence of music, or at least a certain kind of music, as when Islamic thought claims that recitation of the Koran is not music. Adumbration functions frequently as a border-crossing mechanism, allowing one to conceptualize the music of the other through shadows evident in one's own.

That these ontological conditions are not exclusive goes without saying. Music may be embedded as an object or as a process; adumbration, similarly, may be recognizable through the objects it leaves or the processes it unleashes. It is, moreover, the interaction between and among these conditions that makes their metaphysical routes so complex and so difficult to chart. Perhaps these are the reasons why envisioning and mapping music's ontologies are so vital to rethinking music, for the interactiveness of the ontological domains that I examine in this essay results from human experience and everyday practice. The ontologies that I consider here, then, are not those of philosophers, aestheticians, or musicologists, but rather those of individual practitioners of music. Music's ontologies are not, it follows, separable from the practice of music. Quite the contrary, they can be instantiated only through musical practices, for they do not result from abstract categories, that some individuals think about, but others do not. The sections that follow begin to map some of the routes along which the everyday experiences of music yield the ontologies of music.

## II

*My Music / Your Music.* There are many reasons to want music to be one's own. Music assumes many different ontologies when it becomes one's own. 'My music' may be the music one has grown up with; it may be the music that accompanied one through a difficult or especially joyous time; it may be the music one knows best, about which one exhibits a special knowledge or exercises a special control. 'My music' might also belong to one because it contrasts with someone else's, with 'your music'; it might have special meanings, which others don't perceive; it might provide a tool of resistance, a set of actions that one protects against those who don't possess the same music. Claiming a music as one's own recognizes music as an object. The object, music, is bounded and named by selfness, if indeed by nothing else. Music that is truly 'my music' could not, by definition, be a process, for then it might become someone else's. Although 'my music' may be embedded in other activities—dance for teenagers, gospel hymns in the Protestant American South—it is ontologically separable from those activities—inscribed on records, anthologized in hymnals. To become 'my music', it must assume a form one can own.

As an attribute of identity, 'my music' may result from the production or reproduction of music. It is in the composer's self-interest to insist on the identity of his or her music, for it loses all commodity value when it becomes someone else's music. When Native Americans of the North American High Plains (e.g. Flathead Indians) receive songs in dreams, they also acquire personal ownership of the songs, albeit without commodity value, for one individual's songs may, in fact, 'sound' like those of another.[1] It is the experience of dreaming the song, not the song itself, that distinguishes it as belonging to an individual. It may be the case that performances produce personal ownership; scholars collect folk-songs as if they belong to an individual singer, even though many, if not most, of an individual's repertory circulate in a larger community.[2] Ownership of music can be transferred, but this often relies on other ontological concepts. Wagner's *Ring* becomes the San Francisco Opera's *Ring* through specific forms of performance and the acquisition of rights from other owners, say publishers or the Wagner heirs.

'My music' does not assume the form of a single class of objects. What may be 'my music' for one generational group or one socio-economic class or ethnic group may not be comparable to 'my music' in other groups.[3] Wagner's *Ring* belongs to a class of objects different from the San Francisco Opera's. 'My music', furthermore, fails to lend itself to cross-cultural comparison. Ultimately, the ontology of 'my music' is personal, deriving from conditions that have individual meanings and are unlike the conditions for 'your music'. Accordingly, 'my music' cannot be 'your music'. To make it so would devalue it, negating the reasons for possessing it as 'my music'.

*Our Music / Their Music.* Music exhibits a powerful capacity to contribute to social and communal cohesiveness. It contributes to the building of community, but even more powerfully, it articulates the bulwark that distinguishes one commu-

---

[1] See Alan P. Merriam, *Ethnomusicology of the Flathead Indians* (Chicago, 1967) and Bruno Nettl, *Blackfoot Musical Thought: Comparative Perspectives* (Kent, Oh., 1989).

[2] See Roger D. Abrahams (ed.), *A Singer and Her Songs* (Baton Rouge, La., 1970).

[3] See e.g. Susan D. Crafts, Daniel Cavicchi, Charles Keil, and the Music in Daily Life Project, *My Music* (Hanover and London, 1993).

nity from another. Unlike 'my music', however, 'our music' most often functions as a process—indeed, as many processes that embed music within the social fabric. 'Our music' is not so much owned as shared, and it therefore makes sense that most concepts of 'our music' (e.g. folk-music, traditional music, or national music) stress its reproducibility. 'Our music' conveys history, for example, through what Phillips Barry called 'communal re-creation'.[4] 'Our music' derives its social power from its ability to instantiate community, polity, and history. Nowhere has this been more evident than in the modern West, where the ultimate ontology of 'our music' has been national music, which has grounded aesthetic theory and justified racism alike.

'Our music' comes into existence within the group; the boundedness of the music accords with the boundedness of the group itself, and 'our music' even becomes a means of communication for knowing and familiarity within the group itself.[5] The resulting form of musical knowledge tends toward growing specialization, thereby acquiring exchange value *vis-à-vis* 'their music'. Such exchange value is heightened, moreover, precisely because it cannot in fact be exchanged, and therefore the group will attempt to intensify its specialization in order to increase the worth of 'our music'. Members of the drum-making caste of Hindu South India, who have the name *pariah*s in the Tamil language, concern themselves primarily with reproduction of the material culture of time in Carnatic music, thereby using musical knowledge as a means of subverting the hierarchy of caste. Unable to produce the high-caste aspects of music (e.g. to play the *vīṇā* publicly), the *pariah* draws himself ever closer to the musical speciality that literally defines the group.

Because 'our music' increasingly depends on processes that embed music in culture when social organization expands beyond the group, it becomes virtually impossible to define what 'our music' is—that is, what repertories or even pieces it embraces. Group knowledge gives way to political or national ideology. When, for example, Johann Gottfried Herder, Richard Wagner, Theodor W. Adorno, and countless others wrote tracts on 'German music', their motivation resulted from the lack of assurance as to what that really was.[6] What it wasn't, of course, was 'their music'—that is, French, Italian, or Jewish music. For music to be German, boundaries should not be transgressed. In contrast, for music to be Suyá—in other words, to constitute the song practices of the Suyá people of the Brazilian Amazon—boundaries must be transgressed, for Suyá music comes into existence when the Suyá gather songs and other commodities in skirmishes with other Amazonian peoples.[7] Other Native North and South American peoples also assemble 'our music' to distinguish it from 'theirs', using practices

---

[4] Phillips Barry, 'Communal Re-Creation', *Bulletin of the Folk-Song Society of the Northeast*, 5 (1933), 4–6.

[5] See Ernst Klusen, *Volkslied: Fund und Erfindung* (Cologne, 1969).

[6] See e.g. Johann Gottfried Herder *et al.*, *Von deutscher Art und Kunst: einige fliegende Blätter* (Hamburg, 1773).

[7] Anthony Seeger, 'When Music Makes History', in Stephen Blum, Philip V. Bohlman, and Daniel M. Neuman (eds.), *Ethnomusicology and Modern Music History* (Urbana, Ill., 1991), 23–34.

of borrowing and *bricolage* not so vastly different from those of Jesuit missionaries in the so-called age of discovery or hip-hop DJs in Los Angeles and London, or more recently in Bombay and Jakarta. The interaction between 'our music' and 'theirs' depends on the very reproducibility of music's ontologies themselves.

*Music 'Out There' / Music in the Numbers.* Is there music 'out there'? Are there works of music waiting to be discovered? Does music exist anyway, with or without the intervention of human actions to bring about its reification? These are the ontological questions that Platonism presumes to answer; they are also questions that are fundamental to many mythologies. The assumption that music exists prior to being found by composers, performers, or even mathematicians is surprisingly widespread, both culturally and historically. On the one hand, the assumption often lays claim to scientistic explanations for music; on the other, it is often the clearest evidence that explanations for creation have simply been suspended for lack of any way to prove them.

Platonist theories of music's ontologies generally take one of two forms in the West, which in turn derive their distinction from the contrasting ways in which the act of creating or composing music takes place. The first form concerns itself primarily with the materials of music, hence the acts performed upon these by a composer or agent of creation; a *guslar*, or epic singer, in the Balkans, for example, acts on musical formulas in order to combine them into an epic.[8] The second form seeks to explain the existence of musical works—in other words, pieces that obtain and retain their own identity. In Western art-music, notation has become the primary means of retaining an identity—framing it, that is, in a score, which then becomes 'the work'.[9] Western Platonism is not the only source for these two forms asserting that music is 'out there'. Some Eskimo peoples of north-western North America also claim that the universe consists of a finite number of songs, which individuals receive and perform, but eventually release back into the finite repertory bounded by the universe. The identity of the composer is more important in South Indian classical music, even though a given vocal composition, a *kriti*, consists essentially of two related phrases, the *asthāyī* and *antarā*, which are continually performed into works only through the processes of improvisation.

The search for music 'out there' also relies on certain scientific methods, especially mathematics and physics. Neoplatonist concepts of music make claims for a mathematical and physical order that music ultimately articulates when it comes into existence—say, the naturalness of intervals built from lower ratios between pitch differences in a simplified overtone series. The identity of a musical work, it follows, may be increasingly embedded in itself, if, for example, metric patterns and melodic structures reduce to the same mathematical relations.

[8] Albert B. Lord, *The Singer of Tales* (Cambridge, Mass., 1960).
[9] Lydia Goehr, *The Imaginary Museum of Musical Works: An Essay in the Philosophy of Music* (Oxford, 1992).

Music that is 'out there' ends up turned outside-in, the conditions of the universe such as *harmonia* residing in the work.[10]

Accordingly, the finite processes of a universal musical metaphysics may gradually become the processes of history and culture specificity, a case argued for the relation between dissonance and consonance as a Neoplatonist teleology in the West, beginning with the hierarchical relation between the fifth and the octave in the twelfth century and resolving with Schoenberg's emancipation of dissonance in the twentieth.[11] The structures of numbers also inform the political economy of music, the patterns of exchange that form different social forces within musical life and embed music in history in different ways.[12] Music, it follows, links mathematical structures and processes to history, structuring it as a set of procedures performed by those making music. The lack of teleology in myth—for example, the cyclicity in the *Rāmāyaṇa* and *Mahabhārata* texts in Javanese *wayang* (musical drama)—situates the structures of temporal repetitiveness in Javanese music, embedding the harmonic wholeness of the gamelan and its instruments in the interlocking patterns of a music that is an icon for time itself.[13] What's 'out there' ontologically achieves the status of being 'in there'.

*Music in Nature / The Naturalness in Music.* The embeddedness of music in nature is conceptualized as ontologies in vastly different ways. A connectedness between music and nature, none the less, is present in some form in most cultures. At one extreme of a continuum we might construct is the belief that music exists in nature, and that one simply bounds natural phenomena by naming them. At the other extreme music strives toward nature—that is, to emulate nature. I characterize these two extremes by the rubrics 'music in nature' and 'naturalness in music'.

Music's embeddedness in nature often generates a rhetoric of metaphors, and its ontologies come to depend on these. These metaphors may serve to classify by means of a system of representation: for example, when bird-song is perceived as naturally melodic, and then is represented by a singer or composer as a melody itself, say among the Kaluli of Papua New Guinea[14] or by Olivier Messiaen in his *Catalogue d'oiseaux*. Ideally, one might argue, there is no real boundary between nature and its musical representation. The Inuit of circumpolar Canada and Greenland engage in vocal games called *kattajjait*, in which two vocalists, their mouths only centimetres apart, alternately sing patterns that represent geese or other birds into the mouths of their partners. The space between their mouths

---

[10] Cf. David Lewin, *Generalized Music Intervals and Transformations* (New Haven, 1987).

[11] Carl Dahlhaus and Hans Heinrich Eggebrecht, *Was ist Musik?* (Wilhelmshaven, 1987), 43–54.

[12] See Jacques Attali, *Noise: The Political Economy of Music*, trans. Brian Massumi (Minneapolis, 1985).

[13] Judith Becker and Alton Becker, 'A Grammar of the Musical Genre *Srepegan*', *Journal of Music Theory*, 23/1 (1979), 1–43.

[14] See Steven Feld, *Sound and Sentiment: Birds, Weeping, Poetics, and Song in Kaluli Expression*, 2nd edn. (Philadelphia, 1990).

quite literally forms the boundary that dissolves as one vocal chamber shapes the sound produced by another's vocal chords. Music 'sounds like' nature in this ludic representation of nature.

When music strives toward nature, by contrast, there is an implicit admission of this boundary, which the procedures of composition and performance can negate. Such procedures may not, on the other hand, be rallied to overcome, but rather to stylize, the representation itself. In Lévi-Straussian structuralist terms the naturalness in music, originally raw, becomes 'cooked', for its substance is altered to situate it in human society.[15] Accordingly, highly representative musical vocabularies emerge, in which musical parts synecdochically stand in for the whole. Among the Wagogo in south-eastern Africa, for example, communal performance of music may represent entire natural soundscapes, musically produced society thereby sonically supplanting the natural world. When music is too far removed from nature in most societies, a sort of ontological fear sets in, a fear that one is no longer really experiencing music.

*Music as Science.* 'Musica est scientia bene modulandi', according to St Augustine. Pronouncements about music's capacity to be a science—to provide a way of knowing—are often the earliest traces of music's ontologies. They usually pre-date notational systems, though they often provide grounds for using notation to corroborate scientific evidence. If we take 'science' to mean a 'way of knowing', music's scientific potential seems to be a pre-condition rather than a result of systematic cognitive procedures. What is important is that music is a vehicle to help us know. What music helps us know differs dramatically according to the operations in which it is embedded.

When music first appears as a component of scientific operations, its embeddedness is remarkably complex. *Saṅgīta* in early Sanskrit theoretical writings (between *c.*500 and *c.*1000 CE) both identifies other aesthetic practices and embodies a systematic division of itself.[16] The more that extensively scientific operations are performed on music, the more a self-identity (*Musik an sich*, music in and of itself) emerges; yet, paradoxically, that self-identity has increasingly less to do with practice. In the Islamic Middle Ages, scientific writings on music often had very little to do with musical practice, even though some theoretical areas (e.g. rhythmic and metric theory) were initially grounded in practices such as speech and poetic patterns. The ontological wedge between scientific theory and practice, however, does not expand endlessly. Quite the contrary, there is a tension between science and practice, which makes it necessary to employ one as a source for the other. Modern Arabic musical practices still bear a resemblance to modal theory in the eleventh century CE. Contemporary practice, therefore, has not abandoned science as a way of knowing music.

---

[15] Claude Lévi-Strauss, *The Raw and the Cooked: Introduction to a Science of Mythology: I,* trans. John Weightman and Doreen Weightman (New York, 1969).

[16] Lewis Rowell, *Music and Musical Thought in Early India* (Chicago, 1993), 10.

*Music as Language / Music Embedded in Language.* Speaking about music is extra-ordinarily difficult; yet music is interwoven with few human activities as insep-arably as language. That the boundaries between music and language are flexible, permeable, and blurred is evident in the rather widespread identification of speech/song as a proto-musical ontology. Religions that wish to distance themselves from music as a distinct (and distracting) practice do so by insisting that textual and ritual performances employ something akin to song. In secular domains non-musical music that uses words is poesy—again, a larger category that embodies smaller categories which cannot be separated from each other. In everyday practices, too, the boundaries between speech and music broaden to include heightened speech and ritualized metalanguages, which rely on music to make language more than it is.

For eighteenth-century European linguistic philosophers such as Herder, poesy possessed an ontological status of its own, which in turn meant that song enjoyed a privileged aesthetic presence in communication and expression.[17] Since the eighteenth century, Western writers on music have relied on the models of a musical poetics that does not properly recognize music as a descrip-tive tool when attempting to relativize forms of vocal expression in which music and words do not parse easily into bounded categories.

The metaphysical conundrums that result from the inability to unravel the dis-tinctions between music and language are legion. Whereas most observers hold that music communicates, thereby functioning like a language, few agree on how or what music communicates, thereby according it non-linguistic proper-ties. Some individuals 'know what music communicates for them', while others assert that musical languages are so indefinite that they can be made to com-municate anything to anybody. Does music have special semiotic qualities? Or is it precisely because music lends itself to semiotic interpretation that it functions like other humanly constructed systems of signs?[18] The difference between a musical ontology that holds that music communicates nothing and one that holds that it can communicate anything is not great, if indeed there is a difference.

*Die Musik / Musics.* Why should music acquire the hegemonic universality that the German term *die Musik* ('the music') ascribes to it? Why should it possess the relativistic presence that the ethnomusicological term 'musics' accords it? Nom-inalist strategies are extraordinarily important in the politics that music's ontolo-gies often embody.[19] On the one hand, in the German language it is possible to address an abstract ontology only with a definite article, and it is a measure of

---

[17] See e.g. Jean-Jacques Rousseau and Johann Gottfried Herder, *On the Origin of Language*, trans. John H. Moran and Alexander Gode (Chicago, 1966).

[18] Cf. Jean-Jacques Nattiez, *Music and Discourse: Toward a Semiology of Music*, trans. Carolyn Abbate (Princeton, 1990).

[19] For a broader application of nominalist strategies see Nelson Goodman, *Languages of Art: An Approach to a Theory of Symbols* (Indianapolis, 1976).

their abstraction that these concepts have no plural; 'music' alone does not exist, and 'musics' makes no sense. On the other hand, blaming grammar is rather unsatisfying, for few—particularly, few non-Germans—would doubt that *die Musik* derives its contextual referentiality from German history and the hegemonic imagination necessary for the generation of nineteenth-century Romanticism. 'The music' belongs to a privileged group with a specific educational and economic status, no less than art-music practices in South India belong to high-caste Brahmins or élite practices in China belong to an intelligentsia deriving power from Confucian social theories. Circumscribing the ontology of music in the singular not only sells encyclopedias (*Die Musik in Geschichte und Gegenwart*); it provides a basis for imperial power and intellectual control.

The politics of empire are no less evident on a musical map with many musics. If every 'music culture' has 'a music' (indefinite rather than definite article), then the world can be parsed by scholars who figure out one music after another. By recognizing musics, the scholar erects a scaffold for the entire music culture: it's not just that Sri Lanka has 'a music'; it has 'classical musics', 'popular musics', 'folk-musics', 'religious musics', and—quite literally, the unchecked proliferation of plurals goes on. Ironically, the definite-article and indefinite-article metaphysics of music go hand in hand. The UNESCO-sponsored 'Universe of Music' project depended on authors in individual music cultures writing about their own music histories. *Die Musik* occupied a privileged position among all other musics. Were it not, it would be impossible in the 1990s to speak of 'world music' as if it were an ontology of music.

The nomenclature that distinguishes between 'the music' and 'musics' results from an extreme case of understanding music as an object. Naming, in fact, makes it an object, bounding it semantically just as one places it on the musical landscape politically or organizes record stores according to 'music' and 'musics'. Whereas this nomenclature distinguishes between univeral and local phenomena, and between absolute and relative practices, it also provides a place for them in a single linguistic system. *Die Musik*, therefore, objectifies music, bounding it with language because one cannot do so with individual practice or imagination. Similarly, it comforts us to know that Fiji has a music and that *fújì* in Nigeria is a music, not least because these musics are not that easily accessible. Ontologically, these acts of naming and the articles on which they depend make a vast connectedness possible. Indeed, the individual is potentially connected to any and all musical phenomena, simply by following the road signs that lead from the music immediately accessible to the universe of all music(s).

*The Voice of God / The Struggle of the Everyday.* In Ibn Isḥāq's *Life of Muhammad* we encounter one of the most profound and eloquent ontological revelations of God's voice through recitation and musical practices:

[One day] in the month of Ramaḍān in which God willed concerning him what He willed of His grace, the apostle set forth to Ḥirā' as was his wont, and his family with him. When it was the night on which God honoured him with his mission and showed mercy on His servants thereby, Gabriel brought him the command of God. 'He came to me', said the apostle of God, 'while I was asleep, with a coverlet of brocade whereon was some writing, and said, "Read!" I said, "What shall I read?" He pressed me with it so tightly that I thought it was death; then he let me go and said "Read!" I said, "What then shall I read?" He pressed me with it the third time so that I thought it was death and said "Read!" I said, "What then shall I read?"—and this I said only to deliver myself from him lest he should do the same to me again. He said:

> "Read in the name of thy Lord who created,
> Who created man of blood coagulated.
> Read! Thy Lord is most beneficent,
> Who taught by the pen,
> Taught that which they knew not unto men."

(Koran, Surah 96: 1–5)

So I read it, and he departed from me. And I awoke from my sleep, and it was as though these words were written on my heart.'[20]

The revelation of God's voice is direct, mediated only by the vessel of the body that receives and then recites that voice as received. The concept of the human as vessel for the voice of God provides a common ontological moment—indeed, a remarkable metaphysical coupling of God and humans through voice and music. Although divine ontologies separate product and process from each other—the voice of God is an unalterable product, the revelation and recitation as processes assure its unalterability—they nevertheless conceptualize a dependence of one on the other. This dependence, in turn, is realized through a trajectory that begins with God and culminates in the recitation of a voice—in the case of Islam, the recitation (*qirā'ah*) of the words reified as a text always already in performance, the Koran. The sacred becomes the everyday through musical performance.

Ontologies that begin with the everyday generate different trajectories of musical performance, which aspire, so to speak, toward the sacred. Music uplifts the everyday, modulating the voice of quotidian practice into sacred practice. On a daily basis, ritual achieves this function of transforming human voice into the divine. In sacred practices such as pilgrimage, the transformation of the everyday into the sacred is far more extensive; it relies on a virtually complete transformation of the voices of a community of pilgrims into a sacred chorus that moves steadily toward God, metaphorically and literally. The ontological moment for pilgrims, too, is direct and dependent on the vessel of the body, for it occurs when the pilgrims reach the sacred centre, which is a portal

[20] Ibn Isḥāq Muhammad, *Life of Muhammad: A Translation of Isḥāq's Sīrat Rasūl Allāh*, ed. Ibn Hishām (Karachi, 1955), 105–6.

to the sacred that has transcended the everyday. Through the act of pilgrimage and the ritual that reifies the sacred centre of a pilgrimage site, there is an intersection of the divine and everyday trajectories of musical voice, the sacred and the profane.

*In the Notes / Outside the Notes.* Musical notation serves as a recognition that music cannot adequately be notated. Something disappears or changes during the course of oral tradition and performance, and the sounds that notes represent recuperate as much of that sound as possible. The fear of loss drives the technologies of notation. The notes, then, are not music; rather, they are the traces of many performances. These traces may be sounds, as is most often the case in common-practice Western notation; or they may guide the musician to produce sounds, as is most often the case in East Asian plucked-zither notation. Music comes into existence through following the orders embedded in these traces. Because different musicians follow such orders in different ways—because they understand music beyond the notes to be different—music emerges in different ways from its notated traces. Its identity assumes varied forms, whose controversial ontologies lie in the hands of those performing that identity into existence.

The problem of identity that arises from the use of notation further leads to a concern with the possibility that music assumes the form of 'works'.[21] Notational traces not only provide the essence of an identity; they make it possible for that identity, however sketchy, to persist through time and through the acts of many performers. A South Indian *kriti* from the early nineteenth century possesses identity as a work because of a melodic skeleton, the formal-generic constraints of a *kriti* itself (three parts, with structural and improvisational moments built into them), and the historical tradition of melody in Carnatic music. Although performances vary vastly, the conditions for the *kriti*'s identity as a work of music are understood by many.

A different problem of identity emerges when notational traces convey the 'concept' of a musical work. An individual blues piece, for example, exists not as a work so much as a concept. The notational limitations of the blues are merely abstractions; they exist to be superseded during performance. The three-line strophe (AAB) of twelve bars, with its harmonic movement between tonic, subdominant, and dominant, does not specify identity; transcription of a melody is merely a historicizing gesture, which locates one moment of performance in the past. The nomenclature 'Muleskinner Blues' tells us little about the identity of a blues piece. Still, notating many performances of 'Muleskinner Blues', in Mississippi Delta style or in country-western or bluegrass versions, thickly describes the concept of such a piece. With the notes, the nature of the identity beyond the notes becomes ontologically recognizable.

[21] Cf. Roman Ingarden, *The Work of Music and the Problem of Its Identity*, trans. Adam Czeniawski, ed. Jean G. Harrell (Berkeley and Los Angeles, 1986), and Goehr, *Imaginary Museum.*

*In Time / Outside Time.* Music takes place in time. As an aesthetic domain, music is distinctive because of its special relation to time. Music's temporal ontology, it follows, comes to define time through sonic calibration and the physical performance of music. The axioms about music and time are so commonplace that there would appear to be no need to challenge them or even to modify their straightforward logic. And that is not what I intend to do in this section. Still, if there is a commonsensical nature to adages about music and time, it belies a deeper uneasiness about the difficulty of finding representational languages to describe time, hence its presence in determining music's ontologies.

Even the most basic assumption about music, stated in my opening sentence in this section, may not be ontologically valid all the time. Let us take Japanese music as an example; such music does not necessarily take place in time. In Japanese music the notion of emptiness, known as *ma*, is extremely important. *Ma* is silence between sound, a silence, however, whose ontology is not determined by sounds that frame it. Unlike the silence of a rest in Western music, *ma* does not begin when the sound preceding it ends, and it does not cease when sound begins again. *Ma* is perceived and pondered on its own; it defines itself by its own emptiness, its ontology of existing outside time.[22]

Problematizing the temporal metaphysics of music is our uncertain notion of time itself. Even those concepts of time closest to us have the capacity at once to regulate time and undermine it. Modernity, with its insistence on production according to clockwork and its metaphors of human life as distinct periods of regulated production, nevertheless spawns metaphors of time in which many events can happen at the same time in an unregulated temporal cacophony. These translate into the aesthetic genres of modernity—for example, into the novel, in which events happen out of sequence and outside time. Music, too, juxtaposes and scrambles moments of time, in the stretto of a fugue or the sampling and mixing of hip-hop. These acts upon music distort time, and rip it apart, as if its metaphysics were not so teleologically commonsensical. The interlocking cycles of Javanese music also layer time unit upon time unit, creating not a single representation of music in time but a web of voices moving into and out of time.

Music may be ontologically dependent on time, but time is ontologically dependent on music. Music provides an important vehicle for recalling and redeeming time, hence its interpolation of memory. Not only does music help us remember (e.g. the words of a religious text or a popular song), but performance of music often serves as a fundamental act of remembering. The act of remembering in the rituals of Sufism, called *zikr* ('memory'), spiritually and physically moves the believer closer to God through the repetition of the name Allah, as

---

[22] See William P. Malm, *Six Hidden Views of Japanese Music* (Berkeley, 1986); cf. John Cage, *Silence: Lectures and Writings* (Middletown, Conn., 1961).

well as the most basic epithets that themselves recall the essence of Allah.[23] Memory is fundamental to the connections through time to the past that Australian Aborigines imagine into the ontology of music, which in turn instantiate the memory of the ancestral past through time-lines. In the time-lines of Aborigines the past becomes the present; or, more precisely, myth crosses from a timeless state to a condition bounded by song. More than any other aesthetic-spiritual practice, music passes between myth and history, between the worlds before time and the worlds of historical time. It is hardly surprising, then, that song inevitably negotiates between the worlds of myth and history, whether in the Homeric epics[24] or the Hindu epics whose narratives unfold in the performance of South Asian classical music or in Javanese *wayang*. The ontological presence of music in time and outside time makes it possible to remember the past and imagine the future, to cross the boundaries between narratives experienced and those transposed on to other beings, and to embed music in cognitive and spiritual processes of knowing experiences and worlds other than one's own.

*Vom musikalischen Schönen / On the Unremarkable in Music.* Music is not beautiful in many cultures; there's no reason why it should be. Beauty as a condition of music is a construct of modernity, a quality of the exchange value that accrued to it when technologies in the West made it possible to reproduce music as a commodity, a product in which the object, 'beauty', could lodge. As a quality of Western aesthetics, beauty persistently makes an appearance in writings of the eighteenth century.[25] By the end of the nineteenth century, not least because of the intervention of Romanticism, beauty's objectified status had come to permeate aesthetic thought so pervasively that composers were forced to succumb to it or openly to reject it. In the twentieth century beauty has proliferated as a component of modernity, extending beyond the West and asserting its presence in the reproductive technologies of cassette culture[26] or export industries that globalize world musics. For Indian classical music and Javanese gamelan repertories to achieve popularity as music in the West and to gain a position in the exchange of goods between Western economies and Indian or Indonesian export systems, it has been necessary to replace function with beauty. We have turned to world music in no short measure because we are able to imagine that it contains beauty.

In those cultures in which there is no need for beauty, there is also no open exchange of musical products as commodities. Music exists in unremarkable ways, functioning through processes only to be instantiated in the cultural con-

---

[23] Gilbert Rouget, *Music and Trance: A Theory of the Relations between Music and Possession*, trans. Brunhilde Biebuyck (Chicago, 1985).

[24] Lord, *Singer of Tales*.

[25] See Dahlhaus and Eggebrecht, *Was ist Musik?*, 174–86.

[26] Peter Manuel, *Cassette Culture: Popular Music and Technology in North India* (Chicago, 1993).

texts of music.[27] The widespread unremarkability of music results directly from the ontological condition of embeddedness: music is so much part of other social practices that there is no need to separate it from them or to attribute special qualities to it. Among the Hausa of Nigeria, music is so embedded in other cultural activities that there is no need to name it at all, despite the fact that the activities it accompanies have themselves hundreds of different names.[28] In its Javanese cultural contexts music of the gamelan also has an unremarkable existence—indeed, so unremarkable that there is no historical tradition of auditors removing themselves from other activities in order to listen to music attentively.[29] Javanese music is efficacious when it properly accompanies narrative, drama, or the ritual and social practices of court and village. The more extensively a group, community, or society participates in musical performance, the more beauty might serve to encumber its practices and presence.

*Authentic Sound / Recorded Sound.* How does music, as sonic phenomenon and social production, relate to the site of its production? Is that relation confused when the site of production becomes a site of mechanical reproduction? Is a recording music? The technologies that reproduce sound radically confuse the ontologies of music; indeed, few ontologies of music, whether in the modern West or in traditional music cultures, are secure enough to withstand all the metaphysical challenges that recording sets in motion. When late nineteenth-century ethnological expeditions armed with wax-cylinder recording equipment spread across the American West to capture the music of Native Americans before it (and they) disappeared, they reproduced sounds on the cylinders to which the original singers could relate only in alienated ways, imagining even that performers of some kind occupied the space of the stylus itself. Western musicians in the early twentieth century struggled with the identity of music on a recording. Arnold Schoenberg was among those who believed the recording to be an instrument of musical production, not just of reproduction, and composers of futurist music and *musique concrète* alike sought to diminish the distance between sound and music, productive and reproductive ontologies. The local use of technologies of inexpensive recording production and distribution, called 'cassette culture' by Peter Manuel in his study of North Indian music in the final decades of the twentieth century,[30] transforms each owner of a cassette machine into a new type of musician, who may 'play' the music originally performed by others in personal contexts that give it entirely new meaning. Cassette music played in the home or in the intimate circle of family and friends may, therefore, bring the cinema or the temple into the home, recontextualizing ritual according to the technological limits of the cassette itself.

[27] Philip V. Bohlman, 'On the Unremarkable in Music', *19th-Century Music*, 16/2 (1992), 203–16.

[28] David W. Ames and Anthony V. King, *Glossary of Hausa Music and Its Social Contexts* (Evanston, Ill., 1971).

[29] Cf. Sumarsam, *Gamelan: Cultural Interaction and Musical Development in Central Java* (Chicago, 1995).

[30] Manuel, *Cassette Culture*.

Mechanical technologies change the functions and contexts of music, both multiplying the metaphysical notions of what music is and privileging certain forms of musical production over others. Authentic sound is only conceptually possible when technology creates the possibility that something other than an original source of music comes into existence. It is only with technology, moreover, that one can retrieve the original conditions of authenticity. The ethnomusicologist can bring authentic music from the field and play it on a recording in the classroom, but can do so only by implicitly making an ontological claim that objectifies music. Similarly, performers of so-called early music who play on period instruments make ontological claims about the machines that make their instruments, which reproduce an idealized level of imagined sound. Authenticity insists that music can exist as a product of the site of production and reproduction, that the instruments on which music is performed are technologically instantiated in order to become the primary site of music itself. In so doing, the technologies of musical production and reproduction become conflated, blurring into one form, which nevertheless can exist only at a considerable metaphysical distance from the musician—that is, the human body as a site of musical production and an embodiment of music's ontologies.

*In the Body / Beyond the Body*. Fear often attends the removal of music from the body as a site of its production and performance. When recordings reproduce sound, it no longer belongs to the self; its ownership has been transferred with its sound. Control of music, too, loosens when the mechanics of performance take over. It is hardly surprising, then, that many musicians refuse to allow recordings for fear that their souls will be recorded together with the music they perform. It is no less surprising that musical ontologies that concern themselves with the effects of music on the body transfer its performance to sites of 'otherness'. When musical performance became theologically suspect in the history of Islam, for example, this otherness took the form of instrumental music, referred to by the loan words *mūsīqā* and *mūsīqi*, or of other musicians, the *dhimmīs*— that is, protected minorities such as Jews and Christians. 'Hearing' and 'listening' (*samāʿ*) were physically separated from playing and performing, thereby resolving the tension, at least in part, that results from the body's ontological presence in music.

The body creates all sorts of dilemmas in music's ontologies. On one hand, the body is indispensable to ontologies of difference.[31] People with one body type, racially or ethnically determined, make one kind of music; those with another type make another type of music. The fourteenth-century North African polymath, Ibn Khaldūn, coded bodily responses to nature, in order to explain why

---

[31] See Mark Johnson, *The Body in the Mind: The Bodily Basis of Meaning, Imagination, and Reason* (Chicago, 1987).

music on the Mediterranean coast differed from that south of the Sahara.[32] Gender and sexuality, too, lead to different musics, just as they locate music differently in the body.[33] The body, furthermore, metaphysically loosens music from its own autonomy, mapping it on to other physical practices, such as ritual and dance, which in Western terms have 'nothing to do with music'. The fear about music's identity intensifies once discussion of the body as a site for musical production begins. Although we want our musical experiences to be intensely personal—that is, to perceive them as lying within us as individuals—we often don't want to think about them as such; we prefer to deny the possibility of a language to describe the music that resides within. If we turn to the body, then, the fundamental dilemma about music's ontologies resolutely refuses to go away. Can music be about itself? Must it be about other human practices? Do its substances come from within or from without?

### III.  Concluding Where Music Begins: Musical Ontology as Human Practice

I shall not conclude by answering these questions, but I shall claim that they are not merely rhetorical. They are insistent questions, and they interpellate the assumptions that many different cultures make about music. They don't go away, but instead confront us with the constant ontological probing that music-making engenders. The ontologies of music, therefore, do not occupy a philosophical realm of importance only to those who think about music. They reside in the physical and the everyday, the beautiful and spiritual, past histories and myths about the future. They are spread across the entire spectrum of human experience. Thinking about and experiencing music are basic human practices.

The ontological concepts in this essay are not isolated unto themselves; nor are they isolated one from another. Whereas some may predominate in certain cultures, or may even be fundamental to a culture's constructs of what music is or is not, they do not divide the world into different regions. Music's ontologies in the West are no more or less numerous than those of the 'other' cultures and peoples created by the West. Technologies affect virtually all these ontologies, and most of the ontologies discussed here have determined how technologies have come to shape the ways in which humans imagine music. Returning to the metaphysical conditions introduced at the beginning of the essay, we also recognize that none of these stands out as isolated when we examine music's

---

[32] Cf. Ibn Khaldūn, *The Muqaddimah: An Introduction to History*, ed. and trans. Franz Rosenthal (3 vols., Princeton, 1958), vol. 1.

[33] Cf. Susan McClary, *Feminine Endings: Music, Gender, and Sexuality* (Minneapolis, 1991), and Philip Brett, Elizabeth Wood, and Gary C. Thomas (eds.), *Queering the Pitch: The New Gay and Lesbian Musicology* (London, 1994).

ontologies as a complex. Music as object and music as process may suggest conditions that describe music at different stages of production and reproduction, but object and process are none the less dependent upon both production and reproduction. The embeddedness of music in the contexts of time and space, history and culture, moreover, generates the conditions of adumbration, music's connectedness with cultural practices in which it does not directly participate. The interrelatedness of these metaphysical conditions is a striking metonym for music's ontologies.

In conclusion, I return to the plural that served as the point of departure for this essay. For some readers it may well seem that there is a linguistic sleight of hand lurking in my title, or perhaps even a contradiction. If one is going to employ 'ontologies' as plural, shouldn't one also do the same with 'musics'? By retaining the singular 'music', don't I capitulate to the predominant ontological assumption of the West? Yes and no. Yes, because ontologies of music *do* almost always concern themselves with a singular notion of music. No, because that notion of music is internally complex and multiple. The processes that lead to the imagination and construction of a musical ontology assemble it from various metaphysical conditions, but they strive toward an ontology that expresses and resides in some understanding of self-identity. Far from negating other musics and other ontologies, this self-identity depends on them. An individual ontology of music, then, maps the global musical landscape from local perspectives, and imagines what music is according to the conditions that determine those perspectives. While depending on a distinction between self and other, each ontology blurs that distinction; self is understood as entangled with another.

Ontologically, music is more closely imagined and conceived through 'rethinking' than through 'thinking music', and in this sense I should like to think that this essay is not isolated from the others in the present volume. 'Thinking music' privileges one way of understanding music, the cognitive; it proceeds with the assurance that self is ultimately knowable. 'Rethinking music' proceeds only nervously, lacking conviction that any ontological process is ultimately knowable; we rethink music out of the belief that we missed something the first time round. Rethinking music undermines thinking music, and moves beyond it. Far more important, however, rethinking music asks us to situate our understanding of music in other experiences of music-making, the human practices of bringing music into existence through ritual and belief, act and imagination, and, yes, through thought.

# 2

# Analysis in Context

## Jim Samson

### Analysis *contra* Musicology

Categories of knowledge shape our understanding, and are shaped by it. Categories are selective, and their boundaries, like all boundaries, exclude as they select. Categories are also permeable. Since they are motivated in large part by the need to make knowledge manageable or persuasive in particular contexts, they find or create institutions, lodging within them. This makes them vulnerable, and also contingent. They are subject to revision. Even those primary categories of the mind proposed by some idealist theories of knowledge[1] are increasingly viewed within a network of relationships, so that invariants, if they exist at all, are already mediated.

A categorical quest has characterized the relation between modes of enquiry and their objects. Yet the progressive acquisition of knowledge need not of itself lead to this (Kantian) separation. That it has tended to do so in our culture is due above all to the strengthening imperative of instrumental rationality within Western thought and society.[2] That imperative has resulted in a constant marking out of new boundaries, suppressing or 'occulting' previous aspects of knowledge, and at the same time breaking the bonds connecting disciplines and subdisciplines. It is a process both of fragmentation and of reordering, and its tendency is towards a redefinition of the generic. This begs an ancient question about specialized knowledge, one which has an obvious bearing on any analytical enquiry. Does a close bond with the special facilitate or impede our grasp of the generic?[3] There is another, less ancient, but no less relevant, question. Does

---

[1] Ernst Cassirer, e.g., identified space, time, and number as permanent categories of the mind, organized in different ways by different art-forms: see *The Philosophy of Symbolic Forms*, trans. R. Manheim (3 vols., New Haven, 1968; orig. pub. 1955). A more theoretical approach to the imaging of categories is found in George Lakoff, *Women, Fire, and Dangerous Things: What Categories Reveal about the Mind* (Chicago, 1987).

[2] The most sustained application of concepts of progressive rationalization to music is in Max Weber's classic text, *The Rational and Social Foundations of Music*, trans. and ed. D. Martindale, J. Riedel, and G. Neuwirth (Carbondale, Ill., 1958; orig. pub. 1921). Weber's ideas were later adapted by Adorno, notably in *Aesthetic Theory*, trans. C. Lenhardt (London, 1984). For a discussion, see Max Paddison, *Adorno's Aesthetics of Music* (Cambridge, 1993), 135–48.

[3] Conflicting answers span the centuries, Plato echoed by Schopenhauer, Aristotle by Goethe. The Platonic view is that universals are unavailable and unknowable, and that art (at two removes from universals) can offer only a

specialized knowledge become or promote reified knowledge, disengaged from its object? That question is moot when we consider a poetics, since, almost by definition, a poetics implies a separation of knowledge about art from the conditions which made it possible, from context.[4] As a category, it already lays out some of the ground for analysis.

In today's climate of ideas there is an impulse towards integration following this categorical quest. Or if not integration, then at least some crossing of disciplinary boundaries, some sharing of roles. This is by no means nostalgia for a naïve totality, to which specialized knowledge might pay lip-service before taking its separate path. If a totality is acknowledged at all, it is a complex, ultimately unknowable totality, whose quest will implicate specialized knowledge, just as it will implicate the enquiring subject. Musical knowledge can offer us a useful instance. Consider analysis and performance, one of several pairs exemplifying that division of theory and praxis (discourse and discipline) which is formalized by our major teaching institutions, university and conservatory. An extensive literature proclaims the value of interaction between analysis and performance,[5] though for many it has served merely to reinforce their separateness. In recent years, however, attempts at mediation have taken on a new dimension, one which speaks to our way of thinking today. Dialogue, successful or not, is now invited at a level which preserves and even extends the specialized knowledge not just of music analysis, but of other sub-disciplines, including structural linguistics and cognitive psychology.[6] This in turn feeds back to the initial categories, opening a debate about the aims, capacities, and identities of each of them. Institutional inertia may impede the debate, but even our institutions can and do (usually under pressure) engage in renovative self-reflection.

The divides within musical scholarship further exemplify the categorical quest, as they do also the problems of mediation. In particular, quite different stories about music emerge through the categories of German and East Euro-

---

shadowy knowledge of them—hence the potential conflict between truth and beauty. Aristotle, on the other hand, regarded art as a privileged source of knowledge about universals; they may be lit up, as it were, by the particular. Goethe's *aperçu* has something of this meaning.

[4] For a qualification of this generalization, see Alan Swingewood's discussion of Bakhtin in *Sociological Poetics and Aesthetic Theory* (London, 1986).

[5] See, *inter alia*, Wallace Berry, *Musical Structure and Performance* (New Haven, 1989), together with reviews of it by Steve Larson and Cynthia Folio in *Journal of Music Theory*, 35 (1991), 298–309; John Rink in *Music Analysis*, 9 (1990), 319–39; and Joel Lester in *Music Theory Spectrum*, 14 (Spring 1992), 75–81. See also David Beach, 'The First Movement of Mozart's Piano Sonata in A minor, K.310: Some Thoughts on Structure and Performance', *Journal of Musicological Research*, 7 (1987), 157–86; Carl Schachter, '20th-Century Analysis and Mozart Performance', *Early Music*, 19 (1991), 620–6; William Rothstein, 'Heinrich Schenker as an Interpreter of Beethoven's Piano Sonatas', *19th-Century Music*, 8 (1984), 3–28; and Jonathan Dunsby, 'Guest Editorial: Performance and Analysis of Music', *Music Analysis*, 8 (1989), 5–20. This topic is discussed in Nicholas Cook's chapter.

[6] This latter especially so in publications by Eric Clarke, Neil Todd, Henry Shaffer, Stephen McAdams, David Lewin, and Nicholas Cook, notably in the journals *Psychology of Music, Music Perception, Music Analysis*, and *Contemporary Music Review*. See also Peter Howell, Ian Cross, and Robert West (eds.), *Musical Structure and Cognition* (London, 1985). An interesting attempt to carve out a performance discourse which restores the performer's perspective is Chee Yee Jennifer Tong, 'Separate Discourses: A Study of Performance and Analysis' (Ph.D. diss., University of Southampton, 1995).

pean musicology on the one hand and those of Anglo-American musicology on the other. American scholarship in particular draws a clean line between 'theory and analysis' and 'historical musicology'. That line, paralleling in some ways the line separating analytic aesthetics and hermeneutics, is visible in the structures and syllabuses of our academic departments, in our journals, societies, and conferences, and in the descriptions we give of ourselves, when called to account.[7] Professional empires are built, professional communities (some would say 'ghettos') created. Smudging the line has been an energetic, enjoyable pursuit of recent so-called critical musicologists.[8] But it is far from clear that well-sharpened (albeit often fetishized) tools will or should be set aside, even if their applications may need to be reconsidered. Nor is it certain that the dismantling of ghettos will achieve anything more positive than the creation of new ghettos. All the same, it is worth reminding ourselves that this particular division is by no means axiomatic. The academic study of music has been variously disciplined during its relatively short lifetime. Only in the broadest and most recent of generic classifications has it included something called 'analysis'.

Implicit in a good deal of Anglo-American 'New Musicology' is a critique of this divide between music analysis and historical musicology. My purpose here is to focus that critique by scrutinizing one term of the pair, examining its roots, exposing some of its ideological and institutional foundations, and locating both its primary causes and the 'historical moment' of its emergence. By investigating the grounds for an autonomous category of analytical thought, I will (paradoxically) throw into sharp relief the nature of its dependencies. This in turn will raise the question of its legitimation—or at the very least its placing—within our contemporary scholarship. Can it pass muster as a body of specialized, 'professional' knowledge? If so, who and what is this body of knowledge for? And how, anyway, does it sit with developing orthodoxies premissed on the multidisciplinary and the intertextual? The intention, in short, is to problematize music analysis in our changing world. I suggest that it may be especially valuable to do so from within the institution of analysis, and from a position which recognizes its achievements.[9] Confident dismissals from without can so easily carry the imprint of their own institutional prejudice.

## The Institution of Analysis

Debates about history and structure are a little easier to manage now that they have jettisoned some of their ideological freight. Resolving an opposition

---

[7] See e.g. David Fallows, Arnold Whittall, and John Blacking, 'Musicology in Great Britain since 1945', *Acta Musicologica*, 52 (1980), 38–68.

[8] It should be noted, though, that some commentators (notably Leo Treitler and Susan McClary) have attempted to reinforce the line by redefining 'analysis' in a much narrower way.

[9] The 'institution' now has its own infrastructure in Britain as well as in North America, with a society, newsletter, journal, and conference.

between Hegelian–Marxist and structuralist theories is not the imperative it once seemed,[10] and we are liberated into a sharper argument about disciplinary identities, about the scope, limits, and competence of particular modes of enquiry. On the one hand, disciplinary integrity is affirmed. Why should we expect conclusions about functions to be generated from researches into origins? Or generalizations about style (a historical category) to emerge from an examination of structures?[11] On the other hand, meeting-points are identified. Analytical tools do, after all, depend on certain normative categories which emerge from history, just as historical subject-matter properly includes structures. The balance of interests is a precarious one. A search for mutual roots may be in the interdisciplinary spirit of our age, but it is a daunting enterprise, for it has to surmount or accommodate an ethos of professionalism which is firmly entrenched in the academic world. That ethos has promoted esoteric languages which often seem expressly designed both to unite the communities of individual disciplines and to separate them from those of other disciplines, and of course from 'mass culture'. Even more crucially, an ethos of professionalism risks separating disciplines from the underlying (instrumental) questions they pose.

Already in early attempts to formulate a professional discipline of musicology[12] a division between 'history' and 'system' was taken to be fundamental. On the face of it, *Musikwissenschaft*, like other emergent academic disciplines in the late nineteenth century, adopted methods of classification indebted to the natural sciences and to the prevailing positivistic climate of the time. But a more telling model was the new philology of Friedrich August Wolf, and it is that model which provides a key to the underlying agenda. Behind Wolf's project lay a massive attempt to restore the ancients, whose rhetorical topoi had been progressively hollowed out (or parodied) during the eighteenth century. A wedge was firmly driven between the classical and the contemporary, to the disadvantage of the latter. Adler's hugely influential scheme for *Musikwissenschaft* had a similar effect, though naturally the province of the 'classical' had to be redefined. In keeping with its philological inspiration, the youthful science of music effectively distanced the unworthy art of the present from the perfection of a classical canon, and at the same time reduced that classical canon to the conscientious typologies of the new science. Historicism and scientism met in this endeavour, expressly in the terms of 'historical' and 'systematic' musicology.

It is striking that this magisterial attempt to summarize and categorize existing forms of musical knowledge in the late nineteenth century should have excluded any serious reference to the analysis of individual works. Moreover,

---

[10] See Alfred Schmidt, *History and Structure: An Essay on Hegelian–Marxist and Structuralist Theories of History*, trans. J. Herf (Cambridge, Mass., 1983; orig. pub. 1971).

[11] These methodological confusions are especially rife in writings on historically 'locatable' technical features such as the so-called two-key scheme. See e.g. Harald Krebs, 'Alternatives to Monotonality in Early Nineteenth-century Music', *Journal of Music Theory*, 25 (1981), 1–16.

[12] Guido Adler, 'Umfang, Methode und Zeil der Musikwissenschaft', *Vierteljahrsschrift für Musikwissenschaft*, 1 (1885), 5–20.

where analysis does exist within Adler's scheme, it is as an agent of historical rather than systematic musicology, a means of tracing the growth and development of musical styles, again with the implicit aim of validating a classical canon. Adler's categories remind us, then, of the humble scholarly status of music analysis in the nineteenth century. As an activity, it was of course already in place well before he drew up his 'summary'; but it existed principally in the form of what Ian Bent has called 'analytical moments', hosted by other categories of musical knowledge. Its move to autonomy was prepared above all by the ascendancy of the musical work as a cultural concept;[13] and that in turn was closely linked to the rise of music aesthetics (and criticism), to canon formation (with the associated development of text-critical study), to a transformation of function within music theory and pedagogy, and to changing compositional praxes.

It is probably unhelpful to try to draw these several strands into a single figure, such as the 'ideology of organicism' proposed by some commentators as a principal ground for analysis.[14] None the less, it would be difficult to deny the import of this idea. It both grew from and served to validate aesthetic autonomy, that essentialist Enlightenment project which carved out a space for art in the precarious middle ground between sensory perception and intellectual cognition, between *sensus* and *ratio*. From Kant to Croce, the project of aesthetic autonomy—embracing the entire development of modern European art—was deemed to have fulfilled its vital bridging role through a massive investment in the realm of subjectivity. And, as Andrew Bowie argues in a penetrating study,[15] it was precisely the difficulty of 'objectifying' that realm—deriving certainties from it in the absence of any ethical premiss—which made (the emancipation of) aesthetic theory necessary and possible in the first place. Through organicism, rather than mimesis, the aesthetic was presumed to establish a purpose in Nature, healing the division of subject and object by uniting both in the Self. This, however, was not a single shift of paradigm. Lotte Thaler astutely distinguishes between an early 'morphological' and a later 'energetic' organicism, implying, though at no point stating, that the organicist metaphor took its starting-point in a kind of idealized mimesis, where the unities of art would mirror other unities.[16] Only with the development of an inherent (energetic) organicism, purged of context, is art transformed from an idealized image of what the world is to one of what the world might become.

It is that stage which enshrines the work concept and marks the transition to an analytical philosophy of art in general and to music analysis in particular,

---

[13] The major text here is Lydia Goehr, *The Imaginary Museum of Musical Works: An Essay in the Philosophy of Music* (Oxford, 1992).

[14] Joseph Kerman, 'How We Got into Analysis, and How to Get Out', *Critical Inquiry*, 7 (1980), 311–31. See also Alan Street, 'Superior Myths, Dogmatic Allegories: The Resistance to Musical Unity', *Music Analysis*, 8 (1989), 77–124.

[15] Andrew Bowie, *Aesthetics and Subjectivity from Kant to Nietzsche* (Manchester, 1993).

[16] Lotte Thaler, *Organische Form in der Musiktheorie des 19. und beginnenden 20. Jahrhunderts* (Munich, 1984).

though it should be stressed again that, grounded in subjectivity, the unity of the work now reflects the presumed unity or (more accurately) unification of the Self, rather than of Nature or of God.[17] The artwork would transcend the divisions of the self, its individual moments cohering into a whole which presents a sort of utopian *promesse de bonheur*, hinting at the possibility of (by serving as a model for) that chimerical whole which might ultimately reconcile subjective and objective spirit; in short, it could stand for the indivisible Absolute, beloved of idealist thought. There are numerous variants of such idealist aesthetics in the nineteenth century. And there are closet supporters of it among more recent thinkers too, notably those who view the musical work as a kind of sound-image of experience, capable of symbolizing feeling through its forms.[18] What they all share is a commitment to the closure which separates the work of art from the world, and to the consequent capacity of the significant work to draw us into its healing 'real presence'.[19]

The rise of criticism likewise celebrates the autonomy of the aesthetic, marking as it does the replacement of functional by aesthetic judgements. The story related by nineteenth-century music criticism is above all the story of canon formation,[20] without which the entire (apparently antithetical) development of modern art would have been inconceivable. This in turn influenced the mode of critical writing. By the end of the century there was a swerve towards a poetics and a 'structural mode' in at least one strand of criticism, in music as in the other arts. Among the several causes for this was the tendency of the musical canon, like the literary, to promote and respond to the growing importance of the printed text.[21] Through the offices of the published score, the canonized musical work was congealed into a fixed configuration, its forms solidified until they might be equated with those of verbal or spatial works. And around those works an industry of (philologically inspired) textual exegesis began to develop in the later nineteenth century, significantly in circles which remained somewhat apart from the institutions of musical pedagogy. The scholarly tradition represented by Nottebohm and continued by members of the Brahms circle such as Kalbeck and Mandieczewski played a prominent role in this development, one which culminated in that 'science of autograph study' proudly practised by Schenker, himself no lover of institutions.[22] Here again the ground was prepared for a focus on music as text, on work-centred knowledge.

These changes had implications for the categorical quest. In particular, the

---

[17] For Heinrich Schenker it embraced all three.

[18] See e.g. Suzanne Langer, *Feeling and Form* (London, 1953), and Leonard B. Meyer, *Emotion and Meaning in Music* (Chicago, 1956).

[19] George Steiner, *Real Presences* (London, 1989).

[20] For a good case-study see Katharine Ellis, *Music Criticism in Nineteenth-Century France: La Revue et Gazette musicale de Paris 1834–1880* (Cambridge, 1995).

[21] Jerome McGann has explored this for literature in *Black Riders: The Visible Language of Modernism* (Princeton, 1993).

[22] Heinrich Schenker, *Free Composition*, trans. and ed. E. Oster (2 vols., New York, 1979; orig. pub. 1935), i. 7.

translation of criticism into poetics, a development associated with the early years of the twentieth century, brought it within close reach of theory. This was an orientation common to all the arts. But music occupied a rather special position, for it already enjoyed a long tradition of theory, uniquely bridging the historical chasm separating Aristotelian and structuralist poetics. To put it another way, a primary and enduring concern of music theory over many years—the search for systematic rules and laws conditioning the art, where these are derived (inductively) from the art itself—became the primary concern of other art-forms at a very particular historical moment in the early twentieth century.[23] At the same time there is an important conceptual space separating traditional music theory from a structuralist poetics. Within music theory the search for order (and beauty) was not initially directed towards individual musical works, but rather towards what were thought to be generalized properties of music. The later shift to a work-centred perspective was a response to what might be described as a much more general intellectual shift—and one of epochal significance—from doctrinal to rational knowledge.

The effect of this reorientation within music theory (mainly a product of the eighteenth century) was to change the status of the musical work from a prospective to a retrospective object.[24] The work itself became the principal locus of enquiry, its structure transcending the rules of speculative theory, or understood negatively in relation to those rules. There emerged, in short, a structural sense of form in the nineteenth century, given expression through the developing tradition of *Formenlehre*. From early beginnings in theorists such as Adolf Bernhard Marx to later formulations in Riemann, Mersmann, Schoenberg, and Schenker, the idea of a structural sense of form gained unstoppable momentum, sweeping music theory before it, and in the end building on its premiss the entire edifice of a newly independent discipline, music analysis, essentially a discipline of our age. Unity and wholeness, whatever these may mean in a temporal art, were assumed a priori, and the analytical act was their demonstration. The work became a structure, and in that lay its value. It was at this stage of its development that music theory found common ground with the emergence of a structuralist poetics in other art-forms.

It may be worth adding that music analysis began to emerge in rather different guise through the pedagogical theory of the nineteenth century. Major changes in pedagogy resulted from the institutionalization of musical knowledge which accompanied an increasingly professionalized musical life, associated above all with the rise of the conservatories. The transition from craft instruction to the classroom resulted in a measure of divergence between speculative and pedagogical theory in the nineteenth century, the one continuing to

[23] This was by no means confined to formalist and structuralist positions. It was also true of American 'New Criticism' and later of Northrop Frye (see his *Anatomy of Criticism* (London, 1957) ).

[24] This is discussed at length in James Garnett, 'Complexity in Music: Studies in Compositional, Theoretical and Analytical Thought' (Ph.D. diss., Oxford, 1993).

construct an intellectual model of the nature of music, the other formulating rules of composition. Analysis played its part in pedagogical theory, in so-called practical schools of composition, but essentially as an adjunct to composing, to making. And as such, it recovered something of the original function of a poetics. One of several senses in which Schenker and Schoenberg marked important twin turning-points in the emancipation of music analysis was through their (very different) syntheses of these two traditions, such that 'poietic' analysis took its place centrally within speculative theory. It is obvious, too, that the analytical theories of Schenker and Schoenberg drew sustenance from a specific orientation on the part of some nineteenth-century composers.[25] Organicism was at least in part a deliberate strategy by composers.

Music analysis was instituted, then, at the turn of the nineteenth and twentieth centuries, its 'historical moment' arriving rather more than a century after the 'historical moment' of aesthetic theory. A consequence of the project of aesthetic autonomy and the rise of the work concept, the institution of analysis formalized the shift towards a work-centred music theory, one which replaced rules with structures. Moreover, the new conceptual world embodied in analytical theory collided with the rebirth of poetics in the other arts, sharing with that development a (heavily ideological) suppression of context in any explanation of the aesthetic. The converse, incidentally, also followed: a structuralist poetics implicitly freed social history, together with cognitive and ethical values, from aesthetic interference. It goes without saying that this separation of specialized categories from each other and from the social world could never be fully realized. The unified musical work, celebrated by the institution of analysis, was a necessary, valuable, and glorious myth, but it was a myth shaped in all essentials by a particular set of social and historical circumstances. Its status was twofold. As a product of those dominant processes of rationality from whose repressive influence it sought to escape, the unified work was emblematic of a notionally unified bourgeois culture. On the other hand, as an autonomous aesthetic object seeking to articulate areas of subjectivity excluded by those very processes of rationality, the unified work had the potential to oppose and criticize the social sphere. We are bound to ask if it can retain either meaning today.

## Epistemology

While its primary causes were deep-seated, the concrete institution of analysis was initially an achievement of Austro-German theorists, a produce of *Formenlehre*. It was the later transplant of analysis to the North American college circle, however, which ensured its more complete categorical separation not only from

---

[25] Thus Wagner on the *Ring*: '[It] turned out to be a firmly entwined unity: there is scarcely a bar in the orchestral writing that doesn't develop out of preceding motives' (quoted in C. von Westernhagen, *The Forging of the Ring*, trans. A. and M. Whittall (Cambridge, 1976), 65).

metaphysics but ultimately from theory.[26] It remained, of course, heavily dependent on theory; but its aims were distinguishable, its province more specific. The
transformation of Schenker's thought into a straightforward, modern scientific
truth stripped of metaphysical resonance is symptomatic of this later stage of
analytical enquiry, one which subsequently fed through from American to
British analysts, clearly differentiating both from German theorists. And it was
above all this stage, exemplified by the hegemony of so-called Schenkerian analysis, together with the set-theoretic approaches developed by Milton Babbitt and
Allen Forte, that defined analysis as an autonomous category. From our present
perspective, it is useful to question the nature and competence of this category.
Just what kind of musical knowledge is analytical knowledge? Is there a single,
all-embracing category of such knowledge? What conditions must obtain before
we can consider it valid? And how does it relate to other categories of knowledge,
in the natural and social as well as the cultural sciences?

Music analysis proceeds from a premiss which underlies analytic aesthetics in
general: namely, that objects of art share certain characteristics which define
them as art and make them valuable to us, that they are determinate, and that
they represent conceptual unities. In short, it is premissed on a closed, homogeneous concept of the artwork. The most characteristic analytical mode is to
equate concepts with objects, to allow fixed (or closed) representations of the
object to stand for the object. Both the premiss and the mode have been subjected
to critical scrutiny over the last two decades. An important achievement of
recent studies in the ontology of artworks, notably in Lydia Goehr's book, has
been to counter an analytical philosophy of art by underlining the dependent,
culturally emergent nature both of artworks themselves and of discourse about
them.[27] Moreover, the neat equation of concept and object has been undermined—powerfully and influentially—by Morris Weitz's proposal that interpretations of artworks (whose essence is necessarily undefinable) should be
expressed in terms of 'open concepts' whose defining criteria can be neither
precise nor complete.[28] If it were otherwise, Weitz argues, any further creative
development would be compromised. Such anti-essentialist critiques remind us
that closed concepts of an artwork, involving such notions as structure, unity,
wholeness, and complexity, are products of perspectival knowledge. Specifically,
they are products of a particular kind of institutionalized analytic-referential discourse.[29] They cannot be equated with the work itself.

This imposes an immediate limitation on analytical knowledge. In the case of
music, what we analyse is not a musical work, which embodies all kinds of indeterminate areas not at all susceptible to analysis. (The investigation of what we

---

[26] See William Rothstein, 'The Americanization of Heinrich Schenker', in Hedi Siegel (ed.), *Schenker Studies* (Cambridge, 1990), 193–203.

[27] Goehr, *Imaginary Museum*.

[28] See Morris Weitz, 'The Role of Theory in Aesthetics', *Journal of Aesthetics and Art Criticism*, 15 (1956), 27–35,
also his *The Opening Mind: A Philosophical Study of Humanistic Concepts* (Chicago, 1977).

[29] For a discussion of this discourse see Timothy J. Reiss, *The Discourse of Modernism* (Ithaca, NY, 1982).

may call 'nuance' is just one dimension of this, but it is an important one and it remains an underdeveloped corner of the general field of aesthetics.[30]) What we analyse is rather a schematic structure, to use Ingarden's term,[31] schematic in the sense that it is bound to remain less than its realization as a work. Moreover, the schematic structure will itself be a particular, contingent representation, which can make only limited claims to general validity. When we analyse, in other words, we construct the object of our analysis according to certain pre-suppositions. One of the several values of a reception study is to make us aware of this by obliging us to confront other subjects, including historical subjects, since these reveal to us the historical context not just of the work but of the questions we ask of the work. A reception aesthetics thus calls into question one of the central tenets of analysis, the stability of the work's identity, its capacity to make its own statement independent of any recognitional condition. Ultimately it calls into question the very possibility of an ontological essence for the musical work. This is not to deny the value of analysis. Rather, it is to (re)define the boundaries of analytical knowledge by exposing the false identity of concepts and their objects, and by underlining the heavily mediated character of any analytical insight. Within these more limited boundaries there is considerable protection for analysis. Even reception studies usually conclude that the work's identity is not infinitely permeable (if it were so, it would be approachable only by way of intertextual difference), and that determinacy recedes only to certain 'horizons'.[32] The loss of essence need not entail a loss of presence.

This revision of premiss leads in turn to a reassessment of mode. In practice, music analysis has drawn on methods well established in the natural sciences, in that the individual analysis follows from, and defers to, inductively established theory. This is the process known (in philology) as 'seriation', which in turn finds expression in an explicative 'plot'.[33] The analytical insight derives its meaning from a particular theoretical presupposition, which of course begs the question of how we locate the theory. To what does theory defer, given that (at least from the eighteenth century onwards) its reasoning proceeds from the observation of concrete particulars? As George Steiner has shown, the term 'theory' has undergone considerable transformation;[34] but it is as a component of the Cartesian tandem of theory and practice (hypothesis and test) that it has been transferred from the scientific to the aesthetic sphere—and also, incidentally, to the social sciences. Again, that transferral has been widely challenged. It is rather easy to demonstrate that what passes for 'theory' in the humanities is closer to inter-

[30]  See Diana Raffman, *Language, Music and Mind* (Cambridge, Mass., 1993), and the review of Raffmann's book by Stephen Davies, *Journal of Aesthetics and Art Criticism*, 52 (1994), 360–2.

[31]  Roman Ingarden, *The Work of Music and the Problem of its Identity*, trans. A. Czerniawski, ed. J. G. Harrell (Berkeley, 1986; orig. pub. 1928).

[32]  Hans-George Gadamer, *Truth and Method*, trans. G. Barden and J. Cumming (New York, 1975; orig. pub. 1960).

[33]  Jean-Jacques Nattiez, 'The Concepts of Plot and Seriation Process in Music Analysis', *Music Analysis*, 4 (1985), 107–18.

[34]  Steiner, *Real Presences*, 69–87.

pretation, description, and even straightforward belief than to scientific theory in the classic Popperian sense (that is, a source of falsifiable knowledge).[35] The analytical knowledge derived from theory in the arts cannot, in short, be certain knowledge.

The case for music possessing theory in the Cartesian sense may seem initially rather more plausible than that for, say, literature or painting. Music theory, after all, appears to have 'rules', and they are rules which have no validity outside the medium itself. But such rules—even if they appeal to verifiable acoustic realities—are in the end more like culturally conditioned regularities or norms than scientific laws. As Wittgenstein argues, 'they do not amount to a system, and only the experienced can apply them correctly. Unlike the rules of arithmetics.'[36] In any case their explanatory value weakens when we proceed from 'theory' to analytical 'practice'. Since music theory rests on functions, its analytical exemplification involves a reduction from explicit 'surface' to implicit 'structure' (this is by no means exclusive to Schenker), and such a reduction, far from providing an empirical explanation of a work, can only offer an interpretation of it, albeit one which may be constrained by something akin to a rule-governed system. Accepting analysis as interpretation presupposes of course that there will be alternative interpretations, and that in turn means that analytical 'facts' can have no independent or objective existence. Moreover, they are contingent not only on theory, but also on history, in that their authority derives not from the work but from the historically sedimented conventions and schemata which make up a notional tradition of which the work partakes. However 'structuralist' the analysis, it implicitly views the work as the instantiation of a 'type'.[37]

It is worth stressing these contingencies, since the scientific mode (to say nothing of the technical language) of music analysis might lead us to suppose that it stands in a similar relation to the work as does science to the natural world. Indeed, there are explicit claims to that effect in some quarters,[38] and some suggestive proposals in others (notably in cognitive studies) that such a relation is at least not unthinkable, even if it does not yet exist. What is at stake here is less the scientific character of the analytical system (set theory may appear more 'scientific' than Schenker, for example) than the aim and pretension of the analyst. The demarcation lines hinge not on the method, then, nor

---

[35] Karl Popper, *The Logic of Scientific Discovery* (London, 1959).

[36] Ludwig Wittgenstein, *Lectures and Conversations on Aesthetics, Psychology and Religious Belief* (Oxford, 1966), 19.

[37] Some aestheticians have found it helpful to speak of 'tokens' of a 'type', in order to refine for artworks the notion of particulars and universals. See esp. Richard Wollheim, *Art and its Objects* (New York, 1968). See also his *On Art and the Mind* (Cambridge, Mass., 1974), and Joseph Margolis, *The Language of Art and Art Criticism* (Detroit, 1965).

[38] Matthew G. Brown and Douglas J. Dempster, 'The Scientific Image of Music Theory', *Journal of Music Theory*, (1989) 33, 65–106. This is part of a 'Theory Colloquium' which includes replies to Brown and Dempster by Benjamin Boretz, Nicholas Cook, John Rahn, and Richard Taruskin.

even on the nature of the object observed (man-made as opposed to natural, or nature-based), but rather on the role of the observer, who—as analyst—creates a theoretically predetermined and pre-analytic concept of the object to be analysed. It is well known that even within the natural sciences there has been a loss of faith in the stability of objective description over recent decades, amounting in effect to a liberation (or reinvention) of the subject. In music analysis the subject is irredeemably implicated, and a mediating theory can offer only limited protection. It is the recognition of this—the growing awareness that an analysis is integral to both its subject and its object—that has called into question the implicitly scientific basis of music analysis as a discipline. And it is that same recognition which has triggered a renewed interest among Anglo-American scholars in a critical hermeneutics whose foundations were already well established in Continental thought.

It would perhaps be more accurate to say that music analysis as a discipline has increasingly been recognized as itself akin to, if it is not indeed a form of, hermeneutics, with the analyst/subject 'drawn', as Street puts it, 'into the hermeneutic circle'.[39] This implicit redefinition of category locates analysis at some remove from both the presumed subjectivity of aesthetics and the presumed objectivity of the natural sciences. To push it to an extreme, it registers that music analysis is as much a form of self-analysis (raising all the familiar problems of the 'I' describing itself) as an empirical explanation of the other, since the subject can neither be abolished altogether nor congealed into fixity. This accommodation with relativism implies an accommodation with plurality. Raymond Monelle spells this out, arguing that 'the rigorously systematic programme of structuralism leads us, not to the promised land of objective truth, but to the acceptance of plurality'.[40] It becomes of some importance, then, to scrutinize the nature of the images, models, or metaphors used in analysis, since their *modus operandi* defines the gap between our experience and our description of that experience.[41] Indeed, a good deal of recent writing is concerned with deconstructing analytical discourse precisely with that in mind. It goes without saying that this in turn influences both the ambition and the pretension of the analyst, since his or her discourse is now widely recognized as fictive, of itself neither more nor less useful than, say, the fictive programmes of the nineteenth-century critic. In both cases we are given parallels to, rather than explanations of, the musical experience. The sermon is preached, but still proves hard to assimilate. Monelle leaves us with an admonition, urging us to look in the gaps, the spaces, the 'gloomiest clefts and crannies' both within and between analyses. In doing so, he reveals just how powerful the myth of the unified work really is, controlling even those who seek to deconstruct it.

[39] Street, 'Superior Myths', 89.

[40] Raymond Monelle, *Linguistics and Semiotics in Music* (Chur, Switzerland, 1992), 323.

[41] See Nicholas Cook, *Music, Imagination, Culture* (Oxford, 1990), 4.

## Contexts

The failure of the structuralist programme measures the larger failures of aesthetic autonomy and of the 'institution of art'.[42] In revealing the contingencies of music analysis, we reveal not just the fictive character of this and other discourses about music, but the contingent nature of music itself. There are two parts to this, and they need to be unpicked. One concerns music's specificity, the other its autonomy. The recognition that music's 'project of autonomy' was historically produced and contingent brooks little dissension today. Well before the New Musicology, it was a central plank of Adorno's aesthetics, and his commentary in this respect remains persuasive. But we can easily reject music's presumed monadic character (having exposed its ideological roots) and at the same time argue for its specificity. Indeed, there may well be a central irony in this, reaching to the heart of any attempt to write about and explain music. Music, it might be argued, is so utterly and irreducibly specific, its meaning so embedded in its essence, that we are forced to borrow from other systems of thought in order to attempt any kind of description at all. Straddling several categories of thought, it fits uneasily within any, condemning even the most 'scientific' of descriptions to opacity. This, moreover, has always been the case. When contemporary commentators expose the contingency of music analysis, its dependence on models and metaphors drawn from other disciplines—indeed, its essential character as metaphor—they are in fact describing the age-old condition of music theory.

This is apparent from even the most cursory consideration of earlier stages of the categorical quest. Within medieval thought the close relation of music and mathematics, already recognized of course by the Greeks, was formalized and institutionalized by the quadrivium, a category derived originally from Roman pedagogy. Initially that relation stood for an idealized, ahistorical mimesis peculiar to music, where music, through the medium of numbers, might reflect (be equated with) both a natural and an ethical order. Something of that Neoplatonic function was inevitably lost when theological systems of knowledge began to make room for rationalistic and/or historical systems. But the mathematical model, principally through the harmonic series, remained the essential premiss of later developments in harmonic theory. Indeed, it was treated as primary and originating for a rational and functional tonal system, and continued to be so treated by mainstream theorists until well into the present century. It is unnecessary to deny the reality of acoustic laws, or the pragmatic value of mathematically based theory (or, for that matter, the creative power of sound structures based on arithmetic and geometry), in order to see the inadequacy of the mathematical model as a necessary and sufficient cause for tonal music, and

[42] The phrase is Peter Bürger's, in *Theory of the Avant-Garde*, trans. M. Shaw (Manchester and Minneapolis, 1984; orig. pub. 1974).

hence the intrinsic limitations of any attempt to explain (as distinct from inter-pret) music through analytical systems which build from a mathematically based premiss.

Within Renaissance–Baroque thought an alternative categorization of music emerged, one which linked music to verbal language, and (in the eighteenth century) to an *ars oratoria*. Like the mathematical model, the language model was also familiar to the Greeks, and again it survived in one form or another to recent times. Verbal language and rhetoric (or at least some modified form of ora-torical concepts) began to assume increasing significance, then, as explanatory models for music. Through rhetorical effects, codified in terms of genres, tonal types, and (above all) figures, music evoked its responses, even if these were recognized—though not so described—as what Wittgenstein later called a 'secondary sense' of the emotions. They were achieved after all through representation, where the emotion is 'seen in' the artwork.[43] In short, a theory of affections is another form of mimesis. Despite this mimetic basis, however, an important conceptual shift in the purpose of music accompanied the rhetorical model, a shift towards persuasion (rhetoric is, it will be remembered, the art of persuasive speech), and from there towards its classification as a 'fine art' rather than a science. Moreover, as mimesis declined (largely through an emerging problematic of meaning which would culminate in Romanticism), the affinities with verbal language were made increasingly specific, until in due course they found their way into incipiently analytical theoretical systems for the 'parsing' of music.

It is obvious that music does indeed share some of the characteristics of a lan-guage. Indeed, the tendency to describe it as a kind of language ('of the emo-tions and passions') has moved from the reasoned debate of eighteenth-century compositional theory to the informal parlance of music-lovers everywhere. But the limitations of this analogy have become a commonplace of more recent crit-ical writing. The communicative role of music (if it exists at all in any strict sense) is radically compromised by the inseparability of its syntactic and semantic ele-ments, such that it can be neither translated nor paraphrased. Even on a purely syntactic level the analogy will not withstand much scrutiny. Despite the flexibility introduced by the 'preference rules' proposed by Lerdahl and Jackendoff,[44] it remains highly doubtful that one can construct anything akin to a 'grammar' of tonal music. Music may have a 'language character' (as proposed in different ways by Schoenberg and Adorno), but it is not a language.[45] This has not, of course, prevented music analysis from borrowing the labelling systems and some of the methods of linguistics. From Koch's exposition of

---

[43] The implications of 'seeing in' and 'seeing as' are discussed by Wittgenstein in *Philosophical Investigations*, trans. G. E. M. Anscombe (Oxford, 1953).

[44] Fred Lerdahl and Ray Jackendoff, *A Generative Theory of Tonal Music* (Cambridge, Mass., 1983).

[45] See Max Paddison, 'The Language-Character of Music: Some Motifs in Adorno', *Journal of the Royal Musical Association*, 116 (1991), 267–79.

phrase structures and extensions, through Schoenberg's parsing of periods and sentences, to more recent generative theories, such methods have often proved illuminating. But they remain firmly on the level of imported models or metaphors, whose application to an ontological distinct art-form can never prove more than suggestive.

In less explicit ways the visual and spatial arts also served as explanatory models for music, notably through the ascendancy of formal theories of art in the late nineteenth and early twentieth centuries. Such theories, already plotted by Kant's recognition of formal coherence as a prerequisite of the beautiful, were by no means unique to music (Kant, it will be remembered, denied music a place among the 'formative arts'). Their background was a lively debate about priority between different art-forms, usually within the context of all-embracing philosophical systems. The changing hierarchical placement of music within such systems is itself a subject of much interest—one which had a bearing on compositional styles as well as aesthetics in the nineteenth century—but it is not central to my argument. I want simply to draw attention to a paradox underlying formal theories as they have been applied to music. According to such theories, the essence of music was perceived to lie in the formal properties of musical works, separating them off from other art-forms. Yet the formal properties themselves could be described only by recourse to a spatial metaphor. Hanslick's 'motion' remains, as is often pointed out, a virtual property only. It seems that if we are to hear music as form (as opposed to structure or shape), we can do so only by borrowing yet again from without. Effectively, we translate the temporal into the spatial, freezing the work in a single synoptic moment and laying it out for dissection in an imagined, illusory space. This sleight of hand, which assumes an equivalence of formal functions on a single level of signification, underlies the brand of formal analysis developed by Hugo Riemann and Hugo Leichtentritt.[46] It also underpins much of the formal theory of the Second Viennese School, as codified especially by Erwin Ratz.[47] As with the other models and metaphors, the point is not to denigrate such approaches, but to recognize them for what they are. As Dahlhaus put it, 'Spatialisation and form, emergence and objectivity, are interdependent; one is the support or precondition for the other.'[48]

In reviewing these dialogues, it is tempting to see the history of analytical thought as an almost classical Hegelian cycle, where analysis had first to achieve independence before it could achieve self-awareness, and with that an acknowledgement of its dependencies. In its turn, that acknowledgement allowed a much more pro-active engagement with cognate disciplines, amounting (in recent years) to a deep-rooted change of orientation within the discipline. The premiss was questioned fundamentally, even where many of the working practices

---

[46] Hugo Riemann, *Vademecum der Phrasierung* (Leipzig, 1900); Hugo Leichtentritt, *Musikalische Formenlehre* (Leipzig, 1911).

[47] Erwin Ratz, *Probleme der musikalische Formenlehre* (Vienna, 1953).

[48] Carl Dahlhaus, *Esthetics of Music*, trans. W. Austin (Cambridge, 1982), 12.

remained—as they often do remain—largely unaffected. Naomi Cumming has described this sea change aptly as a change of 'root-metaphor', from organicism to contextualism.[49] No longer welded to music theory, analysis was allowed to interact freely with other categories of knowledge, openly embracing the metaphorical status of all discourses on music, and in the process accessing expanding realms of meaning behind the musical text. Analytical insights increasingly took their place within a much larger 'implicative complex',[50] where the selection, emphasis, and grouping of particular musical features would be determined not just by music-theoretic criteria but by the extent of their iso-morphic correspondence to other controlling metaphors. Analysis, ironically enough, found itself influenced by many of those very features it had tried to shake off, including the biographical, social, and literary tropes which had dom-inated nineteenth-century criticism.

It is easy to see how this play of 'secondary subjects' served the purposes of a renewed interest in context. Acceptance of a contextual mode of enquiry promoted acceptance of a contextualized object of enquiry. But it would be inadequate to view this as a return to some pre-analytic, crudely Marxian investigation of context, where immediate social cause (the concern of a social history of music) might be presented as a sufficient condition for a work. The attempts of recent commentators to 'ground' music[51] do of course embrace social cause, but they extend also to what we may call 'social trace' (the imprint of the social world on musical materials themselves) and to the social produc-tion of musical meanings (the subject-matter of a reception history). Where analysis is engaged by this larger enterprise, it characteristically addresses the second of these levels (social trace), though it may do so by any one of several strategies. It may, for instance, make concrete the notion of a 'double root' for the musical work (social and stylistic),[52] typically through homologies of com-positional and contextual constructions; this is in essence the way of a socio-logical poetics. Alternatively it may form one strand, or several, of a 'thick' web of metaphors, metonyms, or allegories,[53] such that the work is encircled by enriching and suggestive layers of possible meaning. Or it may, through the offices of a semiotic theory, make possible a series of stepping-stones linking 'neutral' musical materials to formal, generic, and narrative codes, and ulti-mately—by way of these codes—to the world beyond music. Analysis, in short,

---

[49] Naomi Cumming, 'Analogy in Leonard B. Meyer's Theory of Musical Meaning', in Jamie C. Kassler (ed.), *Metaphor: A Musical Dimension* (Sydney, 1991), 177–92.

[50] The term is Max Black's. See his 'More about Metaphor', in Alfred Ortony (ed.), *Metaphor and Thought* (Cam-bridge, 1979), 19–43.

[51] See e.g. Richard Leppert and Susan McClary, *Music and Society: The Politics of Composition, Performance and Reception* (Cambridge, 1987).

[52] The notion of a 'double root', social and stylistic, was developed for art history especially by Heinrich Wölfflin; see his *Principles of Art History*, trans. M. D. Hottinger (New York, 1950; orig. pub. 1917).

[53] See in particular Gary Tomlinson, 'The Web of Culture: A Context for Musicology', *19th-Century Music*, 7 (1984), 350–62. Also Clifford Geertz, 'Thick Description: Toward an Interpretive Theory of Culture', in *The Inter-pretation of Cultures: Selected Essays* (New York, 1973), 3–30.

may confront, may be absorbed by, or may itself absorb context. Whatever the strategy, the enterprise involves a relocation of analysis, and with it a frank dismissal of the austerities and exclusions of formalism. The emphasis lies rather on *in*clusion, the 'bringing together' of disparate perspectives and separated categories, and that speaks of a postmodern world.

## Analysis and Postmodernism

One of the achievements of reception histories has been to point up a central paradox concerning the 'project' of aesthetic autonomy.[54] It was just when that project came nearest to completion, right on the cusp between classical and modern notions of art, that the domain of the aesthetic was most vulnerable to appropriation. In other words, the more art disengaged itself from the social world (and thus gained—as Adorno saw it—critical acumen), the more easily it could be manipulated by that world, and the less effectively it could adopt a disinterested critical stance. It was, indeed, precisely the inadequacy of its social critique, as Peter Bürger has argued, that marked the true failure of aesthetic autonomy.[55] We might argue further that this failure posed a fundamental challenge to both modernism and formalism, given that both were firmly grounded in, and closely connected by, the project of autonomy. The cultural era of modernism represented the summation of that project, just as formalism represented its most characteristic critical mode. Significantly, a second generation of Frankfurt theorists, notably Jürgen Habermas and Albrecht Wellmer, radically revised Adorno's uncompromising negative dialectics.[56]

Critical theory has highlighted both teleological and cyclic dimensions of the modernist enterprise, and of our subsequent 'condition of postmodernity'. The teleology registers a massive loss of faith in Enlightenment projects, culminating in a crisis of bourgeois culture at the turn of the nineteenth and twentieth centuries. This has been variously characterized as an epochal change of discourse (Reiss), a broken contract between word and world (Steiner), and a deconstruction of the boundary between *sensus* and *ratio* (Derrida). Postmodernism, on this reading, entails both a loss of values and a loss of presence. The cycle, on the other hand, lies in a parallel between modernism and Cartesian rationalism, and between postmodernism and the rise of aesthetics. As Andrew Bowie sees it, postmodernism, like early aesthetics, responds above all to the failure of rationalism to do justice to man's sensuous relation to nature.[57] On this reading, it is a questioning of both rationalism and idealism. What is common to both

---

[54] See the first part of my essay, 'Chopin Reception: Theory, History, Analysis', in J. Rink and J. Samson (eds.), *Chopin Studies 2* (Cambridge, 1994), 1–17.

[55] Bürger, *Theory of the Avant-garde*.

[56] For a discussion, see Alastair Williams, 'New Music and the Claims of Modernity' (Aldershot, 1997).

[57] Bowie, *Aesthetics and Subjectivity*.

readings of postmodernism is a recognition (it may be disillusioning or cathartic) that the notion of a single culture, on which modern art had been predicated, is no longer viable. Where music is concerned, those explosive tensions between the polarized repertories (avant-garde, classical, commercial) of a unified, albeit increasingly fragmented, cultural world were defused with astonishing ease. Disparate musics could apparently coexist without antinomies or force fields.

The recent relocation of analysis cannot be separated from these larger cultural changes. I have remarked already that formalism and modernism were closely tied together, their fortunes controlled by the project of aesthetic autonomy. We might expect, then, that any displacement of modernism by postmodernism would demand a comparable displacement of formalism. The 'opening up' of analysis can in part be understood in these terms. In fact, many of its characteristics find a natural context within critical understandings of postmodernism.[58] There is the parenthetical, once-removed quality attributed to analytical insights, registering that analysis now takes place in a time of 'lost innocence', to use Eco's phrase.[59] There is the democratic embrace by analysis of non-canonic repertories, where nothing is peripheral, and everything is accessed via the multiple codes of a consumer-orientated and media-conscious age.[60] There is the replacement of a single 'master narrative' by a cluster of 'little narratives'.[61] There is the determination to expose the ideological and political character of all discourses, including analysis—to 'de-naturalize' knowledge, as it were.[62] There is the simultaneous affirming and questioning of analytical orthodoxies, an ambivalence which has promoted at times a self-ironizing (even trivializing) tone.[63] In semiotic language, there is a focus on the signifier, and a replacement of the single signified by a recursive intertextuality.

Given these postmodern tendencies, it is worth pursuing a little further, and by way of conclusion, the analogy between modernism and formalism, neither of which has been at all anxious to lie down and die. Their continuing projects are of great value to our culture, not least through their projection of some of those qualities (of the work and of the art) which refuse to yield to contingent explanation. They take their stand, in other words, on presence and greatness. But these projects take on new significance in a postmodern world. Far from

---

[58] Not only analysis, one might argue, but musicology in general. Among the several pleas for a postmodernist musicology is Lawrence Kramer's 'The Musicology of the Future', *repercussions*, 1 (1993), 5–18. Kramer's essential aim is a 'willingness and ability to read as inscribed within the immediacy-effects of music itself the kind of mediating structures usually positioned outside music under the rubric of context'.

[59] Umberto Eco, *Reflections on 'The Name of the Rose'* (London, 1985), 67–8.

[60] This 'post-industrialist' resonance of postmodern culture is stressed by Fredric Jameson in *Postmodernism, or, The Cultural Logic of Late Capitalism* (London, 1991).

[61] The term is Jean-François Lyotard's, in *The Postmodern Condition: A Report on Knowledge* (Manchester, 1984).

[62] This aspect is highlighted by Linda Hutcheon, in *The Politics of Postmodernism* (London, 1989). See also her *A Poetics of Postmodernism. History, Theory, Fiction* (London, 1988).

[63] Terry Eagleton describes the postmodern artefact as 'self-ironizing and even schizoid' in 'Proust, Punk or Both', *Times Literary Supplement*, 18 Dec. 1992.

clearing a path for the rest of our (notionally unified) culture to follow as best it can, today's 'modernist', paradoxically a conservative figure, works in one corner of a plural cultural field. And the same might be claimed of today's 'formalist'. The formalist enterprise, again a conservative one, retains its constituency and much of its potency,[64] but it is now just one of several options open to the wider community of analysts. Before reflecting on some of these options, it may be as well to recall a cautionary lesson of history: it is dangerous to discount the conservative voice.

What, then, are some of the alternatives available to analysts today? For some, a redefinition of the province of music theory will be a prerequisite for any further advance in the professional discipline of analysis. Such a redefinition would step beyond the identification of musical structures, and would focus, rather, on the identification of musical materials, confronting the social nature of those materials and exploring the mechanisms involved in their realization and perception. In other words, music theory, and the analysis which flows from it, would draw context into its discourse, as well as engaging directly with issues of performance and perception.[65] For others, the musical work as object will remain centre stage, but its analytical interpretation will embrace disjunction and indeterminacy, as well as (theories of) chaos and complexity. Such approaches, already actively pursued, appear to defy, even to deconstruct, an 'ideology of organicism'; but that ideology may lurk behind them, providing the yardstick *in absentia* for measures of disunity. For yet others—and they may be a growing number—analysis as a separate discipline (though not as an activity) with lose its identity in a mesh of wider critical perspectives, its tools and practices drawn into and absorbed by those wider perspectives. This is an evident response to the replacement of organicism by analogy, and for many it has represented a liberating process of renewal and discovery within the larger discipline of musicology. Yet there are pitfalls on this path too. Setting aside Eco's timely warning of the dangers of over-interpretation,[66] we might simply note the considerable risks that attach to any conflation of poetic and interpretative functions. In practice, the former are all too likely to collapse into the latter, compromising aesthetic significance, that vital capacity of the significant text (however widely we define its 'author') to make its own statement.

There is transparently a challenge to existing categories in the relocation of analysis expressed by these alternatives.[67] Less transparently, but importantly, there is a challenge to institutions. The challenges will be met—are already being

---

[64] See Derrick Puffett, 'Editorial: In Defense of Formalism', *Music Analysis*, 13 (1994), 4–5.

[65] As David Schwarz puts it, music theory can be 're-figured beyond structural limits'. See his review essay, 'On Music and Disciplinarity' in A. Kassabian (ed.), '*And the walls came a-tumblin' down': Music in the Age of Postdisciplinarity*, special issue of *Stanford Humanities Review*, 3/2 (1993), 179–86.

[66] Umberto Eco, *Interpretation and Over-interpretation*, ed. Stefan Collini (Cambridge, 1992).

[67] Among those studies concerned with directions that the study of music might now take outside the framework of traditional disciplines are Katherine Bergeron and Philip V. Bohlman (eds.), *Disciplining Music* (Chicago, 1992), and Kassabian (ed.), '*And the walls came a-tumblin' down*'.

met—as the dust settles. Yet we need to keep an eye on the larger picture. The debates about formalism and positivism (the two were unhelpfully associated by Kerman) did indeed signal the end of a particular project, one of those mysterious caesuras which punctuate intellectual history and which no amount of context can fully explain. In tackling the present essay, I fall into step with the swelling ranks of commentators impelled to make the effort. Yet even as I do so, I sense that the time is ripe to point beyond a debate that is in danger of growing wearisome. More than twenty years ago, Roland Barthes, through a simple but profound reorientation of critical focus, challenged theory with the 'pleasure of the text'.[68] That challenge was important, for it highlighted motivations rather than methods. The need for criticism is as fundamental as the need for art. Quite simply, it is the need to share our reactions (especially our enthusiasm and excitement), and there are no restrictions on their authentic expression. This is not to say that methods can be altogether divorced from motivations. Channels of criticism become blocked; new paradigms release the flow. But the old formalism, no less than the New Musicology, may take its impetus from pleasure and intensity, and may in turn create that surplus of both which enables the best (the 'highest') criticism. That, if we need one, is a defence of formalism.

[68] Roland Barthes, *The Pleasure of the Text*, trans. R. Miller (New York, 1975).

# 3

# *Beyond Privileged Contexts: Intertextuality, Influence, and Dialogue*

## Kevin Korsyn

### I

One place to begin rethinking music lies at the frontier between text and context, at the threshold where the individual composition meets the surrounding world. Conceiving text and context as a stable opposition promotes a compartmentalization of musical research, dividing the synchronic analysis of internal structure from the diachronic narratives of history. Music analysis treats pieces as closed, static entities, open to history only at the level of abstract paradigms (such as formal archetypes). Since analytical techniques have been developed primarily with respect to autonomous compositions, even music historians, when they analyse music, must use 'internal' methods of analysis, as if the piece were created outside time and then parachuted into history. Thus we inhabit a conceptual space ruled by metaphors of 'inside' and 'outside'. You are either 'inside' the piece, securing its boundaries through 'internal' analysis, or you are 'outside', mapping its position with respect to other closed units. You can alternate between internal and external perspectives, tilting like a see-saw, but you can't occupy both positions at once. The trouble with such binary oppositions, as Jacques Derrida has shown, is that they create 'a hierarchy and an order of subordination'.[1] One side of the opposition dominates or controls the other. This has indeed been the case with analysis and history, although the valorized term depends on who is speaking. Analysts often believe that they occupy the privileged site, since they are inside, in a zone of intimate contact with the work. Historians might reply, however, that their activity is primary, because context is greater than any single text. Rather than taking sides in this perennial debate, however, we should remember Michel Foucault's insight that the same system of thought may generate 'an interplay of simultaneous and apparently contradictory opinions'.[2] The controversy between analysis and history masks an

---

[1] Jacques Derrida, *Margins of Philosophy*, trans. Alan Bass (Chicago, 1982), 329.
[2] Michel Foucault, *The Order of Things: An Archaeology of the Human Sciences* (New York, 1970), 75.

underlying complicity, because both disciplines rely on the text/context dualism. You can't escape the prison-house of the autonomous text by appealing to context, because you're still confined by the same binary scheme. This is the impasse, the crisis, of musical research.

If we want to face this crisis, post-structuralist thought offers new metaphors for conceptualizing discursive space. Instead of conceiving the text as a closed entity, like a country on a map, texts are increasingly viewed as networks or relational events. A decisive step here was taken by Derrida, who showed that the inside/outside opposition that sustains the traditional notion of the closed text is vulnerable to deconstruction. Through his concept of 'dissemination', Derrida set the text in motion, turning a static, singular entity into a dynamic multiplicity, pursuing textual 'grafts' that insert one discourse into another.[3] Meanwhile Mikhail Bakhtin, working in a different tradition, much of the time in internal exile in the former Soviet Union, was advocating a decentralized model of literature, replacing the 'monologic' belief in self-sufficient texts with the study of 'dialogic' relationships. Julia Kristeva, who was among the first to introduce Bakhtin to Western audiences, combined his dialogic methods with insights current in France, including Derridean 'writing'. It was in two essays on Bakhtin[4] that she invented the term 'intertextuality': 'Any text is constructed as a mosaic of quotations; any text is the absorption and transformation of another. . . . In the space of a given text, several utterances, taken from other texts, intersect and neutralize one another.'[5] Once Kristeva had put the term into circulation, it was rapidly appropriated by other critics, including Roland Barthes, Michael Riffaterre, and many more. For many critics, intertextuality came to signify an anonymous, impersonal crossing of texts, marking a shift towards a reader-oriented criticism. In his theory of poetic influence, however, Harold Bloom retained the idea of the author as agent within an intertextual theory in which 'there are no texts, only relations *between texts*'.[6] Other thinkers have called attention to the interaction of texts with non-discursive practices, including politics, economics, class, race, gender, and so on, thus further undermining the autonomy of literary artefacts.

Although music research has sometimes adopted post-structuralist insights, we have been reluctant to face the radical consequences of such thought to reconstitute not only our methods, but even the objects under investigation. Intertextuality, for example, deconstructs the text/context opposition, creating 'a radical resegmentation of literature', as 'the words of one text become "part" of another in a single unit of meaning'.[7] Context invades text. The potential to

---

[3] Jonathan Culler, *On Deconstruction: Theory and Criticism after Structuralism* (Ithaca, NY, 1982), 134–5.

[4] Julia Kristeva, 'Word, Dialogue, and Novel' (1966) and 'The Bounded Text' (1966–7), in *Desire in Language: A Semiotic Approach to Literature and Art*, ed. Léon S. Roudiez, trans. Thomas Gora, Alice Jardine, and Leon S. Roudiez (New York, 1970).

[5] Kristeva, *Desire in Language*, 66, 36.

[6] Harold Bloom, *A Map of Misreading* (Oxford, 1975), 3.

[7] Jay Clayton and Eric Rothstein, 'Figures in the Corpus', in Clayton and Rothstein (eds.), *Intertextuality and Influence in Literary History* (Madison, 1991), 24.

complicate traditional notions of music analysis and history will become increasingly evident as we proceed.

Since in this limited space I can only suggest some directions for further thought, I will not try to be comprehensive. Instead, I will concentrate primarily on Bakhtin, whose concept of dialogue offers crucial insights for any attempt to rethink the text/context opposition. Bakhtin is often called a literary critic, but this term miniaturizes him. He sometimes described himself as working at the boundaries of several disciplines,[8] and the profound scope of his cultural vision invites extensions of his ideas to other fields, including music.

## II

Rather than starting from literature, Bakhtin begins from our experience of language in social life and in the construction of selfhood. Speakers constantly refer to the words of others: we repeat, paraphrase, imitate, parody, and distort what others have said, and do so with various degrees of identification or distance. Bakhtin reminds us that no one is 'the first speaker, the one who disturbs the eternal silence of the universe'.[9] Since 'the word [is] already inhabited',[10] our experience of language is 'the *assimilation*—more or less creative—of others' words (and not the words of a language)'.[11] This dialogic character of everyday language provides a model for understanding literature. Every literary work participates in a complex dialogic chain:

There can be no such thing as an isolated utterance. It always presupposes utterances that precede and follow it. No one utterance can be either the first or the last. Each is only a link in a chain, and none can be studied outside this chain. Among utterances there exist relations that cannot be defined in either mechanistic or linguistic categories. They have no analogues.[12]

A key distinction that Bakhtin makes here is between 'utterance' and 'sentence'. The sentence is a unit of *language*, whereas the utterance is a unit of *speech communication*. Utterances and sentences differ in several crucial ways. While sentences are repeatable, utterances are not, because repeating an utterance in a new context creates a new utterance. Unlike sentences, which can exist as isolated units, utterances always have a history, addressing the 'already-spoken-about' and the 'not-yet-spoken-about'. Since authors take earlier utterances into account while also trying to anticipate the reception of their own discourse, text

---

[8] Mikhail Bakhtin, *Speech Genres and Other Late Essays*, trans. Vern W. McGee. ed. Caryl Emerson and Michael Holquist (Austin, Tex., 1986), 103.

[9] Ibid. 69.

[10] Mikhail Bakhtin, *Problems of Dostoevsky's Poetics*, ed. and trans. Caryl Emerson and Michael Holquist (Austin, Tex., 1984), 202.

[11] Bakhtin, *Speech Genres*, 89.

[12] Ibid. 136.

and context reciprocally condition each other. A sentence could function as an utterance, but only by undergoing several essential changes. Most importantly, it must be framed as an utterance; it must be said by someone and to someone, requiring both an author and an addressee. In penetrating critiques of linguistics, semiotics, and structuralism, Bakhtin contends that linguistics has erred in taking the sentence as the model for all speech-acts, ignoring the utterance, and thus giving a distorted, over-simplified picture of communication, depicting the listener as a passive recipient of a message that would be the same even if the listener were absent. Utterances always presuppose an active listener. We always consider the other as we shape our speech; we anticipate his or her response, interests, and potential objections. Thus 'the word . . . is interindividual'.[13]

With this distinction in mind, we can understand Bakhtin's claim that neither logical nor grammatical analysis can explain the aetiology of utterances. Linguistics can tell us about the structure of sentences, but not about relationships between utterances. What is needed, Bakhtin insists, is a 'metalinguistics' that deals with concrete relationships among utterances as wholes.[14] This allows Bakhtin to undertake the paradoxical task of theorizing about uniqueness, dealing with the unrepeatable event of the utterance, while showing how utterances function in a dialogic chain.[15]

Bakhtin's critique of linguistics has profound implications for musical research, because music analysis has often looked to linguistics as a privileged model. One thinks, for example, of Fred Lerdahl and Ray Jackendoff, who have emulated the work of Noam Chomsky, or writers like Jean-Jacques Nattiez, V. Kofi Agawu, or Robert Hatten, who have drawn inspiration from semiotics. Yet even in theories of the past, the dominance of language models has often been evident. Rameau's theories, for example, reflect attitudes towards language prevalent in his day. Foucault has shown that during the seventeenth and eighteenth centuries, language was analysed as a series of propositions. Propositions link two signs through the verb 'to be': 'The grass is green' links grass and greenness, affirming the coexistence of two representations.[16] For Rameau, the cadence assumes the function of a proposition: the cadence links two harmonies into a unit, just as propositions link two representations. Rameau uses the cadence as the model for other progressions, so that the piece becomes a series of interconnected cadences. His use of interpolated notes in the fundamental bass creates cadences where they are not apparent on paper: this practice parallels the contemporary belief that 'all nominal propositions conceal the invisible presence of a verb'.[17]

---

[13] Bakhtin, *Speech Genres*, 121.
[14] Bakhtin, *Problems*, 201–2.
[15] Gary Saul Morson and Caryl Emerson, *Mikhail Bakhtin: Creation of a Prosaics* (Stanford, Calif., 1990), 33.
[16] Foucault, *Order of Things*, 92–6.
[17] Ibid. 93.

Just as literary history and criticism have been impoverished by their privileging of linguistic models, so reliance on these models has impoverished music analysis. Analysis has focused on features of music that are abstract and repeatable, on musical grammar and logic. Although it considers individual compositions as wholes, and relates the parts of compositions to abstract paradigms, we lack any vocabulary, methodology, or concepts that would deal with concrete relationships among whole compositions. To quote Peter McCallum, this constitutes 'one of the failures of analysis to date: its inability to deal with "third-order articulations", such as musical gesture, stylistic reference, and parody, with any sophistication'.[18]

Faced with this predicament, some have urged us to 'get out' of analysis.[19] Another response to the situation, however, would be to rethink both the activity and the *objects* of analysis, by analysing a relational field rather than a discrete work; certainly such an enrichment of analysis could only benefit music history and criticism. We need something resembling Bakhtin's metalinguistics, that would analyse concrete relationships among musical utterances as wholes.

But here some problems arise. If pieces are relational events or nodes in an intertextual network, rather than closed units, then we must question some of the most basic assumptions of our discipline. To talk about relationships among utterances as wholes involves rethinking the issue of wholeness itself and the relationship of text to context. Although utterances have boundaries, dialogic relationships among them prevent them from congealing into autonomous entities; any unity is relative and provisional. If something 'outside' the text becomes 'part' of the text in a single unit of analysis, then these metaphors of inside and outside become deeply problematic. In what follows, I will explore these issues, examining how intertextuality affects both sides of the text/context opposition. As we shall see, these issues mark the site of deeper ideological problems.

## III

Inter-analysis must rethink the idea of the closed, self-identical, unified piece, since 'the intertext divides the text from itself'.[20] One step towards rethinking unity is to *historicize* the concept. Martha Woodmansee wisely remarks that a continuity of terminology in the history of aesthetics may conceal radical discontinuities, because terms are often redefined and assimilated into new programmes that contradict their original functions.[21] This has indeed been the case

---

[18] Peter McCallum, 'Classic Preoccupations: Instruments for the Obliteration of Analysis?', *Music Analysis*, 9 (1990), 206.

[19] Joseph Kerman, 'How We Got into Analysis, and How to Get Out', *Critical Inquiry*, 7 (1980), 311–31.

[20] Vincent B. Leitch, *Deconstructive Criticism: An Advanced Introduction* (Ithaca, NY, 1983), 98–9.

[21] Martha Woodmansee, *The Author, Art, and the Market: Rereading the History of Aesthetics* (New York, 1994).

with unity, and with the metaphors used to describe it. The pragmatic approach to unity advanced by the classical rhetoricians, for example, contrasts strikingly with organicist efforts to assimilate the work of art to natural processes.[22] An oration was unified and comprehensible only so that it could persuade its audience, whether this entailed convincing a jury to free a client or persuading a senate to declare war.

Terry Eagleton has shown how the idea of unity received a new ideological twist in the late eighteenth century, as the work of art came to be modelled on the human subject:

Conceptions of the unity and integrity of the work of art are commonplaces of an 'aesthetic' discourse which stretches back to classical antiquity; but what emerges from such familiar notions in the late eighteenth century is the curious idea of the work of art as a kind of *subject*. It is, to be sure, a peculiar kind of subject, this newly defined artefact, but it is a subject none the less. And the historical pressures which give rise to such a strange style of thought, unlike concepts of aesthetic unity, by no means extend back to the epoch of Aristotle.[23]

This 'cryptosubjectivity', as Eagleton calls it,[24] explains our investment in artistic unity: it is our own unity as subjects which is at stake. The aesthetic has become a 'surrogate discourse' in which our hopes for the autonomy and freedom of the individual have been surreptitiously transferred to the aesthetic object. Indeed, the more precarious our hopes as real individuals have become, the greater the tendency has been to proclaim art the region where all restrictions on freedom and autonomy are transcended. This tempts us to make inflated claims for artistic unity, attributing to art a fantastic degree of autonomy, beyond the power of any artefact to achieve.[25]

Questioning this fetishization of unity, however, does not mean surrendering to chaos. Rather than creating 'a brave new world in which unity never figures', deconstruction, as Jonathan Culler contends, leads to 'the identification of unity as a problematic figure'.[26] We need new paradigms for analysis, new models that will allow both unity and heterogeneity.

Although musicians today seem increasingly receptive to heterogeneity, the allure of closure may be more difficult to resist than we realize. Feminist musicologists, for example, in trying to focus on societal contexts rather than autonomous texts, have urged us to question unity. In their practice, however, the autonomous musical object seems reluctant to abandon control. Marcia Citron, for example, in her discussion of Cécile Chaminade's Sonata, Op. 21,

---

[22] See Kevin Korsyn, 'Schenker and Kantian Epistemology', *Theoria*, 3 (1988), 1–58; *idem*, 'Brahms Research and Aesthetic Ideology', *Music Analysis*, 12 (1993), 89–103; *idem*, review of Mark Evan Bonds, *Wordless Rhetoric: Musical Form and the Metaphor of the Oration*, *Music Theory Spectrum*, 16 (1994), 122–31; *idem*, 'Schenker's Organicism Reexamined', *Intégral*, 7 (1993), 82–118.

[23] Terry Eagleton, *The Ideology of the Aesthetic* (Oxford, 1990), 4.

[24] Ibid. 169.

[25] See Korsyn, 'Brahms Research' and 'Schenker's Organicism Reexamined'.

[26] Culler, *On Deconstruction*, 200.

takes it for granted that the object of analysis is a single, closed text, which is subsequently contextualized.[27] Alan Street, from a different perspective, has argued that 'the championship of unity over diversity represents nothing other than a generalized state of false consciousness'.[28] Since he offers no alternatives to the privileging of unity, however, his essay reads like an obituary for music analysis.

As I have suggested elsewhere,[29] Bakhtin's concept of dialogue might provide a model for rethinking unity. According to Bakhtin, novelistic discourse is stratified, rather than lying on a single plane; the novel may contain 'several heterogeneous stylistic unities, often located on different linguistic levels and subject to different stylistic controls'.[30] These discursive layers may be 'subordinated, yet still relatively autonomous unities'.[31] The novel represents a new kind of linguistic consciousness that Bakhtin calls dialogic; instead of the closed unity of monologic genres, novelistic discourse creates 'artistic images of languages':

The novelistic hybrid is *an artistically organized system for bringing different languages in contact with one another*, a system having as its goal the illumination of one language by means of another, the carving-out of a living image of another language.[32]

The languages of which Bakhtin speaks here are social languages; for Bakhtin, national languages are never unitary, but are always stratified by the conflicting world-views of their speakers. Bakhtin calls this social stratification of language 'heteroglossia'.[33] In the novel, the languages of heteroglossia enter complex dialogic relationships, as consciousness learns to 'orient itself amidst heteroglossia . . . facing the necessity of *having to choose a language*'.[34]

This dialogic unity is unlike that of a dialectic, in which the dialectic process is realized within a single consciousness. In a lucid commentary on Bakhtin, Paul de Man explains this difference between dialogue and dialectic:

Far from aspiring to the telos of a synthesis or resolution, as could be said to be the case in dialectical systems, the function of dialogism is to sustain and think through the radical exteriority or heterogeneity of one voice with regard to any other, including that of the novelist himself.[35]

Only a specific example, however, will clarify the difference between the closure of a dialectical unity and the openness of Bakhtinian dialogue. Consider

---

[27] Marcia J. Citron, *Gender and the Musical Canon* (Cambridge, 1993), 145–59.

[28] Alan Street, 'Superior Myths, Dogmatic Allegories: The Resistance to Musical Unity', *Music Analysis*, 8 (1989), 80.

[29] Korsyn, 'Brahms Research'.

[30] Mikhail Bakhtin, *The Dialogic Imagination: Four Essays*, ed. Michael Holquist, trans. Caryl Emerson and Michael Holquist (Austin, Tex., 1981), 261.

[31] Ibid. 262.

[32] Ibid. 361.

[33] Ibid. 291–2.

[34] Ibid. 295.

[35] Paul de Man, *The Resistance to Theory* (Minneapolis, 1986), 109.

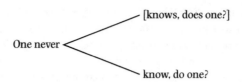

**Fig. 3.1.** An example of double-voiced discourse.

an utterance attributed to Thomas 'Fats' Waller: 'One never know, do one?'
Although Bakhtin never analysed this remark, it compresses into five words the
sort of double-voiced discourse that Bakhtin found in the novel. Calling this
double-voiced may seem puzzling, since we hear only one speaker (Waller) and
one language (English). As we have seen, however, national languages are stratified by social heteroglossia. The two voices in Waller's utterance represent two
social languages. One voice speaks from a dominant social position, and we could
reconstruct it: 'One never knows, does one?' (Imagine this spoken by Margaret
Dumont, the pretentious society matron in the Marx Brothers films.) The second
voice, speaking from a marginal social position (in black dialect) distorts the first
and mocks it, substituting 'know' for 'knows', and 'do' for 'does'. (Figure 3.1 represents this double-voiced quality schematically.) Bakhtin would further classify
this as 'vari-directional discourse', because the two voices pull in different directions, and as parody, because the other's word is treated with hostile intent.[36]
Beneath the obvious humour of Waller's quip lies a subtle form of social criticism; through parody, it displays the coercion involved in the use of the impersonal pronoun 'one'. If I say, for example, 'One so enjoys the weather here at
Palm Beach', I assume an authority for my discourse, as if I were articulating a
universal wisdom rather than merely stating my opinion. Disagreement is ruled
out in advance. Waller's witticism exemplifies the genius of popular, 'unofficial'
language to criticize and subvert 'official monologism, which pretends to *possess
a ready-made truth*'.[37]

Notice that the two voices do *not* merge into a unity, do not collapse into a synthesis. Rather, there is an irreducible heterogeneity here: the utterance displays
a social contradiction, a collision between two social languages; real history
invades the utterance in the form of these contradictions. This is not the dialectical evolution of a single consciousness overcoming otherness; it is not a monologic consciousness reducing difference to sameness. Instead, consciousness
here is multiple. Although Waller's remark is unified syntactically, the social formations to which it points are radically heterogeneous. Bakhtin contends that
this sort of irreducible heterogeneity is at the heart of novelistic discourse,
although different novels exhibit it to different degrees. To imagine the social
voices in the novel as unified would falsify the relationship between art and

---

[36] Bakhtin, *Problems*, 198.    [37] Ibid. 111.

society. According to Bakhtin, ideology suppresses this heterogeneity; the multiplicity of novelistic discourse is reduced to the simple unity of a mono-logic consciousness, because of the 'faith in the self-sufficiency of a single consciousness'.[38]

Here, then, is an alternative to the 'cryptosubjectivity' of aesthetic discourse. Bakhtin replaces the monologic subject with the idea of selfhood as dialogue: 'A person has no internal sovereign territory, he is wholly and always on the boundary; looking inside himself, he looks *into the eyes of another* or *with the eyes of another*'.[39] The unity of the work of art changes into something more complex: 'unity not as an innate one-and-only, but as a dïalogic *concordance* of unmerged twos or multiples'.[40] Although Bakhtin's concept retains some affinities with the idea of cryptosubjectivity, he avoids many of the ideological traps of traditional concepts of unity, because his idea of the unity of consciousness, and conse-quently of the unity of the work of art, is so intricate.

There have been some attempts to apply Bakhtinian concepts to music. Iso-lated Bakhtinian terms, for example, have appeared in discourse about music, but with little awareness of their wider ramifications. Jeffrey Kallberg, for instance, has invoked the concept of double-voiced discourse in a discussion of nineteenth-century piano nocturnes by women composers.[41] Curiously, however, he does not mention Bakhtin, and attributes the term to several femi-nist writers. He seems unfamiliar with Bakhtin's richly imagined typology of dis-course, in which the difference between single-voiced and double-voiced discourse functions not as a binary opposition, but as a continuum with almost infinite degrees.[42] Ingrid Monson has also appropriated the double-voiced concept. Unlike Kallberg, she does mention Bakhtin; but she fails to understand the complexity of the classification. She produces three examples of borrowings in jazz, and classifies all three as both double-voiced and parodic.[43] Not all double-voiced discourse, however, is parodic; moreover, Bakhtin makes an inge-nious distinction between cases in which the parodied material resists what is being done to it, '[exerting] a counterforce against the author's intentions', and parody of a more passive type.[44] I note this not to enforce usage of Bakhtin's ter-minology, or of any particular terminology, but to suggest that Bakhtin has thought more deeply than most about the interaction of languages within an utterance, and his classification of discourse types could enable us to ask new questions about music. Appropriating his terminology, moreover, should include understanding his entire philosophy of language.

Rather than try to apply Bakhtin to music within the limited space available

---

[38] Ibid. 82.                    [39] Ibid. 287.                    [40] Ibid. 289.

[41] Jeffrey Kallberg, 'The Harmony of the Tea-Table: Gender and Ideology in the Piano Nocturne', *Representations*, 39 (1992), 116.

[42] See Bakhtin, *Problems*, 181–269; also Morson and Emerson, *Mikhail Bakhtin*, 123–71.

[43] Ingrid Monson, 'Doubleness and Jazz Improvisation: Irony, Parody, and Ethnomusicology', *Critical Inquiry*, 20 (1994), 283–313.

[44] Bakhtin, *Problems*, 198.

here, I refer the reader to an article of mine[45] in which I offered a Bakhtinian alternative to an analysis by David Lewin.[46] In a discussion of Brahms's String Quartet Op. 51 No. 1, first movement, Lewin identified a scheme of intertextual references, which he characterized as Mozartean and Beethovenian. Lewin's explanation of the relationships among these discourses, however, is dialectical.[47] Against Lewin's monologic vision of a 'dialectic synthesis of musical contradictions', I suggested that the stratified musical languages in the quartet do not merge, do not coalesce; instead, Brahms creates a plurality of unmerged voices. The listener, as a result, undergoes a process of decentring:

[Brahms] dismantles the Beethovenian hierarchy, dissolving the clear opposition of functions that Beethoven had maintained. . . . He dismembers and disarticulates Beethoven's procedures. . . . And by 'placing' Beethoven in this way, Brahms also re-situates the listener, creating a different awareness of self, a different mode of consciousness . . . This is where Lewin's criticism encounters a limit; though he grants Brahms a history, it is a purely musical one. He fails to consider how Brahms's music addresses and constitutes the human subject, and how that subject might both reflect and critique real human subjects. . . . Rather than collapsing into a synthesis, these historical modes fail to coalesce. The non-convergence, the abrasion, of discourses seems to me more essential than any dialectical resolution.[48]

This background may make the idea of heterogeneity seem less alien. Nevertheless, one might object that the subjective feeling of unity in music (or at least in certain repertoires) is so profound that one cannot relinquish it. A dialogic approach, however, would not require us to disregard such feelings. But we would no longer mystify or naturalize the feeling of closure, as if a work of art could really be a free-standing unit. If closure is achieved through conventional means, then the process of closure itself becomes an intertextual event. One can only induce a sense of closure by appealing to conventions, by enacting rituals of closure; thus, paradoxically, the very factors that close a work off, sealing its borders and creating a sense of autonomy, also refer to a plurality of events outside the text.

## IV

Dialogic analysis, then, would reverse the priorities of traditional music analysis. Rather than reducing difference to sameness, in an attempt to secure the boundaries of an autonomous, self-identical text, dialogic analysis would begin from this apparent unity, this *unity-effect*, but would move towards heterogene-

[45] Korsyn, 'Brahms Research'.

[46] David Lewin, 'Brahms, his Past, and Modes of Music Theory', in George S. Bozarth (ed.), *Brahms Studies: Analytical and Historical Perspectives* (Oxford, 1990), 13–28.

[47] Ibid. 24.

[48] Korsyn, 'Brahms Research', 98–9.

ity, activating and releasing the voices of a musical heteroglossia. Turning to music history, I suggest that a similar reversal must happen there. Just as music analysis has generally privileged unity over heterogeneity, so music history has preferred continuity to discontinuity. The historical counterpart of the autonomous text is the ideal of continuous history. Post-structuralist music history must learn to accommodate the 'discontinuities, ruptures, [and] gaps' of which Foucault has spoken.[49]

As Foucault has shown with respect to the history of ideas, historians tend to treat difference as something that must be explained away:

For the history of ideas, the appearance of difference indicates an error, or a trap; instead of examining it, the clever historian must try to reduce it: to find beneath it a smaller difference, and beneath that an even smaller one, and so on until he reaches the ideal limit, the non-difference of perfect continuity.[50]

One assumption that historians rely on to engineer continuity is the idea of a stable, enduring background against which change takes place. This strategy neutralizes and domesticates change by positing a realm of stability as a balance to the world of historical contingency. Change becomes less disruptive, less threatening, because it is the only thing moving against an otherwise immobile historical background.

Another assumption that supports the idea of continuous history has been analysed by Elizabeth Deeds Ermarth, who contends that modern historians view time 'as a neutral, homogeneous medium like the space of pictorial realism in painting'.[51] This belief in a common temporal horizon that explains all historical relationships is a relatively recent invention, one that coincided with the inventions of the Cartesian subject and of perspective in painting. In each case, as Ermarth points out, there is a central point of intelligibility, a privileged position for the spectator. Ermarth's conclusions support Foucault's argument that continuous history 'was secretly, but entirely related to the synthetic activity of the subject'.[52] This relation to the subject leads to the ideological use of history:

Continuous history is the indispensable correlative of the founding function of the subject: the guarantee that everything that has eluded him may be restored to him; the certainty that time will disperse nothing without restoring it in a reconstituted unity; the promise that one day the subject—in the form of historical consciousness—will once again be able to appropriate, to bring back under his sway, all those things that are kept at a distance by difference, and find in them what might be called his abode. Making historical analysis the discourse of the continuous and making human consciousness the

---

[49] Michel Foucault, *The Archaeology of Knowledge and the Discourse on Language*, trans. A. M. Sheridan Smith (New York, 1972), 169.

[50] Ibid. 171.

[51] Elizabeth Deeds Ermarth, *Sequel to History: Postmodernism and the Crisis of Representational Time* (Princeton, 1992), 27.

[52] Foucault, *Archaeology*, 14.

original subject of all historical development and all action are the two sides of the same system of thought.[53]

One consequence of the relationship between continuous history and the subject is the temptation to use the individual consciousness as a source of metaphors for historical processes. For example, Foucault suggests that the tendency to reduce history to pure succession, without allowing for the simultaneity of different temporalities, results from 'the linear model of speech'.[54] Leonard B. Meyer's recent attempt, in *Style and Music*, to assimilate historical change to the psychology of perception may also manifest this ideological use of history; his approach deserves scrutiny here, especially because he explicitly thematizes assumptions that operate implicitly in the work of many music historians.

Meyer attempts to transfer his implication–realization model, which is heavily indebted to cognitive psychology, from its original sphere of analysis to account for historical processes, thus unifying historical explanation and psychology. One of Meyer's guiding assumptions is his 'axiom of constancy':

> To direct attention to change is tacitly to assume that change (especially when it seems anomalous) is what calls for explanation, and correlatively, to take for granted that persistence is the norm of existence. Thus an *axiom of constancy* underlies not only historical interpretation but almost all forms of human comprehension.[55]

I have already analysed this passage at length elsewhere, showing that Meyer's belief that persistence does not require explanation is both a very common assumption among historians and one that is questionable: 'If ideas or institutions reproduce themselves in the same way, resisting the corrosive effects of time and preserving their identities, this could be considered a dynamic process that we should not take for granted'.[56] Change and constancy, as Foucault has shown, are equally problematic.

The controlling metaphor in this passage, which derives from the figure/ground schema of Gestalt psychology, is also problematic. Meyer suggests that change is to constancy as figure is to ground; historical persistence offers a background against which change is legible, as it were, like a figure against a ground. This use of psychology as a privileged model for history, however, may be vulnerable to the objections that Paul de Man raised to the use of phenomenology in Hans Robert Jauss's aesthetics of reception. Since history, to summarize de Man, is not an object in the world, it is not available for sensuous cognition. The expectation, therefore, that the obstacles to historical understanding 'could be mastered by processes that stem from the psychology of perception is by no means certain'.[57] Meyer tries to assimilate historical change to

---

[53] Foucault, *Archaeology*, 12.                                                                    [54] Ibid. 169.

[55] Leonard B. Meyer, *Style and Music: Theory, History, and Ideology* (Philadelphia, 1989), 88; emphasis original.

[56] Kevin Korsyn, review of Meyer, *Style and Music, JAMS* 46 (1993), 472.

[57] de Man, *Resistance to Theory*, 62.

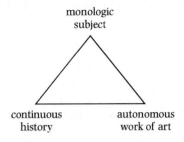

**Fig. 3.2.** The triangle of aesthetic ideology.

an analytical model involving binary oppositions such as implication/realization, congruence/non-congruence, closure/non-closure, and so on. The simple binary options that seem reasonably reliable when an object is within our perceptual horizon become something quite different when we shift to the level of history. To elide the differences between present perception and historical processes suggests that behind Meyer's equation of history and perception lies a subject of history, as if there were a spectator, a subject-writ-large, who perceives the spectacle of historical development as if it were an object of sensuous cognition.

We have already seen how the cryptosubjectivity of aesthetic discourse models the work of art on the hoped-for unity and autonomy of the subject. Now we can extend this idea to history: the unitary, monologic subject is the model for both the autonomous work of art and continuous history. Thus we can imagine a triangle that captures this complicity between music analysis and history: the repression of heterogeneity in analysis parallels the repression of discontinuity in history, and both originate in the repression of otherness that creates the monologic subject (see Fig. 3.2).

V

Discontinuity, according to Hans Kellner, is one of the defining anxieties for the historian; through narrative, historians conceal the intrinsic discontinuity of their subject-matter: 'Narrative exists to make continuous what is discontinuous; it covers gaps in time, in action, in documentation, even when it points to them.'[58] In music history, scholars foster narrative continuity through the use of what I call 'privileged contexts'. These contexts constitute various ways of framing compositions to create historical narratives; they are privileged because historians rely on a limited number of contexts, preferring certain types of frames to others, so that the series of contexts becomes stereotyped and

[58] Hans Kellner, *Language and Historical Representation: Getting the Story Crooked* (Madison, 1989), 55.

predictable, limiting the questions that we ask about music. The composer's *œuvre* and the stylistic period are two of the most obvious contexts that allow historians to organize their narratives, creating discursive unities that reproduce the structure of the autonomous work on a higher level. Another type of contextualization involves comparisons among different arts within the same stylistic period, on the assumption that the products of a given period share a common essence, once again inviting the historian to privilege continuity over discontinuity. The attribution of influence is another framing device that historians favour; by using the arrow of influence to connect one composer to another, historians underwrite 'the homogeneity and continuity' of tradition.[59] The history of genres provides another sort of contextualization; the genre gives the historian's narrative a protagonist, acting as a 'suprapersonal entity' that persists through time, serving the needs of a continuous history.[60]

We tend to take these privileged contexts for granted, seldom doubting the legitimacy of the narrative unities that they foster, just as we seldom doubt the unity of the individual text. To be sure, all these contexts imply a kind of intertextuality; but, as Leitch contends, context 'reduces [intertextuality] in the name of law. Context serves as border patrol.'[61] By establishing a 'proper' frame of reference, historians hope to control the proliferation of meaning. Foucault has spoken of the need 'to disconnect the unquestioned unities by which we organize, in advance, the discourse that we are to analyze'.[62] Among the questionable unities that Foucault mentions are the book, the *œuvre*, 'tradition', 'influence', 'spirit', and even 'literature'. This is not to say that such unities must be banished absolutely, but that they need to be rethought and reconstituted.

Limitations of space permit me to present only one example of a music historian's use of a privileged context, so I will choose an extreme instance for the sake of clarity, and discuss Roy Howat's allegations of Chopin's influence on Debussy.[63] Moreover, to reveal the complicity between analysis and history, I will juxtapose Howat's historical narrative with Jean-Jacques Eigeldinger's analysis of the Chopin Preludes Op. 28.

Eigeldinger presents his analysis as the unveiling of a mystery: the Preludes '[gaze] at us like a sphinx proposing a riddle, one that has remained more or less unsolved'.[64] His answer to the riddle is to analyse the Preludes as a single organic whole, unified by a generative motive: 'Above all, the Twenty-four

[59] Louis A. Renza, 'Influence', in Frank Lentricchia and Thomas McLaughlin (eds.), *Critical Terms for Literary Study* (Chicago, 1990), 186.

[60] David Perkins, *Is Literary History Possible?* (Baltimore, 1992), 3.

[61] Leitch, *Deconstructive Criticism*, 161.

[62] Foucault, *Archaeology*, 25.

[63] Roy Howat, 'Chopin's Influence on the *Fin-de-Siècle* and Beyond', in Jim Samson (ed.), *The Cambridge Companion to Chopin* (Cambridge, 1992), 246–83.

[64] Jean-Jacques Eigeldinger, 'Twenty-four Preludes Op. 28: Genre, Structure, Significance', in Jim Samson (ed.), *Chopin Studies* (Cambridge, 1988), 167.

Preludes are a cycle by virtue of an omnipresent *motivic cell* which assures its unity through a variety of textures.'[65] The motive in question consists of an ascending sixth followed by a descending step (G–E–D (Ex. 3.1*a*) and sometimes G–E–D–C).

Howat suggests that this motive 'may have been intuitively carried over' in Debussy's 'Feux d'artifice'.[66] The motive, which served as 'proof' of unity in an analysis, is now recruited to vouch for influence (see Ex. 3.1*b*). Howat remarks, entirely without irony, that Eigeldinger's motive is 'virtually unstated' in Chopin's Preludes. And indeed, Eigeldinger has to go to extraordinary lengths to

Ex. 3.1*a*. *Melodic shape pervading Chopin's Preludes, Op. 28 (Eigeldinger) (adapted from Howat, 'Chopin's Influence on the Fin-de-Siècle and Beyond', in J. Samson (ed.),* The Cambridge Companion to Chopin *(Cambridge, 1992), 268).*

Ex. 3.1*b*. *Debussy, 'Feux d'artifice', principal motive (adapted from Howat, 'Chopin's Influence', 268).*

Ex. 3.2. *Chopin, Prelude no. 20.*

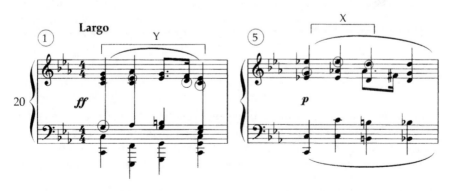

isolate the notes that gratify his desire for unity. Example 3.2 shows his sleight of hand in smuggling the motive into Prelude No. 20; this is by no means an extreme example of his analytical method. The riddle of the Preludes becomes: how can one reduce difference to sameness? Eigeldinger annihilates hetero-geneity, ignoring anything that resists his unitary scheme.

Although Eigeldinger is not alone in analysing the Preludes as a cyclic work, Jeffrey Kallberg has raised some fundamental objections to such a reading: 'These arguments endorse—unwittingly perhaps—the view that smallness of form works to the aesthetic detriment of a musical work.'[67] Perhaps more importantly, Kallberg insists that we remember the generic qualities of the prelude: performers often improvised preludes to larger works, and many nineteenth-century composers wrote preludes to substitute for such improvisa-tions. Chopin himself may have used his preludes to introduce larger pieces; and Kallberg presents suggestive evidence that Chopin may have coupled the F sharp minor Prelude to the F sharp major Impromptu at a concert in 1848.[68] Certainly Chopin did not respect the integrity of his alleged 'cycle', since he often per-formed the preludes outside their published sequence. Kallberg cites a typical Chopin concert programme, which refers to a 'Suite de Nocturnes, Préludes, et Études'.[69]

What Eigeldinger represses, then, is the *intertextual promiscuity* of the Preludes. By fixing them into a frozen, obligatory sequence, he defends against the anxiety that they could function in an indefinite number of contexts, as independent pieces, or as preludes to other works, becoming, in the process, other texts. Eigeldinger turns the text into its own context, making each prelude a prelude to the next, and giving us an object-lesson in how to reify a text.

Howat's historical scheme belongs to the same ideological system. Using Eigeldinger's motive, he creates a continuous history, linking Chopin and Debussy through a unified narrative, assuring us that beneath the obvious discontinuities in their music lies a common tradition. The attribution of influence functions here 'as a benign, even reverential endorsement of humanism'.[70]

# VI

If we hope to escape the tyranny of privileged contexts, we need new models for history; we need paradigms that will accommodate discontinuity, that will authorize new types of narrative. Harold Bloom's theory of poetic misprision, for example, offers an imaginative model for poetic history. Instead of embracing the

[67] Jeffrey Kallberg, 'Small "Forms": In Defence of the Prelude', in Samson (ed.), *Cambridge Companion to Chopin*, 136.
[68] Ibid. 137–8.          [69] Ibid. 138.          [70] Renza, 'Influence', 186.

values of continuous history, Bloom inverts the conventional schema, celebrating the discontinuity of literary history.[71] Although his theory is associated with the phrase 'the anxiety of influence', his concern is not with influence in the sense of tracing allusions from one poet to another. Rather, his subject is 'repressed influence', or 'antithetical influence'; his theory charts the paths by which one poet evades or represses the influence of another. This point is fundamental, but it is too often misunderstood. The anxiety of influence is really a theory of originality.

The paradox, the task around which Bloom's enterprise revolves could be summarized by Paul Ricoeur's splendid question: 'How can I, by starting from another—say from the father—become myself?'[72] Bloom transfers this self/other dialectic to terms of originality and tradition. Neither poems nor people can escape prior models, but an original relationship to the past requires discontinuity as well as continuity. Thus Bloom rejects traditional notions of influence as passive reception, imitation, or benign transmission from one poet to another. Bloom's six 'revisionary ratios' constitute six modes of 'misreading' the precursor, six tropes through which the poet represses anterior poetry.

The appalling difficulty, or strenuous pleasure, in reading Bloom lies in his reversal of the relationship between presence and absence in a poem. Instead of concentrating on what is present, Bloom is interested in '*what is missing in the poem because it had to be excluded*'.[73] This fascination with absence should not be considered a form of imaginative wildness, because Bloom, like Fredric Jameson, wants 'to register a determinate and signifying *absence* in the text'.[74] This 'negative intertextuality', as Jameson calls it, is analogous to the dark matter of the universe, the invisible matter that is known only through its effects on what is seen. Although this notion of absence is refractory indeed, it may seem less alien if we reconstruct the questions that Bloom is engaging here. As I have suggested elsewhere, Bloom is juggling the competing claims of originality and tradition:

Conventional source study tends to dissolve a poem into its alleged sources, without explaining what constitutes a poem's unique claim on our attention. Formalist criticism treats poems as autonomous entities, leaving poems unconnected to history. By showing how poems repress and exclude other poems, Bloom can show how poems become unique, yet relate to tradition, by defending themselves against influence.[75]

The present essay can be read as a belated preface, or perhaps an extended footnote, to my article 'Towards a New Poetics of Musical Influence'[76] in which I attempt to capture Bloom for music. Readers who share my concerns about

---

[71] Harold Bloom, 'The Breaking of Form', in Bloom *et al.*, *Deconstruction and Criticism* (New York, 1979), 15.

[72] Paul Ricoeur, *Freud and Philosophy: An Essay on Interpretation*, trans. Denis Savage (New Haven, 1970), 186.

[73] Bloom, 'Breaking of Form', 15.

[74] Fredric Jameson, *The Political Unconscious: Narrative as a Socially Symbolic Act* (Ithaca, NY, 1981), 137.

[75] Kevin Korsyn, 'Towards a New Poetics of Musical Influence', *Music Analysis*, 10 (1991), 13.

[76] Ibid. 3–72.

conventional musicology may wish to consult it, to see how Bloom might help us to resist the allure of a continuous history.

Here, I have only been able to suggest a few directions for future exploration. As we have seen, rethinking the text/context opposition in music compels us to ask some very fundamental questions concerning the nature of unity, the foundations of music history, and even the construction of selfhood. If we have the courage to pursue these questions, we may discover ways to reinvent and reimagine both our discipline and ourselves.

# 4

# *Autonomy/Heteronomy: The Contexts of Musicology*

## Arnold Whittall

How serious music would have developed without its accompaniment of verbiage is hard to imagine!

Elliott Carter (1972)

## I

Music and language are locked in perpetual symbiosis. The use of words about
music inevitably leads away from abstraction and absolute distinctions: for
example, a composition that is said to be 'non-functional' in the sense of serving
no social or ceremonial purpose can nevertheless be held to 'function' as an
expression of the composer which provokes an aesthetic response in listeners.
Some musicologists prefer to avoid such word-play, believing that it diminishes
the seriousness of their discipline. Others, acknowledging an element of linguistic pluralism that fits well with their modernist predispositions, see no reason
to resist the shifting connotations of such fundamental terms; for example, Carl
Dahlhaus's observation that 'it was the need to understand autonomous, *non-
functional* music that made listeners silently retrace the act of composition in
their minds' follows closely on his identification of the nineteenth-century, bourgeois conception of 'the educative and edifying *function* of music'.[1]

The shift in function identified by Dahlhaus is often regarded as confirming
music's 'autonomy', its capacity to be understood 'in its own right'; and, in turn,
the emergence and persistence of that apparent autonomy helps to explain
the birth and survival of musicology. Before functionality acquired this new
connotation, there was less need to 'silently retrace the act of composition' in
order to 'understand' the music. But the new functionality brought with it the

---

[1] Carl Dahlhaus, *19th-Century Music*, trans. J. B. Robinson (Berkeley, 1989), 50; emphasis added. See also the
discussion in Marcia Citron, *Gender and the Musical Canon* (Cambridge, 1993), esp. 125–8. Her conclusion is that
'functionality is probably inescapable'. Citron also discusses 'the myth of autonomous music' (142), and explores
the value of 'an aesthetic of contradiction' (206).

possibility of distinguishing between listeners capable of understanding the music 'as music' and listeners who were not disposed to explore the technicalities of the compositional process, even when they accepted that music's function was more aesthetic than anything else.

Leon Botstein has argued that what Dahlhaus called the 'educative and edifying function of music' emerged at a time when 'listening [as distinct from performing] became a norm of musical culture', and when 'the capacity . . . to read and "compose" along with what one heard was severely diminished'.[2] A clean line could therefore be drawn between those for whom 'listening was no longer a species of thinking musically; rather, it became an act that helped to verify and vindicate a literary image' (138), and those for whom the 'need to understand' was most fully satisfied not by listening but by study—'silent retracing' writ large. Yet neither musicology nor the wider world of music reception can escape from forms of writing. In Botstein's terms, music in the nineteenth century came to represent 'that to which language could allude' (141), and although he claims that the theoretical and analytical branches of musicology attempted to reverse the 'dependency of music on language' (144), that reversal could never be complete. All forms of musicology depend on language, even if they do not also depend on thinking of musical literacy as more linguistic than musical. The process described as 'musicological listening', or 'structural hearing',[3] is an intellectual activity that craves verbal outlets, if only because 'silent retracing' of the act of composition in the mind alone cannot provide evidence of thought about music accessible to other musicologists.

Even so, this circumstance need not imply that musicology functions best when music itself is deemed 'autonomous'. The exploitation of verbal outlets by musicologists whose prime concern is to explicate specific compositions as more than compendia of particular technical procedures tends inevitably to address matters of meaning (if only of those same technical procedures), and to consider the composition in ways which associate it, directly or indirectly, with the wider world of aesthetics and history. This activity will be dubbed 'interpretative musicology' in the remainder of this essay.

The practice of interpretative musicology serves to complement the exercise of 'structural hearing' which, according to Dahlhaus, 'meant immersing oneself in the internal workings of a piece of music as though nothing else in the world existed. In its original form, it was accompanied by a metaphysic and religion of

---

[2] Leon Botstein, 'Listening through Reading: Musical Literacy and the Concert Audience', *19th-Century Music*, 16 (1992–3), 137; subsequent page references to this essay are given in the text.

[3] By Nicholas Cook and Carl Dahlhaus respectively: see Cook, *Music, Imagination, and Culture* (Oxford, 1990), 152–60, and Dahlhaus, *19th-Century Music*, 95. Dahlhaus's use of the term inevitably intersects with Felix Salzer's, which reflects a concern to train the ear 'to hear not only the succession of tones, melodic lines and chord progressions, but also their structural significance and coherence' (*Structural Hearing. Tonal Coherence in Music* (New York, 1952), p. xvi). For a third term, 'structural listening', see Rose Rosengard Subotnik, 'Towards a Deconstruction of Structural Listening: A Critique of Schoenberg, Adorno and Stravinsky', in E. Narmour and R. A. Solie (eds.), *Explorations in Music, the Arts, and Ideas* (New York, 1988), 87–122.

art. Only in our century, in the name of the same structural hearing, were these mediating factors dismissed as extraneous additives to the acoustic phenomenon.'[4] Such 'dismissals' tended to take the form of writings that were themselves 'extraneous' to the extent of using words about music. Yet it is undeniable that musicological writing, on occasion, has been concerned solely with music's 'internal workings', as if 'nothing else in the world existed'— except the particular, culturally-determined theories of music employed by the writer.

It is in response to the belief that such tendencies in musicology are unhealthy that the cry has gone up to bring back 'the world' into the discipline. The point is not that all writing primarily concerned with 'internal workings'—theory textbooks, for example—should be banned, but that music which belongs to a particular place, time, and compositional persona should not be seriously written about as if it were separate from the world and from all the uncertainties which impinge as soon as we seek to explain cultures as well as the thought-processes of individual human beings.

The problem is to decide how this concern for heteronomy should be expressed. It is one thing for musicologists to approve Rose Rosengard Subotnik's Adorno-inspired observation that 'even as we define problems and relationships in apparent autonomy, we are reflecting complex interactions with society of which we are largely unconscious';[5] it is something else to turn approval into a convincing musicological narrative. It is one thing to accept that critical discrimination should involve more than the circumstance once described by David Lewin—'what the analyst . . . chooses to point out, and the way in which he organizes his presentation, will always reflect a critical attitude towards the piece'[6]—and something else to range persuasively beyond the chosen analytical method and mode of presentation. Even if it is accepted that a more hermeneutic orientation need not involve the total rejection of 'the formalist viewpoints . . . that have been part and parcel of modernist thinking on the arts',[7] the suggestion that the most desirable option for the interpretative musicologist is to embrace an open-minded pluralism, with the aim of balancing the complementary claims of formalism and hermeneutics, creates formidable technical problems for writers seeking to balance narrative flow with methodological credibility. Thomas Christensen presents a widely accepted position when he declares that

It is a formalist prejudice that an artwork receives aesthetic value commensurate to the degree that it can be analyzed as an autonomous entity. But no musical piece is born in a vacuum. Every composition exists along a plurality of continuums: the composer's own artistic development, the historical unfolding of a given genre or style, evolving social and

[4] Dahlhaus, *Nineteenth-Century Music*, 95.

[5] Rose Rosengard Subotnik, *Developing Variations; Style and Ideology in Western Music* (Minneapolis, 1991), 147.

[6] David Lewin, 'Behind the Beyond', *Perspectives of New Music*, 7 (1969), 63.

[7] Richard Taruskin, 'Resisting the Ninth', *19th-Century Music*, 12 (1988–9), 247.

aesthetic forces, and so on. In my mind, any analysis that ignores such processive features needlessly impoverishes itself.[8]

When confronted with such a comprehensive check-list of requirements, however, the aspiring interpretative musicologist may well take comfort in the fact that statements of the case for pluralism are often accompanied by (post)modernist, would-be-deconstructive pleas for doubt, uncertainty, provisionality—for using multivalent interpretation as a counter to the old musicology's decisive single-mindedness.

The effect of this recent explosion of critiques and counter-critiques has been both stimulating and disconcerting. It is still too early to decide whether a critical practice which is 'destabilizing of itself', and which 'sufficiently puts its own world in jeopardy',[9] is either possible or desirable, at least where commentary on the mainstream of Western art-music is concerned. I am all for a writing which 'will undermine and moderate its own voice through its clearer (but never full) hearing of others'; I, too, favour 'tendencies' rather than 'absolutes',[10] and wish to 'encourage multiple border crossings'[11] which efface absolute distinctions between a composition and its cultural contexts. Few will want to promote an impoverished musicology, and the signs are that most professionals have welcomed the initiative embodied in the view that 'musical autonomy . . . is a chimera; neither music nor anything else can be other than worldly through and through'.[12]

Even so, if the fantasy of music's autonomy is now to be confined to theory texts, composition primers, and other pedagogical materials, those who write something else are left with the need to develop appropriate methods to serve an interpretative musicology which might even exploit 'our willingness and ability to read as inscribed within the immediacy-effects of music itself the kind of mediating structures usually positioned outside music under the rubric of context'.[13] Most of the recent writing which goes all or at least part of the way down the road mapped out by Lawrence Kramer is best interpreted as transitional between the old musicology and the new, not least because of its often uncertain handling of analytical procedures once regarded as the preserve of those concerned only with music's 'internal workings'. The following survey of various contributions to this type of writing aims to illustrate the difficulties as well as the rewards of essaying ambitious flights of musicological interpretation at a time when the discipline is in a particularly unstable state and even the most apparently unambiguous texts prove to contain the makings of doubt and uncertainty.

[8] Thomas Christensen, *Music Theory Spectrum*, 15 (1993), 110. See also Christensen's 'Music Theory and its Histories', in C. Hatch and D. Bernstein (eds.), *Music Theory and the Exploration of the Past* (Chicago, 1993), 9–39.

[9] See 'Gary Tomlinson Responds [to Lawrence Kramer]', *Current Musicology*, 53 (1993), 39.

[10] Ibid. 39, 36.

[11] Lawrence Kramer, 'Music Theory and the Postmodern Turn: In Contrary Motion with Gary Tomlinson', *Current Musicology*, 53 (1993), 34.

[12] Lawrence Kramer, 'The Musicology of the Future', *repercussions*, 1 (1992), 9.

[13] Ibid. 10.

# II

No writer on music seems more committed to the principle of autonomy—of 'immersing oneself in the internal workings of a piece of music as though nothing else in the world existed'—than Heinrich Schenker; he therefore poses a challenge, if not a threat, to all aspiring pluralists concerned with the tonal repertory. Schenker's interpretation of compositions as integrally hierarchic and organic (at least when in the hands of the masters) can nevertheless be regarded, not as 'purely musical' in the most literal sense, but as culturally determined by factors outside and beyond music itself. Schenker may have resisted analogies between compositions and either literary or social contexts, yet he was committed to a far wider frame of reference than that provided by aesthetic and cultural elements—that of the cosmos, no less: 'Between fundamental structure and foreground there is manifested a rapport much like that ever-present interactional rapport which connects God to creation and creation to God. Fundamental structure and foreground represent, in terms of this rapport, the celestial and the terrestrial in music.'[14]

Despite his rejection of nineteenth-century harmonic analysis in the tradition of the Abbé Vogler and Gottfried Weber, Schenker embodied a strong nineteenth-century ethos, focusing on the sense of transcendence to which music was held to have privileged access. Since a deep structure represents organic coherence in its most universal form, it embraces a vision of the work of art as a counter to social fragmentation and confusion as much as to religious disbelief and the inadequacies of a purely humanist philosophy. One may not like it, but it is hardly a 'purely musical' affair. Ultimately, it would appear, the only autonomy that concerned Schenker was that of 'the cosmos and its eternal ideas—this alone signifies a life of beauty, true immortality in God';[15] and it follows that the interpretative musicology of tonal compositions can hardly refuse to engage with the implicit transcendence as well as the explicit organicism of Schenkerian theory and practice.

To ignore Schenker where tonal music is concerned is, therefore, to reinforce a commitment to social and cultural 'realities' at the expense of the organic and the transcendent. For example, in their discussions of Chopin's second prelude from Op. 28 (Ex. 4.1*a*), both Rose Rosengard Subotnik and Lawrence Kramer leave Schenker's voice-leading graph of the piece (Ex. 4.1*b*) out of account, since, for them, the prelude is characterized above all by its dis-integration, its resistance to and rejection of all that 'tonality' most commonly implies. For Subotnik, 'harmonic meaning in the sense of recognizable harmonic

---

[14] Heinrich Schenker, *Free Composition*, trans. and ed. E. Oster (New York, 1979), 160. Nicholas Cook, 'Schenker's Theory of Music as Ethics', *Journal of Musicology*, 7 (1989), 415–39, and William Rothstein, 'The Americanization of Heinrich Schenker', in H. Siegel (ed.), *Schenker Studies* (Cambridge, 1990), 193–203, have some relevance to what follows.

[15] Schenker, *Free Composition*, 161.

Ex. 4.1*a*.  *Chopin*, Preludes, *Op. 28 No. 2.*

Ex. 4.1b. *Schenker's voice-leading graph of Chopin, Prelude, Op. 28 No. 2 (Free Composition, Fig. 110, no. 3).*

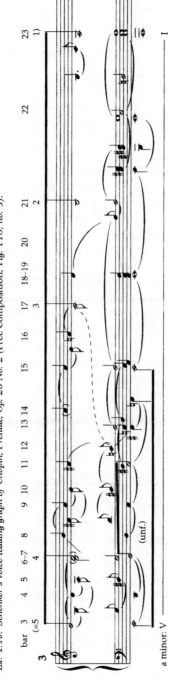

function is not absent in this piece, but by and large, harmonic structure has disintegrated into localized and roughly (though not in every respect audibly) analogous harmonic units.'[16] For Kramer, 'latent continuities can be teased out of the piece . . . but the value of doing so is questionable . . . From a hermeneutic standpoint, the question that needs to be asked of this music is not what deep structure holds it together, but rather what motivates it to keep breaking apart.'[17]

Both writers believe that it is anachronistic to ask questions about 'deep structure' in the prelude; but both are concerned with much more than such aspects of musical autonomy. Subotnik's study forms part of her large-scale exploration of the argument that serious music since late Beethoven profoundly reflects cultural and social fragmentation. Kramer places the music in a cultural framework that includes Géricault and Manet, seeking to identify and elucidate 'the self-haunting incoherence that no Romantic subject can escape, and that must be stabilized in order to bridge the gap between self-absorption and the social/material world'.[18]

Arguably, Subotnik and Kramer have done Schenker a favour by not mentioning an analysis which might have been calculated to support any points they might wish to make about the inflexibility and unreality of Schenker's cosmic conception of tonality in the face of Chopin's most progressive and imaginative thought. Schenker's answer to the forbidden question—'What deep structure holds the piece together?'—has not wholly persuaded commentators generally sympathetic to his aims, and even Marianne Kielian-Gilbert's relatively full defence of the continuity between motive and voice-leading which can be read from Schenker's graph does not answer all criticism of the *Urlinie* itself.[19] The graph[20] (see Ex. 4.1*b*) is at its most defiantly organicist in the way it shows the scale degree 4 of the background projected from the foreground (bar 4) to bar 6, then prolonged across the centre of the piece to bar 17. Schenker asks us to hear the projection of D above G from bar 6 as more fundamental to the piece's coherence than the 'new start' on a B minor chord in bar 8; and it is this strategy which might make his analysis seem more a defiant imposition of an inflexible principle than a revelatory solution to a musical puzzle. Yet, that 'incomplete transference of the forms of the fundamental structure'[21] on which the graph is predicated acknowledges that the harmonic structure of the prelude is (exceptionally) fragmentary, and Kramer and Subotnik have missed the opportunity to contrast the way in which Schenker strives to preserve the unity of a fragment

[16] Subotnik, *Developing Variations*, 134.

[17] Lawrence Kramer, *Music as Cultural Practice, 1800–1900* (Berkeley, 1990), 72.

[18] Ibid. 91–2.

[19] Marianne Kielian-Gilbert, 'Motivic Transfer in Chopin's A minor Prelude', *In Theory Only*, 9/i (Mar. 1986), 21–32.

[20] Schenker, *Free Composition*, fig. 110, a. 3.

[21] Ibid. 88–9.

(the divine harmony remaining triumphantly intact) with the manner in which they celebrate the fragment's disintegration into yet smaller elements, mirroring the 'real world', rather than the cosmos.

If Schenker's cultural conditioning, and not just his theoretical predispositions, his 'purely musical' understanding, encouraged him to resist any impulse to offset organicism by conceding a formal role to the fragmentation of structures (as opposed to their—rare—partial presentation as smaller, incomplete unities), the modernist readings of Subotnik and Kramer conform to the opposite extreme. Subotnik's concern is to locate Chopin—the E major Study as much as the A minor Prelude—within a Romantic reaction to the classicism which had 'aimed at a high ideal of human universality, in which all rational structures would be self-evident'; and she asserts that Romanticism 'gave honest voice to the dawning recognition by modern Western society that such universality did not characterize human reality'.[22] Yet Subotnik, like Kramer, interprets Chopin as if the change consequent on this 'dawning recognition' was already absolute and complete, without even that transitional interaction between well-established and progressive forces which more conventional analysis of Chopin (and much other Romantic music) explores. Without the 'cosmic' perspective of Schenker's attempt to shore up Chopin's music against the ruins of Romanticism, analyses like theirs are severely impoverished.

Interpretative musicologists who actually include a Schenkerian dimension in their work tend to do so either to reinforce a contrast, comparable to that just proposed, or, more radically, to probe Schenker's own work for evidence of latent ambiguity and conflict—failure to live up to its transcendent pretensions. Schenker may also be invoked simply to dramatize a polemical stance, as when Kramer asserts, in a follow-up to his study of Haydn's 'Representation of Chaos', that 'the standard modes of analytic writing and graphic representation . . . are the very picture of the positivist's dream of truth', and claims that there is an 'ineradicable difference between the critical and analytical treatments of the foreground'.[23] Yet Kramer's attempt to separate deep structure from foreground, on the basis that only the foreground has a signifying role, has no analytical justification, since deep structure interacts inseparably with surface structure, and to this extent supports and embodies all aspects of that surface. To argue for tension, rather than integration, between background and foreground is a straightforward modernist ploy, seeking to fragment an integrated form, and the ploy is far more convincing when the possibility of tension between different aspects of structure itself—harmony and motive, for example—is considered. This topic will return a little later on.

---

[22] Subotnik, *Developing Variations*, 151.

[23] Lawrence Kramer, 'Haydn's Chaos, Schenker's Order; or, Hermeneutics and Musical Analysis: Can they Mix?', *19th-Century Music*, 16 (1992–3), 3–17; *idem*, 'Criticizing Criticism, Analyzing Analysis', *19th-Century Music*, 16 (1992–3), 78.

There have been various demonstrations of how response to a tonal structure may be enriched when an orthodox Schenkerian analysis is complemented either by more traditional thematic or formal readings or by contrasting accounts of harmony itself.[24] When Schenker is complemented by a broad cluster of critical responses, the account can become even more richly poised in terms of an interaction between formalist and hermeneutic initiatives. For example, in his study of Beethoven's Ninth Symphony, Nicholas Cook comments that 'it was certainly Schenker's aim, as much as Kretzschmar's, to explain the mutual relationship between part and whole in music'.[25] Yet Cook's point is not simply to demonstrate the differences and similarities between Schenker's formalism and Kretzschmar's hermeneutics, but to contrast both of them, in their essential Romanticism, with his own more modernist stance. Cook complains that 'Romantic interpretations reduce the contradictory elements of the Ninth Symphony to a narrative thread or a series of pictures; absolute-music interpretations reduce them to an architectural plan. And the result in each case is the same: the music is deproblematized, sanitized, shrink-wrapped' (93). Cook's strategy, therefore, is to set a modernist belief that the Ninth Symphony 'is profoundly ambivalent' (101) against those more reductive interpretations, and a major consequence of presenting the argument in this way is to underline the extent to which responses which may at first appear to be concerned with music as an autonomous entity prove to be contextual to the extent that they are culturally determined. Just as the ideas of Schenker and Kretzschmar owe much to the Romantic obsession with (and occasional resistance to) the idea of the organism, so Cook's own concern with ambivalence is a prime characteristic of modernism as both ideology and cultural practice.

A particularly striking example of the use of Schenkerian techniques—albeit in adapted form—as part of a wide-ranging interpretation balancing formalist and hermeneutic initiatives can be found in Timothy L. Jackson's study of Richard Strauss's *Metamorphosen*.[26] It considers manuscript sources and materials as well as the 'finished' score, and also responds uninhibitedly to the special historical circumstances of the composer and his work at the end of Second World War. Jackson's complex, extended argument proceeds to two principal goals: to establish the true source of *Metamorphosen* and to explain the composition's meaning in the light of a 'correct' reading of its structure. Jackson presents documentary evidence to show that *Metamorphosen* originated not, as is commonly assumed, in the waltz 'Trauer um München', but in an unfinished choral setting of Goethe's poem 'Niemand wird sich selber kennen', and he

---

[24] For a notable example of the latter see Christopher Wintle, 'Kontra-Schenker: *Largo e mesto* from Beethoven's Op. 10 No. 3', *Music Analysis*, 4 (1985), 145–77.

[25] Nicholas Cook, *Beethoven. Symphony No. 9* (Cambridge, 1993), 84; subsequent page references to this essay are given in the text.

[26] Timothy L. Jackson, 'The Metamorphosis of the *Metamorphosen*: New Analytical and Source-critical Discoveries', in Brian Gilliam (ed.), *Richard Strauss. New Perspectives on the Composer and his Work* (Durham, NC, 1992), 193–241; subsequent page references to this essay are given in the text.

argues that the composition 'is a Goethean probing of the underlying cause of war, namely of the bestial in man' (195). Jackson believes that 'the recomposition of the incomplete setting of Goethe . . . in the *Metamorphosen* seems to coincide with Strauss's ultimate disillusionment with the National Socialists' (199). In this reading, therefore, a very concrete biographical and historical context is provided for the argument that *Metamorphosen* embodies 'Strauss's essentially tragic view [that] the end result of metamorphosis is not man's attainment of the divine but his descent into bestiality' (195). Jackson underlines the crucial point as follows: 'In Strauss's instrumental meditation Goethe's concept is violently inverted; through self-knowledge, man regresses from the divine to the bestial' (201).

Jackson's narrative is enthralling and compelling; yet one looks in vain for that self-questioning scepticism which a properly modernist interpretative musicology must invoke. For example, Jackson finds no element of paradox in the way he seeks to equate his belief in the music's achievement of convincing closure with the view that the work's philosophical content concerns man's 'ultimate defeat'. It may well be that *Metamorphosen*'s concluding reference to the Funeral March of Beethoven's 'Eroica' Symphony represents Strauss's repudiation of Hitler, as Beethoven repudiated Napoleon. Yet that repudiation itself, in common with the purely artistic triumph that *Metamorphosen* is usually held to represent, might indicate a sense in which man's defeat is relative, not absolute—a 'tragic' ending in the true sense of the word, whereas Jackson's view that 'the end result . . . is man's descent into bestiality' seems more nihilistic than tragic.

A comparable single-mindedness attends Jackson's analysis of Strauss's score. He provides convincing documentary evidence to support his argument that, while the Goethe-setting sketch should be placed 'in chronological proximity to the first *Metamorphosen* sketches' (222), dating from August–September 1944, the earliest sketches with material for 'Trauer um München' belong to October 1944, and extend to January 1945, a period when Strauss was facing an impasse in work on *Metamorphosen* itself. Chronological contiguity creates the possibility of interconnection, and Jackson has no doubt that the E minor/C major progression of the Goethe setting's first bar (Ex. 4.2*a*) is the source of the 'E/C ambiguity' (202) evident in the way *Metamorphosen* moves initially from an E minor triad to C (minor) by way of A major and C flat major (Ex. 4.2*b*). Already the differences might seem more striking than the similarities, but Jackson believes that the similarities are what matter: he believes, in particular, that *Metamorphosen* is fundamentally concerned with middle-ground and background transformations of a single underlying motive—what he terms the 'Metamorphose-motiv'—which is none other than the E/C motion which, in its most background manifestation of all, is held to span the entire work.

It is therefore central to Jackson's interpretation not only that the motive itself is textually meaningful—in the Goethe setting it 'represents the elusiveness of the "self-I"' (209)—but that transformations of it are present, at higher structural levels, in the Goethe setting and *Metamorphosen* alike. Jackson provides voice-leading graphs of both compositions to demonstrate the pervasiveness of motivic transformation, and, bearing in mind his belief that in *Metamorphosen* 'Goethe's concept is violently inverted', it might seem appropriate that the fundamental structures of the two should differ radically. Indeed, although the Goethe fragment ends on the dominant, Jackson is able to read elements of a descending *Urlinie* (Ex 4.2c) which are, in a sense, 'inverted' in *Metamorphosen*'s background (Ex 4.2d). Here, not only is there an ascending *Urlinie* (a concept which Jackson claims to have arrived at independently of David Neumeyer), but the composing out of the 'Metamorphosemotiv' which he seeks to illustrate involves an *Ursatz* which has no structural dominant, no bass arpeggiation. Clearly, then, the structure of Strauss's work involves a metamorphosis of what

Ex. 4.2a. *Jackson's realization of 'Niemand wird sich selber kennen', bars 1–4 (T. L. Jackson, 'The Metamorphosis of the* Metamorphosen', *in B. Gilliam (ed.),* Richard Strauss *(Durham, NC, 1992).*

Ex. 4.2b. *The beginning of* Metamorphosen, *as summarized by Jackson ('Metamorphosis', 203–4).*

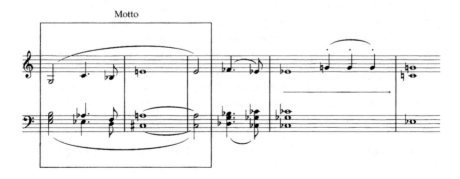

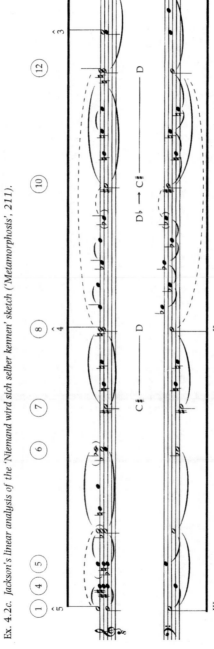

Ex. 4.2c. *Jackson's linear analysis of the 'Niemand wird sich selber kennen' sketch ('Metamorphosis', 211).*

Ex. 4.2d. *Jackson's linear analysis of Metamorphosen: background and middle ground ('Metamorphosis', 212).*

Schenker would have recognized as 'tonality'; and one is bound to ask whether Strauss's apparent concern to 'invert' Goethe in *Metamorphosen* might not have led him, not so much to project an 'inverted' *Ursatz* over the whole work, as to abandon such highly integrated foundations altogether.

Jackson is well aware of the technical minefield created by these issues, and he devotes a long footnote, amounting to an appendix, to a defence of his departures from Schenkerian orthodoxy. He acknowledges that 'the reader may ask why I do not read a structural dominant beginning in m. 377 . . . and extended through m. 389' (238). But the reader may already have asked how far the possibility might be taken of demonstrating a more conventional fundamental structure for *Metamorphosen*: and, if the answer is 'not very far', to question how plausible it is to conclude that a highly chromatic late Romantic composition, even one which sets out to be in some respects a kind of mirror image of its (unfinished) model, is spanned by a single governing background, orthodox or unorthodox. Even if, like Jackson, one accepts that 'many—though not all—of Strauss's compositions are highly organic' (237), the argument that *Metamorphosen* is quite so powerfully integrated at quite so high a structural level, and quite so single-minded in its working-out of its fundamental Goethean associations, strains credulity, on historical as well as technical grounds. Some hint of uncertainty amid all these powerfully urged conclusions seems called for.

The last thing I want to do is propose an alternative, no less definitive 'truth' to Jackson's, since it is precisely the forceful goal-directedness of his argument, his 'anti-modernism', that precludes the admission that he might be offering a counter-structure to some more conventional—even if looser—musical design. Jackson avoids a fuller consideration of those surface motivic and chordal factors which might, in the light of the composer's training and 'history', be felt to represent Strauss's main area of concern. Jackson's fundamental structure for *Metamorphosen* certainly offers a 'counter' to that for the Goethe setting, as described above, but the importance of this symbiotic feature is diminished by the desire to promote parallel unities in two such radically different designs. Ironically, Jackson's main concern is to integrate context, as suggested by documentary evidence and theory-based analysis, as closely as possible, even though the whole edifice depends on the argument that *Metamorphosen* inverts, rather than simply amplifies, the Goethe material. Jackson concludes that while 'Goethe's view of metamorphosis . . . is essentially optimistic' (201), its inversion, the representation of 'man's ultimate defeat' in Strauss's instrumental meditation, is 'definitively achieved only in the final tonic minor chord because it is only in this chord that the largest-scale structural lines resolve' (213).

Clearly enough, it is Jackson's decision to press the connection with 'inverted' Goethe to its limits which determines his apocalyptic reading of *Metamorphosen*. I have already offered the counter-argument that it is possible to hear the tragedy in the work's ending shorn of the nihilistic overtones implied by an analysis like

Jackson's in which a potential pluralism is swept away by an integrating certainty so compulsive that it leaves no room for scepticism or ambiguity. By contrast, I regard Strauss's final dialogue with Beethoven as ambivalent—an acknowledgement of the permanent strengths of German culture as well as a rite of penance in the face of dictatorship and genocide. The dialogue between Strauss and Beethoven is also a dialogue between vice and virtue, weakness and strength, Goethe inverted and Goethe the right way up. The aged Strauss, not unlike the Countess in *Capriccio*, could compose an ending which convinced him personally, precisely because that ending was, in some respects, decisively indecisive, the work's meaning remaining open at the point of formal closure. This, at least, is my Strauss, and a rather different Strauss from Jackson's, who resolves those 'largest-scale structural lines' in *Metamorphosen*'s final chord.

Jackson's work raises major questions for practitioners of interpretative musicology. One could say, to be consistent with the argument of this essay, that the problems which arise from his analysis do so not from its pluralism, its determination to avoid considering *Metamorphosen* merely as an 'autonomous' musical structure, but from its determination to progress beyond pluralism to synthesis. Jackson remains in thrall to the theoretical constraints of his principal analytical technique, even though this involves major modifications of the original Schenkerian precepts. He cannot be accused of offering a 'deproblematized, sanitized, shrink-wrapped' *Metamorphosen*, yet his conclusion seems to be that the work is in no way ambivalent or multivalent.

The most thought-provoking complement to work like Jackson's is to be found in attempts to show that Schenker himself was not, in practice, the pure, organicist Romantic of the now traditional view, but that he actually (unintentionally?) embodied a degree of ambiguity true to the cultural modernism rife in the years in which his most important work was done. The proposal that a shift from a concept of hierarchy to a concept of networks enables the musicologist to balance the claims of motivic and harmonic elements in tonal music in a more accurate, convincing manner has yet to be tested in depth; but it clearly represents an important initiative in the attempt to reinterpret Schenker the 'cosmic' organicist in modernist terms.[27] The principle of 'plural unities' affirms the importance to interpretative musicology of compositions which resist the overpowering strategies of their 'fields of affiliation',[28] while at the same time acknowledging that no composition is ever adequately interpreted by means of a single theoretical principle. A comparable impulse is at work in Kevin Korsyn's reading of Schenker's system as one which 'discloses *both* hierarchical reduplication *and* its opposite, showing both the possibility of a rapport between levels, as when the same motive appears in both the foreground and the middle ground, and a tension or contradiction between levels, as when a dissonance on one level

---

[27] See R. Cohn and D. Dempster, 'Hierarchical Unity, Plural Unities: Toward a Reconciliation', in K. Bergeron and P. Bohlman (eds.), *Disciplining Music: Musicology and its Canons* (Chicago, 1992), 156–81.

[28] Lawrence Kramer's term ('Haydn's Chaos', 8).

becomes consonant at the next'.[29] Korsyn even regards exploitation of this conflict between levels as a way of suggesting an implicit musical irony. With reference to Schenker's discussion of the opening of the third *Leonore* Overture, he
observes that 'although Schenker did not explicitly formulate this notion of simulating the structure of rhetorical irony through a conflict between structural
levels, it is not difficult to elicit it from his texts'.[30]

Korsyn seeks to replace 'the idea of autonomous, self-contained compositions
as closed and static entities' with a concept of the composition as a 'relational
event', whose meaning (in Korsyn's adaptation of Harold Bloom's formula) 'can
only be another composition'.[31] In his work on Brahms, Korsyn argues that it is
the presence of multiple perspectives on tonality itself, irrespective of any wider
hermeneutic factors, that undermines any simplistic formalist interpretation. He
is clear that 'what appears modern—or rather postmodern—in Brahms is his
recruitment of a plurality of musical languages', in the sense of 'a number of
historically differentiated discourses'.[32] He notes the risk for modern musicology
in stressing the variety and even the 'ambivalence' in a composer's work simply
in order to lay the foundations for the demonstration of a higher and more satisfying unity. Korsyn sees Brahms, as Subotnik and Kramer in effect see Chopin,
as embodying an 'astonishing modernism', in compositions which 'become self-
deconstructing, questioning their own closure, subverting their own status as
independent works by constantly invoking other texts'.[33] Korsyn is able to
provide some persuasive evidence that Brahms was less interested in 'fostering
synthesis' than in exploiting 'the irreducible heterogeneity' of 'modes of musical
rhetoric'. For example, in the C minor Quartet, Brahms 'dismembers and disarticulates' Beethoven's procedures, and the sense emerges of the opening of the
quartet as a 'dismantling' of 'the Beethovenian hierarchy'.[34]

All this may suggest that Korsyn conforms to the Subotnik/Kramer strategy
of viewing Romanticism primarily in terms of its most forward-looking cultural
and technical facets. Yet Korsyn does not propose that, in Brahms, tonality itself
is dismembered and disarticulated; rather, he offers a reading of the Romance,
Op. 118 No. 5, in which Schenkerian analysis plays a vital role in showing that
orthodox voice-leading is compatible with the presence of tonal instability, by
way of a 'conflict of levels'.[35] Since Korsyn is committed to the argument that
tonal stability and instability are simultaneous in the Romance, he aims to
demonstrate by way of a voice-leading graph a double functioning whereby the
'conflict' is embedded between what in the foreground is a tonality of D major
(in the piece's middle section) and what in the larger context is a submediant

[29]   K. Korsyn, 'Towards a New Poetics of Musical Influence', *Music Analysis*, 10 (1991), 27.
[30]   Ibid. 69.
[31]   Ibid. 14.
[32]   K. Korsyn, 'Brahms Research and Aesthetic Ideology', *Music Analysis*, 12 (1993), 90.
[33]   Korsyn, 'Towards a New Poetics', 53.
[34]   Korsyn, 'Brahms Research', 94–8.
[35]   Korsyn, 'Towards a New Poetics', 35.

major (of F major). (For Korsyn, there is instability here, since, whereas the A major harmony in bar 8 leads back to F, its return in bar 16 leads on to the D major middle section, thwarting expectations.)

From the perspective of a musicologist like Richard Taruskin, dedicated to finding 'a way out of the formalist impasse', Korsyn is vulnerable to the objection that his '"new poetics" mainly reconfirms conventional judgements'. For Taruskin, Korsyn does not reject 'the comforting autonomy paradigm', but reinforces '"the compelling logic and unity" in pieces'[36]—just as Korsyn accuses Karl Gieringer of doing. Given the character of the Romance it is difficult to see what else Korsyn could have done: and he does at least suggest that 'the compelling logic and unity' of the piece is given an aura of ambivalence by the kind of 'tension or contradiction between levels' which he seeks to demonstrate. The idea needs fuller exploration, not least to examine the possible value of distinguishing between tonal pieces which possess this quality and those which do not. It would also be a good thing if Korsyn were able to expand his Brahms work by tackling larger compositions and by giving ideological and technical elements a stronger historical dimension. A good start might be to challenge Susan McClary's interpretation of 'identity and difference' in Brahms's Third Symphony in terms of the Samson and Delilah story.[37]

## III

Ironically, perhaps, initiatives to promote multivalent musicological interpretation appear to strengthen the possible parallels between tonal compositions and more explicitly modernist, post-tonal works. In the latter case, nevertheless, Schenkerian hierarchies are not available to counterbalance hermeneutic analysis, and while an approach to the 'internal workings' of a post-tonal design exclusively in terms of pitch-class set structure can undoubtedly create the impression of strongly integrated musical forces, the value of pluralism in the interpretation of such works seems even more widely endorsed than is the case with tonal compositions. I will now provide an outline analysis of a short post-tonal work by a major modernist composer, in an attempt to illustrate an interpretative musicology that mediates (up to a point) between 'old' and 'new' concerns. It may appear that I give rather greater weight to matters autonomous than to matters contextual, to technical commentary than to cultural explanation—but I shall do so from a heteronomous perspective, acknowledging the inevitable and delightful confusion attendant on all verbal discourse about music.

---

[36] Richard Taruskin, 'Revising Revision', *JAMS*, 46 (1993), 114–30, pp. 120, 123.

[37] Susan McClary, 'Narrative Agendas in "Absolute" Music: Identity and Difference in Brahms's Third Symphony', in Ruth A. Solie (ed.), *Musicology and Difference. Gender and Sexuality in Music Scholarship* (Berkeley, 1993), 326–44.

   If it is a particular characteristic of modernist composition that it embodies symbiotic interactions which are fundamental to the nature of the work (as structure, texture, expression) and not subordinate to a higher synthesis which can be represented by means of a coherent theory of structural levels, then Elliott Carter's *Scrivo in vento* (1991) is explicitly modernist. My discussion will refer to various texts—the published score, Carter's comments in an interview with Andrew Ford, the sonnet by Petrarch entitled 'Beato in sogno', which includes the phrase 'scrivo in vento', and two commentaries on Petrarch. First, the sonnet itself, preceded by Carter's comment in the score:

*Scrivo in vento*, for flute alone . . . takes its title from a poem of Petrarch who lived in and around Avignon from 1326 to 1352. It uses the flute to present contrasting musical ideas and registers to suggest the paradoxical nature of the poem.

> Beato in sogno et di languir contento,
> d' abbracciar l'ombre et seguir l'aura estiva,
> nuoto per mar che non à fondo o riva;
> solco onde, e 'n rena fondo, et scrivo in vento;
> e 'l sol vagheggio si ch' elli à già spento
> col suo splendor la mia vertù visiva;
> et una cerva errante et fugitiva
> caccio con un bue zoppo e 'nfermo et lento.
> Cieco et stanco ad ogni altro ch' al mio danno,
> il qual dì et notte palpitando cerco,
> sol Amor et Madonna et Morte chiamo.
> Così venti anni, grave et lungo affanno,
> pur lagrime et sospiri et dolor merco:
> in tale stella presi l'esca et l' amo!

Petrarch, RIME SPARSE 212

Blessed in sleep and satisfied to languish, to embrace shadows, and to pursue the summer breeze. I swim through a sea that has no floor or shore, I plow the waves and found my house on sand and write on the wind;

and I gaze yearning at the sun so that he has already put out with his brightness my power of sight; and I pursue a wandering, fleeing doe with a lame, sick, slow ox.

Blind and weary to everything except my harm, which I trembling seek day and night, I call only Love and my Lady and Death; thus for twenty years—heavy, long labor—I have gained only tears and sighs and sorrow: under such a star I took the bait and the hook![38]

   Carter's brief comment invites expansion, along the lines that the poem expresses the poet's overwhelming awareness of mortality, and that paradoxical circumstance in which artists attempt to create something permanent (relatively speaking) out of their own sense of impermanence. Perhaps the poem's most powerful encapsulation of that paradox is the image of gazing longingly at the

---

[38] Trans. Robert M. Durling.

sun, which is seen as a transcendent symbol of light and renewal, despite the knowledge that the sun's cycle is also a potent guarantee of human transience. The paradox is that the poem, the artefact, celebrates (or at any rate acknowledges) its own ultimate impermanance, yet it also endures—the poem has survived its author—in a way Carter neatly spells out when he observes that his *Scrivo in vento* was first performed 'coincidentally on Petrarch's 687th birthday'.

Not surprisingly, I am tempted to pursue the argument that Petrarch's poem is modernist in the twentieth-century sense. To say, as Robert M. Durling does, that 'Petrarch is obscure, he is ambiguous, and he is refined and even precious in his diction',[39] is not to contend that these qualities somehow permeate the very structure of his verse in the way they permeate the very structure of Carter's music—Durling is talking about matters of meaning rather than form. Yet the claim that 'Petrarch explores the experience of love' in terms of oppositions that he does not resolve unambiguously—oppositions 'of eternity and time, stability and instability'[40]—points up the importance of what Durling terms 'impossibilia' to his work; and the persistence of unresolved oppositions, of which 'impossibilia' are a particularly telling symbol,[41] is certainly striking in the context of a musical manner very different from the madrigal style with which Petrarch is commonly associated, and which, in Gary Tomlinson's view, formed one aspect of the dialogue between humanism and mannerism that can be found in such works as Monteverdi's *Il Combattimento di Tancredi e Clorinda*.[42] If Monteverdi's 'Lamento di Arianna' is the archetypal musical formulation of the 'Petrarchan humanist ideal' as synthesis, an unambiguous resolution of oppositions, Elliott Carter's *Scrivo in vento* is truer to that alternative Petrarch who fails to achieve such resolution, despite the clarity of his poetic forms and the consistency of his poetic language.

It might be argued that there is nothing specifically modernist about a composition which relates to texts playing with the paradoxes that inevitably arise when writers juggle with images of permanence and impermanence. From Renaissance madrigals to Romantic tone-poems, composers have devised integrated, synthesized tonal structures to parallel such verbal materials. Nevertheless, as a post-tonal composer, Carter employs a musical language to which synthesis in the traditional sense is alien, and it seems to me that, as modernist, he relishes the opportunity to provide not simply a 'setting' of the sonnet—a musical text that parallels the expressive ebb and flow of Petrarch's 'Scrivo in vento'—but a dislocation, a dialogue in which the main participants are Petrarch and Carter, artists separated by 600 years but linked by a mutual fas-

---

[39] Robert M. Durling (ed.), *Petrarch's Lyric Poems* (Cambridge, Mass., 1976), p. ix.

[40] Ibid. 20.

[41] See the discussion in Sarah Sturm-Maddox, *Petrarch's Laurels* (Philadelphia, 1992), 22–3.

[42] Gary Tomlinson, *Monteverdi and the End of the Renaissance* (Oxford, 1987), 259–60. I am indebted to Tim Carter for the information that Petrarch's 'Beato in sogno' was set to music by Ambrosio Marien (*Il primo libro di madrigali a quattro voci*, Venice, 1580).

cination with paradox. Carter's *Scrivo in vento* may be regarded as a 'relational event', the prime progenitor of which is the Petrarch poem; and the feature which David Schiff aptly terms Carter's 'musical signature'[43]—the all-interval tetrachord (0146)—provides the primary source for those unresolved oppositions for which Petrarch can only use words. But before pursuing the dialogue between similarity and difference which the composer's deployment of this invariant element involves, I want to air more general considerations of form and meaning, bearing in mind the possibility that some if not all of *Scrivo in vento* was composed before Carter became aware that its particular features might be aligned with Petrarch's poem. (This possibility is raised by Andrew Ford's statement that, when he met Carter in June 1991, there was 'a flute piece . . . on Carter's desk [which] has since been given the title *Scrivo in vento*'.[44])

Carter's remark, in his note, about 'contrasting musical ideas and registers' has its equivalent in his further comments to Ford:

In this little flute piece I had the idea that I'd like to have the flute play a series of things in which one bit was in the very lowest register and the next bit in the very highest. And after writing a piece which did that, I decided I didn't know how to begin it. Because you have the flute playing something very slow and quiet in the low register and then you have some very high notes, and it was important to suggest what is the reason that this suddenly happens this way. And so today I wrote a whole beginning which explained all that. (6)

These words seem calculated to characterize a composer who is, as Carter told Ford, 'very concerned with causality' (6). They also create an intriguing problem for the analyst who has not discussed the piece with the composer. Where (assuming it survives) is *Scrivo in vento*'s false beginning? The answer could well be: 'on the last quaver beat of bar 10', since what begins there is in some respects an elaboration of what has gone before; bars 1–5 might then be said to 'explain', to 'cause', bars 10–13, in the sense that they provide the pure form of the (0146) 'signature collection' for the later statement to decorate (Ex. 4.3*a*). As a whole, bars 1–10 might also be held to 'explain' that the piece will not only be concerned with those basic oppositions of register and character mentioned by Carter: in the main body of the piece, the low, slow, and quiet segments and the high, loud segments will both make use of (0146) collections to a certain extent. But the effect of their first deployment, in bars 1–10 (Ex. 4.3*b*), is to underline the evolving contrast between a first segment which is 'pure' signature; a second, overlapping segment, mixing low/long and high/short notes, which preserves the collection and is therefore transitional; and a third segment, predominantly high/short, which resists the collection to the extent that, in order to be generated wholly by intersecting (0146)s, the

---

[43] David Schiff, 'Elliott Carter's Harvest Home', *Tempo*, 167 (1988), 5.

[44] Andrew Ford, *Composer to Composer: Conversations about Contemporary Music* (London, 1993), 2; subsequent page references to this conversation with Elliott Carter are given in the text.

Ex. 4.3a. *Elliott Carter,* Scrivo in vento, *bars 1–18.*

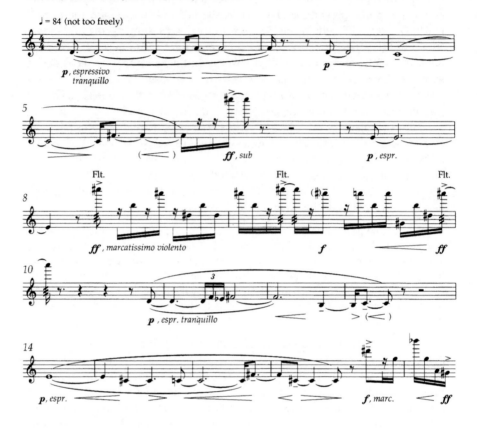

c¹ and d¹ of segment 1 and the e¹ of segment 2 would need to be invoked—a tortuous, far-fetched exercise!

The signature collection serves nevertheless to close the gap between the two types of material, a process analogous to the wind's closing of the gap between the World Trade Centre's towers, as seen from the windows of Carter's Greenwich Village apartment—a phenomenon that Carter described to Ford (2).[45] A force of nature which, in the world outside Carter's apartment (and his composition), is alarming in its untameable power is harnessed to an artistic technique. The composition is about closing gaps, but also about preserving gaps. As a feature of the New York 'world', the closed gap seems to represent instability; but as a compositional process exemplified by *Scrivo in vento*, it serves to stabilize the

[45] Ibid. It is tempting to see *Scrivo in vento* as a late after-shock of Carter's *Concerto for Orchestra* (1969), described by David Schiff as his 'most American vision, evoking an entire continent and a vast heterogeneous society in a state of turmoil', by way of its associations with the prose poem 'Winds' by St John Perse (see Schiff, *The Music of Elliott Carter* (London, 1983), 246).

Ex. 4.3*b*.  Scrivo in vento, *bars 1–10: Carter's 'signature collection'.*

composition's modernist sense of balance, its achievement of equilibrium in the absence of the anchoring force of tonality.

The pervasiveness of the (0146) collection in *Scrivo in vento* is confirmed by its piece-spanning occurrences (differently ordered) and by recurrences which have an almost recapitulatory resemblance to the initial event (bar 10, then bar 73: see Ex. 4.3*c*), as well as by a large number of other well-varied, well-concealed manifestations. Yet this discussion of the work's organizing principles cannot

Ex. 4.3c.  Scrivo in vento: *further occurrences of Carter's 'signature collection'.*

Ex. 4.3d.  Scrivo in vento: *white-note 'modality'.*

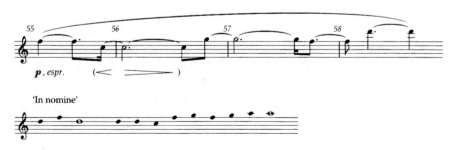

Ex. 4.3e. Scrivo in vento: *mirror symmetry.*

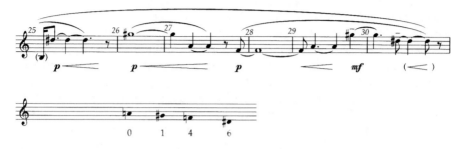

escape all uncertainty, in keeping with an understanding of causality that has as much to do with provoking contradictions as with generating derivations. Moreover, the dialogue Carter sets up between 'doux' and 'rude', smooth and fractured, is less the surface projection of a deep structure than a reality which stands or falls on its own immediate qualities of thought and feeling. There is also a hint of the playfulness proper to serious art in the suggestion of a further layer of dialogue in the music between the topics of 'then' and 'now'. It is as if the Petrarch character speaks first through a reference to chant—the 'In nomine', perhaps?—a white-note modality ripe for black-note contradiction. But although this melodic figure is alluded to intermittently as the piece proceeds (most explicitly in bars 55–8—see Ex. 4.3d—and 73–5), it is more likely that what Carter came to see as the Petrarchan aspect of the music lies in the deeper paradox of a mortal mind aspiring to immortal thoughts—something Petrarch shares with many other poets, but which he articulates with a special passion and eloquence. The only way in which music can translate this notion in sober structural terms is through the exploration of degrees of stability (apparent 'permanence') and instability: and once this translatability is permitted, modernist composers have rich resources at their disposal.

The initial opening-up of *Scrivo in vento* through opposition—'espressivo, tranquillo / marcatissimo, violento'—is balanced at the end of the piece by a narrowing-down which reverses the motion from violent to tranquil. It is clearly important for the interpretative musicologist dedicated to demonstrating modernism not to fall into the trap of assuming that this 'ultimate balancing' is indistinguishable from a synthesizing resolution of contrasts (even the specifically post-tonal kind of synthesis proposed by Edward Cone[46]). Yet it is difficult to deny that this composition is 'unified' by Carter's consistent working with his chosen oppositions. *Scrivo in vento* could hardly aspire to coherence were it not so. More crucially, that coherence embodies (and is likely to have been stimulated by) the opposition between the potential for strict frameworking found in the persistence of a particular pitch-class collection, and the resistance to such strictness in the

[46] Edward T. Cone, 'Stravinsky: The Progress of a Method', *Perspectives of New Music*, 1 (1962–3), 18–26.

musical line as we hear it and think about it. After all, Carter could hardly have brought Petrarch's sonnet into alignment with his (already completed?) music had he not found in it an appealing analogy to the well-established components of his modernist musical language.

Carter's treatment of the essentially modernist strategy of mirror symmetry also suggests that he is particularly interested in the contrasts available between the explicit and the implicit as a way of grounding, though not rigidly determining, his music's dialogue between more fixed and freer elements. For example, at a relatively early stage in the piece there is an explicit mirroring (pitches, not durations) of the (0146) collection. Yet this grows out of a longer melodic phrase (bars 25–30), and therefore 'melody' overrides 'harmony' in the sense that the phrasing seeks to counter the simple symmetry of the pitch content (Ex. 4.3e). Mirrorings of this kind provide evident 'local' consistency, while the more comprehensive balancings between beginning and ending, and the larger tranquil and violent segments, show mirroring extending more freely into the larger-scale formal design of the piece.

There is, of course, a limit to the degree to which a monody can develop ideas of dialogue. It might be a weakness of *Scrivo in vento* that some segments seem to rely on rather routine, ostinato-like gestures; but a context determined by the poetics of paradox suggests that these segments may represent a deliberately 'weak' attempt to assert the topic of inflexibility. The fanciful embodies impermanence when it counters such fixity; so it is the music's subtle play with mirrorings that represents its most creative allusion to stability, and provides a particularly telling analogy to Petrarch's text. In this sense, it may even be that the music from bar 73 to the end presents a more stable rethinking of bars 1–72, and the essential paradox, which anti-hierarchic modernism seems especially well suited to promote, lies in the impulse to make something memorable out of the image of impermanence, that permanent cultural feature of our time.

As should be clear from this discussion of *Scrivo in vento*, my 'pluralism', considering the music not just in terms of its pitch-class content, or even of its purely musical melodic and formal character, but also as a response to a particular poem and a continuation of the composer's dialogue with the landscape and culture of his own time, does not aim to replace unity with diversity, but to balance their competing claims. In linking work to world, it is still the work that dominates, because it represents a triumph over the world: it is a product of the world that transcends its context. Since my discussion remains within the framework of well-established musicological procedures, it may be judged a failure by those who seek to introduce 'an essential uncertainty'. It pursues aesthetic and critical topics, to do with modernism, in terms of structural and technical factors, discussing the ways in which the music's fragments are ordered and balanced by the composer. This interpretation of modernism might be regarded as equivalent to cultural explanation, and it is certainly part of my interpretation of *Scrivo in vento* to propose a continuity between the piece and that persistent Carterian project which makes it possible for Andrew Ford to regard all his mature compositions as 'almost models of society' (6).

Yet, while it may well be possible to set one's critical imagination to work in order to propose a specific cultural explanation of *Scrivo in vento* focusing on topics and concepts which would not be so directly applicable to any other piece, I would prefer to suggest that the specifics are in the music, rather than in the meanings. Attractive though it may be to use Ford's narrative about the closing of the gap between the twin towers of the World Trade Centre on windy days in order to explain the essential character of the piece, such an explanation might be felt to enhance the separateness of the music from the world as much as to subject the piece to the world's powerful and irresistible embrace. After all, as a New York 'jeopardy' piece, *Scrivo in vento* can scarcely compare to Tom Wolfe's novel *Bonfire of the Vanities*.

## IV

When a musicologist interprets other interpreters, there is an inevitable tendency to align, stratify, and synthesize. We are all in the grip of that inescapable binary stand-off between music and language: but just as music is best thought of as interacting with the structures of speech and language rather than as simply opposed to them, so the New Musicology is likely to be best served by the promotion of dialogues—dialogues about compositions, that is, even more than about the nature of musicology itself.

Since at least the time of the Abbé Vogler's *Handbuch zur Harmonielehre* (1802), it has been difficult to think of music as other than multivalent. But it was the shift from tonality to post-tonality—not absolute, of course—that most powerfully reinforced the essential ambivalence of a form of expression that thrives on the polarity of similarity and difference. So, although it has always been true that 'a work of music characteristically underdetermines any unique interpretation of it; that is, a score or a work of music answers to more than one interpretation of it',[47] it can also be argued that any one musicological interpretation will itself be multivalent, if not by definition ambivalent. Even so, a multivalence derived from diverse technical and historical sources will still be inadequate if one accepts the argument that 'the analysis of a work in terms of how the given content was achieved is, and has to be, logically secondary'.[48] What we should seek to interpret, on this view, is 'what it is that has the power to affect us . . . primary aesthetic experience'. 'Internal workings' alone clearly do not meet the case.

---

[47] See Michael Krausz (ed.), editor's introduction to *The Interpretation of Music. Philosophical Essays* (Oxford, 1993), 3.

[48] F. M. Berenson, 'Interpreting the Emotional Content of Music', in Krausz (ed.), *Interpretation of Music*, 66.

The impact of such aesthetic arguments on analysis is most apparent in the current musicological enthusiasm for a revived hermeneutics. Professional journals and conference programmes offer abundant evidence of a strong tendency to go at least as far down the hermeneutic path as is consistent with thinking less about musical material in terms of structural functions and properties, and more about musical meaning in terms of topics and generic models. This thinking, and its associated methodologies, goes some way to justifying the belief that a multivalent analysis can balance the claims of poetics and formalism within a coherent discourse without subordinating works to the power-play of 'fields of affiliation'; it also promotes acknowledgement of the innate cultural modernism of analytical work, whatever the period of music we happen to be concerned with. The aim is to complement a technical discussion which itself acknowledges music's inherent multivalence with a contextual perspective that incorporates as many factors as the analyst's single mind regards as relevant and pertinent. Such a properly modern analysis should recognize the incompleteness of any one methodology (however all-embracing in itself); yet it should not push its embrace of the fragmentary to the point where the ultimate effect of the analysis is simply incoherent. This aspiration to an overall coherence is risky, but only seriously so if it is confused with that lingering coercive desire to say the last, definitive word on what matters about a composition: a desire every interpretative musicologist must acknowledge—and resist.

Musicologists continue their search for a role, even to the extent of asking whether they should still be called musicologists. Given the widespread suspicion of 'music-science', the shift towards a more creative function, as interpreter or even inventor, is understandably attractive. The objective, polemically expressed, is to affirm music's worldliness, to put it back where it belongs in time, place, and thought. At the same time, however, it is possible to counter these potentially decisive acts by displays of sincere, far-reaching uncertainty, in keeping with the deconstructive initiatives prevalent in a culture believing itself to be deep in a postmodernity of supreme instability and relativism.

While few scholars are likely to reject initiatives that seek to give context and even self-doubt a place in interpretative musicology, I sense that there is a less general conviction that narratives of cultural explanation should become the main concern. A deconstructed musicology ceases to be musicology at all if it resists direct engagement with composer and composition, and side-steps the possibility that works of art may be defences against the world as much as products of the world. It is understandable that committed deconstructionists should (single-mindedly) regard the idea of a less monolithic but still work-centred musicology as seeking to achieve the old coercive objectives by only slightly different means. Yet, for that very reason, those same committed deconstructionists, in their zeal to transform musicology into something else, may be reluctant to accept that much, if not all, of what they desire can actually be better achieved from within an enriched musicology than from outside it. If music is indeed 'worldly through and through', as Lawrence Kramer contends, that serves to reinforce the complex tension between its formal and hermeneutic aspects, and in turn to reinforce the difficulty of achieving an interpretative musicology that is adequately plural and adequately coherent. Ironically, it may be the force of these difficulties that will encourage the pendulum to swing back to favour the specializations of 'music-science'. But if that happens, musicology risks finding itself even more out of step with the evolving, enduring relativism of modern culture than is already the case.

# 5

## Going Flat: Post-Hierarchical Music Theory and the Musical Surface

### Robert Fink

Those who go beneath the surface do so at their peril.

Oscar Wilde

One of the hardiest discussion threads on the Internet newsgroup devoted to classical music has been a long-term attempt to answer the perennial question, 'What's the *deepest* piece of music?'[1] Aside from a few jokers (*La Mer?*), most who tackle the question frame it in terms of ideal content, usually extra-musical. They provide lists of pieces that seem 'profound', that appear to deal with meaningful, spiritual, universal issues: Beethoven's Ninth, Bach's B minor Mass, *Parsifal*, Mahler and Bruckner symphonies. An issue that almost never seems to come up is abstract musical structure: the idea that a composition models in some purely formal way a bounded, multi-level, often hierarchical space which provides a sense of depth and complexity independent of any hermeneutic goal.

But the assertion that abstract musical artworks have a surface, and thus also have a hidden interiority and depth, underlies what is perhaps the single most important metaphor of structuralist musical analysis. It is with some trepidation that I reconsider this fundamental assumption, since to give it up would cut one loose from the very foundations of music theory as practised today. It remains undeniable that surface–depth models of music have led to elegant, totalizing representations of musical structure that appeal to many. Still, I intend to argue that, for reasons both technical and political, it may be time to retire the surface–depth metaphor—indispensable as it has been—as we attempt to understand the way music is composed and received now. It is no less true for being platitudinous that we live in an era whose fundamental break with the era of surface and depth is encapsulated by the over-used adjective 'postmodern'.

The following meditation on analytical technique is thus another in a long series of attempts to reconstruct the ideological supports of music theory, both to bring it into line with new cultural politics and, more practically, to allow us

---

[1] Technically the newsgroup is a function of the Usenet; its formal name is rec.music.classical.

to analyse previously intractable repertories. In this sense I am making a sequel to the many reconsiderations of 'organicism' that have appeared in recent decades.[2] As we shall see, the surface–depth metaphor, since it leads to the assumption of musical hierarchy and a theory of structural levels, underpins the most influential claims—Schenkerian analysis and set theory—that all great music has hidden organic unity, no matter how complex, chaotic, or incomplete the listener's experience of its 'surface' may be. In the face of much recent music which, in a peculiarly postmodern way, exalts surface and flouts depth, one might begin to question whether hierarchy is the best index of value in contemporary music—or even in the canonic master-works that submit so satisfyingly to hierarchical music theories.

## I. Axiomatic

I begin with an immediate strategic retreat. I do not think it possible to prove the presence or absence of surface and depth in music. In the face of fundamental disagreement about the ontological status of music itself, an ontological critique of the surface–depth metaphor seems arrogant and naïve, if not simply hopeless. But whether or not music has surface and hierarchical depth, it is an indisputable fact that much of the analytical discourse around music assumes that it does.[3] I would like to take this assumption itself as the basis for a two-part utilitarian enquiry. The first part of this chapter will evaluate the surface–depth metaphor in terms of practical analytical technique. I will present a hyperbolic series of analytical vignettes, from Beethoven to Rochberg, that will attempt to demonstrate that depth models of musical structure become progressively more untenable—or, at least, progressively worse explanations of salient musical experiences—as we approach the contemporary moment. But the cultural work that surface–depth metaphors perform goes far beyond the 'purely' structural; and in the second part of this investigation I will attempt a tentative outline of the way in which hierarchical music theory works as cultural politics, giving this powerful and comforting musical analogy its due as an index to—or even a constituent of—deeply rooted social constructions of individuality, interiority, and class identity.

Unfortunately we cannot plunge directly into either music or the bourgeois

[2] The major landmarks: Joseph Kerman, 'How We Got into Analysis and How to Get Out', *Critical Inquiry*, 7 (1980), 311–31; Ruth Solie, 'The Living Work: Organicism and Musical Analysis', *19th-Century Music*, 4 (Fall 1980), 147–56; Leo Treitler, '*To Worship That Celestial Sound*: Motives for Analysis' and 'Music Analysis in a Historical Context', both in *Music and the Historical Imagination* (Cambridge, Mass., 1989), 46–66, 67–78 resp.; and also Janet M. Levy, 'Covert and Casual Values in Recent Writings about Music', *Journal of Musicology*, 5 (1987), 3–27. For a more focused historical account of organicism *bei* Schenker see William Pastille, 'Heinrich Schenker: Anti-Organicist', *19th-Century Music*, 8 (1984), 28–36, and 'Ursatz: The Philosophy of Heinrich Schenker' (Ph.D. diss., Cornell University, 1985).

[3] For an investigative survey of music's spurious spatial existence see Patricia Carpenter, 'The Musical Object', *Current Musicology*, 5 (1967), 56–87.

ego; it is impossible to elide epistemological considerations completely. What does it mean to say that music has a surface? How does the surface relate to the depths—and how are those depths structured? What does the organization of the depths 'do' to the surface? The axiomatic presentation below is deliberately schematic. It attempts only to erect a quick, provisional framework within which we can address the more fruitful questions of analytical technique and politics.

## 1.  Fear of the Surface

One might begin with the slightly tautological observation that by calling the surface the surface, we have already crystallized an anxiety. For by naming a surface, we conjure up a depth which is, at least at first, hardly more than a lack—an absence. Why is it that what we write down, what we play, what we hear, is somehow both *too much* and *not enough*? It does seem that there is a 'fear of the surface' running through much analytical work, from the canonical studies of Schenker and Schoenberg to the most recent explorations of semiotics and the anxiety of influence. Digital storage of bibliographical information makes a kind of *ad hoc* statistical analysis possible: enter the word 'surface' as a query into the RILM database of abstracts, and the results display certain discursive patterns again and again. The word 'surface' never appears without being shadowed by the word 'depth'; the hierarchic relationship between surface and depth is more important than any feature of the surface itself; in most cases, surface detail is explained as a projection of hidden structural levels, motivically or through voice-leading; the complexity or incoherence of the surface before analysis is often noted, and the promise of analysis is that it will be made to disappear.

This distrust of the surface runs deep in structuralist music theory. Pass over Schenker's reduction theory of tonal voice-leading for the moment—'Every surface, seen for itself alone, is of necessity confusing and always complex'[4]— and take as an extreme but not unrepresentative example Allen Forte's cautionary 1972 discussion of 'Sets and Nonsets in Schoenberg's Atonal Music'. It may be uncharitable to summarize Forte's complex segmentation arguments as 'If you can see it on the surface, it's not there'—but what are we to make of passages like the following?

the augmented triads visible from the notation are not significant structural components and, in fact, are a fortuity of notation or, perhaps, a notational concealment—which would not be untypical of Schoenberg. Nor is it untypical of Stravinsky. Similar passages abound, for example, in *The Rite of Spring*. . . .

About the diverging 'chordal streams' in m. 2, it can be said, without qualification, that

---

[4]  Heinrich Schenker, *Free Composition*, trans. and ed. Ernst Oster (New York, 1979), p. xxiii.

(once again) the 'augmented triads', 'minor triads', and 'chromatic lines' so congenial to the amateur analyst are of no significance in themselves.[5]

Forte is constructing a 'multi-dimensional' deep structure for atonal music, a powerful and clearly very satisfying project which is certainly his right; yet in the process of warding off 'amateur analysts', he has problematized the musical surface to an extraordinary degree. Forte's professionalism has never been in dispute: but I wonder about the cultural implications of turning Schoenberg's seductive, expressive (even expressionist) musical surface into something defensive and threatening: an uninviting morass of pitfalls guarded by 'notational concealment'.

## 2. The Surface as the Edge of the Hierarchy

Forte gives no documentary or anecdotal evidence for disregarding surface manifestations of familiar triadic and chromatic groupings. His argument is purely systemic: if he can come up with a deep structure for this music, we *must* prefer to hear its surface as a projection of that structure, rather than (the only alternative) as a jumble of superficial details. This is the power and the limitation of the surface in structuralist music theory: *surface events must be conceptualized as 'taking place' at the limits of a generative hierarchic structure.* The hierarchy of structural levels generates the surface, organizes its often bewildering complexity, and endows it with 'organic' unity by linking every surface event back to a single deep structure. (Forte: 'Every detail, no matter how minute, is an integral part of the musical conception.'[6])

The relation between generative hierarchies and musical surfaces has already undergone careful epistemological critique by Richard Cohn and Douglas Dempster.[7] They make a convincing case that viewing the musical surface solely as the product of a single generative hierarchy is too limiting; they prefer to consider it as the product of multiple interlocking hierarchies. Neatly reversing Schenker's fetishization of the 'fundamental structure', they relocate the unity of a tonal work in its complex surface—the common foreground of several backgrounds, only one of which is the strict voice-leading hierarchy of Schenkerian theory.[8] Cohn and Dempster's proposal for 'plural unities' certainly offers an

[5] Allen Forte, 'Sets and Nonsets in Schoenberg's Atonal Music', *Perspectives of New Music*, 2/1 (1972), 58, 54.

[6] Ibid. 48.

[7] Richard Cohn and Douglas Dempster, 'Hierarchical Unity, Plural Unities', in Katherine Bergeron and Philip V. Bohlman (eds.), *Disciplining Music* (Chicago, 1992), 156–81.

[8] 'The concept of product networks suggests that, instead of thinking of a complex musical surface as unified by an underlying structural simplicity, we consider the surface as a *solution* to the compositional problem of mutually satisfying the demands of several sets of independent formal operations. . . . What is most potentially unsettling about this view is that the apparently complex musical surface is reconceived as the basis of a composition's unity. It is the surface that 'holds together' underlying diversity by providing a compositional solution to multiple and disparate demands of harmonic, contrapuntal, motivic, and rhythmic operations' (ibid. 176–7).

invigorating alternative to the monadic organicism of the *Urlinie*; but their revisionism does not yet encompass the radical step of detaching the surface from hierarchy altogether.

## 3. The Surface as Impermeable Boundary

To do that would run the risk of the surface falling apart. Plural unities still add up, after all, to unity—they still explain *everything*. It seems that one of the crucial goals of hierarchic music theory is to weld the surface of a musical work into a seamless totality—to provide it with 'structural integrity'. Only if it possesses that quasi-organic integrity can the surface fulfil its key function as the *boundary* between the music 'inside' and a constantly encroaching (non-musical) 'outside'. For Schenker, this epistemological boundary is literally a matter of life and death:

> that art, however, *which is developed into an organic whole through the connection of background and foreground, is so filled with genuine life, it cannot tolerate the encroachment upon itself by non-living, mechanistic systems of immature musical intellectuals.*[9]

Of course, for Schenker the connection of foreground and background is essential, not constructed. Still, one can see how a theory without at least the potential to link the two, and thus explain every last surface event, is not just less ambitious, but defensively useless. Schenker himself makes the analogy between surface and epidermis;[10] the final section of my essay will explore some of the implications of seeing the surface of a musical work as analogous to one's own skin.

## 4. Reductionism, Formalism, Schenkerism

The model of music as a skin-like surface stretched over hierarchically structured depths effectively determines the operation of our analytic methodologies. It demands that theories of musical structure be reductive, since analysts feel obligated to map out structural levels by systematically stripping away surface details. And it effectively guarantees formalism, since its seamless embrace of the musical surface leaves no purchase for extra-musical explanations. (Why search outside the work for significance when every event on the surface is explicable from below and inside?)

The most influential and fully developed reductionist formal theory of music is Heinrich Schenker's theory of long-range linear structure. I will follow Cohn and Dempster, and make it the foil for my rethinking of music. Like them, I see

---

[9] Heinrich Schenker, 'Rameau or Beethoven?,' in Sylvan Kalib, 'Thirteen Essays from the Three Yearbooks *Das Meisterwerk in der Musik* by Heinrich Schenker: An Annotated Translation' (Ph.D. diss., Northwestern University, 1973), ii. 506. The emphasis is Schenker's own.

[10] Schenker, *Free Composition*, 6.

Schenkerian theory as the paradigmatic depth theory of music, and thus the natural backdrop for any reconsideration of music and hierarchy. Unlike them, however, I will tend, especially in the context of cultural politics, to privilege Schenker's original ideological formulations over post-war Anglo-American reinterpretations.[11] Schenker's profound identification with his theoretical structures—and his penchant for interweaving music-theoretical and political polemics—goes a long way towards explaining why it has been so culturally important to us that music have structured depth.

## 5.  Schenker on his Head

I also engage Schenker because the major analytical work that I have done also deals with tracing long-range linear connections in both tonal and post-tonal music.[12] But in formalizing the results, I was forced to discard the covert goal of Schenkerian voice-leading analysis: to uphold hierarchy and totality in music. In many ways my idiosyncratic methodology 'stands Schenker on his head'. Not only do the long-range melodic lines I want to trace *rise*, rather than fall; unlike the *Urlinie*, the constructs I have dubbed 'linear ascents' are irretrievably surface phenomena. Outlining a linear ascent makes a very different statement about a piece than the grand unifying claim of Schenker's *Urlinie*. Identifying two pitches as *Stufen* in a Schenkerian structural descent says that we accept that one 'passes' to the other at some conceptual level; it also makes a powerful explanatory statement about all the notes in between. They and their linear patterns are hierarchically subordinate, prolonging the background linear event—created from it, in fact, through level upon level of voice-leading rules.

Identifying the 'passing' motion of a linear ascent has different implications: the successive '*Stufen*' of its climb are prolonged, but in our listening minds— that is, *dramatically*. Remembering the salient moments where linear progression comes to the fore, the listener leap-frogs between them, tracing linear dramas or 'mechanisms of desire' which ignore the intervening music. Connections are established not by ever more reductive voice-leading constructs, but by our perceptual tendency to link up the high points of musical experience.

Conceptually, the *Urlinie* is a skeleton or foundation which lies beneath the surface of a piece; we dig down to it, stripping away successive layers of elaboration in accordance with our understanding of the rules of strict counterpoint. The linear ascent is much more like a series of energy measurements: it rides on top of the musical surface. I identify a linear ascent by slicing off the high points

---

[11]  For a cogent critique of the epistemological relation between Schenker's theories and those of the so-called neo-Schenkerians, see Eugene Narmour, *Beyond Schenkerism* (Chicago, 1977). This should not be taken as an endorsement of Narmour's larger conclusions, or his implication–realization theories.

[12]  See Robert Fink, ' "Arrows of Desire": Linear Structure and the Transformation of Musical Energy' (Ph.D. diss., University of California, Berkeley, 1994).

of a musical experience and constructing a mechanism to link them. When it works, this method can remain on the surface of the musical work—and still trace its long-range patterns of tension and release.

## II. Hierarchy: Surface–Depth as a Problem of Analytic Technique

The analytical examples that follow are snapshots taken from larger analytical projects; as in any survey of this kind, I will be forced to decontextualize my own analytical readings as I concentrate on the meta-theoretical issue at hand. In each case (except the last) I have tried to highlight the attempt to trace surface ascents by identifying long-range linear connections that do *not* rely on an underlying hierarchy of structural levels. In effect, the examples pose the question: When is it interesting to link notes that are widely separated on the musical surface without explaining everything in between? Can one harness the dynamic tension inherent in the concept of 'prolongation' without first invoking the totalizing claims of generative hierarchies? Can one talk about dynamic tension and prolongation at all, if the music in question radically negates hierarchic depth?

### 1. A Passion for Flying-over (Beethoven, *Missa Solemnis*, Credo)

> Today one flies over the work of art in the same manner as one flies over villages, cities, palaces, castles, fields, woods, rivers, and lakes. This contradicts not only the historical bases of the work of art but also—more significantly—its coherence, its inner relationships, which demand to be 'traversed'.
>
> *Heinrich Schenker*

If one is not going to attempt a totalizing explanation of every linear event on the surface, or appeal to an a priori deep structure to bestow significance on particular abstract progressions, the unmediated surface of a work becomes a bewildering place. In the average symphonic movement there are literally tens of thousands of possible 'events'—at least as many as there are notes, and probably many more. Even if we restrict our attention to linear events—roughly defined as the connections formed, either directly or indirectly, between pitches representing adjacent scale steps—the surface of a piece is a turbulent sea of seemingly random, overlapping lines, from the smallest scale to the largest. Which linear connections are *significant*—eligible to function as events in a musical plot or parts of a musical mechanism like the linear ascent?

There is no axiomatic answer to this question, but some compositional strate-

Ex. 5.1. *The 'Mixolydian ascent'.*

gies push the analyst strongly toward features of the musical surface. For instance, in Beethoven's *Missa Solemnis*, choral tessitura leads us to associate pitches according to a surface variable only intermittently respected by reductionist analysis: the strain inherent in choral high notes.[13] The most obvious sign of a significant linear event in Beethoven is *extremity*. He pushes instruments and voices to their limits. And since those limits are fixed within a single piece, significant melodic events tend to occur and recur at the limits of the sonic spectrum, in the same extreme registers, with the same strained timbres. A visceral linear connection is forged between widely separated melodic events which share a distinctive sound energy—an audible sense of 'high-wire' risk.

To take the specific example of the *Missa Solemnis*: even the best choral sopranos are only really comfortable up to high G; from that point to their absolute top note of B (never broached in Viennese choral music) every half-step creates increasing strain. It is thus no surprise that Beethoven assigns every significant melodic climax in the Credo to the sopranos, consistently forcing them up into that 'danger zone' between A♭ and B, and almost sadistically holding them there for measures on end. The *Missa* was traditionally held to be 'unsingable'. It isn't, but it is quite deliberately *barely* singable. The extremities of physical effort demanded from the soprano section signal the significance of the melodic climaxes in which they participate. On this principle, I take notice every time the soprano line climbs higher than G, and prefer it as the main carrier of linear events.

The choral tessitura of the Credo thus tempts the analyst temporarily to abandon the complex multi-level structures of Schenkerian voice-leading, and to parse the musical surface in a way that may seem, by comparison, rather crude and incomplete. Why not, we ask, simply link up all the high notes, and see what kind of structure they outline? Ex. 5.1 condenses one way of traversing the space above high G in the Credo as an ideal type (*not* a deep structure!) which I call the 'Mixolydian ascent' on the basis of its flattened seventh. The 'rules' encoded in this music example can be verbalized as follows: the successful ascent will traverse at least the third from G to B♭ in the highest register of the soprano voice; in the process it will engage A♭, then decisively repudiate that 'wrong' note for A♮ as leading-tone; and there will be a memorable arrival on high B♭, almost certainly as the fifth of a subdominant triad.

[13] Schenker's concept of 'obligatory register' (*obligate Lage*) does at least admit the 'urge' to return to a particular register as a long-range voice-leading force: his 'basic register' is almost always associated with the first pitch of the fundamental line. (See *Free Composition*, 107–8.)

Ex. 5.2. *Beethoven, Missa Solemnis, Credo: long-range connections.*

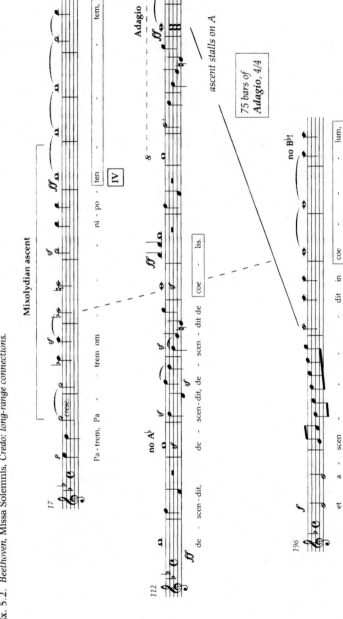

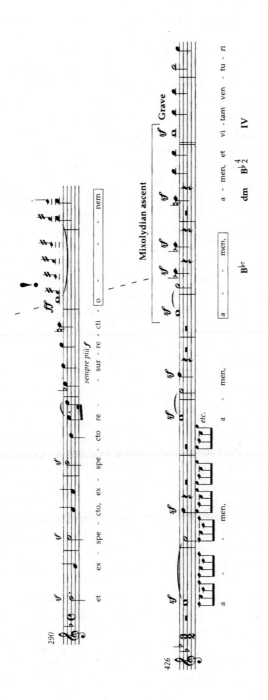

Example 5.2 attempts to diagramme the long-range connections between the five climaxes in the Credo that incorporate either a sustained $a^2$ or $b\flat^2$. A coherent linear 'plot' emerges: a full Mixolydian ascent at bar 17; a dramatic cadence $a^2$–$b\flat^2$ at bars 117–18, without the Mixolydian inflection—a cadence which upon repetition stalls on $a^2$; the retaking of $a^2$ after 75 bars of Adagio at bars 196–201; the retaking of $b\flat^2$ after almost 100 *more* bars at bars 290–4; and a final ecstatic Mixolydian ascent through $a\flat^2$ and $a\natural^2$ to $b\flat^2$ at bars 430–3 (although the rising line can be traced as far back as bar 399).

What justification do we have for postulating a linear connection between these five widely separated passages? Much of the evidence is in the form of a heterogeneous web of surface resemblances, not all of them pitch-based. For one thing, Beethoven's tendency to cap his sustained high notes on the penultimate syllable of a word with a short 'after-beat' that accentuates, incorrectly, the unstressed final syllable: thus in bars 21–4, '[omnipo]ten-*tem*'; in bars 117–18, 'coe-*lis*'; in bars 199–201, 'coe-*lum*'; in bars 294–5, '[resurrecti]-o-*nem*'; in bars 431–2, 'a-*men*'. The connection between the $a^2$s at bar 117 and bar 199 is even more direct: both mis-accented words have the same root—'[descendit de] coe-*lis*' becomes '[ascendit in] coe-*lum*'. (The symmetry is mirrored by the musical setting in the most naïve way.) For another thing, the sense that the sustained $b\flat^2$ at bars 21–4 is somehow left hanging until the long $b\flat^2$ of bars 433–4 picks it up—more than 400 bars later!—is immeasurably strengthened by the simple fact that they both appear as $\hat{5}$ over a blazing E♭ major fortissimo. The point is not whether both passages prolong a single structural IV on some fundamental level; it is that these are the *only two times in the entire movement* that this particular configuration of the musical surface—a sustained *ff* high $b\flat^1$ for the choral sopranos harmonized by an E♭ major chord—occurs.

In forging these linear connections, then, I am appealing not to hierarchy, but to the presence or absence of untransformed sounds on the musical surface. The connection I trace back from the $b\flat^2$ at bars 294–5 to the $a^2$s at bars 117–18 and 199–201 does not depend on a transcendental ear for tonal voice-leading on the largest scale. It does not assign some pitches to a 'deeper' level of structure; nor does it say anything about the intervening music. It is simply a consequence of the surface fact that these are the *only sustained choral notes in the extreme (above $g^2$) soprano register during that 178-bar stretch of music*. Beethoven, a composer with an unparalleled sense of linear strategy, marshals his high notes with extreme care.

The strange progression that underpins the final ascent in bars 431–3 can stand as a concrete reminder of the epistemological gulf that separates the surface Mixolydian ascent from a more traditional linear construct like the Schenkerian *Urlinie*. I consider this $a\flat^2$–$a\natural^2$–$b\flat^2$ motion to be the crucial linear event in the movement, the final resolving step of an abstract ascending line that connects it back to climaxes hundreds of bars before. Yet, in a total inversion of traditional theories of large-scale voice-leading, the linear progression singled out as 'structural' is not supported by the basic tonal functions (that is, caden-tial harmonies), but by a strange burst of non-functional, non-cadential har-monic 'noise'. Beethoven gets to $a\natural^2$ with a brazen trick—a chromatic voice exchange between two inversions of $B\flat^7$ that harmonizes the crucial leading-tone not with the home dominant, but as a non-functional linear $^6_4$. The Mixolydian $\flat\hat{7}$ is wrenched up a semitone, its contrapuntal obligation to descend autocrati-cally overruled. The very arbitrariness of the gesture makes it dramatically strik-ing, and thus important to the linear structure.

Even in a tonal work ultimately ruled by a voice-leading hierarchy, this way of hearing drives a transgressive wedge between the surface and the depths. Now the key moment of linear progression on the musical surface stands out on account of its *divorce* from the fundamental structure. As any Schenkerian will tell you, the $a\flat^2$–$a\natural^2$–$b\flat^2$ progression is, from the point of view of tonal hierarchy, purely decorative: it would quickly be eliminated in even the most cursory middle-ground reduction.

Let me be absolutely clear: Ex. 5.1 is in no sense a 'deep structure' or a 'reduc-tion' of the Credo. In fact, it is not 'in' the Credo at all. It is prolonged, if at all, in our minds; and its dynamism exists there, too—as desire. One might well con-cretize the set of conditions that determines a coherent linear ascent as an abstract melodic line; but the epistemological status of this construct must not be inflated. Unlike the *Urlinie*, whose a priori existence in an ideal and transcen-dent sense generates the entire melodic-harmonic content of the piece, the linear ascent in Beethoven is a mental construct that we infer, during experience, as we attempt to impose pattern and direction on a work's salient melodic climaxes. The fact that in the *Missa* we *can* find a simple linear template that will link together almost all the memorable and puzzling melodic climaxes—make them seem like parts in a coherent mechanism, whose function is discharged when Beethoven finally 'gets it right'—is to my mind a crucial and liberating aesthetic discovery.

## 2. Prolongation versus Hierarchy (Stravinsky, *Symphony in Three Movements*, first movement)

> I doubt whether *The Rite* can be satisfactorily performed in terms of Herr von Karajan's traditions. I do not mean to imply that he is out of his depths, however, but rather that he is in my shallows—or call them simple concre-tions and reifications. There are simply no regions for soul-searching in *The Rite of Spring*.
>
> *Igor Stravinsky*

As long as the focus is tonal music, the decision to split off the musical surface from deep structures based on voice-leading hierarchies is, admittedly, an idio-syncratic one. There is certainly no reason for a Schenkerian reduction of the

Credo to fail; or any a priori reason why the structural levels of such an analysis might not actually buttress some of the deliberately loose 'prolongations' I outlined above. If I display the 'passion for flying over' (*die Leidenschaft des Überfliegens*) that Schenker inveighed against in the quotation from *Free Composition* at the beginning of the previous section, it is because I feel that 'flying over' Beethoven is closer to the contingencies of the listening experience than a painstaking traversal of hidden structural levels. William Pastille argues that Schenker, following the tradition of German idealism, meant his graphs to record a transcendental engagement with the 'underlying models of tonal motion'.[14] He thus had no interest in analyses that appeal to the general experience of listeners untrained in structural hearing. Our more democratic, materialist era may demand a stricter accountability to listener response—and thus to the musical surface.

Still, it is when we shift our analytical focus to post-tonal music that the freedom of manœuvre gained by detaching surface and depth becomes increasingly attractive. Hierarchically minded theorists of post-tonal music confront a persistent 'problem': they must resolve the conflict between a surface that evokes the tonal past—fifth progressions in the bass, half-step melodic 'cadences', directional 'prolongation' spans—and a new pitch language which seems to fracture structural levels.[15] It is not clear whether this new music even has a single deep structure, let alone one capable of fusing surface gestures into an organic totality.

The problem is particularly acute in the neo-classical music of Stravinsky, in which both the vertical and the horizontal dimensions of the musical surface are so complicit with tonality that the presence or absence of a tonal deep structure is a recurring question. In 1926 Schenker himself tried an analysis of a short passage from the *Concerto for Piano and Winds* which was really more like an exorcism.[16] He succeeded in proving—to his own satisfaction—that Stravinsky's voice-leading, though it mimics tonal procedures, fails to create any kind of organic tonal hierarchy: the various prolongation spans just do not cohere at any level.

Still there is *something* about Stravinsky's music that drew Schenker's attention—a similar stunt with, say, Schoenberg's Op. 25 would have been inconceivable. And in the next generation, others ran the same voice-leading diagnostic and got diametrically opposed results. Ex. 5.3*a* reproduces a rather notorious middle-ground reduction of the first 100-odd bars of the *Symphony in Three Movements* which appeared in Felix Salzer's 1952 book *Structural Hearing*.[17]

---

[14] See William Pastille, 'Goethe's Influence on Schenker's Thought', in Hedi Siegel (ed.), *Schenker Studies* (Cambridge, 1990), 37, 42.

[15] See Kofi Agawu, 'Stravinsky's *Mass* and Stravinsky Analysis', *Music Theory Spectrum*, 2 (Fall 1989), 139–41, for a cogent survey of the relevant analytical literature.

[16] Heinrich Schenker, *Das Meisterwerk in der Musik, II Jahr* (repr. Hildesheim, 1974), 37–40; trans. in Kalib, 'Thirteen Essays', ii. 212–16.

[17] See Felix Salzer, *Structural Hearing* (New York, 1962), 218–19, 234–7.

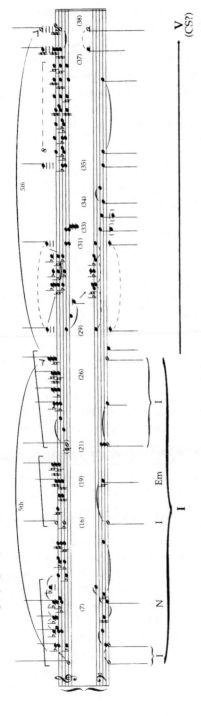

Ex. 5.3a. *Stravinsky, Symphony in Three Movements: Salzer's middle-ground sketch (Structural Hearing (New York, 1952), ii. 236–7, fig. 472b).*

Ex. 5.3b. *Stravinsky, Symphony in Three Movements: Salzer's background sketch (Structural Hearing, ii. 236, fig. 472d).*

Ex. 5.3c. *Stravinsky, Symphony in Three Movements: Joseph Straus's motivic reinterpretation of Salzer's prolongation ('The Problem of Prolongation in Post-tonal Music', Journal of Music Theory, 31/1 (Spring 1987), 11, ex. 6a).*

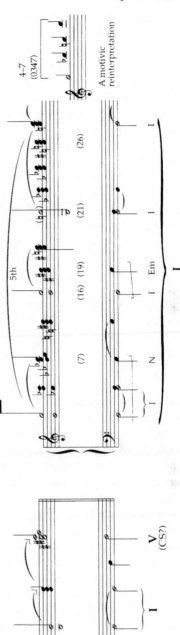

Salzer blithely asserts that the first 108 bars of the symphony are a 'gigantic prolongation of G'. It appears from his graph that he is basing this assumption on the strong sense of directionality and drive he hears on the music's surface. The inexorably rising soprano line over the first 100 bars must have seemed the perfect candidate for explanation as a prolongational 'tension span'. Salzer thus splits the ascent in the soprano line into two spans of a fifth that project traditional tonal functionality: from the opening to just before rehearsal number 29 (R29) the fifth $g^1$–$d^2$ prolongs the tonic; from R29 to R38, the upper fifth, $d^2$–$a^2$, controls a modulation to the dominant. (Salzer's background sketch is Ex. 5.3*b*.)

All this is very neat—ultimately, too neat. One might protest that Stravinsky has not articulated his rising span as two fifths at all. The opening 108 bars present the listener with two surface ascents: first, a $g^1$–$g^2$ octave span which links the G-centred tutti at the opening with its return at R16; and then the clear ascent of a major *sixth* ($g^2$–$e^3$) from R16 to the massive E minor arrival at R29. Nor can the spans of a fifth really help explain what is going on underneath. The polarity of key centres does not involve G (tonic) and D (dominant); it is *E minor* that emerges at R29 as the secondary key area, a compromise axis balanced halfway between the tritone-related poles G and D♭. Nor does Salzer successfully rationalize the unremittingly high level of dissonance in the opening tutti by asserting that what is being prolonged is really the 'polychord on G with the D♭ chord as a secondary chord of fusion'.

The weakness of the connection between Salzer's upper voice spans of a fifth and any putative deep structure—their inability to organize the music into structural levels—was pointed out in 1987 by Joseph Straus.[18] Like most theorists of his generation and training, Straus sees tonal and non-tonal musics as completely disjunct; he is thus impatient with the attempts of apologists like Salzer and Roy Travis to use the concepts of prolongation and reduction to argue 'creatively' for tonal directionality in Stravinsky and Schoenberg. His article seeks to define precisely the conditions under which the concept of prolongation can be invoked to organize a musical texture into structural levels, and then to show that these conditions can never be fulfilled in post-tonal music. Straus carefully details the logical inconsistencies of voice-leading and dissonance treatment implied at every moment by Salzer's graph, and rightly concludes that post-tonal prolongation spans, though they may seem 'superficially attractive', ultimately lack the vital power to create hierarchy that they would possess in a tonal context. He provides an alternative, less ambitious structure for the upper voice—a composing-out of Stravinsky's characteristic [0347] tetrachord—that fits perfectly with the underlying pitch structure (see Ex. 5.3*c*).

One cannot deny the force of Straus's logic: the graphs in *Structural Hearing* simply fail to construct a convincing voice-leading hierarchy for this kind of

---

[18] Joseph N. Straus, 'The Problem of Prolongation in Post-Tonal Music', *Journal of Music Theory*, 31 (Spring 1987), 1–22.

music. Very well. We can relinquish without regret the attempt to 'Schenkerize' Stravinsky.

Yet, Straus may well have the better theory, but it is Salzer who produces the better analysis. Salzer's ascending spans, whether or not they actually prolong anything, seem closer to the way Stravinsky's music is perceived by a listener than Straus's static association of notes according to a motivic pitch-class (pc) set.[19] It appears that a strict hierarchical definition of prolongation imposes its cost: it prevents Straus from discussing the obvious stepwise organization of the musical surface, because the resulting structures look too much like forbidden prolongations. Consequently, it is the older, 'sloppier' theorist who best grasps the dynamic structure of Stravinsky's rising lines.

Ex. 5.4 presents my own analysis of the passage in question: it traces a two-part linear ascent—first $g^1$–$g^2$, then $g^2$–$e^3$—over the first 108 bars of the musical surface. Stravinsky builds his ascending melodic progressions out of a series of tense plateaux—short passages in which repeated melodic cells are energized by complex rhythmic variation. The tension of each plateau is 'discharged' when it jumps up to the next one (Exx. 5.4b–d). The surface linear structure is unusually clear: each plateau is impressed on the ear by its internal repetition, and the plateaux line up, one after another, in an almost unbroken stepwise succession. (Wherever there is a leap, Stravinsky carefully goes back and fills it in.[20]) For me, this ascent is coherent and compelling enough as a surface melodic construct that there is no need to justify it within a totalizing hierarchy of pitch. This is not to say that the $g^2$–$e^3$ span doesn't have something to do with the octatonic tripolarity between G, D♭, and E 'underneath'. But that loose relationship will not necessarily reproduce the structural levels so highly valued in tonal music. The horizontal and vertical aspects of Stravinsky's textures resist being parsed into a hierarchy of deep and surface structure.

Thus the analyst is faced with an unenviable choice: either follow the spans on the surface and play fast and loose with the depths, as Salzer did; or, like Straus, preserve the integrity of the deep structure at the cost of badly misreading the musical surface. And the way out of this systemic trap is to devalue totality and hierarchy. But what presented itself as a temptation with Beethoven now begins to look rather more like liberation. As long as we demand a rigorous, total integration of surface and deep structure, both Salzer and Straus produce readings of the *Symphony in Three Movements* that are 'wrong'. But allow the surface to float free of the depths, and they can both just as easily be *right*. Straus and Schenker are justified in denying that ersatz post-tonal spans can create a prolongational hierarchy; and Salzer and I are justified in listening for them anyway—as long as we don't call it *structural hearing*.

---

[19] To be fair, Straus tries to assert a dynamic drive towards what he calls 'pattern completion' when these pc-sets are composed out horizontally; see ibid. 17–19, and the more extended discussion in his earlier article, 'A Principle of Voiceleading in the Music of Stravinsky', *Music Theory Spectrum*, 4 (1982), 106–24.

[20] For instance, the *fff* leap from G♯ to B after R19 is filled in by the A♭–B♭–B♯ of R22–R28.

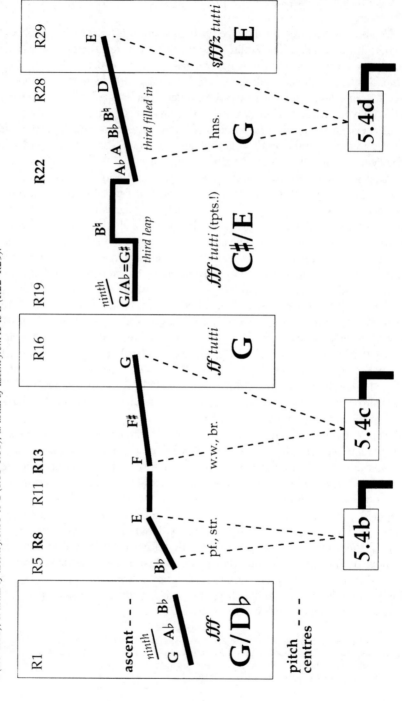

Ex. 5.4. *Stravinsky, Symphony in Three Movements, opening of first movement: a: overview of non-functional ascent from G to E; b: detail of ascent from B♭ to E (R8–R11); c: detail of ascent from F to G (R13–R16); d: detail of ascent from A♭ to E (R22–R29).*

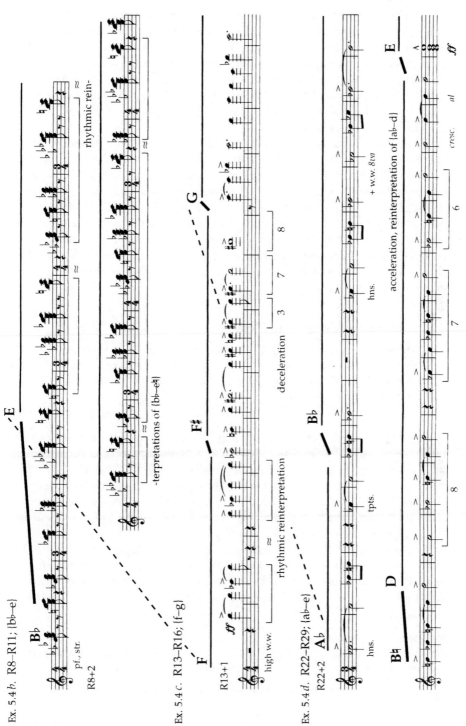

Ex. 5.4 *b*. R8–R11; {b♭–e}

Ex. 5.4 *c*. R13–R16; {f–g}

Ex. 5.4 *d*. R22–R29; {a♭–e}

Schenker despised Stravinsky's music—his exact words were 'thoroughly bad, inartistic, and unmusical'.[21] He noted, correctly, that its voice-leading spans do not work together, that there is thus no basis upon which to construct a real tonal hierarchy and that the whole therefore lacks coherence and depth. (He can't stop remarking on how *simple-minded* it all is.) Those who love Stravinsky have hastened to assure Schenker that the music *does* have coherence and structural depth—of a different kind, yes, but in many ways analogous. And many have laboured hard to make it so.

But we didn't listen to the composer, who defiantly stood by his 'shallows', his 'simple concretions and reifications'. Stravinsky flatly declared that there were no regions for soul-searching in a masterpiece like *The Rite of Spring*. One would not normally think to interpret that comment in terms of structure; but if the regions for musical soul-searching are coexistent with the space mapped out between background and foreground—and I will argue below that they are— then Stravinsky's remark becomes a warning to the music theorist, as well as the conductor. *Flatness*, in both the hermeneutic and the formal domains, is the last thing our theoretical tools equip us to value and explore. But we are in the shallows now.

### Excursus: 'Flatness' in Modern and Postmodern Theory

The first and most evident [difference between high and postmodernism] is the emergence of a new kind of flatness or depthlessness, a new kind of superficiality in the most literal sense, perhaps the supreme formal feature of all the postmodernisms.

*Fredric Jameson*

A brief digression into cultural theory may help to put my polemic in perspective; it will also serve as a *lasciate ogni speranza* to those still looking for deep structures as we cross the threshold of the postmodern. It is indeed remarkable that while music theorists were lovingly cultivating (fetishizing?) theories of depth, observers of both modern and postmodern cultural production were becoming increasingly convinced that *flatness* was its key formal feature.

Consider the influential visual aesthetic of Clement Greenberg, the powerful American champion of abstract art. He claimed that the truly modern feature of abstract expressionist painting was not its elimination of representation, but its stark, anti-illusionistic insistence on the two-dimensional picture plane. If the painting was once a stage, he argues, the backdrop has now become the same as the curtain:

It is not so much the distortion or even the absence of images that we may mind in this curtain-painting, but the abrogation of those spatial rights which images used to enjoy back when the painter was obliged to create an illusion of the same kind of space as that

---

[21] 'durchaus Schlecht, unkünstlerisch, und unmusicalisch'; see *Das Meisterwerk, II Jahr*, 39.

in which out bodies move. *The picture has now become an entity belonging to the same order of space as our bodies; it is no longer the vehicle of an imagined equivalent of that order.* Pictorial space has lost its 'inside' and become all 'outside'.[22]

Greenberg saw the progress of modernism in its becoming 'shallower and shallower'; thus the fractured, foreshortened space of analytical cubism was a precursor of the frank two-dimensionality of action and field painting, where the eye must 'treat the whole of the surface as a single undifferentiated field of interest'. This developmental rubric works, provisionally at least, for one strand of modernist music—it explains the way Stravinsky's 'shallows' presage the undifferentiated flatness of Steve Reich. (As we shall see below, minimalism is the musical example of the backdrop becoming the same as the curtain.) In fact, Greenberg described the effect of 'anti-illusionist' painting—'the abstract picture seems[s] to offer a narrower, more physical, and less imaginative kind of experience'—in language that evokes Stravinsky rather precisely. *Imaginary regions*, whether for soul-searching or for story-telling, have no place in this version of the modernist aesthetic.

The repudiation of depth is a formal link between this brand of modernism and most of what we call postmodernism—even though the two aesthetics disagree violently on almost everything else, especially the related question of representation. René Magritte, for example, clung doggedly, almost perversely, to representational illusions. Yet, as Foucault points out, a surrealist painting like *L'Alphabet des révélations* undermines the very illusions of depth that structure its surface, presenting us with an uncanny spectacle: the surface looks almost the same, but the depth (or the representation of depth) that it constructed has been abolished. We have *perspective* without *depth*: 'Magritte allows the old space of representation to rule, but only at the surface, no more than a polished stone, bearing words and shapes: beneath, nothing. It is a gravestone.'[23] A herald of postmodernity like Jean Baudrillard would say that this gravestone marks the site of a more fundamental disappearance: it is the final resting-place of the Real. All that is left in the postmodern era is the *simulacrum*, the image that represents only itself, the surface that floats free of any reality 'underneath'. Magritte's self-deconstructing surfaces now look suspiciously like a premonition of the postmodern: 'The transition from signs which dissimulate something to signs which dissimulate that there is nothing, marks the decisive turning point.'[24]

The most thoroughgoing exploration of 'postmodern space' has been undertaken by the Marxist literary critic Frederic Jameson, whose magisterial survey, *Postmodernism, or, the Cultural Logic of Late Capitalism*, is perhaps the key

[22] Clement Greenberg, 'Abstract, Representational, and So Forth', *Arts Digest*, 29 (Nov. 1954), 6–8; repr. in *Art and Culture* (Boston, 1961), 133–8; the present quote is taken from Herschel B. Chipp, *Theories of Modern Art* (Berkeley, 1968), 580; emphasis added.

[23] Michel Foucault, *This is Not a Pipe*, trans. James Harkness (Berkeley, 1983), 41.

[24] Jean Baudrillard, *Simulations* (New York, 1983), 12. For a good introduction to Baudrillard's contradictory and often brilliant theories, see Mark Poster (ed.), *Jean Baudrillard: Selected Writings* (Stanford, Calif., 1988).

definition of postmodernism as both an aesthetic and a political reality of contemporary society. He sees the creation of a new, disorienting type of space in postmodern art and architecture—as well as in literary metaphors like the 'cyberspace' of recent science fiction—as an attempt to create a formal representation of the unrepresentable: the incomprehensible structures of multinational capitalism.

Often this new virtual space is radically flat, a presentation of pure, freefloating surface—'depth is replaced by surface, or by multiple surfaces'.[25] Faced with these disembodied surfaces, the consumer of contemporary architecture experiences a vertigo whose production seems to be postmodernism's chief aesthetic strategy:

mounting what used to be Raymond Chandler's Bunker Hill from the great Chicano markets on Broadway and Fourth Street in downtown Los Angeles, [one] suddenly confronts the great free-standing wall of Wells Fargo Court (Skidmore, Owings, and Merrill)— a surface which seems to be unsupported by any volume, or whose putative volume (rectangular? trapezoidal?) is ocularly quite undecidable. This great sheet of windows, with its gravity-defying two-dimensionality, momentarily transforms the solid ground on which we stand into the contents of a stereopticon, pasteboard shapes profiling themselves here and there around us.[26]

There are places in Jameson's work where he seems to argue that all postmodern cultural production possesses this disorienting flatness.[27] Jameson's most systematic definition of postmodern space is somewhat more complex, and comes late in his book. He argues that each of the three stages of capitalist evolution—market, monopoly, and multinational capitalism—creates its own kind of space. The shifts in the phenomenology of space thus reflect discrete stages in the increasing ubiquity of capital. Late capitalist space in particular may have volume, but it lacks depth, because it is implacably hostile to *perspective*, and thus to *hierarchy*:

The new [late capitalist] space . . . involves the *suppression of distance* (in the sense of Benjamin's aura) and the relentless saturation of any remaining voids and empty spaces, to the point where the postmodern body—whether wandering through a postmodern hotel, locked into rock sound by means of headphones, or undergoing the multiple shocks and

[25] Fredric Jameson, *Postmodernism, or the Cultural Logic of Late Capitalism* (Durham, NC, 1991), 12.

[26] Ibid. 13.

[27] Jameson was quite categorical about this in the 1984 essay which provided the title and the first chapter of his book. In a characteristically exhaustive passage, he hammers postmodernism *absolutely flat*: 'Overhastily, we can say that besides the hermeneutic model of outside and inside . . . at least four other fundamental depth models have generally been repudiated in contemporary theory: (1) the dialectical one of essence and appearance (along with a whole range of concepts of ideology or false consciousness which tend to accompany it); (2) the Freudian model of latent and manifest, or of repression (which is of course the target of Michel Foucault's programmatic and symptomatic *La Volonté de savoir* (*The History of Sexuality*) ); (3) the existential model of authenticity and inauthenticity whose heroic or tragic thematics are closely related to that other great opposition between alienation and disalienation, itself equally a casualty of the poststructural or postmodern period; and (4) most recently, the great semiotic opposition between signifier and signified, which was itself rapidly unraveled and deconstructed during its brief heyday in the 1960s and 1970s' (ibid. 12).

bombardments of the Vietnam War as Michael Herr conveys it to us—is now exposed to *a perceptual barrage of immediacy from which all sheltering layers and intervening mediations have been removed.*[28]

Jameson pushes us to re-evaluate the hoariest cliché of music appreciation: If 'architecture is frozen music', then which sounds, exactly, congealed to form Wells Fargo Court—or its pomo Los Angeles neighbour, John Portman's Westin Bonaventure Hotel? ('[A] constant busyness gives the feeling that emptiness is here absolutely packed, that it is an element within which you yourself are immersed, without any of that distance that formerly enabled the perception of perspective or volume.'[29]) There are no more elegant cathedrals of sound in contemporary music, it seems—just the disorientation of being lost in a (multinational, corporate) hotel atrium.

To summarize: theorists like Greenberg, Foucault, and Jameson present us with two characteristic mutations away from the hierarchic space mapped by old-fashioned theories of structural levels. In the first, which we might call 'degraded hierarchy', the background collapses on to the foreground. This 'minimalist' flatness can be loosely opposed to, or bleed into, a second, more radical, 'postmodernist' flatness, in which hierarchy is banished altogether. We either face *perspective without depth*, where 'familiar' surfaces float free from the depths that could structure them; or *depth without perspective*, where the 'barrage of immediacy' that we have always associated with the surface of a generative hierarchy is stepped up until it pulverizes the hierarchy of the 'interior'.

Ultimately, the surface–depth metaphor feels increasingly irrelevant to the new, exotic topographies characteristic of the postmodern work of art. When we recognize new kinds of space in a late twentieth-century piece of music—and we will—shouldn't our analytical models (and the subsequent value-judgments) 'mutate' right along with them?

## 3. Degraded Hierarchies (Reich, *Piano Phase*)

What I'm interested in is a compositional process and a sounding music that are one and the same thing. . . . The use of hidden structural devices in music never appealed to me. Even when all the cards are on the table and everyone bears what is gradually happening in a musical process, there are still enough mysteries to satisfy all.

*Steve Reich*

I would argue that the single most salient feature of musical minimalism—its obsessive repetition—represents a *saturation of aural space*, the formal equivalent of the saturation of physical space that Jameson described above. And, just as in that physical space, the barrage of immediacy—Reich called it 'total sensuous-intellectual involvement'—has the effect of rendering structural hierarchy, the

---

[28] Ibid. 412–13; emphasis added.    [29] Ibid. 43.

Ex. 5.5a. *Steve Reich*, Piano Phase.

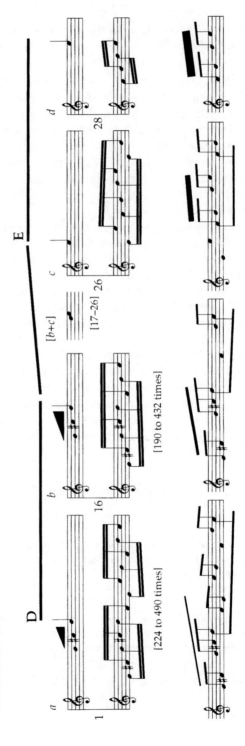

'layers' that mediate and shelter, irrelevant.[30] To demonstrate, I want to examine a ground-breaking minimalist process piece, Reich's *Piano Phase*, from what may seem an unpromising perspective to those familiar with the style: long-range tonal voice-leading.

To be sure, Paul Epstein has done a contrapuntal analysis of *Piano Phase* which describes the way Reich's first melodic pattern realizes complex, varied harmonic implications when shifted against itself.[31] But there are more patterns, and more processes, in the work. If the entire piece (Ex. 5.5*a*) is considered, the primary evidence for a rudimentary linear ascent is obvious enough. *Piano Phase* is built on four patterns of interlocking semiquavers: (a) a twelve-note pattern in 1–15; (b) a shorter, eight-note pattern with the same pitches in 16–25; (c) a new eight-note pattern which overlaps pattern (b) in 17–26; (d) a four-note pattern in 27–32 which is a truncated version of (c).[32] The highest note of patterns (a) and (b) is $d^2$; when Reich brings in new pitch material at bar 17, he begins a gradual switch to patterns (c) and (d), whose top note is $e^2$. In terms of large-scale voice-leading structure, *Piano Phase* is a single ascending step from $d^2$ to $e^2$.

In one sense, the fact that *Piano Phase* starts with $d^2$ on top and ends with $e^2$ on top is enough. As far as I can see, it is the only really convincing way to explain why Reich decided to change the pitch content of his rhythmic processes half-way through the piece—and furthermore, why he chose to replace E–F♯–B–C♯–D with A–B–D–E. In support of this global connection we can also adduce the linear tensions built into the individual patterns themselves. As Ex. 5.5*a* demonstrates, the strongest linear implication of pattern (a) is a continuation of its longest conjunct motion—a B–C♯–D progression that focuses all attention on $d^2$ as soprano note. Repeated more than 400 times, this melodic fragment creates a cumulatively irresistible desire for the next scale step, $e^2$.

Our overall linear impression of the first phase cycle (1–15) is of the rising third, B–D repeatedly coalescing out of an indistinct linear texture, but each time in a new, unique rhythmic configuration. When the two patterns return to complete synchronization at phase 14, the original rising third comes back into focus with a powerful jolt as the primary linear gesture of the piece. It seems quite natural that this energy should be channelled into the rhythmic acceleration at 16: as pattern (b) takes over, B–C♯–D begins to recur almost twice as often (with five, instead of nine, semiquavers intervening). The following cycle (16–25) provides the rising step that 'resolves' the tension; this series of phases gradually carries out the piece's global move from $d^2$ to $e^2$—which is only fully confirmed when the old B–C♯–D pattern fades out underneath. The piece ends with another acceleration: pattern (d) is cut in half so that it can complete its full cycle in only

[30] Steve Reich, *Music as a Gradual Process* (1968), repr. in *Writings about Music* (Halifax, 1974), 52.

[31] Paul Epstein, 'Pattern and Process in Steve Reich's *Piano Phase*', *Musical Quarterly*, 72 (1986), 494–502.

[32] Numbers refer to the numbered pattern combinations in Reich's score (Universal Edition 161561, London, 1980).

four shifts, during which the progression D–E is subjected to the same blurring and ultimate resynchronization that kept us interested in B–C♯–D. Since the other two notes of pattern (d) form the ascending step A–B, rising linear motion comes to dominate the texture completely. Consider *Piano Phase* in terms of the 'implication–realization' models of Meyer and Narmour (Ex. 5.5*a*, bottom line): its four patterns exhibit a progression from the tense balance of rising and falling implications in pattern (a) to the simple upward sweep of pattern (d).

It is when we attempt to place this long-range scale step into a voice-leading hierarchy that the fun begins. If one is disposed to think in terms of tonal functionality, trimming away those last four notes from pattern (d) has far-ranging harmonic implications. Eliminating the e¹'s leaves a¹ as the 'bass' note of this final pattern, and allows us to postulate a vague V–I progression underlying the whole of *Piano Phase*—an attenuated (or is it vestigial?) tonal structure to go along with its wispy linearity. The opening set of pitches, patterns (a) and (b), is tonally ambiguous, but its best reading is probably as a collection centred loosely on E. The progression $\hat{5}$–♯$\hat{6}$–♮$\hat{7}$, like the Beethovenian Mixolydian ascent discussed above, creates a desire for the 'wrong note', the dissonant seventh, to resolve up to the octave. But there is no question of replacing it with a 'real' leading-tone to create an 'authentic' dominant; *Piano Phase* does not project hierarchic harmonic relationships that strongly any more. Reich replaces *hierarchy* with *saturation*: he relies on the tension generated by mass repetition to 'prolong' the weak dissonance of the minor seventh, and to make his quasi-arbitrary move to the e¹–e² octave of pattern (c) convincing. This octave then provides the outer voices of a blurry I⁶₄ chord in A, which duly drops the lower fifth at phase 26a and 'resolves' to the 'root position' of pattern (d).

Ex. 5.5*b*.  *Steve Reich,* Piano Phase: *minimal voice-leading graph.*

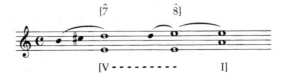

The long-range voice-leading in *Piano Phase* might be represented by the minimal graph shown in Ex. 5.5*b*. This graph achieves the sparse simplicity and temporal compression of the *Urlinie*, but I adduce it here in a quite different spirit. Unlike the Schenkerian background level, this is not a voice-leading construct approached by analytical reduction from the musical surface; this *is* the musical surface (at least in terms of pitch). Ex. 5.5*b* is not background; elemental as it is, it represents a slow-motion progression in the *foreground*. Or rather, it represents foreground and background both. If this 20-minute piece can hold our attention with only a single blurry scale step and a single uncertain bass motion, it can obviously do without a voice-leading hierarchy altogether. The virtual coincidence of background and foreground progressions makes the voice-leading structure of *Piano Phase* almost totally non-hierarchic, totally flat. The backdrop has become the curtain.

I would venture that this collapsing of voice-leading and functional hierarchies is one of the most characteristic features of minimalist tonality—a two-dimensional tonality which seems, even at its most blandly consonant, somehow flat and unreal, without perspective, stubbornly anti-illusionistic. Stravinsky's voice-leading structure did not satisfy Schenker's taste for complex tonal hierarchy, but that music's surface was still complicated enough to make the search for some other generative deep structure, if no longer compulsory, at least plausible. Minimalism is so obviously *flat* that even the most flexible depth theorist must quail before it: what is there on this surface that needs generating or explaining through a theory of structural levels?

Yet we can still describe a linear ascent where it would be absurd to postulate an *Urlinie*. The long-range scale steps of the *Urlinie* make sense only in their usual position at the top of a generative tonal hierarchy that fills in the gaps; a surface with only one scale step categorically denies explanation in terms of generative hierarchy. But, as I pointed out in differentiating my surface linear ascents from their Schenkerian *alter egos*, it is possible to define long-range tensions and connections without reference to an underlying voice-leading hierarchy (that is, tonal 'perspective'). The levels of Schenkerian analysis justify our intuitive sense that classical tonality is a complex structure with hierarchical depth. The looser connections I am interested in pursuing are indifferent to that justification: they describe and link events that we perceive on the musical surface. Since *Piano Phase* is nothing *but* surface, its destruction of voice-leading hierarchy now means that it presents something which Schenker would not have believed possible: long-range voice-leading connections—20 minutes to get from $d^2$ to $e^2$!—without multiple tonal levels underneath.

The problem is not really that Schenkerian theoretical tools don't work here; it is that they *can't* work here, because there is no work to be done. Minimalism's repetitive tonal surfaces already feel unitary, like deep structures, and so they require no 'justification' by a complex hierarchy of diminutions. In this degraded hierarchy, the surface holds *itself* together, and surface linear progressions are the only voice-leading we need. The complete absence of any 'regions for soul-searching' can be taken as a given. As Reich himself points out, the experience of this kind of music is diametrically opposed to the seductive interiority of 'deep' music: 'Musical processes can give one a direct contact with the impersonal.'[33] This is not a contact we normally seek from art-music—or an experience we normally choose to validate by structuralist analysis.

But there are other criteria of value in music besides complexity and hierarchic depth. As a mechanism for 'prolonging' the single scale step $d^2$–$e^2$, *Piano*

---

[33] Reich, *Writings*, 10.

*Phase* is without parallel. The prolongation is accomplished without structural levels, by brute pitch saturation; but it holds our attention simply and effectively. Straus is quite right to insist that in Schenkerian tonal theories, prolongation and hierarchy are inextricably linked: we have been taught that prolongation, and hence large-scale tension and release, cannot exist without generative hierarchy. But I would argue that *Piano Phase*, like most truly 'minimalist' music, uses pitch repetition to redefine prolongation, to *detach prolongation from hierarchy*.

Reich's music pushes the theorist of Western art-music to consider, perhaps for the first time, the implications of using simple repetition to create large-scale tonal connections without structural levels. If prolongation can 'work' without complex hierarchy, we might favour one over the other, exercising a new—and perhaps disorienting—freedom of choice. Do we value *prolongation* as a guarantee of *hierarchy*, and thus depth and integrity in a piece of music? Or do we value *hierarchy* because, traditionally, it has guaranteed large-scale *prolongations*, and thus tension and excitement in a piece of music? Organic unity and hierarchic depth have always seemed somewhat rarefied virtues to demand of music. It may be that the intensity of our long affair with organicism is evidence of a sublimated passion for something much more visceral. Could it be that what we really want is the long-range patterns of tension and release that we thought only organic hierarchy could assure? And would it be so terrible if we got the tension and release without the 'regions for soul-searching'? There are critics and composers who act as if the obvious sensuous pleasure that listeners get from minimal music were some kind of Marcusian 'repressive desublimation'. But listening to two-dimensional music doesn't necessarily make you a One-Dimensional Man—unless, that is, you expect the (*deep*) music you value to mirror—and thus reinforce—your very sense of self (*depth*).

## 4.  Perspective without Depth, Depth without Perspective; or, the Joys of *Heterotopia* (Rochberg, *Music for the Magic Theatre*; Berio, *Sinfonia*)

> The center piece of my *Music for the Magic Theatre* is a transcription, that is, a completely new version, of a Mozart Adagio. I decided to repeat it in my own way because I loved it. People who don't understand think it's by Mozart.
>
> *George Rochberg*

It will not have escaped the reader that *Piano Phase* partakes of both Greenberg's 'modern' and Jameson's 'postmodern' flatness. This overdetermination is not accidental: I would argue that minimal music is interesting precisely in so far as it refuses to be reduced either to modernist asceticism or to postmodern pandering. *Between* modernism and postmodernism, to paraphrase a famous formula of Carl Dalhaus, is where we should look for the epistemological underpinnings of this still-controversial musical style.[34]

But I want to end my analytical survey with a brief consideration of music that trumpets its 'postmodernism'—music characterized by historical referentiality, quotation, and collage. Such pieces display Jameson's 'multiple surfaces' with a vengeance. One suspects that, asked to come up with a musical equivalent to the Westin Bonaventure atrium, Jameson himself would pick MTV; but he might also mention something like Berio's 1969 *Sinfonia*, in which the 'relentless saturation' of aural space takes the form of a hallucinatory excess of musical quotation. The hail of overlapping quotes shatters the musical surface—or, more, precisely, constructs a strange atomized musical space, where there are multiple musical levels, *but each level is itself the surface of another piece*. Bach becomes the 'deep structure' for Schoenberg; Beethoven's Ninth looms up from 'within' *La Valse*; the common 'background' of all Berio's layered surfaces is just another surface: the actual score—*not* a voice-leading 'skeleton'—of the Scherzo from Mahler's Second Symphony. The generative process that Schenker saw moving from background to foreground in a single work now leaps, promiscuously, from work to work—and always from *foreground* to *foreground*.

The 'real' deep structure which generates all of these foregrounds would seem to be nothing less than the history of music itself. (Berio would have us believe that it is the Mahler Scherzo which does the generating, but I am not convinced.[35]) Yet the historical space which *Sinfonia* constructs is completely without temporal perspective: the quotes come in no apparent order, and represent a random, deliberately unrepresentative sampling of the musical past. (To paraphrase Jameson, Berio's piece, like postmodernity in general, is 'historically deaf'.) The multiple surfaces of the *Sinfonia* condense music history into a pulverizing 'barrage of immediacy'—a despairing-exhilarating confession that there is no believable hierarchy of musical styles left.

Pieces like *Sinfonia* that enact the collapse of style hierarchy through radical collage were thick on the ground in the late Sixties; a short check-list might include Lukas Foss's *Baroque Variations* (1967), Arvo Pärt's *Credo* (1968), and Alfred Schnittke's First Symphony (1969–72). But the problem of surface and depth is raised in an equally fundamental way by a contemporaneous work which is dominated by a single, transgressive quotation. When George Rochberg allowed himself to transcribe the Adagio from Mozart's Divertimento, K.287, as the second 'Act' of his *Music for the Magic Theatre* (1967), he created a document as foundational for musical postmodernism as its more famous

---

[34] See Fink, 'Arrows of Desire', ch. 7 for a more detailed critical discussion.

[35] Berio has, bewilderingly enough, claimed that the third movement of *Sinfonia* is not a 'collage', by which he apparently means a totally random assemblage of fragments. He represses this vision of the piece—attractive, to some—and asks us to hear the quotations as sober harmonic commentary on the pitch structure of the Mahler. To get a sense of the party line on this quasi-organic relationship, see the brief discussion in David Osmond-Smith, *Berio* (Oxford, 1991), 53–5, which puts *Sinfonia* in the context of 'purer' works like *Chemins*, *Bewegung*, and *Eindrücke*.

younger cousin, *Sinfonia*. Rochberg's gesture, less flamboyant, less overtly virtuosic than Berio's, was perhaps even more radical, because it was so stark and uncompromising. The presence of Mozart's entire Divertimento movement in Rochberg's score doesn't allow much room for argument. Nor does it leave much space for 'the composer's voice'—a fact of which the composer himself was well aware: 'The presence of the transcription abrogates the 19th to early 20th-century notion of "originality," puts the paraphernalia of its aesthetic completely aside.'[36]

Yet, having delivered this crushing blow to modernist authenticity, Rochberg took pains to reclaim at least a small sliver of the compositional space for himself. In 'No Center', a tortured, stream-of-consciousness essay written two years after *Music for the Magic Theatre*, he characterizes its middle movement as 'a transcription, that is, a completely new version', and adds—cryptically—'People who don't understand think it's by Mozart.' A glance at the score and this apparent self-contradiction starts to make sense. Berio's *Sinfonia* incorporates the untransformed surfaces of many other pieces; Rochberg's second movement incorporates only one other piece—*is* that piece, more or less—but its surface is thoroughly transformed. The rather drab complexion of Mozart's Divertimento (muted strings) is cosmetically enhanced with virtuoso flair: Rochberg adds a new concertante piano part, transposes most of the solo violin line up an octave, reintroduces the pair of horns that Mozart left out, and concocts exotic woodwind doublings that give the whole a glossy surface sheen.[37]

This is more than 'mere' transcription, but not quite recomposition on the scale of, say, Stravinsky's *Pulcinella*. Rochberg does not restrict himself to the pitches of the original, as did Webern in his radical deconstruction of Bach's six-part Ricercare; nor does he limit his additions to orchestrational elaboration in the Stokowski manner. He actually composes new, independent surface details. The only way I can understand Rochberg's paradoxical claim that Act II of *Music for the Magic Theatre* is 'not by Mozart' is as a reminder of what his own renunciation of originality obscures: that the piece is not *all* by Mozart.

In particular, the musical surface is brand new, and it is by Rochberg. But the new lines and voices are purely decorative; they do not alter by one iota the fundamental voice-leading structure. Thus—and here a chasm opens up—the deep structure beneath Rochberg's shiny new surface is still by Mozart. It might be less unsettling if the transcription's new surface details did colonize Mozart's structure, if they added motivic density or created dissonant collections that demanded post-tonal explanation.[38] But they don't. Rochberg's brilliant make-

---

[36] George Rochberg, *Music for the Magic Theatre* (Bryn Mawr, Pa., 1972), composer's preface.

[37] I have discussed this movement at length in my paper, 'Amadeus in Disneyland: Hyperreality, Postmodernism, and Rochberg's *Music for the Magic Theatre*', delivered at the second West Coast Conference on Music Theory and Analysis, Santa Barbara, Calif., 1992.

[38] This rather controversial notion about modernist works by Stravinsky and Schoenberg (among others) has been advanced within the context of Harold Bloom's famous 'anxiety of influence' by Joseph N. Straus, *Remaking the Past: Musical Modernism and the Influence of the Tonal Tradition* (Cambridge, Mass., 1990). This neo-Bloomian for-

over is only skin-deep. Move one reductive step towards the middle-ground level, and the piece isn't by him anymore. (The only remains of *his* piece would be some anomalies of register.) The space within which Rochberg chooses to work is as flat as the surface of a Magritte, and as glossily smooth.[39] It is a gravestone: beneath, nothing—at least, nothing by Rochberg.

This disembodied surface is thus a simulacrum, a sign that dissimulates that there is nothing underneath. And the figure of the gravestone seems even more apropos to Rochberg's 1970s style, which moves past quotation to more equivocal pastiches like the infamous 'Beethovenian' slow movement of the Third String Quartet. Presumably, when Rochberg confined this Adagio to radiant, diatonic A major, he created, *malgré lui*, a traditional tonal hierarchy, with a surface and a deep structure. But such postmodern tonality is, simply by virtue of its music-historical position, volatile and arbitrary. After atonality, a tonal surface, however well-behaved, can never again have the inevitability of 'natural law', and thus can never again give the impression of following necessarily from a single, fundamental, deep structure. (You can induce Pandora to close her box again—but *I* wouldn't turn my back on her for a minute.) One might paraphrase Foucault, and claim that Rochberg's tonal works 'allow the old space of tonality to rule, but only at the surface'. Underneath, the old hierarchy of tonal voice-leading is dead. It *feels* dead, abdicated, since it no longer has the unique ability to guarantee order at the surface for us. Each new surface event is fraught with tension. Isn't it possible at any moment for the style to shift, for atonality to reclaim this space, for the rules of tonal voice-leading to mutate, or even evaporate into the past? Whether or not a collapse actually comes, and whether it is within or between movements, the potential is always there, and always destructive to organicism. If the purpose of structural levels is to guarantee the unity of the musical surface, then an arbitrary hierarchy is functionally equivalent to no hierarchy at all.

The musical space inhabited by composers like Berio, Schnittke, and Rochberg is not the unified hierarchic space of Schenker and Schoenberg; it seems much closer to the absolute chaos of what Foucault called a 'heterotopia':

the disorder in which a large number of possible orders glitter separately, in the lawless and uncharted dimension of the *heteroclite* . . . In such a state, things are 'laid,' 'placed,' 'arranged' in sites so very different from one another that it is impossible to find a common place beneath them all. . . . *Heterotopias* are disturbing, probably because they secretly undermine language [and] because they shatter . . . that less apparent syntax which causes words and things to 'hang together.'[40]

mulation treats Rochberg rather poorly. Straus bases his criteria for 'strength' on systematic recomposition of pitch structures. Rochberg, who slavishly reproduces every note of his original, and whose added notes punctiliously respect the voice-leading rules of the original, doesn't 'misread' at all—and is thus the weakest of weak readers. For a pungent critique of Straus's project, see Richard Taruskin, review of Kevin Korsyn, 'Towards a New Poetics of Musical Influence' and Joseph Straus, 'Remaking the Past', *Journal of the American Musicological Society*, 46 (1993), 114–38.

[39] Rochberg makes the link to surrealism himself in his preface to *Music for the Magic Theatre*, 6.

[40] Michel Foucault, *The Order of Things* (New York, 1970), 48.

For Schenker, tonal voice-leading provides that 'less apparent syntax', and the fundamental structure is, of course, the paradigmatic 'common place beneath them all'. Poly-stylism defies totalizing hierarchic explanations, and embraces incoherence and incommensurability: there will be pitches and musical events on the surface which simply *cannot be related hierarchically* because they function within incommensurate systems that are totally disjunct.[41] This schizoid disintegration of the musical surface is undeniably as disturbing as it is liberating. (*Sinfonia* is not an upbeat piece.) But to demand organic unity from contemporary composition is ultimately quixotic: it is hopeless to insist that music reflect, not the *heterotopia* in which we live, but some one of the many utopias in which we no longer believe.

## III.  Boundaries: The Cultural Politics of Surface–Depth

> The masses, however, lack the soul of genius. They are not aware of background, they have no feeling for the future. Their lives are merely an eternally disordered foreground, a continuous present without connection, unwinding chaotically in empty, animal fashion. It is always the individual who creates and transmits connection and coherence.
>
> *Heinrich Schenker*

> Choke me in the shallow water before I get too deep.
>
> *Edie Brickell and New Bohemians*

Let me make no effort to disguise my polemical intent: the preceding analytical survey was expressly designed to make the surface–depth metaphor look increasingly irrelevant to present-day analytical concerns. The various 'flatnesses' of minimalism and postmodernism might well cause one to ask whether depth is an *essential* property of music, even the most familiar and canonical music. If conceptualizing Beethoven's music as a hierarchically organized space now feels just a little more contingent, then the rather *outré* attempts above to think hierarchically about Rochberg and Reich have served their purpose. But to assume that even the most cleverly constructed practical demonstration I can provide will persuade theorists to abandon *en masse* this most satisfying metaphor for music would be worse than arrogant—it would be culturally naïve. It is uniquely satisfying to construe music as a bounded, hierarchical, and thus unified entity; otherwise the pressures of new musical styles and new cultural theories would

---

[41] It is this radical disjunction that differentiates *heterotopia* from Cohn and Dempster's 'product networks'. They propose to replace the single deep structure of Schenkerian analysis with an interlocking network of multiple deep structures that work together to create a unified surface. I submit that many contemporary musical works replace this single deep structure with multiple deep and surface structures that *do not work together at all*. They propose to replace the oligarchic model of musical structure favoured by organicism with a 'democratic' model where the surface is a 'consensus'. I fear—yes, well, actually exult—that the surface of many postmodern works represents not consensus, but chaos.

have pushed most of us to abandon hierarchic depth models long ago. The following is to be taken as an extremely provisional exploration of a topic that by rights deserves treatment at length: why do depth metaphors for music seem so powerful, so resonant, so *natural* to us? It appears that if we give up musical depth, we risk losing nothing less than the security of our own psychic depths. Our hierarchic theories presuppose that we value music for its ability to provide a structural reflection—and thus a crucial reinforcement—of our own interiority as human subjects.

Even a cursory look at the way in which surface, depth, and hierarchy function within Heinrich Schenker's cultural politics will leave no doubt that he saw musical structure as in some sense correlative to the (threatened) structure of the individual ego. Very early in *Free Composition* he makes the crucial identification: 'Music is not only an *object* of theoretical consideration. It is *subject*, just as we are subject.'[42] If a musical work is a subject, like us, then its structure must necessarily reflect *our* structure. Indeed, Schenker asserts a few pages earlier that 'in its linear progressions . . . music mirrors the human soul'. But the mirroring is only possible because the master-work, like the human psyche, has depth, and is organically unified. The multi-levelled integrity of great art is *uniquely* akin to ours: 'How different is today's idol, the machine! It simulates the organic, yet, since its parts are directed toward only a partial goal, a partial achievement, its totality is only an aggregate which has nothing in common with the human soul.'[43]

Mechano-phobia is a particular obsession for Schenker. In his writings a strange dichotomy opens up: on the one side, the individual human psyche and the organic master-work, equally and totally organized according to strict hierarchy; and on the other, the mass and the machine. In Schenker's Luddite view the machine is a symbol for *lack* of structure, an inanimate, loosely organized heap of parts whose 'totality is only an aggregate'. Time and again, the image of the individual soul calls up its opposite, the mechanized, soulless mass:

Instead of creating substance out of the live source of an idea, the average person absorbs ideas handed down to him only mechanically. He upholds them mechanically all his life and even transmits them mechanically. . . . Thus long before the invention of the machine, the soul of the average person was already a kind of machine.[44]

This constellation of anxieties—fear of machines, fear of the mass, and fear of the collapse of the bourgeois ego—is exhaustively analysed by Klaus Theweleit in his massive study of *Male Fantasies*.[45] Theweleit's observations are particularly apropos because he is dissecting what he calls '*Freikorps* culture', the culture of

---

[42] Schenker, *Free Composition*, 9.

[43] Ibid. pp. xxiii–xxiv.

[44] Schenker, 'Rameau or Beethoven', 501–2.

[45] Klaus Theweleit, *Male Fantasies*, has been published in 2 vols. (1: women, floods, bodies, history; 2: male bodies: psychoanalysing the white terror) by University of Minnesota Press, 1987–9. These are a translation of *Männerphantasien* (2 vols., 1977–8).

right-wing paramilitary groups in the aftermath of the First World War. Schenker was a contemporary and perhaps even a supporter of these 'soldier-males' in their bloody struggle against the working-class uprisings of 1918–23. (His hysterical German chauvinism and extreme right-wing political views are on display in every one of his post-war publications—publications roughly simultaneous with the *Freikorps* novels and memoirs that Theweleit analyses.[46]) Theweleit sees a basic link between the integrity of the bourgeois ego and a fear of machines: 'As bourgeois individuals, we have been brought up to think of our-selves as totalities, and unique ones at that. To the bourgeois mind, this concep-tion of self accords precisely with the notion that we cannot be anything like 'machines', 'mechanically' produced or producing, or even 'products of mass production'.[47] Following Deleuze and Guattari,[48] Theweleit interprets the machine in this context as the emblem of the 'desiring-production' of the un-conscious; the 'flows' of desiring-production are a subject of fascination and intolerable anxiety for the soldier-male, because they annihilate the carefully constructed boundaries of the bourgeois ego.

For Theweleit, the rigid boundaries of this bourgeois ego are completely arti-ficial, built up by centuries of the repressive 'civilizing process':

It seems unlikely that a human desire itself would limit the flowing of its streams or the fluidity of its form . . . in order to assume a fixed, confining external shape. It seems far more likely that the rigidity and permanence of bodily boundaries and psychic systems have been set up by external social constraints and natural adversity—a dam built around flowing desire by hostile forces.[49]

A subject securely ensconced within the pre-capitalist social matrix could afford to have porous ego boundaries, a loose sense of himself as an individual, no real inner world. But the bourgeois subject needs a complex depth and interiority, since in Marx's famous formula, everything solid around him has melted into air. As a functional 'adaptation', the surface of the ego becomes hard, imperme-able; disruptive feelings are walled off:

---

[46] I direct the interested reader to the first issue of *Der Tonwille* (1921). Schenker began this journal of music theory with a rambling, xenophobic, right-wing editorial screed—complete with attacks on democracy, a diatribe against Woodrow Wilson, references to the *Dolchstoss*, and racist revulsion at the supposed posting of Senegalese Negro troops in occupied Germany—under the high-flown title, 'On the Mission of German Genius'. In this context, the dispassionate discussion of 'The Fundamental Structure' that follows takes on a different, somewhat disturbing, cultural significance. See Heinrich Schenker, 'Von der Sendung des deutschen Genies', in *Der Tonwille*, repr. in 1 vol. (Hildesheim, 1990), 3–21. It is strange to realize, given the subsequent history of Schenkerian theories in America, that Schenker himself despised the United States, and all that (he thought) it stood for. The idea of the compatriots of Woodrow Wilson and John D. Rockefeller developing deep insights into German music would, I am afraid, have seemed to him grotesquely absurd.

[47] Theweleit, *Male Fantasies*, i. 211.

[48] See Gilles Deleuze and Félix Guattari, *Anti-Oedipus: Capitalism and Schizophrenia*, trans. Robert Hurley, Mark Seem, and Helen R. Lane (Minneapolis, 1983), 36–42. For a useful gloss on Deleuze and Guattari's famously opaque manifesto, see Brian Massumi, *A User's Guide to Capitalism and Schizophrenia: Deviations from Deleuze and Guattari* (Cambridge, Mass., 1992).

[49] Theweleit, *Male Fantasies*, i. 211.

The man puts on a coat of 'armor.' . . . A lengthy process of 'self-distancing,' 'self-control,' and 'self-scrutiny' ensues—a 'subduing of affect,' an opposition of 'interior' and 'exterior,' of near and far.[50]

A schematic presentation like this does not really do Theweleit justice. His analysis of masculine bourgeois 'character armor' (to use the Reichian term) is grounded in encyclopaedic and close reading of *Freikorps* literature, where inner and outer threats to the bourgeois ego—women, the masses, communism, unconscious desire—are represented by innumerable anxiety-charged images of the rigid soldier-male inundated by floods, waves, muck, and mire—'The Red flood poured its filth over Germany', and so on.

Schenker's fanatical insistence on the total organic coherence of the masterwork seems to be a less virulent reaction to the same chaotic political situation. The hierarchic connection between background and foreground forms a crucial bulwark against the dissolution of both music and the bourgeois ego in a decadent age dominated by egalitarian mass culture. Schenker's mature writings are punctuated by contemptuous dismissals of the 'masses'. He had no patience with appeals by the left wing of modernism to the inner genius of the proletariat: 'Only the genius is connected with God, not the people. Thus we must undo the deification of the masses.'[51] But even in the context of naïve leftist paeans to 'mass art', the passage from the introduction to *Free Composition* that I quoted at the beginning of this section remains shocking—shocking for the way it blithely uses the surface–depth metaphor to dehumanize an entire class of people. The masses are animals, their life is all chaotic surface; only the bourgeois 'individual', who, like the musical master-works he loves, has both foreground and background, can 'create and transmit connection and coherence'. Interiority, structure, hierarchy—these properties not only define the space of the masterwork; they define the psychic space within which we (bourgeois) can experience subjectivity. It is our inner 'regions for soul-searching' that make us—and *not* the masses—truly human.

Schenker was not the only theorist who saw the emerging mass culture of modernity as hostile to old-fashioned bourgeois subjectivity, and thus to the traditions of art. The titles of Ortega y Gasset's two most famous books—*The Revolt of the Masses* and *The Dehumanization of Art*—encapsulate the relation rather neatly. In Schenker's writings the masses are not only indifferent to great art; they are a positive threat: 'the fundamental structure amounts to a sort of secret, hidden and unsuspected, a secret which, incidentally, provides music with a kind of natural preservation from destruction by the masses.'[52] The 'secret of the

---

[50] Ibid. i. 302.

[51] Schenker, *Free Composition*, 159. (Note: this passage was eliminated from the original German edn. My translation differs slightly from John Rothgeb's.)

[52] Ibid. 9. Schenker was fond of this law-of-the-jungle metaphor; witness an offhand remark about hidden motivic parallels: 'The mysterious concealment of such repetitions is an almost biological means of protection: repetitions thrive better in secret than in the full light of consciousness' (ibid. 18).

fundamental structure' is the secret of hierarchy and total organization. Set aside Schenker's confident assumption that these are essential characteristics of 'real' music—characteristics which revealed themselves only to him—and the question arises: What is gained by postulating (that is, constructing) a totalized hierarchic structure for music? In Schenker's case, the motive seems to have been defence. In the face of hostile, dehumanized mass culture, the subjectivity and interiority encoded by great art must be defended behind an impregnable skin: a surface-as-boundary that, though confusing and complex to the uninitiated, possesses the solid integrity of total organization.

Music (and music theory) must be disciplined, organized, if it is to resist being swept away by the flood of mediocrity that is modern mass culture. The site of discipline is, of course, the academy—whether musical or military. Theweleit sees the drill and discipline of military training as a similar defence mechanism for hardening boundaries: the hierarchy of military rank and the total control of military discipline create tough soldiers who will eventually stand firm against the raging mass, both outside (Communists) and inside (the unconscious). To use his terms, *desiring-machines* must be replaced by *totality-machines*:

The desiring-machine of the unconscious is a molecular mass entity composed of organ-machines, well-sprung machines, energy-machines, coupled to partial objects, remnants of this and building-blocks of that: it is pure multiplicity, incapable of agglomeration, but capable of entering every possible association, producing any pleasure. *The technological machine, by contrast, is a molar construction, whose individual components occupy and fulfill prescribed positions and specific functions. Since this machine can be conceived as a hierarchically organized unity, I have called it a totality-machine: a machine that is exemplary in the way it maintains the desire for a specifically constructed individual body.* Within the machine 'instinctual life' is controlled and transformed into a dynamic of regularized functions; it is devoid of feeling.[53]

Schenkerian analysis might, in this context, be seen as a method for constructing musical totality-machines. The point of this comparison is not the invidious hint that hierarchic theories like Schenkerian analysis are somehow 'Fascist' (I am well aware of the subsequent persecution of Schenker, his family, and his disciples by the Nazis). It is, rather, to show how making a totality-machine out of music does powerful cultural work: it provides a way of reinforcing the bounded, interior self, perpetually under attack in modern and postmodern society.

But—and this is the purpose of the entire exercise—what if we relieve music of this burden, and choose to conceptualize and experience musical artworks as pure desiring-machines? It appears that much recent music, abandoning totality and hierarchic depth, has already abrogated the agreement—unilaterally, as it were. 'Remnants of this and building-blocks of that' is a fair description of postmodernist collage works like *Sinfonia* and *Music for the Magic Theatre*. At

---

[53] Theweleit, *Male Fantasies*, 198; emphasis added.

the other end of the stylistic spectrum, the pulsating, saturated surfaces of minimalism are even more radical representations of Theweleit's non-hierarchic 'energy-machines' in sound. I would argue that the mechanical vernacular of 'cycles', 'gates', and 'phases' that pervades minimalist discourse indexes a *pure desiring-production without interiorized subjectivity*—the closest musical analogue to Deleuze and Guattari's desiring-machines of the unconscious that the high-art music culture of the West has ever produced.

Even the music that Schenker himself prized as organic—Bach, Beethoven, Brahms—can easily be experienced as desiring-production. The view of a Beethoven symphony as a chaotic and shifting assemblage of surface 'flows'—transient, intense energy connections between 'partial objects', some in the piece, some in a listening consciousness—may be of little use as a defensive construct. But it does capture the fundamental contingency of musical experience. On the material level, the level of our *non*-transcendental powers of hearing and attention, I perceive (and value!) a Beethoven symphony as exciting, disorganized, and all surface. It feels less like an *ego*—and it makes me feel more like an *id.*

Hierarchic music theories ask us to renounce the pleasures of the surface for the defensive security of the depths. We may not all want to make the exchange.

Perhaps, after all, beauty is only skin-deep.

Even in music.

> Yet now, forsooth, because Pierre begins to see through the first superficiality of the world, he fondly weens he has come to the unlayered substance. But, as far as any geologist has yet gone down into the world, it is found to consist of nothing but surface stratified on surface. To its axis, the world being nothing but superinduced superficies. By vast pains we mine into the pyramid; by horrible gropings we come to the central room; with joy we espy the sarcophagus; but we lift the lid—and no body is there!—appallingly vacant as vast is the soul of man!
>
> Herman Melville, *Pierre, or, the Ambiguities* (1852)

# 6

# The Challenge of Semiotics

## Kofi Agawu

In an influential discussion of the 'place of language in human facts', Ferdinand de Saussure set forth a vision of the science of semiology in which language, social institution' as well as 'a system of signs', was given pre-eminent status:

A science that studies the life of signs within society is conceivable; it would be a part of social psychology and consequently of general psychology; I shall call it *semiology* (from Greek *semeîon*, 'sign'). Semiology would show what constitutes signs, what laws govern them. Since the science does not yet exist, no one can say what it would be; but it has a right to existence, a place staked out in advance. Linguistics is only a part of the general science of semiology; the laws discovered by semiology will be applicable to linguistics, and the latter will circumscribe a well-defined area within the mass of anthropological facts.[1]

The cultural specificity of sign formation ('the life of signs within society'), the mediation of individual as well as group perceptions, the materiality of signs, the existence of rules or constraints governing their disposition, and the recognition of other sign systems from among 'the mass of anthropological facts': these together present an ambitious, broadly based programme for semiology. Although Saussure's own practical concerns effectively reduced the scope of this vision to specific technical problems in linguistic semiology, his statement none the less retains a sense of the potential breadth and diversity of the field.

In an equally influential envisioning of the theory of signs, Charles Sanders Peirce understood semiotics as 'the quasi-necessary, or formal doctrine of signs', from which he immediately deduced the importance of abstraction to the semiotic enterprise. Central to his view of semiotics is the sign, defined in an oft cited statement that lays bare the conditions of possibility of signifying:

A sign, or *representamen*, is something which stands to somebody for something in some respect or capacity. It addresses somebody, that is, creates in the mind of that person an equivalent sign, or perhaps a more developed sign. That sign which it creates I call the *interpretant* of the first sign. The sign stands for something, its *object*. It stands for that

---

[1] Ferdinand de Saussure, *Course in General Linguistics*, trans. Wade Baskin, ed. Charles Bally and Albert Sechehaye (New York, 1959), 16; orig. pub. as *Cours de linguistique générale* (Paris, 1916).

object, not in all respects, but in reference to a sort of idea, which I have sometimes called the *ground* of the representamen.[2]

This tripartite model of sign functioning (interpretant–object–ground) places at its centre what might be called the ongoing invention of interpretants, a complex cognitive process that should discourage hasty statements about what a particular cultural object or expressive form actually 'means'.

Countless books and articles have, of course, been devoted to explaining, refining, or refuting the theories of Saussure and Peirce. It is not my aim to provide a genealogy of those ideas here; rather, I want to emphasize the instability of the terms and concepts that have served to define a startling assortment of theoretical, and especially analytical, activity as 'semiotic', a practice unaffected by the collapse of European 'semiology' (after Saussure) into American 'semiotics' (after Peirce). The *Encyclopedic Dictionary of Semiotics*, for example, runs to three volumes, including 1,621 pages written by 235 scholars covering histories, definitions, and explanations of a bewildering array of topics, some of them plainly semiotic (code, interpretant, meaning, zoosemiotics), others only indirectly but no less pertinently so (ambiguity, Cabbala, noise, truth).[3] In the same spirit, but without the benefit of a team of contributors, Umberto Eco provides a list of 'areas of contemporary research [that] may belong to the semiotic field' near the beginning of his book, *A Theory of Semiotics*. They include zoosemiotics, olfactory signs, tactile communication, codes of taste, paralinguistics, medical semiotics, kinesics and proxemics, musical codes, formalized languages, written languages, unknown alphabets, secret codes, natural languages, visual communication, systems of objects, plot structure, text theory, cultural codes, aesthetic texts, mass communication, and rhetoric.[4] In the light of such diversity, one wonders whether there are any remaining areas of research in the human sciences that have not been, or could not possibly be, touched by the semiotic wand. To say that dealing in signs is a—or perhaps *the*—basic human activity is to say something obvious.

It is against this broad, heterogeneous background that any attempt to assess the challenge of musical semiotics should proceed. For in the twenty years or so of active research in musical semiotics, there is no sign that practitioners subscribe to the same basic tenets. While researchers in other fields do not, of course, adhere slavishly to a handful of founding principles, the diversity of music-semiotic research goes beyond the normal divergences of other research enterprises. While some may read this condition as a sign of a healthy, welcome pluralism, others will question the validity of an intellectual enterprise that has failed to define its basic aims in an acceptably general form from the start.

Consider, for example, the range of reference in Raymond Monelle's recent

[2] *Collected Papers of Charles Sanders Peirce*, ed. C. Harsshorne, P. Weiss, and A. W. Burks (8 vols., Cambridge, Mass., 1931–66), ii. para. 228.

[3] Thomas Sebeok (ed.), *Encyclopedic Dictionary of Semiotics* (3 vols., Berlin, 1986).

[4] Umberto Eco, *A Theory of Semiotics* (Bloomington, Ind., 1976), 9–14.

handbook, *Linguistics and Semiotics in Music*.[5] Although Monelle includes linguistics as well as semiotics in his discussion, he does not always maintain a hard and fast distinction between the two fields. Indeed, the elevated position that Saussure accords linguistics within the general field of semiology suggests that it would be difficult, if not impossible, to escape, at a fundamental level, the intervention of natural language, with its formidable apparatus and its undeniable semantic baggage. Thus Monelle recognizes that questions of musical meaning require engagement with a body of texts by Hanslick, Gurney, Cooke, and others, normally classified under the heading 'aesthetics'. Hard linguistic theory is summarized from the writings of Piaget, Saussure, Chomsky, and Hjelmslev, with reference to ideas such as structure, pertinence, opposition, and generation. Segmentation and repetition, central concerns in any analysis of music, are discussed with a view to clarifying the methods by which we construe musical segments, methods that have sometimes seemed arbitrary or merely 'intuitive'. The writings of Ruwet, Nattiez, Lerdahl and Jackendoff, John Blacking, various computer-based analytical as well as compositional projects, and issues of metalanguage (including the semiotic analysis of analysis) are all given due attention. Predictably, the opening up of a possible semantic dimension takes Monelle into even more heterogeneous territory. Among the issues discussed here are the connections between myth and music, the possible narrative capacity of music, the centrality of markedness as a discriminating device, and the role of conventional topoi in conveying musical ideas within a carefully regulated formal discourse. Monelle even includes a chapter on deconstruction and allegory, styles of thought that would seem fundamentally anti-semiotic in so far as they reject—at least rhetorically—essentialist premises. Monelle's generous, catholic configuring of the field of musical semiotics is logical and cogent, making it difficult for the critic to isolate a core of methodological premises that might sustain a strict definition of semiotics.[6]

Semiotics, in short, applies in every circumstance that music is produced and consumed. It has been adapted to the analysis of the pre-tonal, tonal, and post-tonal repertoires. Moreover, semiotics does not endorse what some feel is an essentially political or commercial distinction between 'high' art and 'low' or popular art. (Monelle, for example, discusses popular song and television commercials alongside works by Beethoven, Liszt, Wagner, and Debussy, among others.) Nor does it insist on a distinction between Western and non-Western music. The crucial question is whether this breadth of application indicates an uncommonly powerful explanatory potential, or whether it is nothing but a sign of generality bordering on the trivially universal.

My aim in this chapter is to reconsider aspects of the challenge posed by semi-

---

[5] Raymond Monelle, *Linguistics and Semiotics in Music*, Contemporary Music Studies, 5 (Chur, Switzerland, 1992).

[6] For two other major mappings of the field of musical semiotics, see Jean-Jacques Nattiez, 'Reflections on the Development of Semiology in Music', *Music Analysis*, 8 (1989), 21–75, and David Lidov, 'Music', in Sebeok (ed.), *Encyclopedic Dictionary of Semiotics*, i. 577–87.

otics with a view not to providing a categorical answer to the question posed in the last sentence but to showing how a few corners of semiotic research may usefully clarify, and perhaps even validate, certain kinds of knowledge about musical works. I shall begin by reviewing one of the oldest and (still) problematic alliances that musicians have had to come to terms with: namely, that between natural language and music. The aim is to summarize some of the enabling conditions for musical signification. After that I shall discuss aspects of semiotic analytical method. Throughout this main part of the chapter, I will insist that unless musical semiotics comes to terms with traditional music theory, it is unlikely to proceed very far methodologically before discovering that it has been engaged in reinventing the wheel all along. A brief final section mentions three areas of musical research in which semiotics might prove particularly valuable.

## Is Music a Language?

The association between music and language goes back to the earliest writings on music theory. It is an association that must appear unavoidable wherever people make (and therefore talk about) music. It is also an association that must feature in any evaluation of the signifying potential of music. There is by now such a vast literature on the subject that further discussion would seem most productive only in carefully circumscribed contexts of specific music(s) and language(s). In what follows, however, I will keep the discussion on a general enough level to sketch a background for later discussion of musical signs. The following are eleven propositions concerning the music-as-language metaphor.

1. *Music, like language and possibly religion, is a species-specific trait of man.*[7] All known human societies make music (and this includes societies in whose languages the word 'music' does not exist), despite the striking differences in material, medium, and situations of production and consumption. Music is thus 'necessary to us'.[8] But whereas the average person's linguistic abilities are sufficient to define what is meant by competence, assessing normal musical competence is a rather more elusive enterprise. And if we focus not on competence, but on performance, on the culturally specific products of our innate capacities, we are struck by the greater differences among musics than among languages.[9] The more radical constructedness and artificiality of music, together with its

---

[7] John Blacking, *How Musical is Man?* (Seattle, 1973), 7.

[8] Gayle A. Henrotte, 'Music as Language: A Semiotic Paradigm?', in John Deely (ed.), *Semiotics 1984* (Lanham, Md., 1985),163–70.

[9] Harold Powers, 'Language Models and Music Analyisis', *Ethnomusicology*, 25 (1980), 38.

dependence on context for validation and meaning, suggest that a semiotics of music cannot simply be formulated in parallel with a semiotics of language.

2. *Unlike language, which functions both as a medium for communication ('ordinary language') and as a vehicle for artistic expression ('poetic language'), musical language exists primarily in the 'poetic' sense, although it can function for communicative purposes.*[10] The distinction between ordinary language and poetic language is obviously not categorical. Yet, despite the existence of sporadic evidence that music may function as an 'ordinary' medium for communication—one thinks of the talking drums of Africa studied by John Carrington[11] or the 'thought-songs' of the Tepehua people of Mexico studied by Charles Boilès[12]—the discursive communicative capacity of music is inferior to that of language. The predominantly aesthetic function of music compares only with certain special uses of natural language.

3. *Unlike language, music exists only in performance (actual, idealized, imagined, remembered).* Partly because of the communicative function of language, which enables, among other things, a distinction between true and false propositions, there is a wider range among the various states of linguistic existence than among those of musical existence. Special uses of language involve performance, and these are thought to differ from 'ordinary' uses. Music, by contrast, is inconceivable outside a context of performance. That all speech-acts are performative acts and that some musicians (such as analysts) have the ability to conceive of music outside a specific context of social performance: these facts do not negate the proposition that the constraints placed upon music-making are special and more severe than those placed upon ordinary verbal behaviour.

4. *Like language, music is organized into temporally bounded or 'closed' texts.* The internal mode of existence of musical works is ontologically comparable to that of verbal texts, whether these be oral texts (such as greetings, oaths, and prayers) or written texts (such as poems, novels, letters, and speeches). Questions about the identity of a musical work are made less challenging by the undeniable fact that every text (or work) has in principle a beginning, a middle, and an end. This is not to dispute the idea that once we move beyond the ontological specificity of the work, our attempts to decode it necessarily reconfigure it as an open text.

5. *A musical text, like a verbal text, is organized into discrete units or segments. Music is therefore segmentable.* Many writings in music theory, especially the great seventeenth- and eighteenth-century treatises on rhetoric and music, devote considerable space to demonstrating this point. Although the explicit aim is often to establish the boundaries of rests, notes, motives, themes, phrases, periods, and sections, the implicit premiss is that these constructs actively engender meaning.

---

[10] Roman Jakobson, 'Language in Relation to Other Communication Systems', in *Selected Writings*, vol. 2 (The Hague, 1971), 704–5.

[11] John Carrington, *Talking Drums of Africa* (London, 1949; repr. New York, 1969).

[12] Charles Boilès, 'Tepehua Thought-Song', *Ethnomusicology*, 11 (1967), 267–92.

That is why some writers pursue analogies between musical structure and letters, words, sentences, and paragraphs. The issue of music's physical segmentability is less interesting, however, than what might be called its cultural segmentability. The two are intertwined, of course, but there is a difference in the degree to which historically specific data are included in the criteria for segmentation. To segment culturally is to draw on a rich, culturally specific body of formal and informal discourses in order to determine a work's significant sense units. Such units are not neutrally derived; nor are they value-free. Already, an explicit metalanguage has emerged. For when analysts invoke 'musical logic' or 'developing variation', with their implications of a 'syntax', they have already made assumptions about the nature of unit-formation. (Incidentally, the idea that the units of tonal music, as opposed to those of post-tonal music and especially the free atonal repertories, are stable, and that the criteria for their determination are transparent, is highly misleading.)

6. *Although segmentable, the musical text is more continuous in its sonic reality or 'real-time unfolding' than a verbal text. Verbal texts rely more on virtual or physical rests than do musical texts.* Here the cultural and chronological limits placed upon the valid domain for testing these propositions is especially apparent, for one can easily cite certain works of contemporary music in which continuity is threatened. (There is always John Cage's 4′ 33″ to challenge any hastily formed notions of continuity.) Still, a case can be made for the greater physical or psychological continuity of tonal music over, say, a Wordsworth poem, because of the ways in which organized (musical) sound 'tyrannizes' whatever it accompanies. One source of the illusion of continuity in music is the far from mechanical approach to punctuation. Whereas, generally speaking, a period is a period in verbal punctuation, the role, or even identity, of a musical cadence is not so self-evident. The linear spill-overs, the continuities across formal boundaries, and the complex hierarchies of closure in tonal music: all these confer on the tonal organism a higher degree of interdependence among its parts, an interdependence all the more striking for having fewer direct semantic resonances outside the work. The auditor of tonal music is thus not allowed enough time to ponder other associations, but must follow a train of thought from its inception to its completion.[13]

7. *A musical segment (phrase, period, sentence, paragraph, section, movement) exists in two interdependent planes, the plane of succession ('melody') and the plane of simultaneity ('harmony'). Language lacks the place of simultaneity.* This proposition is not meant to deny that there are acts of literature or drama in which some form of simultaneous doing occurs, or that there are some acts of music that apparently lack the plane of simultaneity. Yet, even in unaccompanied monodies, an implicit contrapuntal dimension—a dimension populated by silent

---

[13] See also the reference to music's 'structural continuity' in Lidov, 'Musical and Verbal Semantics', *Semiotica*, 31 (1980), 369–91.

voices—brings to view a plane of simultaneity. One could, of course, argue this for language, too, stressing Saussure's insight that meaning is difference, and concluding that language usages subtend a normative background comprising whatever has been excluded or purposefully erased from the reigning foreground. But even this somewhat more refined argument does not challenge the fact that it is hard to imagine the equivalent of a phenomenon such as harmony (or counterpoint or polyphony) in natural language. This plane of simultaneity is one of the factors that makes music untranslatable.

8. *Units of language have more or less fixed lexical meaning, while units of music do not.* To deny music a foundational semantic dimension is not, of course, to claim that semantic meanings cannot be imposed on a non-signifying musical structure. And while language, too, is subject to its share of foundational instability, there is no comparison between such instability and that of music. Deryck Cooke's *The Language of Music* makes a case for investing certain recurring tonal patterns with associational meaning; to the extent that these meanings are plausible within the culture of (European) consumers, his thesis is persuasive.[14] The issue is not that musical configurations lack meaning outside their original cultural contexts, but that it might be more productive to assign meanings on the basis of the kinds of contracts known to exist between composers and their audiences. The absence of lexical meaning for music also has implications for its translatability. According to Henrotte, 'musical styles are not translatable, but the impulses that produce music are';[15] while Émile Benveniste posits a principle of non-redundancy between semiotic systems, according to which 'two semiotic systems of different types cannot be mutually interchangeable'.[16] This 'nonconvertibility of systems with different bases' undermines all arguments for translation, without denying the existence of morphological or expressive resemblances between systems.

9. *Musical and linguistic meaning (or reference) may be extrinsic or intrinsic. But in music intrinsic meaning predominates over extrinsic meaning, whereas in language it is the other way round.* The mode of signification in music has often been conceptualized oppositionally as in the above proposition. Extrinsic reference is familiar from the work of leitmotifs in Wagner, word-painting in Handel, or the depiction of an 'external' reality in Liszt's or Strauss's tone-poems. This mode of signification relies on 'musical-verbal dictionaries'.[17] Leitmotifs, for example, are made to bear the weight of an assigned reference. Similarly, Handel's word-paintings typically aspire to the condition of iconic signs. The point being made is that extrinsic reference is possible only as a result of the intervention of layers of conventional signification. By contrast, intrinsic reference is exemplified by a

---

[14] Deryck Cooke, *The Language of Music* (London, 1959).

[15] Henrotte, 'Music as Language', 169.

[16] Emile Benveniste, 'The Semiology of Language', in Robert E. Innis (ed.), *Semiotics: An Introductory Reader* (London, 1986), 235.

[17] Powers, 'Language Models and Music Analysis', 2.

dominant-seventh chord indexing a subsequent tonic, a melodic gap prescribing a complementary fill, an opening ritornello indexing solo playing, or an antecedent phrase pointing ahead to a complementary consequent. These meanings apparently involve recourse to nothing but internal (or 'purely') musical knowledge.

The extrinsic–intrinsic dichotomy is ultimately false, however, for so-called intrinsic meanings, too, are mediated by various external factors. A dominant-seventh chord indexes a tonic only by the force of a certain conventional practice. (In other contexts, it may index a submediant chord or a completely different tonic by being read as an enharmonic German-sixth chord.) And even if conventional practice rests on certain 'natural' associations (as claimed by some theorists, among them Rameau and Schenker), such universal determinants can function only to the extent that they are mediated by culturally specific factors. A listing of rough equivalents for the extrinsic–intrinsic opposition will make clear the nature of the distinction that several writers have sought to articulate: semantic–syntactic; subjective–objective; extra-musical–musical; extroversive semiosis–introversive semiosis,[18] extra-generic–congeneric,[19] exosemantic–endosemantic,[20] and hermeneutics–analysis. What needs to be acknowledged is not what Dahlhaus called 'the merely intermittent nature of the semantic element in music'[21]—although such acknowledgement would surely go a long way towards correcting the impression that the extrinsic–intrinsic polarity is symmetrical and comparably distributed in the literature—but the inevitable falsity of the proposition.[22]

10. *While the essence of music is play, play forms only a special part of language use.* By denying music an essential semantic component and by stressing its untranslatability—indeed, its autonomy—one is forced to conclude (somewhat tautologically) that music means nothing but itself. This, of course, has been the dominant paradigm in European aesthetics since the mid-nineteenth century, and there is no reason to think that it is about to be superseded.[23] To speak of musical essences, however, is to go against the grain of our current anti-essentialist mood.

11. *Whereas language interprets itself, music cannot interpret itself. Language is the interpreting system of music.*[24] If musical units have no lexical meaning, if the semantic element in music is 'merely intermittent' as Dahlhaus put it, if one cannot 'propositionalize' in music,[25] and if music is ultimately untranslatable,

---

[18] Roman Jakobson, 'Closing Statement: Linguistics and Poetics', in Innis (ed.), *Semiotics: An Introductory Reader*, 147–75.

[19] Wilson Coker, *Music and Meaning: A Theoretical Introduction to Musical Aesthetics* (New York, 1972), 60–88 and 144–70.

[20] William Bright, 'Language and Music: Areas for Cooperation', *Ethnomusicology*, 7 (1963), 28–9.

[21] Carl Dahlhaus, 'Fragments of a Musical Hermeneutics', *Current Musicology*, 50 (1992), 11.

[22] A concise discussion of the extrinsic–intrinsic polarity may be found in Jean-Jacques Nattiez, *Music and Discourse: Toward a Semiology of Music*, trans. Carolyn Abbate (Princeton, 1990), 111–29.

[23] For evidence of this bias, see Bojan Bujic, *Music in European Thought 1851–1912* (Cambridge, 1988).

[24] Benveniste, 'Semiology of Language', 235.  [25] Henrotte, 'Music as Language', 168.

then it is obvious that music cannot interpret itself. Even in the most musical of metalanguages, such as Schenker's graphic notation, there is no escaping the intervention, at a very basic level, of concepts and therefore of language.[26] It is possible to translate a Schenker graph into prose—cumbersome though that might be—whereas it is never possible to translate the 'Eroica' into words. This is not to deny that one piece of music can comment on another (as in genres that use the variation principle or the variation form), or that one section of a work can refer to, and indeed amplify, ideas exposed elsewhere. But these processes can be perceived as such only through the mediation of a metalanguage.

To the question, is music a language?, then, we might answer that while music can be shown to exhibit features describable as linguistic (features of syntax, semantics, and semiotics), it is finally not language, since no linguistic act can substitute for the musical act. Nor is music a system of communication in the ordinary sense, although it can be used to communicate. The question then arises, What is the use of the music-as-language metaphor? I would say that the metaphor is useful to the extent that it forces its users to confront its limitations. Language and music are ineluctably intertwined, of course; what the linguistic analogy does is to provide a more secure basis for framing certain kinds of musical knowledge as semiotic.

## What is a Musical Sign?

One of the most fertile ideas implied by Peirce's definition of the sign as 'something which stands to somebody for something in some respect or capacity'[27] is that of the *interpretant*, 'a sign that in some way translates, explains, or develops a previous sign, and so on, in a process of infinite or unlimited semiosis'.[28] Nattiez bases his theory of semiology on 'the Peircian notion of the infinite and dynamic interpretant'.[29] The interpretant allows us to explain the impulse of meaning formation in any symbolic system. Because of its inherent dynamism, the interpretant further facilitates a proper acknowledgement of plural meanings. But without disputing the validity of the notion that an infinite chain of interpretants is released in every situation in which we try to make sense of a sign or group of signs, we might also acknowledge the advantages of a pragmatic setting of limits for the purposes of analysis; the plain fact is that some meanings are more important than others. To overemphasize the dynamism of interpretant formation is to risk missing the forest for the trees; it is to risk overlooking the

---

[26] On the metalinguistic nature of Schenkerian graphs, see my 'Schenkerian Notation in Theory and Practice', *Music Analysis*, 8 (1989), 275–301.

[27] *Collected Papers of Charles Sanders Peirce*, ii. para. 228.

[28] Sebeok (ed.), *Encyclopedic Dictionary of Semiotics*, i. 387.

[29] Nattiez, *Music and Discourse*, 8.

central fact that both composer- and work-immanent prescriptions ultimately determine the work's strongest meanings.

Let us, then, return to the beginning, so to speak, and consider the nature of the musical sign. In earlier work, both Ruwet and Nattiez expressed considerable scepticism about the value of sign typologies. Ruwet failed to 'see what one gains by considering music as a system of signs',[30] while Nattiez maintained in 1977 that 'a semiotic approach to music made from the standpoint of sign typotogies . . . seems ill-fated from the start'.[31] Since then, a number of studies by, among others, Tarasti, Noske, and Grabocz, have made sensible use of sign typologies.[32] Ruwet's and Nattiez's scepticism is nevertheless valuable in so far as it discourages a facile invocation of 'signs' and associated meanings at too early a stage in the semiological enterprise.

In their most extensive analytical demonstrations of semiotic method, Ruwet and Nattiez employ the notion of musical units rather than musical signs, thus neutralizing the notion of sign and domesticating it for an art that many believe to be foundationally asemantic.[33] Talk of musical units, which allows semiotics to collapse into classical structuralism, is valid and helpful; but it has the disadvantage of derailing the enterprise of searching for musical meanings that arise from specific histories and societies. In what follows, I shall exemplify some aspects of semiotic method, noting the assumptions that support their moves and arguing that units, defined as elementary oppositional elements in a closed structure, subtend 'semantic' meanings whether or not such meanings are made explicit. Sign typologies in fact constrain every semiotic analysis. Differences arise between analysts who acknowledge them explicitly and those for whom they remain implicit in the act of narrating an analysis.

In order to achieve maximum clarity in presenting some basic issues of sign definition in music, I have chosen a highly limited, perhaps somewhat banal text: the melody line of the first six bars of 'God Save the King' (Ex. 6.1a). We will assume for present purposes that this is the work in its entirety. The analyst's job is to make sense of the work's elements and procedures. As will become clear, every single observation I make will be seen to be propped up by an implicit typology or set of typologies.[34]

The work is in F major, in simple triple metre, and is six bars long. Are these features signs? It could be argued that they are. The key of F major dates back at least to the seventeenth century, so that for the analyst who wishes to

---

[30] Quoted in Jean-Jacques Nattiez, 'The Contribution of Musical Semiotics to the Semiotic Discussion in General', in Thomas A. Sebeok (ed.), *A Perfusion of Signs* (Bloomington, Ind., 1977), 123.

[31] Ibid.

[32] See the discussion of these writers' work in Monelle, *Linguistics and Semiotics in Music*.

[33] Nicolas Ruwet, 'Methods of Analysis in Musicology', *Music Analysis*, 6 (1987), 11–36, and Jean-Jacques Nattiez, 'Varèse's "Density 21.5": A Study in Semiological Analysis', *Music Analysis*, 1 (1982), 243–340.

[34] For another semiotic analysis of 'God Save the King', see Jonathan Dunsby and Arnold Whittall, *Music Analysis in Theory and Practice* (London, 1988), 223–5. A Schenkerian graph may be found in David Neumeyer and Susan Tepping, *A Guide to Schenkerian Analysis* (Englewood Cliffs, NJ, 1992), 65.

Ex. 6.1a. *The tune of 'God Save the King', bars 1–6.*

Ex. 6.1b. *Paradigmatic structure of 'God Save the King' based on melodic contour.*

Ex. 6.1c. *Paradigmatic structure of 'God Save the King' based on rhythmic patterns.*

acknowledge part of the historical and cultural baggage of the key signature, there is plenty to invoke in connection with this anonymous but widely distributed work whose earliest known source dates from 1744.[35] Triple meter similarly carries considerable intertextual weight, some of which stems from its dance potential. And the six-bar length suggests a departure from a putative four-bar norm. Some may dispute the value of such a restricted norm despite its firm, normative compositional use from the mid-eighteenth century onwards. If one chooses to hear it in two-bar phrases, one still needs to confront the fact that

---

[35] Malcolm Boyd, 'National Anthems', in Stanley Sadie (ed.), *The New Grove Dictionary of Music and Musicians* (London, 1980), xiii. 56.

there is an odd rather than an even number of two-bar units. Even at this very elementary stage of reading the key signature, metre, and phrase length, one can say that the work signifies, and that each sign conforms to Peirce's notion of 'something which stands to somebody for something in some respect or capacity'.

Although it could be argued that, with the possible exception of the observation about phrase structure, none of the foregoing remarks deals in any significant way with the work's content, the fact that a number of interpretants have been activated already shows that we have broached a dimension of musical meaning, and not just an intrinsic one. Many analysts, however, would consider the real task of making sense of the work as beginning with the determination of its significant units. What are these units, and by what means are they associated in the work?

Exx. 6.1*b* and 6.1*c* rewrite the content of the work to reveal its ordering of patterns. In Ex. 6.1*b* melodic contour determines pattern perception. The six bars of the work form a paradigmatic pattern as summarized in the integer chart to the right of the example. Implicit in this chart—and this is true of all others— is a narrative, which may be made explicit as follows. Unit 1 is followed by a contrasting unit 2. Unit 3 is a transposed version of unit 1 (suppressing for now the change in intervallic content as a result of the transposition). Unit 4 is new, although it retains the rhythm of unit 2, and unit 5 is a transposition of unit 4, with a modification of its rhythm. Unit 6, too, is new, providing further contrast. From the point of view of melodic contour, then, four of the work's six units group in pairs (1, 3 and 4, 5) while the other two, 2 and 6, stand independently.

The observation that unit 2 is 'new', although true from the point of view of melodic contour, may strike some as counter-intuitive: units 2 and 4 share the same rhythm, and their contours are inversely related. If we hear unit 2 as a 'question', unit 4 provides an 'answer'. Ex. 6.1*c* acknowledges the parallels between units 2 and 4 by rearranging the contents of the work on the basis of rhythmic identity. According to this second paradigm, units 1 and 2 expose two successively different rhythmic ideas. Units 3 and 4 repeat the succession exactly. Unit 5 returns to the pattern of units 1 and 3, perhaps even promising to repeat 2 as 6. The most dramatic change takes place in unit 6, where, on the one hand, the expectations set up by the rhythmic patterning are denied, and on the other, an expectation of a change that would bring about a satisfying close is fulfilled. The integer chart shows a reduction in the number of columns from four in Ex. 6.1*b* to three in Ex. 6.1*c*.

We have now developed two competing narratives of the work, one based on melodic contour, the other on rhythmic pattern. Is it possible to synthesize the two sets of results into a larger meaning? We can start by observing that the 1, 2, 3 sequence of units is the same in both narratives. Divergence comes with unit 4, which is interpreted as different from, as well as similar to, unit 2 in Exx. 6.1*b* and *c* respectively. Have melody and rhythm gone their separate ways here, perhaps? If we assume that the disruption of a previously stable pattern is necessary for musical coherence (and therefore meaning), then we could argue that, from a third perspective, the congruence between melodic contour and rhythm is challenged in unit 4. What about unit 5? Here, too, the story told by Ex. 6.1*b* is that the 'new' unit 4 is repeated as unit 5, whereas in Ex. 6.1*c*, unit 5 was understood as the third statement of unit 1. The common point in the two readings is that unit 5 is not new, while the divergence stems from the nature of unit 5's reference. Of course, decisions made about earlier units affect the interpretation of unit 5, for once we have constructed our columns according to an explicit rule, subsequent events fall into place. A great deal, then, depends on the sensitivity of those initial rules, which are presumably formulated not only after some acquaintance with the details of the particular work but with reference to a tradition of parsing. If the method here seems circular, it is also well-nigh unavoidable in analysis.

Exx. 6.1*b* and *c* are further united in reading unit 6 as unique. Here it is easy to pile on a series of *ad hoc* justifications for its uniqueness: coming after a pattern of variations, this last bar of the work articulates the longest-lasting note, thus denoting an appropriate point of rest. Ex. 6.1*b* suggests a connection between units 2 and 6 on account of their uniqueness as paradigms; but here too, and from another point of view, unit 6 would seem incomparable to unit 2 since it lacks a contour. The point is obviously that our perception of a connection or lack of connection between units 2 and 6 will depend on the kind of plot that guides our analysis.

To the demonstration in Exx. 6.1*b* and *c* we may add a third, taxonomic-empirical one in which pitch identity and the corresponding frequency of attack points determine our vertical columns. This third narrative is shown in Ex. 6.1*d*, and is summarized in number form to the right of the example (numbers here refer to successive notes in the work). The narrative suggests a weighting towards the pitch $f^1$, which has six attack points, two more than the next prominent pitch, $g^1$, three more than the next prominent, $a^1$, and five more than the pitch b♭, which occurs only once throughout the entire work. Comparisons with previous taxonomies (Exx. 6.1*b* and *c*) are not especially productive, since the method of determining units is different; but we might observe one salient similarity: two of the three analyses (Exx. 6.1*c* and *d*) show that the work is beginning-oriented. Just as the opening bar of Ex. 6.1*c* returns twice more before the end of the melody, so the first note of Ex. 6.1*d* returns twice more before taking off. The absence of $f^1$ from the succession of units 7–11 in Ex. 6.1*d* is the longest such absence throughout the work. We may interpret this to mean that after $f^1$ has been established as the point of departure (units 1–5), tension is created by its absence (units 6–11), which tension is resolved at the close (units 12–16). The work thus plays out a familiar, perhaps invariant, gesture of large-scale tonal structure. Note also that the uniqueness attributed to the final $f^1$ in Exx. 6.1*b* and *c* is erased in Ex. 6.1*d*, where the final $f^1$ represents the sixth and

Ex. 6.1*d*. *Paradigmatic structure of 'God Save the King' based on pitch identity.*

final appearance of that pitch. The assumption that an f$^1$ is an f$^1$ irrespective of where it occurs, how long it lasts, and how it is approached, will seem deeply problematic to many musicians, some of whom may wish to reject Ex. 6.1*d* out of hand for failing to provide a finer discrimination among f$^1$s in its construction of paradigms.

One principal difference between Exx. 6.1*b* and *c*, on the one hand, and Ex. 6.1*d*, on the other, is that whereas the former define their units with reference to patterns—that is to say, relationally—Ex. 6.1*d* uses absolute pitch identity as its exclusive criterion. Yet one of the most basic features of tonal structure

Ex. 6.1e. *Voice-leading graph of 'God Save the King'.*

is its supreme relationality. Many would contest the meaningfulness of units or signs whose contrapuntal dependencies are suppressed in the determination of columns, and it is for this reason that some would reject Ex. 6.1*d* as being simply unmusical. The view that an explicit, rule-governed approach to segmenting tonal music is likely to produce counter-intuitive ('unmusical') insights is not to be dismissed lightly. To restore musicality to its proper, determining role, taxonomic empiricists must come to terms with traditional music theory, which lays great store by the *ad hoc* prescriptions of musical performance. Analyses convince because they are good performances, not because they are intellectually rigorous. The semiotic challenge is in part to strike a balance between these two, somewhat contradictory impulses.

In discussing Exx. 6.1*b*, *c*, and *d*, we have referred unproblematically to units of structure, units that may be described as signs, and that may be said to refer both internally (that is, to signs elsewhere in the work) and externally (that is, to similar configurations outside the work). But the limitations of Ex. 6.1*d* in particular would seem to suggest that a more musical approach to segmentation would be one that recognized an ongoing, continuous structure whose units are irreducibly relational. Ex. 6.1*e* offers such an interpretation of the work. It is a Schenkerian voice-leading graph based on the a priori view of the work as a single, unfolding structure whose elements compose a simple, deep, diatonic 'song'. Seen this way, none of the notes in the work could stand alone, since each forms part of a context of structural levels. According to this reading, the principal contrapuntal motion is the white-note $\hat{3}$–$\hat{2}$–$\hat{1}$ progression, led up to by means of an ascending progression ($\hat{1}$–$\hat{2}$–$\hat{3}$) and prolonged by means of a preliminary $\hat{3}$–$\hat{2}$–$\hat{1}$ descent to the tonic in bar 4. Further prolongation on more local levels involves operations familiar from species counterpoint: the incomplete neighbour-note prologation of the notes f¹ and a¹ in bars 1 and 3 respectively and the passing motions coupled with unfoldings in bars 2 and 5. To repeat: no note stands as an isolated entity. Any and all groupings of notes are irreducibly connected. Connections are not necessarily contiguous; nor do they exist on the same structural level.

The 'entangled' view of units offered by a Schenkerian reading has the virtue of stressing continuities over discontinuities and of conveying a sense of the life of tones (the organicist metaphor can hardly be resisted). Because this particular graph presents a multi-levelled structure in a single, comprehensive representation (levels are distinguished notationally), it finds little obvious, useful support from the taxonomies presented in Exx. 6.1*b*, *c*, and *d*. In particular, it resists a simplistic reading of salience, since salience here is construed as part of a contrapuntal web of relations. For example, while the note b♭¹ in bar 3 forms the highest pitch in the work (it is the only note that occurs only once in the course of the entire work), it appears as a 'mere' upper neighbour-note in Ex. 6.1*e*. The apparent non-congruence between structural salience152 and what might be called phenomenal salience (as suggested, for example, by durational patterns or frequency of occurrence) is crucial in evaluating the work's semiotic.

I have dwelt on the taxonomic-empirical mode of analysis partly because it is probably the most familiar and explicit method associated with semiology. Although the method itself, especially its mode of graphic presentation, was not new with semiologists—chant scholars had been using something like it before the semiologists came along[36]—it has received a more rigorous demonstration at their hands. By basing its procedures on repetition, it draws on a foundational element of music. Paradigmatic analysis is concrete, precise, and representationally explicit. It also inevitably harbours a narrative or collection of narratives, and these, I have argued, ought not to be suppressed when the method is used.

The question, though, is whether semiotic method explains things better than traditional analysis. What difference might there be between Ex. 6.1*b* and an old-fashioned motivic analysis of 'God Save the King'? The plain answer is, Very little. Semiological analysis dresses up a mode of motivic association in language and a presentational scheme that seem stricter and therefore more scientifically reliable. If one opts for this refinement in metalanguage, then one would of course prefer the semiological method. If one prefers to stress the continuities between the methods of Réti, Alan Walker, and David Epstein and those of semiologists, then one would dispute any claims that the semiotic method is new or that it has a greater explanatory scope. Ruwet imagined the semiological paradigm as a verification procedure, a way of thinking through the analysis, not a way of generating fresh insights. Semiotics is also a discovery procedure, however, for it enables the discovery of significant dimensions of opposition and variance. This may partly explain why, in Nattiez's most recent mapping of the field of semiology, there is a broadening of perspectives, an embrace of questions of criticism, meaning, and hermeneutics.[37] It has become increasingly obvious that only political or institutional interests, rather than epistemological concerns, would lead one to continue to uphold the autonomy of a field of musical semiotics.

---

[36] Powers makes this point in 'Language Models and Music Analysis', 33.

[37] See e.g. Nattiez, *Music and Discourse*.

Nattiez is not the only one among leading semioticians to advocate a reconfiguration of the field of semiotics. As mentioned earlier, Raymond Monelle, in his recent handbook, constructs an even more heterogeneous terrain than does Nattiez. And David Lidov has, since his earliest writings on semiotics, emphasized the importance of coming to terms with traditional music theory, a move that results unavoidably in a broadening of perspectives. Lidov's own analyses resemble those of music theorists, so it is not surprising to find him identifying a potential of semiotics as an opportunity to 'reintroduce questions concerning the status of music as a species of sign' into the general musicological (including music-theoretical) discussion.[38] The challenge of semiotics is inextricably linked with the challenge of music analysis. By clarifying the ways in which we know musical facts, semiotics plays a much needed role in promoting greater self-awareness among analysts. But as long as semiotics remains a framing device with strong metalinguistic pretensions, rather than a framework for generating good musical insights, it will remain an adjunct field.

## Three Areas of Semiotic Research

The foregoing discussion of semiotics has focused on its classical structuralist paradigm. Although it might be argued that all analyses are inevitably propped up by structuralist concerns, there is nevertheless a difference between the pitch-based analytical approaches discussed in the previous section ('hard' semiotics) and some broader perspectives stemming from a more anthropological view of the musical work ('soft' semiotics). This section outlines three areas of musical research which can be strengthened by semiotics. These are music and the emotions, topoi, and song.

First, music and the emotions. As far back as any of us can remember, music has been associated with the emotions. Yet, partly as a result of a powerful vogue for musical autonomy in the aesthetic writings of the last century, and extending to our own day, the subject of music's emotional content has not been a favourite topic of research. Even the great strides in psychoanalytical research made in our century have not resulted in a paradigm shift in our music-analytical behaviour. Yet we need only reread a book like Deryck Cooke's *The Language of Music* to realize that the emotions cannot be properly excluded from any discussion of musical meaning, whether structural or expressive.[39]

---

[38] Lidov, 'Music', 577.

[39] Nor has this fact escaped semioticians such as David Lidov and Manfred Clynes, who have written about the emotions in music. See Clynes, *Sentics, the Touch of Emotions* (New York, 1977) and Lidov, 'Mind and Body in Music', *Semiotica*, 66 (1977), 69–97. For a philosophical treatment, see Malcolm Budd, *Music and the Emotions: The Philosophical Theories* (London, 1985).

Cooke's claim, still unchallenged in its essential aspects, is that some composers and listeners invest certain intervals and (mainly diatonic) scale patterns with certain emotions: major thirds and sixths express pleasure, minor thirds grief, minor sixths pain, and so on. The conjoining of individual intervals produces a basic 'musical vocabulary' that is also invested with meanings. Thus, the ascending 1–(2)–3–(4)–5 in major may express 'an outgoing, active, assertive emotion of joy', the pattern 1–(2)–3–(2)–1 in minor may express 'brooding, an obsession with gloomy feelings, a trapped fear, or a sense of inescapable doom, especially when it is repeated over and over', and the (5)–6–5 in minor, 'the most widely used of all terms of musical language', carries a sense of anguish.[40]

Cooke's 'vocabulary of musical language' is much more extensive than is indicated here, and it is supported by copious quotations from pre-tonal, tonal, and post-tonal works. It forms a closed lexicon in which we can look up the 'meanings' of various inaugural motives. As with any good dictionary, the meanings it gives are not fixed but flexible. And since we are, after all, dealing with an impossible translation from the world of notes to the world of feeling, we need to acknowledge a certain imprecision or suggestiveness in the transfers reported by Cooke. A given term is defined not literally, by what it means, but by the network of connotations, denotations, or associations that it invokes. To speak of a network of feelings is to recognize the existence of secondary emotions. This point is lost on those who criticize Cooke's theory for naïvely specifying the emotions contained in particular works. What Cooke presents instead are the conditions of possibility for a reading of emotions. And it is sometimes the case that a vocabulary item may occur without the secondary and tertiary factors that need to support it.

But although Cooke specifies musical signs, or musical units, he only indirectly hints at how they might succeed each other. In other words, missing from his theory is the second, indispensable stage of an authentic structuralist analysis: namely, a determination of the rules by which units follow each other. A loose syntax is present by default in Cooke's analysis of Mozart's G minor Symphony, but it is clear that a separate syntax of emotions in a tonal work is not viable; emotions are given through tones, and it is the syntax of tones that determines the syntax of emotions. A second limitation of Cooke's project is that, as Monelle remarked, Cooke 'situat[es] his "terms" on the side of nature rather than culture'.[41] This is one reason why Monelle does not admit Cooke's theory into the canon of semiotic studies.

One might ask in what sense the nature–culture dichotomy was strongly present and available to Cooke. I suspect that although, like many other theorists since Rameau, Cooke builds his theory of tonal music on the 'natural' overtone series, his occasional references to non-Western cultures are enough

---

[40] Cooke, *Language of Music*, 115, 141, 146.
[41] Monelle, *Linguistics and Semiotics in Music*, 13.

to suggest that had he been presented with the nature–nurture dichotomy, he might well have opted for nurture. After all, what he is anxious to point out are certain 'habitual propensities' on the part of composers, 'propensities to group certain tonal tensions together in certain ways'.[42] To allow the dominant culture to stand for all cultures, and to imply that what the dominant culture does is 'natural', is an error unlikely to occur—or, at least, in the same totalizing form—in our increasingly pluralistic, relativistic world. A sympathetic reading of Cooke's intellectual prejudices would allow us to rescue his theory for semiotics.

In what sense, then, does Cooke's theory constitute a semiotic theory? If, as Saussure said, semiotics deals with 'the life of signs within society', then Cooke's theory, concerned as it is with European music since the fourteenth century but making frequent references to non-European traditions, fits the prescription. In view of this, it is regrettable that few analysts (as opposed to aestheticians) have sought to build on Cooke's insight, to make his system more rigorous, and to frame its claims in such a way that they are less assailable. It is perhaps not an exaggeration to say that, although nearly four decades old, *The Language of Music* has yet to receive the full, considered critique that it deserves.

A second, related area of research to which semiotics may apply is topos research. No one doubts any more the fact that composers frequently deploy conventionally recognizable patterns, styles, or musical types in an effort to reach their audiences. Some recent writing on both operatic and instrumental repertoires of the Classical period, for example, has drawn on notions of topoi or commonplaces, to enrich our understanding of musical discourse.[43] Like Cooke's vocabulary of emotions, topoi are signs that operate within a closed corpus and in a specifically delimited cultural and musical context. The musical configurations that represent topoi may be defined either in Saussurean terms, as signifiers pointing to a complex of signifieds, or in Peircean terms, as sign situations in which a specific ground allows the objects so isolated to set off an infinite chain of interpretants.

Harder to negotiate, though not perhaps as hard as Cooke's vocabulary of emotions, is the question of a syntax of topoi. It seems clear that in Classical instrumental music, for example, certain topoi occur characteristically at beginnings of pieces, while others are used in closing situations. Since beginnings, middles, and endings are defined in terms of conventional harmonic, melodic, and rhythmic activity, the role of topoi needs to be understood in reference to these more primary dimensions. To recognize this normative congruence—to

---

[42] Cooke, *Language of Music*, 172, 174.

[43] The foundational work is Leonard G. Ratner, *Classic Music: Expression, Form, and Style* (New York, 1980). On operatic music, see Wye Jamison Allanbrook, *Rhythmic Gesture in Mozart: Le Nozze di Figaro and Don Giovanni* (Chicago, 1983). On instrumental music, see my *Playing with Signs: A Semiotic Interpretation of Classic Music* (Princeton, 1991), and Robert Hatten, *Musical Meaning in Beethoven: Markedness, Correlation, and Interpretation* (Bloomington, Ind., 1994).

say, in short, that topoi give a profile to more fundamental structural processes—is in part to recognize the possibility of playing with them, of dislocating a beginning topos from its harmonic attachment, for example. This is only one instance of the sort of play that lies at the heart of music of the Classical period.

One could also read the joint roles of topoi and harmonic/melodic/rhythmic activity in terms of conventional signs. Topoi would then seem to conform to the most famous of Peirce's trichotomies, the icon–index–symbol, with the further possibility of various weighted hybrid structures, including iconic symbols, symbolic icons, indexical icons, iconic indexes, and so on. Semiotics allows us to formulate more precisely the ways in which signs come to have meaning for Classical composers and their listeners. Although this kind of research depends on old-fashioned style analysis, it can be strengthened by semiotics.

A third and final area in which the searchlight of semiotics might prove illuminating is in genres that involve words and music. Consider, for example, the chorus 'All we like sheep have gone astray' from Handel's *Messiah*, based on the following text:

> All we like sheep have gone astray.
> We have turned everyone to his own way.
> And the Lord hath laid on Him the iniquity of us all.

The conjunction of two independent sign systems, music and words, creates a third, song. This account of the compositional process suggests that the resulting alloy should be understood in a multiplicity of ways: how the resulting compound structure signifies and how its two inputs signify, both singly and in conjunction. A semiotics of song prescribes neither a text-to-music nor a music-to-text approach; its sole requirement is that the enabling conditions of each approach be made explicit.

If we follow a text-to-music approach, we may begin by reading the above lines with a view to what Handel is likely to set, and in what way. The grouping of the lines as 2 + 1 in accordance with the rhyme scheme, the first two describing our fallen condition, the last telling where salvation is likely to come from as a result of one person's sacrifice on behalf of the rest of us: this semantic progression finds a direct correlative in Handel's F major to F minor progression. The major–minor succession argues an overall 'depression' in effect, a complicating of positive affects, a dip into less stable—indeed, troubled—emotions. This is, of course, a conventional progression, with a network of associations, which Handel's listeners are invited to interpret. The progression from a positive, bright, happy world to a darker, more grievous, more painful one describes affective states, as Cooke might say, out of which a listener will select but one or two meanings for contemplation. The text-to-music approach, based on familiarity with Handel's routines in the oratorios, will also highlight words with pictorial representational possibilities. The fact of sheep going astray, for example, or of everyone turning 'to his own way', are immediately suggestive of iconic portrayal. Not surprisingly, Handel exploits a number of these opportunities: he chooses the pastoral key of F major to house this chorus, the word 'astray' is set in its initial appearance (which also becomes the paradigm for later appearances) as an extended melisma of some twelve notes, and the motif on 'turned' performs a literal turning motion. At each point in a text-to-music analysis, the semiotician asks the important 'how' question, and is always armed with a series of terms and concepts to help frame answers to that question in the most precise possible way.

A music-to-text approach, on the other hand, begins by recognizing some of the basic structural constraints that Handel would have had to consider in composing one of several choruses within an oratorio. How, for example, would the musical sense of the chorus be sustained? Handel chose a modulatory scheme of a $I-V-IV-(V)-i$ progression, a progression that may or may not be available for interpretation beyond its status as a conventional construct. Such 'natural', or necessary, constraints become objects of semiotic decoding only when they assume a particular, characterizing form within the work. Often, it is those spaces marked by contradictions between the necessary and the contingent that become sites of rich meaning. The idea of sheep going astray, for example, must be enacted within a stylized musical form.

A semiotic approach allows us to specify ways in which words and music 'enhance, contradict, or remain indifferent to each other'.[44] For it is obvious, as already mentioned, that in order to meet the requirements of an extended tonal structure, complete with long-range linear connections and approaches to closure on immediate, intermediate, and remote structural levels, Handel's music must make sense when abstracted from these particular words. For example, the melismas on the word 'astray' and the distinctions among voices conveyed by the phrase 'everyone to his own way', must eventually yield to a cadence. And when Handel brings the voices together in homophonic texture to cadence on 'to his own way' (Ex. 6.2), the effect is faintly comical because of the blatant contradiction between words and music. Against the effect of the text's open message, Handel must intervene in order to effect a simple cadence without which intelligibility of structure cannot be guaranteed. But this apparent contradiction, far from denoting an unusual (or unsuccessful) setting of words, in fact points to the basic condition of song, which, as Lawrence Kramer interprets it, is dissociative and agonic.[45] It is this ongoing tension between words and music, signalled further by the congruences and non-congruences in such dimensions as word accent (the setting of the preposition 'of' three bars from the end is particularly telling) and melodic contour, that determines the basic condition of song. Semiotics allows us to define sharply the conditions of possibility for the construction of meaning. It does not perform a critical or evaluative func-

[44] Kofi Agawu, 'Theory and Practice in the Analysis of the Nineteenth-Century *Lied*', *Music Analysis*, 11 (1992), 30.

[45] Lawrence Kramer, *Music and Poetry: The Nineteenth Century and After* (Berkeley, 1984), 129.

Ex. 6.2. *Handel, Messiah, 'All We Like Sheep', bars 46–8.*

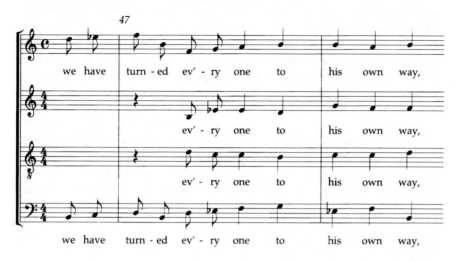

tion, except in a very restricted sense; nor does it specify procedures for the discovery of insightful or musical ways of listening. It serves, in short, as a handmaid.

We could go on and list other areas of analytical research for which semiotics might serve as a valuable thinking-through tool, but this would not significantly enhance the point that semiotics plays an adjunct, metalinguistic role in music analysis. Let me conclude by briefly recalling the arguments made earlier. I began by enacting what is fast becoming a ritual in music-semiotic studies: namely, acknowledging the extraordinary breadth of the field of semiotics. I then proposed ways in which the properties of natural language, a privileged domain in Saussurean and Peircean semiotics, both resemble and differ from those of music. And I discussed the challenge of semiotics in reference first to the taxonomic-empirical method of Ruwet and Nattiez and then to 'softer' areas of semiotic research such as music and the emotions, topoi, and song. Two main conclusions may be drawn from this discussion.

First, the fact that we deal in signs in all our activities as human beings suggests the indispensability of semiotics to our understanding of the world. To be human is to do semiotics. The transition from general semiotics to musical semiotics has not been successfully negotiated, however, because of the special nature of musical art. We may regret the fact that earlier phases of music-semiotic research bypassed the important proto-semiotic aspects of traditional theory, but we cannot escape the non-uniqueness of semiotic method. Even a cursory examination of the analytical demonstrations of semioticians reveals their similarity to familiar brands of music analysis; for example, as I suggested, the pursuit of melodic similarities by Ruwet and Nattiez as a form of paradigmatic analysis is nothing if not a brand of thematic or motivic analysis. Furthermore, for those music theorists who see Schenker's 'motivic parallelisms' as a significant advance over the practices of Réti, Walker, and Keller, the method of the semioticians may well seem crude and old-fashioned. If, therefore, traditional music theory has more powerful ways of explaining tonal phenomena, there can be no justification for a separate, autonomous field of musical semiotics except as a declaration of interest in the political ordering of fields of knowledge.

The second conclusion is that, although the discussion has been confined to a handful of semiotic practices, the wider purview of music semiotics suggests that it may be instrumental in actively promoting interdisciplinarity and pluralism. Again, the imbrication of music's metalanguages in linguistic systems suggests that analytical practice has in one sense been interdisciplinary all along. To say that is also to acknowledge 'traditional analysis' as latently semiotic. If what is desired is a more visible, perhaps more deliberate juxtaposition of such fields as anthropology, literary criticism, art history, or philosophy with musicology, rather than an ongoing adaptation of a few powerful, 'translatable' concepts to music analysis, then interdisciplinarity might prove at best harmless, at worst a retreat from those rich, ultimately untranslatable concepts that play a central role in sophisticated technical analyses of music. As for pluralism, its strength will come from bringing theories into confrontation so that we can compare their explanatory potential. And the pluralistic enterprise could do worse than allow semiotics to play a key role; for semiotics facilitates such comparison by providing a rigorous mechanism for laying bare the enabling structures of any music theory.

# 7

## An Experimental Music Theory?

### Robert Gjerdingen

Aristotle knew his logic. He could ring the changes on premisses major and minor, true and false, universal and particular. Yet he still wrote the following:

In man, the size of the trunk is proportionate to the lower portions, and as a man grows up it becomes much smaller in proportion. In infancy the reverse is found. . . . In other words, all children are dwarfs. . . . The whole groups of birds and fishes are dwarf-like. . . . This is why all animals are less intelligent than man. . . . And the reason, as aforesaid, is that in very many of them the principle of the soul is sluggish and corporeal. And if the heat which raises the organism up wanes still further while the earthy matter waxes, then the animals' bodies wane, and they will be many-footed; and finally they lose their feet altogether and lie full length on the ground. Proceeding a little further in this way, they actually have their principal part down below, and finally the part which answers to a head comes to have neither motion nor sensation; at this stage the creature becomes a plant.[1]

This fine bit of nonsense took root in fertile commonplaces. Any Attic fool knew that there were four elements in the cosmos and four associated humours in all living things. Slight variations in the balance of these humours affected an organism's moods, while gross variations affected its very nature. Aristotle's experience of the world, filtered through these four-square verities, reinforced the apparent rightness of the theory. Feedback between theory and observation assimilated anomaly. Data that ought to have invalidated the theory became reinterpreted as its triumph. Even the most recalcitrant facts only forced a grudging accommodation that, like Ptolemaic epicycles, complexified but did not challenge the received dogma. Aristotle's mastery of logic was no defence against untested or untestable premisses.

The theory of four elements and humours, though surely 'sluggish and corporeal', nevertheless had legs. Much late medieval art testifies that children remained conceptualized as dwarfs for a long, long time. Depictions of children gained verisimilitude only when the new men of the Renaissance, men like Dürer in the north and da Vinci in the south, forced themselves to separate knowing from seeing by introducing objective measurement. When Dürer gazed at a

---

[1] Aristotle, *De partibus animalium*, 686b6–34.

subject through a grid of wire or string, his act of measurement corrected the distortions introduced by the knowledge-driven, highly interpreted perception that characterizes so many of the transactions between the human mind and its environment. Measurement changed seeing, and led to a new knowing.

Today, whenever I attend a meeting of music theorists, I am struck by the conviction with which old beliefs are invoked as eternal verities. 'Tonality', like Aristotle's 'principle of the soul', is asserted as an agent in the world. 'Voice-leading', like Aristotle's 'heat', is given causal force as an explanation of why musical things are the way they are. The waxing and waning of these principles seemingly create music history, govern style, and, 'proceeding a little further in this way', determine hearing itself. Recent attempts to 'problematize' these verities have resulted in complexified dogma. The basic terms of the debate, however, remain unchanged. As a result, music-theoretical discourse has become largely music-exegetical in content. The self-stabilizing, corroborating effect of interdependent premises precludes fundamental revisions, major discoveries, or even accidental breakthroughs.

From this state of affairs one might conclude that music theorists would have little interest in psychological experiments directed toward an objective understanding of music perception. Nothing could be further from the truth. Having presented the work of experimental psychologists to music theorists on many occasions, I can report that music theorists have a passionate interest in this work. The musical illusions, ambiguous musical figures, and artificially modified sounds that are used as stimuli in such experiments have their most fascinated—and perhaps most discerning—audience among music theorists. Why, then, does this considerable interest and fascination have little noticeable effect on the discipline?

It is not, I would argue, because musicians mistrust experimentalists or the notion of experiment as impartial arbiter of conflicting hypotheses. Musicians routinely conduct informal experiments when they evaluate alternative modes of performance. A concert-mistress may test several bowings, comparing each to a learned ideal of Romantic phrasing, or a studio guitarist may ask an arranger which of several voicings he prefers for an upcoming recording session. Even teachers of aural skills conduct batteries of informal experiments in music perception. In college and university classrooms each day, thousands of students give millions of responses to written, sung, played, or recorded musical stimuli.

Although music theory endorses experiment, and grants the presumption that experiments are skilfully performed and accurately reported, the interpretation of experimental results takes place in a no man's land between disciplines with very different histories, mores, central subject-matters, and professional goals. Take, for example, a hypothetical experiment in melodic perception. The psychologist who sets up the experiment may be seeking correlates in the auditory system for some well-studied phenomena in the visual system. The history of that prior research in vision will dictate the outlines of the proposed study in music, and experimental protocols will be employed based on their utility within, and comparability to, a larger body of research in, say, mental representations. For the psychologist, the core of the article reporting the eventual experiment will be the 'results' section, where statistical proofs are adduced to support or refute the relevant hypotheses. Music theorists, by contrast, will probably skip the recondite 'results' section and concentrate instead on the narrative 'discussion' section. There, where the psychologist is permitted licence to speculate, the music theorist will subject to intense scrutiny words often intended as mere musical tokens for general psychological phenomena. Moreover, should the melodic stimuli imply (to the theorist) certain harmonic progressions, the 'laws' of harmony will be brought to bear in criticizing the 'lack of reality' in the experiment. Because the psychologist sought to avoid musical material too tied to a particular place, time, social class, and system of belief, and because he or she failed to frame concepts within guild-sanctioned modes of discourse, music theorists are likely to dismiss the entire experiment as failing to address 'real music'. And they may go on to ask, Why don't psychologists study *real* musical issues? Why, for example, can't they measure how long a tonic can be prolonged?

The measurement of things musical is frequently problematic. For instance, if a music student sings doh–me–soh in response to a written doh–ray–me, how many mistakes should the teacher record? On the one hand, the teacher might have an atomistic view of music cognition and performance in which the student is theorized to have made three independent judgements of pitch (doh, ray, and me), two of which were performed in error. On the other hand, perhaps in the spirit of Deutsch and Feroe,[2] the teacher might have a structuralist view, according to which the student is theorized to have chosen the wrong alphabet ('triad' rather than 'diatonic scale'), three successive tones of which were none the less performed correctly. The number of errors 'observed' thus depends on the theory assumed. For this task, the 'scientific' measurement of error according to, say, cycles per second is no advance, because it engages only the epiphenomena of hidden mental processes.

Psychologists know the pitfalls associated with trying to measure a mental state or process. Their training in experimental method has sensitized them to how easily an attempt to measure $x$ may turn out to be a measurement of $y$, $z$, or some combination of still other factors. Just as musicians learn to respect examples of flawless part-writing, so experimental psychologists learn to value classic experiments that have met high standards of design, procedure, and statistical analysis. They know that such experiments are fiendishly difficult to conceive and both laborious and expensive to carry out. Psychologists, reviewing an

---

[2] D. Deutsch and J. Feroe, 'The Internal Representation of Pitch Sequences in Tonal Music', *Psychological Review*, 88 (1981), 503–22.

experiment proposed by a music theorist, will probably spot the methodological equivalent of parallel fifths, tritones, cross-relations, and odd doublings. They may go on to wonder, Why don't they do a *real* experiment?

To give some specificity to the interpretative rift between music theory and music psychology, let us examine an experiment on the perception of large-scale tonal closure by Nicholas Cook.[3] Cook selected six nineteenth-century compositions, and altered them so that each makes a tonal detour to end in a key other than the tonic. He played the altered and unaltered pieces pairwise to music students, and asked them to rate which of each pair they preferred in terms of four separate descriptors: pleasure, expressiveness, coherence, and sense of completion. The results of these ratings were interpreted to show that the perceptual influence of large-scale tonal closure is 'relatively weak and restricted to fairly short time spans'.[4]

Here music theorists may recognize one of their own, who directly tackled the question, How long can a tonic be prolonged? Real music was used to study a real musical issue. Old dogmas of tonal unity were held up to objective measurement, and apparently found wanting. Moreover, Cook appears to have demonstrated statistically that the effect of large-scale tonal closure is perceptually weak if perceptible at all, a conclusion I personally find persuasive. Psychologists, however, would argue that nothing of the kind was proved or disproved by the experiment. It suffered from problems both of conception and of execution. Let me treat conception first.

Proving the non-existence of a mental state or process is never easy. In evaluating an experiment, psychologists begin with a 'null hypothesis', and then disprove it statistically. That is, they take as a baseline assumption the absence of an effect, and then demonstrate that their data are in fact distributed in a way that is highly unlikely to occur if the null hypothesis is true. If the data instead show no strong reason to reject the null hypothesis, one does not then claim that the null hypothesis is true. In other words, one can only disprove the null hypothesis. Thus, in preference ratings for 'expressiveness', the absence of a significant effect of unaltered over altered versions of live piano performances tells us nothing specifically about the existence or non-existence of large-scale tonal closure. 'Pleasure' is equally uninformative. The apparent co-variance of 'coherence' and 'sense of completion' with the first two factors suggests that something else was being measured than large-scale tonal closure. Indeed, as Cook freely admits, the consistent effect shown by the ratings was a slight preference for the second performance of each piece, regardless of whether it was the altered version or the original.

The problem of the order of presentation is a problem of execution. Cook responded to it by conducting a second experiment in which various subgroups

---

[3] N. Cook, 'The Perception of Large-Scale Tonal Closure', *Music Perception*, 5 (1987), 197–205.
[4] Ibid. 197.

of students heard the pieces played in different orders. But he selected only the two shortest pieces for this revised experiment. And of these, the sole statistically significant result was that the 'coherence' of Brahms's own version of the St Anthony chorale (*Haydn Variations*, bars 1–10) was rated higher than an altered version in which the key of the chorale suddenly leaps down a minor third following the half-cadence. From one rating of 'coherence' in one short piece, are we really to conclude that 'the influence of tonal closure over listeners' responses is restricted to a maximum time scale, possibly on the order of 1 min'?[5] The notion of a function relating the force of tonal closure to time span—a quite reasonable notion, I might add—came from the first experiment. But that experiment demonstrated only the effect of order of performance. Cook asserts the function; the experiments do not support it.

Cook's experiments reveal the manifest difficulties in attempting to apply rigorous methods to poorly defined, culturally contingent phenomena. The number of pieces tested, for instance, was far too small. All the pieces were of different lengths and styles. No tests were done to see if the students could reliably tell if the second performance was different from the first. Students from the first, flawed experiment participated in the second experiment, and were played pieces from the first experiment. The responses of 'no preference' were omitted from the statistics in the first experiment. A human performer, hopefully not the experimenter, executed both versions of each piece, ensuring that large-scale tonal closure was not the sole variable. And the surgeries required to alter each piece varied considerably in their aesthetic effect: in one piece the scar is cleverly concealed, in another it glowers hideously.

I note these shortcomings because Cook has caricatured the more circumspect studies undertaken by professional psychologists as pedestrian efforts based on banal music-theoretical concepts that lead only to a 'psychology of ear training'.[6] Even if this charge were warranted, which it is not, a pedestrian but rigorously substantiated demonstration of the psychological validity of some small facet of music-theoretical discourse would be extremely valuable. Such findings could do far more to create interdisciplinary understanding than unsubstantiated claims about the perceptual nature of an ill-defined tonal mode of listening.

Cook's experiments were well received, perhaps because many in the crowd were only too happy to have someone point out an embarrassing problem with the emperor's clothes. The crowd, of course, was more interested in the critique than the experimental method. In our rush toward fashionable criticism— and I presume no one would wish to be thought 'uncritical'—we must be careful not to let knowing once again outstrip seeing. When Cook[7] cites experiments by

[5] Ibid. 203.
[6] N. Cook, 'Perception: A Perspective from Music Theory', in R. Aiello (ed.), *Musical Perceptions* (New York, 1994), 76.
[7] Ibid. 72.

Clarke and Krumhansl[8] that tested the criteria by which listeners recognized sectional boundaries in one piece by Stockhausen and another by Mozart, his welcome critique of the idolatry of tonal structure goes beyond just emphasizing that changes of texture, dynamics, metre, and other non-tonal features were important cues to sectional boundaries in both compositions. He claims that

> what is strikingly absent from the criteria adopted in the Mozart is any sign of specifically *tonal* features, such as modulations, cadence points, or tonal closure. . . . The conclusion seems inescapable: if people (musically trained people) listen to tonal and atonal music in much the same way, and if atonal music is not very grammatical, then tonal music cannot be very grammatical either.[9]

I was surprised to read that listeners to Mozart seemed to pay no heed to tonal features, and when I referred to the original study, I was even more surprised to see tonal features listed prominently. Clarke and Krumhansl's table 2 has 'Change of key (minor to major)' as its first entry for 'Musical Characteristics Contributing to the Six Boundaries in Mozart's *Fantasie*'.[10] 'Change of key' appears twice more, and is joined by 'Change of harmony (cadence)'. In four of the six recognized sectional boundaries, some listeners specifically made mention of tonal features. The 'inescapable' conclusion to be drawn is not, however, that Mozart's music is thus 'grammatical' after all, but that criteria for selecting sectional boundaries neither prove nor disprove a music's grammaticality. Of course, Cook may have been using 'tonal features' in some special sense, restricting their semantic field to 'tonal features in the sense of Lerdahl and Jackendoff's hierarchical structures'. Nevertheless, vague, discipline-summarizing terms like 'tonal features' and 'grammaticality' simply do not constitute the appropriate objects for the confident manipulations of Aristotelian logic.

Experiments well done provide resistance to theories too enmeshed in networks of self-confirming premises. Careful measurements of what is truly measurable can serve to correct the inevitable distortions of culturally contingent modes of evaluation. In surveying the history of music theory, a cynic might conclude that the discipline has often provided little more than a technical apparatus in support of the current aesthetic doctrine. Yet music theory can and should do more. A thoughtful confrontation between theory and the results of solid experiments fosters real progress in understanding. Rameau, the great eighteenth-century theorist, recast his explanation of harmony in response to the scientific work of Sauveur[11] and other pioneers of acoustics.[12] Riemann, the nineteenth century's most brilliant theorist, engaged in a lifelong dialectic

---

[8]   E. Clarke and C. Krumhansl, 'Perceiving Musical Time', *Music Perception*, 7 (1990), 213–51.

[9]   Cook, 'Perception: A Perspective', 72.

[10]   Clarke and Krumhansl, 'Perceiving Musical Time', 243.

[11]   J. Sauveur, 'Système général des intervalles des sons', *Mémoires de L'Académie royale des sciences* (Paris, 1701), *passim*.

[12]   J-Ph. Rameau, *Nouveau Système de musique théorique* (Paris, 1726).

between Romantic musical practice and the findings of Helmholtz's experiments[13] on auditory sensation.[14] Many in this century—Leonard B. Meyer comes to mind[15]—have made real contributions through interpretations of the work of experimental psychologists. Experiments serve as important goals to refine or reformulate theory, and new theory in turn can provide the conceptual underpinnings for further experiments.

At no time has this idealized interplay between theory and experiment been closer to actual practice than today. A lively, international, interdisciplinary group of scholars and researchers is actively engaged in experiments directed toward questions of harmony, rhythm, metre, timbre, performance, contour, style, emotion, and a host of other topics that lie at the heart of music theory. For example, the music-theoretical work of Lerdahl and Jackendoff[16] has stimulated psychological experiments directed at testing its claims about segmentation[17] and tonal tension.[18] Similarly, the recent melodic theory of Narmour[19] is currently being tested by researchers at Cornell, in particular Carol Krumhansl. These and other studies are collaborative in nature. Theorists and experimentalists have pooled their expertise in the hope of producing results that meet the needs and standards of both disciplines.

The relevance to music theory of some experimental work has been obscured by arcane or newly minted terminology. Not every musician who reads the term 'auditory stream segregation'[20] will recognize that it refers to mental processes central to the experience of voice-leading.[21] Similarly, the musical relevance of 'virtual pitch sensations'[22] is not immediately obvious, even though the concept may be fundamental to questions of perceived harmonic roots and progressions.[23] Yet terminology changes because theory changes. And in the two cases just cited, theory changed because the results of experiments in auditory perception indicated that more precise terms were required. The fact that such developments are occurring outside the traditional confines of music theory should give the discipline pause.

Beyond difficulties in terminology, the work of Bregman on auditory stream

[13] H. von Helmholtz, *Die Lehre von den Tonempfindungen* (Brunswick, 1863).

[14] H. Riemann, preface to *Musikgeschichte in Beispielen* (Leipzig, 1912).

[15] L. B. Meyer, *Emotion and Meaning in Music* (Chicago, 1956); *idem, Style and Music: Theory, History, and Ideology* (Philadelphia, 1989).

[16] F. Lerdahl and R. Jackendoff, *A Generative Theory of Tonal Music* (Cambridge, Mass., 1983).

[17] I. Deliège, 'Grouping Conditions in Listening to Music: An Approach to Lerdahl and Jackendoff's Grouping Preference Rules', *Music Perception*, 4 (1987), 35–60.

[18] E. Bigand, 'Abstraction of Two Forms of Underlying Structure in a Tonal Melody', *Psychology of Music*, 18 (1990), 45–59.

[19] E. Narmour, *The Analysis and Cognition of Basic Melodic Structures: The Implication–Realization Model* (Chicago, 1990).

[20] A. Bregman, *Auditory Scene Analysis: The Perceptual Organization of Sound* (Cambridge, Mass., 1990).

[21] D. Huron, 'The Avoidance of Part-Crossing in Polyphonic Music: Perceptual Evidence and Musical Practice', *Music Perception*, 9 (1991), 93–104.

[22] E. Terhardt, G. Stoll, and M. Seewan, 'Pitch of Complex Signals According to Virtual-Pitch Theory: Tests, Examples, and Predictions', *Journal of the Acoustical Society of America*, 71 (1982), 671–8.

[23] R. Parncutt, *Harmony: A Psychoacoustic Approach* (Berlin, 1989).

segregation and of Terhardt and colleagues on virtual pitch sensations can be difficult for music theorists to evaluate, because they imply a mental faculty capable of finding the 'best organization' inherent in a complex, noisy sensory environment. The analytical orientation of music theory favours firm primary objects (notes, durations, intervals), which can then be manipulated in a musical calculus. By contrast, the perception of an auditory stream—the recognition, for example, that the violas are playing a countermelody—is conditional, emergent, evanescent, and characterized by shades of grey rather than black-and-white certainty. How melodic, for instance, must a viola part be before a listener recognizes it as a countermelody? Must it be played louder? Must the melodic interest of the other parts be attenuated? A little reflection on these questions leads one to realize that a great deal of music perception is contingent, situational, and subject to biases of culture and experience. Can any systematic exploration be made of areas this complex and this resistant to Aristotelian logic?

One promising avenue of enquiry leads to the province of connectionism, or neural networks. Based loosely on the neural architecture of the human cortex, computer simulations of the behaviour of massively interconnected processing units exhibit many of the very qualities needed to find a 'best organization' in a complex environment. Neural networks can 'learn'; they can 'generalize'; they can 'fill in gaps'; they can form 'prototypes'; and they can arrive at global decisions based on an evaluation, weighted by 'experience', of the simultaneous input of hundreds of pieces of information. Take, for example, Bharucha's connectionist simulation of how Terhardt's virtual pitch sensations could be learned through experience with the tones typical of speech and music.[24] In the process of simulating such learning, Bharucha was able to show how the resulting neural system would share with human subjects a peculiar, but highly predictable, response to tones with specially mistuned upper partials. This response requires the system to find a global 'best organization' of stimuli that did not figure in the system's past experience. Likewise, my connectionist simulation of the perception of auditory streams demonstrates the same appearance and disappearance of perceived voices reported in classic psychological studies.[25] The simulation suggests that auditory stream segregation is necessarily multiplex, contingent, and linked to processes of attention.

As analogues of biophysical processes, such simulations neither prove nor disprove particular premises. Other, quite different simulations might also emulate a particular facet of human behaviour. But these simulations do lead us to think about thinking in a new way. The mere existence of simulations that perform complex feats of pattern recognition without a rule-based master program makes it easier to imagine theories of music perception that replace

[24] J. J. Bharucha, 'The Emergence of Auditory and Musical Cognition from Neural Nets Exposed to Environmental Constraints', paper presented at the Second International Conference on Music Perception and Cognition, Los Angeles, Feb. 1992.

[25] R. Gjerdingen, 'Apparent Motion in Music?', *Music Perception*, 11 (1994), 335–70.

the calculus of musical atoms with an emphasis on experience, training, and attention.

Music theory is unlikely to become an experimental science. Not only do its areas of interest have important historical and art-critical components, but, as alluded to earlier, its practitioners are often professionally untrained to meet the specific standards required of researchers in established experimental sciences. Rather than become an experimental science, music theory should embrace experimental science. Theorists should, as many now do, collaborate with psychologists, acousticians, cognitive scientists, neurologists, behavioural scientists, and others who want to join in exploring the many aspects of music. The premises of discourse within the discipline of music theory should be capable of meeting the challenge of translation into domains where inexactitude is never mistaken for subtlety. Our conceptual children will look far less dwarfish if our theoretical gaze is sharpened by reference to the grid of experiment.

## Appendix

As a service to those who might wish to visit the terrain where experiments in music perception receive extended discussion, I have provided the following short bibliographic Baedeker.

### *Journals*

Three scholarly journals devoted to research in music perception and cognition are *Music Perception*, published by the University of California Press, *Psychomusicology*, originally published by Stephen F. Austin State University but now published by Illinois State University at Normal, and *Psychology of Music*, published in the United Kingdom by the Society for Research in Psychology of Music and Music Education. These journals, as well as the many psychological and acoustical journals that publish occasional articles on music perception, can be searched through Psychological Abstracts, a large database available at many college and university libraries either on-line, in CD-ROM format, or in printed form. Those who have never ventured into this domain may be astonished by the sheer volume of work being done on topics of interest to musicians.

### *Books*

Among recent English-language books reporting or summarizing experiments in music perception and cognition are the following:

Aiello, R., *Musical Perceptions* (New York, 1994).
Bamberger, J., *The Mind behind the Musical Ear: How Children Develop Musical Intelligence* (Cambridge, Mass., 1991).
Bregman, A., *Auditory Scene Analysis: The Perceptual Organization of Sound* (Cambridge, Mass., 1990).
Butler, D., *The Musician's Guide to Perception and Cognition* (New York, 1992).
Deutsch, D. (ed.), *The Psychology of Music* (Orlando, Fla., 1982; rev. edn. in press).

Dowling, W., and Harwood, D., *Music Cognition* (Orlando, Fla., 1986).

Gabrielsson, A. (ed.), *Action and Perception in Rhythm and Music: Papers Given at a Symposium in the Third International Conference on Event Perception and Action* (Stockholm, 1987).

Handel, S., *Listening: An Introduction to the Perception of Auditory Events* (Cambridge, Mass., 1989).

Hargreaves, D., *The Developmental Psychology of Music* (Cambridge, 1986).

Howell, P., Cross, I., and West, R. (eds.), *Musical Structure and Cognition* (Orlando, Fla., 1985).

Jones, M., and Halleran, S. (eds.), *The Cognitive Bases of Musical Communication* (Washington D.C., 1991).

Krumhansl, C., *Cognitive Foundations of Musical Pitch* (New York, 1990).

McAdams, S., and Bigand, E. (eds.), *Thinking in Sound: The Cognitive Psychology of Human Audition* (Oxford, 1993).

Serafine, M., *Music as Cognition: The Development of Thought in Sound* (New York, 1988).

Sloboda, J., *The Musical Mind: The Cognitive Psychology of Music* (Oxford, 1985).

Sloboda, J. (ed.), *Generative Processes in Music: The Psychology of Performance, Improvisation, and Composition* (Oxford, 1988).

Tighe, T., and Dowling, J. (eds.), *Psychology and Music: The Understanding of Melody and Rhythm* (Hillsdale, N.J., 1993).

# 8

# Concepts of Musical Unity

## Fred Everett Maus

Unity is a familiar criterion of value for individual musical compositions, especially for eighteenth- and nineteenth-century European instrumental music and related twentieth-century traditions. But recent discussions suggest that the content and status of this criterion may be unclear. Perhaps we do not always know what we mean by 'musical unity'; perhaps unity (whatever it is) is not as important or as central as we have sometimes believed.

Discourse about musical unity has a close association with technical musical analysis. Musical analysis usually tries to display musical unity. The goal may be stated overtly, as when William Mitchell writes, at the beginning of an analytical article, that 'the aim here will be . . . to arrive at a view of the entire work as a unified, articulated structure';[1] or it may be inexplicit, though obvious. Conversely, when music scholars want to demonstrate unity, they typically draw upon analytical description. But it would be wrong to identify discourse about musical unity with music-analytical discourse.

For one thing, if analysis can display musical unity, then it must also have the capacity to display disunity. Any non-vacuous vocabulary for asserting close musical relationships also provides ways of denying those relationships—that is, ways of identifying differences. If one can assert, for instance, that two passages present motivically related material, then, by the same criterion of relatedness, it should be meaningful to assert that a third passage lacks that motivic feature. Consequently, if one wants to display, and perhaps praise, the heterogeneity of a composition, analysis could provide valuable descriptive tools. Analysts do not typically explore this possibility, but I suppose that reflects a habitual commitment to unity, not an inherent limitation of analytical techniques.[2]

---

[1] William Mitchell, 'The Tristan Prelude: Techniques and Structure', *Music Forum*, 1 (1967), 162.

[2] Some of Benjamin Boretz's analyses in *Meta-Variations* in effect propose the disunity of various compositions: 'it may appear that a frequent consequence of the "motivic" approach . . . is that a more complete and coherent description is possible for a local structure regarded *as* a "piece" in itself than is possible for the same passage when it is regarded as *part* of a larger structure.' For his summary of the analyses, see 'Meta-Variations, Part IV: Analytic Fallout (II)', *Perspectives of New Music*, 11/2 (1974), 188–9. Apparently Boretz regards this disunity as problematic. But his analyses show a way that someone who enjoys or accepts a lack of unity might use analysis to bring out the heterogeneity within a composition.

Also, there are critical or theoretical approaches to music other than technical analysis, and they can provide non-technical ways to state claims about unity. Anthony Newcomb's psychological account of Schumann's Second Symphony is a fine example, especially its excellent discussion of the last movement. The movement does not conform to a familiar formal pattern, so some critics find it problematic. But on Newcomb's account, the succession of events makes sense as a sort of psychological fiction, and the events of the last movement are the final stage in a unified psychological progression extending through the whole symphony.[3] If one wants to show, in detail, the unity of a composition, analysis may not always provide the most effective or most appropriate tools. Further, while Newcomb's essay, like conventional technical analysis, describes many details of the music, there may also be ways of thinking about unity that do not require, or invite, explicit verbal description of musical detail.[4]

This potential divergence of analysis and unity is an important issue; actually, it is a pair of issues, since analysis can address disunity, and non-analytical discourse can address unity. Here I shall neglect the first issue, the analytical study of disunity, and focus on questions about the nature of musical unity. In doing so, I shall not assume that valuable discourse about unity must be technical.[5]

Someone might object: 'You can't reach a serious understanding of musical unity without also exploring some possibilities for disunity or heterogeneity in music.' The objection is correct. This is an exploratory essay, not a definitive treatment of unity. But one can also turn this point around and say: 'You can't form a plausible conception of musical disunity or heterogeneity except in light of a plausible conception of musical unity.'

Do we lack such a conception? If unity is a familiar criterion of musical value, why would anyone question its content or status?

---

[3] Roughly, the progression of the whole symphony is from struggle and grief to happiness; but the point about the last movement is that the happiness initially seems unearned, and the movement (or its protagonist) needs to re-establish contact with the sadness of the preceding movement (Anthony Newcomb, 'Once More "Between Absolute and Program Music": Schumann's Second Symphony', *19th-Century Music*, 7 (1984), 233–50).

Though Newcomb's overall unity comes from a dramatic progression, the essay uses analysis as well. Another essay by Newcomb, 'Narrative Archetypes and Mahler's Ninth Symphony' (in Steven Scher (ed.), *Music and Text* (Cambridge, 1992), 118–36), is somewhat less dependent on technical analysis. Perhaps J. K. Randall's 'how music goes' (*Perspectives of New Music*, 14/2–15/1 (1976), 424–517) is at the purely non-analytical end of the spectrum; see n. 37.

[4] At present there is debate among musicologists about whether serious writing about music must always, sooner or later, turn to detailed analytical description of individual compositions. This debate sometimes gets mixed up with the question of whether musicologists should *ever* offer detailed analytical descriptions; I have heard several historians recommend a total ban on analytical description. My view is that analysis and other detailed descriptions are sometimes crucial for various communicative purposes, sometimes unnecessary and intrusive. Perhaps it is embarrassing to have such a bland view, but I regard the more extreme positions as melodramatic.

[5] Having mentioned that analytical language can address disunity, I should mention the obvious additional point that non-technical discourse can also address disunity.

## Three Ways of Questioning Unity

While accepting the traditional view that unity is an important musical value, one might find the notion of unity unclear, or find that standard explications are problematic. So one can ask for a more explicit or more accurate account of musical unity. Or, while agreeing that unity is an important musical value, one might find that analysts or critics have overemphasized unity, at the expense of other values. So one might ask for more discussion of other valuable qualities of music, and perhaps for an account of the relations between unity and those other qualities. Or, more radically, one might question whether the attribution of musical unity is ever appropriate as a critical or scholarly aim.

Richard Cohn and Douglas Dempster have provided a well-known, recent example of the first kind of enquiry.[6] They identify 'the principal and most persistent canon governing our Western aesthetic': 'successful works of art, including the "masterpieces" of Western art music, exhibit unity, coherence, or "organic" integrity' (156). Accepting this canon, they go on to question a more specific assumption about the nature of musical unity. They find that most present-day theorists seek explanations of unity in terms of an underlying hierarchical structure. But this 'yields an incomplete vision of musical unity' (156) in their view; by exploring a tension between hierarchy and motivic pattern in Schenker's thought, they work toward an alternative account. They reconstrue unity, but do not challenge its role as 'the principal canon'.[7]

Joseph Kerman, in 'How We Got into Analysis, and How to Get Out', exemplifies the second kind of enquiry.[8] Kerman accepts the critical pertinence of 'organic unity' for some music, especially in the Germanic instrumental tradition; but he emphasizes the need to 'find ways of dealing with other kinds of aesthetic value in music besides organicism' (30). As Kerman argues, some music from outside the Germanic instrumental repertory may not derive its value from unity; and an exclusive focus on unity is wrong even for 'standard German-masterpiece-type' compositions, since it distracts from other valuable qualities. He concludes that critics need alternatives to the criterion of unity.

The first and second kinds of question about unity can be addressed independently. For instance, Kerman does not seem to worry much about the first topic, the clarity or adequacy of current concepts of unity; he appears to regard 'organic unity' as the one musical quality that can be entrusted to the analysts.

---

[6] Richard Cohn and Douglas Dempster, 'Hierarchical Unity, Plural Unities', in Katherine Bergeron and Philip Bohlman (eds.), *Disciplining Music: Musicology and its Canons* (Chicago, 1992), 156–81; subsequent page references to this essay are given in the text.

[7] Of course, Schenker's own writings provide a spectacular historical example of the same general approach: clearly Schenker found it crucial to improve upon previous accounts of the unity of master-works.

[8] Joseph Kerman, 'How We Got into Analysis, and How to Get Out', orig. pub. 1980; repr. in Kerman, *Write All These Down: Essays on Music* (Berkeley, 1994), 12–32; subsequent page references to this essay are given in the text.

But, of course, the two kinds of enquiry are compatible, and could be pursued together: one could try to rethink the notion of musical unity while also exploring the relation between unity and other musical qualities. Cohn and Dempster provide a simple example: in trying to clarify the canon of unity, they also arrive at recognition of 'a second, independent canon', which they call 'richness'.[9]

The third attitude is incompatible with the others. If music scholars should not describe or explain musical unity, then questions about the correct construal of unity or about its relation to other musical values become pointless. A lack of interest in the unity of individual compositions might result from an overriding emphasis on the cultural and historical contexts of music (the polemical writings of Gary Tomlinson, with their attack on 'internalism', may be an example[10]). Or arguments against the value of unity might come from some general conceptual orientation—deconstructive or postmodernist thought, for instance.[11]

Such a universally dismissive attitude toward the topic of unity seems wrong to me, simply—but decisively—because it conflicts with much of my musical experience. For me, the interesting questions about musical unity come from the first two categories.[12] But I sympathize with the suspicious or sceptical attitudes that can lead to a dismissal of unity, because I find much discourse about musical unity unsatisfactory, mainly in two ways.

First, many statements about musical unity are formulaic and insubstantial. The topic of unity seems to invite dull, unevocative pieties. How can one escape this dullness? In part, no doubt, through close critical attention to the language one uses. That is, writing well or badly about musical unity is an instance of writing well or badly, and success will depend on the linguistic care—and, of course, talent—that any serious writer needs. Obviously, the focus of 'close critical attention to language' varies with the purpose of the writing or speech.

---

[9] The notion of richness is, roughly, the susceptibility of the same musical events to explanation by a number of distinct generative operations. I comment shortly on a problematic aspect of this notion.

[10] See Gary Tomlinson, 'The Web of Culture: A Context for Musicology', *19th-Century Music*, 7/3 (1984), 350–62.

[11] For a large-scale discussion, much indebted to the work of Paul de Man, see Alan Street, 'Superior Myths, Dogmatic Allegories: The Resistance to Musical Unity', *Music Analysis*, 8/1–2 (1989), 77–123. Of course, Street's use of de Man inherits any vulnerability of de Man's philosophical thought; in particular, Street relies on de Man's assertion of a gap between language and phenomena. Richard Rorty gives a trenchant rebuttal of such ideas in 'Two Meanings of "Logocentrism"', in Reed Way Dasenbrook (ed.), *Redrawing the Lines* (Minneapolis, 1989), 204–16; see 211–13. In any case, a reader of Street's essay who is not happy with de Manian formulations will face a formidable task of translation.

As I have formulated the third category, it involves a general distrust of the criterion of unity. I mean to distinguish this from Kerman's more empirical, relativized questioning of unity: Kerman suggests that unity might turn out to be unimportant in some repertories, not that it is *always* unimportant. His claim is based on reflective encounters with music, not on a general philosophical or methodological position.

[12] A bit of autobiography may interest some readers. When I began to think about this essay, I assumed that I would argue, one way or another, for a postmodern account of the heterogeneity and disunity of compositions. In working on it, I learned to separate my negative reaction to much writing about musical unity from my own musical experience, in which unity plays a prominent role.

My second problem with much discourse on unity has to do with the goal of the description. Claims about musical unity, including detailed analyses, tend to be formulated simply as assertions about compositions, without showing the relation of the alleged compositional unity to musical experiences. This exclusive focus on compositions is a serious problem.

## Unity and Experience

My interest in musical unity derives from my experience of listening to music, and I assume that experiences provide the decisive motivation and data for most people who want to think about musical unity.[13] I feel that unity of some kind is important, somehow, in many of my listening experiences; and in thinking about unity, I am looking for a fuller, more precise articulation of that fact. In working toward further articulation, I cannot accept as relevant a description of various properties of a composition 'in itself' unless I can recognize that the description somehow contributes to a characterization of my experiences in interacting with that composition.[14] (Schenkerian analyses are typically incomplete in this way, though they provide stimulating starting-points for working toward an experience of the music, typically a somewhat altered experience.)

This claim, that discourse about unity should somehow characterize musical experience, follows from my general attitude about analytical and critical discourse on music. In general, if I work toward analytical or critical formulations, including formulations about musical unity, I do so in order to communicate with others about my musical experiences, or to clarify for myself the qualities of those experiences. Others may respond by recognizing shared qualities of experience, which may also allow them to sharpen my descriptions; or they may find that their future experiences alter in light of my description; or my descriptions (and perhaps subsequent exchanges) may ultimately reveal differences in experience.

The notion of *recognizing* the relevance of a description to one's experiences is important.[15] Confronted with a demonstration, on the basis of a score, that some kind of musical pattern exists, one may be tempted to conclude that the pattern explains features of one's experiences, even though one does not recognize the pattern as such in listening. The temptation is familiar in analytical reflection on

---

[13] I do not mean that my interest in unity derives from my experiences of listening to music *rather than* the discourse about music I have heard. I am not making some claim about a non-linguistic, originary, or conceptually uncontaminated experience. I mean that my interest derives from my experience of listening to music, as a member of a musical culture, with all the linguistic and other baggage that makes up that culture.

[14] For an excellent general account of criticism as communication about experience, see Arnold Isenberg, 'Critical Communication', in *Aesthetics and the Theory of Criticism* (Chicago, 1973), 156–71. For a fascinating exchange about music criticism and experience, see Kendall Walton, 'Understanding Humor and Understanding Music', and Marion Guck, 'Taking Notice', *Journal of Musicology*, 11/1 (1993), 32–44, 45–51 resp.

[15] Walton, 'Understanding Humor', emphasizes the concept of acknowledging aspects of one's experience.

successful twelve-tone music. On one hand, a twelve-tone piece may seem convincing, unified, and beautiful; on the other hand, the twelve-tone patterning seems undeniable. So, one feels bound to admit, somehow the patterning must explain the experiences, including the feeling of unity. One should resist such hypothetical analytical explanations—not primarily because they are false (though I think they are not known to be true), but because they change the subject of analysis, leading away from the articulation of experienced qualities of music.[16] In my view, musical experiences should be not just the testing ground, but also the main subject-matter, of musical analysis and criticism. If the central task in critical writing about music is to articulate and communicate experience, then that goal should orient one's critical attention to language, in choosing one's own words about music or reflecting on the words of others.

## A Problematic Example

To me, such claims about the central role of experience are obvious to the point of banality. But much scholarly writing about music neglects listeners' experiences. The essay by Cohn and Dempster mentioned above is an instance. It is worth taking some care over a description of it, because it reflects widely shared habits of analytical discourse.

Cohn and Dempster begin with the commonplace observation that a Schenkerian hierarchical account of a composition is a demonstration of unity. But, they point out, motivic patterning operates somewhat independently of prolongational hierarchy. So they borrow from David Lewin the concept of a 'product-network', and regard the surface of a composition as 'a product of logically independent operations' (176).[17] Finally, they conclude that the surface is actually 'the basis of a composition's unity'.

In evaluating this argument, I focus on the conclusion, specifically its appeal to the musical 'surface'. Of course, Cohn and Dempster are not the only writers to take an interest in the surface of music. Writers concerned with musical experiences often emphasize musical surfaces, typically in contrast to underlying structures. In particular, the complaint that analysis neglects experience may be expressed by insisting on the importance of surfaces. Cohn and Dempster appear to acknowledge and address this type of complaint, but actually they do not fully respond to it. Here is what they write:

Analysts are frequently accused of neglecting what is musically valuable when they listen 'beneath' the surface interests of a piece. This objection is disarmed by a product-network

---

[16] Joseph Dubiel, 'Three Essays on Milton Babbitt', *Perspectives of New Music*, 28/2 (Summer 1990), 216–61; 29/1 (Winter 1991), 90–122; and 30/1 (Winter 1992), 82–131, is an imaginative search for realistic descriptions of Milton Babbitt's music, which avoids the temptation to comment primarily on its twelve-tone structure.

[17] However, they do not try to give a clear definition of a 'product-network'.

conception of musical unity, which draws our attention, and the analyst's, back to the surface of the piece as the ground of its unity. (177)

To critics of certain kinds of analysis, Cohn and Dempster reply, in effect, that they have found something to say about the surface; they reply as though any kind of attention to the surface of music will satisfy the objection.

But what is the surface, for Cohn and Dempster? The surface is the meeting-place of various generative schemes. What those schemes have in common is that they lead to the same surface features, and that is the sense in which the surface is the 'ground of unity'.[18] Understanding the surface in this way, one loses, or at least obscures, the connection between surface and experience. Cohn and Dempster do not indicate in any way what it is to hear a composition in terms of any one generative scheme; nor, consequently, can one tell what it might be to hear a composition in terms of several coexisting generative schemes. So the surface, as an object of experience, remains mysterious in their account.

The distinctive features of their account may actually make it harder to understand how one might experience musical surfaces. If a generative scheme is relevant to experience, presumably this is because it attributes various surface qualities—that is, qualities that can be experienced by a listener. But if several different schemes attribute qualities independently, it seems that a particular surface event would be heard as a bundle of uncoordinated qualities. As a general account of ordinary musical experience, this seems strange and improbable.

In their essay Cohn and Dempster never acknowledge experience as a significant topic.[19] In contrast, when Joseph Kerman identifies Tovey as 'a "foreground" analyst par excellence, an analyst of the rhythmic surface of music', he specifically contrasts Tovey's approach with the search for 'backgrounds', which presumably includes the sort of formal generative procedures that Cohn and Dempster evoke.[20] Edward T. Cone, writing of 'healthily hedonistic attention to the musical surface' or 'the direct enjoyment . . . of the sheer sound of an orchestra', obviously intends to direct attention to qualities that the surface has in a listener's experiences.[21] To engage in serious dialogue with such

---

[18] 'It is the surface that "holds together" underlying diversity by providing a compositional solution to multiple and disparate demands of harmonic, contrapuntal, motivic, and rhythmic operations' (177).

[19] In passing, I want to mention another problem with Cohn's and Dempster's location of unity at 'the surface', though it does not bear directly on my main concerns here. The surface grounds unity, they conclude, in that it holds the various generative schemes together; it is what all the generative schemes have in common. But that does not exhaust the role of unity in their account, because it seems that *each* 'set of independent formal operations' for the piece is *also* governed by the 'canon of unity', yielding an account of a unified voice-leading hierarchy, motivic unity, unity of figuration, or whatever. So it is wrong to single out the surface as the unique locus of unity. (This point is reflected in Cohn's and Dempster's title—these 'independent formal operations' yield the title's 'plural unities'—but the point disappears in their peroration on surface.)

[20] Joseph Kerman, 'Tovey's Beethoven', repr. in Kerman, *Write All These Down*, 162. Kerman emphasizes that Tovey's analyses, rather than looking for 'compositorial causes', 'look forward from the music to its aesthetic effect'—experience again (163).

[21] Edward T. Cone, *Musical Form and Musical Performance* (New York, 1968), 98, 89.

claims, one would need to address the role of experience, as Cohn and Dempster do not.

How do Cohn and Dempster believe that one should recognize the unity of an individual composition, if not in listening? The answer emerges when they address 'musical comprehension', which, they write, 'seems best served not by neglecting underlying structure, but rather by shuttling between the surface and underlying compositional parameters. The surface reveals both *what* underlying parameters are compositionally active and *how* they coordinate to generate the surface' (177). It seems likely that the person who 'shuttles between' in this way is analysing a composition, not listening to it. Apparently, for Cohn and Dempster, the basic form of musical engagement, the one that yields 'musical comprehension', is analysis. But a view that gives such centrality to analysis as a self-sufficient activity seems quite academic, in the pejorative sense.[22] Certainly that attitude contrasts with my view, that the main value of analysis lies in its capacity to describe, clarify, and alter listening experiences.

As I have already suggested, the essay by Cohn and Dempster reflects widely shared habits of analytical discourse. Many writers seem to regard analytical experience as the source of musical comprehension, and use the musical surface as a mere source of data, rather than as the place where experience and enquiry should come to rest. What are the alternatives? How can one conceive of musical unity while placing appropriate emphasis on the role of musical experiences?

## Musical Experiences

In the next sections I shall offer some positive claims about musical unity. They are broad claims, responding to a very basic question: when one has an experience of musical unity, *what is it* that is unified? Or, to put the same question differently, what is the bearer of musical unity?

I have already observed that claims about musical unity often appear as assertions about compositions, with no clear relation to musical experiences, and I stated that this is problematic. But what is wrong with such accounts? Is it just the failure to show, in some fairly explicit way, the relation between unified compositions and musical experience? If so, one needs to add more information about the relationship. But perhaps, more radically, there is a problem in the assumption that compositions are the primary bearers of unity.

Despite our prevailing habits of thought, it may be wrong to start an account of musical unity by reflecting on the unity of compositions. But what, besides a composition, could be 'musically unified'? I shall suggest three answers. These answers seem to clarify my intuitions about musical unity, and I propose them as good starting-points for further work on the topic.

---

[22] For better or worse, their position is realistic with regard to the outcome of much professional-level analytical training, which often leads primarily to its own *sui generis* analytical form of musical life.

My first answer is: an experience, a musical experience. One important kind of musical unity, I suggest, is *the unity of a listening experience*, or (in a more precise, if cumbersome, formulation), the unity and distinctness of a particular experience of listening to a composition.[23]

I propose this first answer under the influence of John Dewey's *Art as Experience*. The discussion of art in that excellent book can provide a useful model for thinking about music, specifically, a model that centres on description of experiences rather than objects.[24] In the following paragraphs I will give a brief account of some of Dewey's ideas; for more detail, see the appendix to this essay.

Much of Dewey's book is written in reaction to the tendency to see a gap between high art and everyday life. Dewey wants to show relations and interactions between art and other aspects of life. He identifies, as a 'primary task' in philosophy of art, 'to restore continuity between the refined and intensified forms of experience that are works of art and the everyday events, doings, and sufferings that are universally recognized to constitute experience' (3). To create a context for an account of art, Dewey makes a general distinction between 'experience', which 'occurs continuously', and '*an* experience', which 'is integrated within and demarcated in the general stream of experience from other experiences' (35). Life is not just a continuous flow of 'experience', but 'a thing of histories, each with its own plot, its own inception and movement toward its close, each having its own particular rhythmic movement; each with its own unrepeated quality pervading it throughout' (36). Such distinct experiences are characteristic of interactions with art. Artists seek to create the conditions in which such experiences can occur.

An experience, according to Dewey, is both 'demarcated from' the 'stream of experience' or other individual experiences, hence separate, *and* 'integrated within' experience, hence somehow continuous with, or in contact with, the rest of one's life. Some of the cleverness and depth of Dewey's idea can come out in a paradoxical formulation: to recognize the continuity between art and the rest of life, one must first recognize a particular kind of discontinuity that is possible, and desirable, within everyday life itself. That is, someone who thinks of art as other-worldly, ethereal, and uniquely separate probably overestimates the seamless continuity of the rest of life.[25] Everyday experience already has the

[23] I could make the formulation more precise by referring to 'a performance of a composition', rather than 'a composition'. The role of performance is important, and is, at least, available for consideration when one insists on talking about experiences (since, of course, what a listener experiences is a performance). However, I do not address it in this essay, which already has a full agenda.

[24] Here is a characteristic passage on this point: 'The *product* of art—temple, painting, statue, poem—is not the *work* of art. The work takes place when a human being cooperates with the product so that the outcome is an experience that is enjoyed because of its liberating and ordered properties' (John Dewey, *Art as Experience* (New York, 1980; orig. pub. 1934), 214; subsequent page references to this book are given in the text and the following notes.

[25] There is another, more basic reason why one might think of art as other-worldly: one might think of art objects independently of people's interactions with them. Dewey opposes this way of thinking, of course, as I do.

potential for separation into numerous distinct experiences, each with its own shape and individual qualities. And this separation of experience into experiences need not be a problematic fragmentation. Rather, the formation of distinct, characterful experiences is valuable, a source of pleasure. Further, individuated experiences become memorable, encapsulated, unlike the routine flow of experience in which 'things happen, but they are neither definitely included nor decisively excluded; we drift' (40). Demarcated experiences can become touchstones, points of reference for thinking about the rest of one's experience.[26] Dewey makes the attractive claim that each experience has 'its own unrepeated quality pervading it throughout'. Having, and remembering, experiences gives access to such complex, unrepeated qualities.

Dewey understands an experience to be an interaction between, as he likes to put it, an 'organism' and its 'environment', a process of mutual adjustment. The interaction involves a rhythm of 'doing and undergoing', which we might call, in more routine language, a constant shift between relatively active and receptive roles for the organism.[27]

Dewey's broad emphases, intended for all art, are obviously appropriate in thinking about music. An emphasis on the interaction between music and listener locates unity, along with other musical qualities, in a particularized, contingent event, rather than an ontologically and experientially mysterious 'work' or 'composition'.[28] And with its emphasis on the ongoing, developmental qualities of the interaction, Dewey's approach gives suitable recognition to musical temporality.[29]

Dewey's position yields the following account of one aspect of musical unity. Listening to certain musical compositions, one may have an experience that is demarcated from experience-in-general as a distinct event. This experience consists of interaction between the listener and the music, in which the listener both 'does' and 'undergoes'—that is, construes the music, and responds continuously, on the basis of previous construals, to new sounds. The experience can be described as unified, and the occurrence of such experiences is one reason to associate music and unity.

---

[26] For instance, he writes of 'that meal in a Paris restaurant' that 'stands out as an enduring memorial of what food can be'. Or 'that storm one went through in crossing the Atlantic—the storm that seemed in its fury, as it was experienced, to sum up in itself all that a storm can be, complete in itself, standing out because marked out from what went before and what came after' (36).

[27] I don't suggest that the ordinary formulation is better than Dewey's 'doing and undergoing', just more familiar.

[28] Thus it leaves a natural place for considerations of performance. Emphasis on musical works notoriously neglects the contribution of performance, typically treating the performer's contribution as, at best, a kind of edifying commentary on the work itself.

[29] The importance Dewey grants to 'continuous consummation' suggests a cogent criticism of most professional analytical writing. Standard analytical writing, by proceeding as though the entire piece is already known and simultaneously present, in effect treats listening as a mere means, in which the sense of completion is postponed. That is, as I remarked in relation to Cohn and Dempster, analysis often proceeds as though listening were just a way of acquiring information about the music: the object of analysis, the complete composition, is present only at the conclusion of the listening.

What, in this context, would constitute a verbal demonstration or display of unity? Since the unity belongs to an experience, not a composition, one would have to offer a persuasive description of an experience. The description would provide evidence for a claim like this: a certain composition (perhaps in a certain performance) can interact with a listener to yield a musical experience. The only authoritative way to make such a claim would be on the basis of one's own experience, and the most decisive reason to accept such a claim would be that the description has led one to *have* an experience matching the description.

In relation to any particular description of musical experience, the Deweyan description is very general. Obviously it could be elaborated with an analytical emphasis on technical description, or with alternative, non-technical vocabularies.

## Worlds

Another intuitively attractive answer to the question about the bearer of musical unity is this: the unity belongs to a world (or, one might say, a musical world). Many people feel that listening to a successful piece of instrumental music gives them, in some sense, access to a particular world, which can be visited, explored, perhaps inhabited, perhaps just contemplated. So, for instance, Robert Schumann writes, in reviewing Schubert's Ninth Symphony, of 'the entirely new world that opens before us'.[30]

The idea of a musical world need not be an alternative to the Deweyan notion of 'a musical experience'; rather, it further specifies that notion. Some experiences involve the construction of a world. In such cases, describing that world is an important part of describing the experience.

When might one appeal to the notion of a musical world, distinct from the everyday world one inhabits before and after listening? What about one's experience would make the notion appropriate?

One might refer to a distinct world if the events one follows seem to belong together, and are of a different kind from those in the everyday world. Of course, this would be true for classical music generally, with its special sounds and rhythms, its restriction of relevant information to a small range of audible sensations. A context in which sounds are present only as sounds, not as evidence of the behaviour of physical objects, is very different from our everyday world.

One might also refer to a distinct world if the relevant events seem to be governed by generalizations that hold within that world, but not outside it. This criterion would allow one to think of a large set of pieces—for instance, the entire

---

[30] Robert Schumann, *On Music and Musicians*, trans. Paul Rosenfeld (New York, 1969; orig. pub. 1946), 111.

repertory of tonal music—as making possible the experience of one particular world ('the world of tonality'); but also any smaller group of pieces that could be experienced as stylistically similar could be thought of as occupying its own world ('the world of Baroque music', 'the world of Beethoven's late quartets', etc.). Experiencing an individual piece as a world, in this sense, would involve attention to the generalizations that can be made about events within that one piece, but not about other pieces, even stylistically similar ones.

However, it would be wrong to suggest that the perception of musical worlds arises exclusively from the perception of generalizations that hold within those worlds. Uniformities within a composition may create a sense of a world, but something close to the opposite can also be true: approaching a composition as a world, one may be prepared to accept sharply contrasting kinds of music as somehow relevant to each other.

One can also refer to a distinct world in the context of fictional truths: propositions that elaborate a single fiction can be said to describe a single fictional world, distinct from the actual world and from other fictional worlds. If listening to music sometimes involves the elaboration of a fictional world, then the distinctness of the fictional world in a particular listening experience constitutes a kind of musical unity. For instance, one might hear a piece by imagining a series of fictional motions (rising, falling, converging); these might belong together in a particular fictional world, related perhaps as consequences, commentaries, digressions, and so on.[31]

## Stories

A third answer to the question about the bearer of musical unity is that the unity belongs to a story somehow communicated in or by the music. This is the way that Newcomb addresses unity in his descriptions of symphonies by Schumann and Mahler: in both cases, he tells a story of psychological development, unified *as a story*, and proposes a moment-by-moment embodiment of the story in the music.[32]

Since Newcomb's essays are well known, and the story-like qualities of music are currently enjoying lively discussion, I shall make only a few points about stories and unity.[33] The first point is simply that the association of music with a

[31] Kendall Walton, *Mimesis as Make-Believe* (Cambridge, Mass., 1990), is an impressive study of fictional truths and fictional worlds. Walton's 'Listening with Imagination', *Journal of Aesthetics and Art Criticism*, 52/1 (Winter 1994), 47–61, is, so far, his fullest exploration of the consequences for music. See also Nelson Goodman's lively *Ways of Worldmaking* (Indianapolis, 1978).

[32] See citations in n. 3.

[33] For some interesting recent discussion, see Jean-Jacques Nattiez, 'Can One Speak of Narrativity in Music?', *Journal of the Royal Musical Association*, 115/2 (1990), 240–57; Lawrence Kramer, ' "As If a Voice Were in Them" ': Music, Narrative, and Deconstruction', in *Music as Cultural Practice, 1800–1900* (Berkeley, 1990), 176–213; Carolyn Abbate, 'What the Sorcerer Said', in *Unsung Voices: Opera and Musical Narrative in the Nineteenth Century* (Princeton, 1991), 30–60; Joseph Kerman, 'Representing a Relationship: Notes on a Beethoven Concerto', *Representations*, 39 (Summer 1992), 80–101.

story is a way of attributing musical unity: the parts of a story belong together, somehow, and in associating music and story one is, somehow, transferring that unity to a musical context. Second, as I understand it, the notion of a musical story is not an alternative to the notions of musical experiences or musical world. They are related as follows: a listener may have a unified experience, and that experience may include the imagining of a fictional world, and the events within that fictional world may form a story. Third, it may be that the degree of unity in Newcomb's accounts goes beyond what is necessary for music to have story-like qualities and a related kind of unity. Newcomb's stories involve a single protagonist and a lucid, orderly succession of events. Perhaps music can be experienced as having a story-like unity, even when the fictional characters are less determinate and the motivation of the succession of events is more mysterious.[34]

## Kinds of Unity

I have asserted the importance of musical experience, and offered suggestions about the bearer of musical unity, all in response to my dissatisfaction with the customary focus on unified compositions. Now I want to return to my other problem with much discourse on musical unity: that often, assertions of unity seem like comfortable things to say, pieties or platitudes, rather than evocative or hard-won articulations of experiences. Edward T. Cone's essay 'Music: A View from Delft' provides an example:

The Golden Age of functional tonality . . . witnessed a synthesis of all musical elements into forms as self-sufficient as any that music has ever known. The tension between detail and whole was here brought into equilibrium; musical suspense was under complete control; the shapes demanded by the respective needs of melody, harmony, and rhythm were integrated into a rich, multidimensional whole.[35]

Blandly, Cone cites various aspects of music, and announces their union. Encountering such language, I do not exactly feel that it is wrong—nor right— but mainly that it is easy and unhelpful. A fuzzy, familiar blanket swallows up the music.[36]

How can one avoid such pieties? One way is through linguistic innovation, the creation of fresh kinds of description.[37] But familiar vocabulary may also be capable of leading to clear, fresh perceptions. It is rewarding to linger over the

---

[34] The analysis in Leo Treitler, 'Mozart and the Idea of Absolute Music', in *Music and the Historical Imagination* (Cambridge, Mass., 1989), 191–214, seems closer to my ordinary musical experience, partly because of its unforced, somewhat disorderly quality.

[35] Edward T. Cone, *Music: A View from Delft* (Chicago, 1989), 21.

[36] Kevin Korsyn, 'Brahms Research and Aesthetic Ideology', *Music Analysis*, 12/1 (1993), 89–102, identifies similar passages, including a 'synthesizing' argument by David Lewin. Korsyn, like Cohn and Dempster, proposes to revise the concept of musical unity so that it includes irreducible diversity; he conceives the relevant diversity quite differently. His remarks on this are condensed, not to say enigmatic.

[37] My *locus classicus* is Randall's 'how music goes' (see n. 3). In an attempt to assimilate Randall to familiar categories, one might say that his text is an idiosyncratic study of the contribution of motivic relations to musical unity.

diverse vocabulary that is readily available for descriptions of musical unity: the result is a sharper awareness of different conceptions of musical unity and an ability to use some of the familiar terms with evocative precision.

Here are some terms, all of which summarize qualities related to unity: 'coherence', 'completeness', 'comprehensiveness', 'fusion', 'integrity', 'integration', 'logic', 'organic unity', 'perfection', 'self-sufficiency', 'synthesis', 'totality', 'wholeness'. They differ in that some seem to be species of unity ('coherence', 'fusion', 'wholeness'), while others do not ('logic', 'self-sufficiency'). But the relation to unity is clear in the latter cases as well: when a sequence of musical events is called logical, the point is that the events *go together* in a certain way; an ascription of self-sufficiency suggests a unified whole that is separated from some exterior.

Such terms, used carefully, can indicate related but distinct properties attributed to music. I shall indicate some of the possible distinctions. (In doing so, I revert to formulations that attribute qualities to compositions, despite the alternatives I have recommended in the preceding sections. I am concerned, now, with exploring the nuances of some common assertions about compositions; therefore I shall set aside, but not abandon, my claim that such language may ultimately be unsatisfactory, requiring paraphrase into a more experiential vocabulary.[38])

The non-musical uses of these terms can indicate the potential musical differences. Take a pair that seems close: 'integrity' and 'integration'. 'Integrity' normally refers, in non-musical contexts, to a quality of human character: roughly, a person shows integrity by preserving and acting upon certain central values in a variety of situations.[39] Thus one may show integrity by accepting and responding to the consequences of an initial decision in some series of events, standing by the values that motivated the decision.[40] 'Integration', in non-musical uses, evokes a different psychological trait—roughly, the successful co-ordination of all one's beliefs and desires, without suppression of aspects of oneself or conflict among various aspects. 'Integration' sounds like the result of an act of 'integrating', and thus suggests an accomplishment. 'Integrity' implies commitment, consistency through time; 'integration' implies something more like acceptance of, and perhaps control over, internal diversity.

But it would be more accurate to say that the essay offers to replace conventional discourse about motivic relations with a more evocative kind of writing; as I understand it, the text aims to make standard writing about motivic relations look bad. For commentary, see Joseph Dubiel, 'Senses of Sensemaking', *Perspectives of New Music*, 30/1 (Winter 1992), 210–21.

[38] In fact, many of the following ascriptions invite restatement in terms of fictional truths.

[39] There is a good discussion of integrity in Gabriele Taylor, *Pride, Shame, and Guilt: Emotions of Self-Assessment* (Oxford, 1983), 108–41. Etymologically, and in some earlier English-language uses, 'integrity' has a more general meaning of wholeness or completeness. (The word is related to 'integer'.) Perhaps that is all that some musicians mean when they talk about musical 'integrity'. If so, the word is unnecessary. Rather than accept that dull outcome, I prefer to follow up on the possibility of a precise, resonant musical usage.

[40] That is a sense in which one can assert, for instance, the integrity of Milton Babbitt's compositional work since the late 1940s.

How would such meanings carry over to musical contexts? Beethoven's Quartet Op. 131 provides a fairly straightforward example: it is perhaps appropriate to attribute integrity to the opening fugue, and integration to the whole seven-movement composition. Why? Referring to the integrity of the first movement, one directs attention to its consistent style and material; everything results from a kind of behaviour established at the beginning and sustained throughout, even at the cost of some asceticism. Referring to the integration of the whole composition, one draws attention to the accomplishment of bringing together different kinds of music in a persuasive way. (By contrast, I think it would be odd to refer to the 'integration' of the first movement. What, in that rather restricted movement, has required integration? On the other hand, one might make a subtle point by referring to the integrity of the whole quartet. One might mean, for instance, that the individual movements are relatively limited in their development of material; the limitation may display an ongoing commitment to the value of a final integration.)

Attributions of both integrity and integration, as I have interpreted them, are anthropomorphic: they construe a composition in terms of someone acting purposefully. Interestingly, the two attributions differ subtly in their temporal qualities; this is worth noting, because temporal qualities of music are so crucial. Normally, one perceives integrity by following a series of events or actions, regarding them as expressions of values; as the succession unfolds, each event can confirm or damage integrity. Though integrity is attributed globally, one can perceive it moment-by-moment, and the testing of integrity can create suspense. Integration is a quality of a totality; perhaps it is typically perceived retrospectively, outside the time of listening or, while listening, at or near the end of an integrated series of events. In my experience, the quality of integration in the Op. 131 quartet emerges as the last movement begins: around that time it becomes fully obvious that the preceding movements can be heard as interdependent stages of a dramatic whole.[41]

Here are briefer comments on other terms related to unity. 'Synthesis', like 'integration', implies that potentially discrepant items have been brought into some satisfactory relationship. But 'synthesis' is less clearly anthropomorphic than 'integration'; parts of a person's psyche may be integrated, but not synthesized (at any rate, not in any usage with which I am familiar). Actually, without any further context to specify its meaning, the term 'synthesis' is somewhat vague in a description of music, because of the range of its non-musical uses. (Should one think of Kantian perception or Hegelian dialectic? white light

---

[41] I interpret Tovey as making a similar point about the quartet. In his movement-by-movement description, he reaches the beginning of the last movement, and writes: 'At this point we must survey the keys which have been heard in the course of the work' (Donald F. Tovey, *The Main Stream of Music* (New York, 1949), 292; subsequent page references to this book are given in the text). Suppose that Tovey means to ascribe this retrospection to a normative skilful listener, and grant that Tovey perceives the unity of the quartet partly in terms of key relations: then he is suggesting that the beginning of the last movement leads a listener to call to mind, for the first time, the overall pattern of keys, and thus to perceive, for the first time, a crucial factor in the unity of the music.

or polyester? How does the common opposition of analysis and synthesis figure in claims about musical synthesis?) 'Fusion' is more plainly physical in its connotations, and thus seems to belong to a non-anthropomorphic image of music. 'Logic' evokes a complex range of ideas. It conveys, suggestively, the possibility of language-like relationships abstracted from determinate meanings and, perhaps, from any particular uttering or thinking subject; but of course the meaningful utterances of a particular subject may also be logical. 'Logic' also suggests a temporal quality, an orderly relation of earlier and later events; one can follow a logically ordered succession through time.[42] I suggested above that integrity has similar temporal implications. But one is following something different in the two cases: roughly, in following a succession that displays integrity, one finds, again and again, the preservation of some core value; whereas in following a logical succession, one perceives different things succeeding each other with a sense of non-empirical necessity.

The availability of these distinctions helps to specify the problem with passages like the one I cited from Cone: by rapidly attributing 'synthesis', 'self-sufficiency', 'equilibrium', 'integration', and 'wholeness', Cone blurs the distinctions, reducing the potential of these terms for differentiated meaning. Hence the impression of fuzziness.

## Conceptual Frameworks

It would be possible, and interesting, to continue working out distinctions among commonplace terms for musical unity. But the preceding comments also invite a more basic kind of investigation. The distinctions among these terms seem to display a range of underlying interpretive conceptions, perhaps taking the form of an elaborated fiction or metaphor. An individual term for a kind of musical unity may be the tip of a conceptual iceberg, as when, in attributing integrity to a composition, one may be attributing certain stable, effective values to some agent or agents.[43] If so, then it is natural to move from these individual

---

[42] However, one might also refer to relations between large structures and details as 'logical', in which case the time of the logical reasoning is outside the time of the musical succession.

[43] To whom? Presumably a fictional agent or agents, or perhaps an implied composer. I think both possibilities are realistic, but the attributions may vary. This is a tricky, obscure topic, but here is a sketch of a distinction. Suppose you attribute integrity to four interacting instrumental agents who produce the opening movement of Beethoven's Op. 131. What would they do if they lost their integrity? Most likely, lose their motivic concerns, and therewith their sense of sustained purpose, in a way that offers them greater immediate gratification. Suppose you attribute integrity to the implied composer of that movement. What would he have done if he had lost his integrity? Most likely, something aimed at producing greater immediate pleasure for the audience. The intuition is that the musical agents' purposes concern their own situation, while the composer's purposes concern his relation to the audience (at least, the purposes that are likely to interfere with integrity).

summarizing terms to consideration of broader metaphorical or fictional frameworks.

No doubt organicism is the most familiar metaphorical system for musical unity (or cluster of metaphorical systems), but it is crucial to notice that there are others. Kerman, in 'How We Got into Analysis', persistently refers to 'organic unity', thus failing to note the diversity of conceptions of unity. But Kerman's own historical examples reveal this diversity when they are read independently of his descriptions.[44] As one example of organicism, Kerman mentions the derivation of material from a single theme. He alludes to Hoffmann's review of Beethoven's Fifth Symphony, a composition which, in Kerman's paraphrase of Hoffmann, 'seem[s] to grow from a single theme as though from a Goethean *Urpflanz*' (16). But organic metaphors are quite scarce in Hoffmann's essay. Reading the essay for imaginative language, one is more likely to notice the remarkable description, near the opening, of Haydn, Mozart, and Beethoven leading listeners into three new worlds.[45] The idea that a composer opens up a special world is, as I have already indicated, a distinctive way of asserting the unity of the composer's works, considered collectively.

In another example, Kerman mentions that Tovey ultimately accepted 'the organicist position', and he cites Tovey's analysis of Beethoven's Quartet Op. 131, in which Tovey 'saw tonality inspiring the whole work' (17). Certainly Tovey's account addresses unity, but not through organic metaphors. Here is Tovey's summarizing formulation: 'The whole quartet is a perfect unity, governed by the results of the initial event of that modified first movement which maintained itself in the flat supertonic after the opening fugue had firmly established the key of C sharp minor' (294–5). Probably this 'perfect unity' is best understood in dramatic terms. On Tovey's view, the recapitulation of the second subject in the last movement definitively confirms the large-scale unity of the quartet: the arrival of the second subject in D prompts his claim that 'the wheel has come full circle. The whole quartet is a perfect unity.' Here is his description:

---

[44] Ruth A. Solie, 'The Living Work: Organicism and Musical Analysis', *19th-Century Music*, 4 (1980), 147–56, confines her discussion more strictly to conceptions based on organisms.

[45] The most striking organic metaphor comes in an analogy between Shakespeare and Beethoven, and applies directly to Shakespeare, *not* Beethoven: 'Just as our aesthetic overseers have often complained of a total lack of real unity and inner coherence in Shakespeare, when only profounder contemplation shows the splendid tree, buds, and leaves, blossom and fruit springing from the same seed, so only the most penetrating study of the inner structure of Beethoven's music can reveal its high level of rational awareness, which is inseparable from true genius and nourished by continuous study of the art' (David Charlton (ed.), *E. T. A. Hoffmann's Musical Writings* (Cambridge, 1989), 238–9). The main focus of the passage is Beethoven's 'rational awareness, his controlling self detached from the inner realm of sounds and ruling it in absolute authority'—a political metaphor that does not seem to encourage the addition of botanical figures. The detailed analysis of the symphony is mostly in technical language, interspersed with comments about the listener's 'mood of anxious, restless yearning' (241).

We have now reached this wonderful recapitulation in D major. But a more wonderful stroke is pending . . . [The music moves to the tonic major, and] the whole subject is recapitulated again. The pathos is enhanced by the fact that the tonic major has never before been heard in the whole work. This beautiful gleam of hope and consolation is a typical example of tragic irony; for the ensuing coda is unsurpassed anywhere in Beethoven for tragic power. (295)

Though I am not certain about how to fill out all the details of Tovey's story, it seems that the effect of D major and C♯ major in the last movement depends simultaneously upon the harmonic events of the entire quarter *and* their 'wonderful' placement in a large tragic plot. Presumably, then, Tovey regards the key relation of the first two movements as a conflict that initiates a tragic sequence of events.[46] If this is right, one cannot understand Tovey's sense of the unity of the piece without also understanding his dramatic conception. (And note that Tovey's own summarizing statement of unity does not reveal the model: that is, the phrase 'a perfect unity' does nothing to show that Tovey means 'unified *as a tragic drama*'.)

Unity is a somewhat indeterminate notion, and requires further determination to become evocative in relation to music. Various specific terms for unity, such as 'integrity' or 'fusion', imply more determinate conceptions. And more importantly, various conceptual frameworks, which may be metaphorical or fictional as well as literal, shape musical experience, and reveal the kinds of unity that may be attributed to music.

## Concluding Comments

Though this chapter has been complex, I can state my main conclusions simply. One should not assume that analysis is the same as discourse about musical unity. One should be reluctant to accept claims about unity, or repudiations of the topic of unity, that do not give a central place to musical experience. One should not assume that compositions are the only conceivable bearers of musical unity; the topics of experiences, worlds, and stories may reward further exploration. And the subtleties of vocabularies and conceptual schemes for thinking about, and experiencing, music, are extraordinary, a fine site for further study and invention.

---

[46] Here is a conjecture about a more detailed story. The key relations of the first two movements present an initial conflict. In the last movement, there is an act of recapitulation (resolution) that simultaneously acknowledges the need to address the initial conflict, and seems to do so by confirming the 'emotionally positive' member of the initial pair. But this resolution does not succeed, presumably because of the banal necessities of tonic centricity. A further act of recapitulation seems to solve the problem, retaining the major mode but returning the music to the initial tonic; but this also fails, perhaps because the unprecedented sound of the major tonic is at odds with its function as a return. Failure of these solutions brings on the tragic conclusion.

I shall close by saying something that I hope has been obvious throughout: I offer all these arguments and claims as contributions to an ongoing conversation. I hope they are helpful, and I look forward to the continuation of the conversation with great interest and curiosity.

## Appendix

Here I shall give a bit more detail about Dewey's ideas in *Art as Experience*. I begin with the notion of 'doing and undergoing'.

Of course, the most obvious examples of doing and undergoing involve physical interaction with the environment. Someone lifting a stone will both 'do' and 'undergo', physically altering the position of the object and also perceiving the result, and the two aspects will constantly affect each other.[47] It is easy to extend such an account to, for instance, etching or painting.[48]

But Dewey emphasizes that 'doing and undergoing' are important in all aesthetic experience and all relations to art; in reading, viewing, or listening to art, activity is crucial, even though it may not be overt physical activity. 'To perceive, a beholder must *create* his own experience' (54). The alternative is 'bare recognition', which 'is satisfied when a proper tag or label is attached' (53). Dewey is not very clear or specific about the nature of this 'doing', though he is definite about its importance. But clearly he means that a 'beholder' must actively construe and evaluate, seeking shape and significance, and in doing so must be ready to abandon stereotypes and pre-existing concepts.

Since everyday life always involves some interplay of doing and undergoing, one needs to ask what is added, or what is distinctive, when doing and undergoing constitute an individual experience, and, further, what is added for an aesthetic experience. Not surprisingly, since Dewey's goal is to understand art and aesthetic experience through the general notion of an experience, the second answer is mostly contained in the first.[49]

Dewey seems to propose two necessary conditions for an experience, having to do with awareness of the relationship between doing and undergoing and a sense of completeness. First, an experience occurs only when one constantly perceives the interaction of doing and undergoing—one is aware of the perceptual consequences of one's activity, and aware of the way perceptions lead to further activity. (This contrasts, of course, with a dull, habitual interaction with the environment.) Second, one has an experience only if

---

[47] 'A man does something; he lifts, let us say, a stone. In consequence he undergoes, suffers, something: the weight, strain, texture of the surface of the thing lifted' (44).

[48] 'The hand moves with etching needle or with brush. The eye attends and reports the consequence of what is done. Because of this intimate connection, subsequent doing is cumulative and not a matter of caprice nor yet of routine' (49–50).

[49] It is worth mentioning, especially since Dewey is not clear on this point, that Dewey's notion of an experience does not correspond exactly to idiomatic usage of the term 'an experience'. That is, everything Dewey calls 'an experience' would also be 'an experience' in ordinary usage, but not conversely. Ordinary usage allows 'an experience' to be chaotic, fragmentary, unsatisfying, and unpleasant: for instance, I could say, of being lost in a confusing building when all I want to do is leave, '*That* was an experience!'

Of course this failure to match ordinary usage does not affect Dewey's project, which can be described as the specification of one kind of experience common to artistic and non-artistic contexts.

the interaction leads to a point of stability, a successful adjustment between the organism and the environment, yielding a sense of completion.[50]

What more is needed for an experience to become aesthetic? The answer will imply Dewey's definition of art, since art objects are just objects that are made with the intention that they will provide aesthetic experiences. But on Dewey's account, art and the aesthetic do not have unprecedented qualities that separate them from the rest of life; rather, they possess to a conspicuous degree qualities that, less conspicuously, make up part of everyday life. It seems that an aesthetic experience is just an experience in which one is particularly clearly aware of the interaction of doing and undergoing, and enjoys that interaction partly for its own sake, rather than deriving one's satisfaction solely from meeting a practical goal.[51]

If one's thought and action are not directed exclusively at the production of some practical result, the interaction between doing and undergoing can become more intense, in several ways. Doing can be oriented more to the production of immediately perceptible consequences, rather than relatively delayed effects. Undergoing can focus on perceptible qualities without regarding them as evidence about facts that fall outside the current experience. And when completeness does not depend on accomplishing a practical task (for instance, building a strong stone wall), the sense of completeness can be more continuous, rather than emerging only at the end after a period of somewhat unpleasant suspense.

The last point is important. Here is one of Dewey's formulations on the subject:

In the practice and reasoning of ordinary life . . . the sense of the conclusion or consummation comes, comparatively at least, only at the end, instead of being carried at every stage. This postponement of the sense of completion, this lack of the presence of continuous perfecting, reacts, of course, to reduce means used to the state of *mere* means. (172)

Artists at work can provide clear illustration of 'continuous perfecting':

Fulfilling, consummating, are continuous functions, not mere ends, located at one place only. An engraver, painter, or writer is in process of completing at every stage of his work. He must at each point retain and sum up what has gone before as a whole and with reference to a whole to come. (56)

But, as one would expect, Dewey believes that the sense of continuous consummation should also characterize beholding, reading, or listening.

There is an interesting potential ambiguity in this notion of continuous consummation. A question will bring out the ambiguity. Would the experience seem complete if one

---

[50] Here is the end of the little story about lifting a stone: 'The stone is too heavy or too angular, not solid enough; or else the properties undergone show it is fit for the use for which it is intended. The process continues until a mutual adaptation of the self and the object emerges and the particular experience comes to a close' (44).

[51] This is fairly clear in Dewey's definition of an object of art: 'An object is peculiarly and dominantly esthetic, yielding the enjoyment characteristic of esthetic perception, when the factors that determine anything which can be called *an* experience are lifted high above the threshold of perception and are made manifest for their own sake' (57). Of course, the point about enjoying those factors 'for their own sake' is Dewey's version of the familiar eighteenth-century notion of 'disinterestedness'; but his development in relation to 'an experience' is original and valuable.

stopped at any point before the end, or would it seem fragmentary? Dewey's formulation seems to mandate both possibilities: one continuously 'retains and sums up' the experience *both* 'as a whole' *and* 'with reference to a whole to come'. That is, one should be continuously aware of what the qualities of the experience would be if the present moment were the last, and of what the qualities of the experience might be if the experience continues in various ways.

I find all this marvellously apt as generalization about many musical experiences. For instance, in construing music, it is often fruitful to avoid mere labelling or recognition, resisting classification of the sounds as instances of familiar kinds.[52] Part of an experience can be a continuous awareness of the perceptual consequences of one's interpretive activity, and of the way new perceptions lead to further, new construals. This awareness is enjoyable for its own sake. And throughout a listening experience, one can enjoy the act of 'retaining and summing up what has gone before', both 'as a whole and with reference to a whole to come'. The end of the experience will have a fully satisfying sense of completeness.[53]

General accounts of the nature of art have been considered problematic for several decades, especially when, like Dewey's, they centre on an 'aesthetic attitude'.[54] So it may seem that a return to Dewey's ideas of the early 1930s is a step backward. But in using Dewey's work as a basis for claims about music, one need not endorse the ambitious generalizations that would now be considered problematic. For the musical case it need not matter whether Dewey has given a plausible general account of all art or all aesthetic experience. Nor need one insist on a general account of all music or all musical experience. If Dewey's ideas can lead to plausible claims about some important range of musical experience—common present-day experiences of eighteenth- and nineteenth-century instrumental works—that is sufficiently interesting.

So in my use of Dewey I have hoped to evade issues about essences and definitions. I suggest that Dewey's general description of an aesthetic experience provides a model

---

[52] In music theory, such resistance goes by the name of 'contextual analysis'; it is an important element in Milton Babbitt's thought, and was more fully developed by Benjamin Boretz in *Meta-Variations* (published in *Perspectives of New Music* in several instalments, from 8/1 (Fall–Winter 1969) to 11/2 (Spring–Summer 1973)). The term 'contextual' abbreviates the thought that local events should be interpreted with reference to the context provided by a unique individual composition, rather than a general theory—for instance, a theory of tonal harmony. It is a confusing term, since musicologists also refer to 'contextual interpretations'—that is, interpretations that move beyond the individual work to consider other musical and non-musical factors. So a 'contextual' interpretation, in one usage, insists on the boundary of the individual composition, while in the other usage, it insists on crossing that boundary.

[53] These aspects of a Deweyan account of listening find clear parallels in three essays on music and time written by Benjamin Boretz in the mid-1970s. See 'A World of Times', 'Musical Cosmology', and 'What Lingers on (When the Song is Ended)', all published in *Perspectives of New Music*, respectively, 12 (Fall–Winter 1973, Spring–Summer 1974), 315–18; 15/2 (Spring–Summer 1977), 122–32; 16/1 (Fall–Winter 1977), 102–9. These essays seem to retain a conventional emphasis on the composition, rather than the experience, but Boretz's observations are readily recast in more Deyewan terms. In fact, Boretz is plainly describing the composition 'as experienced'—that is, a particular kind of interaction between listener and music, not a composition 'in itself'. Shortly after writing these articles, Boretz turned his own formulations emphatically toward experience; see 'If I am a Musical Thinker . . .', *Perspectives of New Music*, 20 (Fall–Winter 1981, Spring–Summer 1982), 464–517.

[54] Morris Weitz, 'The Role of Theory in Aesthetics', *Journal of Aesthetics and Art Criticism*, 15 (1957), 27–35, and W. E. Kennick, 'Does Traditional Aesthetics Rest on a Mistake?', *Mind*, 67 (1958), 317–34, are classic attacks on the project of defining art. Kennick goes on, somewhat as I do, to suggest that traditional aesthetics can be used in an anti-essentialist spirit.

for a satisfying description of musical experiences—that is, of what some musical experiences can be, for some listeners. And the occurrence of such musical experiences, as a result of the interaction of listener and music, constitutes one important kind of musical unity.[55]

---

[55] At the risk of redundancy, let me be clear here. I am not saying that the occurrence of an experience shows the unity of the composition. Rather, the unity of an interaction that can be called 'an experience' is one important kind of musical unity.

# 9

## How Music Matters: Poetic Content Revisited

### Scott Burnham

Only connect.

E. M. Forster

### I

The idea that music is graced with poetic content is as old as the mythical history of music itself. Orpheus, after all, was the ultimate poet, and it was not simply the words he sang, but rather his musical skills as singer and player that could move even the inorganic world to sympathy. The choruses of ancient Greek drama brought music, words, and dance together (or, rather, chose not to separate them) in order to represent something like the concerted mores of contemporaneous society when faced with the action on the stage. But if the Greeks thus felt that music, in conjunction with poetry, communed with and about nature, as well as human nature, it is only at the outset of the nineteenth century, the threshold of our modern aesthetic values, that artists and thinkers began to seek in instrumental music itself something higher than poetry, something to which poetry might now aspire.

This attitude toward music was of a piece with the general Romantic notion that human life was no longer closely tied to nature, and that only music remained as the symbolic locus of this bond. The union of music and nature was aptly symbolized in German Romantic literature by the fabled Aeolian harp and in Continental music theory by the overtone series and tonality. Romantic thought treated both music and nature as hieroglyphs of a more innocent, golden age of humanity, a time when man was united with nature, and language with music. But now man and his language were felt to be irrevocably sundered from nature and music. Perceiving themselves as having lost the living connection, artists were now confined to sending music (and words after it) into the gulf that separated the reality of the modern age from cherished ideality. Music was indeed the sound of that gulf—it thus symbolized both the presence and the absence of the ideal. Music's invisibility, temporal transience, and unarguable immediacy combined to create a symbolic language truly befitting an ideal presence no longer as ubiquitous as the light of day but now concentrated in the mystery and power of the visitation.

Allegedly in league with the *Ding an sich*, privy to the hidden impulses of the will, music was now a conduit of transcendent revelation, paradoxically direct and indirect, internal and external, immediate yet in need of semantic mediation, Orphic rather than prosaic. Music was thought to affect its listeners at an intensely personal level while being strikingly impersonal, engaging both the faceless many and the individual, as something which was, at the same time, universal and highly individual, invisible and concrete. Music's nearest correlate in these particulars was the 'word of God', which could address an entire congregation in the same terms and yet hold a distinct meaning for each member.

All this might seem to indicate a corrosion of faith in human language, rather than a sudden conversion to the power of music—yet, if anything, the Romantics granted language an enhanced ability to capture spiritual intimations. But whereas verbal language had to be purposefully muddied, made obscure and elliptical, fragmented, and—in a word—problematized, in order to achieve the desired form of aesthetic communication, music had only to continue its reflexive, largely hermetic discourse. Given the Romantic predilection for the suggestive fragment, the 'sentimental' approximation, and the intimation, music became the premier modality of Romanticism, for its referential moorings remain invisible, and, like the stars, leave only points of light, which listeners are free to construe into meaningful constellations. It is important to remember that behind this view of music the notion of language lingers on; music is here ennobled as a kind of ideal language, perhaps even a primal language. Thus there is a pointed irony in the Romantic projection of music as a wordless, therefore supreme, art: whereas verbal language is said to have lost some of its power in the face of music, the concept itself of language has in fact gained greater power by providing music with an epistemological, if not ontological, status.

Music and language become configured within a mutual exchange: music provides language with a modality fitted to the Romantic aesthetic ethos, and language provides music with a grounding, with a default modality that sets music apart and defines its special quality. In other words, music is only a *kind* of language, whereas verbal language *is* language—yet, music is a higher language. And if Romantic thought is wont to treat language and music as the now separate components of a former, pre-lapsarian unity—with music now shading up toward the ideal, and language down to the real—we might add that they are still attracted each to each other. For music conceived as the language of revelation still unfailingly provokes a verbal reaction, if only to ensure that it is indeed a revelation by verbally intimating what it might be a revelation of. Thus, music no longer in need of words now seems more than ever in need of words. This paradox can be formulated as follows: language lets music speak in its own voice (allows it a voice that is 'beyond words'), even while it insists on lending music *its* voice (by translating what music is saying). The obligatory assurance that words can never do justice to the revelation that is music has never stopped anyone from the attempt, and in fact stages the attempt, which is after all the central challenge for the Romantic literary artist: how to fit the reality of words to the revelation of ideality. Understood in this way, our verbal relationship to music is fundamentally poetic.

The new conception of music as a privileged form of commerce with the realm of the spirit contributed to an acute shift in attitude toward music in the criticism of the early nineteenth century. No longer did critics make rule-based material demands on pieces of music; pieces of music now made spiritual demands on critics. A. B. Marx conceived of the spirit, in the critic and in the musical work, as that greater whole which combines and transcends its several parts: namely, reason, imagination, and emotion. '[B]eyond the intellect's mere recognition of the form of a work and beyond a work's merely sensuous, and general, excitation of feeling, a higher essence reveals itself.'[1] To connect with this higher essence and thereby successfully interpret a musical work, the critic must approach the work with an 'intimate surrendering of the entire soul'.[2]

And here the hermeneutic impulse begins to flourish in music criticism. In accordance with the views of Friedrich Schleiermacher, Marx would claim that understanding a piece of music requires a certain amount of divination, and that this is warranted by the very nature of humankind. As Hans-Georg Gadamer explains, 'This is, in fact, Schleiermacher's presupposition, namely that all individuality is a manifestation of universal life and hence "everyone carries a tiny bit of everyone else within himself, so that divination is stimulated by comparison with oneself".'[3] To speak in the language of Marx, it was now incumbent upon the listener to fathom the spirit of the composer, as expressed in the soul of the musical work—and this is most readily achieved by consulting one's own spirit, one's nearest resource for understanding the spirit of another. Music encourages listeners to reach within themselves, understanding in their own way the spiritual experience of music by finding their own language to convey it. Music—and the understanding of music—now falls under the rubric of spirit and its divination, once the intellectual preserve of biblical hermeneutics. And again we are confronted with the analogy of the word of God, with the attempt to understand something felt to be greater than oneself, yet somehow within oneself.

The subjective basis of this secular religion was predictably abandoned in our own century, as critics fled from the twilight vagaries of spiritual divination into the comfortable rigours of formalism and structuralism. The logic of structured

[1]  Adolph Bernhard Marx, 'Etwas über die Symphonie', *Berliner allgemeine musikalische Zeitung*, 1 (1824), 183.
[2]  Ibid.
[3]  Hans-Georg Gadamer, *Truth and Method* (New York, 1982), 166.

expression now began to hold sway over the act of expression itself, the aesthetic artefacts of human emotional life understood first and foremost as structures, their examination (best left to specialists) safely removed from any contaminating emotional implications. Yet many were the hard-edged, heady joys of discovery, as the emotional rewards of interacting with music were apparently transferred from the shared connection of understanding to the power of explanation. Hegelian notions of the concretion and apperception of ideality suffered under a kind of Kantian backlash as structuralist theorists, in their own version of the search for lost universals, felt they were close to descrying the very shape of human cognition, of our window on the world. Characteristically, the metalanguages now employed to deal with music moved away from verbal language to more formal languages. From this new point of view, the construction of a dramatic programme for a work of instrumental music could only seem a childish exercise, a fairy-tale version of what the music is really about.

## II

The characterizations I have offered of nineteenth-century hermeneut and twentieth-century formalist are to some degree caricatures of historical narrative, and to claim a fundamental dichotomy between the two types on the basis of method alone would be misleading. For the assumptions about music underlying each position remain largely the same, in that both pledge obeisance to the power of the musical work and to its integrity. One might say that if the Romantic hermeneut has religion, the formalist of this century has a church: both honour the idea of the autonomous, sacrosanct work, but there is now much more in the way of institutionalized priestcraft.

Even their methods are more similar than recent polemics would have us understand. At first blush, it seems clear that hermeneutic interpretation is premissed on being provisional and contingent, while latter-day analysis is premissed on achieving closure—but in actual practice, much about analysis is provisional, and much about hermeneutic interpretation achieves closure. Perhaps the perceived difference has to do with the historical foundation of the two disciplines: hermeneutic criticism is unambiguously allied with the *Geisteswissenschaften*, the human sciences, while theory-based analysis has roots both in the human sciences and in natural science. Detractors of analysis often assume that it attempts to fly solely by the lights of the (now outmoded) view of essentialist science, the view that music is like a natural object which could one day be explained, if only our science were good enough. But if theory-based analysis is in some sense modelled on scientific discourse, its actual practice is much closer to hermeneutic interpretation, for it involves a back-and-forth motion between the world of the work and the experience and tendencies of the analyst. In the best analysis, there is always an open feeling that the musical work can change one's analytical presuppositions, or—at the least—can participate in a dialogue with those suppositions.

Thus the practice of analysis is not really the powerful, science-like tool that Joseph Kerman describes with the following words: 'Its methods are so straightforward, its results so automatic, and its conclusions so easily tested and communicated that every important American critic at the present time has involved himself or implicated himself centrally with analysis.'[4] Here analysis is clearly being counterpointed to a developing idea of hermeneutic and historically aware criticism, and is thus being made to look like the machinery of hard science (or what hard science used to be thought to look like before it became obvious to scientists that it is much more like a hermeneutic activity, where object and subject talk to one another—in fact, science might more readily find a model in the practice of musical analysis than vice versa).

And if analysis is closer to hermeneutic interpretation than we generally imagine, some of the explicitly hermeneutic approaches of this century can be said to share the positivist concerns more often attributed to analysis. Arnold Schering, for example, promoted detailed literary readings of the works of Beethoven, interpretations that appear to partake of the hermeneutic spirit. Yet what Schering offers is not hermeneutic understanding, but rather an explanatory key. Such a key is presumed to unlock the musical work and often takes the form of a kind of text underlay. The excitement in this critical approach is something like working a crossword puzzle or reading a detective story for the first time: one is led to assume that a solution awaits, if only one knew how to read the clues. And the clues include not only suggestive aspects of the music, but scraps of attributive evidence from Beethoven's notebooks or conversations or from the shelves of his library. These are led to the witness stand as if to provide factual, evidentiary legitimacy for what might seem to be unforgivably fanciful readings of the musical works. Yet it is precisely the reliance on this sort of evidence which, far from giving the hermeneutic impulse legitimacy, in fact blows the cover of this would-be hermeneut, revealing the positivist impulse underneath: music is treated as something that needs to be explained, something that primarily encodes some other order of experience, and, like all codes, demands to be broken, and is not satisfactorily negotiated until it is translated.

The results of such readings can be bracing, and can indeed open up new paths for listening—but they are ultimately prescriptive, and have little to do with the hermeneutic impulse of the nineteenth century. For in compulsively seeking evidence from outside the work and outside the critic, practitioners of this type of poetic criticism are precisely denying, eschewing, or otherwise avoiding the spiritual connection of one interior experience to another. The basis of

[4] Joseph Kerman, 'How We Got into Analysis, and How to Get Out', *Critical Inquiry*, 7, (1980), 321.

interaction with a musical work has shifted from personal truth to reasoned argument, from a matter of conviction to one of convincing. But whatever their motivation, or their method, the stories they tell often resonate in ways similar to those of the previous century's critics: in the end, what makes us want to entertain such accounts at all is not the positivist evidence the critic may compile, but the way the resulting story (however arrived at) poeticizes something we feel to be real in the way we take in the piece. What is disturbing is to have such a reading presented in the form of a scholarly argument—as if it were more important to determine what a piece means than what it can mean. As soon as a privileged version of a piece's meaning is determined in this way, the piece is stopped dead in its tracks as a viable artwork that might continue to approach us; it is no longer permitted to meet us half-way, for now it has become definitively situated, rendered a museum of its own meaning, its listeners reduced to curators or collectors.

Truly hermeneutic interpretations, on the other hand, are more invested in connecting than collecting. The opposition of these two verbs, 'to collect' and 'to connect', yields more than the opportunity of an alliterative pairing: they indicate two different ways of interacting with and therefore conceptualizing the artwork. We cannot connect with a work that has been closed off; our only option is to collect such works, to own or possess them. When we are in the business of connecting with an artwork, however, we assume that the work is open. This distinction reveals a better way to characterize the difference between the prevailing nineteenth-century standpoint and that of our own century, for the operative dichotomy is not between the explicit poetic critic and the explicit formal analyst, but between surveyors of the open work and purveyors of the closed work.

A comparison of Schering's approach with that of an apparently antithetical contemporary, Heinrich Schenker, helps the point. Despite the polar difference in their methods, they both rely on the concept of the closed work: Schering's explicit use of the word 'key' to denote what he was providing for the works of Beethoven is reminiscent of the attitude of Schenker, who described his analysis of the 'Eroica' as being the first to portray the work in its true content.[5] And if Schering's poetic approach has an implicit positivist basis, Schenker's analytical system can be said to have an implicit poetic basis, in the form of fundamental metaphorical takes on music that are picturesque and even poetically resonant.[6] His notion of *Tonwille*, for example, is one such poetic conceit. Thus we can speak of the implicit poetic basis of explicitly formalist analysis and the implicit positivist basis of explicitly poetic criticism. This ironic dialectic between Schenker

[5] Heinrich Schenker, 'Beethovens Dritte Sinfonie zum erstenmal in ihrem wahren Inhalt dargestellt', in *Das Meisterwerk in der Musik*, vol. 3 (Munich, 1930), 25–84.

[6] Some of these have been imaginatively explored by Brian Hyer, in 'Picturing Music', a talk presented at the New England Conference of Music Theorists, Connecticut College, 10 Apr. 1994. On the subject of implicit metaphors embedded in the language of music analysts, see Marion A. Guck, 'Analytical Fictions', *Music Theory Spectrum*, 16/2 (Fall 1994), 217–30.

and Schering is emblematic for the first half of the twentieth century: formal-ism emerges within the domain of poetic criticism, and poetics lie submerged within formalist analysis. Both standpoints, poetic understanding and formal explanation, are active components of the landscape of musical thought, but now the poetic has been consciously repressed in favour of the formal, as the vision of the closed work begins to dominate the horizon.

It is no doubt clear from my rhetoric up to this point that I have been clearing the ground for a defence of the standpoint of the open work and the possibility of connection. I would not wish this to be perceived, however, as the position of a disgruntled *laudator temporis acti*. For I am not advocating a wholesale return to what Thomas Sipe has called the 'metaphorical' stage of music interpreta-tion.[7] I am not asking us to deny what we have learned from more recent modes of interacting with music that have come to bear the stigmatizing label 'formalism'. Instead, I am asking us to recognize that we have never truly abandoned the notion of poetic significance in music. This involves acknowl-edging the poetic content and applicability of our analytic assumptions, as well as the analytic utility of our poetic observations, allowing the poetic and the analytic to mingle freely, as mutually enhancing perspectives, rather than covertly and stiltedly, as they have under the systematic oppressions of academic balkanization.

I would like to illustrate such an approach by elaborating, at times analytically, on the type of poetic approach to music broadly associated with nineteenth-century criticism. This means turning to the music of Beethoven. For if any one composer can be said to be implicated in each stage of the historical and con-ceptual dialectic adumbrated above between music and language, formalism and poetic hermeneutics, and open and closed conceptions of the musical work, it is Beethoven. His music played a motivating role at the outset of poetic criticism, forcing music critics to complete the paradigm shift toward the organic artwork already negotiated by literary critics. And the first order of business of almost every subsequent new approach in both analysis and criticism has been to step up to the implied challenge of his music. In what follows I propose to examine the yield of a poetic approach to Beethoven's music, in order to identify the aspects of musical engagement it alone seems willing to address.

# III

What has Beethoven's music been heard to tell us? There has never been much doubt that Beethoven's music has in fact been trying to tell us something. In the daunting range of interpretations and analyses that surround his instrumental

---

[7] See Thomas Sipe, 'Interpreting Beethoven: History, Aesthetics, and Critical Reception' (Ph.D. diss., University of Pennsylvania, 1992), ch. 2: 'The History and Taxonomy of Beethoven Criticism'.

music, Beethoven has steadily assumed what I have called a 'telling presence'.[8] Inheriting a style that enjoyed widespread comprehension and, indeed, claims to universality (it became, in the hands of German music theorists of the later nineteenth and early twentieth centuries, the essential basis of all Western music), Beethoven has generally been heard to narrate across the grain, seemingly in an effort to convey something above and beyond the syntactical and affective conventions of the Classical style. From E. T. A. Hoffmann's intimation of the terror of the supernatural and A. B. Marx's claims for the expression of transcendent *Ideen* to the rather more mundane literary readings of Schering and Owen Jander, a powerfully compelling voice has consistently been heard to speak from and even above this music.[9] Yet Beethoven's voice may more accurately be said to narrate *through*, or *with*, the Classical style. This is especially true of the middle-period works, where Beethoven rhetorically marks the syntactic junctures of the underlying form in such a way as to shape those junctures into the highest peaks of an intensely dramatic topography, and consequently lend sonata form a power beyond that of a stylistic norm. The mythic power of these realizations of the form creates a broader, deeper appeal than an aesthetic appreciation of stylistic mastery and wit: sonata form now takes on the aspect of an ethos, anchored in the moral bedrock of the age. Poetic assessments of the content of Beethoven's music, by directly addressing this moral dimension (arguably the foundation of his music's perennial appeal), can provide terms in which the music hits home, terms which register its most obvious heft, and permit its 'message' to be both plain and profound.

To elaborate this point, I would like to consider a famous passage in Beethoven's Fifth Symphony: namely, the appearance of music from the Scherzo in the Finale, in order to understand how such a moment engages poeticizing critics at the level of a profound statement about the human condition. At the very least, the passage makes problematic certain Classical-style formal conventions; the radical incursion of the Scherzo into the Finale affects the form at both intra-movement and inter-movement levels. For one cannot explore the return of the Scherzo theme in the Finale without first considering the connection between the last two movements. It would seem that the theme of the Finale and the transition from the Scherzo are inseparable: the Finale needs an introduction which makes the baldest display of C major fanfare both possible and effective; and, conversely, the tensions generated by the transition passage demand a resolution both straightforward and weighty.[10] The theme needs to be heard to work against something, otherwise its musculature is rendered absurd. This

---

[8] In *Beethoven Hero* (Princeton, 1995), 144 ff.

[9] It is thus no coincidence that Beethoven's music is the subject of much recent work in musical semiotics, notably including that of Kofi Agawu, *Playing with Signs: A Semiotic Interpretation of Classic Music* (Princeton, 1991), ch. 6, and Robert Hatten, *Musical Meaning in Beethoven: Markedness, Correlation, and Interpretation* (Bloomington, Ind., 1994).

[10] Rudolph Réti regards the entire Scherzo as an *Auftakt* to the Finale; see Réti, *The Thematic Process of Music* (Westport, Conn., 1951), 185.

inseparability provides, perhaps, the most direct motivation for the return of the Scherzo music immediately before the recapitulated theme.

But there are other factors at play here. Beethoven achieves several things by bringing the Scherzo theme and its transition back specifically during the retransition of his Finale. First, he carries off one of his favourite ploys for making the recapitulation more momentous: he introduces a quieter passage fraught with anticipatory tension. He had already done this with great effect in the first movement, when the music's sails fall slack after having ventured into a windless, quietly ominous stretch of F sharp minor; one also recalls the first movement of the 'Eroica' with its *sotto voce* tremoli and famous horn call. In all these cases the recapitulation is heard to *impend*: its arrival becomes a matter of dramatic urgency, even necessity.

Second, Beethoven prepares the entrance of the Scherzo theme in the Finale in a way that emphatically marks it as the result of a disjunction. Although it takes place as the second stage of a lengthy dominant pedal-point whose ultimate role is that of a retransition (bars 132 ff.), it appears only after the first stage breaks off completely—the music does not work itself to the Scherzo theme the way it works itself, in the first movement, to that F sharp minor sonority. Instead, the Scherzo theme is what materializes after the music of the development has reached a *non plus ultra*.[11] This process is worth tracing. The attainment of the pedal-point at bar 132 is perhaps the most climactic moment yet in the Finale (not including the drama of its very opening, of course). This is a grandiose passage, and when Beethoven introduces the two chromatic chords in bars 141–3, G major is stabilized as a chord of resolution, an effect immediately consolidated by the retarding arpeggiations which follow. In fact, the dominant is now so laden with monumentality that it slows to a stop, too heavy to move. The almost faceless grandiosity and obtuse immobility of this dominant is strange, and it does nothing to encourage the business of recapitulating. For Beethoven could hardly follow such an excess of splendour with the recapitulation of the similarly splendid first theme[12]—this would surely be piling surfeit upon surfeit, and would deaden the listener's sensitivity to the overall feeling of triumph, a deleterious possibility that worried Berlioz and Oulibicheff in connection with this Finale.

The Scherzo citation which follows recreates the necessary precondition for the splendour of the opening theme, while serving harmonically to transform the stable dominant into an unstable dominant seventh.[13] The bare Gs that precede the Scherzo theme turn the previous wash of sound into a

---

[11] In this regard, its entrance bears some similarity to the arrival of the 'new theme' in the 'Eroica' first movement, which is also prepared by a climactic section that cannot be continued but can only break off.

[12] Schenker makes this observation as well; for him, the return of the Scherzo creates a parallelism with the transition to the Finale that is much more effective than a direct link of the fortissimo of the recapitulation with the fortissimo of bars 132–53. See Heinrich Schenker, *Beethoven V. Sinfonie* (Vienna, 1925), 65.

[13] Again, see ibid. In Schenker's analysis, the Scherzo provides Beethoven with a passing seventh, transforming a composed-out dominant into a dominant pedal-point.

simple yet concentrated drip, and the repeated note begins more pointedly to bear the expectant aspect of a dominant (as any repeated single note will tend to do in a tonal context, given the overtone structure). Altogether, the entire scene is one of high drama: the sudden disappearance of all that sound, now funnelled into the iterations of a single pitch, creates a musical void, a palpable absence. When the Scherzo theme enters, it does more than resolve a dominant: it offers something familiar, if not entirely reassuring, to fill the aching space.

How do specifically programmatic interpretations of this symphony tend to construe this moment? The metaphor most often pressed into service for the return of the Scherzo theme is that of an unsettling visitation from the past. Indeed, for several such commentators the return of the Scherzo theme takes on the presence of a ghost: Hermann Kretzschmar likens it to the spirit of Banquo appearing at Macbeth's feast table. The comparison is apt, for, like Banquo's ghost, the Scherzo theme suddenly materializes at a point of high revelry. In Paul Bekker's view, the victory hymn (at the end of the development) reaches a climax and then breaks off suddenly, 'as if startled by the threats of a ghostly apparition . . . [G]loomy images hold the soul in thrall and wake memories of the hopeless struggles of the past. But the present is more powerful.'[14] Readings of this music as apparitional work well with the harmonic identity of the passage: as part of an extended dominant pedal-point, the Scherzo theme's harmonic status as a tonic is undermined; it is a dominant-heavy C minor, which, like a ghostly projection with no certain grounding in substantiality, all too readily recedes into the twilight dominant now heading toward the dawning rays of C major. The image of a ghost captures with some precision the ambiguous status of this dominant-heavy tonic, the way it makes a show of corporeal stability while functioning at a broader level as a 6–4 suspension of dominant harmony. There could be no questioning C minor's stability back in the actual Scherzo, for there it is the fundamental tonic to begin with (although it wouldn't be particularly far-fetched to interpret, retroactively, the Scherzo itself as dominant-heavy, as part of a process by which C minor begins to be undermined so as to collapse into a dominant that will then lead to a redeeming C major[15]).

More important than any homology between the metaphor of the ghost and the harmonic process of the passage is the emotional *mise-en-scène* to which such readings appeal. They invoke a nexus of related concepts: the past is associated with gloom, terror, and possibly remorse (remember Macbeth and Banquo); the past invades the present, becomes present itself (as an incorporeal ghost), challenging but not overcoming the power of the real present.[16]

---

[14] Paul Bekker, *Beethoven* (Berlin, 1911), 190.

[15] Such a reading might interpret the four movements as enacting a large-scale teleological harmonic progression: i–VI– $i_4^6$–V–I, with the Scherzo and transition as the $i_4^6$–V component.

[16] It is in the imposing shadow of this interpretive tradition that Réti's reading of the Scherzo as an expression of 'utter optimism' seems so luridly wrong, and can only be invoked as the exception that proves the rule. See Réti, *Thematic Process*, 185.

It is apparent that for these listeners, Beethoven's repetition of musical material from a previous movement represents much more than a means of organic coherence, drawing its motivation instead from a palpable psychological scenario.

The twentieth-century critic Donald Francis Tovey offers a less supernatural, more strictly psychological, version of this incursion of past into present, one which can lead to a sophisticated view of the nature of narration in this symphony and in the Classical style. When we hear the return of the Scherzo, Tovey claims, 'we cannot forget that the terror is passed'. Beethoven cites the Scherzo 'as a memory, which we know for a fact but can no longer understand' (that is, we know it happened, as a historical fact, but we can no longer be directly affected by it, no longer understand it as a present source of terror). Thus the Scherzo citation 'confirms the truth of the former terror and the security of the present triumph'.[17] Tovey is clearly not haunted by the Scherzo's return. Instead, he treats its appearance as an act of narration: a previous terror is now recollected from the vantage-point of a secure present. This could provide us with an important insight into the function of the Classical-style recapitulation as a locus of narration, a place from which earlier musical events may be cast into a kind of past tense. For Tovey, the recapitulation of Beethoven's Finale replays the terror and denouement of the entire symphony, now as a memory.

Sir George Grove touches on some musical aspects of the recapitulated Scherzo theme that support hearing it as a memory rather than as an actual return. He mentions the fact that the return of the Scherzo theme is no literal reprise, but actually represents something like a continuation of the last form of the theme, as it appeared within the Scherzo itself.[18] The oboe in particular transforms this theme into a more retrospective version (see bars 172–207). This relates to the way the oboe is used in the first movement. At the very end of that movement, the oboe sighs along as the first theme is heard one last time, transformed by the lyric winds and the tonic pedal-point into an almost wistful memory, which is then obliterated with fortissimo cadential blasts. And at the first fermata of the recapitulation the oboe sounds its famous cadenza, which sums up the line played by the oboe over the recapitulated theme. The oboe is thus given a narrating role throughout the symphony, as a 'voice-over' that signals retrospection.[19]

Why use the voice of the oboe at these spots? We might invoke the old adage:

---

[17] Donald Francis Tovey, *Symphonies and Other Orchestral Works* (Oxford, 1989), 59. In a similar vein, A. B. Marx refers to the return of the Scherzo as a 'menschennothwendige Rückerinnerung' (*Ludwig van Beethoven: Leben und Schaffen*, vol. 2, 3rd edn., ed. by Gustav Behncke (Berlin, 1875), 68).

[18] Sir George Grove, *Beethoven and his Nine Symphonies* (London, 1896), 170.

[19] The voice of the oboe at these moments seems to meet Carolyn Abbate's brilliantly stringent requirements for the creation of a musical 'past tense'. See her *Unsung Voices: Opera and Musical Narrative in the Nineteenth Century* (Princeton: Princeton University Press, 1991), 52–60.

'That which was hard to bear is sweet to remember'.[20] The oboe's bitter-sweet timbre and lyrical persona offer the emotive presence of a first-person narrator, and the resultant music serves as a metaphor for how we emotionally take in a 'memory we know for a fact but can no longer understand'. Tovey's distinction between knowing and understanding, past tense and present tense, and memory and current experience, enriches the way we experience the business of formal return in this symphony, and suggests the sophisticated narration that can take place within Beethoven's heroic style, always assumed to be the quintessential model of straightforward enactment. For we are now encouraged to hear Beethoven's voice not simply as the unfolding of some one-dimensional dramatic process, but as including the resonant space of another dimension, the oblique and potentially ironic dimension of memory and narration. Such a reading points the work toward our experience of consciousness, allows it to be more complex yet still directly accessible. This is indeed a hallmark trait of such poet-icizing observations: the music remains open to a level of experience that is profound, yet this connection can be made and felt without recourse to the specialized language of a professional.[21]

It may seem curious to proffer this claim in reference to one of the foremost professional critics of our century; for this reason, I would like now to turn to a very different witness, the novelist E. M. Forster. Whereas Tovey downplays the perceived terrors of the Scherzo theme in favour of issues of form, memory, and narration, Forster, in a well-known episode from *Howards End*, is wonderfully specific about the nature of the terror heard in the Scherzo and its return. His reading addresses a distinctly moral conflict, and ultimately calls into question what Tovey deemed 'the security of the present triumph'. The richness of Forster's interpretation will surely excuse an extensive quotation:

[T]he music [of the Scherzo] started with a goblin walking quietly over the universe, from end to end. Others followed him. They were not aggressive creatures; it was that that made them so terrible. . . . They merely observed that there was no such thing as splendour or heroism in the world. After the interlude of elephants dancing, they returned and made the observation for the second time. Helen could not contradict them, for, once at all events, she had felt the same, and had seen the reliable walls of youth collapse. Panic and emptiness! Panic and emptiness! The goblins were right.

. . . as if things were going too far, Beethoven took hold of the goblins and made them do what he wanted. He appeared in person. He gave them a little push, and they began to walk in a major key instead of in a minor, and then—he blew with his mouth and they were scattered! Gusts of splendour, gods and demi-gods contending with vast swords, colour and fragrance broadcast on the field of battle, magnificent victory, magnificent

---

[20] 'Quae fuit durum pati, meminisse dulce est', from Seneca, *Hercules Furens*, line 656. Seneca's opposition of sweet to hard is governed at least partially by the combination of alliteration and assonance afforded by the two opposed terms, *durum* and *dulce*.

[21] Though I have chosen to explore Tovey's observation in terms of narration and musical form, the experience Tovey speaks of does not depend on such specialized speculation.

death! Oh, it all burst before the girl, and she even stretched out her gloved hands as if it was tangible. Any fate was titanic; any contest desirable; conqueror and conquered would alike be applauded by the angels of the utmost stars.

And the goblins—they had not really been there at all? They were only the phantoms of cowardice and unbelief? One healthy human impulse would dispel them? . . . Beethoven knew better. The goblins really had been there. They might return—and they did. It was as if the splendour of life might boil over and waste to steam and froth. In its dissolution one heard the terrible, ominous note, and a goblin, with increased malignity, walked quietly over the universe from end to end. Panic and emptiness! Panic and empti-ness! Even the flaming ramparts of the world might fall.

Beethoven chose to make all right in the end. He built the ramparts up. He blew with his mouth for the second time, and again the goblins were scattered. He brought back the gusts of splendour, the heroism, the youth, the magnificence of life and of death, and, amid vast roarings of a superhuman joy, he led his Fifth Symphony to its conclusion. But the goblins were there. They could return. He had said so bravely, and that is why one can trust Beethoven when he says other things.[22]

The ramifications of this passage range widely, proceeding from Forster's imaginative take on the Scherzo and Finale to a concise statement of the Beethoven ethos (why one can trust Beethoven, and how music can even qualify as a form of communication to which trust and belief are meaningful reactions). One can quickly take account of the more obvious metaphorical cor-respondences with the music: the dynamics and instrumentation (quiet bas-soons) bring to mind a goblin, not some more imposing monster;[23] the registral shape of the theme suggests that the creature walks across some large expanse. But Forster makes this expanse encompass the universe, and notes that the unassuming mien of the goblins is what renders them so terrible (a point embed-ded as well in the adverbial understatement: 'They *merely* observed that there was no such thing as splendour or heroism in the world'). The message of doubt is thus delivered not with Nietzschean thunder, but as something small and insinuating—as if doubt were so close by that it had no need to raise its voice. Yet this small voice of doubt knows the range of the universe, and traverses it as a habitude.

The Scherzo and Finale, taken together, are heard as the projection of the forces of doubt and faith, a brave acknowledgement of the void leading to an affirmation available to all: 'Any fate was titanic; any contest desirable.' Beethoven himself is deemed the moral agent of this affirmative impulse, for he is said to appear in person during the transition to the Finale; he is identified not with the goblins but with their dispersion, not with devilish doubt but with

---

[22] E. M. Forster, *Howards End* (New York: Vintage, 1921), 33–4.

[23] Forster's image of the goblin is reminiscent of Wilhelm von Lenz's whimsical view of the scherzo's return within the finale as a gnome who has been left behind in the bowels of the earth and has not yet heard the general rejoicing. See Lenz, *Beethoven: Eine Kunst-Studie*, Part Four: *Kritischer Katalog sämmtlicher Werke Ludwig van Beethovens mit Analysen derselben*, Third Part, Second Half: Op. 56 bis Op. 100 (Hamburg: Hoffmann & Campe, 1860), 76–7.

godlike affirmation.[24] This pretence not only confirms the usual image of Beethoven as a moral force, but situates him with the listener (in this case Helen) on the same side of the struggle.

But the drama does not end with the beginning of the Finale. The fineness of Forster's feeling for the musical process is again in evidence when Helen experiences the return of the goblins within the Finale. Unlike most commentators, Forster gives special consideration to the passage preceding the return of the music from the Scherzo: Helen notes that it is 'as if the splendour of life might boil over and waste to steam and froth'. This is not an inapt assessment of the way the dominant is presented at this point in the development. As noted above, this dominant is reached climactically, in bar 132, and it sounds as the issue of the entire development. But instead of leading to the tonic of the recapitulation, as one might reasonably expect of a dominant retransition, this dominant is itself tonicized (by the chromatic chords in bars 141–3) and then prolonged by a process of arpeggiation which broadens, grandly, to a halt.[25] The point of interest, in formal terms, is that all this grandiosity is expended not on the returning tonic but on the key area of the retransition. In this sense the passage may indeed be heard as a wasteful bit of revelry, splendour allowed to boil over.

And then a goblin reappears, with 'increased malignity'. Again Beethoven intercedes, dispelling 'panic and emptiness' with triumph and splendour. But Helen's goblin is not merely a phantom of fear, as in the readings of Kretzschmar and Bekker; it was really there. This, for Helen, is what Beethoven gives us to understand by bringing the Scherzo theme back in the Finale: although the goblins are ultimately dispersed, the point is that they do in fact appear at the very height of the Finale's affirmative celebrations. And this is what constitutes Beethoven's bravery, for he acknowledges the void at the heart of life's fullness, and then morally overpowers it with 'vast roarings of superhuman joy'.

And yet we are left, ultimately, with the presence of doubt. For one remembers—with Helen?—that no such noise was necessary to convince one of doubt. The possibility arises that we might hear the fabled affirmation of the heroic style as the overwrought exertion of bad faith, in that Beethoven overemphasizes closure and return. He narrates the form in such a way that we hear ultimate affirmation as a noise simply deafening us to the sound of doubt. Rose Rosengard Subotnick makes a similar point when she observes that Beethoven's rhetorical emphasis of primary structural junctures in effect questions the self-evidence of those junctures.[26] But while this may be read as evidence of bad faith in the underlying Classical-style form, we must also remember that in the

[24] This is similar to the view of Alexandre Oulibicheff, who hears the affirmative music of the finale as presaging Beethoven's own 'immense gloire posthume' by prevailing over the evils of earthly existence signified by the scherzo. Oulibicheff, *Beethoven, ses Critiques et ses Glossateurs* (Leipzig: Brockhaus, 1857), 206.

[25] Schenker, op. cit., 65, observes that this dominant is not a pedal point but a composing out.

[26] Rose Rosengard Subotnick, *Developing Variations: Style and Ideology in Western Music* (Minneapolis, 1991), 279.

main the effect is compellingly affirmative. That is, in so far as we hear Beethoven *narrating* sonata form, we may detect bad faith; but in so far as we feel the music as the enactment of a narration, and feel ourselves impelled along by this enactment, we feel we are experiencing actual affirmation. We can hear the noise of his rhetoric—'the vast roarings of superhuman joy'—as an attempt to make evident what is no longer self-evident, and we can also hear this noise as a transformation of the self-evident into the exalted. This leaves us with a tension not easily resolved, a tension not only at the foundation of the heroic style, but at the foundation of human faith and doubt: such music might in fact register as the sound of belief, taken as a complex mental state that, in some deep sense, is the sworn companion of doubt. This paradoxical juxtaposition is nowhere so evident as when the Scherzo music returns amid the noisy revelry of the Finale, and Forster's metaphorical reading thus allows us to hear the moment as so much more than the coherence-generating return of earlier material: it lays bare a central quandary of Beethoven's heroic style. For now this music is heard as symbolic of a struggle between faith and doubt that goes beyond the usual uncomplicated scenario of faith simply triumphing over doubt. And thus Tovey's scenario of memory and narration is here trumped and deepened; the irony is not simply that of the present moment retrospectively engaging, and being engaged by, the past—the ironic presence of the past—but of the most exalted and engaging affirmation imaginable being at the same time an expression of the power of doubt.[27]

Finally, Forster's interpretation merges the symphony's Scherzo and its Finale into one complex process, bringing us back again to the issue of Beethoven's use of Classical-style form. What are the implications for musical form of the Scherzo theme's reappearance? Remember that the transition to the Finale is generally heard as the grand denouement of the entire symphony, a passage into the light and triumph of C major, dispelling the gloom and oppression of C minor. By replaying this transitional passage, however condensed, within the retransition to the Finale's recapitulated theme, Beethoven embeds the process of denouement of the entire work within the ethos of sonata form. This works in two directions: the dramatic turning-point of the entire symphony can be heard to be recapitulated within the Finale, and the entire symphony can be heard to be conceived within the broadest reaches of the sonata-form impulse. This is because the transition to the Finale sounds like a Beethovenian retransition, an impression retroactively corroborated by the use of another version of the same music

---

[27] Thomas S. Grey interprets E. T. A. Hoffmann's reaction to the closing moment of the finale in nearly identical terms: 'Hoffmann's verbal "transliteration" of the closing measures into words . . . seems calculated to drive home the disconcertingly obsessive quality of the coda, a compulsive repetition belying some inner doubt' (*Wagner's Musical Prose: Texts and Contexts* (Cambridge, 1995), 94). And Nicholas Cook notes a similar irony in the Ninth Symphony: 'Beethoven's last symphony proclaims the ideals of universal brotherhood and joy; that is unmistakable. But at the same time, and just as unmistakably, it casts doubt upon them.' Later, Cook concludes that 'we . . . have to keep before us . . . the image of a Beethoven who was both earnest and ironical' (*Beethoven: Symphony No. 9* (Cambridge, 1993), 104–5).

as an actual retransition within the Finale. The recapitulation of the Finale is thus an echo of the grand resolution of the symphony, and the syntax of formal return is given a rhetorical significance beyond that of symmetry or the restoring of balance—it is now understood that a recapitulation can be made to bear the weight of an overwhelmingly dramatic resolution. By relating the sonata form of the Finale to a larger, overarching process that is marked so unmistakably as one of triumph after adversity, Beethoven indicates how high he has raised the stakes of sonata form. The idea of return ascends from a self-evident convention of syntax and style to the realm of mythic archetype—sonata form is heard as a musico-formal process that can invoke the broadest and most profound moral concerns of humankind. Thus transformed into a vehicle of mythic expression, the Beethovenian sonata form becomes a voice of human significance, telling the grand themes of quest, renewal, and closure.[28] It is at this level that poetic criticism seeks to meet Beethoven's music.

## IV

That Beethoven's works often build to a denouement somehow larger than life is a recurrent asseveration of poetic critics. The Ninth Symphony and the text of its Finale combine to provide another, even more transcendent example of this process. As in the Fifth Symphony, the Finale encompasses a resolution momentous enough to be said to serve the entire symphony. Specifically, the dissonant $V^9$ at the end of the 'Seid umschlungen' section of the Finale (bars 650–4) leads to a climactic resolution (the double fugue), a process that Leo Treitler has deemed the denouement of the entire symphony.[29] In the long-range harmonic progress of the movement, this dominant is surely what we have come to think of as a structural dominant; it follows an extended subdominant area (the G major 'Seid umschlungen' section), thus taking part in a large-scale cadential motion, and it also brings about the only dominant-activated return to D major from an extended section in another key (the return to D from the episode in B flat is worked through a chromatic modulation centring on the pitch F♯). This moment acts as something of a continental divide—from this point on, everything seems to flow downhill toward the ending. As James Webster puts it, in his comprehensive and convincing reading of the Finale as through-composed, 'the tonal and motivic forces move with increasing urgency toward a simple, definitive, and satisfying state of closure.'[30]

As an illustration of how a poetic approach can enrich a reading of the entire

---

[28] For an account of how poetic criticism has engaged the first movement of the 'Eroica' Symphony in the terms of a quest plot, see my 'On the Programmatic Reception of Beethoven's Eroica Symphony', *Beethoven Forum*, 1 (1992), 1–24.

[29] Leo Treitler, *Music and the Historical Imagination* (Cambridge, Mass., 1989), 64. For other, similar assessments of this passage see Cook, *Beethoven: Symphony No. 9*, 104.

[30] James Webster, 'The Form of the Finale of Beethoven's Ninth Symphony', *Beethoven Forum*, 1 (1992), 62.

symphony, I would like to consider this denouement as the marriage of a musical event and a poetic image: namely, the text 'über[m] Sternen[zelt] muss er [ein lieber Vater] wohnen' and the pulsing minor-ninth dominant. The image of the 'starry vault' will help us understand more completely just how this passage functions as a denouement of the entire symphony; we will find that in this case a poetic image not only renders the musical process very precisely, but suggests as well a deep-seated rationale for that process.

To begin, I will associate the presence of the twinkling stars specifically with the pitch B♭. Three things happen at once in bar 650: the chords in the winds start pulsating, the strings begin their tremoli, and the B♭ becomes dissonant when the E drops to A in the bass, a move that transforms the diminished-seventh sonority to a dominant seventh with minor ninth. The combination of pulsating winds and an acute, yet registrally removed, dissonance gives the stars of Schiller's text their twinkle. This effect is particularly enhanced by the place-ment of the dissonant B♭, high and away from the A in the musical space, yet not the highest note—in this way it enjoys a special status of dissonance, producing a vague sense of atmospheric disturbance without calling pointedly for resolu-tion, as it would were it at the very top of the texture.

Analysts love telling pitch stories, and the story of B♭ in the Ninth Symphony is a favourite.[31] In the first movement, D minor falls into B flat at the repetition of the first theme, anticipated by the bassoon's drop to B♭ from D in bar 49, the first of many dramatic drops of a major third throughout the symphony. The use of B flat for the repetition of the first theme establishes a kind of parallelism between the two keys, a relationship which is deepened when the second theme as well appears in B flat major rather than the more normative relative major, F. At the point of recapitulation the pitch B♭ is made distinctly problematic: its resolution to A is elided in the famous chord at bar 313. B flat major and D minor, as chords and as keys, seem somehow mutually permeable; their interactions are heard not to require the usual modulatory engineering.

After a Scherzo in which the B♭ might be said to recede back to some of its nor-mative roles as a flat-sixth scale degree in D minor,[32] the slow movement shows what an extended residence in B flat would indeed be like. From the prologuing seconds of its opening to the final quiet iterations of B flat major, this movement lives in an air of ideality and relaxed serenity (note the regal time scale of the theme and its echoes, and the effusively detailed embroideries of the theme's sub-sequent variations). Like the unveiling of a Grail, the second theme of this double variation reveals the quiet flame warming the entire movement; this vision is approached and left through mystical transitions whose agent is G♭/F♯ (the major third on the other side of D). A dramatically articulated falling major third is

---

[31] See e.g. the role of the B♭ as interpreted by Réti, *Thematic Process*, ch. 1: 'The Thematic Plan of the Ninth Symphony'.

[32] Most notably in the retransition to the Scherzo's recapitulation in bars 248 ff. and in the inflected flat-sixth degree effecting the return to D minor from the trio's D major drone (bar 530).

again heard in bar 133 (F to D♭), initiating a short harmonic excursion that seems about to expound some central secret of this realm, but instead flows on to an exultant tonic 6–4. In short, there is nothing earthbound about this movement; all is burnished mystery and musical beatitude.

The *Schreckensfanfare!* An earthly brace of trumpet and drums utterly shatters the peace of the third movement, shredding B♭'s veil of serenity with a raucously dissonant A. Holding the B♭, D, and F over into the first sonority of the Finale thus makes thematic the clash of ideal and real; and it is the 'real', the A of the trumpet and drums, that is initially heard as a dissonant intrusion. We cannot live in B♭; the dissonant A signals our return to earth and its vulgar parade. How will B♭ and A continue to interact throughout the movement? What will be the issue of this clash of ideal and real?

To address this question, we jump ahead to the famous moment at the words 'vor Gott'. The falling major third sounds once again, now as a Beethovenian *non plus ultra*: here, finally, is the majestically rivetting, transporting presence of which all the other falling thirds gave but distant and echoed reports. The drop in the bass from A to F transforms the upper-voice A from a tonicized dominant to a luminous third; the F major sonority is not so much arrived at as revealed. Hearing through the process of that transformed A brings one to a very palpable symbol of the awe-inspiring presence of the deity: because of the tonicizing G♯s and the directional sweeps of the semiquavers, we accept the A as a stable goal tone—and then it suddenly becomes a stream of light suspended in the midst of a vast, bottomless space. The effect is vertiginous, breath-taking, truly a moment of epiphany, of presence.

The music which follows treats this epiphanic F major sonority as a dominant of B flat; in the symbolic key relationships we have been establishing it would thus serve (and quite appropriately given the text 'steht vor Gott') as the threshold of the ideal realm. But as if the B flat realm that is here associated with God is simply inaccessible within the context of this movement, we drop (and I mean drop) from the magnificent illumination of its dominant (and the pitch A) all the way down to the extreme depths of the orchestra, to a subterranean croak in the contrabassoon worthy of an Alberich. The vision of the throne of God vanishes, and we are back in the *ici-bas*, where the sudden, total removal of blinding light has made it seem darker than ever. And now the key of B flat, source of divine utterance one movement ago, finds itself on the lips of every street-crier: Beethoven's juxtaposition of a Turkish march both with the 'Ode to Joy' theme and with the celestial similes of this stanza of Schiller's poem creates a burlesque of the ideal. We have thus dropped from an exalted A to a debased B♭, reversing the terms of these two pitches in the opening *Schreckensfanfare*. This is clearly one way to resolve the conflict of ideal and real: simply drag the ideal down, and make it walk the streets.

Only at the starry denouement is the B♭ put in its place and cosmic order reestablished. Here at the fulcrum of the entire symphony Beethoven's music defines the relation of ideal to real with a musical-poetic symbol; the stars show us our true relation to the ideal represented by B flat, and the pitch B♭ finds its place within the overall tonal context of D minor-into-D major. At the outset of the Finale, we learned that we cannot live in B flat, and the later attempt to bring B flat down to earth in the Turkish march resulted in burlesque. At Beethoven's denouement, the pitch B♭ appears at an impossible distance, making the stars shimmer, giving life and significance to the heavens. This B♭ transforms the dissonance between ideal and real into a vast space across which something none the less seems to transpire, for the twinkling stars propitiate belief in a benevolent beyond. If the B♭ of the Turkish march was a grotesque ideal, this B♭ furnishes a 'sentimental' ideal: this is Schiller's sense of an ideal that can only be yearned for, never realized, and as such provides a fundamental aesthetic and ethical orientation.

The text Beethoven sets at this clarifying point in the music amounts to a credo: 'über Sternen muss er [ein lieber Vater] wohnen'. Yet the word 'muss' is revealing: this is a faith willed from within, not dictated from without (*ex cathedra*). As the musical texture pulls itself up in a slow ascent from 'Ihr stürzt nieder' to 'über Sternen muss er wohnen', we hear something like the sound of Beethoven's 'muss', the sound of faith striving from within to carry intimation ('Ahnest du den Schöpfer, Welt?') over into certainty.[33] Reflecting back on Forster's interpretation of the Fifth Symphony, we might say that much of Beethoven's music is about this 'muss'; perhaps this is the Beethovenian 'muss' of which Adorno speaks.[34]

As Nicholas Cook points out, a corollary text to this passage in the Ninth is that famous entry in Beethoven's conversation book, the paraphrase from Kant: 'The moral law within us, and the starry heavens above us'.[35] The devotional music in G major followed by the successive ascending stations to the minor-ninth sonority makes us feel the connection between the moral law within and the stars above, and leads us to the force of the Beethovenian credo: *these* stars are projected from the earth, this faith kindled from within. For William Kinderman, the E flat major chord in bars 643–6 is a monolithic symbol of the deity;[36] we can go on to say that its transformation into a diminished seventh serves to place the deity in relation to us, that is, in 'the starry heavens above us'. The rising harmonic monoliths immediately preceding the denouement are willed declarations of faith, the shimmering stars a sign of divine presence. And the ideal which has been sought in so many ways throughout the symphony is suddenly here, now, unimaginably remote, yet as visible as the stars. This is how

[33] Maynard Solomon speculates that Beethoven's choral treatment of the word 'muss' suggests doubtful queries about the presence of the deity (*Beethoven Essays* (Cambridge, Mass., 1988), 30).

[34] Theodor W. Adorno, *Musikalische Schriften IV: Moments Musicaux; Impromptus* (Frankfurt, 1982), 31 (in the essay entitled 'Schubert').

[35] Cook, *Beethoven: Symphony No. 9*, 104.

[36] William Kinderman, 'Beethoven's Symbol for the Deity in the Missa Solemnis and the Ninth Symphony', *19th-Century Music*, 9/2 (1985), 116.

Beethoven comes to conceive of the ideal: namely, from the standpoint of the real. As mortals we cannot reside in the ideal realm, but we can at least work for the privilege of believing in it and letting it guide us, both from within and from above. Like much of what we have come to admire most about Beethoven's music, the musical effect and its poetic conjunction are utterly simple, probably even banal; yet they work at a profound level.

By the lights of this interpretation, the Ninth can be heard as a kind of theodicy. If it doesn't explicitly 'justify the ways of God to man', it does make a clarifying statement about the relation of God to man; it weighs in with a statement about the relation of the ideal and the real, clearly a major preoccupation of the early nineteenth century and its Romanticism. And the decisive stroke in this reading, the revelation that acts in the manner of a dialectical synthesis, transcending the thesis of the slow movement (the real pulled up to the level of the ideal) and the antithesis of the Turkish march (the ideal pulled down to the level of the real), is also the major syntactic juncture of the Finale. As in the recapitulation of the Fifth Symphony Finale, the syntax of formal return is here made monumental, and is heard to take on a moral force. This is a point we could not have reached without a poetic reading of the piece: not only are we given something to ponder regarding how Beethoven's music interacts with the Classical style, but we are also invited to see how tonal music can be understood to sound and explore values, and not just to value and explore sounds.

## V

What is striking about writers who practise poetic interpretation is their urge to get directly to the business of how music affects them; one gets a sense of why it might be important to listen to music. Latter-day analytical methodology, in distancing itself from this type of poetic impulse, prefers to make music primarily an object for academic discourse, and has done so admirably. Yet we might now complain, with Seneca, that 'we are learning not for life, but for school'.[37] For after experiencing and talking about what these works can be for us, the level at which they can engage us, can we then imagine seriously entertaining the claim that we are somehow better off if we posit that a work like the 'Eroica' Symphony is first and foremost about some musical *Grundgestalt*? How is this not just as presumptuous as claiming it is about Napoleon or about Beethoven himself? A satisfactory answer to these questions would entail finding a perspective from which such a claim about the *Grundgestalt* was not just unproblematic, but represented an improvement over the competing claims of poetic or biographical content. The basic commitment of any such perspective would be towards maintaining the illusion that the piece is ultimately about itself, or about

---

[37] 'Non vitae, sed scholae discimus' (L. Annaeus Seneca, *Ad Lucilium Epistulae Morales*, vol. 2, ed. L. D. Reynolds (Oxford, 1965), 447 (from the 106th Letter).

music. And this of course sounds the aesthetic compact of absolute music: music shall no longer sing of things directly and broadly vital to humanity, but shall maintain its transcendental authority by virtue of its autonomy, its ability to be conceived as a world unto itself. The idea of the closed work sits well with this view, for here music itself becomes a closed world, a monad.[38]

The extreme positions of both poetic and formal analysis are equally danger-ous: as critics, we should not concentrate only on the autonomous claims of music; nor should we focus only on some spot beyond those claims. Even Marx recognized that music, though expressive of transcendent *Ideen*, still prosecutes its own claims, and that some things happen not in the service of an *Idee* but because of musical necessity.[39] And a recent attempt at musical interpreta-tion in the name of cultural hermeneutics has been charged with making music 'speak too plainly'.[40] Music does not speak plainly—if it did, it wouldn't be music. Thus it simply won't do to deny music's autonomy or to portray the very idea of its autonomy as the mere dupe of ideology. Music is hardly so trans-parently simple. With this, it may well please us to conclude that the implied question here—'What is music about?'—can only lead to an impasse. But there is an alternative. We might shift our question from inherent properties of music to ways of relating to music; we might ask, 'What are we about when we are about music?'

Under this new directive, let us first look again at the analytical position which posits that music is largely about itself. What is it about us that allows this view? I would argue that it is our training as musicians that encourages us to treat music as a language with its own claims, for an 'as if' notion of autonomy is an indispensable corollary to the act of learning to use this language. The study of music often takes on the self-sufficiency and absorbing intensity of a game: we learn rules, protocols, calculated risks, all of which can be negotiated with a limited intervention of verbal language. And this manner of interacting with music remains one of the great appeals of Schenkerian analysis, in which the language of music is used to comment on music, in which, as Joseph Dubiel points out, we are asked to apply musical metaphors like 'passing tone' to entire sections of music, in order to hear them in a new way.[41] Because music can be used in this way as its own metalanguage, analysis which exploits this pos-sibility can be deeply satisfying and meaningful for the hands-on musician. With this in mind, the automatic, exclusive consignment of analytical models like the *Grundgestalt* to the ideological paradigm of absolute music turns out to be

[38] In this regard we should remember Schenker's claim that philosophers would do well to look to the absolute nature of music as a heuristic model for the mystery of the universe (Heinrich Schenker, *Counterpoint* (New York, 1987), 16).

[39] Marx, *Ludwig van Beethoven: Leben und Schaffen*, 3rd edn. (2 vols., Berlin, 1875), i. 286.

[40] Roger Parker, 'High Hermeneutic Windows', review of Lawrence Kramer, *Music as Cultural Practice, 1800–1900* (Berkeley and Los Angeles, 1990), *Journal of Musicological Research*, 12 (1992), 251.

[41] Joseph Dubiel, 'What Did Schenker Mean by Prolongation?', paper presented at 'Critical Perspectives on Schenker: Toward a New Research Paradigm', University of Notre Dame, Notre Dame, Ind., 20 Mar. 1994.

overwrought and simplistically reductive, for Schoenberg himself would probably have thought of the *Grundgestalt* in the manner of a guild practice, a regulative, 'as if' conception of music helpful to composers and analysts, to those who propose to 'think in music'.

If the act of analysis thus engages one's sense of oneself as a musician, then the act of poetic criticism may be said to engage one's sense of oneself as a poet. By this I do not mean that poetic critics write poems or somehow rely on a training in poetics. Rather, I refer to the process through which one engages a non-verbal, emotional and/or aesthetic stimulus by trying to express it for oneself in words: this is a poetic act. The excerpt from *Howards End* is helpful here, because in it Forster actually stages the act of poetic interpretation. His character, Helen, brings her own state of mind, her own anxieties and predispositions, into the concert-hall, and hears the music say something to her personally. What it tells her carries no small authority: 'she read it as a tangible statement, which could never be superseded.'[42] Helen's reading of the music is thus presented as truth. But this truth is not about the music; nor is it, strictly speaking, about Helen. Rather, it is a truth *for* Helen. If it is about anything, it is about Helen's interaction with this music. It is truth not in any positivist sense, but in the sense of personal conviction, born of the merging of aesthetic and ethical force. We may call it 'poetic truth'.

As poetic critics, we behave like Helen: we put into play our own values, our individual sensibilities, as well as our inherited view of the music as an object of study, our susceptibility to and knowledge of the historical and cultural circumstances surrounding the music and its reception. Extensive programmes and other more isolated metaphors, whether directly inspired or intertextually suggested by an interpretive tradition, are poetic attempts at consolidating one's experience with the music at a given time, recording the interaction between the world of the piece and the world of the listener. Verbal interpretations thus act as a way of embodying the musical experience of an active listener, a way of making the music into a truth for the listener.

Those poetic interpretations that attain the status of a *sensus communis* about a musical work often invoke a broadly compelling ethical component, as in interpretations of Beethoven's heroic style as the triumphant overcoming of personal suffering. As we observed above, such readings register something like the direct impact of a work; they record its most obvious, yet also most profound, effects. But the validity of any poetic interpretation, regardless of its level of general acceptance, rests on its grasp of what it is that keeps one listening, what it is that convinces one of the importance and vitality of the listening experience. Hearing a piece of music as a powerful cathexis of one's own emotional and/or ethical preoccupations can have the effect of a deliverance, as in the act of psychotherapeutic projection. And the verbal transcription of this sense of connection with

---

[42] Forster, *Howards End*, 34.

the music provides closure (to invoke again the psychotherapeutic model), a way to complete and then integrate the experience.[43]

But in thus granting the power and satisfaction of poetic interpretation, we should not put out of mind the types of claims about music's autonomy that underwrite music analysis. Analysis and poetic criticism are not either/or alternatives. One might go further and claim that we *need* to understand music as music, as an autonomous language, if we want to grant it the power to speak of other things: we could not reasonably expect something without its own voice to comment on anything. Something without its own voice would at best be a mouthpiece for something else, and this is what is so unsatisfying about the ascription to musical works of literary keys, in which the music becomes little more than a code, its interpretant a cryptographer.

In short, precisely because music is musical, it can speak to us of things that are not strictly musical. This is how we hear music speak: not by reducing it to some other set of circumstances—music is simply not reducible to any other circumstances, whether cultural, historical, biographical, or sexual, and any attempt to make it so has only a cartoonish reality—but by allowing it the opacity of its own voice, and then engaging that voice in ways that reflect both its presence and our own, much as we allow others a voice when we converse with them. Thus we are far from abandoning the idea of music's immanence, for we reckon with it continually.

Analysis and poetic criticism are thus mutually enhancing, if we allow that we all harbour a sense of music as music as well as a sense of music as speaking to us of things that are not necessarily musical.[44] Our ways of being about music include both treating music as itself and treating it as a privileged form of utterance about things other than itself. And yet we are too advanced these days to speak of 'the music itself' without the qualifying addition of quotation marks, just as earlier analysts thought themselves too advanced to speak of 'poetic content'. But must we forbid the analyst the illusion that he or she treats of music itself? And must we forbid the poetic critic the illusion that music treats of himself or herself? For if we now accede to the view that these beliefs are in fact

---

[43] The model of psychotherapy has much to offer as a way to understand poetic readings of music. Music is becoming a more popular therapeutic modality, and the so-called Guided Imagery and Music (GIM) technique, developed by Helen Bonny, actually encourages patients to verbalize imagery as they listen to music.

[44] From the analysts' camp one detects a happy conjunction of these two impulses in the work of Ernst Oster, e.g. 'The Dramatic Character of the Egmont Overture', *Musicology*, 2/3 (1949), 269–85; repr. in David Beach (ed.), *Aspects of Schenkerian Theory* (New Haven, 1983), 209–22, and in some recent work of Carl Schachter, e.g. 'The Triad as Place and Action', *Music Theory Spectrum*, 17/2 (Fall 1995), 149–69. Both these analysts start from a securely Schenkerian standpoint, and then interpret their analyses in order to address meanings and values that are not expressible in the terms of a musical metalanguage. This may also be the place to mention an important earlier article on the subject of metaphor and analysis, Marion A. Guck's 'Musical Images as Musical Thoughts: The Contribution of Metaphor to Analysis', *In Theory Only*, 5/5 (1981), 29–42. Written from the perspective of a music theorist and analyst coming to grips with her students' stubbornly metaphorical impressions of musical processes, Guck's study explores how metaphors (mostly physiological in this case) can link musical processes with 'what is most important to us', and how they act as an efficient, succinct form of communication about those processes.

illusions (and, like other tenets of post-structuralist theory, this view has the signal advantage of being impossible to prove otherwise), are we to scoff at those who continue to fly by these lights, simply because we 'know' that they are not the fixed stars we once took them to be? To do so would be like scoffing at someone who assumes he is standing still on a flat surface, when everyone knows he is on a rapidly spinning sphere.

For these illusions simply mark the ways we are when we are about music, the ways that music takes part in our reality, that its mystery partakes of our own great mystery. We assume that we have the authority to speak about music and that music has the authority to speak about us—otherwise, why bother with it? Such 'as if' assumptions collectively form a primary condition of our intellectual interaction with music. Whether we analyse or criticize, poeticize or formalize, we are attempting to bring intuitive knowledge about music's imposing role in our lives into line with other kinds of knowledge, other things that are important to us. The bridge between music and these other realms is as tenuous, as hopeful, and as universal as the words 'as if'. Thus the fundamental imperative empowering all these approaches to music is one and the same: 'only connect'.[45]

Returning to an earlier concern of this essay, we might now conclude that we can reclaim the open work by being open about the ways we connect with it, by embracing the ways of the poet and those of the musician. And if we let music say as much as it can, if we acknowledge that it finds, among other things, the level of our deepest selves, are we not acting in the spirit of the poet Orpheus, who coaxed a lost self from the underworld? For this is what we share with that legendary musician from the dawn of our sonorous age: we too have never left off discovering how music matters.

---

[45] I would like to thank Richard Taruskin for encouraging the idea that poetic criticism and music analysis are, at bottom, the same activity.

# 10

# *Translating Musical Meaning: The Nineteenth-Century Performer as Narrator*

## John Rink

### 'Historical Performance': Theory or Practice?

Some research into 'historical performance' studies the past at the expense of the present, aiming to discover 'what was done' in bygone eras rather than to guide the modern performer.[1] This chapter, by contrast, has a practical goal: it enlists both historical and analytical evidence in an effort to capture the 'spirit' of a work as a prelude to live performance. Not only does it complement recent speculative writing on what historical performance 'should' entail and how analysis 'should' inform performance; it also casts light on nineteenth-century performance practice in particular, which remains relatively uncharted research territory. Past forays into this domain have typically concentrated on 'factual' matters like editions and instruments, virtually ignoring such issues as how composers conveyed 'meaning' (defined in any number of ways) in the score and how contemporary performers translated it into sound. By broaching these issues in terms relevant to this day and age, I shall show how the performer of nineteenth-century music can bring the score to life as a narrator of the expressive message inherent therein.[2]

I have written elsewhere that it is the performer who 'determines the music's essential "narrative" content by following indications in the score as to "plot",

---

[1] 'Positivist [performance practice] scholarship is interested in letter, not spirit . . . , the goal being avowedly to determine "What was done", not "What is to be done", let alone "How to do it". Direct application to actual performance is not the primary aim of such studies. They are not "utilitarian" but "pure research"' (Richard Taruskin, 'The Pastness of the Present and the Presence of the Past', in Nicholas Kenyon (ed.), *Authenticity and Early Music* (Oxford, 1988), 201).

[2] My references here and later to 'innate' meaning presuppose the definition of criteria (stylistic and otherwise) for the determination thereof. (See John Rink, 'Authentic Chopin: History, Analysis and Intuition in Performance', in John Rink and Jim Samson (eds.), *Chopin Studies 2* (Cambridge, 1994), 236 n.) Even though an interpretation will vary with the occasion, performers *must* commit themselves to a particular inferred 'meaning' in a given performance if the playing is to have any sense of conviction. Weighing up options on the concert platform is simply not viable.

and, as in the enactment of any "plot archetype", by shaping the unfolding tale on the spur of the moment in an expressively appropriate manner'.[3] This kind of 'narration'—a particular legacy of nineteenth-century performance practice— involves the creation of a unifying thread, a *grande ligne* linking the constituent parts of a performance into a rhythmically activated synthesis.[4] Vital for intelligible, effective performance, it means giving the music a sense of shape in time by devising a hierarchy of temporally defined musical gestures from the small to the large scale. While playing, the performer engages in a continual dialogue between the comprehensive architecture and the 'here-and-now', between some sort of goal-directed impulse at the uppermost hierarchical level (the piece 'in a nutshell'[5]) and subsidiary motions[6] extending down to the beat or sub-beat level, with different parts of the hierarchy activated at different points within the performance.[7]

To link the narrative thread that guides a performance to a verbal narrative— a story in words—would miss the point of the metaphor.[8] The narrative I am referring to is musically constituted: a time-dependent unfolding of successive musical events, palpably linked to produce a coherent 'statement' embodied in sound alone, which is of course the principal expressive medium available to the instrumentalist. This is not to suggest that musical *meaning* is itself defined in one and only one way;[9] but any communication thereof by the performer will take place largely via sensory experience, just as the codes devised by the composer to represent it in the score are themselves conceived in sound.

[3] John Rink, 'Chopin's Ballades and the Dialectic: Analysis in Historical Perspective', *Music Analysis*, 13/1 (1994), 112.

[4] William Rothstein comments that the performer synthesizes a musical narrative 'from all he or she knows and feels about the work; listeners, in turn, will construct their own narratives, guided by the performer' ('Analysis and the Act of Performance', in John Rink (ed.), *The Practice of Performance: Studies in Musical Interpretation* (Cambridge, 1995), 237). See also Jonathan Dunsby, *Performing Music: Shared Concerns* (Oxford, 1995), 82 ff.

For information about the *grande ligne* in nineteenth-century performance practice (and especially its relation to Schenker's *Urlinie* concept), see Thérèse Malengreau, 'De la "grande ligne" romantique à la ligne fondamentale de Schenker', in the forthcoming proceedings of the Third European Conference on Music Analysis, Montpellier, Feb. 1995.

[5] Erwin Stein, *Form and Performance* (London, 1962), 71. Performers might represent such an impulse as a physical gesture, tracing a contour with arm and hand as if to say, 'The piece goes like *this*'.

[6] For a discussion of gesture in performance, see Patrick Shove and Bruno Repp, 'Musical Motion and Performance: Theoretical and Empirical Perspectives', in Rink (ed.), *Practice of Performance*, 55–83.

[7] Both anecdotal and psychological evidence indicates this constant interplay between hierarchical levels. See respectively Louis Kentner, 'The Interpretation of Liszt's Piano Music', in Alan Walker (ed.), *Franz Liszt: The Man and his Music* (London, 1970), 202; and Eric Clarke, 'Generative Principles in Music Performance', in John Sloboda (ed.), *Generative Processes in Music* (Oxford, 1989), 1–26. Clarke's use of hierarchical 'tree diagrams' to depict knowledge structures in performance is particularly noteworthy.

[8] Note, however, the terms in which Wilhelm von Lenz describes Liszt's powerful performance rhetoric: 'Liszt does not merely *play piano*; he tells, at the piano, the story of his own destiny' (*The Great Piano Virtuosos of our Time from Personal Acquaintance*, trans. Madeleine R. Baker (New York, 1973), 1).

Some performers do construct imaginary stories to guide their interpretations, but that is not what is being described here.

[9] See n. 2 above; cf. Gary Tomlinson, 'The Historian, the Performer, and Authentic Meaning in Music', in Kenyon (ed.), *Authenticity*, 115–36. See also Anthony Pople (ed.), *Theory, Analysis and Meaning in Music* (Cambridge, 1994).

That this was recognized by nineteenth-century composers such as Liszt (the focus of much of this chapter) can be seen in the preface to his *Album d'un voyageur* (1842), where he acknowledges using 'the most appropriate rhythms, motions, and figures to express the fantasy, passion, or thought that inspired them'. What Liszt calls the 'architecture of sounds' conveys the sense of the music[10]—particularly in performance, which has unique powers to communicate in the original expressive idiom rather than some foreign (verbal) language.

Nevertheless, a different 'translation'—from notation to sound—must occur when constructing a musical narrative for performance, and to achieve this is by no means straightforward, even in repertoire from the mid- to late nineteenth century, where an 'apparent continuity of tradition'[11] often seduces musicians into making perilously false assumptions about 'stylistically correct' interpretation. Although it smacks of the glib imperatives of some historical performance specialists, only one conclusion can be drawn: to make sense of the music in whole or in part virtually requires an understanding of original compositional and interpretative contexts and criteria—not in order to achieve a putative authenticity (a chimerical if not downright naïve goal, despite the continuing allegiance of some to that aim[12]), but to provide essential terms of reference for 'meaningful' modern-day performances.

But contextual awareness, however necessary, is not sufficient to achieve the synthesis described above, which requires a broader interpretative vision to make the music cohere in time. Time—or the manipulation of time, timing—is the crucial ingredient, the *sine qua non*, of performance, and not just of nineteenth-century music (which is dogged by particular temporal problems—about how to relate sections,[13] shape a line with rubato,[14] or treat the notorious metronome markings in some composers' scores). Of music's principal expressive parameters—timing, dynamics, and articulation—it is both the most elusive and

---

[10] 'La première [partie de l'*Album*] comprendra une suite de morceaux qui . . . prendront successivement les rhythmes [*sic*], les mouvements, les figures les plus propres à exprimer la rêverie, la passion ou la pensée qui les aura inspirés. . . . ce n'est pas sans justesse qu'on l'a défini: une architecture de sons' (Franz Liszt, 'Avant-propos', in *Album d'un voyageur* (Vienna, 1842), 5). All translations in this chapter are mine except where indicated.

[11] Robert Winter, 'Performing Practice: After 1750', in Stanley Sadie (ed.), *The New Grove Dictionary of Musical Instruments* (3 vols., London, 1984), iii. 53. This 'continuous tradition' follows the dawn of modern performance practice *c.*1840—in particular, the development of present-day instruments and playing techniques, the growing distinction between composition and performance, and the rise of 'interpretation', with one artist responding to and recreating another's work.

[12] See e.g. Peter Seymour, 'Oratory and Performance', in J. Paynter *et al.* (eds.), *Companion to Contemporary Musical Thought* (2 vols., London, 1992), ii. 914. Rink, 'Authentic Chopin', demonstrates how historical information and analytical enquiry can shape an interpretation without eclipsing the performer's artistic vision, thus achieving a different 'authenticity'.

[13] See Jon Finson, 'Performing Practice in the Late Nineteenth Century, with Special Reference to the Music of Brahms', *Musical Quarterly*, 70/4 (1984), 457–75. See also John Rink, 'Performing in Time: Rhythm, Metre and Tempo in Brahms's *Fantasien* Op. 116', in Rink (ed.), *Practice of Performance*, 254–82.

[14] See Richard Hudson, *Stolen Time: The History of Tempo Rubato* (Oxford, 1994); David Rowland, 'Chopin's *Tempo Rubato* in Context', in Rink and Samson (eds.), *Chopin Studies 2*, 199–213; and Edward F. Kravitt, 'Tempo as an Expressive Element in the Late Romantic Lied', *Musical Quarterly*, 49/4 (1973), 497–518.

(ironically) the very key to performing nineteenth-century repertoire, which exploits time to highly dramatic ends. Whereas the prevailing model for musical performance in the eighteenth century was oratory, in the nineteenth it was drama: indeed, a particular nineteenth-century performance rhetoric can be defined not according to the Classical tradition adapted, say, by Mattheson, but with regard to explicitly dramatic properties exploiting familiar rhetorical devices—structure, gestures, figures, inflections, emphases, pauses—to new and different ends. This rhetoric is implicit in Richard Taruskin's description of 'vital' performance in terms of 'fluctuations of tempo and intensity' and other 'dynamic qualities', which, he says, explains 'why romantic music—and romantic performance practice—are more richly endowed than any other kind with crescendos and diminuendos, accelerandos and ritardandos, not to mention tempo rubato and a highly variegated timbral palette'.[15] A case in point is Wagner, for whom 'the sublime was associated particularly with the fluctuant, dynamic aspects of his music—its waxing and waning, its harmonic fluidity, its oceanic, infinitely evolving *forma formans*'.[16]

Another such example is Liszt, whose 'constantly fluctuating tempi'[17] in certain compositions reflect his idiosyncratic performance style. Violently opposed to the rigidity of musical time inspired by the metronome's invention,[18] Liszt excoriated 'up-and-down', 'windmill'-like conducting, telling his orchestral players 'not to keep strictly to his beat (*sich nicht allzu streng zu seinen Tact zu halten*)',[19] but to employ the rubato for which his piano playing was renowned. His commitment to flexibility of timing extended from early on (at a lesson in 1832 he taught that 'one must not stamp music with a uniform balance, but speed it up or slow it down with spirit and according to the meaning that it possesses'[20]) to late in his career, when, in 1870, he wrote: 'A metronomical perfor-

---

[15] Taruskin, 'Pastness of the Present', 160.

[16] Ibid. 185. See Kravitt, 'Tempo', 503, about Wagner's use of tempo. Nicholas Cook explores the Wagnerian tradition of 'flexible declamation' as practised by Wilhelm Furtwängler in 'The Conductor and the Theorist: Furtwängler, Schenker and the First Movement of Beethoven's Ninth Symphony', in Rink (ed.), *Practice of Performance*, 105–25, esp. 122 ff.

[17] Alan Walker, *Franz Liszt*, Vol. 2: *The Weimar Years 1848–1861* (London, 1989), 270.

[18] See George Barth, *The Pianist as Orator: Beethoven and the Transformation of Keyboard Style* (Ithaca, N.Y., 1992), regarding the fundamental changes in musical time-keeping that the metronome engendered.

[19] Quoted in a review, signed 'H', in the *Niederrheinische Musik-Zeitung für Kunstfreunde und Künstler*, 1/18 (1853), 140–1. Compare the following passage from Liszt's preface to his symphonic poems (Weimar, 1856): 'It is not enough for a composition to be beaten out regularly and performed mechanically and more or less correctly: no composer can be satisfied with this kind of performance or recognise it as a faithful interpretation of his thought. The vital nerve (*nerf vital*) of good symphonic playing lies in understanding, which the conductor above all must possess and communicate' (Preface to *Ce qu'on entend sur la montagne*, trans. Humphrey Searle (London, 1976), p. viii). See also Liszt's letter to Richard Pohl (Weimar, 5 Nov. 1853), in La Mara (ed.), *Letters of Franz Liszt*, trans. Constance Bache (2 vols., London, 1894), i. 175, where he attacks the 'imperturbable beating of the time' typical of some conductors: 'In many cases even the rough, literal maintenance of the time and of each continuous bar | 1, 2, 3, 4, | 1, 2, 3, 4, | clashes with the sense and expression. There, as elsewhere, *the letter killeth the spirit*'.

[20] 'On ne doit pas imprimer à la musique un balancement uniforme, mais l'animer, la ralentir avec esprit et selon le sens qu'elle comporte' (lesson given to Valérie Boissier on 31 Jan. 1832, described in Madame Auguste Boissier, *Liszt pédagogue: leçons de piano données par Liszt à Mademoiselle Valérie Boissier à Paris en 1832* (Paris, 1927), 35). Else-

mance is certainly tiresome and nonsensical; time and rhythm must be adapted to and identified with the melody, the harmony, the accent and the poetry'.[21] Based on a principle of 'free declamation', his distinctive rubato occasionally led to charges of 'excessive rhythmic fluidity',[22] but it always remained 'intelligible',[23] consisting (as Carl von Lachmund observed)

of subtle variations of tempo and expression within a free declamation, entirely different from Chopin's give-and-take system (*Eilen und Zögern*). Liszt's rubato is more a sudden, light suspension of the rhythm on this or that significant note, so that the phrasing will above all be clearly and convincingly brought out. While playing, Liszt seemed barely pre-occupied with keeping in time, and yet neither the aesthetic symmetry nor the rhythm was affected.[24]

To capture this flexible declamation, Liszt experimented with notation in the *Album d'un voyageur* and other early works,[25] indicating very brief pauses (marked =), small decreases in tempo (——), and, occasionally, tiny accelerandos ( ⊏⊐ ) in accordance with the 'sense' or inflection of the music at that point. After renouncing his virtuoso career in the late 1840s, he streamlined the expression markings in his music, assimilating the tempo fluctuations crudely but valiantly notated in earlier works into the essence of the score, to be read out by the interpreter according to context, stylistic norms, and, to some extent, personal taste. Given the importance that Liszt assigned to them, it is tempting to insist that modern performers must convey these 'innate' tempo fluctuations—as part of the music's implicit rhetoric—for effective performance to occur. A rational but subtly expressive flexibility of tempo would transcend both the arbitrary, indulgent liberties of late nineteenth- and early twentieth-century performers and the more rigid approach to tempo that followed later in this century,[26] enabling the music's 'spirit' to be communicated more in keeping with original intentions, and thus, perhaps, with greater cogency.

Declarations of what the performer must do—however inflammatory—might also be made regarding the poetic content of Liszt's music. Many of his works are of course directly tied to literature, but sometimes problematically. Not only did his 'translations' from literature to music attract the 'reproaches of aesthetic purists',[27] but, as Schoenberg asserted in 1911 in a provocative—some would

---

where (61) we read of Liszt: 'Il chante, ses phrases musicales l'inspirent et dans sa verve il les déclame comme un grand acteur, cherchant avec ses doigts à atteindre l'expression juste.'

[21] He goes on: 'But how [to] indicate all this? I shudder at the thought of it' (letter to Siegmund Lebert, Villa d'Este, 10 Jan. 1870, in *Letters of Franz Liszt*, ii. 194).

[22] Berlioz, *The Memoirs of Hector Berlioz*, trans. and ed. David Cairns (London, 1969), 551.

[23] Carl Czerny's judgement (*c*.1845), quoted in Rowland, 'Chopin's *Tempo Rubato*', 208.

[24] Carl von Lachmund, *Mein Leben mit Franz Liszt* (Eschwege, 1970), 62, quoted in Jean-Jacques Eigeldinger, *Chopin: Pianist and Teacher as Seen by his Pupils*, trans. Naomi Shohet with Krysia Osostowicz and Roy Howat, ed. Roy Howat (Cambridge, 1986), 122 n.

[25] Most of the pieces in question were composed *c*.1837–8.

[26] For discussion, see Taruskin, 'Pastness of the Present', and Kravitt, 'Tempo'.

[27] Carl Dahlhaus, *Nineteenth-Century Music*, trans. J. Bradford Robinson (Berkeley and Los Angeles, 1989), 149.

say outrageous—article, they often amounted to little more than 'second-hand poetry': 'instead of exclusively allowing his own visionary form, the poet in himself, direct musical expression', Liszt 'suppressed the poet in himself'; his 'real, inner personality, therefore, pervades his work to a smaller degree . . . than ought to be the case'.[28] In short, claims Schoenberg, his 'translations' can be stilted: although Liszt considered music a 'poetic language more apt perhaps than poetry itself' for expressing the transcendent, the inexplicable, the inaccessible,[29] he intones it at times with a foreign tongue, sometimes slight, sometimes pronounced distortions[30] in syntax, inflection, and turn of phrase affecting the accent and even the meaning.[31]

Where Liszt does succeed in capturing the 'spirit' of poetry without stifling the life of the music, allowing it instead to speak in its own terms, with its own internal musical logic,[32] he embodies that 'spirit' in specific parameters (motives, harmonies, melodies, textures, timbres, and so on) and, above all, in certain processes which act out the music's drama, all of which expressively connote more than the sum of their parts. One of these processes—the 'transformation of themes'—is a particularly vital narrative strategy, as Carl Dahlhaus suggests:

Liszt himself explicitly drew the conclusion that it is not so much musical themes and motives themselves as the transformations they undergo and the relations made to pertain between them that determine the 'speechlike' aspect of instrumental music: 'It is precisely the unlimited alterations which a motive may undergo—in rhythm, key (*Modulation*), tempo, accompaniment, instrumentation, transformation, and so forth—that make up the language by means of which one can express thoughts (*Ideen*) and, as it were, dramatic action (*dramatische Handlung*).'[33]

This, insists Dahlhaus, leads to a simple conclusion: 'Liszt's "literarization" of music . . . *should be analyzed from the vantage point of structure*. . . . It is not "lit-

---

[28] Arnold Schoenberg, 'Franz Liszt's Work and Being', in *Style and Idea*, ed. Leo Stein, trans. Leo Black (London, 1975), 443–5, *passim*. I am grateful to Alexander Goehr for drawing this essay to my attention.

[29] 'A mesure que la musique instrumentale progresse, . . . elle tend . . . à devenir non plus une simple combinaison de sons, mais un langage poétique plus apte peut-être que la poësie elle-même à exprimer tout ce qui en nous franchit les horizons accoutumés; tout ce qui échappe à l'analyse; tout ce qui s'agite à des profondeurs inaccessibles de désirs impérissables, de pressentiments infinis' (Liszt, 'Avant-propos', 5).

[30] In performance Liszt could more than compensate for these, given his unrivalled skill as a communicator. See William S. Newman, 'Liszt's Interpreting of Beethoven's Piano Sonatas', *Musical Quarterly*, 58/2 (1972), 206; compare Clara Schumann's appraisal, quoted in David Rowland, *A History of Pianoforte Pedalling* (Cambridge, 1993), 118.

[31] One of many works that rebut Schoenberg's claims is 'Vallée d'Obermann' (to which we shall return), the subject of which 'really "possessed" the composer', hence the 'absolute conviction' palpable throughout (Humphrey Searle, *The Music of Liszt* (London, 1954), 23).

[32] Dahlhaus, *Nineteenth-Century Music*, 361–2, writes that 'neither the existence nor the nonexistence of a program has the slightest bearing on whether a work does or does not have an internal musical logic'. (The comment concerns Richard Strauss, but applies generally.)

[33] Ibid. 242. The internal quotation is from Franz Liszt, 'Dornröschen. Genast's Gedicht und Raff's Musik gleichen Namens (1856)', in Lina Ramann (ed.), *Gesammelte Schriften* (6 vols., Leipzig, 1882), v. 172. My thanks to Rena Mueller for providing this information. (The quotation has been slightly modified to conform more closely to Liszt's original.)

erarization" per se which is "poetic", but rather the substance that attaches to a work of music when the composer succeeds, as it were, in picking up the *thread* of a major work of literature.'[34]

The implications of this for the performer are equally simple: to construct a musical narrative initially requires close study of the score—'structural analysis'[35]—in order to reveal its particular message or meaning, as a preliminary to translating it into sound. This sort of 'reading', which will vary from performer to performer,[36] itself derives from the interpretative ethos of the mid- to late nineteenth century, when, according to Dahlhaus, 'structural hearing meant immersing oneself in the internal workings of a piece of music' to an almost metaphysical expressive end.[37] That it had to do with more than the ostensibly systematic, objective analytical results often sought these days can be seen in an excerpt from Pivert de Senancour's epistolary novel *Oberman* from 1804 (which inspired the work to be studied below) stating that when music is played in a 'manner which is not just technically correct, but which is faithful to its spirit, if the player really feels the music', the listener will be transported to a different plane—thus indicating how profoundly a sensitive musical 'narration' could affect its auditors.[38]

The case-study that follows focuses on Liszt's 'Vallée d'Obermann' to show how the modern performer can construct such a narrative. After describing the three literary epigraphs that were published with the work and defining its essential structural properties, I shall sketch the hierarchical set of gestures that constitute the narrative thread, alluding to the precursor version of the piece to demonstrate how the more refined harmony, thematic material, and form of the second version shape the course of musical events—that is, the narrative itself. The goal is to articulate a rhetoric of performance suitable for this music and possibly other nineteenth-century repertoire, responding to the piece in terms sympathetic to original contexts and its expressive *raison d'être*.[39]

---

[34] Dahlhaus, *Nineteenth-Century Music*, 149–50; emphases added. (Compare Louis Köhler's review of the *Années de Pèlerinage: Suisse* in *Neue Zeitschrift für Musik*, 43/7 (1855), 69.)

[35] By this I refer not to particular techniques or methodologies (e.g. Schenker analysis), but to a more broadly conceived, flexible analytical approach directly relevant to the performer. For discussion, see John Rink, review of Wallace Berry, *Musical Structure and Performance*, in *Music Analysis*, 9/3 (1990), 319–39.

[36] There are no absolutes in this realm, apart from every performer's need for total commitment to an interpretation (see n. 2 above). For discussion see Rink, 'Authentic Chopin'.

[37] He goes on to say: 'In its original form, it [structural hearing] was accompanied by a metaphysic and a religion of art. Only in our century, in the name of that same structural hearing, were these mediating factors dismissed as extraneous additives to the acoustic phenomenon' (Dahlhaus, *Nineteenth-Century Music*, 95).

[38] 'S'il [le ranz des vaches] est exprimé d'une manière plus juste que savante, si celui qui le joue le sent bien; les premiers sons vous placent dans les hautes vallées, près des rocs nus et d'un gris roussâtre, sous le ciel froid, sous le soleil ardent' ([Etienne Pivert de] Senancour, *Oberman* (2 vols., Paris, 1804), i. 263–4; trans. from Peter le Huray and James Day, *Music and Aesthetics in the Eighteenth and Early-Nineteenth Centuries* (Cambridge, 1981), 539). The excerpt comes from the lengthy 'troisième fragment', 'De l'expression romantique, et du ranz des vaches', which Liszt later used as an epigraph before 'Le Mals du pays' in his *Années de Pèlerinage: Suisse*.

[39] For the sake of argument, the ensuing discussion presupposes (idealistically!) that the pianist has perfect technical control of both the music and the modern instrument on which the piece will be played.

## Reading the Score

'Vallée d'Obermann' has variously been described as a 'gigantic poetic meditation', an 'earlier *Verklärte Nacht*', an act of 'self-confession (*Selbstbekenntnis*)', and
the 'Ur-type of ultra-Romantic music'.[40] Liszt himself called it 'gloomy', 'hyper-
elegiac', and 'the monochord of the inexorable loneliness of human suffering',[41]
freely acknowledging its inspiration from Senancour's novel, the main character of which, 'in self-imposed exile in Switzerland',[42] suffers debilitating self-
doubt and existential pessimism. Oberman's emotional crisis serves Liszt as an
'associative inner programme',[43] the epigraphs relating (by his own admission)
to the book's 'central elements'.

The first version, composed between 1835 and 1838, was published in two
roughly contemporaneous editions: Richault's *Première Année de Pèlerinage*
(1841) and Haslinger's three-part *Album d'un voyageur* (1842), the latter of
which, originally planned for 1840, had already been superseded by the artistically more ambitious *Année* volume when it finally appeared.[44] By 1852 Liszt had
substantially 'corrected, expanded, and transformed' the set, having 'arrived at
last at that point where the style is adequate to the thought',[45] and three years
later—when the reworked *Années de Pèlerinage: Suisse* was published by Schott—
he repudiated the *Album d'un voyageur*, excluding it from a catalogue of his
works.[46]

Liszt made changes not only to the musical text of 'Vallée d'Obermann', but
also to the epigraphs, moving the long 'De l'expression romantique . . .' elsewhere in the set, and adding to the remaining excerpts from letters 4 and 63 in
*Oberman* a third brief passage, from Byron's *Childe Harold's Pilgrimage*, which
renders more explicit the self-doubt and alienation felt by the 'exiled' protagonist

---

[40] Respectively, Jean-Jacques Eigeldinger, 'Les Années de Pèlerinage de Liszt', *Revue musicale de Suisse romande*,
33/4 (1980), 154; Searle, *Music of Liszt*, 27; Walter Rüsch, *Franz Liszts Années de Pèlerinage: Beiträge zur Geschichte
seiner Persönlichkeit und seines Stiles* (Bellinzona, 1934), 23; and A. H. Cornette, *Liszt en zijne 'Années de Pèlerinage'*
(Antwerp, 1923), 21.

[41] 'Obermann könnte man das Monochord der unerbittlichen Einsamkeit der menschlichen Schmerzen
nennen. . . . Das düstere, hyper-elegische Fragment "la Vallée d'Obermann" . . . bringt mehrere Hauptmomente
des Werkes von Sénancourt worauf auch die gewählten Epigraphen hinweisen' (letter to Franz Schott, Weimar,
18 May 1855, quoted in Edgar Istel, 'Elf ungedruckte Briefe Liszts an Schott', *Die Musik*, 5/19/13 (1905–6),
46).

[42] William H. Hughes, 'Liszt's *Première Année de Pèlerinage: Suisse*: A Comparative Study of Early and Revised
Versions' (D.M.A diss., University of Rochester, 1985), 151.

[43] Márta Grabócz, 'Die Wirkung des Programms auf die Entwicklung der instrumentalen Formen in Liszts
Klavierwerken', *Studia Musicologica*, 22 (1980), 318.

[44] The complicated history of the *Album d'un voyageur* is traced in György Króo, ' "La ligne intérieure"—the Years
of Transformation and the "Album d'un voyageur" ', *Studia Musicologica*, 28 (1986), 249–60; see also Searle, *Music
of Liszt*, 23 ff. The composition date is proposed by Alexander Main for the entire set of *Impressions et poésies*
(of which 'Vallée d'Obermann' formed part) in 'Liszt and Lamartine: Two Early Letters', in Serge Gut (ed.), *Liszt-
Studien 2: Kongreßbericht Eisenstadt 1978* (Munich, 1981), 137–9. Other commentators have suggested a date of
1837–8 specifically for 'Vallée d'Obermann'.

[45] Letter to Carl Czerny, Weimar, 19 Apr. 1852, in *Letters of Franz Liszt*, i. 131.

[46] See his letter of 17 Jan. 1855 to Alfred Dörffel, ibid. i. 231.

(whether Oberman, Senancour, or Liszt himself).[47] As for the music, the first version's extravagant decoration and virtuosity, both of which inhibit the music's progression, give way in the greatly streamlined second version to a tighter emotional focus and more dynamic use of structure, whereby a sense of flow is created from within, the expressive content having been absorbed into the notes themselves.

The basis of this inner dynamic—and indeed the music's drama in general—is the 'transformation of themes' process referred to above.[48] One musical theme, analogous to one human character, undergoes an emotional metamorphosis in what Márta Grabócz calls an 'evolutionary form (*Evolutionsform*)' based on a single cell most baldly stated in bar 1 of the *Album* version.[49] Both Grabócz and William Hughes independently identify four main sections in the piece. Figure 10.1 depicts the structure discerned by Hughes, who in both versions isolates two rhythmically distinct forms of the theme (A and B, respectively in minor and major keys),[50] while Table 10.1 summarizes Grabócz's semantic chart of the second version, which, in keeping with the *Sprechende Prinzip* that she deems prevalent in this period, dissects the work according to four isotopes.[51] These differ from both the five isotopes assigned by Eero Tarasti[52] and yet another four designated elsewhere by Grabócz,[53] and although this discrepancy undermines their credibility, the essentially static vision of the music of Grabócz and Tarasti is in fact more troubling. Despite their professed attention to 'evolutionary form' and rhetorical process,[54] the performer would be hard pressed to make much practical use of their analyses, as all the activation of the music in time remains to be done. Hughes's blow-by-blow description is more helpful in that regard,[55] but a grasp of the whole—a 'broader interpretative vision' or *grande ligne* to guide the narrative—is still lacking.

[47] Interestingly, these epigraphs were not included in the edition of 'Vallée d'Obermann' that was published separately in 1855 (the *Années de Pèlerinage: Suisse* came out both as a set and as individual numbers), which suggests that the music had to stand on its own, the poetry providing only a frame of reference.

[48] Márta Grabócz (*Morphologie des œuvres pour piano de Liszt: Influence du programme sur l'évolution des formes instrumentales* (Budapest, 1986; revd. ed. Paris, 1996), 143) calls this process 'un des principaux modèles dramaturgiques chez Liszt'. Compare Hughes, 'Liszt's *Première Année*', 153; see also Karen S. Wilson, 'A Historical Study and Stylistic Analysis of Franz Liszt's *Années de Pèlerinage*' (Ph.D. diss., University of North Carolina, 1977).

[49] Grabócz, 'Die Wirkung', 302. Various authors (including August Stradal, Richard Stein, and Grabócz herself) have linked this motive—a descending third, G–F♯–E, played ♩ ♩  ♩ —with two questions in the first epigraph: 'Que veux-je? Que suis-je?'

[50] Hughes, 'Liszt's *Première Année*', 154, 156.

[51] Grabócz, *Morphologie*, 141–8, 178. Notwithstanding the problems identified below, Grabócz's analyses are perceptive and often persuasive.

[52] Eero Tarasti, 'The Case of *Obermann*: Franz Liszt and Marie d'Agoult in Switzerland', in Jan Stęszewski and Maciej Jabłonski (eds.), *Interdisciplinary Studies in Musicology* (Poznań, 1993), 96 ff.

[53] Grabócz, 'Die Wirkung', 318–19.

[54] Grabócz (*Morphologie*, 145) traces this from *exposition* through *développement/intrigue/noeud* to *dénouement/résolution*, defined by the successive *variations de caractère*, i.e. thematic transformations. Note that both Grabócz and Tarasti use an over-deterministic verbal medium to pin-point the work's meaning, as opposed to the more suggestive, *musical* mode of expression available to the performer. (See p. 218 above.)

[55] Hughes, 'Liszt's *Première Année*', 151–201. Compare the diachronic outline in Michèle Biget, 'Écriture(s) instrumentale(s). Liszt: La Vallée d'Obermann', *Analyse musicale*, 21 (1990), 90.

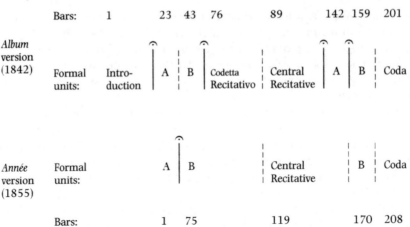

**Fig. 10.1.** 'Vallée d'Obermann': formal outline, versions 1 and 2 (after Fig. 9.1 in Hughes, 'Liszt's *Première Année*', 156).

Before unravelling the narrative thread as I see it, I shall first demonstrate the mediation between poetry and music not as Grabócz and Tarasti do, but by proposing salient intertextual references previously overlooked by commentators. Not only is 'Vallée d'Obermann' linked through the epigraphs to notions of impotence, exile, and alienation, but there are also specific musical allusions to the archetypal Romantic work expressing these ideas: Schubert's song 'Der Wanderer' (composed 1816),[56] which Liszt transcribed for piano in 1837–8, around the time of the first version of 'Vallée d'Obermann'. The intertextual connections include the A–C♯–B reaching-over motive at the climactic 'wo bist du?' in bars 54–5 of Schubert's song, found throughout both versions of 'Vallée d'Obermann' at expressively significant moments and as one of two 'basic shapes' (Ex. 10.1*a*); the progression from an augmented-sixth chord to the tonic at the same point in the Schubert and at the end of Liszt's second version, bars 215–16 (note that E major is the goal tonic in both pieces; see again Ex. 10.1*a*), as well as in bars 68 and 70–1; and the melody and accompanying augmented-sixth progression at another crucial moment in 'Der Wanderer', bars 20–2, where the singer (literally 'der Seufzer') asks 'wo? immer wo?', quoted in the second version of 'Vallée d'Obermann' at bars 178–9 (compare also 173 and 195), the registration, texture, and arpeggio figuration of which recall the parallel passage in bars 20–3 of Liszt's transcription (Ex. 10.1*b*).[57] Both the ubiquitous reaching-

---

[56] The second and third versions were written in 1818 and 1822 respectively; the text is by Georg Philipp Schmidt, although the title is Schubert's. Both Eigeldinger ('Les Années', 147–8) and Tarasti ('Case of *Obermann*', 91) stress the importance of 'wandering' and 'pilgrimage' to the Romantic imagination, but, like other authors, do not observe the musical links between 'Vallée d'Obermann' and 'Der Wanderer' that I adduce below.

[57] Links also exist between Liszt's transcription and the *first* version of 'Vallée d'Obermann', including the tempo marking ('Lento assai') and the *recitando* indications early in both pieces. It is difficult, however, to establish anteriority. The first version lacks both the expressively significant augmented-sixth harmonies and the 'wo? immer wo?' motive (although augmented sixths do occur in bars 58, 59, and 170).

Table 10.1 Summary of Grabócz's semantic chart

| *Syntagmatic axis:* | first thematic complex | second thematic complex | third thematic complex | fourth thematic complex |
|---|---|---|---|---|
| Structural function | theme and rhetorical development | theme and formal variations | motto and 'development' | theme and formal variations |
| Bars | 1–74 | 75–118 | 119–69 | 170–216 |
| Key | opposition of tonic axis (E minor–G minor–B♭ minor– D♭ minor [sic]) and subdominant axis (A minor– C minor–E♭ minor–F♯ minor) | C major and modulation | C♯ minor, D minor, E minor and modulation | E major |
| Tempo and expression marks | Lento assai, *espressivo*; Più lento, *dolcissimo* | Un poco più di moto ma sempre Lento, *pp, dolcissimo* | *Recitativo, pp, trem. appassionato ff; agitato molto;* Presto *ff tempestuoso* | Lento, *dolce, una corda; dolce armonioso; sempre animando sin'al fine fff* |
| Semes or classemes | lamenting-reciting and lugubrious | pastoral-*amoroso, bel canto* | storm semes, macabre semes, fanfare semes | *bel canto,* pathetic, pastoral-pantheist semes |
| Semantic isotopes | macabre quest | pastoral-*amoroso* | macabre struggle | pantheist |

Ex. 10.1a.  *A–C–B motive: (i) Schubert, 'Der Wanderer', bars 54–5; (ii) 'Vallée d'Obermann', bars 1–2, 9–10, 25–6, 169, 171, and 215–16.*

(i)

(ii)

over motive and these other harmonic and melodic elements, which are concentrated in the final section (in other words, when transcendence *seems* possible, after the recitative's turbulent *Verklärung*, but is nevertheless threatened by the implied questions: 'wo? immer wo?', 'wo bist du?'), serve as palpable indications of the music's expressive content, readily accessible to contemporary and modern listeners alike.

Ex. 10.1b. *'Immer wo' harmony/melody: (i) Schubert, 'Der Wanderer', bars 20–2; (ii) Liszt, transcription of 'Der Wanderer', bars 20–3; (iii) 'Vallée d'Obermann', bars 178–9, 173, and 195.*

(i)

(ii)

(iii)

Other devices convey meaning more subtly than these quotations, however, and the pianist's task is to discern them (whether consciously or not) and devise a temporal basis for projecting them. Both Grabócz and Tarasti identify such 'meaningful' parameters as motives, themes and thematic variations, tonal construction, phraseology, cadences, 'gestural shifts', and register;[58] while Michèle Biget singles out timbre as an 'agent of compositional process'.[59] To this list could be added an element of more direct relevance to the performer but often ignored in the literature on performance: *contour*, of both individual musical lines and the broader expressive gestures traced by different parameters at various hierarchical levels within the music—in other words, the 'goal-directed impulses' mentioned above, which together define the performance's topography. The following remarks will focus on contour in three passages— the opening, the recitative, and the final section—followed by consideration of large-scale shape and timing.

## Opening

The second version of 'Vallée d'Obermann' lacks the first version's 22-bar introduction, instead launching directly into the doleful theme, which, according to Liszt, should be 'very strong and very accented (*sehr stark und sehr accentuirt*)' in performance.[60] To gauge the extraordinary effect of this radical opening requires sensitivity to contemporary harmonic vocabulary and syntax, and awareness of Liszt's changes to the first version. (See Ex. 10.2*a*.) The unstable tonic in the first two bars (the root is absent, the harmony clouded by dissonance) and the bold, tonally ambiguous progression in bars 1–8 from E minor through G minor to B flat minor (versus the straightforward i–III–V motion in the *Album* version) immediately capture the mood of uncertainty conveyed in the three epigraphs.[61] A second indecisive idea (derived from the reaching-over 'basic shape') enters in bars 9–10 and leads to incrementally greater levels of intensity, building towards a climax at bar 20 (*rinforzando*), whereupon the register plummets and the music grinds to a halt, with searching 'questions' ('Più lento') thereafter in bars 26–33. Thus an important pattern is forged from the start, based on a gradually mounting degree of intensity directly followed by retraction—in short, a kind of oscillation not unlike that embodied both registrally (Ex. 10.2*b*) and temporally (Ex. 10.2*c*) in the left-hand theme at the opening, as well as in the innumerable dynamic swells that shape the music when

---

[58] Grabócz, 'Die Wirkung', 305, and *Morphologie*, 144; Tarasti, 'Case of *Obermann*', 99 and *passim*. Compare Liszt's remarks, quoted above, about his use of 'rhythms, motions, and figures' to express thought and emotion. Both reasons of space and the cogency of Grabócz's analyses prevent me from elaborating on the semantic role of such parameters.

[59] Biget, 'Écriture(s)', 94.

[60] Reported in Wilhelm Jerger, *Franz Liszts Klavierunterricht von 1884–1886 dargestellt an den Tagebuchaufzeichnungen von August Göllerich* (Regensburg, 1975), 140. Liszt also told Göllerich that bars 75 ff. and 180 ff. should be played 'nicht zu langsam' (ibid. 116), while bars 20–5 should be 'extremely broad (*ungemein Breit*)' in tempo (ibid. 140). In the context of this study, it is noteworthy that Liszt's comments concern tempo and dynamic emphasis.

[61] For discussion of the opening, see Allen Forte, 'Liszt's Experimental Idiom and Music of the Early Twentieth Century', *19th-Century Music*, 10/3 (1987), 212–14, and R. Larry Todd, 'The "Unwelcome Guest" Regaled: Franz Liszt and the Augmented Triad', *19th-Century Music*, 12/2 (1988), 109 (see also 96).

Ex. 10.2. 'Vallée d'Obermann'. (a) theme A in versions 1 and 2; (b) registral contour of theme A, bars 1–8; (c) temporal oscillation in theme A, bars 1–8, based on author's performance.

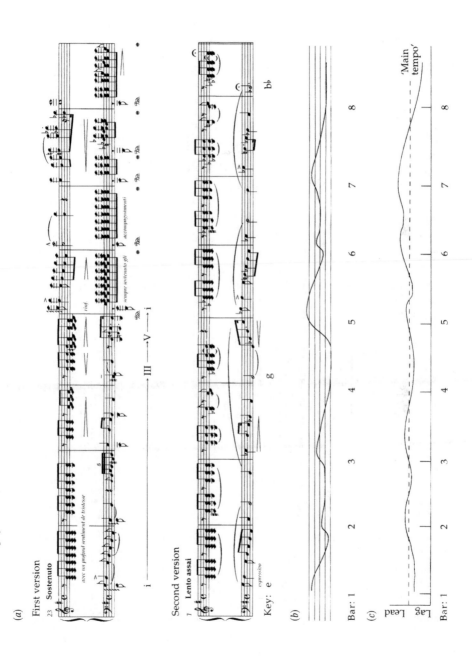

Ex. 10.3. *'Vallée d'Obermann'*: (a) comparison of registral contour in bars 139–41 and 161–9; (b) registral and temporal oscillations in cadenza, bar 169, based on author's performance.

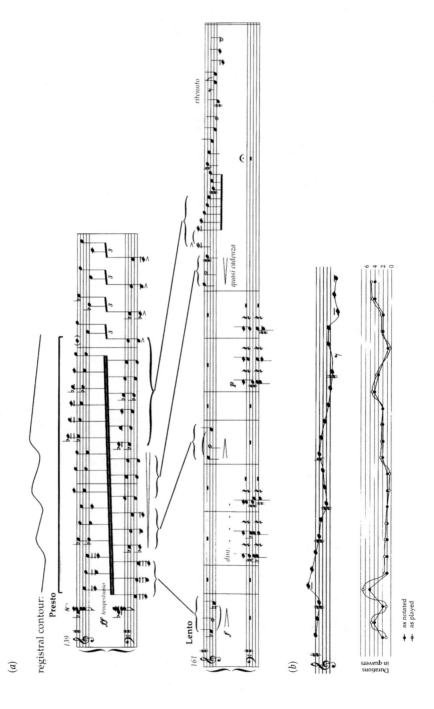

played.[62] Emotional flux characterizes the rest of the first section, which proceeds in phases defined by tempo changes (*rall., poco rit., rit.,* and 'Più lento'), the warmer *dolcissimo* at bar 51, the return of the questions at bar 59, and the *dolente* coda, with its final *pesante* articulation of the theme deep in the bass, the *lunga pausa* preparing for the transcendent second section in bar 75 (marked 'Un poco più di moto ma sempre Lento', *pp, dolcissimo,* and *una corda*), where the 'B' version of the theme first enters, in C major. Here too we find phases of intensification and relaxation, the registral compass, rhythmic activity, and harmonic momentum increasing or decreasing in sweeps of varying magnitude, and the tempo fluctuating correspondingly, with the 'collapse' in bar 118 precipitating the recitative.

## Recitative

The energy level stays extremely high in bars 119–60, despite even greater swings between registers, rhythmic units, textures, harmonies, and so forth as the descending-third 'basic cell' is worked and reworked in both hands. The Presto at 139 ff., marked *ff* and 'tempestuoso', finds the motive in a zigzag pattern moving sequentially higher, tensions culminating with the extended, *fff* statement at 148 ff. After violent registral shifts in bars 151–5, the music winds down in bars 156–9, with the sudden stop on a first-inversion F minor chord in bar 160 (versus the anticlimactic Neapolitan sixth, F *major*, in the earlier version) both unexpected and, in its futility, something of a blow after the stormy *Verklärung* just completed. Here follows not so much a transformation of themes as a transformation of contour, the shape from the earlier Presto returning in a nine-bar augmentation (marked 'Lento') leading to a cadenza, which, as the tempo slows, culminates with the A–C–B 'basic shape' from 'Der Wanderer'[63] (Ex. 10.3*a*). In essence, the expressive contour in these nine bars

---

[62] Tarasti ('Case of *Obermann*', 94–5) considers the theme 'a sort of "iconic" image of the valley' in the title, and 'the use of various registers throughout the piece illustrate[s] the peaks and abysses of those landscapes' in Senancour's novel. A more convincing 'iconicity' will be posited below, however.

Oscillation in dynamics colour bars 1–8, e.g., with swells (i.e. ⟨ ⟩ ) over the tripartite quaver units in the right hand and over the two-bar melodic ideas in the left. Throughout the piece similar swells shape the ubiquitous ♩ ♩ ♩ and ♪♩ ♪ rhythmic units, as well as the accompanimental patterns accelerating from ♪♫ through ♪♫♫♫ to 🎵🎵 .

As noted in the captions, the graphs in Exx. 10.2*c*, 10.3*b*, and Fig. 10.2 are based on my own performance of 'Vallée d'Obermann'; they simulate MIDI-derived diagrams, but were sketched free-hand in an admittedly less 'scientific' but perhaps more 'musical' fashion. No doubt they would vary from one rendition to another on my part, although it is worth noting that psychological research indicates a remarkable consistency of expressive micro- and macro-structure when a performance strategy has been thoroughly worked out by the player. It goes without saying that different contours would emerge from other pianists' interpretations; however, Alfred Brendel's reading (Philips 420 202-2) also features considerable temporal flux, whereas Pascal Rogé's (Decca SXL 6485) is more metronomic—and in my view much less vital than Brendel's.

[63] The shape is stressed even more in the alternative ending sketched in Liszt's manuscript and reproduced in the Henle edition. Compare also the cadenza in the first version (bar 141), which starts similarly, though at twice the speed, but then descends in an uninflected harmonic minor scale to middle C, followed by B. Thus, both the 'wo bist du?' motive and the registral oscillation of the later version are lacking.

acts as a microcosm of the foregoing recitative's unceasing fluctuations, the flexible timing of the cadenza making all the more poignant the line's 'vocal' folding and unfolding—its registral undulation—as it approaches the final section (Ex. 10.3*b*).

## Apotheosis

Whereas in the first version theme A returns in E minor after the cadenza,[64] the second version states the B theme in E major in perhaps the most consolatory passage in the piece (one of only two relatively stable moments), the registration's rich colour and the flowing rhythm providing a balm after the *tempestuoso* recitative. Liszt keeps the mood *dolce* (see bars 170, 175, and 180) until the *sempre animando sin' al fine* in bar 188, which marks the start of an inexorable drive towards the end. Before this, however, as well as after, a state of flux affects the course of events, with a particularly pronounced retraction in bars 184–7 (where the left hand alludes to the A theme), before which an aspirational, ascending form of the B theme is heard for the first time.[65] Another new shape enters in bar 204, where, at the peak of rapture, the linear descent from the theme returns in a much extended, accelerated version sweeping beyond the more confined registral compass of the original. Accompanied by an exultant sequential progression, it offers the second and last moment of stability in the work; as we have seen, the final bars are clouded by harmonic uncertainty and by the 'wo bist du?' motive, the fifth in the treble adding to the open-ended feel.[66]

## Constructing a Musical Narrative

Even this brief sketch of 'Vallée d'Obermann' reveals the patterns of oscillation or flux variously manifested throughout the work. What remains is to depict these more vividly, which I shall do by tracing an 'intensity curve'[67]—that is, a graphic representation of the music's ebb and flow, its 'contour' in time, determined by all active elements (harmony, melody, rhythm, dynamics, etc.) working either independently, in sync, or out of phase with one another to create the changing degrees of energy and thus the overall shape. As an analytical tool,

---

[64] The theme's recapitulation in E minor makes the *Verklärung* seem pointless in retrospect.

[65] In the first version, unlike the second, ascending patterns occur much earlier, destroying the effect of the eventual apotheosis. The 'Wanderer' quote at bars 178–9, discussed above, also injects a sense of doubt ('wo? immer wo?'), as do its anticipation and echo.

[66] Grabócz (*Morphologie*, 147) notes the blend of '*glorification*' and '*intonations macabres*' in this '*coda "aliénante"*', while Todd (' "Unwelcome Guest" ', 109) claims that the augmented triad 'strengthens the motivic cohesiveness of the work'.

[67] This concept was first proposed by Wallace Berry in *Structural Functions in Music* (Englewood Cliffs, N.J., 1976), although it had various precursors—e.g. the work of Manfred Clynes, described in n. 68 below.

the intensity curve has limitations, not least the difficulty of defining and objectively quantifying intensity, but from the performer's viewpoint the construct
is powerful:[68] there are parallels between it and the 'intonatory curve'—or
'intonation contour'—of a spoken narrative[69] (one of the models for performance in the nineteenth century and beyond, as suggested earlier), and implicit
in the concept is the *grande ligne* which, I have been arguing, lies behind the
coherent performance of much Romantic and post-Romantic repertoire.

Taking into account the work's evolutionary form and emotional metamorphosis, and indeed all the processes identified above, an intensity curve can be
drawn as an oscillating line expanding in amplitude and period as the piece pro-
gresses (see Fig. 10.2), achieving an overall ascent despite the many instances
of retraction at various layers of the hierarchy implicit beneath this upper-level
manifestation. To some extent the curve reflects a plot archetype exploited in
much nineteenth-century music, which, like the eighteenth-century impro-
visatory style that partly inspired it, typically involved a succession of alternat-
ing affects, a systematic juxtaposition of opposites.[70] In 'Vallée d'Obermann',
however, it plays a quite distinctive role in the music's synthesis in time and in
the conveying of its particular expressive message.

Perhaps the most striking conclusion to be drawn concerns the relationship
between the different contours within the work's hierarchy: the intensity curve
at the uppermost level (again, the piece 'in a nutshell') closely corresponds in its
incessant fluctuations to the 'iconic' thematic and temporal contours of bars 1–8
(as shown in Exx. 10.2*b* and *c*), the up-and-down zigzag used sequentially in bars

[68] It is hardly coincidental that the intensity curve was conceived by an accomplished pianist and conductor,
whose *Structural Functions* depicts rhythmic and metric impulses in the form of conducting gestures. Berry used it
as an analytical device rather than a means of representing musical performance, but, given its attention to such
features as timing, generation and relaxation of momentum, relative high and low points, etc., its descriptive powers
in respect of performance are profound, likewise its potential as a *prescriptive* tool in performance pedagogy. Compare
the use of gesture described in n. 5 above, which teachers continually exploit to demonstrate to students the shape
of phrases.

The intensity curve concept is echoed in recent psychoacoustic research by Neil Todd, who posits 'integrated
energy flux' as a determinant of musical expression. Todd synthesizes tempo, dynamics, and other components of
expression through a series of filters to produce a hierarchy of integrated energy profiles in the form of 'rhythmo-
grams', which can be likened to intensity curves. (For discussion, see Eric Clarke, 'Expression in Performance: Gen-
erativity, Perception and Semiosis', in Rink (ed.), *Practice of Performance*, 24.) One important difference, however, is
that Todd's approach is 'knowledge-free'; i.e. it is based simply on the combined acoustic properties of the various
components, whereas an intensity curve relies upon the analyst/performer's musical judgements to prioritize the
elements according to their *relative*, contextual importance.

Perhaps even closer echoes exist in the research of Manfred Clynes, who has devised a 'sentograph' to measure
'essentic forms' (which, he claims, characterize basic emotions and embody the structurally defined source of
meaning in music). Subjects produce 'pressure curves' by pressing rhythmically on the sentograph while music is
being played or imagined, thus registering its emotional progression. (For discussion, see Shove and Repp, 'Musical
Motion and Performance', 72–5.)

[69] This point is elaborated in Rink, 'Chopin's Ballades', 112.

[70] This was certainly true of Liszt's playing, the rhetorical force and dramatic logic of which Madame Boissier,
for one, attributed to shifting emotional states and expressive variety. See for instance *Liszt Pédagogue*, 17–18, 39,
and esp. 87–8: ' "La musique doit être variée" dit-il, "et les mêmes nuances, expressions, modifications ne doivent
pas se répéter; les phrases musicales sont soumises aux mêmes règles que les phrases dans un discours; on défend
de répéter les mêmes mots, il ne faut pas que la même tournure d'expression reparaisse, cela fatigue." '

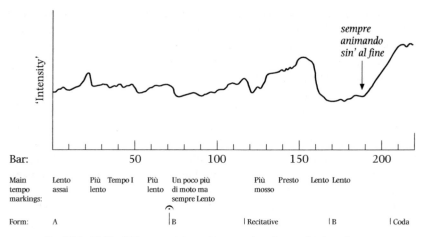

**Fig. 10.2.** 'Vallée d'Obermann': intensity curve, based on author's performance.

139 ff. and greatly augmented at the end of the third section (seen in Ex. 10.3), and indeed the various other oscillations—not least the omnipresent dynamic swells—located throughout the piece and identified in my analysis. What is more, when the music is played with the flexibility of tempo depicted in bars 1–8 and 169 and advocated in general by Liszt—namely, increases or decreases like those explicitly marked in the first version and absorbed into the second; that is, 'subtle variations of tempo and expression within a free declamation' determined by 'the meaning that the music possesses'—the performance as a whole literally *resonates*,[71] driven by a continual flux in all elements, an inner pulsation which, like a human pulse, like human breathing, speeds up or slows down in increasingly agitated or relaxed states. In short, the topography of the performance as represented here offers a musical counterpart to or enactment of the emotional quest of Senancour's protagonist, creating a structural homology between his *vacillation* on the one hand and the music's *oscillation* on the other, a resonance not only within the music as music, but with the poetic meaning it attempts to convey. Surely this explains why 'Vallée d'Obermann' is such a resounding masterpiece:[72] Liszt at once achieves an internal musical logic *and* translates poetic meaning into sound not in a 'second-hand' fashion but with 'absolute conviction', the unity between parts and whole paralleled by a unity between the music's aesthetic aims and their structural manifestation. By activating that

---

[71] *Webster's New Collegiate Dictionary* (Springfield, Mass., 1974) defines resonance as 'a vibration of large amplitude in a mechanical or electrical system caused by a relatively small periodic stimulus of the same or nearly the same period as the natural vibration period of the system'. Here, the resonant 'system' is the 'monochord of human suffering' referred to by Liszt.

[72] The first version, by contrast, is undermined by what Hughes ('Liszt's *Première Année*', 172) calls an 'oddly naïve, almost melodramatic' succession of moods, which 'pass in front of the listener as static tableaux' (195).

structure in time, by following the fluctuating *grande ligne* that guides the musical narrative, the performer acts out the music's drama, communicating a kind of meaning which can only be heard, which exists in sound alone, and taking the listener on an expressive journey up and down the emotional peaks charted by the musical materials themselves.

There is a brief epilogue to this discussion. As an old man, Liszt refused to hear 'Vallée d'Obermann' in entirety (the one time he relented caused great distress[73]), and he recommended that August Göllerich conclude his performances of the piece after the first section, in bar 74, before the first hint of 'reconciliation' in the C major passage.[74] Furthermore, he sanctioned Eduard Lassen's reworking of 'Vallée d'Obermann' for piano trio (dubbed 'Tristia' by Liszt himself[75]), adding to the (undated) manuscript a passage allowing the piece to conclude, albeit in open-ended fashion, after the first section, and drafting a new 21-bar introduction, an 8-bar transition to the 'second movement' (marked 'II' in the score), and another conclusion to close the piece *ad libitum* before the recitative,[76] all of these passages possessing the vague, disconcerting quality of Liszt's late style. Not only do the various changes highlight the fluidity of the 'work concept' as understood by Liszt, but through their negating effect they elucidate the meaning of the 1855 version as described here: whereas in the published composition the tortuous progression through conflicting states leads to transfiguration and eventual apotheosis, the later versions deny the possibility of transcendence, relegating the protagonist to permanent alienation, an exile so absolute that the emotional quest embodied in the music can never really end.

This chapter has approached general issues through the prism of a specific work in order to portray the hierarchical structure of performance and to cast new light on nineteenth-century interpretation in particular, offering guide-lines enabling modern performers to recover at least in part the essential qualities of an original dramaturgy. Just as the communication of 'meaning' lay at the heart of a nineteenth-century performance rhetoric, so it must guide modern performances of that music if they are fully to persuade modern listeners—if 'resonance' is to occur. By 'reading' the score and attending to those elements that bear meaning (themes, motives, rhythms, etc.), and then by constructing a temporal framework for their projection, the performer assumes the role of narrator, tracing a *grande ligne* to mediate between the poetic and the structural,

---

[73] See August Göllerich, *Franz Liszt* (Berlin, 1908), 119.

[74] See Jerger, *Franz Liszts Klavierunterricht*, 140.

[75] This subtitle is probably derived from either Ovid's 'poetic epistle' *Tristia* or Berlioz's eponymous pieces for choir and orchestra, published in full score in 1852 (with two lines from Ovid printed on the cover) and dedicated to Prince Eugène Sayn-Wittgenstein, nephew of Liszt's consort Carolyne. See David Charlton (ed.), *Hector Berlioz. New Edition of the Complete Works*, vol. 12b (Kassel, 1993), pp. ix–xii. I am grateful to Dr Charlton for providing this information.

[76] Full details are given in Wolfgang Marggraf, 'Eine Klaviertrio-Bearbeitung des "Vallée d'Obermann" aus Liszts Spätzeit', *Studia Musicologica*, 28 (1986), 295–302. The latter 'drafts' referred to here exist only in Lassen's hand, but (Marggraf assumes on the basis of stylistic evidence) were originally Liszt's own.

to recount the drama within the notes. The performer's use of analysis to reveal the 'spirit' of music not only re-validates the close study of musical scores in this post-structuralist era; it also broadens our understanding of what 'historical performance' might properly involve, at the same time providing a salutary reminder that not all critical interpretations elucidate music as sound. Only the performer has control over the sounding aspect of music, and critical, historical, or analytical judgements may bear little or no relation to music's process. That does not of course deny their value; but it serves to highlight the special powers that performance has to communicate musical meaning, to embody the narrative that recounts an emotional destiny almost beyond human comprehension.

# 11

# Analysing Performance and Performing Analysis

## Nicholas Cook

### I

More than anything else, I suppose, it was Wallace Berry's book *Musical Structure and Performance* that marked the emergence of 'analysis and performance' as a recognized subdiscipline within music theory.[1] Yet Berry's book reads more like the summation than the opening-up of a field. It represents not so much a cross-disciplinary exercise—the attempt to forge a relationship between two fundamentally different activities—as an attempt to incorporate performance within the existing intellectual framework of theory. Berry's very language locates the intersection of analysis and performance firmly on the theorist's turf; his aim, says Berry, is to investigate 'how . . . a structural relation exposed in analysis can be illuminated in the inflections of edifying performance'.[2] In this way the direction is always *from* analysis *to* performance, and Berry reiterates this to the point that you almost wonder if, deep down, he really believes it. He refers to 'the path from analysis to performance', and elsewhere to 'the path from analysis to interpretive decision',[3] he speaks of 'the findings of analysis and consequent outlets in performance', and of such findings being 'in turn' expressed in performance.[4] And the parentheses say it all when he refers to 'principles of

---

[1] Wallace Berry, *Musical Structure and Performance* (New Haven, 1989). A bibliography of the analysis and performance literature may be found at the end of Cynthia Folio's article 'Analysis and Performance of the Flute Sonatas of J. S. Bach: A Sample Lesson Plan', *Journal of Music Theory Pedagogy*, 5 (1991), 133–59, pp. 154–9. A number of more recent publications are cited in the present chapter. To these may be added Marie Rolf and Elizabeth West Marvin, 'Analytical Issues and Interpretive Decisions in Two Songs by Richard Strauss', *Intégral*, 4 (1990), 67–103; Carl Schachter, '20th Century Analysis and Mozart Performance', *Early Music*, 19 (1991), 620–6; George Fisher and Judy Lochhead, 'Analysis, Hearing, and Performance', *Indiana Theory Review*, 14/1 (1992), 1–36; Cynthia Folio, 'Analysis and Performance: A Study in *Contrasts*', *Intégral*, 7 (1993), 1–37; and Charles Burkhart, 'Mid-bar Downbeats in Bach's Keyboard Music', Carl Schachter, 'Chopin's Prelude in D major, Op. 28, No. 5: Analysis and Performance', and Elizabeth West Marvin, 'Intrinsic Motivation: The Relation of Analysis to Performance in Undergraduate Music Theory Instruction', all in *Journal of Music Theory Pedagogy*, 8 (1994), 3–26, 27–46, and 47–57 respectively.

[2] Berry, *Musical Structure*, p. x.

[3] Ibid. 10, 2.

[4] Ibid. x, 218.

structure (and hence of realization in performance)'.[5] Performers, it seems, have a great deal to learn from analysis; the possibility of a reciprocal process of learning is apparently not considered.

This prescriptive conception of the relationship between analysis and performance is by no means unique to Berry; Eugene Narmour provides an even more extreme instance. In his article 'On the Relationship of Analytical Theory to Performance and Interpretation',[6] Narmour asserts that 'It is obvious that if formal relations are not properly analyzed by the performer, as well as carefully delineated in the performance itself, then many negative consequences follow'.[7] As illustrated in relation to a few bars from *Der Rosenkavalier*, his procedure is first to analyse the music; next to derive from this an 'analytically justifiable recreative interpretation',[8] which he presents in the form of an annotated score; and finally to assess a selection of existing recordings against his annotated score. On this basis, he produces what might be termed a 'buyer's guide'; the best buy, by a comfortable margin, turns out to be Karajan's recording. For Narmour, then, this recommendation is very much more than just a personal critic's choice. 'Of course', he says, 'in an art like music there can never be any such thing as *the* definitive performance.' But he immediately adds: 'The point, however, is that, given the analytical theory applied in example 9 [his annotated score], we can say *more or less objectively* that . . . certain performances are subtly though demonstrably better than others.'[9]

According to Tim Howell, the general tone of music-theoretical writing about performance is 'authoritarian'.[10] The word certainly seems to fit Narmour's article; he frequently stipulates what the performer *must* or *must not* do, judging one performance *correct* and another *incorrect*. Bernstein, for instance, makes an 'obvious mistake' when he crescendos in bars 128–9 of the first movement of Haydn's Symphony No. 83.[11] Julius Katchen's handling of motives in Brahms's Intermezzo Op. 118 No. 1 is 'inexplicable'; his performance 'lacks analytical insight and therefore perceptual consistency'.[12] And in a footnote, Narmour exclaims in exasperation that 'Sometimes conductors do utterly inexplicable things that make no sense at all',[13] instancing a performance of the *Rosenkavalier Suite* by André Previn. Such a sentiment may be understandable enough. But what is striking about it from a methodological point of view is the readiness

[5] Berry, *Musical Structure*, pp. xi–xii.

[6] Eugene Narmour, 'On the Relationship of Analytical Theory to Performance and Interpretation', in Narmour and Ruth Solie (eds.), *Explorations in Music, the Arts, and Ideas: Essays in Honor of Leonard B. Meyer* (Stuyvesant, NY, 1988), 317–40.

[7] Ibid. 319.

[8] Ibid. 334.

[9] Ibid. 334–5; emphasis added.

[10] Tim Howell, 'Analysis and Performance: The Search for a Middleground', in John Paynter *et al.*, *Companion to Contemporary Musical Thought* (London, 1992), ii. 692–714, p. 709.

[11] Narmour, 'Relationship', 325.

[12] Ibid. 319.

[13] Ibid. 333.

with which Narmour is prepared to abandon the attempt to understand what performers do; theory, it seems, is not committed to understanding performers in the way it is to understanding composers. (Have you ever heard a theorist say, 'Sometimes composers do utterly inexplicable things that make no sense at all'?) The assumption that theory exerts some kind of hegemony over performance is so entrenched that Narmour simply doesn't consider the possibility that the failure to understand what a performer does might be a reflection on the theory rather than on the performance.

The prescriptiveness of Narmour's writing reflects a prescriptiveness that is characteristic of, and even perhaps definitive of, music theory as a whole. A conspicuous example is Fred Lerdahl's article 'Cognitive Constraints on Compositional Systems',[14] which offers among other things the rare instance of an explicitly negative critique of a composition (Boulez's 'Le Marteau sans Maître'). Like Narmour's article, Lerdahl's was published in 1988, and the two work in rather similar ways. Both assume that there should be a more or less linear relationship between the manner in which a composer conceives a composition and the manner in which a listener perceives it. But whereas Narmour's focus is on the role of the performer as a link in this communicative chain, Lerdahl's aim is to specify the conditions that must be fulfilled if there is to be conformity between 'compositional grammar' and 'listening grammar'. And, like Narmour, he ends up by measuring existing music against the stipulations of his theory, using this as a basis for aesthetic evaluation. The result is to write off not only the Darmstadt avant-garde and minimalism, but also huge swathes of non-Western and popular music. It turns out that 'the best music' must necessarily involve pitch hierarchies, diatonic scales, and a triadic pitch space; it must, in fact, be 'based on "nature"'.[15] It could almost be Schenker talking.

Like Schenker (who was also prepared to turn his theory to the purposes of negative critique[16]), Lerdahl possesses the rigour of extremism; he is not afraid to pursue his principles to their logical conclusions, however counter-intuitive or even occasionally offensive they may be. I cannot be the only theorist to have a sneaking suspicion that much of what he says makes sense—perhaps more of it 'than I had bargained for', to borrow Lerdahl's own words.[17] The trouble is that you can't pick and choose among Lerdahl's conclusions; they are all of a piece. In other words, if you can't accept *all* Lerdahl's conclusions (and how many of us can?), then it is no good simply attacking his logic, because there is nothing wrong with it. Instead, it is necessary to question the basic framework of his argument. And this framework is that of structuralist music theory, which is to say the whole of music theory as generally understood today. My aim in this

---

[14] Fred Lerdahl, 'Cognitive Constraints on Compositional Systems', in John Sloboda (ed.), *Generative Processes in Music: The Psychology of Performance, Improvisation, and Composition* (Oxford, 1988), 231–59.

[15] Ibid. 256, 257.

[16] See his analyses of Reger's Variations and Fugue on a Theme of J. S. Bach, Op. 81, and Stravinsky's Piano Concerto: Heinrich Schenker, *The Masterwork in Music*, ed. William Drabkin, ii (Cambridge, 1996), 106–17 and 17–18.

[17] Lerdahl, 'Cognitive Constraints', 256.

chapter, then, is to focus on the issue of analysis and performance not so much for its own sake, but for what it can tell us about music theory in general. My central proposition is that a theory which does justice to performance will be at the same time a theory aware of its own performative qualities; in a nutshell, we need to think about what our theory *does* as much as about what it *represents*. Or so I shall argue.

## II

Lerdahl's 'Cognitive Constraints on Compositional Systems' is based on the generative theory of tonal music (GTTM) that he developed in conjunction with Ray Jackendoff,[18] and GTTM is in turn based on structural linguistics. More specifically, it is based on Chomsky's distinction between competence and performance: that is to say, between the abstract knowledge on which any rule-based system depends and the use of that knowledge in any given situation (the production and reception of speech in Chomsky's case, of music in Lerdahl and Jackendoff's). Seen from this perspective, performance—including, of course, musical performance—becomes an epiphenomenon of competence; as Lerdahl and Jackendoff put it, 'In our view it would be fruitless to theorize about mental processing before understanding the organization to which the processing leads.'[19] This movement *from* competence *to* performance, *from* abstract knowledge *to* practical realization, constitutes Lerdahl's and Jackendoff's basic explanatory paradigm, and Narmour's, and indeed that of all structuralist thinking.

In this way, Lerdahl and Narmour both eliminate the musician as an individual, and replace him or her by a theory whose input is some kind of musical text and whose ultimate output is an aesthetic judgement;[20] like all music theorists, perhaps, they explain music without musicians. But perhaps the most striking example of this kind of elimination of the musician as an individual is represented by the work of Eric Clarke, Neil Todd, and other proponents of the generative approach to musical performance.[21] Their outstanding success in explicating some of the cognitive schemata underlying musical performance has come at the expense of interpreting 'expression'—traditionally seen as the core of performers' individuality—as itself an epiphenomenon of structure; performers introduce rubato and other deviations from the notated music, they claim, in order to project or bring out (in a word, to *express*) its underlying struc-

---

[18] Fred Lerdahl and Ray Jackendoff, *A Generative Theory of Tonal Music* (Cambridge, Mass., 1983).

[19] Ibid. 4.

[20] Lerdahl is careful to explain that the constraints which he outlines in his article constitute a necessary, but not a sufficient, condition of high aesthetic value ('Cognitive Constraints', 255).

[21] For overviews of this literature see Eric Clarke, 'Generative Principles in Music Performance', in Sloboda (ed.), *Generative Processes in Music*, 1–26; and Henry Shaffer and Neil Todd, 'The Interpretive Component in Musical Performance', in Rita Aiello (ed.), *Musical Perceptions* (New York, 1984), 258–70.

ture. And this structuralist interpretation of the word 'express' is really no different from the well-established Schenkerian usage according to which, for instance, compositional design 'expresses' structure. In each case, the effect is to explain expression away, and with it the performer; the music is seen as expressing nothing but itself. The result is to give a psychological interpretation to Hanslick's metaphysical model of musical autonomy.

The concept of 'expression' provides a convenient means of introducing an important critique of this kind of structuralist thinking. Judith Butler has written that 'There is no gender identity behind the expressions of gender; that identity is performatively constituted by the very "expressions" that are said to be its results.'[22] We can generalize Butler's point—which Suzanne Cusick summarizes as 'gender is as gender does'—by saying that we tend to explain individual behaviour (including gender-related behaviour) as an epiphenomenon of social structure.[23] And Butler's argument is that this is to put everything back to front; it is individual behaviour that gives rise to social structure, not the other way round. But her point goes a bit further than this. When she refers to 'performativity', Butler is invoking speech-act theory, which emphasizes the extent to which linguistic meaning subsists in what language does, rather than what it represents; this is by virtue of what is referred to as its 'illocutionary force'.[24] What she is saying, then, is that there is no such thing as gender identity independent of the behaviour that 'expresses' it; it is a matter of what your behaviour *is*, not what it represents. And there is an obvious affinity between this and the argument recently advanced by Philip Bohlman for seeing musicology as a 'political act'; as he puts it, musicology 'not only describes but prescribes through its acts of interpretation'.[25] Musicology, in short, doesn't just reflect practice; it helps mould it.

But I want to be more specific and suggest that if we change just one of its words, Butler's maxim becomes directly applicable to music theory: 'structure', it would now read, 'is performatively constituted by the very "expressions" that are said to be its result'. There is an almost banal sense in which this is true of Schenkerian theory. Schenker's concept of structure being ontologically prior to its compositional 'expression' is rooted in nineteenth-century metaphysics; if it retains plausibility today, this is largely because of the *rapprochement* between Schenkerian theory and structural linguistics. And in this context it is very much to the point that speech-act theory, which Butler invokes, is intimately linked with the pragmatist critique of structural linguistics, which focuses on the distinction between competence and performance on which (as I said) GTTM is based. It has been repeatedly pointed out that this distinction 'provides its

---

[22] Judith Butler, *Gender Trouble: Feminisim and the Subversion of Identity* (New York, 1990), 25.

[23] See Suzanne Cusick's discussion of Butler's argument, Ch. 21 below.

[24] The definitive exposition of speech-act theory is J. L. Austin, *How to Do Things with Words* (Cambridge, Mass., 1962); for a convenient, if limited, thumb-nail sketch see Lawrence Kramer, *Music as Cultural Practice, 1800–1900* (Berkeley, 1990), 6–9.

[25] Philip Bohlman, 'Musicology as a Political Act', *Journal of Musicology*, 11 (1993), 411–36, p. 432.

proponents with a protective belt that surrounds their grammatical theories and makes them empirically impenetrable to psycholinguistic counterevidence';[26] if experimental data don't conform to the predictions of a theory of grammatical competence, this can always be put down to performative factors (for instance, constraints on cognitive processing). In this way, pragmatists claim, structural linguistics is unscientific because it is irrefutable. Indeed, according to Roy Harris, it represents a pseudo-science, an illegitimate abstraction from the actual circumstances of language use; seen from such a perspective, the idealized grammar known as 'competence' is, in reality, no more than a collection of 'strategies for understanding and producing sentences'.[27] Instead of reducing performance to a play of abstract structures, then, the pragmatist approach takes it to be a source of signification in its own right.

What would happen if a corresponding critique were applied to the language we traditionally use to describe 'performance' in its specifically musical sense? According to this language, we do not have 'performances' but rather 'performances *of*' pre-existing, Platonic works. The implication is that a performance should function as a transparent medium, 'expressing', 'projecting', or 'bringing out' only what is already 'in' the work, with the highest performance ideal being a selfless *Werktreue* (itself, as Butler might point out, uncomfortably reminiscent of nineteenth-century conceptions regarding the natural role of women[28]). Adopting the Butler/Harris approach, we might want to see what music psychologists refer to as performance 'expression'—the unsystematized transformation of notated pitches, dynamics, and articulation—as an aesthetically foundational aspect of music; structure, as defined by conventional analysis, would then constitute a means of representing or conceptualizing these 'expressive' characteristics, an attempt to capture their trans-situational properties. And more generally, what we call musical 'works' might be regarded along the same lines: that is to say, as means of representing or conceptualizing performances.[29]

Now such a formulation might perhaps seem more applicable to jazz (where interpretation of 'standards' foregrounds the performance rather than the piece) or to many non-Western traditions than to the Western art tradition; after all,

[26] Morten Christiansen, 'The (Non)Necessity of Recursion in Natural Language Processing', in *Proceedings of the Fourteenth Annual Meeting of the Cognitive Science Society* (Hillsdale, NJ, 1993), 665–70, p. 666.

[27] G. Lackoff and H. Thompson, 'Introducing Cognitive Grammer', paper presented at the Berkeley Linguistics Society, 1975; quoted by Edwin Hantz, 'Studies in Music Cognition: Comments from a Music Theorist', *Music Perception*, 2 (1984), 245–64, p. 247. The argument I am presenting at this point is condensed from my article 'Perception: A Perspective from Music Theory', in Aiello (ed.), *Musical Perceptions*, 64–95, pp. 76–8.

[28] The story of the legitimation of music as composition at the expense of music as performance could clearly be told in gendered terms; it would link the Hegelian identification of the Ideal as male (versus the particular as female) with the historical circumstances under which women became established in the sphere of performance long before they did in the sphere of composition.

[29] In effect I am paraphrasing Richard Baumann's argument that the study of performance need not 'begin with artful texts, identified on independent formal grounds and then reinjected into situations of use. . . . Rather, . . . Performance becomes *constitutive*' of the text (*Verbal Art as Performance* (Rowley, Mass., 1977), 11).

the social practice of Western art-music is organized round works, to say nothing of the aesthetic and analytical literature. At the same time, the bewildering variety of versions in which many established works exist (the slow movements of Corelli's Op. 5 sonatas, for instance, or Liszt's *Mazeppa* and its multitudinous avatars) demonstrates how permeable the distinction between works and performances has often been in the Western tradition.[30] Even within the canon of master-works, the performance-orientated formulation is in many ways a more accurate reflection of musical reception than the traditional model of the relationship between work and performance. The advertising pages of any CD magazine show that it is generally the performer as an individual who is marketed, rather than the work; consumers buy Beethoven or Rachmaninov, but as often as not it is Alfred Brendel, or David Helfgott, who motivates the purchase. (Perhaps the canon might be defined as a set of works so familiar that they function more as medium than message.) But I don't think we should look upon this as something that admits of an either/or solution; just as it is impossible fully to understand the reception of Beethoven's or Rachmaninov's music without taking into account the musicians who perform it, so it would be absurd to try and understand Brendel's or Helfgott's playing without reference to *what* they play.

Instead of assigning either work or performance priority over the other, then, the best course is to see them as having a relationship of dialogue with one another.[31] Lawrence Rosenwald expresses this well when he says that the piece exists 'in the relation between its notation and the field of its performances'.[32] Seen in this light, composers and performers collaborate in the creation and maintenance of the repertory.[33] Signs of a corresponding reorientation can be detected in some current writing on analysis and performance; there is a new emphasis on the mutuality of the analyst/performer relationship, as against the hegemonic relationship assumed by Berry and Narmour.[34] Joel Lester speaks of the desirability of a 'reciprocal discourse' between theorists and performers; as he puts it, 'Performers could enter analytical dialogue *as performers*—as artistic/intellectual equals, not as intellectual inferiors who needed to learn from theorists.' (It is the theorists, he says, who need to listen to performers.[35]) And as

---

[30] For Corelli's Op. 5 see my 'Heinrich Schenker, Anti-historicist', *Revista de Musicologia*, 16 (1993), 24–36. For a general discussion of the issue see José Bowen, 'The History of Remembered Innovation: Tradition and its Role in the Relationship between Musical Works and their Performances', *Journal of Musicology*, 11 (1993), 139–73.

[31] Although I am not specifically invoking Bakhtin, my argument at this point might usefully be read in the light of his account of utterances (see Kevin Korsyn's chapter, 4 above).

[32] Lawrence Rosenwald, 'Theory, Text-setting, and Performance', *Journal of Musicology*, 11 (1993), 52–65, p. 62.

[33] For a fuller discussion see my article 'Music Minus One: Rock, Theory, and Performance', *New Formations*, 27 (1995–6), 23–41.

[34] A major stimulus to this development seems to have been Berry's book itself; practically every published review (and there were many, by Lester, Clarke, Rink, and Larson and Folio among others) criticized its prescriptiveness.

[35] Joel Lester, 'Performance and Analysis: Interaction and Interpretation', in John Rink (ed.), *The Practice of Performance: Studies in Musical Interpretation* (Cambridge, 1995), 197–216; there are many resonances between the present chapter and Lester's. Among writers calling for the analysis of performances rather than simply of compositions are Rosenwald ('Theory, Text-setting', 63) and Jonathan Dunsby ('Real Music', *Newsletter of the Society for*

long ago as 1985, Janet Schmalfeldt actually provided an idealized instance of such a dialogue; her article 'On the Relation of Analysis to Performance: Beethoven's Bagatelles Op. 126, Nos. 2 and 5'[36] takes the form of a conversation in which Schmalfeldt the analyst and Schmalfeldt the performer trade insights with one another. It is noticeable, however, that the two Schmalfeldts tend to lecture one another rather than interact freely, and one is ultimately left with the impression that the analyst-Schmalfeldt holds all the cards. (Rosenwald comments shrewdly that the performer-Schmalfeldt's encomium to analysis 'feels a bit too much like a Puritan conversion-narrative'.[37])

Schmalfeldt readily admits that there are areas where the analyst-Schmalfeldt's and the performer-Schmalfeldt's concerns do not intersect; as she puts it, 'it is one thing to consider how we might some day realize a score, and it is quite another thing to perform the work.'[38] This eminently sensible remark exemplifies a second strategy for escaping the prescriptiveness of the Berry/Narmour approach: what might be called the model of partial intersection. Another example comes from Jonathan Dunsby, according to whom 'Understanding and trying to explain musical structure is not the same kind of activity as understanding and communicating music'.[39] He explains this in terms of what he calls

a rather simple distinction, one which is often overlooked, between interpretation and performance. A particular analysis may well lead to the conviction that a particular kind of interpretation is essential, but how to convey that interpretation to the listener in performance is a different matter.

Dunsby's approach is very much along the lines of Schenker's well-known distinction between the musical effect and the manner of its realization in performance. This avoids the blatant prescriptiveness of the Berry/Narmour approach to the extent that it allots an area of creative freedom to the performer. Yet it still vests ultimate authority in the analyst, who (at least in Schenker's eyes) remains responsible for defining what the work *is*; for, as Schenker puts it, 'Performance must come from within the work; the work must breathe from its own lungs—from the linear progressions, neighboring tones, chromatic tones,

*Music Analysis*, 4 (Jan. 1993), 8–9, p. 9); and there is a growing literature which attempts to provide exactly that. (One example among several is my chapter 'The Conductor and the Theorist: Furtwängler, Schenker, and the First Movement of Beethoven's Ninth Symphony', in *Practice of Performance*, 105–25; see in addition José Bowen's chapter, 19 below.)

[36] Janet Schmalfeldt, 'On the Relation of Analysis to Performance: Beethoven's Bagatelles Op. 126, Nos. 2 and 5', *Journal of Music Theory* 29 (1985), 1–31.

[37] Rosenwald, 'Theory, Text-setting', 61. Equally pointedly, Lester refers to Schmalfeldt's 'imbalanced dialogue: her pianist-persona is learning to play the pieces, but it is obvious from her prose that her analyst-persona has studied them long and hard' ('Performance and Analysis', 198 n. 1).

[38] Schmalfeldt, 'Relation', 19.

[39] Jonathan Dunsby, 'Guest Editorial: Performance and Analysis of Music', *Music Analysis*, 8 (1989), 5–20, p. 7. For a philosophical commentary on the distinction between critical and performance interpretation, see Jerrold Levinson, 'Performative vs. Critical Interpretations in Music', in Michael Krausz (ed.), *The Interpretation of Music: Philosophical Essays* (Oxford, 1993), 33–60.

modulations.' And he adds: 'About these, naturally, there cannot exist different interpretations.'[40]

But the main problem with this approach, as I see it, is that it continues to look for a one-to-one mapping of analysis and performance on to one another within the areas of their communality; John Rink describes this as 'too simplistic a translation from analysis to performance'.[41] It may be unwise to use the word 'translation' at all in this context, for it suggests the possibility of a smooth transformation from the one to the other, an unproblematic transference of analytical content into the domain of performance. On the other hand, Rosenwald points out that, in its primary application to language, the idea of translation is by no means as simple as this might suggest: 'we do not know the original,' he says; 'do not and cannot know it *in se*, and . . . come to know it precisely by means of reflecting on its translations.'[42] And as Fred Maus points out in his commentary on Rosenwald's article, 'in this process of exploration the distinction between "making" and "finding" meanings is obscure.'[43] Translated (and I do mean translated) back into terms of performance, this argument suggests once again that performance should be seen as a source of signification in its own right. It does not simply 'express', 'project', or 'bring out' originary meaning—meaning which, in Rosenwald's words, we cannot know *in se*. If we come to know the original 'precisely by means of reflecting on its translations', then it follows that performance is a source of musical meaning. Put like this, it seems almost too obvious: how could performance be anything else?

# III

From this perspective, one is bound to look askance at the dualism implicit in such traditional statements as 'only when one has reached the point where one feels completely certain of how the piece must go should the realization process commence'.[44] (Berry condenses this into seven words when he writes of

[40] From Schenker's unfinished 'Entwurf einer "Lehre vom Vortrag"', quoted and translated by William Rothstein, 'Heinrich Schenker as an Interpreter of Beethoven's Piano Sonatas', *19th-Century Music*, 8 (1984), 3–28, p. 10. This analytically based sense of 'interpretation' needs to be distinguished from two other usages: Schenker's pejorative use of the term to signify arbitrary and personal performance and a usage more characteristic of the performance literature proper, according to which it refers to performance at the highest level; Cortot e.g., says that 'If you love her [music] to the extent of dedicating your life to her service . . . [y]ou will have become an interpreter, not merely a performer' (Jeanne Thieffry, *Alfred Cortot's Studies in Musical Interpretation* (London, 1937), 16).

[41] Review of Berry, *Musical Structure*, *Music Analysis*, 9 (1990), 319–39, p. 321.

[42] Rosenwald, 'Theory, Text-setting', 62.

[43] Fred Maus, 'Response to Rosenwald', *Journal of Musicology*, 11 (1993), 66–72, p. 69.

[44] Joan Allen Smith, *Schoenberg and his Circle: A Viennese Portrait* (New York, 1986), 106. paraphrasing Kolisch. Similar statements may be found in such writers as Erwin Stein ('The performer must have a crystal-clear conception of the music he is going to play' (*Form and Performance* (London, 1962), 19) ) and Hermann Scherchen, according to whom 'the alpha and omega of conducting' is 'the capacity to conceive an absolutely ideal performance in the imagination' (*Handbook of Conducting*, quoted in Christopher Wintle, 'Analysis and Performance: Webern's Concerto Op. 24/II', *Music Analysis*, 1 (1982), 73–99, p. 74). Stein's reference to the performer's need to have 'a whole

'proceeding from conceptualization to realization in performance'.[45]) The dualism to which I refer is between abstract conception, on the one hand, and concrete realization, on the other; and it reappears in the related maxim that 'after the intellect has finished work, the instinct must take over. In performance the analysis must be forgotten.'[46] (Again, this is reflected in Berry's remark that 'The analytical comprehension of structure is usually assimilated to a submerged level of consciousness'.[47]) A performative approach to performance, if it may be called that, would instead stress the inseparability of intellectual and bodily knowledge, the way in which the one informs the other;[48] in this light, a far more realistic attitude is embodied in Glenn Gould's statement that 'the ideal way to go about making a performance . . . is to assume that when you begin, you don't quite know what it is about. You only come to know as you proceed.'[49]

And this has practical implications for the relationship of analysis and performance. Berry suggests that

the analysis that ultimately guides performance is distilled: it is a selective determination along inferred lines of structure that are a basis for the reasoned, reasonable unity to which the analytical enquiry ideally leads, and which in turn is expressed in illumined, illuminating performance.[50]

In other words, you complete the analysis, and then you decide on appropriate performance 'interventions' on the basis of that analysis. ('Intervention' is one of Berry's favourite terms, and it is again highly dualistic; the implication is that performance is something like 'flying by wire', with the option of manual override in case of emergency—that is to say, should structure be endangered.) And this approach exactly complements the traditional piano teacher's approach of which Ralph Kirkpatrick wrote, 'Their admonition was, Learn the notes and then put in the expression.'[51] But if analysis and performance are to be seen as interlocking modes of musical knowledge, then they should be pursued simultaneously and interactively, not in succession.[52] Or to put it another way, analysis should be seen as a means of posing articulate questions, and not, as Berry

---

piece of music in a nutshell in his mind' (*Form and Performance*, 71) links this conception with, on the one hand, Schoenberg's conception of musical space and, on the other, the nineteenth-century tradition of statements about conceiving an entire composition as a single, simultaneous image that were (fraudulently) ascribed to Mozart and Beethoven, and that occupy an important place in Schenker's *Der freie Satz* (*Free Composition*, trans. and ed. Ernst Oster (New York, 1979), 128–9).

[45] Berry, *Musical Structure*, 217.

[46] Benjamin Britten, foreword to Stein, *Form and Performance*, 8.

[47] Berry, *Musical Structure*, xi.

[48] See in this connection Robert Walser, 'The Body in the Mind: Epistemology and Musical Semiotics', *College Music Symposium*, 31 (1991), 117–26.

[49] Tim Page (ed.), *The Glenn Gould Reader* (London, 1987), 287; cited and discussed in Jonathan Dunsby, *Performing Music: Shared Concerns* (Oxford, 1995), 39, 46. I have advanced a similar argument in relation to composition in *Music, Imagination, and Culture* (Oxford, 1990), 204–16.

[50] Berry, *Musical Structure*, 218.

[51] Ralph Kirkpatrick, *Interpreting Bach's 'Well-Tempered Clavier': A Performer's Discourse of Method* (New Haven, 1984), 128. Kirkpatrick continues: 'My admonition is to learn the notes and understand their relationships, and then to draw the expression out.'

[52] For a concrete illustration of what this might entail, see the previous chapter by John Rink.

suggests,[53] as a source of answers; in Howell's words, 'The role of analysis in this context is one of raising possibilities rather than providing solutions.'[54] Yet another way of saying the same thing is that analysis contributes (as I would maintain it always does[55]) as process, not as product, which is why, as Howell says, 'Reading someone else's analysis, even if specifically targeted as "performer friendly", is almost the equivalent of asking someone to practise on your behalf'.[56] Or to rephrase it in terms of pragmatics, what matters about analysis is not so much what it represents but what it does, or more precisely what it leads *you* to do.

What might be called 'structurally informed performance', as urged by Berry or Narmour, aims, then, at a more or less literal translation of the product of analysis. I have no wish to deny that such a style of performance is possible, or indeed that it may be a valid option (although such structurally informed performance can all too easily verge on the patronizing or, to use William Rothstein's word,[57] pedantic). But the point is precisely that it is an *option*, which is to say that there are other options, and this is something that cannot be formulated in terms of the dualistic language of 'expressing', 'projecting', and 'bringing out' structure. In statements that I have already quoted, Berry refers to structurally informed performance as 'edifying', 'illumined', and 'illuminating'; the real point, however, is not so much the implicit value-judgement, but the fact that he has no other language for talking about performance. And I would maintain that the tenacity of the structuralist paradigm in writing about music is as much a linguistic phenomenon as a conceptual or ideological one.

A revealing example of the tenacity of this paradigm is provided by Robert Wason, in his commentary on Webern's Piano Variations, and specifically on the performance indications that Webern communicated to Peter Stadlen, who gave the first performance.[58] In the article that he wrote on this topic, Stadlen (whose purpose was largely polemical) denied that there is any significant coincidence

---

[53] 'The analysis which informs interpretation affords a basis—the only basis—for resolving the hard questions both of general interpretive demeanor and of those elusive refinements of detail which make for performance which is both moving and illuminating' (*Musical Structure*, 223).

[54] Howell, 'Analysis and Performance', 709.

[55] Nicholas Cook, 'Music Theory and "Good Comparison": A Viennese Perspective', *Journal of Music Theory*, 33 (1989), 117–41, p. 129.

[56] Howell, 'Analysis and Performance', 702. Although this point is well taken, it does rather depend what kind of 'reading' is involved. An adequate reading of an analysis, as of a literary or musical text, involves a process of recreation in experience; it involves making 'somebody else's' analysis your own. (As Fisher and Lochhead put it, 'For the performer encountering an analysis by someone else, it may provide the basis for an inner hearing as the performer comes to own the analysis' ('Analysis, Hearing', 36).) Were it not so, there would be little point in publishing analyses.

[57] William Rothstein, 'Analysis and the Act of Performance', in Rink, *Practice of Performance*, 217–40. As Rothstein puts it, 'to perform the analysis is not to perform the piece' (229); he focuses on situations where the performer needs to conceal structure, rather than bring it out.

[58] See Robert Wason, 'Webern's *Variations for Piano*, Op. 27: Musical Structure and the Performance Score', *Intégral*, 1 (1987), 57–103, and Peter Stadlen, 'Serialism Reconsidered', *The Score*, 22 (1958), 12–27. Peter Stadlen's performance score, incorporating Webern's annotations, is published as UE 16845 (Vienna, 1979). If Webern 'felt so sure that there always was, at least in music, just one way of doing things' (Lehrigstein, quoted in Wintle, 'Analysis and Performance', 75), then these annotations should presumably be considered integral to the piece, at least as Webern intended it.

between the serial structure and Webern's performance indications. Wason disagrees; he argues that both serial structure and performance indications are correlated with the phrase structure, so that there is an indirect connection between the two. But what causes him embarrassment is what might be called the 'melody line' of the first movement—that is to say, the sequence of notes at the top of the texture. Webern instructed Stadlen to bring out this line; yet it cuts right across the serial structure. Wason can do no better than conclude, lamely, that 'the derivation of these "melody" notes is itself an interesting phenomenon for future study, although . . . it has so far eluded explanation'.[59] He salvages as much as he can from this failure by concluding that such indications, which 'point to structural features not immediately retraceable to the row . . . produce a tension against the structural segmentations, *while certainly assuming their existence*'.[60] But this sounds suspiciously like a convoluted way of saying that the two have nothing to do with one another.

Rosenwald suggests that such a situation might be the norm, rather than the exception, when he remarks that 'perhaps we could get a livelier dialogue between performer and analyst if the performer were prepared, on analytic grounds, to make a case for the performance of unstructural or antistructural detail'.[61] Certainly it would be an interesting theoretical task to define general situations in which performing 'against' the structure is an appropriate strategy, whether because 'The music is so clear that the interpreter may occasionally phrase *against* formal segmentations of the music without placing that dimension of the music in jeopardy of total loss',[62] or because a piece is too well known and needs defamiliarizing (as might be argued of Mengelberg's performances of the Ninth Symphony, or Roger Norrington's for that matter). But by asking the performer to make the case 'on analytic grounds', Rosenwald perpetuates the classic theorist's strategy of shifting the dialogue between analysis and performance on to the theorist's turf; in this way the dialogue he asks for is already rigged. Following Jennifer Tong, I would like to counterpose not so much the analyst and the performer but rather the 'writing' and the 'performing' musician, or, perhaps more precisely, music as writing and music as performance.[63] And by this I mean to suggest that what is at issue in thinking about performance isn't so crucially a complementarity of respective analytical concerns (in Rosenwald's terms, accommodating the imperatives of

[59] Wason, 'Webern's *Variations*', 95.

[60] Ibid. 101–2; emphasis added.

[61] Rosenwald, 'Theory, Text-setting', 63.

[62] Wason, 'Webern's *Variations*', 102. Characteristically, Wason continues 'although obviously one must have a clear understanding of just what one is "playing against" '.

[63] Jennifer Tong Chee Yee, 'Separate Discourses: A Study of Performance and Analysis' (Ph.D. diss., University of Southampton, 1995). My thinking on analysis and performance has been tangled up with Tong's for the past four years, and I would like to thank her for an influence on my views as expressed in this chapter which I find hard to quantify. Jean-Jacques Nattiez, too, stresses the centrality of writing in the constitution of analysis: 'there is no analysis except that which is *written*, that which has a material presence' (*Music and Discourse: Toward a Semiology of Music*, trans. Carolyn Abbate (Princeton, 1990), 70).

structure and of surface to one another) as the sheer incommensurability of writing and playing.

Seen this way, musical performance involves negotiating between the demands of physical gesture and sound (we can classify these under the heading of 'playing') and those of notation and its associated verbal traditions ('writing'). We might speak of translation between these incommensurable media, but only in Rosenwald's strong sense of 'translation' that emphasizes the semantic friction inherent in the process. This is because the media of writing and those of playing have very different structural characteristics. A score represents the concretization of the contingent, a singular encounter between sound and notation (it is generally only in improvisation that music begins genuinely to resemble the rule-based structures of grammar). And the language use that is aligned with and implicated in performance—let us call it the 'literature of performance'—has its own logic and agenda; this is what gives rise to the characteristic divergence between theory and practice. An illustration of this is the concept of 'compensating rubato'—a nineteenth-century pedagogical generalization from the Baroque or early Classical maxim that a melody, however freely played, should be supported by a rhythmically fixed accompaniment.[64] Empirical studies have repeatedly shown that, regarded as a description of practice, this 'theory' is simply wrong; it does not reflect what performers do.[65] But that is because its aim is to *modify* what performers do; it is not a description, but a prescription. And in this sense it is comparable to old-fashioned grammar books, which prescribed 'correct' usage, rather than to the abstract grammars of structural linguistics;[66] its meaning resides in its illocutionary force.

There is a general principle at work here. We tend to justify the prescriptive application of models and theories on the grounds of their descriptive validity; in effect, Narmour claims the right to judge the quality of performances because he claims that his theoretical model is a valid description of cognitive processes.[67] But the aim of a prescription, unlike that of a scientific description, is to perturb the phenomenon to which it applies; it is (to appropriate Berry's word) an intervention. It follows that the significance of a prescriptive model (such as 'compensating rubato') lies precisely in the gap between theory and practice. And I take this to be emblematic of the relationship between music as writing and music as playing, of which Howell writes that 'from this apparent conflict

---

[64] For a general account see Robert Philip, *Early Recordings and Musical Style: Changing Tastes in Instrumental Performance, 1900–1950* (Cambridge, 1992), 38–44. The basic idea is that any accelerando must be 'paid back' by a corresponding rallentando, or vice versa, whether within the bar or within some higher-level metrical unit.

[65] The classic study is John McEwen, *Tempo Rubato, or Time-variation in Musical Performance* (London, 1928); see the discussion in Philip, *Early Recordings*, 44–9.

[66] See Roy Harris, *The Language Myth* (London, 1981).

[67] Psychologically based writers such as Clarke and Todd, by contrast, scrupulously avoid this kind of leakage from description to prescription; it is this, as much as anything else, that marks their work as something distinct from 'music theory' as generally understood.

between the rational and the instinctive comes a highly creative force'. He continues: 'If this essay has any didactive purpose for performers then it is to encourage them to exploit this creative force, to play off intuitive responses against analytical perceptions in order to shape an interpretation.'[68] It is almost like creating a spark through the juxtaposition of two opposed electrical poles.

**IV**

What is true of the literature of performance is equally true of the literature of analysis as a whole (and, as I previously suggested, if *this* essay has any didactive purpose, it is to use the analysis of musical performance as a model for the performativity of analytical writing in general). In this context, the term 'literature' is more than rhetorical; analysis is a genre of literary production, whose master narrative was for a century and a half the ideology of organicism, but has increasingly become the logic of disciplinary identity. For the autonomy of music theory as a discipline is predicated on the meaningful abstraction of music from context; and if it is true (as who has not on occasion uneasily suspected?) that 'talk about music eclipses music itself as the most fascinating object in the academic firmament',[69] then there is every reason for reading music theory for its performative—and indeed, what might be called its political—content. What, to take a specific example, does an article like Lerdahl's 'Cognitive Constraints on Compositional Systems' actually *do?* By subordinating the production and reception of music to theoretically defined criteria of communicative success, it creates a charmed hermeneutic circle that excludes everything from critical musicology to social psychology. It slips imperceptibly from description to prescription, so reinforcing the hegemony of theory. In this way, while the literary genre of Lerdahl's article is the scientific paper—a genre predicated on the transparent representation of an external reality—its substance lies at least equally in its illocutionary force. To repeat Bohlman's words, it 'not only describes but prescribes through its acts of interpretation'.[70]

But my main point is a more basic one about what we do when we do theory. I want to suggest that there is an evolving consensus on what might be called a 'performative epistemology' of music theory—the idea, to put it in a nutshell, that one should make analysis true *through*, rather than true *to*, experience.[71] David Lewin expresses this clearly when he writes that analysis is 'not an *aid* to

---

[68] Howell, 'Analysis and Performance', 698.

[69] Scott Burnham, 'Musical and Intellectual Values: Interpreting the History of Tonal Theory', *Current Musicology*, 53 (1993), 76–88, p. 76.

[70] See n. 25.

[71] I have tried to sketch some of the background for such an epistemology in 'Music Theory and "Good Comparison"', esp. 123–35. See also Kendall Walton, 'Understanding Humor and Understanding Music', and Mark DeBellis, 'Theoretically Informed Listening', in Krausz (ed.), *Interpretation of Music*, 258–69, 271–81; also Marion

perception, or to the memory of perception; rather, we are *in the very act* of perceiving'. (More extravagantly, he refers to the products of analysis as 'ski tracks tracing the poetic deeds that were the perceptions themselves'.[72]) Maus expresses the same idea with specific reference to Rosenwald's gloss on the concept of translation: 'perhaps', he says, 'analyses . . . could be regarded as translations. That is, analyses can be seen, not as pale copies of a determinate original, but as ways of exploring musical compositions in an ongoing process in which there is no point in distinguishing between making and finding the qualities of the music.'[73] The last point, to which I have already referred, is crucial; Maus is suggesting that musical meaning is emergent, that it arises out of the mutual interaction of musical texts and critical commentaries. And something of the same is conveyed by Dunsby's reference to the need to 'recognize the inevitability of the coexistence of music and discourse, and not shy away from it into the retreats of fragmentary subdisciplines, with mute performers, and arid commentators'.[74]

This performative perspective on analysis constitutes the best defence against the principal charge laid against it by the godfathers of the New Musicology, Joseph Kerman and Leo Treitler: analysis, they say, is interested in music only in the pursuit of abstract generalization, whereas criticism represents a direct, passionate involvement with individual works of music in all their singularity.[75] In Treitler's words, which refer specifically to Schenker's book on Beethoven's Ninth Symphony,

Schenker's purpose was to demonstrate the unity of the work and the necessity of its constituent moments, and to display it as exemplification of a theory. This amounts to the *explanation* of the work in the strict sense that its events are seen to follow with the force of deductive logic. My purpose . . . was the illumination of the work in its individuality. I take this to be a permanent difference between analysis and criticism.[76]

Treitler depicts Schenker as translating the objects of musical experience into abstract theoretical categories, resulting at best in the 'pale copy of a determinate original' to which Maus refers (and at worst in an abstraction, Dunsby's 'arid commentary', that cannot be meaningfully related to the sound and fury of Beethoven's music). We need to remember that Treitler was writing in 1980, before the recent move towards understanding Schenker in his historical context; fifteen years later, Treitler's words appear curiously anachronistic, describing what now seems a perverse way to read a text that is so opaque, so

Guck, 'Rehabilitating the Incorrigible', in Anthony Pople (ed.), *Theory, Analysis and Meaning in Music* (Cambridge, 1994), 57–73.

[72] David Lewin, 'Music Theory, Phenomenology, and Modes of Perception', *Music Perception*, 3 (1986), 327–92, pp. 381–2.

[73] Maus, 'Response to Rosenwald', 70. See also Ch. 8 above.

[74] Dunsby, *Performing Music*, 46.

[75] On Kerman, see Ch. 9 above.

[76] Leo Treitler, 'History, Criticism, and Beethoven's Ninth Symphony', originally published in 1980 (*19th-Century Music*, 3, 193–210), and repr. in *Music and the Historical Imagination* (Cambridge, Mass., 1989), 19–45, p. 32.

full of ideological and polemical content, so motivated by a passionate involvement with music and a no less passionate conviction of its importance to society, as the Ninth Symphony monograph. Put simply, Treitler is outlining an unprofitable way to read a text that is rooted in and communicates so singular a vision, and audition, of Beethoven's music. And of all the works of the Western art tradition, the Ninth Symphony is the one that most dramatically illustrates the extent to which music acquires meaning from the sedimentation of successive layers of commentary. In its wealth of striking literary images, in its fervent advocacy of the 'absolute music' tradition, and in its attempt to erase Wagner from that tradition, as well as in its documentation for all time of a now defunct style of performance, Schenker's book constitutes an irreversible event in the reception history of the Ninth Symphony.[77] In Maus's terms, the Schenker monograph signifies at least as much by virtue of what Schenker makes of the Ninth as by what he finds in it.

But I want to make a more general point regarding what Treitler contrasts as 'explanation' and 'illumination', corresponding (in his terminology) to 'analysis' and 'criticism' respectively. According to Treitler, criticism focuses on 'the unique qualities of individual works, rather than the system that makes the uniqueness of works possible'.[78] Now a theoretical system is something like a ruler; it is an instrument against which individual phenomena may be measured. Or, more accurately, a theory is a calculus of possibilities, a grid of virtualities, against which a given musical concretion stands in all its specificity. Once again, it is the gap between theory and practice, between analytical model and music, that is all-important; it marks the point beyond which the music cannot be subsumed within the systematic and predictable. Theory, in other words, is the means by which the individual is rendered perceptible *as* an individual. And it follows from this that the 'illumination' of the individual, by which Treitler sets such store, is possible only to the extent that it is measured against (or explained in terms of) some kind of theoretical model. In Carl Dahlhaus's words, 'A piece of theory, explicitly or implicitly, provides the starting point for each analysis. The notion of a description without assumptions is a phantom; if it could be realized, it would not be worth the trouble.'[79]

Of course, Dahlhaus is using words differently from Treitler. For Dahlhaus, an analysis 'implies theoretic thoughts without aiming at a theoretic system. It attempts to do justice to the particular and unrepeatable; the general, the theory, is but a means and instrument for the attempt to understand the unique individual case.'[80] In short, Dahlhaus's 'analysis' means the same as Treitler's 'criticism', except that Dahlhaus is open about the role that theory must play in any

[77] See Nicholas Cook, 'Heinrich Schenker, Polemicist: A Reading of the Ninth Symphony Monograph', *Music Analysis*, 14 (1995), 89–105.

[78] Treitler, 'History', 34.

[79] Carl Dahlhaus, *Analysis and Value Judgment* (New York, 1983), 8.

[80] Ibid.

attempt to account for the individual, whereas Treitler is not. Consequently Dahlhaus offers a continuum, an infinite gradation of shades, between what he calls 'theoretically and aesthetically oriented analysis',[81] where Treitler sees a black-and-white distinction, a 'permanent difference between analysis and criticism'. And because Treitler sees what he calls 'criticism' as being fundamentally performative—a process leading to the experience of illumination shared between writer and reader—his black-and-white approach leads him to posit exactly the opposite of what he calls 'analysis'[82]; hence the disjunction between theory and experience that Treitler conveys when he writes, again with specific reference to Schenker, that 'An analysis is a demonstration that, and how, a particular piece is an instance of a sound system whose conceptual structuring is described in a theory (it would correspond more or less to an explanation in science)'.[83]

To assert that analysis is not performative—that it does not have meaning by virtue of what it does—is necessarily to assert that it has meaning by virtue of what it represents; there is no other alternative. So, for Treitler, any validity an analysis might have must derive from its status as an objective representation of reality, and this of course makes it an easy target for epistemological critique. What I would like to claim is that analysis should not be understood, or at least should not be primarily or necessarily understood, in this way. But there is a problem with this: analysts not infrequently write as if they were indeed engaged in the objective representation of some kind of reality. The most concise expression of this is Schenker's famous assertion that 'I was given a vision of the urlinie [*sic*], I did not invent it!'[84] But a better indicator, perhaps, than what analysts explicitly assert is the conclusions that they draw from their work, and in particular conclusions regarding aesthetic value. As Dahlhaus says, if 'no *Ursatz* is to be found notwithstanding persistent analytic efforts, then Schenker does not hesitate to issue an aesthetic verdict';[85] the basis of this is precisely Schenker's

---

[81] Ibid. 9. Similarly Fisher and Lochhead refer to 'theory-driven' and 'piece-driven' analysis, a distinction which they link with an earlier debate between Edward Cone and David Lewin ('Analysis, Hearing', 6).

[82] Compare Treitler's discussion of competence and performance ('History', 34). His insistence on the analysis/criticism dichotomy sits oddly alongside his insistence on the falsity of Schenker's analysis/hermeneutics (or absolute/referential) dichotomy; as he says, 'the very inability of the purists to maintain their purity is a clue to the misdirected nature of the dichotomy' (ibid.).

[83] Treitler, *Music and the Historical Imagination*, 310. It is interesting to see how Treitler uses words to lift Schenker out of his own context and inscribe him within the neo-positivist milieu of East Coast America in the 1970s (he is actually pastiching David Lewin); can you imagine Schenker speaking of the Ninth Symphony as 'an instance of a sound system'?

[84] As trans. by Sylvan Kalib in 'Thirteen Essays from the Three Yearbooks "Das Meisterwerk in der Musik" by Heinrich Schenker: An Annotated Translation' (Ph.D. diss., Northwestern University, 1973), 218; less memorably, if more accurately, trans. John Rothgeb as 'I *apprehended* the Urlinie, I did not *calculate* it!' (Schenker, *Masterwork in Music*, ii. 19). A less concise but no less trenchant formulation comes from Wilhelm Furtwängler, according to whom 'Schenker forged a platform, revealed a condition, that is objectively present, beyond all historical tests, beyond all simple subjective preferences, and which, properly grasped, will be just as demonstrably certain as other contemporary scientific judgments' ('Heinrich Schenker: A Contemporary Problem', *Sonus*, 6 (1985), 1–5, pp. 3–4).

[85] Dahlhaus, *Analysis and Value Judgment*, 9.

belief that his theory represents a reality external to the individual work. And the same applies to the articles by Lerdahl and Narmour which I discussed earlier; both writers issue aesthetic verdicts on the basis that their theories represent actual processes (or at any rate outcomes) of cognition. Aesthetic prescriptiveness, then, is a sure sign of what might be called the 'paradigm of representation'.[86]

To draw aesthetic conclusions from an analytical model of music is to claim, whether explicitly or not, that the aesthetically significant aspects of the music are captured by the model. And that is exactly what, according to Dahlhaus, one should never claim: 'Aesthetic criteria,' he writes, 'singly or jointly, never offer sufficient support for judgment of a musical work. Any attempt to base music criticism on flawless rationality would have to run aground or lose itself in sectarianism.'[87] What is revealing, however, is that at another point in the same book Dahlhaus makes exactly the kind of aesthetic claim that he here says should never be made. It comes in the context of an attack on attempts to reduce aesthetics to reception history. He writes:

It is an error to grant to a 'group norm' which considers a pop tune the essence of music and a Beethoven symphony a hollow din equal aesthetic privileges as to the opposite 'group norm'. The factual judgments underlying the 'group norms' are not equally founded. A listener capable of doing justice to a Beethoven symphony is generally equipped to cope with the musical issues of a pop tune, but the reverse is not true.[88]

I do not know what specific kind of popular music, if any, Dahlaus had in mind when he wrote this. But his argument turns on the assumption that the analytical categories appropriate to a Beethoven symphony, which can in general be extrapolated from conventional notation, are sufficient (more than sufficient) for the analysis of popular music; what he is in essence saying is that anything pop can do, Beethoven can do better. This assumption is of course wrong; it is notorious that many of the most salient aspects of popular music—timbre is only the most obvious—slip between the categories of notation-based analysis. (The point is not that Beethoven is better than pop—or, for that matter, the opposite—but that they are different.) Dahlhaus, then, has fallen into the very trap he described: reducing the music to a set of criteria, and using these as the basis of an aesthetic judgement.

Where did Dahlhaus go wrong? His error is, in a sense, a linguistic one, in the same way that religious fundamentalism is, at core, a linguistic error. Fundamentalism arises from the false belief that language can circumscribe and contain reality, from which it follows that what cannot be said does not exist.

---

[86] There is an obvious parallel between what I am calling the paradigm of representation and Wittgenstein's 'picture' theory of meaning; see Joanna Hodge, 'Aesthetic Decomposition: Music, Identity, and Time', in Krausz (ed.), *Interpretation of Music*, 247–58.

[87] Dahlhaus, *Analysis and Value Judgment*, 34.

[88] Ibid. 6.

Dahlhaus's error is the same: he assumes that what cannot be said in the language of common-practice analysis does not exist, and consequently issues an aesthetic verdict against popular music. It is in this sense that Schenker, Lerdahl, and Narmour (along with all other analysts who issue aesthetic verdicts) can be said to be fundamentalists.

But I would not wish this to be misunderstood. While I think we should always be suspicious of aesthetic verdicts issued by analysts, I do not mean to imply that analysis is misconceived by virtue of being framed within the paradigm of representation. Roger Scruton has written that music criticism (which, for him, subsumes analysis) 'consists of the deliberate construction of an intentional object from the infinitely ambiguous instructions implicit in a sequence of sounds'.[89] In other words, it involves, if not exactly *making* the qualities of the music (to borrow Maus's words), then finding or inventing metaphorical constructions that represent salient aspects of it. And the key word here is 'metaphorical'; analyses represent music, but the mode of that representation is fundamentally metaphorical. This is not to deny that some analyses, some theoretical approaches, are more susceptible to empirical confirmation or refutation than others; music theory ranges from the scientific to the fantastic, and it is sometimes hard to know where to place a given approach on this axis (Schenkerian analysis is a conspicuous example). But there seems to be a general principle that the more 'scientific' an analytical approach is (in the sense of being open to empirical confirmation or refutation), the less well adapted it is for the complex, and often ill-defined, circumstances under which we use analysis to interrogate music and our experience of it.[90] For this reason the primary significance, or truth value, of analysis must lie in its potential for realization in the perceptual or imaginative terms of Lewin's 'poetic deeds'. An analysis, we might say, is like a promise: it is an action disguised as a statement of fact. And seen this way, the scientific truth value of analysis becomes at best secondary, and at times simply irrelevant.[91] Because he insists on treating analyses as if they were bad science, and nothing more, Treitler misreads them in the same way as someone who complains that the events in a novel didn't actually happen.[92] Historical facts are not ruled out of novels, of course. But they are not the basis of what Jeffrey Kallberg calls the 'generic contract'.[93]

Paradigms are closed; what they cannot say, they deny. That is why I have associated the paradigm of representation with fundamentalism. But avoiding fun-

[89] Roger Scruton, 'Understanding Music', *Ratio*, 25 (1983), 108–9.

[90] Robert Gjerdingen refers in Ch. 7 to 'the manifest difficulties in attempting to apply rigorous methods to poorly defined, culturally contingent phenomena' (p. 165)—the point being, of course, that it is 'poorly defined, culturally contingent phenomena' with which music theorists are mainly concerned.

[91] See DeBellis, 'Theoretically Informed Listening', 280–1.

[92] For a parallel perspective on New Musicological misreadings of analysis (focusing on Lawrence Kramer), see Scott Burnham, 'The Criticism of Analysis and the Analysis of Criticism', *19th-Century Music*, 16 (1992), 70–6.

[93] Jeffrey Kallberg, 'The Rhetoric of Genre: Chopin's Nocturne in G Minor', *19th-Century Music*, 11 (1988), 238–61.

damentalism in talking about music does not mean that we have to get away from representation; indeed we cannot, because our language for music is a language of representation. What it means is recognizing that our language for music is not monolithic, but draws its signification from any number of alternative representations of music, each of which constitutes sound as a different intentional object. Each 'music view', as it might be called, captures different aspects of actual or potential experience; each allows generalization across a different range of contexts. If we have a problem with this linguistic pluralism, it arises from the general tendency to identify the representation with what is represented—in short, the tendency towards fundamentalism. The consequence is the positing of a dominant representation that denies the possibility of alternatives. And that is where what I have called a performative perspective comes in. If we think of analysis, or for that matter any musicology, in terms of what it does and not just what it represents, then we have a semantic plane that can accommodate any number of metaphorical representations of music. We can negotiate between different meanings, however different the representations upon which they draw. And the result is to alleviate the greatest danger attendant upon the alignment of words with music, which is that of premature closure.

## V

In analysis, then, as in everything else, our words constantly threaten to run away with us. By way of conclusion, I shall cite a concrete example where, by invoking an implicit paradigm of representation, analytical language creates a meaning of its own, accomplishing cultural work that its author perhaps never intended. In a recent publication,[94] Cynthia Folio describes how the playing of Thelonius Monk, Ornette Coleman, and Eric Dolphy is animated by polymetric tension. She shows how linear progressions and motivic repetitions combine with surface rhythms to articulate a multiplicity of metrical planes that are superimposed upon the underlying metre of the music. The following commentary on Thelonius Monk's recording of 'Bags Groove' gives a flavour of her approach:

Beginning in the third bar, the metric accents create a 3/4 against the basic 4/4 played by the rhythm section. (To add to the complexity, two of the quarter-note beats in Monk's superimposed 3/4 meter are grouped into three's by the quarter-note triplet figures.) This 3/4 against 4/4 is an expression of the ratios 4:3 (at the level of the bar . . .), and 2:3 (at the level of the half note . . .).[95]

Wherein lies the paradigm of representation? Its explicit trace lies in the word

[94] Cynthia Folio, 'An Analysis of Polyrhythm in Selected Improvised Jazz Solos', in Elizabeth West Marvin and Richard Hermann (eds.), *Concert Music, Rock, and Jazz since 1945* (Rochester, NY, 1995), 103–34.
[95] Ibid. 113.

'expression': to say that the music 'expresses' the ratios 4 : 3 and 2 : 3 is to assign ontological priority to the abstract relationship as against its realization in sound.[96] That may seem a lot to read into one little word. But the resulting image of Monk, Coleman, and Dolphy weaving their solos in and out of a hierarchy of metrical levels contributes powerfully to the sense of almost frightening complexity that Folio conveys when, for instance, she writes of one of Dolphy's solos that

the proportion . . . of 7 : 4 has already occurred several times as a motivic element in the long, eleven-minute improvisation. At this point, late in the solo, he further subdivides this seven into three's, so that seven 3/8 bars are implied over the 4/4 (thus, the time signature of 21/8); in other words, four is divided by seven which is divided by three.[97]

And she adds that 'It is no coincidence that this solo is from *Last Date*, the last recorded album before his death, thus representing his most mature style'.

What is this analysis saying? Its overt content is straightforward enough. Folio is demonstrating what might be called the music's potential for perceptual realization, spelling out the various metrical constructions which it is capable of supporting, and aiming thereby to articulate the inner tension that the music conveys to the listener. One might say that she is showing how jazz musicians create local regularities, impressing the sense of an alternative or supplementary metre into the surface of the music. But this unproblematic formulation misses the dimension of meaning which the paradigm of representation brings to Folio's analysis. For deriving the musical surface from an underlying polymetrical structure—which is what is implied by saying that it 'expresses' polymetre—creates a much more mysterious impression: it is as if the musicians possess a rhythmic sensibility that enables them to track each metrical level separately and simultaneously, moving at will from one to another. Indeed, Folio reinforces this suggestion by citing a Ghanaian master drummer's statement that 'all master drummers are trained from childhood to hear all parts at once, not just one part at a time, or even the composite rhythm'.[98] And she remarks that 'some non-Western cultures are apparently better at perceiving many rhythmic layers at once' (better, that is, than Westerners).

All the components for the cultural work to be accomplished by Folio's analysis are now in place: the emphasis on complexity, the interpretation of this complexity as arising from the realization in sound of an abstract polymetrical structure, and the suggestion that it involves a degree of sensitivity that can be

---

[96] For an interesting perspective on such language that has yet to be assimilated into the mainstream of theoretical thought, see Gerald Balzano, 'Measuring Music', in A. Gabrielsson (ed.), *Action and Perception in Rhythm and Music* (Stockholm, 1987), 177–99.

[97] Folio, 'Analysis', 128.

[98] Ibid. 110. There is a parallel with the claim, in the Western musicological literature, that keen listeners can hear four or more independent contrapuntal lines; I have discussed this (with references) in *Music, Imagination, and Culture*, 35.

traced to the non-Western roots of jazz. (In the case of the Dolphy example, one might also note Folio's mention of the solo's unusual length, and the fact that it belongs to his last and most mature period—the late style, in other words.) What is taking place is, of course, an exercise in academic canon formation, and it has two rather contradictory components. One is the emphasis on the otherness, the exotic nature, of jazz improvisation; there is a parallel here with Kofi Agawu's observation that Western transcriptions of African music, with their multiplicity of shifting and superimposed time signatures, create 'an impression that . . . confirms the complexity of this music, a complexity in turn necessary to the construction of its difference, its "exotic" status'.[99] But the exotic easily becomes the marginal, and the major component of Folio's interpretation involves assimilating jazz improvisation firmly to dominant models of academic musical interpretation. Indeed, her final conclusion is that 'The growing number of analyses [of such music] confirm the notion that much of the motivic and structural coherence so characteristic of "composed" music is present in this improvisational art form'.[100] We are left with a reassuring impression that Western analytical methodology—*our* analytical methodology—possesses a truth value which crosses cultural boundaries; it *must* represent something that really is out there!

It is the paradigm of representation that is primarily responsible for all this cultural work. To say simply that jazz musicians sometimes play against the beat, creating the local sense of another metre, will not serve to admit their music to the academic canon, however complex the effects to which such practices give rise. To derive the surface of their music from an underlying abstract structure, on the other hand, is to render it directly comparable with the master-work tradition of Western tonal music; in essence Folio is constructing for jazz improvisation a metrical equivalent of the Schenkerian concept of 'creation from the background',[101] with all its connotations in terms of genius and the music-theoretical canon. And the difference between these two strategies, which is definitive of the paradigm of representation, is the abstraction of structure from lived experience. Again, African music provides a useful comparison. John Chernoff asserts that, in the transcription of African polyphony, it is impossible 'to notate without assigning different metres to different instruments in the ensemble'.[102] However appropriate as a description of the sound, such a transcription will inevitably give rise to the impression of unfathomable complexity to which Agawu refers; what sort of minds must these musicians have that they can internalize polymetrical structures beside which *The Rite of Spring* pales into insignifi-

[99] Kofi Agawu, *African Rhythm: A Northern Ewe Perspective* (Cambridge, 1995), 189.

[100] Folio, 'Analysis', 133. For a more general discussion of what he calls ' "classicizing" strategies for legitimating jazz', see Rob Walser, 'Out of Notes: Signification, Interpretation, and the Problem of Miles Davis', *Musical Quarterly*, 77 (1993), 343–65, 347.

[101] See Schenker, *Masterwork in Music*, ed. Drabkin, i. 113–14.

[102] John Chernoff, *African Rhythm and African Sensibility: Aesthetics and Social Action in African Musical Idioms* (Chicago, 1979), 45.

cance? But there is a fallacy here. The transcription totalizes the experience of the individual musicians making up the ensemble; it abstracts the music from the social process in which it is embedded—the process of making music together through complementary perceptions and mutual accommodations. It creates the image of something that never existed as a reified, abstract structure, thus signifying as much by virtue of its difference as its similarity to the experience it stands for.

Like all languages, the language of analysis signifies simultaneously on multiple levels. Our words summon up representations that are always metaphorical (whatever else they may be), at the same time that they accomplish or register perceptual or imaginative experiences. Reading analyses for their combination of representational content and illocutionary force brings about an enhanced awareness of what we do, and what we *can* do, when we do theory. In this context it is worth remembering that the great abuses of science have generally resulted from the claim that science merely reflects what is out there; maybe the most useful sense in which analysis, theory, or musicology can be 'critical' is in the sense of being self-critical—of being actively aware, to repeat Bohlman's words again, of its prescriptive as well as its descriptive potential.[103] But there is another reason why being aware of what our words can do—that is, adopting a performative perspective—is indispensable in today's climate of analytical, theoretical, and musicological pluralism. The paradigm of representation, in so far as such representation is understood as more than metaphorical, brings with it that dogmatic partisanship that characterized music theory only a few years ago, when to believe in (for instance) Schenkerian analysis implied the obligation to reject all other approaches as false. If today, by contrast, we are content to let a thousand theoretical flowers bloom, then the only epistemological basis for this must be a conviction that each approach creates its own truth through instigating its own perceptions, bringing into being a dimension of experience that will coexist with any number of others. Performativity, in short, is the foundation of pluralism.

[103] I would like this to be read in the context of Ch. 22, by Ralph Locke, and vice versa.

# 12

## Composer, Theorist, Composer/Theorist

### Joseph Dubiel

*This has been a surprisingly difficult essay to write. I began it thinking that, as a prac-*
*titioner of musical composition and theory, I must have plenty to say about the subject.*
*After a while, though, I found myself almost at a loss to identify the subject. Exactly*
*what is the issue about combining composition and theory? What is it that's supposed*
*to be special about the composer/theorist? To me, the combination of activities is as*
*natural as can be: wanting to write music has always involved wanting to explore ideas*
*about how to write it and how it is heard, and I honestly cannot think of any*
*theoretical work that I've ever done or encountered that seemed valid 'as theory' yet*
*irrelevant to composition.*

*Somebody sees an issue in the combination, though. And I don't particularly mean*
*the editors of this volume; the words of the title they have suggested, in which the issue*
*is implicit, are certainly not their invention. The implication of these everyday terms—*
*permit me to be extremely literal-minded—is that there are composers, who do com-*
*position the way it's ordinarily done; and there are theorists, who do theory the way*
*it's ordinarily done; and then there are composer/theorists, who, if they are anything*
*but composers and theorists alternately, must do one or both of these things in a special*
*way, a way that calls for explanation (if not indeed for defence).*

*If this is the idea, then my first obligation must be to figure out what the differences*
*between composer/theorists' composing and theorizing and the normal versions of*
*these activities are supposed to be. I say 'figure out' because my own experience won't*
*tell me; but in a way I'm afraid I know. On the one hand, ordinary composers are sup-*
*posed to write their music without thinking about it in the ways in which com-*
*poser/theorists do; that is, ordinary composers aren't just keeping quiet about some*
*thinking that they and composer/theorists both do, but that only composer/theorists*
*try to convey to other people. On the other hand, ordinary theorists are supposed to*
*want to know things different from what composer/theorists (and perhaps also com-*
*posers) want to know; that is, some of the things that theorists want to know would*
*be of no use to composers if composers did know them, and might even be a hindrance.*
*(Conceivably there are things composers need to know that theorists don't, too—things*
*like how long a bass clarinettist can be expected to play on a single breath at a given*
*dynamic level in a given register, and what dispositions of other instruments will allow*

*the bass clarinet's line to be heard; theorists don't disclaim knowledge of this sort, but they rarely exact it of each other in professional contexts or offer it as explanatory of events in compositions.)*

*What these suppositions together come to is a denial that composers need or want accurate information about music, at least some of the time.[1] Indeed, a more extreme account of the vocational difference would have it that an occasional outright falsehood may be of use to the composer, even though believing it would be beneath the theorist. This view might leave room for a special discourse, including such falsehoods, that might be called 'compositional theory' in a gesture of indulgence to those whose activities depend on occasional self-deception.*

*These ideas seem dubious to me; it is not easy to understand how they can enjoy the credence that they undeniably do in some quarters of our musical culture. Beyond this, I feel obliged to say, such ideas are offensive to me: taken to their logical end, they make me out to be too intellectually concerned to be a real composer, yet too uncritical to be a real scholar. There is nothing appealing about an intellectual project that would oblige me to engage these ideas (or even to document them).*

*But without these unfortunate ideas, what is left as a subject for this essay? All I can think to do is report on the interface between composition and theory as I experience it—which is to say, as a normal state of affairs, even, perhaps, as the state of affairs in contrast to which the division of activities stands in need of explanation (if not indeed of defence). Such, at any rate, is the conception of the project that I have to adopt in order to carry it out. I will try to write from the standpoint of what I actually do, referring to the received notions I have just exposed only when I think they will help to clarify my views (which is to say, rarely).*

Imagine walking in on Beethoven at work. He taps middle D♯ a few times on his piano, with evident interest and perhaps a trace of amusement. You can't hear anything amusing in his D♯s, though. In fact, you can't hear much of anything at all in them. Obviously Beethoven has something in mind that you don't, that lets him hear something in his D♯s that you can't. What does he have in mind?

The easiest thing to suppose he has in mind is the music surrounding these D♯s, the context from which, presumably, they get their sound; in which case his hearing of them is effectively an advance version of yours when the piece is done. So it might be. But perhaps he has in mind only his idea of how the D♯s themselves are to sound. He might be hearing D♯ as a sour note, say, and the rhythm of his tapping as a commonplace, so that the figure curiously combines oddity and plainness. This he could do while still in the dark about most details of what comes before. His work on the rest of the passage would be guided by his sonic image of the D♯ figure: he would use this image as a point of comparison for the

---

[1] Compare Joseph Kerman's 'If bad theory can lead to convincing music, the need for good theory is less than overwhelming' (*Contemplating Music: Challenges to Musicology* (Cambridge, Mass., 1985), 104). Presumably Kerman does not apply this standard to determine the need for musicology or criticism.

sounds that the figure took on from various candidate passages in which he tried embedding it, until he hit on a passage in which the figure sounded as he had imagined it.

It is important to understand (and difficult to explain) that in the latter case as much as in the former Beethoven is *hearing* something: hearing something different from what you hear, rather than merely thinking something different from what you think about what you and he both hear. He is thinking, to be sure; but his thought strikes him in the phenomenology of the D♯s, not just in a belief about them. Part of what makes the latter kind of hearing hard to describe is the difficulty of saying exactly *what* it's a hearing *of*. Most of what it's of isn't there yet; it's like a projection of a hearing of the complete passage down into a single detail—but without the complete passage. Such a hearing is an act of will more than it is a response to anything. It cannot be conveyed to someone else except through the creation of something that will elicit it.

No matter which sort of sonic image Beethoven has in mind as you look in on him (and no matter how fictional the supposition that there ever was such a moment as the one we have imagined), it is certain that he engaged in both kinds of aural imagining sometime during his composing of the Violin Concerto. Both kinds, and many kinds in between; for the clean separation we have drawn between them is as fanciful as any other aspect of our scenario. The activity of composing involves occupying various positions in the range between hearing what you've got and imagining what you want, and moving every which way between them.

And even the mental activities at the extremes of the range are not necessarily distinct. We cannot draw a boundary between 'hearing what's there' and 'imagining something', because hearing sound as music always involves imagination, always involves reading something into the sound, ascribing characteristics to it beyond its immediate acoustical properties. (Even to hear the D♯ tapping as inane is to interpret it.) The two possibilities we considered for Beethoven—hearing the D♯ figure as it is embedded in the opening passage of the concerto and imagining it as an as yet unrealized opening passage should make it sound—alike involve this kind of reading in. The difference they illustrate is between doing it in response to the context in which the figure is embedded and doing it just by virtue of a conception of the figure.

Beethoven's job, we might say, is to turn the latter kind of hearing into the former—by devising musical configurations likely to elicit, from a ready listener, a hearing like the one he has preconceived. As the first such listener, he must be intensely concerned to know the difference between the two kinds of hearing: to know whether, as he tests a possible opening passage, he hears the D♯ figure as he does in response to the context he has created for it or just by virtue of his prior conception of it. Only thus can he tell whether he has accomplished what he intends—has he made D♯ a right 'wrong note', or has he just got himself used to it? But meanwhile he needs his preconceived hearing of the figure to be as vivid and specific as possible, as much like a 'real' hearing as it can be, if it is actually to be realizable with the sonic materials available to him.[2] From the standpoint of their content, as opposed to their aetiology, Beethoven needs his responsive musical experiences and his willed ones to be continuous with one another.

This description of Beethoven's work is slanted in several respects, of course. It represents the score that he produces as his means of conveying his hearing to us—a view that, while hardly mistaken, is admittedly partial. We might with equal justification represent his production of the score as the goal, to which any conceptions entertained by him are among the means. This latter view is preoccupied with our having access only to the product, not to the conception behind it—or, more temperately, with our having access to the conception behind it only in so far as we choose, as a matter of interpretation, to regard our preferred hearing of the work as meant by its author. Musical scholars have with justification been chary of commitment to the composer's intentions as their objects of study (although their equal chariness toward their own hearings suggests evasiveness more than realism as the motive). But this attitude is not obviously helpful in an exploration of compositional thinking. With the observation that we are concerned to understand two reciprocal aspects of musical invention—the imagining of a way for music to sound and the imagining of music to sound that way—this issue might be left in the background for a while, to be resumed explicitly at later points.

Another respect in which our discussion is slanted will concern us immediately. We have gone quite far to represent the hearings in question as hearings specifically of the D♯ figure. Even when concerned with how the sound of the figure is determined by its surroundings—which must mean, by a hearing of its surroundings—we have projected all our hearing on to the D♯ figure itself. This may have been warranted by our initial conceit, which is warranted in turn by the extraordinary degree to which this figure isolates itself from its surroundings as a 'stroke'. But even if we imagine the figure isolated as Beethoven's initial idea for the work, still his realization of this idea would be precisely a matter of letting this hearing of the figure become a way to hear its surroundings (by providing surroundings to elicit this hearing). Accordingly, if we want to speak of a hearing of the D♯ figure, we will do well to realize that this hearing occurs not only at the time of the figure, but at other times as well—that it consists largely in hearings of other passages, to which we compare, connect, and contrast the figure in various ways. To get the full measure of Beethoven's 'idea' of the D♯s, we will want to identify it in part with the idiosyncratic nature and extensive scope of these comparisons, connections, and contrasts.

And so we should enquire: When else in the movement as we know it are we

---

[2] Failure along this line is perfectly possible—there may just be no way to get the imagined sound. Moreover, modification of the image in the process of realizing it is virtually inevitable. But I think my discussion contains no mistakes resulting from its simplification of these matters.

hearing the sound of the D♯ figure? What aspects of what other passages give the figure its sound? What sounds are given to other passages—or exacted of them—by their relation to this figure?

We begin with the music preceding the figure's appearance. The sound of the figure is, first of all, the sound of intrusion on a small band playing with pleasantly understated squareness—a squareness imparted largely by the tonic-and-dominant drumbeats framing the winds' more flexible phrases. The intrusion takes the form of a deadpan imitation of the drumbeats, on a very unsquare pitch, by the most improbable instruments (to imitate the drum, to make their entry by imitating the drum). This pitch, difficult to interpret in itself, comes to sound even odder in the inconsequent sequel, wherein its resolution is repeatedly omitted as ostentatiously as it is implied. In the face of such equivocation, it ceases to be clear whether a resolution of it is still called for.[3]

This is all the more true as, in every respect except pitch, the sense of intrusion fades through the phrase. The string basses mediate between the upper strings and the timpani, timbrally and registrally—and they get their pitches exactly right. As the phrase continues, they gradually dissipate the figure's distinctive rhythm, while the upper strings recall the woodwinds' parallel thirds (and their upper-voice descent from the vicinity of the fifth and sixth degrees). The strings' cadence thus seems to close all the music since the beginning, not just since the violins' peculiar entrance; the band's initially self-contained period has been extended by the strings into a sentence.

This degree of registral, timbral, rhythmic, and motivic synthesis makes it hard to know whether the pitch D♯ remains an issue. How can it not be, sounding as odd as it does? Yet the music makes no mention of D♯ for an amazingly long time after this cadence.[4] Undoubtedly this protracted silence on a subject that we cannot forget is as much the 'idea', as much a part of the image, as any of what we have discussed. If *this* can be part of the D♯ figure's sound (and if it is not part of the sound, then exactly when did this description get off the subject?), then really we can say that the sonic image of the figure takes in everything—not a bad conclusion, for our purposes.

---

[3] Nor, of course, is it certain what its resolution should be. Beethoven first wrote it as E♭ (see Gustav Nottebohm, *Zweite Beethoveniana* (Leipzig, 1887), 533). Hearing the note as D♯ seems easier than hearing it as E♭, in the absence of even an implication of the B♭ for whose sake E would supposedly be altered; and whatever idiomatic advantage the voice leading E♭–C♯ in bars 10–11 may have over D♯–C♯ is undermined by the succession E♭–B, as opposed to D♯–B, in bars 12–13. Moreover, hearing the note as a form of D makes for the most piquant contrariety to the timpani at the beginning. But any choice must be understood as local and qualified, as both hearings remain relevant on the largest scale.

[4] To my ear the E♭ in bar 30, in the plunge to ♭VI, is quite unevocative of our D♯s—especially as this passage is assimilated to the tonic minor, whose status (at least in this part of the piece) is precisely that of a field of chromaticism unconnected to D♯ (if not, indeed, opposed to it). During the D minor version of the second theme, the replacement of the Neapolitan II⁶ in bar 59 by the ordinary II⁶ in the parallel position in bar 63 is so understated as to be almost difficult to notice, let alone to hear as an allusion to D♯. In both these cases, the unambiguousness of E♭ is the main disqualification.

But what experience is supposed to count as hearing the D♯ figure through vast spans of music that make a point of not referring to D♯—as *hearing* it, not merely maintaining a proposition about it in memory while listening to what follows?[5] One experience could be that of hearing the violins still in charge of the drums' figure at the major articulation in bar 43—indeed, as the leaders of the battery when the orchestra once more becomes a band: they introduce the rhythm in bar 42, on the dominant note (the one that the strings *could* get right early on), and remain responsible for it after the drums and horns (and the still-mediating basses, pizzicato) join them. When the drums, now with horns *and* trumpets, reclaim their figure in bar 50, they follow the violins' lead in confining themselves to the dominant pitch, and the figure retains the slight inflection of '—, two, three, four, one' that it acquired when the violins drew it out of the weak-beat-to-strong-beat figure of bars 35–41.

Along these lines, the D♯ figure is effectively audible in the distinctive use of the orchestra through the concerto's entire ritornello: nothing is initiated by the strings except forms of the figure (bars 10 and 42) until the figure's harmonized and resolved return (bar 65), after which the strings lead the tutti (in what might be considered the normal manner) into the cadence of bar 77 and the theme that ensues. It is audible as well in the subtle defamiliarization of the four-square drum rhythm—indeed, it is audible in this initially trivial figure's seeming to be a rhythmic motive at all, but more particularly in the figure's gradual development of an up-beat orientation and an unexpected degree of identification with its weak beats. This process takes in: the low strings' dissolution of the motive into weak-beat attacks (especially second-beat) in bars 14–17; the avoidance, after this dissolution, of any distinct articulation of weak beats (especially second beats) through the theme of bars 18 ff. and the otherwise utterly contrasting theme of bars 28 ff.; the regeneration of the motive in bar 42, from the weak-beat figure that elaborates the half-cadence of bar 35, with a distinct inflection toward the following down-beat; and, after D♯ is recovered and resolved, in hearty strong-beat romping until it is time for the soloist to enter. Needless to say, the solo violin enters in the rhythm '——, two, three, four, one'; thus do the rhythmic and orchestral issues come together with the fact of the piece being a concerto.[6]

Where the D♯ figure does not leave traces is in pitch; what sustains the

---

[5] Tovey's reading, sensitive to the general issues, is underworked in this respect: 'The mysterious unaccompanied D sharp near the beginning of the Violin Concerto is unharmonized, and flagrantly avoids explanation until a later harmonized passage explains it as an example of sweet reasonableness' ('Normality and Freedom in Music', in *The Main Stream of Music and Other Essays* (New York, 1959), 197). We are left to ask: Is this all it takes? Can an isolated odd pitch really await 'explanation' without effect on the intervening music?

[6] Beethoven's restraining of the orchestral strings allows the solo violin to be the first (sometimes the only) string instrument to play most of the major themes: bars 102 ff., 148 ff.—but not the minor-mode version of the latter theme, bars 152 ff., which the orchestral violins do play in the ritornello. The one theme that is introduced by the orchestral violins, in bar 77, is never played by the soloist.

*audacitá* of leaving D♯ alone for such a long time, and after such rough treatment, is the transfer of its charge to every other aspect of the sound.[7] This constitutes the ripest sort of example of a single moment's sound spreading out through 'comparisons, connections, and contrasts' of 'idiosyncratic nature and extensive scope' that the sound induces us to make, and on our making of which it depends. Rather than feel—as we well might—that our effort to speak constantly of hearing is here extended to the breaking-point, we can feel that we have followed a continuous path from a hearing of a single moment to a way of hearing the whole. A *way* of hearing: a peculiar set of concerns, a peculiar ontology (or at least taxonomy) of musical entities, configured by a peculiar network of relationships among them, with which we approach the work; and we can consider ourselves to be responding to Beethoven's invention as much in our adoption of this frame of mind as in our attention to the particular sounds that elicit and reward it.

This is perhaps an exaggeratedly theoretical way to put something commonsensical (though rarely said in any form). What strikes and intrigues us about a piece of music is as much a matter of how we shape ourselves to the music as of what is presented to us *as* music. The *sense* of the music—a good word, as ambiguous between *conception, perception*, and *feeling*—inheres both in the music's particulars and in the frame of mind that suits the perception of them.

In Beethoven's Violin Concerto, this sense includes a puzzled preoccupation with an oddity, presented in marked isolation but with no trace of boisterousness or burlesque—with so little trace, indeed, in such an air of serenity and steady progress, that the puzzled preoccupation is chiefly with whether preoccupation is appropriate. Perhaps the piece can be trusted to make things come right—perhaps there isn't even a problem; either way, it keeps its own counsel. D♯ sounds just wrong enough that we must be mystified as to why it doesn't sound *really* wrong; so the degree to which it is absorbed into the flow may actually be the most unsettling thing about it. The sound of and about the figure transcends the distinctions we might ordinarily make between ha-ha funny, strange funny, and not funny at all; finally, this sort of everyday psychologizing can't touch the passage.[8]

---

[7] It is difficult to stop exclaiming about Beethoven's deft handling of his hot potato, and I can restrain myself only to the extent of displacing this continuation to a footnote. The next stage in the assimilation of the D♯ figure comes with the second theme in the exposition (bars 144 ff.). The theme is in A major—the modulation having been accomplished with the aid of D♯, of course, though without allusion to the rhythm—so that the retained dominant note is D♯'s resolution, E; and now the rhythm is gone—the violin plays only a trill. (The soloist's next long trill, in bars 205 ff., is then the occasion for the reintroduction of the figure, in a new form, with the 'wrong' pitch in the bar following the four beats, that calls forth a new series of developments.)

[8] It's no wonder that practising musicians get impatient with such psychological descriptions. It isn't because we're bound and determined to confine ourselves to technical language (the Peter Kivy theory about us); it's that an account of the 'sense' of a passage isn't going to seem right unless we can understand how it's a sense *of* the notes. A sense that comes over us in the presence of the notes won't do; we need to feel that the notes somehow induce it. When we talk about what we experience largely by way of the musical configurations that we think cause it, we're being true to our impression, not evading it. (Maybe this technique of description by implicit explanation is why we're willing to let our descriptive practice be called 'analysis'.)

The frame of mind in which such a thing can be perceived, in which such a sense can be attributed to the sounds through such peculiar classification and relation of the sounds, is not less remarkable than the perception itself. The music is as much a matter of how our hearing is shaped by what we are given to hear as of what we are given to hear in this way. Accordingly, if we want to understand the Violin Concerto, from our point of view or from Beethoven's, we need to understand both these facets of the experience: *what* we hear and *how* we hear, creating each other and reacting upon each other. To appreciate Beethoven's invention we need to recognize that he imagined a frame of mind, as well as the notes and rhythms to go with it, a range of musical characteristics to listen for and relationships in which to place them: a way of hearing.

I'm just talking about how things sound in context, you could say. Yes; but why 'just'? Do we know so much about how a context can influence a sound? About what aspects of sounds can constitute a context for other sounds? Do we think that there is essentially one way in which this happens, or that there are a lot of ways—perhaps even as many ways as there are hearings?

My fiction tries to raise these questions by concentrating on a single musical figure of which we can easily imagine several sharply different hearings—at the extremes, our blank, puzzled hearing of it as we overhear Beethoven, and his intricate, excited hearing of it as he works. Because the fiction is of composition, we can easily see that it need not be the case that either of these hearings is created by an actual context; Beethoven's hearing could just as well be made up whole and used to guide the creation of a context. Therefore a hearing of the figure is to be attributed not to a context as such, but to a mental configuration that determines how the figure is heard. A mental configuration of this kind might be taken on in response to a presented context—this is presumably what *we* do in listening to Beethoven's Violin Concerto—but it might also be taken on all by itself, as a matter of invention, inspiration, or will. The mental configuration itself will be the locus of contextual influence, no matter how external its origins may be.

It is to account for experiences of music that we postulate the existence of such mental configurations; we have no direct access to them.[9] We postulate them at various levels of specificity and individuality: very general ones to account for our experience of music as more than noise, more specific ones to account for our hearing of such attributes as 'tonic' and 'dominant' in many pieces, and still more specific, indeed highly idiosyncratic, ones to account for our perception of

---

[9] Diana Raffman has asserted this point clearly. Her 'The Meaning of Music', in Peter A. French, Theodore E. Uehling, and Howard K. Wettstein (eds.), *Philosophy and the Arts*, Minnesota Studies in Philosophy, 16 (Notre Dame, Ind., 1991), 360–77, and, more elaborately, her *Language, Music, and Mind* (Cambridge, Mass., 1993), ch. 3, seek to establish that the percepts she calls 'musical feelings' (emphasis on *musical*: tension, relaxation, metrical stress, the way it seems when a suspension resolves) are the *explananda* of musical theories, and structural descriptions are the postulates meant to explain these feelings.

'puzzled preoccupation with an oddity, presented . . . in such an air of serenity and steady progress, that the puzzled preoccupation is chiefly with whether pre-occupation is appropriate' in Beethoven's Violin Concerto.

Once postulated, such frames of mind can be conceived of as possible objects of knowledge themselves. A wish to know about them motivates us to regard the sound of music as something other than an experience in itself: as evidence for the characteristics of these mental configurations. Different sounds heard in a given musical configuration mean different mental configurations; we know the mental configurations by their fruits. And plainly there are people whose busi-ness it is to know the configurations—including at least music theorists (whose business, if not this, is a mystery to me).

Whether anyone's business is purely among the fruits is debatable. Obviously some people prefer to think so. To the most committed of them, mere acknowl-edgement of the mental configurations' existence apparently can be irritating. Acknowledgement brings with it the recognition that one's own ways of hearing must also be *ways*, which recognition undermines the convenience of imagining oneself as 'just hearing', while the other guy labours under the sway of a theory. Fundamentally, I find this position as false as can be—especially when elaborated by the fantasy that refusal to look into the matter will preserve one's purity: I see application far beyond the intended one (to literary theory) in Terry Eagleton's remark that 'Hostility to theory usually means an opposition to other people's theories and an oblivion of one's own.'[10] It may be that recogniz-ing the possibility of other viewpoints does not necessarily aid in acting on one's own; but surely maturity resides in not finding it an *impediment*. To Roger Sessions, the deep contrast between 'the composer', who is, 'in his nature as such, a man of faith and conviction', and 'the critic or theorist, who is essentially . . . a skeptic', does not entail the existence—or the desirability—of 'pure types' of either.[11]

What we can respect in this contrast is its identification of the composer's essential concern to know *the sounds*, to know them *as* sounds, regardless of their potential as evidence about mental configurations—to *have* the experiences that the postulations of music theory are meant to explain. The theorist has an addi-tional concern: to characterize ways of hearing, using the sounds they make pos-sible as sources of information about them. But no less is required of the theorist, as a *listener*, than of the composer. Only by hearing music precisely and intensely can a theorist even have access to the explananda of music theory. Only in an acute awareness of the content of a hearing can there be a clear idea of what a theory of that hearing is supposed to account for.

What is it to know how something sounds? There is a lot to it, and it isn't easy to talk about. One mistake is easy to make: to think of knowing how something

[10]   Terry Eagleton, *Literary Theory: An Introduction* (Minneapolis, 1983), p. viii.

[11]   Roger Sessions, 'The Composer's Craft', in Edward T. Cone (ed.), *Roger Sessions on Music: Collected Essays* (Princeton, 1979), 5.

sounds as a yes-or-no matter—especially in settings in which we feel that our standing as competent musicians may be at stake. *Of course* we know how it sounds! The existence of reasonably successful music theories—ones whose predicates are accurate and useful enough to have become virtually 'observational' for many of us—is often, paradoxically, a threat to clear understanding. There come to be aspects of how things sound that are categorical: either the predicate applies, or it does not. This is particularly likely for those predicates that can be closely correlated with features of sound that are notated, as drilled in the oddly named practice of 'ear-training'. We can be indignantly assured about knowing a major second when we hear one. But a particular interval, in a particular place in a particular piece, under a particular hearing—this is something else again (in as literal a sense as this quaint expression ever enjoys).

How does the interval from Beethoven's D♯ to the following C♯ sound, after all? *Does* it sound like a second?[12] Well, in a sense: if C♯ is a minor second below D, and D♯ sounds like an off version of D (by way of the timpani), then the interval from D♯ to C♯ must sound like some version of the interval from D to C♯. But not in another sense: the succession written as D♯–C♯ can of course be taken as a 'homonym' for the descending diminished third E♭–C♯, which, if the E♭ were part of a Neapolitan chord, would be a relatively idiomatic succession—one that calls for further action less urgently than D♯–C♯ does. Though there is little motivation to hear E♭ while the pitch in question is sounding, there may be enough incentive to hear this voice-leading to make the scale-degree size of the interval seem indeterminate. Certainly it will be desirable to recognize a reference to this interval in the bass succession E♭–C♯ at the crux of the development section, when the tonicized VI of G minor is reinterpreted as the Neapolitan of D to bring about the return of the tonic. By contrast, there is never any remotely comparable working-out of the succession D♯–C♯, although there are of course many of D♯–E.[13]

There is a deeper sense in which the answer is less clear still. Inasmuch as D♯ does sound like a specific alteration of D (as opposed to just a distortion of it), it is an alteration whose import is presumably an intensified sense of motion toward E (and a concomitant disruption of the sense of C♯'s proximity to it). And whether you hear D♯ as moving, out of register, to E a major seventh below it or hear it as moving to an E implicit in the following harmony or as moving to some later E in the appropriate intervallic relationship to it, or hear any kind of

---

[12] If the following discussion beings to seem picayune, think about how you would answer a student who said to you, 'I don't know whether I'm hearing it as a major second or a diminished third: how can I tell?' (And recall Beethoven's hesitation over the spelling of the note in question, mentioned in n. 3 above.)

[13] D♯–E is worked out in tonicizations of E minor—the local application of the D♯ diminished-seventh chord to II in bars 69–71 that follows the recovery of D♯ in bar 65 (and several parallel places), and more remarkably the short excursion of bars 400 ff. In the latter place, the going theme's scale in the bassoon tops out with middle C♯ and D♯ in bar 401, and is eventually answered by a version in the low strings that tops out with C♯; I am emboldened to mention this by the bassoons' involvement in the D♯s in the recapitulation (bar 376), and the progression through both these passages to the bassoon's starring role in the movement's coda (bars 523–9).

indeterminacy among these possibilities, you are hearing D♯ as not exactly moving to C♯, or C♯ as not exactly D♯'s successor, within a single voice. In which case the interval from D♯ to C♯ isn't exactly an *interval* at all.[14]

At the very least, this interval has a sonic identity that transcends the options made available by the going theory—a theory that we none the less have excellent reason to believe applicable to the piece (including the reason that it helps us to articulate this escaping of its categories as part of the piece's sound). And this is at the least: we haven't begun to go beyond pitch, even though we have already had occasion to contemplate the continuity between so-called dimensions of sound that is central to this movement's continuity. Even superficially, the low, loud, gritty sound of C♯'s chord heightens our uncertainty about whether D♯ is resolved or not: this noisy thing is *right?* and D♯ was *wrong?* Perhaps: even these rough, effortful bass strokes *correct* those quiet violin strokes in the direction of quiet drum taps?

This is a long demonstration of my short statement that there's a lot to knowing a sound. And it is only for a single interval, remember; think back over the range of sounds peculiar to this piece that we have discussed. To get much of anywhere in this knowing, you have to be able to be struck by many aspects of the music's sound, to be open to impressions of it that you would never think to listen *for*—impressions of it, we might say, that come to you outside any 'theory of music' you would consciously entertain.

In attributing great skill at this to Beethoven (which is part of what I have been doing since the beginning of the chapter), I may not seem always to have emphasized this openness as such. That is, I may seem to have emphasized connectedness and organization of musical reasoning in my account of his 'way of hearing': the powerful and idiosyncratic paths of 'comparison, connection, and contrast' from D♯s to violins playing drums to the articulation of weak beats to the preparation of the soloist's entrance. I intended the intellectual construction to give some idea of what the listening configuration must be like—to show that the network of relationships goes *this* way and not *that*.

But now my interest is in another aspect. If the mental configuration, as modelled by this network of relationships, is so peculiar, then it is not obvious how we could bring much of it to the piece with us ready-made. What would we have been doing with such a highly specific conceptual and perceptual structure all this time—just keeping it in reserve until the right piece came along? How many others do we have on ice? It is easier to think of this configuration as being in large measure elicited from us by the piece, created in us through our listening

---

[14]  Schenker might well have denied that it was an interval, for exactly this reason (given that it is not a harmonic interval either). Under David Lewin's productive conception of 'the interval from *s* to *t*' as the trace of an imagined motion from *s* to *t* (whose canonical exposition is in his *Generalized Musical Intervals and Transformations* (New Haven, 1987)), the interval from D♯ to C♯ might well be constructed from several other intervals, rather than intuited directly.

(so that what we bring to the piece is the *capacity* to adopt it). The singular sound (and sense) of the music perceived under this mental configuration gives reason to believe that our responsive capacities are being specially shaped to the occasion.

Benjamin Boretz has a way of talking about this that puts the progression from general to specific in the foreground. He calls 'the mental configuration that interacts determinately with the received sound so that the piece acquires certain properties as a piece, uniquely traceable to its being heard in a certain way' a theory—an *attributive* theory. Such a theory, he is quite clear, 'isn't *descriptive or explanatory* of anything; what it does is ascribe properties to, and thereby determine, what there is'.[15] It may be tendentious to call the 'mental configuration' itself a theory—at least in the sense of an explicit symbolic representation of conceptual structure. But if we want to emphasize the other-than-automatic, other-than-innate conceptual structure itself, under which a musical phenomenon is known—known through a determination of what entities it comprises, how they are selected and arranged, by what relationships they are organized, and so on—and if musical phenomena are known only in the hearing of them, then there is considerable warrant for doing so.

In any case, Boretz's framework allows him a strong statement about the transformation wrought upon such a frame of mind by its exercise. The 'mental image of the character . . . of [a] passage' formed under an attributive theory, through which the passage takes on a specific identity, is itself transformed by the reception of the passage through it, in a process that Boretz calls 'semantic fusion'.[16] Thus, with respect to any actual hearing of a passage, the way of hearing provided by the frame of mind brought to the encounter will turn out to have been generic at some level—will indeed be *rendered* generic by comparison with the specific experience that it engenders. While a theory, in the sense of a shaping frame of mind, must always be there in order for music to be made of sounds, it will also always, in so far as it can be reconstructed as a general *frame* of mind, fall short of the music whose perception it enables.

The import of this philosophizing is often recognizable, at least to me, in the simultaneously contentious and frustrating quality of interesting analyses of

---

[15] The first quotation paraphrases a definition that Boretz develops in the context of reading and only later transfers to music; I have adapted it by substituting 'sound' for Boretz's 'print', 'piece' for 'text', and 'heard' for 'read'. Both quotations are from 'What Lingers On (, When The Song Is Ended)', *Perspectives of New Music*, 16/1 (1977), 104. The implicit contrast between 'attributive theory' and 'descriptive theory', which attempts to represent attributive theory or the hearings it engenders, is made explicit in his 'Musical Cosmology', *Perspectives of New Music*, 15/2 (1977), 127. More recently, Boretz has reiterated that no text adequately captures an attributive theory, and warned against the ascriptive use of (necessarily) descriptive discourse, in 'Experiences with No Names', *Perspectives of New Music*, 30/1 (1992), 272–83, esp. 281–2.

[16] Boretz, 'What Lingers On', 104. As in the passage cited above, the point is made for reading and extended to music by analogy: 'Now I plow that mental image back into a close reading of the appropriate pages of print, and there emerges within my mental landscape the determinate feel of a unique, transformed text, as received print is filtered through the filtering image I had adopted. And as that text is made to be what it now is by being so filtered, it in turn transforms what that mental image was, emerging bonded in what I want to call a *semantic fusion*.'

music. The contentiousness will lie in an analysis's introduction of concepts that, at least as conscious elements of my frame of mind, I may never have considered myself to need. It would not surprise me if some readers felt this way about my worrying of the interval from D♯ to C♯ a short way back: was I suggesting that you had hitherto been *missing* something if you had never been seized with the inadequacy of the concept of the major second? The frustratingness lies in the failure of whatever is offered in addition to touch the experience as it really seems: after all that fuss, the description still doesn't get it. I expect this always to be the case. As soon as some conceptual work enhances a sensitivity, the reapplication of this enhanced sensitivity to the sounds at hand will yield something that gets beyond what the concepts provided for. Or at least it should: the possibility of keeping one's hearing entirely within one's set of ear-trained concepts, I can deplore, but not discount.

This means that anyone—composer or not—who cares to dismiss any analytical account of any musical passage from any point of view will always have the means ready to hand. Rightly so, if the account is offered as a representation: then it will miss many of the qualities of any particular hearing. That's what representations *do*. Analyses of music are more likely to be valuable as consciousness-raising exercises—or as the tools for such exercises—than as renderings of the content of musical experiences. What they might help to raise consciousness *about* is what goes into a hearing, what there might be to listen for, that no one had thought to listen for (perhaps even while listening for it); what they won't do is transfer the sense of the music, or any appreciable slice of it, into another medium.

If, as I have already said—and as I will keep saying, because it may be my most important point here—the crucial condition for any increase in musical knowledge is to keep yourself ready to be struck by aspects of sound that you aren't listening for, then the value of analyses will ultimately be their value as ear-openers.[17] The value of theories will be in their facilitation of such analyses, and in their making explicit the range of possibilities for what might be heard and the openness of hearing to change. To make the point stick, I'll allow myself this flashy way of putting it: the reason to *do* theory is to protect yourself against believing too much in any *particular* theory.

What has to be kept clear, though, even under this formulation, is that this hearing in particular ways, and this fine-tuning of the ways through experience, isn't some kind of fooling around, just by virtue of its having such a substantial

---

[17] Nicholas Cook has been saying so a lot lately; see, at least, his 'Music Theory and "Good Comparison": A Viennese Perspective', *Journal of Music Theory*, 33/1 (1989), 117–41, and 'Perception: A Perspective from Music Theory', in Rita Aiello with John A. Sloboda (eds.), *Musical Perceptions* (Oxford, 1994), 64–95. Elsewhere in his writings he can be quick to dismiss the possibility of such transformations of hearing, particularly when the concepts in question seem to him excessively 'technical' or 'musicological'. Well, it's a hard subject to think clearly about. In any event I would be happy to have this chapter read in the context of the ideas about composition that run through his *Music, Imagination, and Culture* (Oxford, 1990); both parallels and virtual oppositions can be found, resulting, I think, from substantial alignment of outlook and difference of purpose.

introspective component. When you write music, you're staking something on your way of hearing. You're *acting* on your perceptions, proposing that the way you hear things hangs together well enough to be accessible to other people—and indeed to be recoverable to yourself. This is the common point to Boretz's talk of the 'coherence-gambles' taken by composers and Milton Babbitt's less racy (but, in the event, perhaps more dangerous) claim that 'every musical composition justifiably may be regarded as an experiment, the embodiment of hypotheses as to certain specific conditions of musical coherence'.[18] There is such a thing as not being borne out in one's expectations.

What I'm talking about is not the tedious and silly—and widely cherished—idea that we awful theory-minded composers write our music 'according to theory', without an idea of how it is going to sound (and that this is the essential 'trouble with modern music').[19] This view, on the kindest reading, misses the point that compositional experiments, like any other experiments, test *predictions*, expectations of particular outcomes. (So do wagers.) A well-considered prediction is apt to anticipate alternative outcomes as well, naturally, with suppositions about what they would mean; but what is up for testing is always some idea of what *will* come out—in the musical case, of how it *will* sound.

What I'm talking about is something that should be perfectly familiar to you if you are reading this book, even if you do not write music; or that can be made familiar if we admit another creative activity besides musical composition to the continuum of experimentation, in order to get a clearer view of the relevant notion of prediction and confirmation. When you write a paragraph in an essay (and surely you've done that), you mean something by it, and intend and expect that your meaning can be read into it by someone else. Sometimes you find yourself mistaken in this expectation: other people don't take your text the way you meant it. Or, more to our present point, you *yourself*, on rereading it the next day, find that it doesn't say what you wanted it to say—that an essential assumption is not conveyed, that too much attention is drawn to a subsidiary point by a colourful word in which you indulged yourself, that the sequence of thoughts is not the best one to make each thought understood. The attributive theory of the passage under which you wrote the passage[20] is not borne out by the experience you now get when you read the passage. Knowing what you want to find in the

---

[18] Milton Babbitt, 'Twelve-Tone Rhythmic Structure and the Electronic Medium', *Perspectives of New Music*, 1/1 (1962), 49, repr. in Benjamin Boretz and Edward T. Cone (eds.), *Perspectives on Contemporary Music Theory* (New York, 1972), 148. Benjamin Boretz, 'Meta-Variations: Studies in the Foundations of Musical Thought' (Ph.D. diss., Princeton University, 1970), 561, repr. in *Perspectives of New Music*, 11/2 (1973), 191. There is a problem, I believe, with the notion of 'coherence' in both these quotations; it seems to me to run together an attribution of intelligibly projected character (hanging together *as something*) and one of projected character as intelligible (following a reasonable course). A proper address to this would require another essay the length of this one; I scratch the surface in 'Senses of Sensemaking', *Perspectives of New Music*, 30/1 (1992), 210–21.

[19] William Benjamin has even found a way to hold this view while subscribing to something like my notion of theory: he thinks that 'the music of the post-war avant-garde is not, as is commonly supposed, a music in which theory precedes practice; it is the first music in history which is not preceded by an unconscious theory' ('Schenker's Theory and the Future of Music', *Journal of Music Theory*, 25/1 (1981), 170).

[20] Recall that Boretz defined his concept of attributive theory in the context of reading (see nn. 15 and 16), and that the idea of 'reading in' was helpful to us in getting started with Beethoven.

passage, you may even thrash about a bit *trying* to read the passage according to your theory of it, and find that the passage just doesn't lend itself to being read in that way.

You might summarize your findings thus: 'That doesn't say what I thought it did.' This would not necessarily impugn your knowledge of English; your paragraph could fail in this way even though your grammar's fine and you've used all the words idiomatically.[21] At most, it would impugn some finer-grained conception of the passage, under which you read the passage in some way in which you now find that the passage doesn't lead someone to read it, not even yourself.

How this matches the musical case should be obvious. There are levels of knowing what a text says, just as there are levels of knowing how a passage sounds. You can know what the words mean and how the sentences work (just as you can know how this interval sounds in these registers of these instruments), while in some more specific and demanding sense you do not know: you thought that this passage would define itself more sharply by contrast with the preceding passage, say; but something you thought would set it off doesn't have that effect after all. You can no longer perceive something that you thought you could perceive in the passage; the frame of mind in which you imagined the passage is not sustained by the passage you've created—not even for you, with all your interest in perceiving the passage that way.

This sort of experience, literary or musical, is the refutation of a theory, as empirical and decisive as anything else blowing up in your face. I don't know why music scholars have been so hesitant to recognize this, and therefore hesitant to invoke this kind of experience as evidence for or against musical theories. I know what the reason is *supposed* to be—that this sort of evidence is inappropriately 'subjective'—but I am unimpressed. The perception that the needle on a dial moves from 0 to 3 is subjective, too (because it, too, is a perception). It is said that people can agree on perceptions like this more easily than on ways of hearing a piece; yes, of course, because this is such a *crude* perception: only a few aspects of the dial's appearance matter, and the dial is designed to make them easy to observe and report. If more aspects (and less predictable ones) mattered, then differences of sensibility would be more significant. But this difference between coarser perceptions and finer ones is a difference of degree—not a difference between two realms of being, an 'objective' one and a 'subjective' one.

From this point of view, what characterizes enterprises like physics is the extremely small number of theories that practitioners ever bring to bear on a set of data at one time—the small number of them and the concomitant coarseness

---

[21] Another possibility is that the experience would change your ideas of grammar and idiom, or of where these categories leave off. (For a mind-stretching assault on these boundaries, see Donald Davidson, 'A Nice Derangement of Epitaphs', in Ernest LePore (ed.), *Truth and Interpretation: Perspectives on the Philosophy of Donald Davidson* (Oxford, 1986), 433–46.) The situation described in the text can occur, however—that is all I need.

of the differences between them. In enterprises like music, the discriminations we are able to make, and thus are obliged to consider, include extremely fine ones. Concomitantly, there can be enormously many different theories to consider, with enormously many possible areas of difference (and of overlap).

Finally the fear of 'subjectivity' seems to depend on the belief that you can hear something 'any way you want to'. But can you? I wonder what musical experience leads anyone to think so. I'm fairly sure it isn't composition—because what composition chiefly teaches you is that, with all the interest you may have in perceiving something a certain way as you write it, you in fact *can't* always perceive it the way you'd like to. (Similarly for essays!) Often you come up against something awfully like empirical resistance—and back you go to the drawing-board. That's why I've placed so much emphasis on testing your own hearing against your expected hearing, and within that context, so much emphasis on negative experiences. It is in these that resistance is felt.

Of course, it is always open to you to regard such a 'negative experience' as a positive one: as an instance of hearing something that you didn't expect, rather than an instance of not hearing something that you did expect. In most cases, your imagined hearing will have fallen short of absolute hallucination anyway; on hearing your passage a little more responsively, a little less according to your preconception, you will discover yourself to have imagined nothing in particular about some aspect of the sound. In such cases, the feedback you get from working with the material isn't anything so categorical as confirmation or disconfirmation of what you imagine; it is refinement of your image to a sharper one. You notice the sound more precisely than you had preconceived it. You can thus consider your 'hypothesis' (which is a sonic image) to have been outclassed and upgraded, rather than to have been falsified as such. You now know better how your passage sounds—and this is what you really want to know, not whether, as a yes-or-no matter, it sounds the way you thought it did.

In short, there are more good things that can happen to your hypothetical sonic image than just verification of it—some of them even flowing from experiences that, under a schematic rendering of composition as experimentation, might count as falsification of it. I emphasize the schematic nature of the model that misses these possibilities, to avoid travesty of actual practice in the natural sciences; a schematic model is all I have been trying to apply, with the idea that any eventual impasse might itself be informative. Composition may involve predictions of a certain kind, tested against experiences which bear them out to varying degrees; but the gains in knowledge that result are not necessarily best understood in terms of confirmation or disconfirmation of these hypotheses.

And as the hypotheses go, so go the theories that they instantiate. When your hearing of a specific passage changes, so also must your *way* of hearing it. This being the case, the 'theories' that are ways of hearing are theories of remarkable instability and diversity—perhaps enough instability and diversity to differentiate them from the other conceptual structures we are wont to call theories, enough to make us doubt once more the utility of conceiving of them in this way. Once again, this is fine with me: all that I've really wanted this conception of these theories to do is to stand behind the conception of hypotheses that we needed in order to work the model of composition as experimentation to an edifying breakdown.

If the preceding derives its account of theory from the experience of compositional invention, it still may not quite get us away from the question of whether what an inventive composer does is theorizing, whether it is so only by some trick of definition, or whether it is something else entirely. What will get us away from that question is another question: who cares? We can say that composition includes theory in the sense that it is work to develop knowledge of sound and to develop therewith the conceptual frameworks that alone make such knowledge possible; we can say that it doesn't include theory in the sense that it isn't particularly concerned to *formulate* this framework. And we learn something about the facts of the matter by looking at it in both these ways and by looking back and forth between these ways. We learn, that is, by looking at the activities of musical invention *in the context of* what is indisputably theory. What more do we gain by deciding—which is to say, by *making up* a sense in which theory 'really' is or isn't taking place?

The composition now on my desk, a piece for solo voice, begins with a long section in a confined low register. Its persistence in this register provides a backdrop for a single blip in the upper register, one meant to seem relatively unmotivated by what precedes it (despite there being plenty of *time* for a motivation to have been worked up) and, more crucially, to subside with minimal after-effects. Part of what I had in mind was to hold off, for a long time or even for ever, those moves that would most obviously count as 'picking up' this discontinuity (such as moving in earnest to the register it opened and later integrating the registers).[22] Rather, I wanted the music to dwell for a long time within the sound, the after-resonance, of this anomalous thing's having occurred, to enter its next section without any explicit address to this anomaly, and, if ever it did resolve the contrast, to do so offhandedly, not by any specific reference to the event. This is a lot of verbiage to describe a relatively straightforward avoidance of one obvious thing; I spell it out to emphasize how it might be important for the piece's first section to persist for a long time in unusually confined conditions.

---

[22] To answer an obvious question: no, I wasn't thinking about the Beethoven Violin Concerto, which I began to think about for purposes of this paper long after I wrote the opening of my piece. It is interesting, though, to notice how the model of an initial odd event creating a problem that must be tended to—a model often instantiated in Beethoven's middle works—dominates the accounts of pieces that we give in 'analytical' contexts; I may well have been reacting against this.

Against this first section's registral situation, a number of contrasts might conceivably be set. (I now speak hypothetically, and will return to the actual course of events in my piece later.) Perhaps the most obvious contrast would be created by comparable passages in other parts of the voice's range. For purposes of such a contrast, the first section's narrowness of range would emerge as a specific resource, since a relatively large number of other comparably narrow registral bands would be available.

My harping on narrowness of course suggests another kind of contrast, namely one between wide and narrow ranges—or, to characterize it in another way, between passages with definite registral locations, such as the opening, and passages whose registral identity is defined by the very difficulty of identifying them with a particular register. In this context, the degree to which a section's registral identity is complicated by internal registral motion—the degree to which such motion might mark a section as characteristically diffuse, rather than remaining an isolated blip, as in the first section—is an area of finer variation suggested by the material at hand.

There are many other possibilities, needless to say, most of them considerably harder to describe than these, in so far as they might be more complex intrinsically and more intricately dependent on the specifics of this piece. But these two will permit me to make a general point of great importance.

It is hard to imagine a very satisfactory piece that did not exploit at least these two kinds of contrast. I would never want to call it impossible (not least because I can imagine deriving some compositional stimulus from the problem), but I can surmise that the piece would have to be a peculiarly epigrammatic one to hold back from exploring either of these types of contrast and still seem to have worked out its premises. Supposing, in any event, that both these kinds of registral contrast do come into play in a piece, how might they interact?

One way, relatively simple to conceive, is: hierarchically. I use the word loosely; what I have in mind is the possibility of a piece being organized on the largest scale by one of these contrasts, with the other contrast mediating. Thus a piece's major articulations might be made by its arrival at narrow registral bands in various parts of its range, and these passages might be diversely connected and inflected by intervening passages of the no-fixed-abode type (or left unconnected by the pointed absence of such passages). Alternatively, the contrast between registral focus and registral diffusion might be the fundamental one, and various narrow passages, whatever their registral location, might all count alike chiefly as instances of the narrow. These two possibilities do not neatly exclude one another, of course; in particular, the second scenario's equation of all the narrow passages *as* narrow is already implicit in the first scenario's definition of its essential motion from one narrow passage to another. The difference between the two would be a matter of different *uses* of registral contrast to articulate the piece's flow. But in two pieces that 'ranked' the two kinds of registral contrast in opposite ways, the spaces of registral possibility would themselves seem to differ.

I must allow again, and emphasize, that these two are only the broadest and most oversimplified schematic possibilities. If you have been asking impatiently, 'But couldn't it also be some other way?' at every point in my exposition of them, then you have a good sense of what I'm talking about. Even in a relatively one-dimensional musical domain like register, different organizations and uses of the possibilities create different senses of what the possibilities are. And even in such a straightforward domain, there is no such thing as a 'natural' ordering of contrasts. Now for the observation I have been driving at: a sense of how various dimensions of contrast are to be laid out (again I choose 'sense' as indeterminate between 'conception', 'perception', and 'feeling') is, to my way of thinking, one of the essential kinds of idea for a piece. (It need not be a preconception; it may evolve throughout the process of composition.)

Accordingly I want any discipline that purports to concern itself with musical ideas to make itself useful by promoting clarity and flexibility about such configurations and reconfigurations of a work's range of possibilities. In this sense, the theory of *music* interests me less than the theories of *pieces* (or of *hearings* of pieces); or rather, the theory of music interests me chiefly as a body of aids to and constraints on the formation of such smaller, more idiosyncratic theories.

I imagine these theories as something like articulated ontologies for the music to which they apply—sets of possible entities, configured by possible relations, open to choice. They are *like* ontologies in their power to affect what will count as entities in given contexts, to improve upon, to render inadequate and perhaps outright inapplicable, the more general systems of categories that are supposed to cover bodies of music. They are not quite like ontologies, though, in that I scarcely expect them to cover all the possibilities at hand. I expect them to be partial and changeable. I say this even while holding the elaboration of one of them, the discovery beyond previous imagining of what it is like to hear things *this* way, to be a high ambition.

I do not imagine such theories as rhetorics or aesthetics, in the sense in which rhetorics and aesthetics embody recommendations for the use of the entities and relations that constitute them. These theories may have something to say about what would happen if such-and-such entities were deployed in such-and-such a way—what the effect would be, what further possibilities would be implied, and so on. But in no sense do they tell a composer—tell me—what to choose. They tell me what to do only in the sense of telling me what things there *are* to do and what it takes to do them. And even at this (as I keep saying), they can be wrong: they can prove not to be quite up to this specific situation in this evolving piece.

Having made these general comments, I want to return to my hypothetical contrasting systems of registral contrast, and through them to my actual composition in progress. Despite the reservations I have expressed about the schematic nature of these contrasts, they are in fact quite useful for describing my piece. (And I should add that, because the piece is for solo voice, contrasts of register loom especially large in its realm of possibilities.) The main complication comes from their interaction with issues raised by the blip, as I began to suggest, so that the issue of 'compact' and 'diffuse' becomes more ramified. It can be asked of any local discontinuity to what degree it is a blip or, conversely, to what extent it works to constitute its section as diffuse; and of every diffuse passage to what extent its diffuseness may be qualified by a degree of focus on a particular register. In any event, in so far as these simple contrasts do apply, their relationship is quite unhierarchical—pointedly so, I believe (and hope). That is, I expect both kinds of contrast to fan out from that long, low, narrow opening passage; and I expect neither kind of contrast to settle distinctly into subsuming or inflecting the other—although I expect it often to be an issue whether this will occur, and I expect a listener's impressions of it to fluctuate from time to time in the piece.

And now perhaps I can make intelligible the experience that has mainly motivated my telling this story of my piece. In the course of my work, it became clear that never after the opening section would there be another section so long and so narrowly defined—not remotely. (I should add that this will be all the more conspicuous because the passage is also sharply restricted in its use of pitch and in the vocabulary of the text, and that it is reinforced by a slow tempo, although this tempo is not unique to the opening.) As I say, it became clear, it struck me; I noticed that I noticed. I can't say that I had an uneasy feeling about it, but I had *some* feeling besides the feeling that it was obviously right for the piece to have this characteristic. The source of the feeling, I now believe, lay in my not knowing—not having conceptual, besides auditory, access to—most of what I have just said about the registral relations within the piece, the account of the piece under which it is reasonable for one disproportionately long, stereotyped section to stand as the common focus of two divergent sets of contrasts. I did not see how it was reasonable for this arrangement to work. Under any conception of it that I could have formed at the time, I would have expected the piece to sound unbalanced, with its opening section unanswered by any commensurable one; or I might have expected it to sound perversely didactic, which a section expounding premises standing apart from many subsequent divagations (an image of musical form which may not displease as it should: scholars seem inordinately fond of it); or it might seem unbalanced *and* perversely didactic.

And yet, as I say, I wasn't in any sense afraid that the piece was failing along these lines. It seemed (and still seems) just fine to me. But looking on my work and seeing that it was good didn't close the matter for me (as it reportedly does for some creators)—on the contrary, it forced me to consider that I didn't really see *how* it was good.

This was in no sense a compositional inhibition; it was an occasion for curiosity. Here I had a chance to learn a way for a piece to work that I had never previously entertained—the way outlined in the preceding pages, to understand which I had to invent (or recognize) some new ways to define and relate entities in the domain of register. In other words, I had experienced the reverse of what people so often claim to worry about when they imagine composers thinking: far from restricting myself to writing what I understood, I had found my understanding opened by my interest in a compositional inclination I felt but did not understand. With this I have also happily reversed the picture I drew earlier of compositional experience refuting a theory; for such clashes occur not only when a passage one composes inexplicably sounds *wrong*: in this instance, the clash between experience and preconception forced an expansion in my conscious ideas about what might sound *right*.

*This, finally, is my issue: do people think that theories tell composers what to do? They don't tell me! People might expect theories to do this, if they think of theories the way analysts sometimes try to use them, as tools to show that what a piece does (or what a composer does) is the right thing to do, or the best. If theories can tell an analyst that (or support an analyst in saying that), then presumably they can tell a composer, too. But nothing is more misleading than the notion that music theory produces hypotheses about what will sound good; or that it should aspire to produce such hypotheses; or that it would have to produce such hypotheses in order to be of value, which it isn't because it doesn't. Music theory's only possible hypotheses are about how various configurations are likely to seem when embedded in various contexts and received in various frames of mind. Good and bad come after that, depend utterly upon it, and are the province of no 'theory'.*

*What do theories tell me? Not what to do; but what there is to do. Not what moves will sound good; but how each possible move will sound. Not 'If you do it this way, it will work'; but 'If you do it this way, it will sound so-and-so—and whether you want that is up to you'.*[23] *And* tell *me is not quite right: they let me find out, or help me find out; and they contribute to the conception of myself and what I'm doing that helps me to keep doing it.*

*So I'm identifying musical theories as the source of my expectations of the effects of the configurations that I might create, as 'ways of hearing'. I could with equal justification speak of these frames of mind as attitudes or moods—perhaps with more justification, since I often find that, in the kind of discipline required to enter, sustain, develop, and act on them, and especially in the kind of vulnerability they sometimes show to attenuation and disruption, they are more like states of affect than like the maintenance of propositions. They are so, too, in their inaccessibility to abstract articulation—in their necessary flight from such articulation as they shed their generality in use. On the other hand, they are most recognizably theories in this sense: that they seem subject not just to dissipation but to falsification, even crashing falsification, in a way that makes them seem much more like opinions than like feelings. Strangely,*

---

[23] The distinctions made here are explored from a different point of view in my ' "When You are a Beethoven": Kinds of Rules in Schenker's *Counterpoint*', *Journal of Music Theory*, 34/2 (1990), 291–333.

*however, they seem never really subject to confirmation; or their confirmation is of relatively little interest, as compared with the actions they make possible or the extensions and refinements of them that they permit and by which they are left behind. What the failures and successes of these theories alike depend on is readiness to respond: to hear what you're not listening for, as I have said, and thus also to realize when you are hearing more than you were listening for. Whatever intellectual activity promotes and recognizes this, I regard as music theory and as part of composition. Anything else is someone else's problem.*

# Part II

# 13

# *The Institutionalization of Musicology: Perspectives of a North American Ethnomusicologist*

## Bruno Nettl

What is it that comes to the minds of musicians, music students, lovers of all types of music, members of the academic professions, when they hear or read the word 'musicology'—or 'Musikwissenschaft' or 'musicologie' or 'musicologia' and so on? To some it suggests fascinating books and lectures from which one learns things one has never suspected about the music and composers one loves. To others it conjures up a kind of police force which sees to it that one learns about composers and their works, long past and perhaps distant, things quite irrelevant to one's musical life in the present. To yet another audience, it is the voice of authority, a branch of knowledge that tells you what in music is good and worthy of hearing and what is bad and to be avoided. Then again, it is a profession whose members promulgate the strange view that all music from everywhere is worthwhile and should be known to all. And on top of that, it is a body of literature that explains how one should, or should not, perform certain well-known and well-loved works of music. At one moment, musicology is seen as largely irrelevant to the creation and practice of music, as merely a kind of musical outcropping of fields of knowledge (such as history, sociology, psychology, anthropology, physics) with quite different subject-matter. But the next moment someone will assert that musical practice in any society is inconceivable without a sense of musical scholarship. In certain quarters, musicology represents the centre of the cultural complex of musical thought; in others, the world of music might be better off without it.

This variety of viewpoints may sound like a version of the parable about the blind men and the elephant, but it reflects some of the debates that have long dominated the field of music scholarship. For just over a hundred years, a rather large group of scholars and teachers have considered themselves to be musicologists, but they have often disagreed on the meaning and implications of the term. In the sense of the *Oxford Universal Dictionary on Historical Principles* (also known as the 'shorter *OED*'), musicology has become an institution, 'an established law, custom, usage, practice, organization, or other element in the political or social life of a people (1551)'.[1] Applying the concept of institution to musicology, 'political or social life of a people' may be converted to 'musical life of a people', or perhaps 'political and social life of the musical profession'; but in any event, the purpose of this chapter is to examine ways in which musicologists have promulgated laws and customs, established usages, engaged in practices, and formed organizations.

Over the last century musicology, largely in North America and Europe, has developed a unique shape and a characteristic structure in its approach to its subject-matter, in its social relationship to the world of music and to the academic world, and in its internal organization. These features result from the cultural and historical contexts in which musicology grew as it developed from a field into a fully fledged discipline. In these pages, using both historical and ethnographic approaches, I wish to consider musicology (mainly in Western culture and from an essentially North American perspective) as an institution by commenting on the musicological discipline, on the profession of musicologists, on the organizations that serve the field, and on some of the issues, canons, and paradigms that dominate musicology, concentrating on the relationship between historical musicology and ethnomusicology.

## Field and Discipline

It seems to me that musicology is distinguished from other humanistic disciplines in its theoretical (if not always *de facto*) inclusion of all imaginable kinds of research into music. The other arts have not developed similarly holistic disciplines. There is in the English-speaking world no 'artology', no 'dramatology' or 'literaturology'; nor are there analogues of the French *musicologie* for other arts; there are such terms as *Kunstwissenschaft* (sometimes translated in dictionaries as 'aesthetics') and *Literaturwissenschaft*, but they have little present-day currency. While academic departments of musicology in North America and Europe usually take (or at least claim) responsibility for a variety of musicological endeavours beyond the history of 'serious' Western music, the various kinds of study of visual art are more commonly distributed among departments as varied as art, communications, advertising, anthropology, sociology, and philosophy.

If one were asked to name a single event signalling the establishment of musicology, it would have to be the publication, in 1885, of Guido Adler's well-known article outlining the content and organization of the field.[2] There is no need here to summarize it; suffice it to recall that Adler sees 'Musikwissenschaft' as con-

---

[1] *The Oxford Universal Dictionary on Historical Principles* (Oxford, 1955), 1018.

[2] Guido Adler, 'Umfang, Methode und Ziel der Musikwissenschaft', *Vierteljahrschrift für Musikwissenschaft*, 1 (1885), 5–20.

sisting of a historical and a systematic branch; that the latter includes a category, 'Musikologie', which presages the comparative musicology that turned into ethnomusicology, but that ethnomusicological concerns were also addressed in aspects of the 'historical' branch; that systematic musicology included aesthetics, theory (and by implication psychology and acoustics), and pedagogy; and that there are several well-defined aspects of historical study. The intention is clear: all types of scholarship in music are, and properly ought to be, part of musicology. In a sense, considering the way this article is presented, Adler claims to define the discipline.

But of course there is a prehistory, which Adler recognized. The epochal article itself begins: 'Die Musikwissenschaft entstand gleichzeitig mit der Tonkunst' (Musicology began simultaneously with the art of music),[3] clearly using 'Tonkunst' to mean a musical system with specific and replicable intervals—something, it now turns out, so characteristic of music that it is virtually a cultural universal. He goes on: 'Alle Völker, bei welchen man von einer Tonkunst sprechen kann, haben auch eine Tonwissenschaft' (All peoples who can be said to possess musical art [i.e. *Tonkunst* should perhaps be translated as 'art music'] also have a theory of music).[4] (I believe that 'music theory' is the correct interpretation of 'Tonwissenschaft', and am encouraged in this view when he continues to the effect that this is so even when no really developed musicological system appears). Adler is trying to be generous to various historical periods and cultures; each has a musicology, he implies, to explain its own music. But to a musicology to which he himself could subscribe, Adler seems to have expected a system that was not tied to one culture, but within which all musical cultures could profitably be studied. If every culture had *a* musicology, then it was Adler's article that defined what one might call *the* musicology. And since Adler's time, while the definitions of musicology found in dictionaries and encyclopaedias vary considerably, very few of them avoid commitment to the comprehensive definition of the field. The question is whether musicologists have, in their hearts, subscribed to the intent of these definitions.

Following cultural anthropologists, ethnomusicologists have for some time maintained (and properly so) that each culture has its system of perceiving and classifying the universe, and that each culture is thus likely—perhaps certain—to have its own musicology.[5] The world's systems of musical thought may or may not coincide with Adler's idea of a holistic, comprehensive discipline. In the cases listed in the last reference, we find explanations of local or native or national musics, identifying relationships to the rest of culture and perhaps to the supernatural forces that govern the world. When I worked in South India and identified myself as a musicologist, local musicians—and perhaps even the population

---

[3] Ibid. 5.                                                                               [4] Ibid.

[5] Alan P. Merriam, *The Anthropology of Music* (Evanston, Ill., 1964), 31–2; Hugo Zemp, 'Aspects of 'Aré'aré Music Theory', *Ethnomusicology*, 23 (1979), 5–48; Bruno Nettl, *Blackfoot Musical Thought: Comparative Perspectives* (Kent, Oh., 1989), 170–3.

as a whole—accepted the concept, and had a fairly definite idea that it entailed something rather different from the Euro-American conception.[6] If musicologists in the Western world today oscillate between the concept of 'music' as a universal phenomenon and the notion that the world of music consists of a group of discrete musics, Adler in his article already felt the ambiguity between a world of culture-specific musicologies and a musicology that encompasses all cultures and all approaches to music. These are two ways of looking at the world of music scholarship, but Adler also implies that they represent a chronology, with the musicologies of the individual cultures being eventually replaced by a universal, comprehensive discipline.

Some major landmarks, intermediate stops of a sort, preceded the comprehensive outline of 1885. One such is Walther's encyclopaedic dictionary of 1732,[7] which for the first time attempts to list concepts and artefacts as well as persons. Rousseau's *Dictionnaire* of 1768[8] provides comprehensiveness in another sense, introducing the beginnings of a world-wide perspective of music. The year 1776 produced the twin histories of music by Charles Burney and John Hawkins, parallel yet contrasting.[9] Self-conscious histories of European music with an emphasis on England, they nevertheless presented views that are compatible with Adler's. Burney begins his volume with an apology ('The feeble beginnings of whatever afterwards becomes great or eminent, are interesting to makind'), followed by a section of some 400 pages on the music of antiquity.[10] Burney divides this large chapter into separate sections each of which coincides with one or more of the categories in Adler's outline: theory, history, ethnography, aesthetics, and organology.

In issuing his clarion call for a musicological discipline in 1885, Adler was preceded by the man who was to become his senior collaborator in editing the *Vierteljahrschrift für Musikwissenchaft*, Friedrich Chrysander. Almost two decades earlier, Chrysander had issued a periodical, *Jahrbücher für musikalische Wissenschaft*,[11] a work somewhat unwieldy in organization and without a totally clear purpose. But Chrysander's preface to the first volume (only two were published, in 1863 and 1867) heralds the founding of a comprehensive musicological discipline, recognizing its magnitude and diversity and maintaining that all its members would agree on the desirability of a common publication: 'Wie sehr

---

[6] Some typical larger works by Indian musicologists include Swami Prajnanananda, *Historical Development of Indian Music, a Critical Study* (Calcutta, 1973), and R. Rangaramanuja Ayyangar, *History of South Indian (Carnatic) Music from Vedic Times to the Present* (Madras, 1972).

[7] Johann Gottfried Walther, *Musicalisches Lexicon* (Leipzig, 1732).

[8] Jean-Jacques Rousseau, *Dictionnaire de musique* (Paris, 1768).

[9] Charles Burney, *A General History of Music from the Earliest Ages to the Present Period, to which is prefixed, A Dissertation on the Music of the Ancients* (London, 1776–82); John Hawkins, *A General History of the Science and Practice of Music* (London, 1776).

[10] On the interest in the music of the ancients as a driving force of nineteenth-century scholarship, see Vincent Duckles, 'Musicology at the Mirror: A Prospectus for the History of Musical Scholarship', in Barry S. Brook, Edward O. D. Downes, and Sherman van Solkema (eds.), *Perspectives in Musicology* (New York, 1972), 40–1.

[11] *Jahrbücher für musikalische Wissenschaft*, ed. Friedrich Chrysander, 1 (Leipzig, 1863).

auch die auf dem grossen Gebiete der Musikwissenschaft thätigen Kräfte in Aussichten und Bestrebungen auseinander gehen mögen, darin sind sie sich einig, dass ein gemeinsames Organ wünschenswert, vielleicht unentbehrlich sei' (However much the forces working within the large field of musicology might diverge in their approaches and purposes, they are united in the belief that a common organ of publication is desirable, perhaps essential).[12] And indeed, this volume includes essays on sound and tuning, on Tinctoris's musical terminology, on early German folk-song, on the origin of 'God Save the King', and on what would now be considered conventional historical topics. For its time, this was an admirable collection, but clearly much thoughtful progress was made between its publication and that of the far more comprehensive, forward-looking *Vierteljahrschrift für Musikwissenschaft*.

Chrysander's preface sets out a comprehensively conceived musicology, but only by implication. By 1885 it had been made explicit; European musical scholarship had added a significant, if small, component, harbinger of the central tasks of the later ethnomusicology. Consider the contents of the first two volumes of the *Vierteljahrschrift*. There are twenty-three fully fledged articles (not including review essays); twelve of them are conventionally historical in the European realm, seven might be regarded as belonging to systematic musicology, and four are about non-Western or vernacular European music. I believe that what was crucial in making a holistic musicology out of music history was the addition of the kinds of work done by ethnomusicologists. It required the establishment of ethnomusicological studies, in the sense of an interculturally comparative perspective, a relativistic approach, and a commitment to the study of the world's musics as aspects of human cultures. That such perspectives were not absent before the 1880s is readily suggested by the (greatly diverse) interests of many scholars of the late eighteenth and early nineteenth centuries.[13]

By the 1880s, several factors combined to provide a critical mass. They include the technology of tone measurement and the establishment of the cent system,[14] the invention of recording,[15] and the increased availability of performers of non-Western music in Europe.[16] Also, there were political developments related to the increased sense of nationhood and ethnicity in Central and Eastern Europe, the virtual completion of the colonial process marked by the Berlin congress of 1885 (in which Africa was divided among a group of European colonizing nations), and the self-conscious development of socio-cultural anthropology. Thus the

---

[12] Friedrich Chrysander, 'Vorwort und Einleitung', ibid. 9.

[13] See, for some famous examples, Rousseau, *Dictionnaire*; Johann Gottfried Herder, *Volkslieder* (Berlin, 1778–9); and later, Raphael Georg Kiesewetter, *Die Musik der Araber* (Leipzig, 1842).

[14] Alexander John Ellis, 'On the Musical Scales of Various Nations', *Journal of the Royal Society of Arts*, 33 (1885), 485–527. This is usually cited as a landmark, but the concept (though not the term) was already suggested by Hermann Helmholtz; see e.g. his *On the Sensations of Tone*, trans. A. J. Ellis (London, 1885), 46.

[15] See Oliver Read and Walter L. Welch, *From Tin Foil to Stereo*, 2nd edn. (Indianapolis, 1976), 7–12; Kay Kaufman Shelemay, 'Recording Technology, the Record Industry, and Ethnomusicological Scholarship', in Bruno Nettl and Philip V. Bohlman (eds.), *Comparative Musicology and Anthropology of Music* (Chicago, 1991), 277–92.

[16] See e.g. Carl Stumpf, 'Lieder der Bellakula-Indianer', *Vierteljahrschrift für Musikwissenschaft*, 2 (1886), 406.

publication of the first scholarly dissertation on a non-Western musical culture by Theodore Baker (1882),[17] of Tylor's book *Anthropology* in 1881,[18] of A. J. Ellis's famous study and Adler's seminal article, both in 1885, and the first field recordings in 1889[19] and the first monographic article presenting a systematic laying-out of musical culture by Stumpf in 1886,[20] all within a few years of each other, provided with suddenness the ethnomusicological ingredient needed for developing a musicology.

Here I will digress briefly to ask why the comprehensive musicology was developed under the almost exclusive leadership of scholars who were ethnically German. It seems to me that the institution of musicology as we understand it today resulted from the coming together, a century ago, of two ideas: (1) that all kinds of musical research were to be carried out under its banner, with the implication that all musics and all approaches are coeval; but (2) that this research was to be carried out under the leadership of scholarship growing out of what has clearly been the most valuable music, the music most worthy of universal dissemination—German music. The notion that music in its most serious sense is a German art became widespread in the nineteenth century. Interestingly, it is still around, as suggested by Albrecht Riethmüller, who in a lecture of 1993 quotes a scientist-colleague's question: 'Die Musik ist doch deutsch, oder etwa nicht?' (Music is a German phenomenon, isn't that so?).[21] Riethmüller traces this sentiment to the nineteenth-century intellectual climate of Germany, and I wish to add only the thought that if comprehensive musicology (in contrast to culture-specific musicology) was a German idea, this may relate to the feeling that Germans were somehow the owners of all music, and responsible for it all.

The self-alignment of musicologists has always revolved around border conflicts and issues of emphasis. The formal definitions have virtually always been holistic. Here is a short survey. An ordinary dictionary: 'a study of music as a branch of knowledge or field of research';[22] and a major unabridged dictionary: 'the systematic study of music'.[23] An older standard music dictionary: 'the scholarly study of music';[24] and its later revision; 'the scholarly study of music, wherever it is found historically or geographically'.[25] Or a respected textbook for graduate students: 'that branch of learning which concerns the discovery and systematization of knowledge concerning music'.[26]

These are relatively recent publications. But as far back as 1914, in the first

---

[17] Theodore Baker, *Über die Musik der nordamerikanischen Wilden* (Leipzig, 1882).

[18] Edward B. Tylor, *Anthropology: An Introduction to the Study of Man and Civilization* (New York, 1881).

[19] For discussion, see Shelemay, 'Recording Technology', 280, 288.

[20] Stumpf, 'Lieder der Bellakula-Indianer'.

[21] Albrecht Riethmüller, *Die Walhalla und ihre Musiker* (Laaber, 1993), 23.

[22] *Webster's Seventh New Collegiate Dictionary* (Springfield, Mass., 1976).

[23] *OED Supplement* (Oxford, 1976).

[24] Willi Apol, *The Harvard Dictionary of Music*, 2nd edn. (Cambridge, Mass., 1969), 558.

[25] Don Randel (ed.), *The New Harvard Dictionary of Music* (Cambridge, Mass., 1986), 520.

[26] Glen Haydon, *Introduction to Musicology* (New York, 1941), 1.

volume of *Musical Quarterly*, Waldo Selden Pratt says that 'musicology must include every conceivable discussion of musical topics'.[27] Otto Kinkeldey, writing in Oscar Thompson's *International Cyclopedia of Music and Musicians* describe it as 'the whole body of systematized knowledge about music'.[28] Some definitions seem to go beyond what is normally regarded as music, such as Paul Henry Lang's statement that 'Musicology unites in its domains all the sciences which deal with the production, appearance and application of the physical phenomenon called sound'.[29] Again, Friedrich Blume, speaking inspirationally to a group of students embarking on musicological careers, described musicology as 'knowledge of and research in the field of empirical music, no matter how far we may extend our concept of music. It embraces all fields of musical activity in all periods of history, and all peoples and nations.'[30]

Beside the many definitions stressing a comprehensive field of music research, there are a few that suggest a more limited view. In a short textbook of 1942 Fellerer does not define musicology outright, but says, 'so sind Akustik, Tonphysiologie, Tonpsychologie, Musikaesthetik, Musiktheorie, Musikgeschichte [but not ethnomusicology] die Hauptgebiete der Musikwissenschaft geworden' (thus have acoustics, physiology of music, psychology of music, musical aesthetics, music theory, and music history developed into the principal fields within musicology).[31] The ethnocentrism in this statement may derive from the period of its publication. But later, in the *Riemann Musiklexikon*, musicology is described as 'wesentlich Wissenschaft von der Musik in ihrer Geschichtlichkeit (essentially music scholarship using a historical perspective)'.[32]

In restating and extending Adler's definition as put forward in the 1885 plan (as well as undertaking to make major theoretical statements about the nature of musicology), Charles Seeger was one of the few who claimed the role of successor to Adler. He too makes clear the comprehensive character of the musicological discipline in this very complex but rational definition:

Musicology is (1) *a speech study*, systematic as well as historical, critical as well as scientific or scientistic; whose field is (2) *the total music* of man, both in itself and in its relationship to what is not itself; whose cultivation is (3) *by individual students* who can view its field as musicians as well as in the terms devised by nonmusical specialists of whose fields some aspects of music are data; whose aim is to contribute to *the understanding of man*, in terms both (4) of human *culture* and (5) of his relationship with the *physical universe*.[33]

[27] Waldo Selden Pratt, 'On Behalf of Musicology', *Musical Quarterly*, 1 (1915), 1–3.

[28] Oscar Thompson (ed.), *International Cyclopedia of Music and Musicians*, 7th edn. (New York, 1956), 1218.

[29] Paul Henry Lang, 'The Place of Musicology in the College Curriculum', *Proceedings of the Music Teachers National Association*, 29 (1934), 144.

[30] Friedrich Blume, 'Musical Scholarship Today', in Brook *et al.* (eds.), *Perspectives in Musicology*, 16.

[31] Karl Gustav Fellerer, *Einführung in die Musikwissenschaft* (Berlin, 1942), 9.

[32] Hans Heinrich Eggebrecht, 'Musikwissenschaft', in *Riemann Musik Lexikon: Sachteil*, 12th edn. (Mainz, 1967), 615.

[33] Charles Seeger, *Studies in Musicology 1935–1975* (Berkeley, 1977), 108; emphasis original.

Seeger not only defines but also characterizes musicology; for example, it should contribute to the understanding of humanity, and be carried out by individuals who work as both musicians and scholars. He provides a diagram which goes far beyond Adler's statement of musicology's interdisciplinary relations.[34] But in the definition itself, he clearly follows Adler's lead.

Seeger's writings, and even more the charisma with which he delivered his papers and lectures, were enormously influential in American musicology in the period since 1950. So too have been the organizations of North American schol-ars, the American Musicological Society and the Society for Ethnomusicology, both of which were in large measure founded by Seeger. In the United States, the character of musicology has reflected an ambivalence between two approaches, the one driven by tension between historical and ethnomusicological scholarship and scholars—a tension about which I'll say more below—and the other by insistence on musicology as a unified field. Seeger shared in this ambivalence. The word 'musicology' is prominent in the title of his only book, whose contents range widely over all types of musicology. But in his mature decades, he associ-ated himself principally with ethnomusicologists and their concerns.

To my knowledge, the only major musicological organization that has under-taken to define the discipline is the American Musicological Society. Why did American scholars in particular feel this need? Perhaps because Americans desire definitive definitions of everything (beginning with the US Constitution); more likely because of the need for American musicologists to compete and to define their place within the spectrum of musical professions and their training grounds in the academy. In any event, the American Musicological Society seems in 1955 to have subscribed to, and promulgated, the following definition:

Musicology is a field of knowledge, having as its object the investigation of the art of music as a physical, psychological, aesthetic, and cultural phenomenon. The musicologist is a research scholar and he aims primarily at knowledge about music. With this primacy he differs from the composer . . . and the performer.[35]

Here too there is no departure from the comprehensive approach, unless one were to interpret the word 'art' (of music) as restrictive, accepting the implica-tion that some music is not an art, or that certain aspects of the cultural complex of music are not relevant to music as an art and thus not in the purview of musi-cology. (The definition does not, for example, speak of 'the science of music' or 'the business of music'.) But I doubt that this kind of exclusion was intended; rather, the word 'art' seems to me to be there to add emphasis and dignity to the definition.

---

[34] Charles Seeger, 109, 114, 123; see also Anthony Seeger, 'Styles of Musical Ethnography', in Nettl and Bohlman (eds.), *Comparative Musicology*, 342–55.

[35] Archibald T. Davidson *et al.*, 'Report of the Committee on Graduate Studies', *Journal of the American Musico-logical Society*, 8 (1955), 153.

## The Shape of Musicology

Since the time of Chrysander and Adler, musicology has included all kinds of music and all types of musical research, but they have not been included on equal terms. The boundaries have been clear and ample, but within the boundaries the shape of the field has varied, in part by period (in the history of musicology), in part by region. As an example, let me briefly compare three landmarks in the West, Adler (1885), the AMS Committee (1955), and Joseph Kerman's *Contemplating Music* (1985),[36] and then comment on the situation in the United States, Germany, England, India, and China in the period since 1950.

In the Western world, the shape of musicology often consists of contrast between centre and periphery (a contrast that may have geographic, stylistic, conceptual, or methodological bases). Adler's outline and the first two volumes of *Vierteljahrschrift* exhibit a remarkable even-handedness among the various domains of musicology. It seems unlikely that Adler himself felt that all music was equally worthy of study; through his life, he mainly devoted himself, after all, to the Austrian musical heritage. Still, his autobiography, published in 1935,[37] suggests that in his view of the discipline he avoided this issue. He distinguishes between two equally valuable tasks of musicology: pure scholarship and practical involvement with practising musicians.[38] He provides a two-page outline of the workings of music history (specifying that it applies to 'christlich-abendländische', or Christian-Western music), and in a few additional sentences notes the congruency of musical style periods with cultural trends, the influence of social structures, and the typical shape of a period from inception to climax to decline. He ends the chapter with a sentence on the development of musicology, clearly assigning to it two areas of concern: (a) music history and (b) comparative musical anthropology (encompassing the entire world). Throughout, the book asserts Adler's vision of the musicologist in the dual role of scholar and teacher.

One can easily see Adler's even-handedness in the first volume of the *Vierteljahrschrift*, for it gives almost equal space to historical and systematic musicology, the latter including ethnomusicological materials that occupy one-sixth of the whole. Similarly, the beginnings of the *Journal of the American Musicological Society* (*JAMS*) may make clear the conception of musicology held by American scholars some sixty years later. The first ten volume (1948–57) contain (fortuitously) approximately 100 articles. Of these, 84 deal with historical subjects in Western music (only seven of them about American music). Nine are about other kinds of music (including non-Western and folk-musics), five involve

---

[36] Adler, 'Umfang, Methode, und Ziel'; Davidson *et al.*, 'Report'; Joseph Kerman, *Contemplating Music: Challenges to Musicology* (Cambridge, Mass., 1985).

[37] Guido Adler, *Wollen und Wirken: Aus dem Leben eines Musikhistorikers* (Vienna, 1935).

[38] Ibid. 34.

systematic musicological subjects, and three are on more general issues of musicology at large. Within the body of historical subjects (allowing for the difficulty of finding borders between periods), 19 articles are on medieval music, 31 on the Renaissance, 14 on the Baroque, 13 (including several of those on American subjects) on the second half of the eighteenth century, and only 4 on the nineteenth and twentieth centuries. The boundaries of musicology are clearly broad; but it is obvious that there is a centre of concentration—the history of European music to *c.*1700—with everything else being peripheral.

(Incidentally, the proportion of non-historical subjects in *JAMS* decreased slightly over the ten-year period. This trend has sometimes been blamed on the need for *JAMS* to coexist with *Ethnomusicology*, the two journals together being seen as the successor to the *Vierteljahrschrift*. But the ten-year period under consideration actually precedes the founding of *Ethnomusicology*, which did not change from a newsletter to a journal until 1958.)

If North American musicology even before 1960 exhibited an increasing emphasis on the history of European music to *c.*1880, thereby de-emphasizing recent, popular, and non-Western music and, in particular, studies in systematic musicology, this may be related to the growing association of musicological research with institution of higher education and, most importantly, with conservatory-like schools of music. The principal task of such institution is the teaching—and indeed, the advocacy—of the Western art-music tradition. Much happened in the hundred or so years between the apocryphal statement of a former president of Harvard—'there is no such thing as musicology, one might as well talk about grandmotherology'[39]—and the prosperous ten-professor departments of musicology at such universities as Michigan, Indiana, Illinois, and UCLA.

The earliest music research was not typically the business of universities. Early American music scholars were often librarians (was Alexander Wheelock Thayer the first?), editors (Theodore Baker, Carl Engel), or professional authors. It is true that the comprehensive concept of musicology as presented by Charles Seeger had a short-lived inception at Berkeley in 1914.[40] But the first meeting of the New York Musicological Society consisted of nine scholars (George Dickinson, Carl Engel, Gustave Reese, Helen H. Roberts, Joseph Schillinger, Charles Seeger, Harold Spivacke, Oliver Strunk, and Joseph Yasser), of whom only two, Dickinson and Reese, held teaching positions. Until *c.*1950, the largest, most productive group of music scholars was the distinguished staff at the Library of Congress. The first American journals for which musicologists habitually wrote, *Musical Quarterly* and *Notes*, were not particularly directed to college teachers.

---

[39] This assertion, which I heard quoted at a lecture decades ago, is familiar to a number of my colleagues in North America, but appears to live only in oral tradition. Whether the supposed speaker objected to the establishment of yet another discipline, was ridiculing the idea of doing serious research on music, or simply disliked the term is not clear.

[40] Ann M. Pescatello, *Charles Seeger: A Life in American Music* (Pittsburgh, 1992), 52–8.

In view of this, it is interesting to find, in American music scholarship of *c*.1935–60, something like the balance between historical, systematic, and ethnomusicological studies suggested in Adler's 1885 article. And it is equally interesting that this balance was later to give way to a greater emphasis on historical studies.

In Kerman's more recent survey of the field, the only sector of systematic musicology discussed at any length is music theory. Ethnomusicology is examined at some length (though in a chapter on 'cultural musicology', an aspect of historical musicology as Kerman sees it), but is found to be relevant to true musicological concerns only is so far as it is concerned with truly worthwhile music.[41] In grappling with questions of definition, Kerman suggests that the term 'musicology' has come to have 'a much more constricted meaning [than in Adler's conception] . . . the history of Western music in the high-art tradition'.[42] In his book he proposes to contemplate the alternatives—the broad and the narrow—but seems to come down squarely on the narrower side, reflecting (or leading?) the norm of the musicological population in North America.

To be sure, a look at music scholarship in North America between 1950 and 1990 indicates an enormous increase in the amount of study devoted to non-Western and folk-musics, and beginning around 1980, to popular musics, all subject-matter ordinarily reserved for ethnomusicologists. The influence of the social sciences, and particularly of anthropology, has all along been a significantly potent force in American (and European) ethnomusicology, and it has come to play an important role in historical musicology in North America as well. Thus, while many who explicitly call themselves musicologists (and are in fact historians of Western music) have moved increasingly to a canonic centre in terms of the repertories they study (the proportion of publications on Bach, Beethoven, and Mozart, for example, has significantly increased since *c*.1970), in the kinds of approaches they follow they have moved closer to ethnomusicology.[43]

The subjects and methods of articles in *Die Musikforschung* and the surveys of courses given at universities listed in that journal suggest that the boundaries of musicology in West Germany have been broad, but that as regards its shape the field has increasingly moved to historical study of European music. The complementary journal published in the former DDR, *Beiträge zur Musikwissenschaft*, took a broader approach, including articles on the sociology of music and on certain non-Western musics. Although important changes have occurred in recent years, the history of musicology in Great Britain parallels that of the United States and Germany. *Music and Letters*, at one time—perhaps still—the

[41] Kerman, *Contemplating Music*, parts of chs. 3 and 5.

[42] Ibid. 11.

[43] For both illustration and commentary, see Katherine Bergeron and Philip V. Bohlman (eds.), *Disciplining Music: Musicology and its Canons* (Chicago, 1992); Susan McClary, *Feminine Endings* (Minneapolis, 1991); Ruth A. Solie (ed.), *Musicology and Difference* (Berkeley, 1993); and Rose Rosengard Subotnik, *Developing Variation: Style and Ideology in Western Music* (Minneapolis, 1992).

central journal of British musicology, has in its articles been essentially limited to the history of art-music in Western culture. British scholarship has produced major monuments of folk-music research, but usually not within the context of the musicological establishment. Much research into non-Western and popular musics has been carried out in Britain, but the former has frequently been regarded as an aspect of social anthropology, while the latter, as suggested in the journal *Popular Music*, is the subject of a discipline of its own, or part of sociology, or yet again, part of an interdisciplinary field sometimes called 'critical theory'.[44]

A glance at the shape of musicology in these Western nations suggests movement from serious attempts to maintain equilibrium among the two, or three, or several branches of the discipline as defined by Adler to a classical centre of concentration with occasional forays to a periphery of non-Western, folk-, and, for that matter, contempor-ary music, involving anthropological, psychological, or sociological approaches. Resistance to this structure is provided by the establishment of subdisciplines or competing fields such as ethnomusicology or the less widely accepted socio-musicology and psycho-musicology, as well as by the assumption of some of the functions of systematic musicology by music educationalists. Musicologists work within this structure, which has provided the terminology for many institutions such as university departments. Examples include the recent division of musical studies at UCLA into departments of 'musicology' (i.e. history of Western music) and of 'ethnomusicology and systematic musicology', the University of Washington's three separate divisions ('musicology', 'ethnomusicology', and 'systematic musicology'), and the traditional separation of 'musicology' (history of Western music) and 'ethnomusicology' (in the School of Music and the Department of Folklore respectively) at Indiana University. Some German institutions follow a similar plan. Historians of Western music came to be associated with the main term, musicology, and other specialities were terminologically treated as subsets.

What about the rest of the world? In Eastern Europe, the nation with the strongest tradition of musicology is probably Hungary, where the number of musicologists active in folk-music studies matches those in conventional history. Folk-music scholars have generally avoided terminological separation, and many scholars have been active in both historical and ethnomusicological studies.[45] Chinese scholarship, a field with a long independent history, has moved towards a synthesis with Western approaches, maintaining separate subdisciplines for the study of different musics; but Chinese scholars are suspicious of the way in which Western scholars (actually, if not by their definitions) divide up the world for study by different musicological subdisciplines.[46] There is, for example,

---

[44] Lawrence Grossberg, Paula Treichler, and Cary Nelson (eds.), *Cultural Studies* (New York, 1992); Richard Middleton, *Studying Popular Music* (Milton Keynes, 1990).

[45] These assertions are impressionistic statements based on informal perusal of bibliographies and publications.

[46] Isabel Wong, 'From Reaction to Synthesis: Chinese Musicology in the Twentieth Century', in Nettl and Bohlman (eds.), *Comparative Musicology*, 49–51.

ambivalence about the need to separate Chinese and Western music because of the need for different methods of research and the value-judgement that this separation implies.

A 'fully developed musicological system', in Adler's words, that has maintained its independence from Western-style musicology may still be found in India. Musical scholarship there has a history of over two millennia, and began, as it did in Europe and China, with what is best described as theoretical writing. The picture in the late twentieth century is one of considerable integration of areas of musical activity ordinarily separated in the West. In South India it is expected that a distinguished performing musician will have some intellectual and research interests. The relationship of musical scholarship to traditional philosophy and cosmology is maintained; music history and theory (which is expected to have practical consequences) are not formally distinguished. On the other hand, the study of non-Indian musics, if carried out at all, is definitely peripheral in terms of the significance attached to it; so too is the study of tribal and folk-musics. Popular music research has hardly been broached by Indian scholars.[47]

Thorough understanding of the various musicologies in the world and their relationship to their musics is an important task for the future.[48] In the most populous musicological world, in Western Europe and North America, musicology is a discipline whose broad definition has been consistent in its comprehensiveness, but whose shape has changed as a result of tensions among its components and in the world of music, and between 'pure' scholarship and activism. In the course of a century, it has become an institution; no one doubts that there is such a thing as musicology. It is no longer anything like grandmotherology.

## Who Are the Musicologists?

We won't resort to the self-study surveys once popular among certain groups of psychologists, sociologists, and educationalists. There seems to be no reliable history of typical personal backgrounds; so let me make a few informal observations. Some patterns provide insight.

Perhaps most significant is the association of the musicologist with the field of practical musicianship. Art historians are only rarely competent painters or sculptors; theatre historians do not come from the acting profession; and historians of literature are infrequently from the ranks of novelists and poets. But I have often heard it said that 'the musicologist must first of all be a musician'.

[47] See Charles Capwell, 'Marginality and Musicology in Nineteenth Century Calcutta', in Nettl and Bohlman (eds.), *Comparative Musicology*, 228–43; and also a number of the essays in Stephen Blum, Philip V. Bohlman, and Daniel M. Neuman (eds.), *Ethnomusicology and Modern Music History* (Urbana, Ill., 1991); also Pradip Kumar Sengupta, *Foundations of Indian Musicology: Perspectives in the Philosophy of Art and Culture* (New Delhi, 1991).

[48] For a conspectus of musicological activity in virtually all parts of the world since c.1800, see Stephen Blum, 'European Musical Terminology and the Music of Africa', in Nettl and Bohlman (eds.), *Comparative Musicology*, 5–10.

And the AMS Committee on Graduate Studies warns: 'The first and foremost pre-requisite is practical musicianship, the basis of which is love and aptitude for music and the ability to think and speak in music as a language. Thus the student should be able to sing or play well and, whatever his principal medium, be able to play the piano and sing readily at sight.'[49] Most musicologists are indeed practising musicians to a substantial extent, and a good many are superb performers.

In North America, serious study of musicology usually begins in graduate pro-grammes into which students hopefully come with a background in music per-formance and theory, as well as languages and knowledge of history and related fields. Actually, they frequently come with a reasonably strong musical back-ground, but little else. My purpose is not to be critical of this situation, which I present here only to point out the fact that musicologists come to their field with both the advantages and the biases of the performer. This is part of the basis for the role of advocacy in the profile of the musicological profession, and for the concern with researching music worthwhile to the musical profession. The fact that musicologists are themselves musicians, but perhaps not among the best, may have something to do with attitudes among performers and composers: musicologists, they believe, should be supporting them and their efforts, but in practice act as a kind of police, requiring them to toe the line in their knowledge of insignificant music and in their adherence to authentic performance practice.

The situation in other parts of the world seems to me to be somewhat but not wholly parallel. An informal survey of German musicologists revealed that they typically took an interest in musicology somewhat earlier in their educational careers than did their North American counterparts, that they were somewhat more likely to take a turn at studying composition, and that their formal back-grounds included more emphasis on the humanities, particularly literature. Chinese music scholars—even those of traditional Chinese music—often come from the study of performance of Western music.[50] Indian music scholars start out, and continue, as performers.

It is interesting to compare the backgrounds of ethnomusicologists with those of music historians. The most obvious characteristic of ethnomusicology at large is the role of anthropology in the backgrounds of its practitioners. This is espe-cially true in the United States, perhaps most because the founder of American-style anthropology, Franz Boas, took a special interest in music. However, a considerable number of the leaders in ethnomusicology in the twentieth century came from anthropological backgrounds. Alice C. Fletcher, whose work began well back in the nineteenth century, was an outright anthropologist; George Herzog, first a music student, received a Ph.D. in anthropology; so too did

---

[49]  Davidson *et al.*, 'Report', 153.

[50]  Isabel K. F. Wong, personal communication. I am grateful to Ms Wong for important insights into the nature of Chinese musical scholarship from papers to be published.

Richard Waterman, David P. McAllester, Alan P. Merriam, John Blacking, Charlotte J. Frisbie, Anthony Seeger, Steven Feld, Daniel Neuman, Christopher Waterman, Adrienne Kaeppler, Norma McLeod, Marcia Herndon, and others. A good many also received their degrees in folkloristics, whose assumptions and methods approximate those of anthropology. All in all, many ethnomusicologists of all sorts have a substantial background in anthropology.

But a survey of ethnomusicologists would probably reveal that 80 per cent see themselves as musicologists of a sort, or at least as associated principally with the field of music. The rest, however, who consider themselves to be anthropologists, have provided far more than their share of the intellectual leadership of the field.[51] And this is responsible for a major characteristic of musicology since 1950: the tension between the concept of musicology as a single, comprehensive discipline and the split, if you will, into two musicologies, one about 'good' music, the other about the rest. (It is not lost on ethnomusicologists that radio stations playing exclusively Western classical music call themselves 'good music stations'.)

In fact, ethnomusicologists do not regard themselves simply as students of all musics outside Western art-music. They define themselves (though they have dozens of published definitions[52]) as students of music in culture, or as students of music from an anthropological perspective, or of music in oral tradition, or of music from an intercultural comparative perspective. But in fact, everybody has thought of them through most of their history as students of the world's strange music, the music of the downtrodden and those outside the establishment. Such a definition even appears in an influential book, Jaap Kunst's *Ethnomusicology* (the first book to use this word in its title), in which the author says: 'Western art and popular music do not belong to its field.'[53]

The tension between musicology as a comprehensive discipline and its shape with Western art-music at the centre is also reflected in the attitudes towards musical backgrounds. Most historians of art music perform this music; not many come from the worlds of jazz or popular music, and there are indeed few from non-Western societies whose performing backgrounds involve Chinese, Japanese, Indian, or Persian music. Although the earliest ethnomusicologists—the likes of Hornbostel, Stumpf, Densmore, and Herzog—came from this classical tradition as well, recently they have come more from popular music and jazz, and that is true even of those whose eventual fields of study have nothing to do with

---

[51] Among major works we can cite only a small selection: Alan P. Merriam, *The Anthropology of Music* (Evanston, Ill., 1964); John Blacking, *How Musical Is Man?* (Seattle, 1973); David P. McAllester, *Enemy Way Music* (Cambridge, Mass., 1954). During the 1930s, a series of articles by George Herzog provided the principal leadership for American ethnomusicologists. See Bruno Nettl, 'The Dual Nature of Ethnomusicology in North America: The Contributions of Charles Seeger and George Herzog', in Nettl and Bohlman (eds.), *Comparative Musicology*, 266–76.

[52] See Alan P. Merriam, 'Definitions of "Comparative Musicology" and "Ethnomusicology": An Historical-Theoretical Perspective', *Ethnomusicology*, 21 (1977), 189–204.

[53] Jaap Kunst, *Ethnomusicology, A Study of its Nature*, 3rd edn. (The Hague, 1959), 1. Actually, this sentence ends Kunst's first paragraph, which is otherwise a rather broadly conceived definition of ethnomusicology.

those genres. From the literature and from personal knowledge, I mention only Richard Waterman (and his son, Christopher Waterman), Alan Merriam, Steven Feld, Artur Simon, Albrecht Schneider, Thomas Turino, and Stephen Friedson. Nevertheless, a background in Western classical music continues to play a role, and the attitude of historical musicologists towards ethnomusicologists is sometimes affected by their musical association. My own interest in eighteenth- and nineteenth-century European music has made historian colleagues more willing to trust (are we talking about tameness?) my ethnomusicological work. Music historians have mentioned with satisfaction the love for performing chamber music on the part of scholars such as Kunst and Wachsmann. And in general the identity of musicologists, their reputation, and their interrelationships are affected by what may be called their 'musical ethnicity', the music that they consider their own.

## Organizations, and Some Remarks on Systematic Musicology

Soon after the publication of Adler's seminal article, musicologists of all types began to form organizations, which played a major role in subsequently institutionalizing the field. The history of musicology is in good measure the history of the Internationale Musikgesellschaft (1899–1914), the Gesellschaft für Musikforschung (reconstituted in 1946), the Royal Musical Association (founded in 1874), the International Musicological Society (founded in 1927), the International Council for Traditional Music (1945–  ), the American Musicological Society (1934–  ), the Society for Ethnomusicology (1955–  ), and many others. In the lives of musicologists, at least in North America, these organizations play important roles. Publishing in their journals rather than in others may be indispensable for maintaining an academic position and receiving indefinite tenure. Holding office is the reward of, but also coeval with, scholarly accomplishment, and many scholars' lives are built around the trips necessary to attend annual and regional meetings. Occasionally musicologists equate the direction presumed to be taken by a society—for instance, decisions made by a journal editor or a programme committee—with the true direction in which the discipline is moving. In North America, the conflicts in music research are in part played out in the interrelationship of societies, as in the determination of joint meetings, the relative prominence of each society in these, and the mutual courtesies.

One general characteristic of these societies (excepting SEM and ICTM) has been their tendency to begin with a broad approach to the field, an approach that is gradually narrowed, in part due to the formation of specialized societies for ethnomusicology. More curious is the role of systematic musicology (or, in Adler's scheme, the *rest* of the systematic area)—acoustics, psychology, sociology, and aesthetics. In the United States of the 1970s and 1980s, musicological study at academic institutions was carried on in four units (though few institutions actually had all four): history of (Western) music, ethnomusicology, systematic musicology (including what sometimes came to be known as psycho-musicology, socio-musicology, and acoustics), and music theory—the methodology of analysis and its application outside historical and social contexts. The last three would have been united in Adler's scheme. In American institutions, however, these four do not consider themselves to be equally musicological. Historical musicology is the centre, 'musicology' *par excellence*; ethnomusicology is sometimes included as true musicology and sometimes as an adjunct 'interdiscipline'. Music theorists consider themselves increasingly as not belonging to a musicological field at all, but as practitioners of a separate discipline, and associate themselves most closely with composers; they established their own society, the Society for Music Theory (which has its own journal), in 1978. But the other branches, which alone retain the term 'systematic', receive little attention in academic institutions; they often associate themselves most closely with music education, and do not have a unitary organization.

One may well ask why psycho-musicology and socio-musicology—fields that might be expected to prosper in the technologically sophisticated and scientifically oriented Western society of the late twentieth century—have not become more prominent. How is it that they account for a larger proportion of activity in Eastern Europe? I admit that measuring the relative prominence of these fields is problematic, considering the overlapping of disciplines (psycho-musicological studies, for instance, are often carried out in departments of psychology). But the lack of interest in such studies in the central musicological organizations and in ethnomusicology seems to me to result from two characteristics of musicologists: music historians and ethnomusicologists are suspicious of examination of music outside cultural and historical contexts, and they see themselves as advocates for certain musics—the 'best', or their own, or the neglected. Hence they are uncomfortable with subjecting music and musical activity to the examination of 'hard' or even 'soft' science.

Consider the role of psychological and acoustic and, for that matter, pedagogical and aesthetic issues in the *New Grove* and *MGG*. In both reference works, each field has a single major article, but the treatment is more often historical than conceptual, and little is said regarding the intercultural aspects of the subject at hand. The authors appear to be addressing audiences of outsiders—historians of Western music—more than scholars in psychology of music, acoustics, philosophy, or music education. Thus 'Education in Music' in the *New Grove* is a truly admirable article, but nevertheless devotes 54 pages to the history of music teaching as against only four to a section entitled 'conceptual aspects'.

If the existence and interaction of societies are a major factor in the direction of musicology, an even greater one may be the relationship of the major departments of musicology at universities. In the United States, the extremely complex hierarchy of universities and colleges plays a major role in higher education and in society at large. Where one has been educated determines a great deal of one's life as scholar, professional, businessman, or politician. Polls resulting in rankings play a large role, and departments compete for great scholars, talented students, and funds, in part by pointing to their relative stature; and colleagues are sometimes pitied in conversations at national meetings if their departments have lost major figures, been forced to decrease their student body, or have sunk in the rankings. Departments sometimes compete by presenting unique profiles, such as an emphasis on early music performance in one, on integration of historical musicology and ethnomusicology in another, on separation and high degrees of specialization in a third, on the influential role of music theory in a fourth, and so on. There is no doubt that a large part of the institutionalization of musicology in the twentieth century has involved the competitive interaction of its institutions.

## Canons, Paradigms, and Issues

For musicology to exist as an institution, as a recognizable entity in the intellectual and academic world, is it enough for it to have a definition, a general shape with centre and periphery, and organizations? I suggest that a discipline ought also to be defined by a group of shared beliefs upon which there is broad agreement, and, by the same token, of issues which are the abiding subject of controversy. But are there things which musicologists everywhere, and from 1885 on, have believed? There is little literature to provide concrete data, and what follow therefore are some very personal interpretations of the current state and history of the discipline.

In recent years, musicologists have written much about canons, and many have looked critically at the power exercised by canons and those who represent them.[54] Ordinarily, the term refers to the works of music that are selected for study or required as basic knowledge. Randel[55] suggests that approaches and methods are also ingredients of a musicological canon, and Bohlman[56] discusses the ethnomusicological use of canons. The nature of canons is determined by criteria derived at least in part from social, economic, and political aspects of culture; this much the authors of the mentioned works agree upon. Perhaps understandably, they usually shy away from listing the specific contents of musicological canons.

---

[54]   See esp. Bergeron and Bohlman (eds.), *Disciplining Music*; Solie (ed.), *Musicology and Difference*, and of course Kerman, *Contemplating Music*.

[55]   Don Michael Randel, 'The Canons in the Musicological Toolbox', in Bergeron and Bohlman (eds.), *Disciplining Music*, esp. 12–14.

[56]   Philip Bohlman, 'Ethnomusicology's Challenge to the Canon: The Canon's Challenge to Etthnomusicology', in Bergeron and Bohlman (eds.), *Disciplining Music*, 29–33.

Is not a canon the content and methodology that one expects all musicologists to control? Let me take American musicology since *c.*1950 as an example. Until quite recently, graduate students specializing in the history of European art-music needed to know little about American music, non-Western music, and systematic musicology. But students of American music had to know the European counterpart, and so did students of non-Western music. The few students of systematic musicology seemed to me to have been required to know something of all these musics. In recent years, graduate student music historians have been urged to present some knowledge of non-Western music, but none of systematic musicology. The concentric-circle structure is obvious.

But look at the music historian's preparation. In some institutions, the faculty distributed lists of works to be known at comprehensive examination time. Their content was usually weighted rather heavily towards Renaissance and Baroque music, and less was expected for the twentieth century. Concentration, in any case, was on detailed knowledge of individual works, with emphasis on harmonic structure, and less on their cultural context or relationships to those of other composers. In the comprehensive examinations of one department, students selected six works in advance, and presented analyses of them. At the first oral preliminary examination in musicology at Indiana University in 1949, the candidate is said to have been asked to play all the principal themes of the Beethoven symphonies on the piano (the committee made him stop after the first three symphonies, we are told). Identification of styles and composers is of course a major requirement. Entrance requirements to graduate programmes often include the writing of a fugue exposition, but not similar control over other complex techniques of composition such as sixteenth-century counterpoint or serial techniques.

In ethnomusicology, canons are harder to identify. Yet in the 1960s it seemed to me that one had difficulty associating with one's colleagues at meetings of SEM, for example, if one did not have some knowledge of (1) Native North American music, (2) music of sub-Saharan Africa, (3) classical music of India, and (4) principles of gamelan music. These areas constituted, at least for a time, a kind of informal canon of musicologically developed areas that enabled people in such a diverse field to communicate. Again, at meetings of the International Folk Music Council in the 1950s, knowledge of the Anglo-American repertories (particularly the Child ballads) and of Hungarian folk-music and the methods used by its scholars seemed to me to be assumed.

If there are canonic works and composers and repertories, are there also canonic techniques? Compared perhaps to biological and chemical sciences, there are few. In one department in which I studied, and in another in which I later taught, virtually the only requirements imposed on all musicology students of all types were a course on bibliographical control and one on techniques for transcribing medieval and Renaissance music. Somewhat similarly, in one ethnomusicology programme a student was first of all required to learn to transcribe recordings into notation; beyond that, each determined his or her individual course of study.

Certain musicological works (historical and ethnomusicological) constituted a canonic centre of the literature, and one had to have read these or at least heard of them to be a proper member of the profession. To be sure, these would vary by nation and over time. In North America during the 1950s, the books in the so-called Norton series (by Reese, Bukofzer, Einstein, and Austin[57]) occupied such a position; so did certain reference books with substantial content—for example, the major encyclopaedias, the major thematic catalogues, the major journals, and perhaps some respectable syntheses of music history. One also needed to have looked at the major complete-works editions. In German institutions in the 1950s, it was my experience that students lacked much in the way of guidance in establishing a canon of musicological literature, but surely knowledge of the Bücken *Handbuch*[58] would be assumed.

In ethnomusicology, the notion of a canon of scholarly works may be easier to define, possibly because there is no analogue to the music historian's repertorial canon. In the 1970s and 1980s, ethnomusicologists in the United States were particularly expected to have control of literature about the field as a whole—something expected far less frequently of music historians—and the principal works would surely have included Charles Seeger's essays[59] and Merriam's 1964 book.[60] By 1990, one could speak of a canon of model ethnographic works typically including those of Steven Feld and Anthony Seeger.[61]

If there are canons, are there also shared beliefs that go beyond the definition of the field? Or shared values? Or, for that matter, typical issues on which controversies focus? Here a fairly clear distinction between ethnomusicologists and historians emerges. In my view, the contrast was most clearly expressed in an informal debate between two scholars about the purposes of the two subdisciplines. The historian ended his talk by insisting that evaluation and judgement, and in the end the scholar's own aesthetic judgement of musical composition and performance, are the central concerns. The ethnomusicologist stated that 'evaluation has no place in musicology'.

In practice, the lines are not so sharp, but it seems clear to me that music historians are very much concerned with the excellence of the music they study. If, indeed, one cannot make a case for the outstanding merit of this music, one tries to show its association with other great music—it influenced, or was influenced

---

[57]    The original series included Curt Sachs, *The Rise of Music in the Ancient World, East and West* (New York, 1943); Gustave Reese, *Music in the Middle Ages* (1940); idem, *Music in the Renaissance* (1954); Manfred Bukofzer, *Music in the Baroque Era* (1947); Alfred Einstein, *Music in the Romantic Era* (1947).

[58]    Ernst Bücken (ed.), *Handbuch der Musikwissenschaft* (Wildpark-Potsdam, 1927–32).

[59]    Seeger, *Studies in Musicology 1935–1975*.

[60]    Merriam, *Anthropology of Music*.

[61]    Steven Feld, *Sound and Sentiment* (Philadelphia, 1982); Anthony Seeger, *Why Suyá Sing: A Musical Anthropology of an Amazonian People* (Cambridge, 1987).

by, a great master; or the composer wrote other, greater music; or he was the teacher or a relative of a major figure; and so on. The criteria of greatness or excellence in music have always been hard to identify; it's a case of 'je ne sais quoi'. Yet complexity (in a quantitative sense) and magnitude play a major role, as they do in the world of music-lovers at large. Outright popularity (for instance, the composers represented in 'pops' concerts) accomplishes the opposite for musicologists; until quite recently, they proudly stayed away from the likes of Tchaikovsky, Offenbach, and Grieg.

In trying to analyse what it was that determined the areas of interest of ethno-musicologists, I found myself looking at two principal approaches. One group (though I won't try to explain how individual choices were made) represented the view that all music was equally worthy of study, and it should all be done. This seems to me to have been the position of Alan Merriam, who in a conversation *c.*1975 told me of the many areas of the world in which his students were working. He even wanted to expand the representation, and he wished to be sure that I understood that Western art-music was included. The other group, by contrast, tended to look at the world of music as more variegated, and thus had reasons for this or that preference.

What kinds of reasons? At one time, questions of origin determined interest; origins of music, yes, but even more, music that could be regarded as 'original', ancient, uninfluenced by other, especially Western music. Clearly the principal one in the early part of the twentieth century, this criterion has waned, but has still not been totally abandoned. It was the notion that what could tell us about origins was worthy of study that dictated the great interest in tribal and rural folk-musics which dominated ethnomusicology through perhaps the 1950s, with the result that more complex cultures were sometimes treated by authors as if they were tribal. In mid-century, emphasis moved to the study of Asian classical systems, in part as a response to the interest on the part of all musicologies in developing the performance of little-known music, both 'early' and non-Western, in part to the desire of the ethnomusicological profession to show that it could compete with historical musicology, as it were, on its own ground. Then, during the last quarter-century, questions of political ideology have provided an impetus for the study of popular urban musics, of the relationship of musics, of cultural mixes, and of contemporary art-music culture from an ethnomusico-logical perspective.

If there are shared beliefs about what is worthy of study in each branch of our discipline, there are also beliefs as to how music 'works' and how scholarship intersects with these workings. Historical musicologists are disinclined to accept polygenesis, instead assuming that similarities in thematic content or compositional procedure indicate contact or 'influence'. They are not often willing to accept coincidence as an explanation of musical similarities, and thus ascribe significance almost automatically to motivic similarities within and among pieces by one composer or even among composers. For instance, they are very concerned with 'borrowings'. They accept the notion that in Western music, composers often write music 'about' other music, by quoting, writing variations, or parodying styles; and they argue the merits of individual cases. These beliefs are likely to be well-founded, and I mention them not to criticize them but rather to point out their role in determining the focus of research.

*[margin note: not critical, but still skeptical]*

One thing that seems to me to have determined the direction also of historical musicologists is interest in origins. They must know when, how, and by whose hand a work originated, and what influences led to it. Despite the recent growth of reception-history studies, they have been less interested in the history of a work after its creation than in its inception. They have tended to participate in major ritualistic activities, such as the publication of a composer's *opera omnia* or the performance of a composer's entire corpus of works. Governments and foundations have been particularly inclined to support such ceremonial projects. Music historians have used the musical work, especially the master-work, as the principal focus for research and presentation.[62] Other shared beliefs involve the integrity of periods, the insights one can gain from biography, the overwhelming validity of chronological approaches, and the significance of using the works of a single composer (rather than, to give an artificial example, the works written or performed in one city during one year) as units of study. My purpose is not to be critical of these approaches; they may be the best ones for realizing the goals of musicology. Yet the neglect of other possible approaches—looking at history by starting with the present and working back, or emphasizing the history of (say) themes or motifs rather than compositional procedures, or charting histories of works throughout their lifetimes—shows that musicology, as an institution, has fostered particular methods and practices, beyond simply engaging in 'the scholarly study of music'.

*[margin note: but again, it is]*

Influenced by both historical musicology and anthropology, ethnomusicology has sometimes provided analogues to Western music history, but more typically, it has taken an opposing stand. With a few notable exceptions, ethnomusicologists have paid little attention to individual musical works and their fate (sometimes to the chagrin of non-Western master musicians); they have rarely concentrated on specific musicians, despite the fact that when they make generalizations about the music of entire cultures, their data may be the statements and performances of only one or a very few musicians or consultants. With the exception of folk-music scholars (who had ceased their efforts by the 1960s),[63] they have rarely attempted to document entire repertories, to collect all the songs of one singer or all the pieces by one composer. Rather, they have looked at a musical society as it exists in one time-frame.

---

[62] Walter Wiora, *Das musikalische Kunstwerk* (Tutzing, 1983).

[63] e.g. Bertrand H. Bronson, *The Traditional Tunes of the Child Ballads* (Princeton, 1959–72); Deutsches Volksliedarchiv (ed.), *Deutsche Volkslieder mit ihren Melodien* (1935–74); or in a different sense, Béla Bartók, *Hungarian Folk Music* (Oxford, 1931).

The contrasts have been so pronounced that one might consider historical musicology and ethnomusicology (both of which, in principle, have interests in history and in the place of music in society) as representing the diametrical opposites between which most music research is played out: synchronic–diachronic, art-music–functional music, the élite–the entire society, dynamic music–static music, personalized–anonymous, individual–societal, origins known–origins unknown, music as sound–music as culture.[64] Yet none of these oppositions, in my view, really defines the differences between the two branches of musicology.

Throughout the period since *c*.1960, music scholars in North America (and elsewhere) have debated the relative advantages of maintaining specialized existences as historians, ethnomusicologists, and theorists, or of merging into an integrated, Adlerian unit. Should there be a single, overarching organization or a single, holistic training curriculum? Or should there be three societies which meet together? Or always separately? Following a celebration of Adler's article in 1985,[65] I detected a tendency towards unification, more evident in the flow of ideas than in the development of organizations. Music historians refer increasingly to anthropological literature, and even to ethnomusicology, in finding models for research and interpretation;[66] ethnomusicologists are more inclined to include Western art-music in their publications and courses.[67] Whether this is a definitive closing of ranks or a faddish diversion is yet to be seen. Nevertheless, it is an indication that musicology—in North America and in Western Europe—continues as a discipline claiming all types of research on music.

Since its inception in the prehistoric eras of Adler's first sentence, and since its official European emergence in 1885, musicology has become an institution both in the academy and in the world of music. It is like other academic disciplines—history, literary history and criticism, sociology, anthropology, economics, physics, microbiology—whose institutionalization can readily be argued and documented. Its uniqueness seems to me to involve two of its characteristics. One

[64] Discussion, explicit but more often by implication, of these oppositions is found in virtually all writings about the field of musicology. See particularly, however, Seeger, *Studies in Musicology 1935–1975*, 1–15, and Gilbert Chase, 'A Dialectical Approach to Music History', *Ethnomusicology*, 2 (1958), 1–9.

[65] A number of events marked the anniversary of the publication of Adler's seminal article. At a symposium, 'Umfang, Methode und Ziel der Musikwissenschaft 1885–1985', held in Geras, Austria, 22–6 Apr. 1985, eight papers dealt in some way with Adler's work. A joint meeting of the AMS, SEM, SMT, and CMS was held in Vancouver, Canada, 7–10 Nov. 1985; Adler's vision of a comprehensive discipline of music research was echoed in the major plenary session, at which the presidents of the four societies read papers indicating the contributions of their various fields.

[66] See e.g. Peter Jeffery, *Re-envisioning Past Musical Cultures: Ethnomusicology in the Study of Gregorian Chant* (Chicago, 1992); Gary Tomlinson, *Music in Renaissance Magic* (Chicago, 1993).

[67] For ethnomusicological perspectives on central institutions of Western art-music in the United States, see Henry Kingsbury, *Music, Talent, and Performance: A Conservatory Cultural System* (Philadelphia, 1988), and Bruno Nettl, *Heartland Excursions: Ethnomusicological Reflections on Schools of Music* (Urbana, Ill., 1995).

is its holistic nature, mentioned frequently in these pages. A second is its involvement with the practice of music, which it affects more than the scholars of other arts affect their subjects. Musicology, an institution in the world of music, plays a significant role in determining the actions and judgements of composers, performers, and the musical public.

# 14

# *Other Musicologies: Exploring Issues and Confronting Practice in India*

## Regula Burckhardt Qureshi

The ingenuously generic title of this chapter[1] instantly and effectively invokes a complex problematic that has variously constrained Western music scholarship both outside and within the bounds of its own conventions. Aspects of this problematic are currently motivating critical initiatives in Western musicology.[2] They are also challenging anew the explicitly other-oriented scholarship of ethnomusicology.[3] A strong sense of engagement, linked to the current rethinking of Western intellectual foundations (to which this volume clearly contributes), characterizes these diverse initiatives for confronting, and juxtaposing, music scholarship and otherness.

Is rethinking music possible while critically invoking, thereby entering the confines of, established musical categories? The notion of 'Western' music and, by implication, musicology is used here for convenience, but not without awareness that the totalizing implications of the term itself contribute to a world-wide dichotomizing strategy that juxtaposes the West versus 'the Rest', and then easily essentializes them as 'own' and 'other'.[4] Furthermore, the notion of Western music/musicology arbitrarily conflates obvious geographic-historical discontinuities, while also excluding major musical practices, creating further domains of otherness. This is not the place to deconstruct the peculiar historicalgeographic conglomerate that makes up 'Western', or to identify the

---

[1] Fortuitously suggested by the editors of this book. My thanks go to Mark Everist, Jason Sinkus, and David Gramit for their contributions to this project.

[2] See e.g. the contributions to this issue by Ruth Solie and Philip Bohlman in Katherine Bergeron and Philip V. Bohlman (eds.), *Disciplining Music: Musicology and its Canons* (Chicago, 1992).

[3] See e.g. the contributions by Line Grenier and Jocelyne Guilbault, ' "*Authority*" Revisited: The "Other" in Anthropology and Popular Music Studies', *Ethnomusicology*, 34/3 (1990), 381–97; Thomas Turino, 'Structure, Context, and Strategy in Musical Ethnography', *Ethnomusicology*, 34/3 (1990), 399–412; Stephen Blum, 'Response to the Symposium Papers: Commentary', *Ethnomusicology*, 34/3 (1990), 413–21.

[4] The project of articulating the imperialist foundations of Western civilization has been pioneered by Edward W. Said in *Orientalism* (New York, 1978) and *Culture and Imperialism* (New York, 1993) and by other literary scholars of non-Western origin like Gauri Vishwanathan, *Masks of Conquest: Literary Study and British Rule in India* (New York, 1989), and Sara Suleri, *The Rhetoric of English in India* (Chicago, 1992).

exclusionary practices that result in 'music', but only to acknowledge that what follows is inevitably dependent on the arbitrariness of both.

Clearly, to explore issues surrounding this topic requires delving beneath the brittle surface of discipline and academic argument, and beyond the sonic universe of music, own and other. In the absence of essences, what follows reflects my own engagement: a broadly generic, personal exploration leads to a consideration of specific issues in my encounters with otherness in 'Indic Musicology'.[5]

## Musicology and Otherness

Considering otherness raises foundational questions, because it challenges the ubiquity of the self and its ideational foundation, including its ways of construing music. Moving from the essentializing 'What is a musicology?' to the exploratory 'What can a musicology be?' gives rise to new alternatives that put the questioner's musicology itself in question.

What, then, are other musicologies? The musicology of others? The musicologies of other musics? Or simply alternative ways of knowing music? If musicology is a way of construing music, how is musicology a response to music and an articulation of musical reception? How is it an intellectual paradigm, informed by the priorities of a *Weltanschauung*? And how is it situated socially, how subject to political agendas? In light of all this, how does it become an intellectual-artistic canon, a prescriptive set of rules for generating music, a tool for sonic control?

Musicology also articulates authorial agency. This raises the questions: Whose musicology? And for whom? Other exists in relation to self, hence one's own musicology offers an exegetical starting-point that becomes an acknowledgement of agency: who is asking, and from what culturally informed assumptions? It took until the middle of this century for Western scholarship to acknowledge the intellectual existence of cultural others; and only at the end of the century have humanists come round to examining their own positionality *vis-à-vis* cultural production that takes place within an expansionist polity and global economy.[6] Given the inevitable filter of our cultural *habitus* and intellectual strategies, informed and articulated through our personal vantage-point and tactics, the best that we can here aspire to is to ask 'What are other musicologies to us?', from a conscious position of our own cultural particularity.

A self-critically open position not only toward other musicologies, but also toward those who create and use them, is the next crucial step in a cross-

---

[5] Adapted from Harold S. Powers's 'Indic musical historiography' ('India, Subcontinent of', in Stanley Sadie (ed.), *New Grove Dictionary of Music and Musicians* (London, 1980), ix. 77.

[6] See Grenier and Guilbault, ' "*Authority*" Revisited'.

cultural experiment of situated musical thinking. Logically, we ask the same questions of intellectual and social relevance regarding their vantage-point and constituencies as authors, patrons, and institutions. But what are our data? Whom do we ask? What are the 'sources' of other musicologies?

To begin with, we encounter the 'other' musicologically within the precincts and legacy of our own musicological enterprise. Deeply embedded within print culture and heir to a positivist historiographic model of scholarship, musicology has helped to shape a scholarly hierarchy of musical otherness in its own image, privileging written over oral, and past over present sources, and always in search of music in notation.

Even more profound, and thus more insidiously transparent, is the impact which dominant paradigms of social-cultural otherness have had on concepts and processes of music scholarship. In line with post-Enlightenment universalist and nineteenth-century dialectical and evolutionary notions of culture, otherness is tied to a set of dichotomies that include a pre-rational or irrational, feminized, dependent 'rest' versus the rational, dominant, imperialist West. Particularly relevant to music is the expression of such otherness through what is considered transitory, ahistorical orality versus essentialized, historicized literacy, including that of scholarship itself.

There may be reasons for this in music scholarship particularly. For in light of this paradigm the written 'scholarly record' might even be viewed as an ongoing rescue operation of a subject that remains incorrigibly oral-aural; if so, this could in part account for musicology's initially hostile response to ethnomusicology, with its scholarly embrace of orality in music.

## 'Other Musicologies' Within

Internally, Western music scholarship has channelled otherness through a positivist hermeneutic of canonicity[7] which, I believe, was further intensified by the post-World War II consolidation of the discipline in North America.[8] Half a century later, the reconsideration of this hermeneutic is well under way, spearheaded, interestingly, by constituencies of 'others' within Western musicology itself. The development of a critical musicology, supported by feminist and gay–lesbian scholarship, is beginning to reshape the scope of Western musicology toward a dehegemonized pluralism that opens up space for 'difference'

[7] Initially explored by Joseph Kerman in *Contemplating Music: Challenges to Musicology* (Cambridge, 1985), and William Weber in *The Rise of Musical Classics in Eighteenth-Century England: A Study in Canon, Ritual, and Ideology* (New York, 1992).

[8] The cultural shift of musicology's epicentre from a nation-based Europe to a 'Western civilization'-based North America has yet to be examined epistemologically and through the dynamic of European *émigré* culture. For a promising beginning, see Reinhold Brinkmann's paper given at the conference on European Émigré Musicologists, held at Harvard University, 1994.

among musical-cultural insiders.[9] Another dehegemonizing influence comes from the expansion of popular music and culture studies, challenging musicology to expand its élite focus beyond 'art' music.[10] These moves toward acknowledging others within the discipline also bring conceptually closer musicologies of cultural, social, and racial others.

Seen from within the musicological establishment, the branch of music scholarship explicitly designated to address global musical 'difference' has from the beginning been relegated to the margins of the discipline, despite its initial inclusion in a comprehensively global and comparative blueprint for musicology.[11]

Pertinent to the entire musicological edifice, postcolonial scholarship is addressing the crucial issue of an imperialist legacy of orientalism and exoticism, both within and outside the domain of music. Supported by the colonial experience, an intellectual succession of paradigms has generated for Western civilization a master narrative of the masters which has lived mostly unacknowledged within conservative humanist disciplines like musicology.

In one sense the very development of a separate specialization for 'ethnically' marked music, and its place at the margins of the unmarked category of Western music, perpetuates the colonial relationship. But in another sense, because of its relative isolation from traditional musicology, ethnomusicology has also been free to extend beyond music and address itself directly to issues of cultural otherness by drawing from other disciplines, mainly anthropology.

## The Western Study of Musical Others

A review of Western musicological responses to other musics clearly reflects changing conceptions of non-Western peoples, although a generic Western élitism *vis-à-vis* Others appears constant across different theoretical frames. Since the antecedents of at least two centuries remain implicated in the Western gaze toward musical and musicological Others, it may be useful to briefly profile major intellectual frames that have contributed to that gaze.

Though heavily overlaid by later models, the rationalist–naturist vision of Natural Man associated with Rousseau (and later Thoreau) continues to offer an idealized primitive version of undifferentiated Others and of their music, as is articulated in Rousseau's own works.[12] More persistent is the evolutionist–

---

[9] The role played by 'the dominated fractions of the dominant class' can be ground-breaking (Pierre Bourdieu, *Distinction: A Social Critique of the Judgement of Taste*, trans. Richard Nice (Cambridge, 1984)), 316.

[10] John Shepherd is a protagonist, along with others connected with British cultural studies. See 'Popular Music Studies: Challenges for Musicology', *Stanford Humanities Review*, 3/2 (1993), 17–35. See also John Shepherd, *Music as Social Text* (Cambridge, 1991).

[11] Foundational as it is, Guido Adler's scheme of musicology soon became relegated to disciplinary invocations; see for instance 'Musicology', in Stanley Sadie (ed.), *New Grove Dictionary of Music and Musicians* (London, 1980), xii. 838, and 'Musikwissenschaft' in *M.G.G.* (Kassel, 1961), ix. 1210.

[12] See Jean-Jacques Rousseau, *Dictionnaire de Musique* (Paris, 1768).

comparative model, for it both contrasts and organically connects the complementary notions of primitive and civilized, simple and complex, early and late, always from the implicit vantage-point of Western culture and cognition as the top of an evolutionary pyramid, music included. Thoroughly Eurocentric, but differentiated as well as dynamic, social evolutionism offers a developmental continuum for societies and cultural production that provided the first global scheme for music scholarship. In addition, scientific empiricism offered tools to compare, rank, and control the world's tonal systems.[13]

Reacting to the foundational opposition between Western and primitive, the paradigm of cultural relativism engenders the notion of different cultural logics, supported by linguistic and cognitive models.[14] But the priority for scholarship as culturally neutral science was difficult to give up, as is expressed in the emic–etic distinction.[15] The most powerful reaction against evolutionism was based on the logic of functional value in an organicist notion of societies as functionally interrelated wholes, and of 'expressive culture' as serving social and individual needs. Foundational for ethnomusicology, functionalism has been the model especially for behaviourist interpretations of Other societies.[16] Élitism lingers, however, when complex 'art' musics are exempted from the crude functionality of Gebrauch.[17]

A mentalist reaction to functionalism as well as a refinement is structuralism which postulates that social as well as cultural patterns articulate universal mental structures. While this is in effect an egalitarian model, accessing those structures for Others has been based on Western interpretational privilege.[18]

Finally, the Marxist model, globally true to its 19th-century origin, focuses on links of production and exploitation within and between Western and Other societies, with culture taking an epiphenomenal place, though 'Cultural Marxism'

[13] Curt Sachs is perhaps the last and most articulate protagonist of this musically as well as socially untenable paradigm for music. See *The Rise of the Ancient World, East and West* (New York, 1943).

[14] See B. L. Whorf's *Language, Thought and Reality* (New York, 1957), and Harold C. Conklin's 'Hanunoo Color Categories', *Southwestern Journal of Anthropology*, 2 (1955), 339–44.

[15] See William Sturtevant, 'Studies in Ethnoscience', *American Anthropologist*, 66 (1964), 99–131, and Marvin Harris, 'Emics, Etics and the New Ethnography', in *The Rise of Anthropological Theory: A History of Theories of Culture* (New York, 1968), 568–604, and 'Emics and Etics Revisited', in T. Headland, K. L. Pike, and M. Harris (eds.), *Emics and Etics: The Insider/Outsider Debate* (London, 1990), 48–61. See also Frank Alvarez-Pereyre and Simha Arom, 'Ethnomusicology and the Emic/Etic Issue', *World of Music*, 35/1 (1993), 7–33; Max Peter Baumann, 'Listening as an Emic/Etic Process in the Context of Observation and Inquiry', *World of Music*, 35/1 (1993), 34–62; Marcia Herndon, 'Insiders, Outsiders: Knowing our Limits, Limiting our Knowing', *World of Music*, 35/1 (1993), 63–80.

[16] Founded in British social anthropology, especially through the work of Bronislaw Malinowski (*Argonauts of the Western Pacific: An Account of Native Enterprise and Adventure in the Archipelagoes of Melanesian New Guinea* (London, 1932)) and Alfred R. Radcliffe-Brown (*Structure and Function in Primitive Societies: Essays and Addresses* (London, 1952)). Alan Merriam posits an essentially functionalist 'anthropology of music' in his ground-breaking work, *The Anthropology of Music* (Evanston, Ill., 1964).

[17] This categorization is particularly well articulated in the German musical category of *G (Gebrauchs)-Musik*, as distinct from *E (Ernste)-Musik*, but also *U (Unterhaltungs)-Musik*.

[18] Claude Lévi-Strauss's encompassing works are foundational, and include an evocative musical example. See *The Elementary Structures of Kinship*, trans. J. Bell (Boston, 1969); *The Raw and Cooked*, trans. John and Doreen Weightman (New York, 1969), and 'Bolero de Maurice Ravel', *L'Homme*, 2 (1971), 5–14.

has developed a differentiated view of culture, including music, as a site of resistance.[19]

Today, decentring initiatives of post-structuralism, feminist criticism, and post-colonial studies are invalidating 'grand theory', but established intellectural practices survive beneath the post-modern challenge that is only beginning to forge semantic links across disciplinal boundaries. In the academic realm of music, particularly, high–low, own–other, art–utility dichotomies have been enshrined in the division between musicology as a classical humanist discipline that studies 'up' and ethnomusicology as a residual cross-discipline that approaches music socially and studies 'down'. But, as the present volume makes eloquently clear, increased participation in each other's conversations is generating conditions for 'crossing over' and sharing in a theoretical engagement that can lead to the respectful acknowledgement of other logics of representing musics.

## How 'Other' is Ethnomusicology?

Within the residual remains of an élitist separation of Others, ethnomusicology has, during its brief history, attained a mediating and synthesizing eclecticism that arises in part from its coexistence with a number of disciplinal environments. The central paradigm of ethnomusicology draws from both musicology and anthropology, somewhat like folklore holistically encompassing both 'text' and 'context' of music, but also uneasily situated between them. As well, ethnomusicology is uneasily situated between its Western frame of reference and its culturally different musical subjects. The primary response by ethnomusicologists to both problematics has been musical participation through applied study, for 'making music together'[20] with those subjects creates encounters with music in its context, while also offering an experiential escape from cognitive dissonance between Western music students and Other music-makers.

The ethnomusicological adaptation to the learning model of Western performers also extends to the explanatory verbal categories that are used within a culture to make sense out of its music, both inherently and through connections with extra-musical signification and referents. In fact, such cultural-musical immersion naturally leads ethnomusicologists to acquire empathetic identification with musical meaning systems as they are attached to performance. Words about music may become central in the musical discovery process, but they don't

---

[19] Raymond Williams's work and work emanating from British cultural studies have typically been applied musically to Western popular and subculture music. See Williams, *Marxism and Literature* (Oxford, 1977); Reebee Garofalo, 'How Autonomous is Relative: Popular Music, the Social Formation and Cultural Struggle', *Popular Music*, 6/1 (1987), 77–92; and Simon During (ed.), *The Cultural Studies Reader* (New York, 1993).

[20] Schutz's evocative title appropriately implies the connecting power of such experience even across cultures. See Alfred Schutz, 'Making Music Together: A Study in Social Relationships', *Social Research*, 18/1 (1951), 76–97.

stand alone, literally or affectively; for the primary verbal communication is oral, and thus inevitably interactive.[21]

Major work in ethnomusicology has been to convert such oral, person- and situation-specific knowledge into written '(ethno-)musicologies', interpretively constructed for scholarly dissemination. Clearly directed toward cultural outsiders, such writings validate the scholar's expertise *vis-à-vis* her Western peers. These are documents of musical mediation rendered in an alien conceptual language. As such, they inevitably open up questions of authorial voice and agency, even when they embody the author's struggle in encountering musical otherness. Whose significations are being articulated here? And are the resulting representations 'indigenous musicologies' or Western appropriations?

These questions acquire further relevance in light of the persistent ancillary agenda of ethnomusicology to record and document musical cultures, thereby isolating musical products, including musicologies as the means of explaining music apart from living contexts and agents. Historically linked to the destructive effects of Western encroachments, especially on Aboriginal American cultures, 'salvage ethnomusicology', like its anthropological forebear, is an ultimate strategy of cultural control; but there are various collaborative initiatives to restore that control.[22]

Current ethnographic critiques of Western scholarly essentializing *vis-à-vis* cultural 'others'[23] highlight how even cross-culturally derived, 'emic' approaches to decoding musical signification remain subsumed within, and therefore intellectually controlled by, the metatheory of the searcher's own musicology. While it may not be possible to escape one's own metatheory any more than one's enculturation, emergent strategies are moving away from essentializing toward a relational scholarship by calling for dialogue, for 'co-thinking one's own historicity', for acknowledging the situatedness of one's own as well as the other's musicology, for an emic mutuality that allows one to sustain 'a sense of meaning in the face of otherness'.[24]

Ethnomusicologists are increasingly engaging with the challenge of such mutuality, aided by a shift of focus toward the study of diverse musical cultures at home, and also by an increasing—or increasingly acknowledged—cultural diversity among scholars themselves. The resulting engagement with musical identity as a socially situated process contributes toward putting into serious question notions of a definitive musicology for any musical culture. In practice,

---

[21] A good verbal representation of this musical-verbal-affective learning process is James Kippen's account in *The Tabla of Lucknow* (Cambridge, 1988).

[22] Perhaps the best example is Beverly Diamond's extensive, careful collaboration with native partners in creating a work on native instrument collections that is totally unassuming and reception-oriented. See her *Visions of Sound: Musical Instruments of First Nations Communities in Northeastern America* (Chicago, 1994).

[23] Johannes Fabian's 'culture garden' syndrome; see Johannes Fabian, *Time and the Other: How Anthropology Makes its Object* (New York, 1983).

[24] The fact that these words were written by a historical musicologist shows concretely how this conversation has begun to extend across the two fields. See Gary Tomlinson, *Music in Renaissance Magic: Toward a Historiography of Others* (Chicago, 1992).

to extend the notion of diversity of musical knowledge challenges any single authority on a particular music, not only among scholarly outsiders, but among music constituencies within the musical culture itself.[25]

## Other Texts, Other Musicologists

Implicit in this and other discussions on musicology is the Western assumption that scholarly authority is invested in written texts. Implied further is a notion that such authority is in some sense distinct from music-making practice, a knowledge not so much 'of', but 'on' or 'about' music, and directed to a constituency of knowledge-seekers. In light of this, do indigenous music literatures constitute musicologies? And what about oral musicologies?

If 'musicology' broadly means making verbal knowledge about music accessible or creating verbal knowledge about music, then this can take place orally as well as in writing. In many cultures normative, interpretive texts live in memories, and their transmission is from one memory to another. In that process, words are of course not separate from the transmitter's purpose of dissemination, and even once received, remembered knowledge remains personal knowledge. Written texts extend beyond that personal nexus through their materiality, which also invites recontextualizations over time, including those by interpretive scholarship itself. Does this make written texts on music more definitive than oral ones? The question of their relationship is particularly relevant in societies in which musical knowledge is transmitted orally as well as in writing. Coming from a divided scholarly tradition that associates 'other' primarily with 'oral', it is also an epistemologically tainted question. For written texts are certainly the bedrock of Western musicology and its traditionally developmental search for historical essences.

On the other hand, the fact that the predominantly participatory and presentist approaches of ethnomusicologists have tended to neglect written texts also plays into the built-in historicism of traditional musicology. But there is more to this omission. Approaching music literatures poses the pragmatic challenge of acquiring another culture's scholarly literacy, including the mastery of discrete scripts.[26] Furthermore, textual traditions are situated within larger epistemological frames with which they articulate as much as with musical practices; they are also socially contingent, often as culturally privileged voices of élite erudition, not necessarily linked to milieus of musical practice. Above all, texts can be treated as objects that remain ontologically intact, available for use as docu-

---

[25] The first generation of ethnomusicologists was peopled by pioneers who became 'sole representatives' for 'their' music, often until their own students could join them. Outstanding examples are Mantle Hood, David McAllester, and Bruno Nettl.

[26] This point may sound trivial, but a script can pose a formidable handicap to full participation in a culture's written world, and Western publishers have little use for its texts.

ments of a musical past and its achievements. Such characteristics match well with the élitist purview of Western art-music scholarship and its humanist paradigm of historical-philological interpretation.

The same humanist paradigm has long extended to the study of non-Western literatures through the scholarly tradition that arose from a confluence of classical and oriental studies in nineteenth-century Europe. Music was included within the culture-historical scope of 'Eastern High Civilizations', which in the main comprise East and South Asia and the Near East. Embedded in a culture-historical matrix, music scholarship focused on a search for origins and cultural authenticity, and thus privileged foundational texts in classical languages—mainly Chinese, Sanskrit, Arabic, and Persian. These antecedents are reflected in a shared epistemological orientation that characterizes the Western treatment of texts in otherwise highly diverse musical traditions.[27]

At present, particularly in North America, 'area studies' extend to a more broadly societal scope, influenced by empiricist social science; but a literary-linguistic core remains, now increasingly in the service of disseminating practical as well as conceptual expertise in cultural otherness. Most important is the concomitant shift toward engaging indigenous literati and the emergence of indigenous scholars as specialists in their own culture.

Today, orientalist writings on music face the challenge of an extensive post-colonial critique of orientalist scholarship and its foundation in Eurocentric hegemony, although our subject has to date received marginal attention.[28] What complicates the matter is that this very scholarship is inevitably implicated in current indigenous constructions of high culture and notions of music. Indigenous participation in orientalist scholarship begins with the usually unacknowledged contributions to the works of great orientalists who were able to extend the extractive enterprise of Western colonialism to their projects. In these highly unequal collaborations, indigenous experts served as sources of essential linguistic and cultural knowledge; the process also offered them exposure to Western intellectual priorities.[29] Active indigenous participation in this scholarship, however, has hinged on acquiring Western language competence, which also implies a degree of intellectual Westernization through colonial schooling. Thus trained, indigenous scholars joined the orientalist conversation, writing about their musical concepts and practices in relation to Western evolutionary, empiricist, or historicist interpretive goals.

---

[27] For reviews of the scholarship in these areas (though of uneven scope and quality) see Helen Myers (ed.), *Ethnomusicology: Historical and Regional Studies* (New York, 1993), and of course relevant articles in the *New Grove*.

[28] Edward Said, the acknowledged founder of this critique and a fine interpreter of music, strictly Western and classical; see his *Musical Elaborations* (New York, 1991). That he neglects the topic of music in his orientalist critique is a reminder not only of music's marginality, but of its ambiguous intellectual status within the Western academy, to which Said clearly belongs.

[29] The resulting scholarly editions, translations, and interpretations of 'other' musical texts rarely reveal the obvious extent of indigenous participation involved in orientalist scholarship from its colonial beginnings. For an example see A. Daniélou and N. R. Bhatt, *Textes des Purana sur la Theorie Musicale* (Pondicherry, 1959).

For Western readers, these literatures present an uncomfortable double exposure, refracting their own paradigms as crudely colonial and dated, their interpretive use perhaps estranged into an 'other' logic. Seen from the ideal of a Western-style, but indigenous, culture-sensitive, historical-analytical musicology, these are seen as 'historically conditioned flaws' in an otherwise salutary 'combination of traditional lore and analytical methods'.[30] But as indigenous voices, these writings predictably articulate conditions of subalternity, as well as of interdependence, which emerge from a scholarly interaction lacking both intellectual and musical reciprocity. Perhaps (ethno)musicologists have not found it easy to relate to the uncanny intersubjective enmeshment of their colonized counterparts that generates compliance as well as resistance to Western intellectual domination.[31]

How do 'other' voices speak today, post-colonially, under national independence, and, at the same time, under the continuing hegemonic foundations of global Western expansion? The question calls for addressing the contemporary role of indigenous musicologists in the cultural nationalist projects of their countries, including the institutionalization of knowledge about music. Here modernist goals of defining national music and its historical antecedents interface with decolonizing agendas for documenting and preserving musical diversity, along with goals of dissemination and pedagogy. No less than their Western counterparts, 'other musicologists' today need to be seen as writing within, and against, broader intellectual contexts that are linked to 'other' centres of power, and addressing 'other' constituencies in their languages, literally as well as figuratively. 'Other' understandings and uses of Western orientalist concepts are integral to such indigenization, as is their rejection. Most obviously, orientalist humanism is being put in the service of musical historiography as a site for articulating 'nation through narration'.[32] Western readers are thus challenged to see their 'own' concepts become part of a particular musicological otherness.

To confront these transformations is not unproblematic for musicologists of any stripe, for they blur the very boundaries on which the quest for 'other musicologies' is founded. Could this help to account for the somewhat striking lack of interest among Western scholars in contemporary musicologies and their indigenous authors? Some ethnomusicologists do struggle to extend to contemporary textual traditions their interactive sense of live musical and verbal

---

[30] Powers, in his pioneering 1965 consideration of this literature: 'Indian Music and the English Language', *Ethnomusicology*, 11/1 (1965), 1–12.

[31] C. Capwell's interpretive work on S. M. Tagore makes an eloquent beginning: 'Marginality and Musicology in Nineteenth-Century Calcutta: The Case of Sourindro Mohun Tagore', in Bruno Nettl and Philip V. Bohlman (eds.), *Comparative Musicology and Anthropology of Music: Essays on the History of Ethnomusicology* (Chicago, 1991), 228–43.

[32] The phrase and concept is adapted from Homi K. Bhabha, *Nation and Narration* (London, 1990). Western historical musicology, too, has its historical foundations in nationalist projects, as does historiography more generally.

processes, but this is often problematic. For while written texts can be treated as objects or fixed statements that remain ontologically intact, they, like oral texts, resist interpretation without the participation of their indigenous creators and interpreters. In today's climate of expanding academic cosmopolitanism, such participation is increasing, supported particularly by a growing indigenous élite of scholars who share current comparative, transnational Western thinking.[33] This trend, however, continues to leave marginalized the majority of those 'other' musicologists who work locally and in local languages, interpreting their own music theoretically and historically to their own audiences. Encountering such textual musical authorities constitutes a test that many ethnomusicologists continue to fail. Is it because such encounters are a confrontation with 'difference' in our use of musicological language and concepts, and not only of language, but more profoundly of agenda and underlying assumptions, even, and especially, where our terms and concepts may be shared, but not their connection with our respective musical and knowledge base.[34] Indeed, an important, as yet little explored factor unique to cross-cultural scholarship in music is precisely the continuing discontinuity between indigenous and Western musical frames of reference. For Western scholars, such 'other' colleagues can become conceptually disturbing interpretive interlocutors in their relationship with the textual or musical 'raw material' and their own interpretations.

Given these profound disjunctures, the question one is left with is: Are other musicologies possible? Or are music scholars arrested within their own paradigms and their particular position *vis-à-vis* hegemonic forces that drive their validation? In a spirit of opposition to globalizing answers, even in the negative, this 'power-knowledge' or 'power-music' question can only be considered situationally and pragmatically, in relation to particular, local practices, but also to dominant classes and political dominance. Included in these pragmatic, situational considerations must be the outsider's own interpretive practices. To acknowledge the contingent, non-essential quality of one's scholarship may not come easily, particularly to those of us trained in the tradition of Ranke. Instead, suspending judgement or 'not knowing'[35] becomes the starting-point for a negotiation of meanings that needs to encompass self and other in their relevant contexts. Intellectually, such a relational approach should make possible an interpretive pluralism that encompasses the possibility of plural agency on both sides and across the self–other divide. An example is the collaboration between Indian and Western Sanskritist-musicologists working on foundational treatises relevant to music history.[36]

---

[33] This élite is far stronger in the humanities generally, but music is increasingly being drawn in.

[34] See Powers, 'Indian Music and the English Language', and Bonnie C. Wade, 'A Guide to Source Materials: Bibliography', in *Music in India: The Classical Tradition* (Englewood Cliffs, NJ, 1979), 213–20.

[35] See Beverley Diamond Cavanagh, ' "Not Knowing" and the Study of Native Music Cultures: Introductory Comments', in *Ethnomusicology in Canada* (Toronto, 1990), 57–61.

[36] The Indian inititative to hold conferences on major treatises like the *Sangita Ratnakara* (Benares, 1993) is symptomatic of this collaboration.

Another approach to that divide, yet to be addressed explicitly, is through the dimension that distinguishes 'other' musicologies from 'other' scholarship generally: music. How does the focus on music—rather than literature or history—mark scholarly encounters with otherness? Problematic as cross-cultural musical encounters may be, they also offer to those who are mutually 'other' a domain of valued experience that they can share. With its potential to set its participants apart in a special way, the shared focus on music creates a constituency *vis-à-vis* other verbal disciplines that also has the potential of setting them apart. Perhaps the aestheticization of performance permits the coexistence of different paradigms and agendas, by harmonizing them into a *summum bonum*. Is music less a tool of power that divides than are words—or more so, but of a power that joins? And does creating and reading texts on music therefore differ from creating and reading other texts?

Such crucial questions are difficult to extend to the practice of musicology, own or other, as long as the study of musical texts in mostly synonymous with the study of a musical past and distinct from the study of a living musical praxis, including its texts. Furthermore, scholarship on music, including ethnomusicologists' writings on oral musical knowledge, is generally seen as an activity of control, an intervention into—or at least a slowing down of—the flow of orally negotiated meaning, thereby establishing and disseminating norms through the reified form of visually represented words, the written source. But by this very process scholarship is also a source of encoded musical content, words about music that can speak to those who share a commitment to the musical constituency within academic scholarship. The sense of such a constituency may arise from a Western ideology about music; but the cross-cultural experience of many ethnomusicologists supports the notion of music's potential to mediate otherness, even among scholars. One way to enhance this potential would seem to be a willingness among musicologists to expand intellectual boundaries in order to make space for music to speak along with and through words, thereby creating another kind of pluralism.[37] Adding the voice of music to speech about music has long been a serious goal of ethnomusicology;[38] to pursue it in the service of cross-cultural imperatives will require new kinds of creativity and collaboration.[39]

[37] John Blacking's Cambridge Studies in Ethnomusicology initiated the process of adding recordings to books, followed by the Chicago Studies in Ethnomusicology with CDs.

[38] See the foundational formulation of Charles Seeger in "Towards a Universal Music-Sound Writing for Musicology', *Journal of the International Folk Music Council*, 4 (1957), 63–6, and *Studies in Musicology 1935–1975* (Berkeley, 1977).

[39] Recent initiatives by Anthony Seeger and Stephen Feld and others are addressing the collaborative use of sound media. See Anthony Seeger, 'Ethnomusicology and Music Law', *Ethnomusicology*, 36/3 (1992), 345–59; Stephen Feld, 'The Politics of Amplification: Notes on "Endangered Music" and Musical Equity', *Folklife Center News*, 15/1 (1993), 12–15; J. McKee, 'Opening Up the "Oz of Archives": Mickey Hart and the Endangered Music Project', *Folklife Center News*, 15/1 (1993), 3–7; *The Spirit Cries: Music from the Rainforests of South America and the Caribbean* produced by Mickey Hart and Alan Jabbour (1993); *Voices of the Rainforest*, produced by Mickey Hart with field recordings and research done by Steven Feld (1991); K. Signell, *Voices of the Rainforest* (recording review), *Ethnomusicology*, 41/2 (1995), 165–7.

Independent of all its complexities, and regardless of tools and procedures, the process of actually engaging with others and other musicologies is also, in my experience, inevitably a process of recognizing how foundational premisses constrain one's scholarship and, eventually, how scholars, as 'theorizing subjects', are themselves constituted by such premisses. Furthermore, if we acknowledge the subjecthood of others, we must acknowledge that they are likewise constrained, and that 'no subject is its own point of departure'.[40] Can a regimen of thought be challenged beyond these premisses? Do they invalidate the autonomy or agency of the musicological subject? And does this put into question the possibility of change in foundational thinking about music and its scholarship?

## Challenges of Otherness: Approaching a Nineteenth-Century Treatise on Hindustani Music

With these questions in mind, and in an attempt to ground this highly abstract set of thoughts in a particular challenge of musicological otherness, I shall now sketch my own preliminary encounter with an important recent treatise on Indian music which embodies substantial links both to the classical music theories of the past and to the regional practice of élite music of pre-independence India. It is also a highly personal, multivalent document. Elsewhere I have attempted to sketch an appropriate composite of relevant contexts within which to situate this complex treatise and have also presented an overview of the work in relation to a set of received cultural and religious models.[41] Here I deliberately avoid making those categories my frame of reference so as to highlight a process that tends to become submerged in generalization and abstraction: the process of personal, individual engagement which is the testing-ground for any claims of respecting otherness. If the resulting account appears disorderly, if not chaotic, this is a deliberate strategy to expose the encounter process before it is interpretively normalized into coherence and consistency—a move that has been inspired to some extent by the recent anthropological debate on ethnography:[42] this move should also test in practice what I consider a problematic expectation of mutuality in historical encounters, hermeneutic preparedness notwithstanding.[43]

[40] See Judith Butler's seminal discussion of this issue in 'Contingent Foundations: Feminism and the Question of "Postmodernism" ', in J. Butler and J. W. Scott (eds.), *Feminists Theorize the Political* (New York, 1992), 3–21.

[41] See R. B. Qureshi, 'Whose Music? Sources and Contexts in Indic Musicology', in *Comparative Musicology and Anthropology of Music: Essay on the History of Ethnomusicology* (Chicago, 1991), 152–68.

[42] See James Clifford and George Marcus (eds.), *Writing Culture: The Poetics and Politics of Ethnography: A School of American Research Advanced Seminar* (Berkeley, 1986).

[43] For a rigorously thoughtful consideration of this issue, see Gary Tomlinson, 'Ideologies of Aztec Song', *JAMS* 48/3 (1995), 343–79.

*Ma'dan-ul-Mausiqi*, or *Mine of Music*, by Hakim Muhammad Karam Imam first surfaced in Indian music studies in 1959–60, in the form of an English translation of three excerpts selected from two much larger chapters for their interest to Indian music scholarship after independence. The venue was the journal of the country's Central Sangeet Natak Akademi (Academy of Music and Dance) located in Delhi and charged to preserve, promote, and study the country's musical heritage and history. Until other journals became established, mainly the *Journal of the Indian Musicological Society*, the Academy's publication was the central voice for disseminating scholarship and information about Indian music in English. The journal articulates the policy of the Academy to recognize and document important artists and to generate research on the structure and history of traditional music and dance.

The excerpts, translated with accuracy and a pleasant flair by Govind Vidyarthi, were selected to address two dominant topics of concern to the musical architects of India's national culture. One is the theoretical foundations of music, with the particular aim of identifying a normative, encompassing system that can account for the existing tonal structure and compositions within it, past and future. Such foundations are enshrined and articulated in writing within centuries-old lineages of treatises on music. The other is the history of musical practice, particularly the diverse communities of hereditary musicians who have constituted the living musical links to those theoretical foundations. Well articulated for decades before independence, the goal of creating and refining a 'History of Music' for India as a nation is here furthered by featuring these excerpts in English. They are presented as discrete, succinctly entitled chapters, though in the original they form part of actual chapters that are much longer and more diverse (compare Fig. 14.1 below).

Published in accordance with the book's chapter sequence, the first excerpt is entitled 'Melody through the Centuries'.[44] It offers a music-historical perspective which is oriented around major patrons and geographically on centres of patronage. Lineages of musicians are identified as the originators and bearers of distinct styles. Cutting across both foci are successive inventories of musicians associated with particular centres and patrons. Strikingly, they are discussed and arranged in categories that are both musical and social. Musicians are identified by instrument, dance, and genre specialization, as well as by social rank and gender. Three kinds of hereditary professional identity serve as the most persistent musical diagnostic for style; but they also overlap musically, as do members of the two major religious communities, Hindu and Muslim. Despite its title, the selection is clearly focused on the agents of music-making, rather than on 'melody' itself.

Much the same domain is addressed in the translator's second selection enti-

---

[44] Hakim Muhammad, Karam Imam, 'Melody through the Centuries', trans. Govind Vidyarthi, *Sangeet Natak Akademi Bulletin*, 2/12 (1959), 13–26, 42.

tled 'Effect of Ragas and Mannerism in Singing',[45] but here the focus is on the extra-musical effect of ragas by asking after the basis of the legendary impact of ragas on humans and nature. This, like the first selection, encompasses a prechronological past; here that past embodies supernatural foundational standards of effectiveness against which later musicians are compared and increasingly found wanting.

The topic of the raga system is addressed in a third excerpt entitled 'Ragas and Raginis';[46] it describes the divinely generated genealogical model of raga creation which is also linked with iconographic identities (*ragamala* paintings) for each male raga and its five female raginis. The author then presents a different version of the model that includes offspring ragas (*putras*), along with performance times and seasons for each raga; but he also notes inconsistencies between them, and with practice as he knows it.

Thanks to their linguistic accessibility, these translations have, particularly for Western scholars of Indian music, become a primary source of historical information on nineteenth-century musical practice, especially about musicians, genres, and instruments.[47] The excerpts, however, lack any interpretive context for situating their composite idiom and content. The translator simply presents them as the voice of a Lucknow courtier at the court of Wajid Ali Shah writing in 1856. Considering the existence of an accessible published version of the entire treatise since 1925,[48] scholars have made surprisingly little use of the work's complete text. One reason may be the surprising omission by the translator of any reference to his Urdu source. But the most obvi-ous barrier, even to Indian scholars of post-independence schooling, appears to be the Urdu script and the Persianized language of the text itself. Given that the primary historical music literature is in Sanskrit, and the primary educational and publishing media are Hindi and English, India's national and official language respectively, music scholars are primarily equipped to use these languages[49]—hence the Sangit Natak Akademi's translations of Urdu texts on music into English and into Hindi as well.[50]

The book entitled *Ma'dan-ul-Mausiqi*[51] was published in Lucknow, then India's acknowledged centre of Urdu culture, of feudal patronage for literature and

---

[45] Hakim Muhammad, Karam Imam, 'Effects of Ragas and Mannerism in Singing', trans. Govind Vidyarthi, *Sangeet Natak Akademi Bulletin*, 2/12 (1959), 6–14.

[46] Hakim Muhammad, Karam Imam, 'Ragas and Raginis', trans. Govind Vidyarthi, *Sangeet Natak Akademi Bulletin*, 2/12 (1959), 49–58.

[47] See e.g. Daniel Neuman, *The Life of Music in North India: The Organization of an Artistic Tradition* (Chicago, 1980), 87–9; Peter Manuel, *Thumri in Historical and Stylistic Perspectives* (Delhi, 1989), 57; and Allyn Miner, *Sitar and Sarod in the 18th and 19th Centuries* (Noetzel, 1993), 42, 67, 69, 119, 124, 142.

[48] Karam Imam, *Ma'dan-ul-Mausiqi* (Lucknow, 1925).

[49] In Pakistan, where Urdu is the national language, music scholarship has yet to flourish institutionally and to be supported educationally.

[50] Perhaps the most important of these is the translated Hindi version of Vilayat Husain's *Sangitagnon ke Samsmaran* (New Delhi, 1959), later repudiated by the author for its considerable editing; see Amal Das Sharma, *Musicians of India, Past and Present* (Calcutta, 1993), 105.

[51] A short treatise entitled *Raz-un-Nisa* ('The Secrets of Women') is appended to the main text of the book.

music, and of support for the nationalist movement with its commitment to music as national culture.[52] Lucknow was also a centre of publishing and education, both established on British models. The strong ties of support there of India's founding musicologist, V. N. Bhatkhande, led to the pioneering establishment of his music college, in the year after the publication of *Ma'dan-ul-Mausiqi.*[53] In his preface, Muhammad Chaudhri Muhammad Abdul Ghani, the editor of the book, calls for published works on the science of music with its 3,000-year history in India.[54] Pointing to the difficulty of understanding the classical music literature in Sanskrit, and even later works in Persian, he hails this book as the first publication of a historical source in Urdu. One of the few university-educated Muslims at the time, and also the Honorary Secretary of the British Rationalist Press Association, he deplores the absence of music in school and university curricula and the difficulty of accessing the oral knowledge of illiterate master musicians.

Clearly, this publishing effort was motivated by the nationalist agenda of music education with its Indologically based goal of establishing an Indian musicology founded on authentic texts through their publication.[55] This is further supported by a reference in the preface to an initiative by 'outsiders'— perhaps Bhatkhande himself—to publish the manuscript, which then prompted its owner and a group of his associates to undertake the task on their own. But Abdul Ghani also specifically relates the nationalist musicological agenda to his and his readers' Muslim identity. In the introductory convention of praising God and the Prophet, he thanks the Creator for endowing the universe with melody. He also justifies music as acceptable in Koranic interpretation, in addition to invoking research by Europeans and Indians proving its importance.

Local roots form another aspect of the book's constituency; it is linked to Sandila, one of the feudal towns near Lucknow. The book begins with an invocation to its soil and saints, whose descendant, Syed Wajid Ali, owned the decaying manuscript and sponsored its publication with the support of other local gentry.[56] As a personal, collective venture, *Ma'dan-ul-Mausiqi* thus documents North Indian regional-cultural and feudal participation in the shaping of an Indian musicology that had its primary centres in Bengal and Maharashtra.[57]

---

[52] Well articulated by P. L. Deshpande, foreword to B. R. Deodhar, *Pillars of Hindustani Music*, trans. Ram Deshmukh (Bombay, 1993), pp. vii–xv.

[53] Named Marris College after the British governor of the province, the thriving college today bears the name of its founder; see Sobhana Nayar, *Bhathkande's Contribution to Music* (Bombay, 1989), 186 f.

[54] Chaudhri Muhammad Abdul Ghani, preface to *Ma'dan-ul-Mausiqi*, pp. iv–vii.

[55] One of Bhatkhande's major agendas was the publication of music treatises; see Pandit Vishnu Narayan Bhatkhande, 'A Comparative Study of Some of the Leading Music Systems of the 15th, 16th, 17th & 18th Centuries', *Journal of the Indian Musicological Society*, 3/2 (1972), 1–61, and 3/3, (1972), 1–52; see also Sobhana Nayar, *Bhatkhande's Contribution to Music: A Historical Perspective* (Bombay, 1989).

[56] Syed Wajid Ali, 'Invocation', in *Ma'dan-ul-Mausiqi*, pp. i–iv.

[57] See Nayar, *Bhatkhande's Contribution.*

Perhaps most important, the publication points to the multi-centred process of negotiation across linguistic and cultural difference that preceded the post-independence consolidation of the musicological narrative in the service of a national classical music. In 1925, the use of Urdu was part of the thrust toward Indian writing about music in the 'mother tongue' of Hindi / Urdu articulated by Bhatkhande himself; Urdu as well as Hindi were by then widely used institutional languages sanctioned by the British and supported by the nationalist movement.[58] This brings into focus the need to consider the personal and institutional enmeshment with colonial rule of those involved in resurrecting the manuscript of *Ma'dan-ul-Mausiqi*; after all, the editors' background includes government service and personal patronage by the British governor as well as British higher education and publishing.

The complex publishing context of *Ma'dan-ul-Mausiqi* is directly implicated in the text itself. Unlike musicologists approaching treatises with the goal of discovering theoretical grounding for musical norms,[59] this musically untutored editorial team had a personal commitment to disseminate a contribution to such knowledge drawn from their own literature. From this commitment flowed a strictly preservationist approach to the text of the insect-threatened manuscript, though hardly to the manuscript itself, once copied.[60] The editor also claimed textual fidelity, respecting what he considered the author's peculiar writing and compiling style.[61] Readers are thus left not only without editorial mediation between the manuscript and the copy at hand, but also without scholarly interference in the highly multi-vocal, multi-layered 'conversation' which the author carries on in the pages of the book. The author's own table of contents gives an impression of the voice, scope, and style of this text (see Fig. 14.1 for a simplified translation).

Using the English translations as an accessible point of departure, a review of the selections in the context of the whole treatise confirms the highly formalized, yet personable narrative style, and the free and sometimes casual use of historical sources which range in identification from a specific work to an anonymous agency or at least a group of authorities. In one sense, this is a compilation from older texts; at the same time, the writing is permeated by the author's evaluations and personal comments based on his experiences and rationales. Most

[58] See B. R. Deodhar, 'Pandit Vishnu Narayan Bhatkhande and his Works', in *Pillars of Hindustani Music*, 38–50, p. 48. For the complex developments around each of these agencies see David Lelyveld, 'The Fate of Hindustani: Colonial Knowledge and the Project of a National Language', in C. Breckenridge and P. van der Veer (eds.), *Orientalism and the Postcolonial Predicament* (Delhi, 1994), 189–214.

[59] See Bhatkande, 'Comparative Study', 2, and H. Powers, 'Reinterpretations of Tradition in Hindustani Music: Omkarnath Thakur Contra Vishnu Narayan Bhatkande', in J. Katz (ed.), *Panels of the VIIth World Sanskrit Conference* (Leiden, 1987), 11.

[60] To date, I have not been able to trace any information about the manuscript in Lucknow or Sandila, but more avenues, possibly to *emigré* Muslims now in Pakistan, remain to be explored.

[61] Ghani, preface to *Ma'dan-ul-Mausiqi*, p. vi.

1. Musical sounds (*Sur*)
   *Divine and human music-makers; sound according to *shastra*; sound systems and instrument classification; creation of tones (*sur*), scales and modes; altered tones, ornaments; *sargam*, notation charts

2. Raga
   *Effects of ragas then and now; nature of raga; *alap*, correct and bad singing, *raga–ragini* classification, two methods; combined and invented ragas, tunes (*dhun*); inventions by Amir Khusrau; ragas by ancient experts, song genres to present

3. Different Ragas according to *Mat*
   Different raga–*ragini* systems (*mat*); their associated times and seasons; raga classes

4. Tala, Indian and Persian
   Pakhawaj drumming, origin and method; rhythm (*lay*); time cycles (tala); Persian tala and verse metres

5. Dance
   Inventors Mahadeo/Kankayya; method and compositions; expressive miming (*bhao*)

6. Twelve *Maqam*, i.e. Ragas of Iran
   Origin, system and elements, comparison with ragas

7. Wondrous Traditions regarding the Science of Music
   Stories of musical origins, ethos, and practice of ancient and contemporary musicians

**Fig. 14.1.** *Ma'dan-ul-Mausiqi*: Author's Table of Contents[62] (translated portions marked with asterisk)

striking is an apparent absence of a single perspective, sometimes even a lack of focus, and certainly of consistency; this also affects the ordering of topics and their signification. This is most evident in the eclectic listing of divergent classificatory and explanatory models for musical concepts, categories, and practices. And while the author literally has the last word in most sections and subsections, ultimately he leaves contradictions to God's judgement in a recurrent concluding formulation.

At the same time *Ma'dan-ul-Mausiqi* presents a whole that is culturally clearly situated, principally through language and style. Karam Imam's Urdu is considerably Persianized, in both vocabulary and structure, to the extent that he even pluralizes purely Hindi terminology in Persian, creating such hybrids as *rag-ha* and *tal-ha*.[63] The entire organization of the book, as well as all numbers and charts, follows Persian conventions. Perhaps most important, but rendered generic in the English version, are the rich cultural, social, and religious associations that this work shares with Persian and Urdu prose-writing in general: a reference frame that invokes God and Prophet Muhammad and refers to the

---

[62] Karam Imam, Hakim Muhammad, *Ma'dan-ul-Mausiqi*, 8–12.
[63] See headings for chs. 3 (ibid. 167) and 4 (181).

wisdom of other prophets like Moses and David and to contributions by Greek scholars like Pythagoras and Hippocrates. More generally, the author supports points by citing appropriate verses, especially from the Persian classics, but also from current Urdu poetry. The prose is ornate and formal, following classical precepts of discourse between cultivated gentlemen. Chapters and sections begin by invoking imagery of classical Persian poetry richly connotational: the 'garden of discourse', a self-chosen realm of deeply meaningful experience and striving; the 'singing nightingale', a seeker with a message and an eternal quest, never fulfilled; the 'branch of meaning', his firm but temporary support.[64] Clearly, discourse on music is here embedded within a cultural horizon and deportment that Urdu uniquely articulates.

Topically, too, the semantic field 'Urdu' permeates signification within the textual content of the work; this essentially means introducing models derived from the Persian cultural orbit. Correspondences with Arabic-derived metres of Urdu and Persian poetry figure prominently in the explication of rhythm. Structure and performance practice of *khayal* and other genres are linked to Sufi verbal performance. And to explain the historical roots of much specifically Indian musical practice, the author repeatedly invokes Amir Khusrau, thirteenth-century poet, Sufi, courtier, and founding figure for musical practices that implicate Persian antecedents and influences, especially for *ragas* and instruments.[65] Most prominently, a separate chapter presents the Persian *maqam* structure as a parallel to the Indian raga system.[66]

Most important, the author explicitly acknowledges drawing from several treatises written in Persian, mostly from the seventeenth and eighteenth centuries, but also including writings of his own time.[67] For literate members of the feudal North Indian élite, especially around the royal court at Lucknow, Persian was the language not only of polite society but also of classical literature, knowledge, and historiography. At the time of Karam Imam's writing, the scripts and conceptual vocabulary of Sanskrit were accessible to Brahmin specialists, while Hindi, written in a similar script, was yet to be widely disseminated through British policy. In this respect, *Ma'dan-ul-Mausiqi* belongs in a lineage of Indo-Persian treatises that represent Muslim patronage and perspectives since the Mughal Empire but contain translations of Sanskrit treatises as well as court chronicles of music-making. Indological scholarship and Indic musicology have generally neglected these writings, essentially because of their non-Indian

---

[64] See e.g. the opening of ch. 1 (ibid. 13) and esp. ch. 2.

[65] This claim is made for the sitar, although it is a much more recent development, implying that Amir Khusrau serves here as a metaphor for Indo-Persian syncretism; see R. B. Qureshi, 'Sufi Music and the Historicity of Oral Tradition', in S. Blum, P. V. Bohlman, and D. Neuman (eds.), *Ethnomusicology and Modern Music History* (Urbana, Ill., 1991), 103–20.

[66] Outlines of the *maqam* system were prevalent in nineteenth-century works on music, even including S. M. Tagore's *Hindu Music, from Various Authors* (Calcutta, 1882), pp. iv–v.

[67] His two major sources are *Sangit Sar* from the period of Akbar the Great and *Rag Darpan* (1665) by Faqirullah, both discussed in Najma Parveen Ahmad, *Hindustani Music in the Seventeenth and Eighteenth Centuries* (Delhi, 1984).

linguistic-cultural origins.[68] And where they serve as sources for otherwise inaccessible Sanskrit treatises, their cultural-intellectual horizon could be ignored. Considering that the entire cultural-intellectual horizon represented by Urdu has been Other to the community of present-day Indian music scholarship, its members may have found that horizon irrelevant to accessing treatises like *Ma'dan* as normative historical information on music.

Still, how this matrix of otherness contributes to the musical content being presented is a question of relevance that extends beyond this particular treatise and its Persian sources. For all Urdu and Persian music treatises also share a focus on an Indian musical past whose foundations precede their own presence in India. Those foundations are contained and re-articulated within a body of Sanskrit treatises that form part of the widely cast 'Shastric' canon of Brahminical scholarship. Indeed, it was to make the contents of these foundations accessible to Muslim patrons of music in their own classical language that Persian compilations and translations of Sanskrit treatises on music were produced. Authorship was usually assigned to the work's patron, whether he was the sole or actual writer or not, a convention that is found among authors of writings in both Sanskrit and Persian, and even Hindi.[69]

*Ma'dan-ul-Mausiqi* therefore is also the end of a chain of repositories that represent musical knowledge according to the 'Indian Shastra' (*shastr-e-Hindi*).[70] As articulated via various Persian predecessors,[71] this knowledge comes with its own cultural reference frame and terminology that needs explication for the Urdu reader, particularly of the superhuman forces linked to the creation and meaning of music. Topically and pragmatically, the author of the treatise identifies Hindu gods, offers vignettes of their actions, and also provides guidance on pronouncing Sanskrit-derived terms. Particularly striking in this process is the absence of juxtaposition of the two religious frameworks, Hindu and Muslim, as own and other. Instead, there is easy topical movement across the two, and a consistent strategy of identifying parallels and analogies between them. How Sanskrit-based musical knowledge is mediated though Persian predecessors is a crucial aspect of *Ma'dan-ul-Mausiqi*'s Muslim-based syncretic musicology of Indian music.

One notable connection with Sanskrit treatises is formal, and reaches back to the foundational thirteenth-century *Sangita Ratnakara* through its model seven-

---

[68] So has the Persian-Islamic branch of orientalist scholarship, since these works address a topic of entirely Indian origin.

[69] Well-known examples are the Sanskrit *Man Kutuhal*, authored by Raja Maharaja Pratap Man Singh of Gwalior, the Persian *Rag Darpan* by Faqirullah, Governor of Kashmir, and the Hindi *Sangit Sar* compiled by Maharaja Pratap Singh of Jaipur (1800); something of a parallel is the scholarly practice of colonial administrators of leaving their 'native collaborators' of Indological works unnamed.

[70] Throughout this treatise, and in preceding Persian treatises, the term *hindi* (Indian) is used as a parallel to *farsi* (Persian), never the terms Hindu or Muslim.

[71] Among 'many Persian treatises' Karam Imam names *Rag Darpan* and *Rag Sar, Sur Sagar, Naghmat-e-Asifi, Khulasat-ul-Aish, Risala-e-Amir Khusrau,* and *Risala-e-Tansain.* See Imam's introduction to *Ma'dan-ul-Mausiqi,* 5.

chapter structure which was widely emulated in successive treatises.[72] Imam's own reference to his work as 'Seven Chapters on the Science of Music' confirms the connection.[73] A comparison between the two outlines (see Fig. 14.2) presents striking parallels, but with telling culturally based modifications in *Ma'dan-ul-Mausiqi* to accommodate Muslim-Persian practice (ch. 3) and theory (ch. 5), and with an eclectic final chapter conveying a set of foundational narratives about musical instruments and legendary music-makers (ch. 7).

|  | *Sangita Ratnakara* | *Ma'dan-ul-Mausiqi* |
|---|---|---|
| Ch. 1 | Sound System | Sound System |
| Ch. 2 | Raga | Raga |
| Ch. 3 | Performing Practice | Raga (including Muslim ragas and performing practice) |
| Ch. 4 | Compositions (vocal, including poetic metre) | Tala (including Arab-Persian metric system) |
| Ch. 5 | Tala | Dance |
| Ch. 6 | Instruments | *Maqam* (Persian modal system) |
| Ch. 7 | Dance | Historical narratives of instruments and musicians |

**Fig. 14.2.** Seven-Chapter Outlines of *Sangita Ratnakara* and *Ma'dan-ul-Mausiqi*

To create this amalgam, however, the author also had access to non-Persian sources for accessing Sanskrit foundational works. Among writings consulted he mentions several 'trusted Hindi books of old and recent times', including the Sanskrit treatise *Sangit Darpan* and the Hindi work *Sangit Sar*, both of which are partly structured on *Sangita Ratnakara*.[74] But the real key to the author's contact with Shastric musical knowledge is the person he praises as his teacher and as the most learned music scholar of the time, Babu Ram Sahai. Throughout *Ma'dan-ul-Mausiqi* Sahai's expertise is invoked relating to raga theory and its foundational connections to Hindu cosmology. A non-Brahmin Hindu acculturated to Persian-Muslim feudal life, Sahai was also teacher of the king's father-in-law,[75] and clearly contributed to the dissemination of Scripture-based musical knowledge among élite amateurs, in a culturally eclectic courtly milieu well

[72] *Sangita Ratnakara* was widely called 'Seven-chaptered'; Harold Powers, too, follows the same structure in his remarkable 'India' treatise in Stanley Sadie (ed.), *New Grove Dictionary of Music and Musicians* (London, 1980), ix. 69–166; for a discussion of the treatise see 88.

[73] See author's introduction to *Ma'dan-ul-Mausiqi*, 8.

[74] *Sangit Darpan*, by Damodara, dates from 1625 (see Saraswathi Mahal Series, 34 (Tanjore, 1952)); *Sangit Sar*, a compilation by Maharaja Pratap Singh, from 1800 (ed. Poona Gayan Samaj (Poona, 1910–12). Karam Imam also lists *Ratan Mala* and *Sur Sagar*; see Karam Imam's introduction to *Ma'dan-ul-Mausiqi*, 5.

[75] It is he who recommended Karam Imam for a position at the court in 1853; see Karam Imam's introduction to *Ma'dan-ul-Mausiqi*, 7.

known for its extensive patronage of outstanding musicians, and for performing nobles, including the king himself.[76]

The impetus among musical literati of this mid-nineteenth-century feudal environment to introduce standards of Shastric purity to contemporary music-making, to learn the 'science of music' in addition to the art of its performance, and to draw on ancient sources for that purity is a musicological agenda of considerable weight that runs quite counter to the much-documented exclusive involvement in 'song and dance' by Wajid Ali Shah's court and by nobles in the region. Perhaps the well-known British condemnation of the Lucknow court and subsequent destruction of it easily obscures the ongoing, if locally marginal British involvement in promoting Scripture-based, authentic Indian culture and its dissemination through literacy.[77] Karam Imam's explicit choice of Urdu, as the language 'prevalent among the general population',[78] fits this mission, particularly because the British had been promoting Urdu, and at that very time elevated it to succeed Persian as official language of their colonial government.[79] While the colonial dimension remains unarticulated in *Ma'dan-ul-Mausiqi*, the author does mention his extended stay outside Lucknow as a revenue official in the British Government, because it enabled him to have contact with great performers and also to see historical manuscripts in the nearby feudal-musical centre of Banda.[80]

Finally, *Ma'dan-ul-Mausiqi* is also explicitly a musicology that contains much living musical knowledge 'passed on orally outside of ancient books'.[81] Karam Imam clearly identifies himself as an amateur musician taught by great masters and as a discerning listener to all the eminent musicians of his time. His notion of oral knowledge is not static, however: Imam also claims profound musical knowledge as the inventor (*naik*) of several new ragas evolved out of established ones. His experiential vantage-point of practice rather than theory finds expression in the personal comments that permeate the multiple domains of the book, in which ancient Scriptures and their theoretical knowledge are considered in relation to present-day musical practice, which is itself highly diverse and fluid. It seems that this is a multiply 'other' musicology that establishes a linear time sequence, but not a developmental one; a centre, but not an exclusive one, an appreciation of theoretical norm and system, but not an unbending one.

---

[76] For a retrospective view of Lucknow and its court life see Abdul Halim Sharar, *Lucknow: The Last Phase of an Oriental Culture*, trans. and ed. E. S. Harcourt and F. Hussain (London, 1975).

[77] A development spearheaded by the Indicologically inspired 'Bengal Renaissance'; see Capwell, 'Marginality and Musicology'.

[78] See introduction to Karam Imam's *Ma'dan-ul-Mausiqi*, 8.

[79] All-India British rule followed the defeat of the 1857 uprising and deposition of the last Mughal emperor.

[80] One of the first British accounts of Indian music arises from Captain Willard's participation in musical life at the court of Banda; see William Jones and Augustus Willard, *Music of India* (Calcutta, 1793).

[81] See Karam Imam's introduction to *Ma'dan-ul-Mausiqi*, 6.

The feudal musical life of the Lucknow region, with its eclectic patronage and cultural inclusiveness, appears congenial to Imam's musicological posture, as the book itself indicates. A careful reading of the introduction, however, also reveals a far more powerful decentring influence: the British annexation of the kingdom of Avadh in 1856, followed by the lived trauma of the Great Rebellion in 1857 and the disappearance of the entire courtly world of Lucknow. While 1856 is the year generally assigned to *Ma'dau-ul-Mausiqi*, references in the text indicate that the work could only have been completed after these momentous events. The author names musicians now serving the king in exile, and says that Lucknow's residents have become afraid to hold musical performances for fear of displeasing the new British rulers.[82] And in his introduction he deplores the loss of his entire social and cultural world on the destruction of the kingdom, citing a poignant verse: 'All that I have seen was but a dream, all that I have heard, but a story.'[83]

What was the impact of a loss so immediate and total on all that Karam Imam had seen? Does this vision account for the seamless blend of his lived experience with accounts drawn from earlier treatises?[84] And for whom is the story told? *Ma'dan-ul-Mausiqi* is not the first Indian account of courtly musical life written immediately after its destruction;[85] but it is also a treatise on music that articulates a cosmopolitan Muslim position on music in a style addressed to feudal literati, while at the same time fitting a primarily colonial agenda of spreading indigenous knowledge through vernacular education and printing in Urdu.[86]

Such are the implications drawn by the assessing outsider; what the author's own words overwhelmingly convey is an impact that is deeply emotional, for at the centre of his loss is also a personal bereavement: the death, in the same year as the kingdom's demise, of his younger brother, who shared his devotion to music.[87] Karam Imam writes with great intensity and eloquence of his personal devastation, and situates his writing of the book in the time of his bereavement. Given the intimate orality of musical transmission, did this death put an end to Karam Imam's sharing of his own oral knowledge, and so

[82]  See 'Melody through the Centuries', 26 and 42. Karam Imam describes himself as residing in the province, not the kingdom, of Awadh. For sources on Lucknow during this period see Mirza Ali Azhar, *King Wajid Ali Shah of Awadh* (Karachi, 1982), and Veena Talwar Oldenburg, *The Making of Colonial Lucknow 1856–1877* (Princeton, 1984).

[83]  This verse remains well known today, See Karam Imam's introduction to *Ma'dan-ul-Mausiqi*, 8.

[84]  The blend is most striking in the final chapter, where episodes from his own experience are included with famous stories of hallowed musical founding figures.

[85]  A Delhi courtier wrote such a retrospective immediately after the destructive 1738 invasion of Delhi by Nadir Shah; see Dargah Quli Khan, *Muraqqa'-i Delhi, The Mughal Capital in Muhammad Shah's Time*, trans. Chander Shekhar and S. M. Chenoy (Delhi, 1989).

[86]  The British had conferred the status of 'official language' on Urdu already in 1837; see Lelyveld, 'Fate of Hindustani'.

[87]  In the Islamic year 1472 (1855–6); according to the editor, Karam Imam had earlier lost his wife and adopted child.

motivate his writing—the suggestion is rooted in a similar basis for other, comparable writings.[88]

This brings the exploration of otherness in Imam's musicologies to a realm of emotions that Western 'topographies of the self' would perhaps assign to the domain of personal sentiment in an inner–outer dichotomy.[89] Here, however, a unified notion of sentiment strikingly permeates the different frames of Karam Imam's book. That notion relates directly to the assessment of musical value: music must be correct, but is it effective, does it evoke affect? That the author's meaning of 'effective' is moving to tears emerges clearly when, in a dispute between two masters, he juxtaposes 8,000 memorized *dhrupad* compositions with one improvised 'melody for weeping'.[90] The outcome of numerous musical contests throughout the book affirms that music is most outstanding because it affects most deeply, regardless of artistry.

Two aspects of this musical ethos are striking: one is its affective link with Muslim musical expressions through Shi'a and also Sufi songs; Karam Imam identifies the 'melody for weeping' with reciting *marsiya*, laments for the Islamic martyrs which flourished under Lucknow's Shi'a kings. Significantly, they were also his own first introduction to music.[91] The second aspect is a completely performative orientation to reception as a measure of musical quality, hence a commitment to the intimately personal roots of any consensus on musical excellence. Accordingly, musical innovation figures strongly in *Ma'dan-ul-Mausiqi*, alongside the mapping of received traditions.

Between convention and individual assertion, musical practice and theory, past purity and present degeneration, Sanskrit and Persian translations, literary linguistic particularism and musical inclusiveness of communities and religions, whose authorial voice speaks, and to whom? This question of agency is addressed in multiple ways in the author's own autobiographical introduction, a remarkably direct conversation with the reader about his antecedents and goals for the book. But there is also the issue of textual authenticity, given that there is only one copy extant. Questions of authorial ambiguity suggest themselves, like the sequencing of sometimes tenuous thematic links between topically diverse parts of single sections, or regarding the status and authorship of addenda within the text. The presence of textually and linguistically diverse footnotes raises further questions about authorship, especially in conjunction with the necessity to re-copy original manuscripts due to climatically induced physical deterioration

---

[88] One example is a fine Urdu manuscript, *Tarikh-e-Mausiqi* ('History of Music'), (unpublished, Hapur, 1918) by Ali Muhammad, a hereditary master who states that he turned to writing down his knowledge because his only son had died.

[89] See Arjun Appadurai's evocative 'Topographies of the Self in Hindu India', in C. A. Lutz and L. Abu-Lughod (eds.), *Language and the Politics of Emotion* (New York, 1990), 92–112. Also see Renato Rosaldo, *Culture and Truth: The Remaking of Social Analysis* (Boston, 1989).

[90] In the twenty-seventh story of ch. 7, p. 240. The masters, in fact, appear to be the author's two teachers: one is a Hindu expert on musical learning, the other a Shi'a expert on musical elegies.

[91] See Karam Imam's Introduction to *Ma'dan-ul-Mausiqi*, 4.

which is common to probably most Indian manuscripts. These textual characteristics need to be considered in light of received transmissional practices of layering and synthesizing textual content. What emerge are authorial notions distinctly 'other' to what animates Western musical scholarship and creativity in general.[92]

In exploring *Ma'dan-ul-Mausiqi* as a uniquely authored work, I join Indian art historian Partha Mitter in considering colonial art anti-hegemonically, 'away from paradigms, to unravel individual motives',[93] in order to gain distance from the depersonalized, textualist historiography whose tools and results I use, including Indological notions of authenticity and a Shastric focus on the descent of knowledge.[94] Recognizing the inevitability of taking recourse to interpretive categories, of whatever provenance, serves as a reminder to those of us who would transcend foundational frames and 'positions' that a white, female anthropologist, socialized and trained in the Western classical canon and personally and musically connected to Lucknow will remain 'always already constituted by those positions', because they are what enable her to interrogate, 'replay, and resignify' them in the first place.[95] Encountering others as subjects who are likewise constituted clearly requires willingness and hard work to engage with the frames and positions, musical and other, that constitute them as subjects, but with a focus on both our ability to transform our notions and be transformed by theirs.

This willingness needs to extend to the fully formed theoretical frames that serve the pre-emptive synthesizing of master narratives, own and other. The goal is not only to hear voices of difference and accept contradiction, but to savour the inevitably personal flavour of both sources and scholarship in what is still an ongoing search for other musicologies, in Hindustani music and elsewhere.

---

[92] See J. A. B. van Buitenen, 'Written Texts and their Preservation', in Edward C. Dimock Jr. *et al.*, *The Literatures of India: An Introduction* (Chicago, 1974), 33–55 and Lewis Rowell, 'Śāstra', in *Music and Musical Thoughts in Early India* (Chicago, 1992), 119–43; also Powers, 'India' treatise in *New Grove*, ix. 69–166.

[93] Partha Mitter, *Art and Nationalism in Colonial India 1850–1922* (Cambridge, 1994), 7.

[94] See Sheldon Pollock, 'The Theory of Practice and the Practice of Theory in Indian Intellectual History', *Joural of the American Oriental Society*, 105/3 (1985), 499–519.

[95] Judith Butler, 'Contingent Foundations, 9.

# 15

## The History of Musical Canon

### William Weber

One of the most fundamental transformations in Western musical culture has been the rise of a canon of great works from the past. At the end of the sixteenth century, it was unusual for music to remain in circulation for more than a generation; those works that did persist remained isolated from each other, or formed part of pedagogical traditions known by a small group of learned musicians. By the end of the nineteenth century, old music had moved from the musician's study to the concert-hall: it had become established in repertories throughout concert life, dominating many programmes, and was legitimated in critical and ideological terms in which the society as a whole participated. That so many major cities have given great civic prominence to opera and concert-halls devoted chiefly to the musical classics—from London's Royal Albert Hall to New York's Lincoln Center to Los Angeles' Music Center—tells us how central this relatively new tradition has become within Western culture.

Music historians have not been quick to interest themselves in the subject—indeed, to recognize that it exists at all. The performance of old music and the idea of musical classics have simply been taken for granted; to ask why, or even when, these practices began has been so far from disciplinary convention that it would seem more than a bit perverse. While a variety of scholars have studied editions or repertories of old music in specific contexts in fruitful ways, such topics have yet to attract much interest in the field as a whole, or to be defined in broad terms, either temporally or conceptually.[1] Joseph Kerman was the

---

[1] Jacques Chailley, *40,000 Years of Music: Man in Search of Music*, trans. Rollo Myers (London, 1964); Percy Young, ' "Ancient" Music in Eighteenth-Century England', *Music & Letters*, 60 (1979), 401–15; H. Diack Johnstone, 'The Genesis of Boyce's *Cathedral Music*', *Music & Letters*, 56 (1975), 26–40; Christoph Helmut Mahling, 'Zum "Musik-betrieb" Berlins und seinen Institutionen in der ersten Hälfte des 19. Jhts.', and Klaus Kropfinger, 'Klassik-Reception in Berlin (1800–30)', both in Carl Dahlhaus (ed.), *Studien zur Musikgeschichte Berlins im frühen 19. Jht.* (Regensburg, 1980), 22–102, 301–80 resp.; Walter Wiora (ed.), *Die Ausbreitung des Historismus über die Musik* (Regensburg, 1969); Erich Reimer, 'Repertoirebildung und Kanonisierung: Zur Vorgeschichte des Klassikbegriffes, 1800–35', *Archiv für Musikwissenschaft*, 43 (1986), 241–60; Herbert Schneider, *Rezeption der Opern Lullys im Frankreich des Ancien Régime* (Tutzing, 1982); J. Peter Burkholder, 'Museum Pieces: The Historicist Mainstream in Music of the Last Hundred Years', *Journal of Musicology*, 2 (1983), 115–34, and 'The Twentieth Century and the Orchestra as Museum', in Joan Peyser (ed.), *The Orchestra: Origins and Transformations* (New York, 1986), 409–34; Joseph Horowitz, *Understanding Toscanini* (New York, 1986); Lawrence Levine, *Highbrow/Lowbrow: The Emergence of Cultural Hierarchy in America* (Cambridge, Mass., 1988). My writings on the problem include *The Rise of Musical Classics in*

pioneer in taking up the problem of canon in such a fashion, though writing chiefly for a literary readership.[2] Recent works by Katherine Bergeron and Philip Bohlman and by Marcia J. Citron have put the problem centre stage by using it as a vehicle to raise major issues about musicology as a discipline and the role of gender in music history.[3] The case is now put: that musicologists have been slow to recognize the problem of canon, because it is so embedded in their assumptions about music, and controls so much of what they do. If we are to understand the canon historically, we must become sceptical of it, and free ourselves from its authority, its ideology, and the whole manner of speech that surrounds it. Only by questioning this tradition can we understand either its musical or its social foundations.

But none of the works mentioned is principally concerned with studying the problem of canon chiefly from a historical perspective, and that has limited the discussion seriously. Because they start from a compelling set of contemporary issues, they essentially look backward, framing the problem in terms that are specific to our time. This tends to make the canon seem far more unified, unchanging—indeed, monolithic—than it tended to be through most of its history; during the second half of this century, classical repertories have dominated concert and opera programming (or at least key areas thereof) much more than was ever the case previously.

Musicologists therefore need to get serious about the historical aspects of canon if they are going to understand its evolution. Very simply, they must start working forwards from the late Middle Ages, trying to see when, where, and why the idea of musical classics—or rather, a changing array of such notions—arose, to become established at the core of musical culture. Once we do that, we begin to see that the components of the canon were much less consistent and well ordered than is usually assumed; we find that it was unified chiefly by its own ideology. Music historians have as yet only a hazy idea about any of these matters, and even that hazy idea generally grows out of the ideological baggage of the canonic tradition more than out of any empirical study of the problem. They do, however, actually know more about the subject than many realize,

Eighteenth-Century England: A Study in Canon, Ritual and Ideology (Oxford, 1992); 'The Contemporaneity of Eighteenth-Century Musical Taste', Musical Quarterly, 70 (1984), 175–94; 'Mentalité, tradition, et origines du canon musical en France et en Angleterre au XVIIIe siècle', Annales E.S.C., 44 (1989), 849–75; 'La Musique ancienne and the Waning of the Ancien Régime', Journal of Modern History, 56 (1984), 58–88; 'The Eighteenth-Century Origins of the Musical Canon', Journal of the Royal Musical Association, 108 (1989), 100–14; 'Lully and the Performance of Old Music in the 18th Century', in Herbert Schneider and Jérôme de la Gorce (eds.), Congress for the Tricentennial of the Death of J. B. Lully, Heidelberg/St. Germain-en-Laye (Laaber, 1991), 581–90; 'Wagner, Wagnerism and Musical Idealism', in David C. Large and William Weber (eds.), Wagnerism in European Culture and Politics (Ithaca, NY, 1984), 28–71; and 'The Classical Repertory in Nineteenth-Century Symphony Orchestras', in Peyser (ed.), Orchestra, 28–71.

[2] Joseph Kerman, 'A Few Canonic Variations', Critical Inquiry, 10 (Sept. 1983), 107–26, repr. in Robert von Hallberg (ed.), Canons (Chicago, 1984), 177–96.

[3] Katherine Bergeron and Philip V. Bohlman (eds.), Disciplining Music: Musicology and its Canons (Chicago, 1992), see esp. Don Randel, 'The Canons in the Musicological Toolbox', ibid. 10–22; Marcia J. Citron, Gender and the Musical Canon (Cambridge, 1993).

since the extensive research of the last several decades has, along the way, dredged up important pieces of information that pertain to it—repertories, academic practices, eulogies to dead composers, and so on.

The problem of tracing the origins and development of a musical canon presents a challenging agenda of research for music historians. We need to re-establish systematically what kinds of old works remained in repertories, libraries, editions, and anthologies, how they acquired certain kinds of authority in musical life, and what social and cultural roles they played within society as a whole. This should be done not for individual composers—the crutch of traditional musicology—but rather by studying collections separately, as idiosyncratic entities, and then together, as a complete musical context in a particular period. This would involve not only obtaining much more extensive information about repertories but, even more important, learning how to interpret such materials—tasks that have rarely been attempted as yet.

One of the hazards of such work is that the words 'canon', 'classic', and 'masterpiece' slip much too easily from the tongue. The notion of the 'great composer' is so engrained in modern musical culture that we use the terms instinctively for any period, essentially in ahistorical terms. By smuggling them back into the past, we blind ourselves to the particular ways in which people respected either living or dead musicians for their work. In 1641 John Barnard, minor canon at St Paul's Cathedral, spoke of 'master-peeces' in the preface to his collection of English church music; but he meant something quite specific and identifiable: pieces by master composers of the Chapel Royal. He did not bring to the term the rich ideological construction that modern musical culture has built upon it.[4] Thus, instead of declaring perforce that one piece or another was a classic, we need to look carefully into the context of its reception and perpetuation; we need to define the terms—musical, social, ideological, and semiological—in which the society considered musical works part of a canonic tradition.

Modern musical culture, let us remember, gets along just fine by calling its great works 'classical music', and one can only wonder whether the fancy new term 'canon' is necessary. There is value in bringing it into use, however, in part because literary scholars have developed a highly productive field around it, but most of all because it suggests the complete construct of activities, values, and authority that surrounded the music. If 'classics' are individual works deemed great, 'canon' is the framework that supports their identification in critical and ideological terms.

The term 'canon' potentially has very broad meanings: it can refer to anything deemed essential to a society or to one of its parts in establishing order and discipline and in measuring worth. As used in theology, law, and the arts, it denotes both broad assumptions and specific practices, both the nature of dogma and the way its application is to be judged. As Katherine Bergeron has suggested, in

---

[4] John Barnard, *The First Book of Selected Church Musick* (London, 1641), 1.

music the term applies not only to the lists of great composers, but also to the most basic precepts of how music functions as a discipline, dictating how 'the individual within a field learns, by internalizing such standards, how not to transgess'.[5] We shall see how the idea of great composers and great works in fact grew directly out of the traditions that governed the craft of music—most important of all, sacred polyphony.

## Major Types of Canon

It is therefore evident that we need to distinguish between three major kinds of canon in musical culture. One kind is a *scholarly* canon, whereby music is studied in theoretical terms. The oldest scholarly canon in music began in antiquity: philosophical and scientific consideration of music, such as that discussed in treatises and taught in the medieval quadrivium. This tradition remained for the most part separate from both musical pedagogy and performance until the eighteenth century; it was a high academic tradition not often practised by musicians. Modern ideas of canon did not grow out of this tradition; if anything, they came about through disillusionment with it, brought about by empirical thinking on music.[6] The scholarly canon became transformed fundamentally at the end of the eighteenth century, as scientific and philosophical study gave way to new theoretical study of harmony and early music. In the modern period this aspect of musical canon has had a much closer relationship with musical performance; in the field of early music it has changed performing practices fundamentally.

The *pedagogical* canon formed part of the tradition of sacred polyphony, and was based in the musically most prominent cathedrals and chapels. First and foremost, it involved the emulation of works by master composers of a previous generation, and as such it linked the teaching of music with the compositional process, at least among certain of the more learned musicians. That is indeed a major aspect that defined this kind of canon: it was known primarily by the most accomplished musicians and some of their patrons, and therefore had a limited public. Academic compositional practices such as the *stile antico*—the process of writing in older styles, done as much for study as for performance—were closely related to emulation of old works. We must remember that none of these practices was focused upon the performance of old works, since the *stile antico*, like the composition by emulation, mingled new and old styles. This tradition took on many new dimensions during the nineteenth century. Canon formation

---

[5] K. Bergeron, 'Prologue: Disciplining Music', in Bergeron and Bohlman (eds.), *Disciplining Music*, 5. See also von Hallberg (ed.), *Canons*, esp. Barbara Herrnstein Smith, 'Contingencies of Value', 5–40; Charles Altieri, 'An Idea and Ideal of a Literary Canon', 41–64; and Gerald L. Burns, 'Canon and Power in the Hebrew Scriptures', 65–84.

[6] See further discussion of this problem in William Weber, 'The Intellectural Origins of Musical Canon in Eighteenth-Century England', *JAMS* 47 (1994), 488–520.

around the music of Haydn, Mozart, Beethoven, and Brahms made the process of emulation even more common and explicit than before; even the less tutored public became somewhat aware of the sources from which composers derived their models. Moreover, the rediscovery of works from the Middle Ages and the Renaissance opened up vast new historical reference-points and stylistic possibilities.

The final major kind of canon, the *performing* canon, involves the presentation of old works organized as repertories and defined as sources of authority with regard to musical taste. I would argue that performance is ultimately the most significant and critical aspect of musical canon. While editions and anthologies figured significantly within the pedagogical and critical aspects of this problem, what emerged as the core of canonicity in musical life, beginning in the eighteenth century, was the public rendition of selected works.[7] Celebration of the canon has been the focus of its role in musical culture; although some canonic works are not performed, they have for the most part been part of specialized pedagogical canons. We shall see that a performing canon is more than just a repertory; it is also a critical and ideological force.

Thus a performing canon is a much broader phenomenon than a pedagogical canon. It is usually more widely known, is based chiefly in public contexts, and has a more prominent ideological framework. The two kinds of canon co-exist and interact extensively—they are ultimately interdependent—but in the modern period it has been the performance of great works that has been centre stage.

'Until the beginning of the nineteenth century . . . all music of a previous age was a dead letter, and of no interest to anyone,' wrote Jacques Chailley in 1964.[8] Let us be wary of such sweeping statements. Music historians have none the less assumed that a canon—loosely defined—first arose in Germany and Austria under the influence of the Romantic movement, revolving around reverence for the canonic trinity of Haydn, Mozart, and Beethoven. The intersection of Romantic philosophy with the cults of these composers has tended to encourage this assumption. But the wealth of archival work on the preceding three centuries done in the last several decades has unearthed information that raises serious questions about such a dating. As we shall see, there were important antecedents to the canon practised in the previous 300 years that must be defined in some terms as canonic. I would argue that a pedagogical canon arose in the sixteenth century, and that a performing canon emerged in England in the course of the eighteenth century, and to a more limited extent in France as well.

I do not have the space in which to sort out these big problems here. But let

[7] On the role of anthologies, see Citron, *Gender*, 32–3.

[8] Chailley, *40,000 Years of Music*, 17. He, of course, was mostly concerned with interest in medieval music, which was indeed a rarity until well into the nineteenth century.

me suggest the following periods as a tentative set of guide-lines for the evolution of musical canon in Western art-music:

(1) 1520–1700: the rise of a significant pedagogical canon, chiefly in the study of works by Josquin Desprez, Palestrina, and Frescobaldi, but with only isolated examples of old works in regular performance;

(2) 1700–1800: the emergence of performing canons separately in Britain and France, based upon repertories given authority in both musical and ideological terms, but with still fairly limited critical definition in published form;

(3) 1800–1870: the rise of an integrated, international canon that established a much stronger authority in aesthetic and critical terms, and that moved to the centre of musical life *c.*1870;

(4) 1870–1945: a stable, though not untroubled, relationship between canonic repertories and contemporary music by which first concert programmes, then opera repertories, were dominated by the classics, but new works none the less maintained considerable prominence;

(5) 1945–1980: an extreme, indeed intolerant predominance of classical over contemporary music in both concert and opera repertories, paralleled by the rise of independent organizations led by composers for the performance of new works;

(6) 1980–  : a limited but still significant re-emergence of taste for new works, chiefly in avant-garde artistic circles separate from traditional concert-halls and opera stages.

We will now look more deeply into the nature of this history by discussing what can be taken to be the four main intellectual bases of canon: *craft*, *repertory*, *criticism*, and *ideology*. In so doing, we will discover some important continuities that run through the evolution of musical canon since the sixteenth century.

## Aspects of Canon: Craft

The idea of a musical classic emerged from respect for the master composer, for the mastery of his *craft*, his ability to compose artfully, especially in learned idioms. The roots of musical canon in craft traditions bound it intimately to the polyphonic tradition. If one can speak of any distinctly musical principle lying behind the authority of musical canon in the last four centuries, it has been the desire to maintain respect for the discipline of contrapuntal technique. Thus have the models of Palestrina, Corelli, J. S. Bach, Mozart, Brahms, Schoenberg, and Carter been invoked against intellectually less ambitious composers in succeeding generations. This does not mean that canon is by definition only very learned polyphony; rather, it brings to bear upon both composition and taste the necessity for certain elements of rigour in voice-leading and textures. In fact, the learned tradition has interacted closely with more popular musical genres in productive ways in many periods, offering testimony to its adaptability, and establishing canonic models in the process. C. P. E. Bach idealized his father, |while adapting the *style galant* to more polyphonic purposes; Liszt paid tribute to Beethoven, while turning early nineteenth-century instrumental virtuosity to more complex purposes; and progressive rock composers such as Brian Eno and Frank Zappa drew upon the classics of the avant-garde in trying to raise the level of taste in their field. In all these cases one can find a creative tension between the more and the less learned kinds of tastes, mediated by canonic models.

The notions of the master composer and the 'masterpiece' originally had canonic implications of a disciplinary, but not a historical, nature. What happened in the sixteenth and the seventeenth centuries was that this tradition extended itself in the longer awareness of master composers—especially that of Palestrina—in a pedagogical canon. Then, during the eighteenth century, the tradition of craft became much more closely allied with performing canons—in England for Corelli, Purcell, and Handel, and in France for Lully and Rameau. Corelli's concertos were both studied and performed, as were Lully's operas and trios transcribed from his arias. During the nineteenth century the value of craft remained a powerful force in the writings of Romantic musical thinkers. Robert Schumann played the pedagogue to younger composers in invoking canonic models: 'There is always a difference between master and disciple. The quickly tossed-off pianoforte sonatas of Beethoven, and still more those of Mozart, in their heavenly grace, exhibit the same degree of mastery that do their deeper revelations.'[9]

When, in the course of the eighteenth and early nineteenth centuries, these notions took on canonic implications, they provided an important line of continuity between the epochs before and after the rise of performing canons, and also between the musical past and present generally. That may be why, even though the rise of musical classics transformed musical taste so profoundly during the late eighteenth and nineteenth centuries, none the less there was remarkably little sense of a major contradiction between new music and old in regard to musical discipline until militant avant-garde groups arose in the late nineteenth century, and even then they did not deny the classics categorically. The notion of craft was inclusive rather than exclusive: it gathered together a tradition of defining what was often called the 'perfection' of music, whether it be new or old. This also meant that the emerging canon did not go very far back: prior to the middle of the nineteenth century it was unusual to find even printed reference to a composer active before Palestrina or Tallis, much less a performance of a work of such antiquity. The traditions that undergirded the continuity between old and new repertories could not absorb works in unusually old or different styles, at least until canonic repertories and authority became so

---

[9] Robert Schumann, *Of Music and Musicians*, trans. Paul Rosenfeld (New York, 1946), 74.

firmly established by the late nineteenth century that more far-flung specialities could appear.

For the same reason, the application of musical craft to canon became focused as much upon collegial notions of great composers who shared common training and musical excellence as on cults of individual composers. The composers whose works remained in performance in eighteenth-century France and England came in large part from the royal courts, and the growing professionalism and pride of place among these musicians was one of the foundations of early tendencies toward canon. By the same token, the idea of a common canon based in orchestral and chamber-music concerts underlay the reverence for Haydn, Mozart, and Beethoven, and then, by extension, for Schubert, Schumann, and Brahms. While individual cults emerged around some key figures— Handel, Beethoven, and Wagner perhaps most prominently of all—they none the less emerged within a strong sense of collegial musical standards. We shall see, however, that individual works, or groups of works, entered repertories based upon quite individual performing traditions.

Marcia Citron has discussed the role of craft in canon in an interesting way, showing how the professionalism of musicians—a set of self-imposed expectations—determined what kinds of music men and women wrote, and therefore whose music became canonic.[10] Her argument is convincing that, until recently, with some important exceptions, women composers have tended to write in the intellectually less ambitious and less canonically oriented genres. The problem is pertinent as well to composers in popular musical life, film music particularly.

But however central the tradition of the musical craft was to the evolution of canon, it possessed limited ability to engage the larger society. In the early eighteenth century, neither preserving old scores, emulating respected works, nor learning to compose in antiquated styles meant much to people interested in hearing or playing works written in the manner of their day. While by 1850 some concert-goers had learned about the emulative exchanges among the classical composers, they remained a distinct minority compared with those who flocked to keep hearing *The Barber of Seville* or *The Messiah*. Musical craft was an inward-looking, ultimately professional discipline, and it could not stand alone in the establishment of a powerful canon.

## Repertory

The second of our principles of musical canon, repertory, has not yet been the subject of much extensive study or analysis.[11] Music historians have only just

---

[10] Citron, *Gender*, esp. ch. 3: 'Professionalism', pp. 80–119.

[11] K. M. Mueller, *27 Major American Symphony Orchestras: A History and Analysis of their Repertoires, Seasons 1842–43 through 1969–70* (Bloomington, Ind., 1973); R. L. and N. W. Weaver, *A Chronology of Music in the Florentine Theater, 1590–1750* (Detroit, 1978); Weber, *Rise of Musical Classics*, ch. 6: 'Repertory of the Concert of Antient Music'.

begun to investigate programmes in opera or concert life at all systematically, and for that reason we are at something of a loss when we try to evaluate the roles that old works played in musical life. To be able to do that confidently, we need far more comprehensive study of repertories both in institutional contexts—royal chapels, orchestras, and opera-houses, for example—and in *ad hoc* presentations—benefit concerts especially. Moreover, we need to look much more closely into the structures of concert programmes, analysing the sequences of genres, performers, and composers, and asking what musical and social practices made old works become increasingly common in the conventions by which programmes were put together. An old work did not appear on a programme simply because people thought it was great; its selection was filtered through an array of conventions, circumstances, and tastes, factors that are often difficult to reconstruct. Tall order though this may be, it is necessary for music historians to attempt it if we are going to understand the evolution of canonic repertories between the eighteenth and twentieth centuries.

The kinds of editions and performing practices employed are a nagging, often insoluble problem in such research. Can one trust the performance of an opera aria by Handel in the 1870s to have been anything closely approximating the renditions he supervised? In the usual absence of performing parts, it is ultimately necessary to treat the problem in fairly basic terms, asking about the size of performing bodies, and assessing how strong the tendency might have been to adapt old works to modern practices. As a rule of thumb, private clubs of serious performers and listeners usually altered works much less than performers of public concerts designed for celebrative purposes.[12] At any rate, where performing parts do exist, musicologists need to go beyond just searching for the *Urtext* of a work, and take seriously the changes that were made. Different things could be done to a piece at any one time, and much can be learned from close investigation of adaptations.

During the early stages whereby canon was formed in music, repertories of old works were not established as a common corpus, but rather through the evolution of separate performing traditions, and that tendency has persisted to a certain degree ever since then. Even though all works were perceived within the collegial, craft-like notion of canon, many had traditions quite their own. Practices of keeping old works in use longer than normal grew up largely independent of each other, and often for different reasons. In eighteenth-century England, for example, William Byrd's masses and motets persisted as a kind of learned music in daily performances in cathedrals and college chapels, while Purcell's *Te Deum* and *Jubilate* remained as festive works in the much more public, annual choir festivals, and Corelli's concertos hung on in both public and pedagogical roles, chiefly in the meetings of amateur music societies. Similarly, in Germany and France arias from operas or cantatas by Jomelli and symphonies

---

[12]  Percy Lovell, ' "Ancient" Music in Eighteenth-Century England', *Music & Letters*, 60 (1979), 401–15; Winton Dean, *Handel's Dramatic Oratorios and Masques* (London, 1959).

by Viotti made occasional appearances in programmes throughout the nineteenth century, with little direct relationship either with each other or with the emerging repertory of works by Haydn, Mozart, and Beethoven. On a certain plane, each of these examples was a separate tradition.

One cannot say that a performing canon existed in any period until a term arose by which to define—indeed, give authority to—a repertory of old works. Prior to 1700 it was by no means unknown for pieces to embed themselves in the customary of a feast or in the repertory of a choir, but such works bore little relationship to one another, and there was no term by which to refer to them. They were perceived in reference to the specific musical or social context within which they persisted, rather than according to any concept of a canonic nature. There were, of course, terms for practices for composing in outdated styles—*stile antico* and *prima pratica*—but they meant something quite different from performing actual works from an earlier period.

The first term for a canonic performing repertory, 'ancient music', made its appearance in England during the 1690s, and became established by the late 1720s. While some authors used it to denote the music and music theory of antiquity, it was used principally to denote music of the sixteenth and early seventeenth centuries. The term became prominent in musical life when, in 1731, the name of the Academy of Vocal Music was changed to the Academy of Ancient Music, and with the founding of the Concert of Antient Music in 1776, it was redefined to mean any music more than about two decades old.[13] A French counterpart, *la musique ancienne*, emerged in the 1740s; since no music remained from before the time of Lully, the term referred to music written by him and his successors at the court, and to the *petits*- and *grands-motets* that Michel Delalande composed for the Chapelle Royale, which were performed at the Concerts Spirituels from their founding in 1725 to the end of the 1760s. The word 'classical' was occasionally used in England to denote great works of music from the past as early as the 1770s, and by the 1830s had emerged as the standard term for canon throughout Europe. There is much work to be done on the language, the semiology, of the classical music tradition as it evolved between the late eighteenth and early twentieth centuries.[14]

The process by which repertories of old works evolved was not self-conscious or unified. Most important of all, repertories were not built up as a set of revivals of old works from a distant past. Until after the middle of the nineteenth century, few works were brought back after long periods of complete disuse; the great majority of old pieces had been performed at least sporadically since the time of their composition, so were involved in some kind of ongoing performing

---

[13] Weber, *Rise of Musical Classics*, 23–36, 46–7, 52–3, 56–7, 168–70, 194–7.

[14] In the article 'Classical' in Stanley Sadie (ed.), *The New Grove Dictionary of Music and Musicians* (London, 1980), iv. 449–51, e.g., Daniel Heartz restricts his discussion to literary ideas of the classic and classicism; he never discusses the canonic uses of the word that have been so basic to the vocabulary of musical life in the nineteenth and twentieth centuries.

tradition. When a work was revived after a long time, it was usually because it was related to a genre or a composer for which there was an active tradition, and its performance therefore did not really constitute a revival. For example, the Concert of Antient Music performed a few of the works which Handel composed in Italy just after the turn of the eighteenth century—the *Dixit Dominus* of 1707, for example, performed in 1785—that had not been performed since that time, but the focus of the programmes on Handel made this no great novelty.

One cannot over-emphasize the diversity of canonic repertories. Different kinds of concerts offered quite different components and had quite different canonic implications. For example, the Academy of Ancient Music and the Concert of Antient Music might have similar names and be without parallel anywhere else in Europe during the 1780s or 1790s, but they offered remarkably different programmes. The Academy had a much less esoteric repertory than the Antient Concert; it served up sentimental ballads, and offered only the best-known Elizabeth madrigals or late Baroque opera arias, works of the sort that the other series provided in great variety.[15] Likewise, in the second half of the nineteenth century, the Conservatoire Orchestra of Paris served as a musical museum or, as some contemporaries described it, a temple; it performed few works by living composers and no Italian opera, featured choral sacred music, and in general reflected a far more rigid sense of canon than any of the similar orchestral societies in the major capital cities. The Philharmonic Society of London, by contrast, built a canon of *bel canto* opera selections, alongside symphonies of Beethoven and opera selections by Cherubini and Rossini.[16]

Thus a repertory of old works was not a unity; it was the sum of component parts that served different musical tastes and constituencies. In the 1790s the Concert of Antient Music looked to its connoisseurs with arias from little-known operas of Handel, and kept its less learned clientele (people there to see the royal family) happy with resounding, militaristic choruses from *Judas Maccabaeus*. In the 1850s the Gewandhaus Orchestra of Leipzig likewise served its intellectual clients an impressively varied array of symphonies by Haydn, Mozart, and Beethoven, together with arias by Gluck and Cherubini, but tried to draw crowds with recent violin concertos and popular selections from Mozart and Weber operas.[17]

---

[15] Programmes of the Antient Concert are to be found in the holdings of a variety of libraries of *The Words of the Music Performed at the Concert of Antient Music* for each season; those of the Academy for the 1790s are in the collection of Mr Christopher Hogwood.

[16] Arthur Dandelot, *La Société des concerts du Conservatoire de 1828 à 1897* (Paris, 1898); Edouard Deldevez, *La Société des concerts du Conservatoire de Musique, 1860 à 1885* (Paris, 1887); Myles Birket Foster, *The History of the Philharmonic Society of London, 1813–1912* (London, 1912); George Hogarth, *The History of the Philharmonic Society of London from its Foundation, 1813, to its Fiftieth Year, 1862* (London, 1862); Richard von Perger and Robert Hirschfeld, *Geschichte der k. k. Gesellschaft der Musikfreunde in Wien* (Vienna, 1912). On the policies of the Conservatoire, see esp. Deldevez, *La Société*, 385.

[17] At the Gewandhaus in Leipzig, between 1781 and 1881, 612 opera selections were performed, 92 opera overtures, but only 221 symphonies (see Albert Doerffel, *Geschichte der Gewandhausconcerte zu Leipzig* (2 vols., Leipzig, 1881–4)).

There was such great variety in the old works performed in different places that one should not think of 'canon' as a universally authorized play-list. It is usually best to think of a period as possessing a set of interlocking canons, rather than a single one; it is even more important to avoid speaking of *the* canon. The ideological burden of the classical music tradition—its effort to enforce its authority—makes one think that there was a single, identifiable list; but upon closer inspection we find a great variety of practices at any one time in different contexts, affected by performing resources, institutional characteristics, and social traditions.

On the broadest plane, the opera differed fundamentally from the concert in the evolution of canon. Only in a few instances did clearly defined repertories of full-length operas remain on-stage for long periods of time before the middle of the nineteenth century. A few works of the late eighteenth century—Gluck's most of all—remained on-stage in Paris until the 1820s, but not after that. Several of Mozart's operas persisted, as did *Fidelio* and *Der Freischütz* in places, but in most places a diversified repertory of German opera had to wait for the leadership of Wagnerian producers later in the century. Probably the largest early operatic repertory to become established was that of works by Rossini, Donizetti, and Bellini that remained in use in many places (centrally in the Théâtre Italien in Paris, for example).[18] Yet it was probably not until the early twentieth century that opera repertories consisted primarily of works by dead composers, as had come about in orchestral and chamber-music concerts by the 1860s.

Repertories of operatic excerpts were far more widespread than complete works: that is where opera persisted most significantly before 1900. Throughout the nineteenth century it was the practice for most orchestral concerts (by 'symphony' orchestras, as it was put even then) to offer opera arias or major scenes or acts; one suspects that such pieces were a major drawing-card. But operatic excerpts were canonized very differently from symphonies or concertos—they were viewed more in popular than in learned terms, with respect but not spiritual awe directed at the composers. While the busts of Bellini and Donizetti were often enshrined on the walls of concert-halls along with those of Haydn and Beethoven by the 1870s, they represented quite different and separate canonic traditions. Mozart and Weber related more closely to this canon than to that of instrumental music, since they were known more for their operas than for their instrumental works.

Works were perceived in canonic terms in large part by the roles they played in repertories and in programmes, and we need therefore to look more closely at the ways by which these frameworks were constructed. The most basic unit of analysis here is the genre: programmes were organized in terms of genre, usually

---

[18] Frédérique Patureau demonstrates an emerging operatic canon in *Le Palais Garnier dans la société parisienne, 1875–1914* (Liège, 1991). Information on opera repertories can be found in concise form in such works as Albert de Lasalle and Ernst Thorirau, *La Musique à Paris* (Paris, 1863).

with strict conventions as to their order, so as to provide contrast within the musical experience. Jeffrey Kallberg has defined genre perceptively in terms of what he calls a 'generic contract' between audience and composer, a set of expectations from which either party can attempt to reinterpret conventional practice; and something of the same kind of thing went on in regard to programmes.[19] We need to ask how old works entered into these contracts—how they found niches in the complex of conventions—and what that meant about their role in musical life.

Prior to the middle of the nineteenth century, a canonic repertory was generally built around a major musical figure: such cultic heroes gave shape and authority to the evolving canonic tradition in the first periods of its development. Palestrina stood at the centre of the works by master composers at the Sistine Chapel in Rome from the 1560s on.[20] He then had a special status, shared to a certain degree with William Byrd, in the programmes of the Academy of Ancient Music until the society transformed its repertory in the early 1780s.[21] Handel was the focal point of the programmes of the Concert of Antient Music and British music festivals. And Beethoven played a similar central role at orchestral concerts during the nineteenth century. But a dominant figure is not evident in repertories after about 1870: one senses that by that time canon had become so firmly established at the core of musical life that no one composer was needed to given structure to canonic repertory.

Still, a great figure always formed part of a larger collegial definition of canonic repertory: in the Academy works by Lassus, Marenzio, and Gibbons were grouped around those of Palestrina; and in nineteenth-century orchestral concerts Haydn, Mozart, and Beethoven were joined by Weber, Cherubini, and Viotti and a great variety of other composers. Frequently a composer might be known for a single piece: a Gloria in polyphonic style by the Sicilian Emanuele D'Astorga (1686–?1757) was performed widely in the eighteenth and nineteenth centuries even though during his lifetime he was known chiefly for cantatas written in a more recent idiom.[22]

The order in which genres tended to follow each other on concert programmes was a matter of custom that had profound implications for how the music was perceived and valued. Overtures and symphonies—terms often used interchangeably right into the nineteenth century—by tradition served as openers to concerts, pieces designed to bring the audience to attention as people settled into the hall, or as finales to long programmes which listeners often left early. Such

---

[19] Jeffrey Kallberg, 'The Rhetoric of Genre: Chopin's Nocturne in G Minor', *19th-Century Music*, 11 (1988), 238–61.

[20] Anthony Cummings, 'Toward an Interpretation of the Sixteenth-Century Motet', *JAMS* 34 (1981), 43–59; Jeffrey Dean, 'The Repertory of the Cappella Guilia in the 1560s', *JAMS* 41 (1988), 465–90; letter to *JAMS* 42 (1989), 671–2.

[21] Fragmentary collections of the programmes of the Academy in its early period are to be found in the Leeds Public Library, the Bibliothèque Nationale, and the British Library.

[22] Weber, *Rise of Musical Classics*, 178, 184–5; 'Amanuele D'Astorga', in *New Grove*, i. 663–4.

positions on programmes had belittling social implications, but one finds symphonies in such spots for much of the nineteenth century. In 1807 the Gewandhaus Orchestra made a drastic break with convention—the contract—when it played Beethoven's 'Eroica' Symphony just after intermission, following it by a scene from a popular opera, and subsequently gave a kind of canonic status to this and a few other works that were played in this spot (the oratorios of Handel and Haydn and a symphony by Peter Winter especially).[23] That symphonies none the less usually remained in their usual spot suggests a limitation to the social 'autonomy' which the genre is often said to have achieved in the Romantic period. Even at as serious an institution as the Paris Conservatoire, Mozart's symphonies remained mainly at the start or the end, except for a few times during the 1850s.[24]

## Criticism

The third principle of canon, criticism, was distinguished from repertory in fundamental fashion by Joseph Kerman, in his pioneering article of 1983. He argued that while repertory is limited to the performance of old works, canon defines the works intellectually and from a critical perspective: 'A canon is an idea; a repertory is a program of action.'[25] Thus, simply performing works does not in and of itself establish them as part of a canon; the musical culture has to assert that such an authority exists, and define it at least to some degree in systematic fashion.

But Kerman pressed the distinction too far: 'Repertories are determined by performers, and canons by critics.'[26] The statement is simplistic: we cannot write off musicians as shapers of the canon. Kerman does not take seriously enough the role played by the tradition of craft in the critical process, a set of principles and standards—indeed, contracts with the public—in which musicians played a major role. Canonization was more than a literary process, a separating-out of musical wheat from chaff in the intellectuals' favourite sheets. It was influenced by a complex variety of social forces, ideologies, and rituals that can often be quite difficult to sort out. In some instances the literati simply gave their intellectual blessing to works that were already revered for different reasons—Leigh Hunt or Stendhal, for example, writing on Rossini in the 1820s, or French royalists who made Rameau their hero long after the Parisian public had made his music their own. This problem aside, Kerman's distinction is an essential tool for historical study of musical canon. We need to use it to enquire how in the

---

[23] The scene that concluded the programme was 'Ah padre mio', from Franc Federici's popular opera *Zaïra*. Programmes of the Gewandhaus Concerts, 29 Jan., 5 Feb. 1807, Museum of the City of Leipzig.

[24] See Dandelot, *La Société des concerts . . . de 1828 à 1897*, and Deldevez, *La Société . . . 1860 à 1885*.

[25] Joseph Kerman, 'A Few Canonic Variations', *Canons*, 177.

[26] Ibid. 182. See as well his *Contemplating Music* (Cambridge, Mass., 1984), 70–2, 207, 215, and Citron, *Gender*, 16–17.

eighteenth and early nineteenth centuries the performance of old works took those crucial steps first from canonic learning to performing repertory, and then to a complete, critical, ideological canon.

Kerman warns us against using 'criticism' too narrowly, focused too much upon reviewing and not enough upon a discourse, the broadly defined process by which participants in musical life consider works of music. What is essential is that the product of canonization is the bestowal of authority upon certain pieces of music. If repertory constitutes the framework of canon, the critical discourse empowers it, endowing old works with authority over musical composition and taste. This can be done in oral just as much as in written form; the point is that it must be stated publicly and categorically, and reinforced by images and rituals. Only if canonic authority is thus articulated and reinforced will it establish the power that it requires to act as a central determinant of musical culture. This authority must reach out over musical life as a whole; it cannot be simply the principles of the musically learned. That is why I argue that there was a pedagogical, rather than a performing, canon in the sixteenth and the seventeenth centuries.

We must never forget that many factors other than criticism came into play in the establishment of works in repertories. For example, Handel's *Occasional Oratorio* hung on in large part because it was written to celebrate the government's victory over the Jacobites in 1745; critics of the second half of the eighteenth century saw it as an inferior work, and much preferred the pieces he wrote in Italy, few of which stayed in the repertory.[27] The length and instrumentation of a piece often played significant roles in whether it lasted or not; Purcell's *Te Deum* and *Jubilate* may very well have become standard repertory at musical festivals because it was short but imposing and demanded no special players.[28]

The relationship between music history and music criticism is another problematic subject. The writing of history about great works of art is by no means essential to canon. Prior to the late eighteenth century, canonic traditions in the arts generally were essentially ahistorical, for the great works of poetry and sculpture were regarded as timeless, and were not studied in historical context—indeed, to do so would have meant questioning their universality. Musical canon emerged with close links to music history because it appeared at a time when such principles were weakening and when historical writing was becoming a vogue in almost all the arts. As I have argued elsewhere, musical canon arose in the eighteenth century in part because the authority of what Frank Kermode has called the 'metropolitan' canon in literature was breaking up.[29] Thus, much of the leadership in establishing the canon came from music historians such as

---

[27] See Robert Price, 'Observations on the Music of George Frederick Handel', the concluding section of John Mainwaring's *Memoirs of the Life of the late George Frederick Handel* (London, 1760), 177–81 and n.

[28] I owe the latter point to Donald J. Burrows.

[29] Weber, 'Intellectual Origins'.

Charles Burney and François Fétis. But, as Carl Dahlhaus has argued, in the nineteenth century the canon was essentially normative, not historical, and the principle of historical accuracy was not a major determinant in public concert life until the early music movement of the last several decades.[30] History served more as a means than an end within the emerging canon. It emerged as an unavoidable element in musical commentary, but ultimately in a subordinate capacity, providing ammunition for fighting wars of taste and a rationale for defining musical norms.

Dahlhaus goes too far, however, in saying that the writing of music history arose *after* the components of the canon had been established, and that it therefore served to legitimate, rather than define, their authority. In Germany and Italy quite impressive works—the history of opera written by Estaban de Arteaga in the 1780s most strikingly of all[31]—were written well before old works were performed frequently in those countries. Music history had its own history; in many respects it developed in its own terms, separate from canon, and accordingly exerted influence upon the development of repertory.[32] It was Fétis, for example, who, by virtue of his roles as both historian and concert impresario, brought music of the Renaissance and the Baroque into repertory and into canon.

## Ideology

In ideology we come to the final, by far the most outward-looking, principle of musical canon.[33] In and of itself, the critique of canonic value usually concerns a relatively limited portion of a community, since it presumes knowledge and intellectual engagement, and involves a demanding analytical process. Canons none the less obtain ideological justification that legitimizes their choices and the grounds of these choices, on bases that command wider, stronger allegiance within society. This has gone particularly far in music, for the power of the classical music tradition since the late eighteenth century has derived from the lofty claims made for its authority. We shall see how the musical canon has been defined variously as a *moral*, a *spiritual*, and a *civic* force; these have been the

---

[30] Carl Dahlhaus, *Foundations of Music History*, trans. J. B. Robinson (Cambridge, 1983), 95–100.

[31] Estaban de Arteaga, *Le rivoluzioni del teatro musicale italiano dalla sua origine fino al presente* (3 vols., Bologna, 1783–8). It was published in translation in Leipzig in 1789 by J. N. Forkel, and in an abbreviated version, *Les Révolutions du théâtre musical en Italie*, in London in 1802.

[32] For a broad treatment of early music histories, see Lawrence Lipking, *The Ordering of the Arts in Eighteenth-Century England* (Princeton, 1970). For examples of this kind of journalistic history, see the *Almanach musical* (1773–81), the *European Magazine* of the same period, and the major music journals of the early nineteenth century—the *Quarterly Music Magazine and Review*, the *Harmonicon*, the *Revue et gazette musicale*, the *Allgemeine Musikzeitung*, and the *Allgemeine wiener Musikzeitung*.

[33] For discussion of ideology in music, see Leonard B. Meyer, *Style and Music: Theory, History and Ideology* (Philadelphia, 1989), chs. 6–8.

terms in which the classical music tradition has been defined on the most fundamental plane.

The ideology of the musical canon has had a *moral* dimension throughout its history. It grew from a reaction against commercialism, against the development of publishing and concert life as manipulative enterprises that were seen to threaten standards of taste. A critique of the ways in which commerce was supposedly degrading musical values—'musical idealism', as I have termed it[34]— appeared as far back as early eighteenth-century England, notably in Arthur Bedford's book of 1711 *The Great Abuse of Musick*, and recurred in relatively similar forms throughout the nineteenth century. It identified the canon as morally and socially purifying, as a force for the good on the highest plane. Because the great master-works were thought to stand above the money-making side of musical life, they could help society transcend commercial culture and thereby regenerate musical life.

The canon has been seen as a *spiritual* force in both sacred and secular terms. Whereas religious idioms figured only secondarily in the canon of modern literature, music's roots in sacred polyphony pointed it in such a direction from the start. Palestrina's sacred style was established as a pedagogical model, and the music of the Elizabethan masters as a part of cathedral repertories. The performance of Delalande's motets in the Concerts Spirituels, justifying musical entertainment on holy days, brought the sacred canon into a secular context, and thereby established one of the key traditions in modern concert life. The performance of Handel's oratorios after his death had a similar impact, but yielded a much more self-consciously spiritual ideology in a wide range of performing contexts. Romantic musical thinking then interpreted the primarily secular repertory of the early nineteenth century in religious terms, and, one might say, spiritualized it.

Notions of the canon as a moral and a spiritual force have been closely related to one another, and together to the tradition of musical craft. The polyphonic tradition and its diverse offshoots have been defined ideologically as the bulwark of solid craftsmanship, good taste, and a lofty order of musical experience. We likewise find these themes in Bedford's polemics against theatre songs and in the attacks made against opera medleys during the 1840s by proponents of the 'classical' repertory. Bedford pointed to Byrd's psalm settings as models whereby to purify taste, and Viennese critics to Beethoven's symphonies and sacred works.[35] These ideological themes together built an authority for the canon that reached out beyond the limited numbers of people active in learned musical life, or indeed in musical culture as a whole.

In the course of achieving this authority, canon naturally took on a *civic* role within society. The rise of the public as a political force independent of the

[34] Weber, 'Wagner, Wagnerism'.
[35] William Weber, *Music and the Middle Class* (London, 1975), ch. 4.

monarch in eighteenth-century Europe made cultural life in general, and music in particular, central to a new definition of community. The governance of musical life became an intimate part of governance of society itself, since a greater concentration of the élites of society gathered together in musical activities than in any other area of life. It was in this context that old, rather than new, works became the focus of major occasions; performing *Messiah* became a means of celebrating the social and political order in times of trouble, England in its constitutional crisis of 1784 and Vienna in the revolution of 1848, for example. For the same reason, cities today have put up major opera-houses or concert-halls in their centres: great works from the past have come to symbolize society's highest moral and spiritual values, as well as its stability.

Musical life also constituted a civic community in its own right from the eighteenth century on, and the canon evolved within this context. The shift of patronage and leadership from monarchs and a few top aristocrats to the broad upper-class public as a whole raised the question of who within the musical world had authority, and on what basis. Any major event in musical life—a new hall, performer, or opera production—became a matter of public concern, involving the community as a whole, and accordingly there was uncertainty as to whether anyone in the public had privileged opinions by virtue of expertise. From the start of the century in England and France it became common to refer to 'connoisseurs' as men—seemingly not women—who were presumed to have special knowledge and critical judgement, chiefly in evaluating vocies and instrumental ability. Initially their judgements were not regarded by any means as sacrosanct, since periodicals often disparaged them, and implied that, ultimately, the public knew more about these matters than did the connoisseurs. This happened because there were no indispensable functions for connoisseurs, such as their colleagues in the plastic arts performed—historical attribution and financial assessment in the growing market for paintings.[36]

But connoisseurs took on much firmer authority as canons became more central to musical life during the first half of the nineteenth century. One of the most basic presumptions established in the classical music tradition by the middle of the nineteenth century was that listeners needed to learn about the great works and great composers—indeed, be educated in the subject. Knowledge born of simple involvement in the musical community was now deemed insufficient. Periodicals promoted themselves in this educational fashion, as the learned interpreters of the classical music tradition; programme notes of a fairly sophisticated kind became routine at the more sophisticated kinds of concerts. Likewise, the leaders of the central classical music institutions—in London, for example, the directors of the Concert of Antient Music,

---

[36] See William Weber, 'Learned and General Musical Taste in Eighteenth-Century France', *Past and Present*, 89 (1980), 58–85; Citron, *Gender*, 178–80.

the Philharmonic Society, and finally the Musical Union—set themselves up on a lofty plane as guardians of the canonic tradition. The learned men of musical life now played much more central, powerful roles in musical life than they had a hundred years before.

The authority of the connoisseur was essentially based upon ideology, and in such terms that the nature of intellectual authority within musical life was reshaped. Repertory was defined by learning and criticism, and the product was legitimated by ideology. Only through the last of these stages did the canon achieve its central role in musical taste and in the culture as a whole. In retrospect, its proponents succeeded in stunning fashion, for it is remarkable that a culture that had focused so intensively upon recent works by living musicians should have turned around to put old ones foremost.

Canonic ideology brought about the ideas of 'popular' and 'classical' music, and a formidable hierarchy of genres. Such distinctions had been by no means unknown in musical life, of course; works were seen as either mundane or artful, and differences might be discerned within each category. But there was no clear, ideologically articulated ranking of genres; opera was presumed to be both highly sophisticated and still accessible to all members of the upper classes. By the middle of the nineteenth century, a much more systematic hierarchy of genres had emerged. Chamber music, focused on the quartets of Beethoven, had become accepted as its pinnacle, followed by the symphony, the concerto, and then lesser genres such as the overture and the suite, and finally popular genres—waltzes, sentimental songs, marches—that were marginal to the formal concerts in which works from the classical music tradition were performed.

The ideology of musical canon was manipulated to social and political ends from its very start: the classical music tradition never had social autonomy. Its authority was wielded chiefly as an assertion of cultural supremacy by the more learned publics within musical life over those less learned, a division found in large part within the upper classes themselves. Yet, in broader respects, this tradition did support the predominance of Western élites over all the lesser classes; subscribers to the leading operas and symphony orchestras, who have passed their places down in their wills, have contributed greatly to the rigidity and social divisions within modern mass society.

How far has a deconstructionist point of view, such as that expressed here, taken us? How sceptical should we become of the hallowed traditions received from the Romantic tradition? On the one hand, musical canon must be seen as much less unified, continuous, and coherent than is often assumed; just why some works persist cannot always be attributed to reasoned musical judgements. Most important of all, canonic authority has often been manipulated for the purposes of snobbery and social élitism. On the other hand, a historical perspective on the evolution of musical canon suggests the continuity of the tradition of craft, a respect for the disciplined, artful construction of music. Naïve though it may sound, a deconstructionist can ultimately keep the faith in the classical music tradition. To maintain a balance between these two perspectives demands that we integrate theory and empiricism, in order to avoid the blinding extremities found among some practitioners of each approach.

# 16

## The Historiography of Music: Issues of Past and Present

### Leo Treitler

I begin with my uneasiness over the title of this book. The prefix 're-', like the word 'new' as in 'new Left', 'New Historicism', 'New Philosophy of History', 'New Musicology' stands for a narrative, now so widely recited as to constitute a modern mythology, of oppression followed by liberation (from the 'hegemony', 'tyranny', 'patriarchy', 'authoritarianism', etc. of traditional disciplines—taken in the double sense of Foucault's *Discipline and Punish*[1]), and attended by an ethos of exhilaration in new-found freedoms. But, paradoxically, the liberation argot that is switched in at the sign of the word 'new', as though by the striking of a computer function key, is itself the sign not only of an imposed radical discontinuity, but also of an encroaching new orthodoxy that threatens to constrain freedom. There is a risk that—not for the first time in our history—the guiding principles for musical scholars have befallen us, rather than having been adopted by us, no less than fashions in dress, architecture, or food.

In any case the prefix 're-' is hardly necessary, or even appropriate; for the historical study of music has hardly been conducted on the grounds of serious reflection about historiographical principles in the first place. It is not so much a matter of 'rethinking' the historiography of music as of thinking it.

Yet the political alertness that finds the theme of patriarchal authoritarianism and hegemony in the descriptions by traditional historians of 'coherent' and 'unified' cultures or historical processes of organic and evolutionary development, together with the stylistic alertness to the production of unified, coherent texts that describe such cultures, have jointly identified a powerful cultural value that is translated into historiographic principles that mutually support one another. There is no doubt something to this link between style and content, and it was an interesting suggestion of Carl Dahlhaus to break the circularity that it entails by adopting the narratives of Proust and Joyce as models for new history in place of those of Sir Walter Scott, which served nineteenth-century historians.[2]

---

[1] Michel Foucault, *Discipline and Punish* (New York, 1979).
[2] Carl Dahlhaus, *Foundations of Music History* (Cambridge, 1983).

To be sure, there is a great deal of rethinking nowadays about historiography in neighbouring disciplines: literary criticism—with its 'New Historicism' which focuses attention on the historical nature of the work of art[3]—and history—with its 'New Philosophy of History' which focuses attention on the artistic nature of the work of history, to put it positively, and on the failure of the idea of history as an objective account of what happened in the past, to state the negative.[4] These 'new' orientations have indeed leaked through to musical studies, and created some of the central issues in recent work that some authors are pleased to identify as 'New' musicology.

Postmodern scepticism about the rule of objectivity has placed the historical object in danger of fading, and the practice of both the contextualism of 'New Historicism' and the scepticism and relativism of the 'New Philosophy of History', taken to their extremes, can hasten and augment that tendency. Through the former, the historical object can be so densely contextualized as to be camouflaged into invisibility; through the latter, it can disappear in the brilliant glare of idiosyncratic virtuoso writing that seizes upon the discovery of the inventive side of history. Under the New Philosophy of History, the text of history can become opaque to its objects and instead call attention to itself. Under the New Historicism the object of history can become transparent to its contextual meaning, which then becomes the focus of attention.

In musical studies the historical object—in so far as it is music itself—might be thought to have greater possibilities of persevering in so far as it has an autonomous presence contemporaneous with the work of the scholar—for example, in so far as it has an existence in the world of performance, but also in so far as it has a presence as music in the consciousness of the scholar. But the idea of an autonomous presence for the work of music is currently under concerted attack from precisely those two orientations as they are represented in musical studies.

The discovery that the study of music has been grounded on the premiss of the autonomous work and the recognition that this premiss is refuted by the fact that the musical work, like its composer and its reception, is deeply embedded in the culture in which it participates and to which it contributes have been followed too quickly by the dogmatic imposition of an obligatory, absolute abstinence from the autonomy concept and the adoption of that ban as one of the main banners of 'new' musical studies. Engagement with the musical work in its autonomy is the beginning, not the end, of historical interpretation. The relationship between the investigating scholar in the present and the historical object in the past is not fixed, but ever changing. It is a relationship of reciprocal influence, whereby each can change in response to engagement with the other. But

---

[3]  See John H. Zammito's review essay, 'Are We Being Theoretical Yet? The New Historicism, the New Philosophy of History, and "Practicing Historians" ', *Journal of Modern History*, 65 (1993), 783–814. Further literature is cited there.

[4]  See n. 3.

it depends absolutely on an autonomous role for each. It has been likened to a dialogue (Bakhtin) and a tennis match (Gadamer). But dialogue is false unless each participant both speaks out of his or her own autonomy and is subject to change during the course of the dialogue and as a result of it.

The great historian of art Erwin Panofsky is perhaps best known outside his field for the conceptions developed in his anthology *Meaning in the Visual Arts.*[5] The centrality of those conceptions to his work, and to his view of humanistic study in general, is made manifest in this elucidation of the book's title: the 'real objects' of the humanities are the meanings that are embodied in the works that are its material objects. But the apprehension of a work's meaning begins in the fact that, 'whether or not it serves some practical purpose, and whether it is good or bad, it demands to be experienced aesthetically. . . . We do this [i.e. experience it aesthetically] when we just look at it (or listen to it) without relating it, intellectually or emotionally, to anything outside of itself. . . . Only he who simply and wholly abandons himself to the object of his perception will experience it aesthetically.'[6] But this central idea did not prevent Panofsky from developing a theory of meaning in the visual arts under the rubric of 'iconology' that is very closely parallel to the contextualism of the New Historicists.[7] Indeed, he begins his exposition of this theory with a justification of the need for contextual interpretation of all human behaviour and its products as a basis for understanding, that anticipates in all essential respects the anthropologist Clifford Geertz's development of his concept of 'thick description', a conception that is acknowledged to be at the core of the New Historicism and of the New Musicology.[8]

If we do not accept such a provisionally autonomous status for the musical work, we risk reducing it to a sign and rendering it transparent to the (extra-musical) meaning whose explication will have become the ultimate aim of musical study; that is, for all practical purposes, we risk its disappearance as an aesthetic object once it has done its job of signifying. That may be a risk the scholar is willing—even eager—to take, but then it should be with the determination that it is worth the risk. The choice is one of the most critical ones facing music scholars today.

With the movement of historiography into the foreground of a newly theory-conscious domain of historical criticism in the arts, the agenda of discussion has itself changed.

'Music Historiography', so begins the *New Grove* article under that title, 'is the writing of music history.' That is putting 'music history' in the category of a literary form, genre, or medium. 'Writing music history' evokes the title of a highly influential, symptomatic book in the field of anthropology, *Writing Culture.*[9] The

---

[5] Erwin Panofsky, *Meaning in the Visual Arts* (Chicago, 1965).

[6] 'The History of Art as a Humanistic Discipline', ibid. 11, 14–22.

[7] See ibid. ch. 1: 'Iconography and Iconology: An Introduction to the Study of Renaissance Art'.

[8] Clifford Geertz, *The Interpretation of Culture* (New York, 1973), ch. 1.

[9] James Clifford and George Marcus, *Writing Culture* (Berkeley, 1986).

essential thesis of that book is that 'culture' is a figment (read 'mental invention') of the writing anthropologist, rather than some sort of organization or practice of particular social groups that are studied and described by anthropologists. This orientation has provoked concern that it devalues ethnography as a necessary component of anthropological work which distinguishes it, for example, from sociology. By the same token, it is possible to read in the opening of the *New Grove* article on music historiography the implication that what we call 'music history' is actually the product of the synthetic or creative activity of music historians who write, rather than some actual set or sequence of events, style conventions, works, performance practices, social conditions, and so on. This suspicion would be strengthened, for example, by consulting the *New Harvard Dictionary of Music* on 'History of Music', which, after a brief introduction, launches into an exposition about the *periods* of music history, a conception that is surely an artefact of writing music history, not a given about the historical world. The problem that the topic of historiography poses today is that of serving the competing interests of history and historiography, for we do not know, as we once thought we did, where the boundary between the two lies; we are not as certain as we once were that we can tell them apart.

There is a continuity from reality to representation and from history to historiography. They are not pairs of distinct, and especially not opposing, categories. That is not said as a statement of confidence in the stable survival of the historical object in the transformation from reality to representation. The kinds of hazards to such survival that the object confronts in transmission constitute a subject that must be high on the agenda of the study called 'historiography'. And that draws attention to the extension of historiography one step further: to the historical study of the writing of history, absolutely essential as a subject of research and pedagogy. This entails a study of the values and interests, the literary modes, and the social functions in accordance with which histories have been written throughout the ages, and the analysis of the resulting histories in terms of the influence of these factors on them.

History is always slow to recognize the cultural meanings of its accounts. Perhaps that is in the nature of things, and must always remain so; for it is at least conceivable that efforts to do history and historiography simultaneously within the same project will be counterproductive, that the historical object will be obscured rather than illuminated by explicit attention to the means employed to represent it. There is a real question as to whether history would survive the effort to catch up. The alternative is to work with a sensitivity to the interests and conventions that are embodied in the models that we have inherited and the habits that we have acquired, a sensitivity that would be sharpened by the sort of historical-historiographical study that I propose. With such a sensitivity we would be in a position to choose, in particular cases, whether we intend to convey the meanings that are embodied in the language and forms that we employ in our historical accounts.

I can illustrate this with reference to historical accounts of Gregorian chant that have been in European music-historical literature since the eighteenth century, and in particular to efforts to fit those into accounts of medieval music in general. The very labels 'Middle Ages' and 'medieval' carry with them an idea of distance—psychological, cultural, aesthetic, stylistic—which was embodied in the feelings of the people of the Renaissance who devised them to express a consciousness of their own fundamental difference from a cultural epoch that they regarded as past. This perception of the Middle Ages as distant and other continues to be manifested directly in the connotations of the word 'Medieval', which can include 'old-fashioned', 'primitive', 'irrational', 'superstitious', 'cruel', and so forth. But music historians have attributed double meaning to chant, not only as cultural other but also as source.

European music history has been understood since the Romantic era to begin in the Middle Ages with Gregorian chant, unlike the history of art and literature, which claim ancient Greek patrimony.[10] Gregorian chant is the oldest European music that we know, and by virtue of that priority it has been granted the presumptive right to be regarded as the progenitor of European music. Thus scholars have long been engaged in the identification of quintessentially 'European' principles in that music, even to the extent of identifying them with principles that dominate the music of Beethoven, the all-time paragon of European music.[11] This works both ways: the definition of what is 'European' is informed by the traits of the chant that has come down as 'Gregorian', and the traits of European music that have been identified as such since the nineteenth century operate tacitly as teleological ideals for the recognition of those traits in chant. This double role continues to affect both large-scale accounts and detailed descriptions of the music, bringing into play a music conception that was not held by its contemporaries.

When we approach historical narrative with the expectation that it is true in a way in which narrative fiction is not, it is not only because experience tells us that this is the case (perhaps it does not), but because our understanding of, and ability to read, either is based on the contrast. We read narrative fiction as the creation of an imaginary world and narrative history as the representation of a real world. Different rules obtain, and we appreciate each for the way in which it creates, or re-creates, its world. If the difference is not observed, history and fiction will 'collapse back into myth and will be indistinguishable from it, as from

---

[10] See my essay 'The Politics of Reception: Tailoring the Present as Fulfilment as of a Desired Past', *Journal of the Royal Music Association*, 116 (1992), 280–98. In this regard music historiography has promulgated a music-historical version of the broader view of 'Europe' as a medieval creation. Thus the historian Hermann Hempel wrote: 'Europe arises out of the Middle Ages; indeed it was first the Middle Ages, but also, already the Middle Ages, that created Europe' (Europa stammt aus dem Mittelalter, aber auch: schon das Mittelalter hat Europa geschaffen) ('Europa und seine mittelalterliche Grundlegung', *Die Sammlung*, 4 (1949), 15.

[11] Ibid.

each other'.[12] Historians do sometimes forget that difference, in fact, and the result can be hard to distinguish from myth.[13]

The *New Grove* definition, which is a good beginning, directs attention to properties of the written medium and to the influence that they can have on the apperception of its object, intentional or otherwise: a tendency to objectify it—to bring it within a synoptic purview as a coherent, closed thing, to render it permanent, and to render what is said confirmable (or disconfirmable). On the other hand, it also directs attention to the ways in which the object is formed and constrained by the conventions and vocabulary of written language and by the logic, the aesthetic, the poetics, or the rhetoric of the mode of representation—for example, narrative as against structural analysis. Awareness of the action and influence of the medium of representation provokes the question of its social function (e.g. as foundation myth or as expression of cultural identity or as assertions about relations of power) and the way that this influences the representation. Much of the content of this book is addressed to such influence.

When historiography addresses itself to such dimensions of writing history, its domain is not any longer the writing of history, but a body of knowledge and a literature about such writing.

What, then, do we mean by 'history', that historiography has as its object? We employ the word in multiple ways: to signify a body of knowledge about the past, the written accounts or literature that incorporate historical knowledge, and the academic-scholarly discipline that organizes such knowledge and its producers, such writings and their writers. But, like it or not, we need and use the word to designate the past itself, apart from the knowing or writing about it—the things that happened or were done or made, the people that inhabited the past, the things that they thought, to which historical knowledge and historical accounts have reference, as when we say 'This feels like the coldest day in history', or 'Today the institution of apartheid becomes history', or 'The rest is history'. If we go even further and say 'This day will go down in history', or 'this is a historical day', we have reference to the status and value that the past has for us. We speak, in that sense, of 'making history', a conception that is now cheapened by the daily announcement as I write this that the New York Stock Exchange has made history today—that is, it has reached its highest values ever. History is sometimes taken to be synonymous either with existence altogether or with earth-bound, time-bound existence, as when there is talk in apocalyptic or postmodern tracts of 'the end of history'. But that also means 'the end of change'. History means continuity and change.

History is also the narrative of what happened in the past—it is, after all, a kind of story. This etymological identity of story and history is reflected in

---

[12] Louis O. Mink, 'Narrative Form as a Cognitive Instrument', in Robert H. Canary and Henry Kozicki (eds.), *The Writing of History: Literary Form and Historical Understanding* (Madison, 1978), 129–49.

[13] For a particularly clear case, see Treitler, 'Politics of Reception'.

languages that use a single word for our words 'history' and 'story': *historia* (Latin), *storia* (Italian), *histoire* (French), *Geschichte* (German). Every story is historical, and every history is a story. This reflects the fact that we cannot just know the past; we know pasts in relation to presents and futures. Narrative is how we know temporality. Hayden White writes: 'Narrative is the necessary means of symbolizing events about which their historicality cannot be indicated. A chronicle makes statements about events without symbolizing them. But this method does not represent the meaning of historical events in the absence of symbolization.'[14]

If we speak of 'doing history', we have reference to producing knowledge, understanding, or interpretation and literature about the past; and in so far as we think of history as a literary genre, its sense as narrative has had the greatest influence on our thinking. Books bearing titles of the form *The History of X* are expected to be narratives about their subjects through time. With regard to the study of the history of music, this expectation has been formed and reinforced in perpetual cycles by the basically narrative outlines of academic courses and the textbooks that are written for them and that therefore have a lasting effect on the historical sense of their consumers. The privileged narrative dimension of this genre is that of temporal succession, and the emphasis has been on origins, linear continuities, and change, often seen from the vantage-point of goals and narrated in terms of progress toward them. The implied dynamic of continuity and change is that of causality of a kind associated with organic growth, so that the developments that are traced have an aura of inevitability about them. History that laid claim to causal explanation as the motor of its narrative progression could claim to be scientific, and that claim could be bolstered by the parallel claim that to know the nature of a thing, you must know its history. Before the currency or vogue of New Historicism, this philosophical idea was known simply as 'historicism'.[15] What I have described here is a paradigm for music history that I shall call 'scientific', for the reasons just given. Characteristic of this genre are passages like the following, which carries an entire chapter in highly compressed form: 'When Emma's funeral music (in Weber's *Euryanthe*) . . . announced through its transformation at the end of the opera that the sinner is redeemed, the seed was planted from which, at Wagner's hands, the whole form of Music Drama was to grow.'[16]

The following passage depends on imagery from a *routier*, rather than from a handbook of botany. The effect is the same: the image generates without effort the causal interpretation that is wanted: 'Instrumental music in the early 17th century was in a different stage of development from vocal music. Vocal music had to assimilate the new technique of monody . . . but instrumental music for

---

[14] Hayden White, *The Content of the Form* (Baltimore, 1986), 3.

[15] It has been critically examined by Karl Popper in *The Poverty of Historicism* (New York, 1961). See also my essay 'The Present as History', in *Music and the Historical Imagination* (Cambridge, Mass., 1989), 95–156.

[16] Alfred Einstein, *A Short History of Music* (New York, 1956), 164.

the most part had only to continue along the path that had already been marked out before the end of the Renaissance.'[17]

Comparisons between chronologically separated moments can be made without the use of any such narrative machinery, as in the following passage:

The distinction between Beethoven and Mahler is that between dialectics and dualities. . . . The essence of dialectic lies in its ability to transform duality into a *process*, one achieved by seeing the poles of a duality subsumed as aspects of a larger meaning. . . . Mahler does not abandon this deeply embedded cultural tradition of dialectics, but he massively emphasizes the unmediated poles of his musical dualities.[18]

If narrative were brought into such an exposition, it would be for its own sake (e.g. if the word 'abandon', which is the one hint of narrative in the passage, were amplified to make that element more prominent). The conveying of the information does not require it. But even at the historiographic level itself there is a temptation to narrativize the changes from Einstein and Grout, through the several versions of Palisca, to Johnson, telling of a declining prominence of the narrative vehicle. It seems unlikely that we shall ever be able—or wish—to resist such temptations altogether, to shed entirely the idea that history entails, among its features, the representation of some part of our world in motion through time, and that in trying to understand some aspect of the present, one thing we are bound to do is investigate its past, speculate about its future, and incorporate it all in some kind of a story. We are bound, that is, not by the ineluctable course of events or by epistemological priority, but by the experience of taking in our life as we live it and by aesthetic temper.

This is demonstrated at the moment, for example, by intense research activity aimed at narrativizing the changes in European art-music around 1800, characterizing the changes in highly detailed ways and assessing causes in ways far less simplistic and redundant than had been done earlier this century. Similar research activity aims to narrativize the extraordinary musical creativity on numerous fronts that is evident in Carolingian Europe—activity that has been characterized as amounting to the formation of the European music culture.[19] It is not just that these are studies of particular periods of music history; the

---

[17] Donald Jay Grout, *A History of Western Music* (New York, 1960), 297. In the 2nd edn. of 1972 the first sentence of the passage has been removed. In the 4th edn. of 1988 (revised by Claude Palisca) the corresponding passage reads thus: 'Instrumental music did not escape the spell of the recitative and aria styles, but they made less of a mark than did the practice of the basso continuo. The sonata for solo instruments *was particularly susceptible* to vocal influences, and, of course, the keyboard accompaniment to treble instruments particularly fell into the basso continuo texture easily. The violin, which rose to prominence in the seventeenth century, tended naturally to emulate the solo singing voice, and many of the techniques of the vocal solo and duet were absorbed into its vocabulary' (emphasis added). The trope of a predestined course of development leading to an inevitable outcome is gone, but the music that is the object of the narrative is still presented as the passive object of some unspecified force that is driving the narrative. In the 5th edn. (1995) the second sentence has undergone a small change that shows the author adjusting the narrative dynamics: 'The sonata for solo instruments, especially, *surrendered* to vocal influences' (emphasis added).

[18] Julian Johnson, 'The Status of the Subject in Mahler's Ninth Symphony', *19th-Century Music*, 18 (1994), 109.

[19] e.g. in my essay 'Inventing a European Music Culture—Then and Now', in John Van Engen (ed.), *The Past and Future of Medieval Studies* (Notre Dame, Ind., 1994), 344–61.

narrative dimension, the representation of that particular part of the world in motion, is an important contribution to the historical understanding.[20] The story itself is the object of study. The very liberation ethos that has so many disciplines in its thrall just now derives its rhetorical and moral force from an implicit narrative—a sort of historiographical *Egmont*, of which the present moment is the happy ending.

If there is any reason to address the subject of the historiography of music anew, it must be to ask, in the altered circumstances of the present, what we now take the domain of music history to be, and what kind of knowledge we aim for and can manage to generate about it.

As I was trying to collect my thoughts about these difficult questions, there appeared in the *New York Review of Books* a review by the biologist Richard Lewontin of the most recent survey of sexual practices in the United States.[21] At the end of his account Lewontin bears down on the fact that any such survey can be based only on the reports of whatever sample of the population is chosen, and when the subject is an aspect of human life that is so vulnerable to every shade of boastfulness and grandiosity, denial and shame, self-inflation, myth, and moral imperatives, the reliability of such reports is hardly assured. Sure enough, judging from the one test that can be run for the reliability of the data, there must have been gross misreporting by the respondents taken as a group.[22]

It is in his reflections on this situation that I find a resonance with my own thoughts on trying to write again about the historiography of music. 'How, then, can there be a "social science?" ' he asks. 'The answer, surely, is to be less ambitious and stop trying to make sociology into a natural science. . . . Each domain of phenomena has its own grain of knowability.'[23]

At one time music history, too, pretended to a kind of scientific knowledge—in particular, the ambition for scientific history with its confusing quest for causal knowledge based on a vain belief in the lawfulness of music-historical succession and a naïve cult of objectivity. Now the generally acknowledged

---

[20] Adding to the sophistication of studies of this sort is the new attention being given to the concept of influence, with a view to understanding its dynamics. See Joseph Straus, *Remaking the Past: Musical Modernism and the Influence of the Tonal Tradition* (Cambridge, Mass., 1990), and Kevin Korsyn, 'The Aesthetics of Influence', *Music Analysis*, 10 (1991), 3–72.

[21] Richard Lewontin, 'Sex, Lies, and Social Science', *New York Review of Books*, 20 Apr. 1995. The book is *The Social Organization of Sexuality: Sexual Practices in the United States* by Edward O. Laumann, John H. Gagnon, Robert T. Michael, and Stuart Michaels (Chicago, 1994).

[22] The test is simply that if everybody had told the truth, the total number of male partners reported by women should have been more or less equal to the total number of female partners reported by men. As it was, for every 10 male partners reported by women, men reported 17.5 female partners. This is not impossible, because the sample was not a closed population; both men and women could and, no doubt, did choose partners outside the sample. But then the sample cannot be regarded as representative. If all the world's population had been surveyed and the same results had been obtained, it would be quite certain that many respondents were dissimulating. Either way, this result makes it doubtful that anything definitive can be learned from the survey.

[23] Lewontin, 'Sex, Lies', 29.

failure of this misjudgement of music history's proper 'grain of knowability' has prepared the way, it seems, for a new assessment, which demands equally close scrutiny: the pretension to anthropological and/or sociological knowledge, not just as possible modes of music-historical knowledge, but as obligatory and exclusive ones. The claim to exclusiveness and obligatory status alone should, on the lesson of the previous failure, be sufficient to raise the red flag of caution.

It is worth following the parallel a bit further. Lewontin notes that there is good and sufficient reason to *want* to know about patterns of sexual practice in the age of the AIDS epidemic. But it seems that the wish to have such knowledge has led the investigators to look the other way when it comes to the need for an independent evaluation of the reliability of their conclusions. The importance of the question stands in as criterion for the plausibility of the answers. The need to know persuades the questioner that he has the knowledge. Similarly, now that our present historical situation has created a demand for a different kind of music-historical knowledge, the question 'How can we have it?' must also be aired. Now that we have lost our *naïveté* and know that we do not establish history merely by means of objective research and the rules of reason, but that we create it, we need to be aware of the interests that lead us to create it in particular ways.

A historical understanding of music requires that we both understand how music is in history and understand the history in music. Understanding the history in music can only follow the understanding of music in history and is its consummation. Music embodies its historicity in a multiplicity of ways, perhaps most importantly in its disposition toward the music that is its past. Joseph Straus begins the first chapter of his interpretation of modern music's embodiment of its past with these sentences:

Music composed in the first half of the twentieth century is permeated by the music of the past. Traditional sonorities, forms, and musical gestures pervade even works that seem stylistically more progressive. But no easy accommodation is possible across the stylistic and structural gulf that separates the traditional tonal music of the eighteenth and nineteenth centuries from the new post-tonal music of the twentieth.[24]

This passage introduces a theory about an 'influence of anxiety' worked by Classical and Romantic music on the music of modernism, following Harold Bloom's theory of influence through struggle in literature, a theory that is drawing considerable attention from music scholars because of its superiority in depth, richness, and plausibility to the shallow concept of influence as an internal moving force of historical development, which used to be switched on at the first sight of musical resemblances (this has the questionable corollary that where there is no palpable resemblance, there has been no influence).

---

[24] See Straus, *Remaking the Past*, 1.

Music embodies its historicity when, through its institutions, its functions, its traditions and conditions of performance and transmission, its technologies, its relationships with the other arts, it enacts or mirrors the societal and cultural patterns and practices and the prevailing ideologies that constitute the historical contexts of its creation. Music may then be interpreted as an item of history from which we may read other aspects of history—the historical, social, and psychological contexts in which music was created and by which it was conditioned.

An issue under intense discussion at the moment is whether, in addition to these external factors, music's internal patterns and structure can also be understood to reflect its wider historicity. At issue is nothing less than the question of whether the historical understanding of music is totally dependent on extra-musical matters, or whether historical understanding of *music* is possible and, if so, what it entails. Then musical works would themselves be interpreted as items of history in the same ways. They would not, then, be simply inert records of the conditions of their creation; it would be important to see them as having been active participants in the dynamics of those conditions.

While this has now become a central question, it was not thought worthwhile or possible to interpret music in such ways as long as music was regarded as abstract and ineffable under formalist, transcendental theory.

Theodor Adorno issued a challenge to interpret the music of Mozart in this way,[25] which has been taken up by Susan McClary in one of the most radical ventures in the historical interpretation of music to appear in recent years.[26] Citing this challenge as the epigraph for her essay, McClary first interprets tonality as articulating 'a social world organized by means of values such as rational control and goal-oriented striving for progress—the values upon which leaders of the upwardly mobile bourgeoisie traditionally have grounded their claim to legitimacy, authority, and 'universality"' (135). She then interprets sonata procedure in terms of its 'emphasis on problems of identity and alterity [highlighting] confrontation and eventual resolution. Conflict and struggles for dominance for purposes of establishing and maintaining all-valued self-identity become essential preoccupations in this style (and, one might argue, at this moment in history)' (136–7). Concerto format 'enacts as a spectacle the dramatic tensions between individual and society, surely one of the major problematics of the emerging middle class' (138). Summing up, 'the problematics addressed in tonality, sonata procedure, and concerto are the familiar issues of the late eighteenth century: the narrative construction of identity and the threat of alterity, the relationships between individual freedom and collective order,

---

[25] Theodor Adorno, *Introduction to the Sociology of Music* (New York, 1976), 70: 'Of all the tasks awaiting us in the social interpretation of music, that of Mozart would be the most difficult and the most urgent.'

[26] Susan McClary, 'A Musical Dialectic from the Englightenment: Mozart's Piano Concerto in G. Major, K.453, Movement 2', *Cultural Critique*, 4 (1986), 129–69; subsequent page references to this article are given in the text.

between objective reason and subjectivity, between stability and dynamic progress' (138–9).

McClary characterizes a critical passage in the movement under investigation in terms of the 'willful deviance' of the piano (with which Mozart is identified), interpreted as 'the individual voice, heroic in its opposition to the collective force', but also as 'flamboyant, theatrical, indulgent in its mode of self-presentation', then as 'a histrionic, exhibitionistic, romantic artist/child. . . . It has situated itself as "Other," rather than as collaborator, with respect to the orchestra's narrative. . . . Nothing less is at stake than the foundations of social order' (146–7). 'The rebellious piano and its adventure come to occupy center stage' (157). Regarding an ambiguous situation in the recapitulation, the author leans toward the interpretation that 'the organic necessities of the individual are blatantly sacrificed to the overpowering requirements of social convention. . . . The social norm comes to the fore and stamps out the deviant strain. . . . If eighteenth-century musical procedures purport to be based on the premise that harmony between social order and individual freedom is possible, then this version of the moment shows the authoritarian force that social convention will draw upon if confronted by recalcitrant nonconformity' (151). 'Mozart is speaking to us from *inside* the Enlightenment, from which vantage point its contradictions are all too real. He is enacting the unsolvable dilemmas and paradoxes within an ideology that champions both social harmony and individual freedom' (159).

From an essay of Lawrence Kramer's I cite a second interpretation instancing the theory of musical works as stagings of cultural feelings and enactments.[27] Kramer aims to demonstrate 'the possibility of understanding a musical work as a concrete effort to *affect the cultural forces*, both material and ideological, amid which it is produced and received' (305). A point of focus is 'the *disruptive* effects of [music's] own meanings' (ibid., emphases added)—in the case of *Carnaval* meanings that challenge established forms of social, intellectual, and sexual authority. The aim is 'to show in detail how the compositional procedures of the music ramify [the metaphor of the quasi-improvisatory grouping of short pieces], continually inviting the listener to think about the interrelations of festivity, art, and gender' (305–6). There are three themes: 'The disunity of the socially constructed self', 'Cross-dressing and the mobility of gender', and 'The woman in the mirror' (306). I quote the author's brief account of the third:

*Carnaval* combines its concerns with gender and identity by forming a network of musical mirror-images. Technically, each image consists of a symmetrical grouping in which a structural unit, large or small, receives a suggestively placed and expressively heightened repetition [e.g. '*Chiarina* emphasizes harmonic progression from a subdominant F minor to a tonic C minor; *Estrella* complements this gesture by emphasizing progression from a

---

[27] Lawrence Kramer, '*Carnaval*, Cross-Dressing, and the Woman in the Mirror', in Ruth A. Solie (ed.), *Musicology and Difference: Gender and Sexuality in Music Scholarship* (Berkeley, 1993), 305–25; subsequent page references to this article are given in the text.

dominant C major to a tonic F minor' (315). In addition the right hand of *Chiarina* begins with an upward third motion A♭–C while the right hand of *Estrella* begins with a downward sixth motion A♭–C]. Culturally, the proliferating network of images serves to release and empower feminine energies, in keeping with nineteenth-century representations of the mirror as the sphere of feminine privilege. Before the mirror, women may do for themselves affirmatively what men do to women appropriatively: they may gaze with pleasure that constructs the thing it sees. (306).

From a theoretical point of view these authors are articulating a very important principle of music historiography. So here is the place to ask whether it is the urgency of the principle itself that supplies the force of the interpretation. There are questions about both examples. In the first, the theme of 'deviance' in the piano's behaviour is wrung out of the characterization of the movement's motto as being 'non-paradigmatic' on account of its five-bar length and of the piano's 'tendency to depart radically from the keys defined by the orchestra' into 'irrational' harmonies. Those and other interpretations of character and meaning are supported by reference to a 'shared musical code of the time' and an 'eighteenth-century Semiotics'.

But Mozart often composed phrases of odd lengths. They were thought normal enough in his time to merit description in Heinrich Christoph Koch's *Versuch einer Anleitung zur Composition* (1782–93), where we find rules for making just such a phrase as that one in K.453, without any hint that they are abnormal.[28] The harmonies characterized as 'irrational' can, in every case, be shown to be fully rational and coherent within the norms of the tonal system, even as normal as modulations by fifths.[29] To be sure, here and elsewhere Mozart was able to create strong effects through his manipulations of that system; but then no one has proposed to regard his music as bland. The claims about 'eighteenth-century Semiotics' would be well moderated by this passage from Wye J. Allanbrook's essay ' "Ear-Tickling Nonsense": A New Context for Musical Expression in Mozart's "Haydn" Quartets':[30]

Recent scholarship has rectified the false impression that writers in the tradition of the Baroque doctrine of the affections [that is the 'semiotic code' to which McClary is presumably referring]—Mattheson et al.—not only retained the confidence that the passions could be codified, but had codified them thoroughly. Such attempts were, in fact, rare, and often idiosyncratic; the confidence didn't produce the cook-book. (9)

Concerning the other example, while the attentive listener can indeed hear in the opening of *Chiarina* a bass-led progression from F to C, that would be com-

---

[28] Part 2: 'The Mechanical Rules of Melody: The Way in which Melody is Connected with Respect to the Mechanical Rules'. Ch. 2: 'Extended Phrases'. Repr. in Oliver Strunk, *Source Readings in Music History*, rev. edn., Leo Treitler, gen. ed. (New York, in press).

[29] See Harold S. Powers, 'Reading Mozart's Music: Text and Topic, Sense and Syntax', *Current Musicology*, 55 (1995), 5–44. Powers points out, too, that it is not always the piano that leads into remote key areas, it may be the orchestra as well. That makes the proposed scenario too simple for the music as it is.

[30] *St. John's Review*, 38 (1988), 1–24; subsequent page references to this article are given in the text.

pared, at the opening of *Estrella*, with a harmony on F which is inflected for one measure each to the supertonic and the dominant (with a bass motion of a half-step to E and back to F)—hardly a mirror of the first progression. But there can be disagreements about how to label a chord progression. What seems hard to imagine in any case is that the experience of the music would lead to reflection about the imagery of the woman in the mirror and all that it means for the culture of the time—that is, that the 'music's own meaning' would have the 'disruptive effect' that Kramer claims.

Is that really what is claimed in both cases? In another of Kramer's publications, his proclamation 'The Musicology of the Future',[31] he indicates that it is musical experience he is talking about, but that 'what we call musical experience needs to be systematically rethought, that the horizons of our musical pleasure need to be redrawn more broadly, and that the embeddedness of music in networks of nonmusical forces is something to be welcomed rather than regretted' (10–11). The reference to the woman in the mirror, with all that the image evokes, is presumably part of the redrawn 'musical experience'.

Here is a fundamental question raised by these interpretations: if postmodern theory would put aside the aestheticization of music that was a project of the early nineteenth century (this will be reviewed further on), then how can postmodern historical interpretation be based on musical analysis that claims to reveal musical *experience* which, no matter how broadly drawn, arises from those aesthetic conceptions? This contradiction is not evaded by musical analysis that is superficial and unengaged, that lacks the conviction of hammer-and-tongs analysis, as though to avoid entrapment in the aesthetic.

These comments apply especially to McClary's interpretation of Mozart K.453. The scenario that is sketched is presented, really, as a programme. It gives concrete content to the music's aesthetic content, and it seems to avoid the appearance of preoccupation with the aesthetic by offering only analysis sketches. As in the other case, the question of the real status of the interpretation as historical is left hanging.

For the question arises in both cases about the *participation* of the music in the society or the culture in the sense of the interpretations, and it is perhaps the most important question. Has the case really been made that the mirror relationship of the harmony of *Estrella* and *Chiarina* represents 'a concrete effort to affect the culture amid which it is produced and received', as Kramer puts it? If music is to be understood, as McClary proposes, as 'social discourse', was anyone listening to the slow movement of K.453 in that sense? No evidence or even suggestion is offered to that effect by either author. That is what makes these proposals seem precariously close to interpretations that are driven by little more than the need to make them. In both cases what is being proposed is not really a picture of music interacting with the society or culture of its time, but another

---

[31] *Repercussions*, 1 (1992), 5–18; subsequent page references to this article are given in the text.

way of reading musical works which, like so many blotters, have soaked up the conditions of their time but which, as we read them, are nevertheless considered in their autonomy, as inert records.

The real difference between the scientific conception of music history and the hermeneutic one is in the historiographic model they follow: the narrative (diachronic) or the systematic (synchronic). Each provides its own way of reading musical works historically. They do not compete with respect either to verisimilitude or to the degree to which they bring history to life. Despite the claims made for it, the hermeneutic mode does not really have the advantage of interpreting music in its *engagement with* the culture and society in which it participates. It is simply another way of deciphering autonomous musical works against the background of some pattern—here of culture or social organization or political forces, there of harmonic/contrapuntal dynamics or of formal conventions or of graduated style differences through the historical continuum. They are not different in form or verisimilitude from the sort of nineteenth-century hermeneutic that interpreted Beethoven's Ninth Symphony in images drawn from Goethe's *Faust*. They are different in reflecting what their respective hermeneutic cultures have sought to find in music: then Faustian aspirations, struggles, and conflicts, now politics and gender issues. Neither can support a claim to reveal what music is *really* about, a notion that would make no sense from a postmodern viewpoint in any case.

These patterns constitute arcana of different kinds, called upon to buttress the claims of the corresponding modes of interpretation to true representation of music, and the new hermeneutic model is proposed with an authoritarianism at least as explicitly forceful as the old: 'From a postmodernist perspective, music as it has been conceived of by musicology simply does not exist,' writes Kramer in 'The Musicology of the Future'. As effortless as such new exegesis has been, it nevertheless entails the analysis of the interior of works, the music itself. This leaves the interpreters in a contradictory position, for they must, at least temporarily, entertain the very conceptions that they programmatically reject.

The contradiction is recognized and thematized in a more radical call to renounce the 'internalist engagement of the critic', a 'close reading of the notes', 'the internalism and formalism that have dominated musicology'; to recognize that 'categories such as "work", "art", "the aesthetic", even "music" itself are not truths given us by the world through which we and others must always conceive musical utterances but are themselves cultural constructions darkly tinted for us with modernist ideology'.[32]

This caveat from Gary Tomlinson seems the more relevant, the more the parallels between these efforts toward a hermeneutic model of music history, with its claim to exegetical knowledge, and the older scientific model, with its claim

---

[32]    Gary Tomlinson, 'Musical Pasts and Postmodern Musicologies: A Response to Lawrence Kramer', *Current Musicology*, 53 (1993), 18–40; subsequent page references to this article are given in the text.

to causal knowledge, become clear. Interpretations, writes Tomlinson, that 'identify the "work" as the locus of the new musicology, . . . making it the primary (almost exclusive) matrix of its own meanings' (20) amount to a renewal of 'internalism and aestheticism, both carrying still the potent charge of nineteenth-century transcendentalism', and constitute a 'sleight-of-hand that decontextualizes . . . [the] contextualism' (ibid.) that was to be its starting premiss. His radical proposal is that we should 'move away from the whole constraining notion that close reading of works of music, of whatever sort, is the *sine qua non* of musicological practice. This notion has repeatedly pulled us back toward the aestheticism and transcendentalism of earlier ideologies' (21–2). In effect, Tomlinson argues for the rejection altogether of the idea that music, considered as aesthetic objects—musical works, that is—should be made the object of music historiography. This means that music history would be *sui generis*: that its forms and contents would not be dependent in any way on the historian's appreciation, interpretation, or analysis of instances of music; that the historian's experience of music would be irrelevant to his or her history of it; and that his or her history of it would not aim toward the better interpretation or criticism or analysis of instances of it. By comparison with the postmodern branch represented by the two interpretations that gave rise to this discussion, this conception is clear about its stance and its aims; nor does it share their internal contradictions.

But we should be aware of its consequences. It would restore the music historian's cool, distanced stance *vis-à-vis* music—for example, the distrust of internal evidence and connoisseurship—during the ascendancy of scientific music history, and it would re-legitimate under a new dogma the rupture that scientific history opened between music history and those subdisciplines that work toward the interpretation of music—criticism and theory. That is to say, it would undermine the postmodern ambition to break away from 'modernist manœuvers' in just those ways. In an essay first published in 1990 I wrote: 'My belief is that we have no access to music as a historical item, we have no possibility of historical knowledge of music, unless we take account of its beauty, its expressiveness, its power to move people, in its time, in the present, and in between.'[33] I addressed it originally to the modernist paradigm of scientific music history. It is ironic to be addressing it now in these postmodern directions.

It is in any case not easy for music historians to accept that the knowledge we wish to produce could be altogether independent of the 'close reading' of instances of music. Tomlinson's programme is more easily proclaimed than followed. I turn again to my experience of attempts at historical understanding of Gregorian chant for exemplification. The historical record contains many direct and indirect references to something like the introduction of Roman chant into

---

[33] Leo Treitler, 'History and Music', *New Literary History*, 21 (1990), 299–319; repr. in Ralph Cohen and Michael Roth (eds.), *History and . . . : Histories within the Human Sciences* (Charlottesville, Va., 1995), 209–30.

the Frankish regions of the Carolingian Empire during the reigns of King Pepin and his son, the Emperor Charlemagne, in the eighth and ninth centuries. In contextualizing this process, we have become aware that it is ensnared in the politics of empire, and that contemporary talk about it reflects a consciousness of strong cultural differences between Rome and the Frankish North. It even betrays apprehensions of those differences in nationalist or racist and gendered terms, apprehensions that survive in modern interpretations.[34] We learn a great deal by developing this evidence. But there is also music—Roman and Frankish versions of the same ritual items—surviving from this process, and close reading of it is indispensable to the interpretation of the historical record. It is the only way to give content to the apprehensions of the music and its performance that we learn about from other sources. Despite the risks, it seems inconceivable that we would want to eschew an intense engagement with the interiority of that music in order to be faithful to the demands of postmodern historiographic ideology.

I have chosen a medieval topic to make this point not only because of my own interests, but also by way of urging that current arguments about these matters are far too constrained by their focus on music and thought about music from the period *c.*1800 to the present.

The negatively charged key words in Tomlinson's critique—'work', 'internalism', 'aesthetics', 'transcendentalism'—have their own historical context, in the light of which they must be read. It is a story that has been told and retold recently, and that can be easily summarized.

Before the late eighteenth century music was in the service of the institutions of Church and State. It was regarded as part of the social world, to whose welfare it contributed through its participation in religious, political, and domestic rituals. It was considered significant by virtue of its dependence on non-musical institutions, on the natural world, and on language and the language arts. In the late eighteenth century this view of music began to be supplanted by one that regarded 'the aesthetic object as purposeless and the subject (the viewer, the reader, the listener) as disinterested. . . . This new view held that the only purpose of art was to be beautiful and to be experienced as such.'[35] 'Music should no longer derive its value or meaning from anything other than itself, . . . from its inner and private soul. Music . . . is its own end.'[36] From these ideas emerged the conception of music as absolute and autonomous, and the idea of the aesthetic.

Under these conceptions the aesthetic principles that were drawn upon for the discussion of music were those of formalism and transcendentalism. 'Formalism'—understood as the doctrine that music's content and meaning are con-

---

[34] See my 'Politics of Reception'.

[35] Sanna Pederson, 'A. B. Marx, Berlin Concert Life, and German National Identity', *19th-Century Music*, 18 (1994), 87–107, pp. 87–8.

[36] Lydia Goehr, 'Writing Music History', *History and Theory*, 31 (1992), 182–99, p. 191.

tained within or comprised by its musical elements alone, its notes and all their properties and patternings, as opposed to the idea that meaning arises out of any sort of reference outside the music itself (e.g. the doctrine of mimesis), out of the relation to a listener (e.g. the doctrine of catharsis), or out of music's 'connection to the ordinary world of concrete significance'[37]—formalism, so understood, is a doctrine that arose in the early nineteenth century (at least a generation before Hanslick, who is mainly associated with it in modern accounts) as one aspect of a complex process of making music autonomous. Its contribution to that process was to 'move music's meaning from its exterior to its structural interior'. It must be understood as complementing, in this project, the philosophy of transcendentalism, which aimed to 'raise music to the level of universal, spiritual meaning',[38] symbolic of human experience and consciousness, but in only the most abstract sense. This process had its economic aspects as well, by the way—public concerts, music publishing, the entrepreneurial activity of the composer—and its mythological aspect—the image of the artist in the garret.

Nowadays formalism and transcendentalism are not understood to be at all related, except as antagonists. This is a consequence of their separation when 'formalism came more closely to be tied to positivist and scientifically-styled theorizing',[39] something brought about only in the second half of the twentieth century, mainly by music theorists in the United States.[40] To read the theoretical writings of Heinrich Schenker, for example, in the light of a formalist conception within that partnership can be quite revealing. The degree to which the attempted separation has succeeded, and whether it will last, can be questioned.[41]

The distinction here is of little consequence, however, for the postmodern position urged by Tomlinson. For both before and after the separation of formalism and transcendentalism, music was autonomized, aestheticized, and dehistoricized or decontextualized. And that is what postmodern theorizing is challenging.

It is fuelled in this by new and valuable research bearing on the historicization of the doctrines of autonomy and the aesthetic themselves, and on the elevation of the symphony as the supreme embodiment of these doctrines and as the core of a musical canon.[42] Having been declared autonomous and rendered independent of its earlier institutional connections, music 'subsequently flourished by being simultaneously perceived both as purely aesthetic object *and*

[37] Ibid. 192. Goehr's essay presents a most succinct and valuable account of the subject under discussion here, which owes much to it. For a brief résumé of theories of musical significance that prevailed during successive eras of post-medieval European history, see Dahlhaus, *Foundations of Music History*, ch. 2: 'The Significance of Art: Historical or Aesthetic?'

[38] Goehr, 'Writing Music History', 192.

[39] Ibid. n. 20.

[40] See Marion Guck, 'Rehabilitating the Incorrigible', in Anthony Pople (ed.), *Theory, Analysis and Meaning in Music* (Cambridge, 1994), 57–73.

[41] See Marion Guck, 'Analytical Fictions', *Music Theory Spectrum*, 16/2 (1994), 217–36.

[42] Pederson, 'A. B. Marx'; subsequent page references are given in the text.

as an available medium for furthering certain social projects. For example, just as music attained status as high art, music instruction and musical organizations were seized on to help consolidate a middle-class society by means of appreciating music for its own sake' (88). The idea of music's autonomy, absolute status, and aesthetic character came to be appropriated in the second quarter of the nineteenth century as a German—especially North German—property, and as both an instrumentality and a sign of North German seriousness, inwardness, and spirituality, and through that of the North German character and its superiority to French and Italian light-headedness. This is Sanna Pederson's central thesis. It calls into question the claim to appreciate music 'for its own sake', and by implication taints the conceptions of autonomy, absolute music, and the aesthetic with political-ideological projects that have little relevance for the evaluation or interpretation of music today.

The critical writing of A. B. Marx also had a more local political aim: that of establishing Berlin as a musical centre in competition with Leipzig. This suggests a local political motive for what has heretofore been presented as though it took place in an abstract, aesthetic space: the universalization and spiritualization of music. The idea of the musical work as both a historical and an aesthetic object is accordingly neither self-evident nor in the nature of things. It has a history; it was formed under certain circumstances; and it came to serve certain extra-musical ends. Music is here presented in its social, cultural, and political roles, not through exegesis of its interior but through a reading of its surroundings and connections.

But where does this leave the historian in presenting the history of the music? There is a risk that this discovery will be taken to render the conceptions of early Romantic philosophers and critics suspect, to invalidate the interpretation of music from *c*.1800 in terms of that conception, and to dismiss its constituent concepts from the vocabulary of concepts relevant to the interpretation of music today. If A. B. Marx appropriated a theme that had been articulated since the late eighteenth century in writings by the likes of Hoffman, Schlegel, Tieck, and Wackenroder, this does not mean that his motives are immanent in their conception. To claim that would be to commit the positivist-historicist fallacy of mistaking the origin of a thing for its nature. What this research exemplifies is the historiographic principle that in historical understanding, music evolves from the moment of its creation to the historian's present. If the idea of the autonomy of symphonic music served German nationalist self-interest and mythology, that does not render the idea false, or taint the music, or render the study of the music in the aspect of its autonomy invalid. The idea of aesthetic autonomy is not *inherently* tied to political thought of a particular kind—nineteenth-century German thought about an 'aesthetic state',[43] even though it was appropriated

---

[43] I have borrowed this phrase from the title of Josef Chytry's book *The Aesthetic State: A Quest in Modern German Thought* (Berkeley, 1989). I quote from Lydia Goehr's review: 'The quest for the aesthetic state reflects humanity's

for a programme of political action in the musical arena. But then what? The author says nothing, and in saying nothing seems to offer us simply an exposé for *its* own sake.[44]

As long ago as 1982, W. J. T. Mitchell wrote, in his introduction to the important anthology *The Politics of Interpretation*, of 'a number of questions which are frequently begged when the issue of a politics of interpretation is raised. The first of these is: so what? What follows from the discovery that an interpretive practice is politically loaded? What effect does the demonstration that an interpretive procedure is not innocent have on its claims to truth? . . . There is considerably more to the politics of interpretation than the negative moment of unveiling concealed ideology.'[45] That should be the beginning, not the end, of discussion.

There is an implicit link between the research of Pederson and the historiographic position of Tomlinson. The concepts that Tomlinson wants excluded from the foundations of historical interpretation are the very ones whose authenticity is challenged by Pederson's research.

Perhaps there are in this material complex the makings of a fuller historical understanding that might serve as one kind of model, addressing the following topics: the formation of the music concept of the early Romantics; the social, cultural, and political factors in its formation; the musical properties to which their conception responded, apprehended through the descriptive (analytical) modes of their time and ours; the ideological meanings that attached to their music concept; the reception of those meanings by scholars today and the significance

desire to achieve a polis or a community that is morally, politically, and spiritually harmonious.' And, contrary to the suggestion that aesthetic ideas derive their force from their service to a political goal, it is the 'unity, beauty, and harmony of works of art, the ability on the part of artists/geniuses to transcend mundane reality', among other factors, that 'turn out to provide the models crucial to the formation of the political concepts of freedom, community, revolution, and judgment' (*Journal of Aesthetics and Art Criticism*, 50 (1992), 261). I am grateful to Professor Goehr for pointing out the relevance of this book to me. Important as Pederson's demonstration of the historicality of the concepts of autonomy and the aesthetic in nineteenth-century Germany is, it tells us nothing about the historicality of those concepts at their inception in the eighteenth century. For that the reader is referred to Martha Woodmansee, *The Author, Art, and the Market* (New York, 1994). There the interpretation is placed on far more material grounds, and is far less preoccupied with ideology, which, after all, always has something of an idealist bias. See also Gene H. Bell-Villada, *Art for Art's Sake and Literary Life: How Politics and Markets Helped Shape the Ideology and Culture of Aestheticism 1790–1990* (Lincoln, Nebr., 1996).

[44] In an earlier paper, 'On the Task of the Music Historian: The Myth of the Symphony after Beethoven', *repercussions*, 2 (1993), 5–30, Pederson also addresses the relation between aesthetics and politics in critical-historical writing in the nineteenth and twentieth centuries. Here she extends the linkages among the theme of German nationalism, the German symphony with the Beethoven symphonies as models, and the idea of autonomy to the idea of the masculine, and thence to the chain of dualities which that implies (most explicit here is the duality of 'civilization', a superficiality associated with the French, and *Kultur*, which is German). The clearest statement of a conclusion here is the following: 'Historians can refuse to let their histories perform their former function in relation to identity and instead make us recognize how complex our idea of history has become.' She rejects Carl Dahlhaus's exemption of music history from such distrust, and rightly so. But this essay, too, ends with a hovering implication that as long as we operate our music history and music criticism with aesthetic concepts that we inherit from the Romantics ('modernism'), we will continue to celebrate German national unity. That charge would have to be substantiated, not just levelled.

[45] W. J. T. Mitchell, *The Politics of Interpretation* (Chicago, 1982), 1–7.

of the ideological tensions that we have seen between the two eras. Above all, a fuller historical understanding would assimilate the categories of the musical and the extra-musical that were created with the theorizing of the early nineteenth century, which have repeatedly been set apart from one another since—most recently by the New Musicology.

In reviews of New Musicological writings, and in introductions of such writings themselves, it has become almost ritually binding to explain that such writing has been made possible by the release of music study from two formerly controlling strategies of thought, formalism and positivism. These, too, must be understood in view of their own histories and the histories of their influence on music studies. In the absence of such a historical presentation, they have been misleadingly characterized for the musicological public, and in consequence the nature of their influence on historical interpretation has not been well understood.

The influence of positivism on music historiography has come principally through its identification of causal knowledge as the exclusive mode of objective, corrigible (either right or wrong) knowledge, the only kind of knowledge worth having from a positivist point of view. That has had a bearing on music historiography in two ways: on the determinist and linear-diachronic emphases of scientific music history (schools, styles, and genres of composition linked through chronologically paced chains of implicit causal relations) and on the rules for relating 'Evidence and Explanation'[46] (the historian's conclusions are essentially presented as theories about the causes that were operative in bringing the evidence into being—they are steps in a process of causal explanation[47]).

However, since the publication of Joseph Kerman's *Contemplating Music*, a watered-down notion of positivism has gone into the label 'positivistic musicology', applied to that branch of musicological activity that entails 'the presentation of the texts of early music and of facts and figures about it',[48] a branch that claimed the greatest attention of musicologists because of its claim to the certainty that positivism is said to demand. It is only with the demise of positivism, so goes this line of diagnostic thought, that musicologists have been freed for the work of interpretation that was precluded under its dominion. But this is a misleading description of the relations among the activities of editing and interpreting and the concepts of positivism and factuality. Editing the music of other cultures—whether earlier Western or non-Western cultures—is potentially one of the most risky interpretive acts the musicologist can perform—as much so as

---

[46] This is the title of a famous essay by Arthur Mendel, published in *International Musicological Society Report of the Eighth Congress, New York 1961* (Kassel, 1962), 3–18.

[47] See the discussion of this problem in my essay 'On Historical Criticism', in *Music and the Historical Imagination*, 82–92.

[48] Joseph Kerman, *Contemplating Music* (Cambridge, Mass., 1985), esp. ch. 2: 'Musicology and Positivism: The Postwar Years'; quotation from p. 42.

any performance if it is not done mindlessly.[49] The degree of certainty that it allows can be extremely limited. As for factuality, it is always good to recall the etymological root of the word 'fact': the Latin *factum*, 'made', as opposed to *datum*, 'given', or simply gathered.[50] The interpretive aspect of the establishing of facts loses its prominence only at the lowest level of factuality.

On another front, positivism has been influential in the field to which the interpretation of musical works from the inside has been consigned by default under both modern and now postmodern paradigms of music history, the field of music theory. It was, as I have already suggested, only with the recasting of formalism in the middle of this century according to positivist standards for music-analytical language and reasoning that it became separated from its former symbiotic relationship with transcendentalism. But that has been a matter of hardly more than a generation, so to cast formalism as an entrenched obstructive force *vis-à-vis* interpretation that is now stepping out of the way is to mislead at both ends of the chronology.

The task now, as is being widely acknowledged, is to re-historicize music, to return it to the world of signification wherein we can plumb its meaning. To this task the quarrel with positivism and formalism, which threatens to throw the baby out with the bathwater, is largely irrelevant; for they do not bear all the responsibility for the neglect of interpretation. And the concepts of autonomy and of the aesthetic are not hostile, but are, rather, necessary to interpretation of any depth beyond that of superficial impression. They do not stand as obstacles to the development of the social and cultural meanings of music, but as the means to assure interpretations that are rich and have depth. That is, present needs call for a realignment: the re-aestheticization as well as the re-historicization of music. No dogma, old or new, should be allowed to oppose their union.

---

[49] See my review essay on Kerman's book, 'The Power of Positivist Thinking', *Journal of the American Musicological Society*, 42 (1989), 375–402.

[50] See my *Fact and Value in Contemporary Musical Scholarship* (Boulder, Colo., 1986), 30–4.

# 17

# Reception Theories, Canonic Discourses, and Musical Value

## Mark Everist

The study of music has always been rooted in the study of history, and music history balances precariously between an account of musical compositions and an account of musical cultures.[1] In the 1970s and 1980s, an enthusiasm for histories based on musical compositions, coupled with a leaning towards formalist analytical procedures, had the effect of dissolving the history of music into a series of more or less unrelated critical readings. Despite this popularity, the hegemony of text-based, formalist criticism is now as much under threat from a study of history as were such procedures in literary scholarship in the late 1970s.[2] An alternative to formalist criticism need not be an old-style literary or musical history that chronicles canonic genres and composers with household names. Nor need it trade in historiographical constructs and value-judgements based on criteria that are never made explicit. A return to history could be marked by a discourse in which canonic boundaries are transcended, in which musical cultures are seen as important as musical works, and in which the subjects of history could be allowed to speak a language that it is the historian's task to translate.[3] A critical history such as this would address questions of canon, value, and reception. In this chapter I will argue that texts and docu-

[1] In literary studies these two tendencies are identified as intrinsic and extrinsic approaches to the writing of history. See Lee Patterson, 'Literary History', in Frank Lentriccia and Thomas McLaughlin (eds.), *Critical Terms for Literary Study* (Chicago, 1990), 250; and for a consideration of histories of music from a similar perspective, Mark Everist, 'The Miller's Mule: Writing the History of Medieval Music', *Music & Letters*, 74 (1993), 44–53.

[2] Such challenges come from a variety of directions, and take various forms. The historicization of key theorists has challenged the validity of certain analytical procedures as teaching tools for the twenty-first century. Awareness of the challenges to formalism in literature and a growing distrust in the value of scientific claims have led to a general dissatisfaction with the productivity of formalist procedures (see two of the three papers that constituted the round table 'Análisis musical: modelos sistemáticos versus modelos históricos' at the 1992 meeting of the International Musicological Society: Laurence Dreyfus, 'Musical Analysis and the Historical Imperative', and Nicholas Cook, 'Heinrich Schenker, Anti-Historicist', *Revista de Musicología*, 16 (1993), 11–23, 24–36 resp. The organicist (and historicized) background of many analytical procedures was identified nearly two decades ago; see Ruth Solie, 'The Living Work: Organicism and Musical Analysis', *19th-Century Music*, 4 (1980), 147–56.

[3] The clearest statement of such a procedure is Clifford Geertz, 'Art as Cultural System', *Modern Language Notes*, 91 (1976), 1473–99. Margaret Bent specifically evokes the idea of translation as a way of engaging with the past in 'Editing Early Music: The Dilemma of Translation', *Early Music*, 22 (1994), 373–93.

ments which articulate the reception of a work are similar—in many cases identical—to those that are responsible for imparting value to the work, and hence for its inclusion in, or exclusion from, the canon. This argument will be supported by an examination of a theory of reception, considerations of canon, and the identification of points at which the two interact.

## Theories of Reception

Theories of reception move historical enquiry away from questions of production and composition and towards issues related to response, audience, and what Carl Dahlhaus, following Walter Benjamin, called the 'after-life' of musical works.[4] Reception *history* is often invoked in the study of music, and the German *Rezeptionsgeschichte* is frequently allowed to stand in its place. This much abused term, in music at least, signifies performance history, 'critical reception'—which usually means the study of journalism—and scholarly or theoretical responses to music. Such reception histories are concerned with the reconstruction of a record; the idea of an account of, for example, *Don Giovanni* or the 'Eroica' Symphony that describes the various stages of the work's reception is a familiar one. As will be seen, however, such a critical practice may not develop the full potential of the surviving documents.[5]

Theories of reception embrace not only what is familiar as reception history, but also more traditional questions of influence, and perhaps such better-known subdisciplines as reader-response criticism and affective stylistics.[6] These involve more than just a chronicle, and prompt the consideration of questions of value and evaluation. One important preliminary distinction needs to be made: between 'effect' and 'reception'. It is impossible to avoid the German terms for these two words, especially given the inadequacy of their translations. In reception theory, *Wirkung* (effect) focuses on the textual and musical aspects of the

[4] Carl Dahlhaus, *Grundlagen der Musikgeschichte*, Musiktaschenbücher: Theoretica, 13 (Cologne, 1977), trans. J. R. Robinson as *Foundations of Music History* (Cambridge, 1983), 155; page numbers refer to English trans. The reference to Benjamin is to 'The Task of the Translator', *Walter Benjamin: Illuminations*, ed. Hannah Arendt, trans. Harry Zohn (New York, 1968), 71.

[5] The literature on *Don Giovanni* and the 'Eroica' Symphony is vast. For recent work on the former, see Sabine Henze-Döhring, 'E. T. A. Hoffmann-"Kult" und "Don Giovanni"-Rezeption im Paris des 19. Jahrhunderts: Castil-Blazes "Don Juan" im Théâtre de l'Académie Royale de Musique am 10 März 1834', in *Mozart-Jahrbuch 1984/5 des Zentralinstituts für Mozartforschung der Internationalen Stiftung Mozarteum Salzburg* (Kassel, 1986), 39–51; Karin Werner-Jensen, *Studien zur 'Don Giovanni' Rezeption im 19. Jahrhundert (1800–1850)*, Frankfurter Beiträge zur Musikwissenschaft, 8 (Tützing, 1980); Katharine Ellis, 'Rewriting *Don Giovanni*, or 'The Thieving Magpies" ', *Journal of the Royal Musical Association*, 119 (1994), 212–50. For the latter, see Scott Burnham, 'On the Programmatic Reception of Beethoven's *Eroica* Symphony', *Beethoven Forum*, 1 (1992), 1–24; Thomas Sipe, 'Interpreting Beethoven: History, Aesthetics and Critical Reception' (Ph.D. diss., University of Pennsylvania, 1992).

[6] Two useful overviews of the wide range of activity that has been subsumed under the rubric of 'reception theory' are Susan R. Suleiman, 'Introduction: Varieties of Audience-Oriented Criticism', in *The Reader in the Text: Essays on Audience and Interpretation* (Princeton, 1980), 3–45, and Robert C. Holub, *Reception Theory: A Critical Introduction* (London, 1984), 53–146.

process, while *Rezeption* (reception) addresses the reader—in the broadest sense, the recipient of the text.[7]

In literary criticism, distinctions between *Wirkung* and *Rezeption* are sometimes hard to make. However, the nature of the musical enterprise polarizes these differences in a way that clarifies them attractively. As part of a study of the history of *Don Giovanni* in the nineteenth century, we might consider within the domain of *Rezeption* the various records of the work left by E. T. A. Hoffmann, Berlioz, Beethoven, Chopin, Schumann, Kierkegaard, Gounod—and just about the rest of the musically literate world.[8] If we were to consider questions of *Wirkung* or effect, on the other hand, we might be interested in the state of the work, the language of its libretto, its relationship to Mozart's Prague and Vienna versions of the opera, and how the narrative portions of the work were preserved—as *secco* recitative, accompanied recitative, spoken dialogue. We might also be interested in the ways in which other pieces of music and literature became associated with the composition, and the effect that such associations might have had on the dramatic structure of the opera. Not only can we begin to distinguish between *Wirkung* and *Rezeption*, but we may also start to see how the two ways of thinking might interact. The following questions could usefully be considered in this context: What exactly *was* the *Don Giovanni* known to Berlioz and Gounod when they wrote their accounts of the work? Was the Mozart that they knew the same as ours, or the same as Mozart's? How should this affect the way we evaluate their readings of the work? Analysis of the interrelation between *Wirkung* and *Rezeption* is a powerful tool when used to answer these questions, and in the presentation of a history of music that gives space to questions of reception.

Despite a highly respectable pedigree, reception theory seems to have little exposure in literary criticism as currently practised.[9] In a gauge of literary criticism in 1988—McLaughlin and Lentriccia's *Critical Terms for Literary Study*—there is no entry for reception, and the word appears only once in the index;

---

[7] The two terms are distinguished with great care by Holub, *Reception Theory*, pp. xi–xii. It is unfortunate that the two terms are left undistinguished in Robinson's translation of Dahlhaus, *Grundlagen der Musikgeschichte*: 'The relatively new fields of *Rezeptionsgeschichte* and *Wirkungsgeschichte* have not yet found their way into Anglo-American academic parlance, but as it is merely a matter of time before they do I have avoided circumlocution and written simply "reception history" for both' (*Foundations*, p. x). It is unclear from the German edition of Dahlhaus's book whether or not he would have accepted the distinction between *Wirkung* and *Rezeption* outlined by Holub and adopted here.

[8] Hans Engel, 'Mozart in der philosophischen und ästhetischen Literatur', *Mozart-Jahrbuch* (1953), 64–80; Erdmann Werner Böhm, 'Mozart in der schönen Literatur: Ergänzungen und Forsetzung', *Mozart-Jahrbuch* (1959), 165–87; Karl Gustav Fellerer, 'Zur Mozart-Kritik im 18./19. Jahrhunderts', *Mozart-Jahrbuch* (1959), 80–94; *idem*, 'Zur Rezeption von Mozarts Oper um die Wende des 18./19. Jahrhunderts', *Mozart-Jahrbuch* (1965–6), 39–49; Herbert Schneider, 'Probleme der Mozart-Rezeption im Frankreich der ersten Hälfte des 19. Jahrhunderts', *Mozart-Jahrbuch* (1980–3), 23–31; Erich Valentin, 'Mozart in der französischen Dichtung (zum 200. Geburtstag Stendhals)', *Acta Mozartiana*, 30 (1983), 71–4.

[9] Such approaches to scholarship are dismissed by some, however, as 'fashionable terms such as "intertextuality", "reception-theory" *and the rest*' (David Fallows, 'Howard Mayer Brown (1930–1993)', *Early Music*, 21 (1993), 507; emphasis added). While the unfashionable nature of reception theories is clear from the present chapter, intertextuality was identified as a characteristic as early as Northrop Frye, *Anatomy of Criticism: Four Essays* (Princeton, 1957; repr. 1990) by Catherine Belsey, *Critical Practice* (London, 1980; repr. 1991), 26. What 'the rest' refers to is unclear.

Jauss's name appears just twice, once wrongly in the context of reader-response criticism and once paired with that of Wolfgang Iser.[10] Fashionable in the late 1960s and 1970s, reception theories in literature—so closely linked to the idea of literary history—were nearly eclipsed in the 1980s. In music, on the other hand, studies of reception are popular. Even before the emergence of a theoretical position in literature, writings about the performance and criticism of music were common. Investigations of performance and response are plentiful today, especially where materials are extensive. In the study of the music of nineteenth-century France, for example, newspaper reports from the 1820s onwards challenge the information management of the best-organized scholar. The study of journalistic criticism has emerged as one of the most popular research paradigms in the study of reception in music in the last twenty years. Although much of it is highly sophisticated, in its most extreme form, this tendency can produce publications that do little except document and reprint newspaper criticism.[11] When we come to look more broadly at the sites of musical reception, we will see just how narrow this perspective really is.

If investigations of reception are popular in music, there may exist a correlative disinclination to consider the theoretical dimension of the subject. Such disinclination can take the form simply of omission: not a reluctance to countenance a theoretical framework, but a clear one-sidedness of approach that is the result of an inadequate or insufficiently reflective critical practice— examinations of music journalism are often cases in point. Occasionally, disinclination verges on outright hostility. The 1992 meeting of the American Musicological Society in Pittsburgh programmed a special session that claimed to assess the nature of 'the discipline of reception-history itself'.[12] The first of the speakers made plain his view that he (in fact he said *we*) had no need of *theories* of reception, whether they came from Hans Robert Jauss or from anyone else. This is akin to a session on historiography without mention of Hayden White, on influence without Bloom, on tonal theory without Schenker, or on *Formenlehre* without Riemann.

Despite the popularity of using documents of reception in music, it cannot be said that there have been no theoretical engagements with the subject.[13]

---

[10] Lentriccia and McLaughlin (eds.), *Critical Terms*, 67 and 220.

[11] Some of the most sophisticated work in reception that depends primarily on the press for its source material is Robert Bledsoe, 'Henry Fothergill Chorley and the Reception of Verdi's Early Operas in England', in Nicholas Temperley (ed.), *The Lost Chord: Essays on Victorian Music* (Bloomington, Ind., 1989), 119–42, and Jann Pasler, '*Pelléas* and Power: Forces behind the Reception of Debussy's Opera', *19th-Century Music*, 11 (1987–8), 147–77. An example of an attempt merely to reproduce newspaper criticism with minimal commentary is Marie-Hélène Coudroy, *La Critique parisienne des 'grands opéras' de Meyerbeer: Robert le diable, Les Huguenots, Le Prophète, L'Africaine*, Études sur l'Opéra français du xixe siècle, 2 (Saarbrucken, 1988).

[12] *Abstracts of Papers Read at the Fifty-Eighth Annual Meeting of the American Musicological Society 4–8 November 1992, Pittsburgh Pennsylvania*, ed. Laurence Dreyfus (Madison, 1992), 13.

[13] There is no entry for 'Reception' in *The New Grove Dictionary of Music and Musicians*, ed. Stanley Sadie (20 vols., London, 1980) or in *The New Grove Dictionary of Opera*, ed. Stanley Sadie (4 vols., London, 1992). There is, however, a succinct and useful entry by Patrick T. Will in *The Harvard Dictionary of Music*, 2nd edn., ed. Don Randel (Cambridge, Mass., 1986), 682. One awaits the arrival of *Die Musik in Geschichte und Gegenwart* at the letter 'R' with interest.

Dahlhaus devoted an entire chapter of his 1977 text *Fundamentals of Music History* to 'Problems in Reception History'; and an interesting debate sprang up *c.*1980 in the pages of the journal of the Berlin Institut für Musikforschung between Dahlhaus and Friedhelm Krummacher. (The principal point of disagreement between Krummacher and Dahlhaus is one to be developed at the end of this chapter.)[14] These contributions were characterized by a focus on theory. There is, however, little consideration of the work of the scholars' literary colleagues. Although specific examples are mentioned in passing, one gets little sense of the beginnings of a new historiography of music that seems to be implied by much of the discussion. Some may view this as a rather unsatisfactory state of affairs: on the one hand, examinations of large amounts of material related to reception in music—which are generally unsullied by theory—and on the other, weighty theoretical discussions that rarely impinge on specific musical and cultural phenomena, let alone the day-to-day practice of musicology. This has only begun to change in the last few years, and it is in that light that this chapter is written.

A fundamental point of contact between music history and reception theory is the early theoretical orientation of Hans Robert Jauss. It is important to distinguish between Jauss's work in 1967 and, for example, that of 1973 and later. Jauss's 1967 essay 'Literary History as a Challenge to Literary Theory' should serve as the starting-point for an understanding of Jauss's work;[15] and it is unfortunate that Dahlhaus, for example, should have started from the 1973 article on Racine and Goethe, in which we can already see the beginnings of Jauss's retreat from the central concept of the 1967 essay: the horizon of expectations (*Erwartungshorizont*).[16] Dahlhaus, it should be said, is not the only one to essentialize in this way.[17] The result is that it is quite possible for different readings of Jauss to yield conflicting or diametrically opposed opinions. For the purposes of this chapter, and in pursuit of an unshifting focus, it is Jauss's early work in reception theory that is under consideration.

---

[14] Dahlhaus, *Foundations*, 150–65; Friedhelm Krummacher, 'Rezeptionsgeschichte als Problem der Musikwissenschaft', *Jahrbuch des Staatlichen Instituts für Musikforschung Preußischer Kulturbesitz* (1979/80), 154–170; Dahlhaus, 'Zwischen Relativismus und Dogmatismus: Anmerkungen zur Rezeptionsgeschichte', *Jahrbuch des Staatlichen Instituts für Musikforschung Preußischer Kulturbesitz* (1981/2), 139–42.

[15] Hans Robert Jauss, 'Was heißt und zu welchem Ende studiert man Literaturgeschichte?', inaugural address at the celebration of the sixtieth birthday of Gerhard Hess (Rector of the University of Konstanz), University of Konstanz, 13 Apr. 1967; published as *Literaturgeschichte als Provokation der Literaturwissenschaft*, Konstanzer Universitätsreden, 3 (Konstanz, 1967; 2nd edn. 1969); repr. in *Literaturgeschichte als Provokation* (Frankfurt am Main, 1970), 144–208, and in Rainer Warning (ed.), *Rezeptionsästhetik*, Uni-Taschenbücher, 303 (Munich, 1975; 2nd edn. 1979), 126–62; partially translated (chs. 5–12) as 'Literary History as a Challenge to Literary Theory', *New Literary History*, 2 (1970–1), 7–37; retranslated in full under the same title by Timothy Bahti in *Toward an Aesthetic of Reception*, Theory and History of Literature, 2 (Minneapolis, 1982), 3–45.

[16] Jauss, 'Racines und Goethes Iphigenie—Mit einem Nachwort über die Partialität der Rezeptionsmethode', *Neue Hefte für Philosophie*, 4 (1973), 1–46; repr. in Warning (ed.), *Rezeptionsästhetik*, 353–400. Jauss's developing approach to the subject is outlined in Holub, *Reception Theory*, 53–81.

[17] See e.g. Sipe's starting-point in 'Interpreting Beethoven', 6; Hans Robert Jauss, 'The Poetic Text within the Change of Horizons of Reading: The Example of Baudelaire's "Spleen II" ', in *Toward an Aesthetic of Reception*, 139–85.

In the 1967 essay, Jauss adumbrates three principal ideas: (1) that history should stand at the heart of literary study; (2) that a theory of reception—embodied as the horizon of expectations—is at the heart of any thinking about literature; and (3) that the outcome of such a procedure is a new sort of literary history.[18] At this level, it is not difficult to see how one could substitute 'music' for 'literature', 'musical' for 'literary', and reach similar conclusions. Indeed, Jauss's starting-point has interesting analogies with the study of music in the last decade of the twentieth century. In his analysis of literary criticism in the late 1960s, he identifies two trends, which he characterizes—following convention—as Marxism and formalism. To reduce a very complex argument to manageable proportions, and to terms that have a certain musicological resonance, we could identify the two positions as, on the one hand, a broadly historical approach that the West German Jauss saw as threatened by Marxist blandishments, and, on the other, an analytical or formalist perspective. It is difficult to read Jauss's introductory comments without being struck by the similarity between his image of a Marxist–formalist division of the discipline and the historical musicology–theory and analysis division of music that so many rightly find pernicious.[19] Reading Jauss's essay through to its conclusion, the possibilities for music study grow in significance, and many of its central concerns, especially the horizon of expectations, become concepts without which sophisticated historical and cultural work in music becomes increasingly difficult.

The horizon of expectations is associated with the recipient of the cultural artefact. The term 'recipient' attractively avoids the specificity of 'audience', and opens up other equally important locations of reception. Jauss says:

The coherence of literature as an event is primarily mediated in the horizon of expectations of the literary experience of contemporary and later readers, critics, and authors. Whether it is possible to comprehend and represent the history of literature in its unique historicity depends on *whether this horizon of expectations can be objectified.*[20]

This may be taken as an invitation to examine the points of intersection of synchronic and a particular sort of diachronic history, and to treat each juncture as of equal epistemological importance. In other words, the horizon of expectations embodies the relationship between *Wirkung* and *Rezeption* alluded to above.

The beginning of the Finale of Sibelius's Fifth Symphony may serve as an example. This passage has elicited two competing interpretations. First, Donald Francis Tovey, writing in the second volume of his *Essays in Musical Analysis*, published in 1935:

The bustling introduction provides a rushing wind, through which Thor can enjoy swinging his hammer. While he swings it there are sounds of a cantabile trying to take form. Thor's hammer swings us into C. . . .

---

[18] Jauss, 'Literary History as a Challenge to Literary Theory', 18–19.

[19] Although identifying both approaches as positivist, Joseph Kerman accepts without question that the two 'disciplines' are separate (and treats them separately), in a manner that itself, in its acknowledgement of two separate spheres of activity, might be seen as positivist (*Musicology*, Fontana Masterguides (London, 1985), 31–59).

[20] Jauss, 'Literary History as a Challenge to Literary Theory', 22; emphasis added.

In due course we reach the key of G flat. In this dark region the whole process . . . is resumed, but pianissimo. And so we eventually come to E flat, where, without change of tempo, Thor swings his hammer in 3/2 time, the cantabile attains full form and glory, and the symphony ends with the finality of a work that knew from the outset exactly when its last note was due.[21]

This can be compared with an entry in Sibelius's diary for 21 April 1915, eight months before the work's première on the composer's fiftieth birthday, but more than six months after the original conception of the music:

Today at ten to eleven I saw 16 swans. One of my greatest experiences. . . . They circled over me for a long time. Disappeared into the solar haze like a gleaming silver ribbon. . . . Nature mysticism and life's *Angst!* The fifth symphony's finale-theme [which he quotes] . . . ![22]

Three days later, Sibelius continued:

The swans are always in my thoughts and give splendour to my life. . . . Nothing in the whole world affects me—nothing in art, literature, or music—in the same way as do these swans and cranes and wild geese.[23]

These two reactions to the same music evoke very different images. Tovey evokes the strength of Wodin's oldest son, the strongest of gods and men, in an interpretation characterized by myth, physical power, violence—even murder—, triumph, and glory. He evokes figures from Norse mythology that are curiously at odds with those who populate the legends of the composer's own country, Finland. Sibelius, by contrast, calls forth nature, autobiography, and specific musical reference encased in a series of self-reflective observations.

To interrogate the *Wirkung*, or effect, of this symphony is to observe that the composer's own response takes place within the context of compositional endeavour. By the middle of 1915, the Fifth Symphony, as Hepokoski points out, 'appears to have been little more than two or three scattered tables of potential themes that still needed weeding, developing, and binding together'.[24] Tovey, by contrast, responds to a work that has gone through three completed versions, publication, and a range of European premières; Tovey himself had conducted the Scottish première.[25] It could be said that Sibelius was responding to a highly unstable text, whereas Tovey could rely on a performed, published version. Although by the 1930s, the Fifth Symphony had achieved a certain international status, critics' wishing to comment more widely on Sibelius's music faced

---

[21] Donald Francis Tovey, *Essays in Musical Analysis*, Vol. 2: *Symphonies (II), Variations and Orchestral Polyphony* (London, 1935), 128–9. A discussion of the organicist implications of the last sentence of this quotation is outside the scope of this chapter, but this is one respect in which Tovey could be admitted to the discussion of the organicism implicit in the work of Réti and Schenker (Solie, 'Living Work').

[22] James Hepokoski, *Sibelius: Symphony No. 5*, Cambridge Music Handbooks (Cambridge, 1993), 36.

[23] Ibid.

[24] Ibid. 41.

[25] Mary Grierson, *Donald Francis Tovey: A Biography Based on Letters* (London, 1952), 298.

technical problems in acquainting themselves with his scores. The effect that this had on critics' views of Sibelius's music is difficult to judge. Cecil Gray reports as follows:

Not only are performances of Sibelius' more important works exceedingly rare . . . but miniature scores of them—up to the time of writing [some time before Gray's publication date of 1931]—amount to no more than two in number, the Fifth Symphony and the String Quartet (*Voces Intimae*), Op. 56. It is, moreover, impossible to procure full scores of his other large works, or even the inevitably inadequate pianoforte arrangements of them at any musical circulating library or public institution. Even the music section of the British Museum Reading-Room possesses only the first three symphonies and a handful of miscellaneous works forming a selection so utterly unrepresentative and arbitrary that it is only charitable to suppose that they were chosen completely at random.[26]

The condition and accessibility of the composition, then, are equally important elements in its *Wirkung* or effect.

Issues of reception also pose wider questions. This example enables us both to anchor the Sibelius interpretation closely to the compositional process and to focus on the position of Sibelius in Great Britain in the 1930s. In acknowledging the importance of Sibelius, by including essays on two of the symphonies in his series, Tovey was typical of his time; he saw Sibelius as a popular composer—a composer described by Gray as a household name.[27] But Gray differed from Tovey in also observing that Sibelius's reputation depended almost exclusively on two works:

*Finlandia* is in the repertoire of every orchestra and brass band, and *Valse Triste* is to be heard in every picture-palace, restaurant, café, tea-shop, and cabaret in the civilised world, from San Francisco to Cairo, and from Stockholm to Cape Town. At the same time . . . the great mass of his work . . . has been . . . consistently and steadily ignored . . . by every section of the musical community . . . in every country in the world, apart from Finland.[28]

What we are witnessing in the accounts by Gray and Tovey is an important point in the reception of Sibelius, an emphasis that attempted subtly to shift his significance from that of a merely popular composer to that of a composer of stature. It was Gray's stated task to introduce his readers to the symphonies and symphonic poems of Sibelius, whereas Tovey restricted his essays to two of the symphonies. Constant Lambert went as far as to compare the Fourth Symphony with Schoenberg's *Pierrot Lunaire*.[29] Indeed, the final section of his final chapter in *Music Ho!* is called 'Sibelius and the Music of the Future'.[30] But the backlash was not far away. As early as 1939, a report in the *Musical Times* suggested that

---

[26] Cecil Gray, *Sibelius* (London, 1931), 9–10.
[27] Ibid. 7.
[28] Ibid.
[29] Constant Lambert, *Music Ho!: A Study of Music in Decline* (London, 1934), 323.
[30] Ibid. 326–32.

'a scholarly counterblast [against uncritical views of the composer] is badly needed in the case of Sibelius.'[31]

## Canonic Discourses

The comparison of these two responses to an identical passage suggests a distinction between *Wirkung* and *Rezeption*. It also shows how, as the discussion of reception opened up and began effectively to 'objectify the Horizon of Expectations', questions arose of the composer's standing—in short, of Sibelius's position in the canon. In contrast to theories of reception, issues relating to canon have been at the centre of literary scholarship for at least twenty years. Questions of canon have stood behind some of the most public literary disagreements in the United States; the so-called Great Books debate[32] and the reform of the Standford curriculum are just two well-known examples.[33] Even in Britain, issues surrounding the teaching of English literature in the National Curriculum have their basis in a critique of the canon.[34] Music study, however, has been less than willing to engage with some of these important questions; indeed, it is easy to detect a clear resistance even to acknowledging the term 'canon' itself. In a review recently published in a musicological journal is a disapproving statement to the effect that the 'modish' term 'canon' is a poor alternative to 'classic'.[35] While such a view might have been congenial to Sainte-Beuve or T. S.

[31]  Robert Lorenz, 'Afterthoughts on the Sibelius Festival', *Musical Times*, 79 (1939), 13–14; cited in Harold E. Johnson, *Sibelius* (London, 1959), 181.

[32]  This debate has kept recurring during the twentieth century. The most recent catalyst has been Allan Bloom, *The Closing of the American Mind: How Higher Education has Failed Democracy and Improverished the Souls of Today's Students* (New York, 1987). For a useful, although poorly documented, history of the debate, see William Casement, 'Some Myths about the Great Books', *Midwest Quarterly: A Journal of Contemporary Thought*, 36 (1995), 203–18. For two liberal critiques of the issue, from different perspectives, see Dinesh d'Souza, 'Multiculturalism 101: Great Books of the Nonwestern World', *Policy Review*, 56 (1991), 22–30, and Eugene Garfield, 'A Different Sort of Great Books List: The 50 20th-Century Works most Cited in the Arts-and-Humanities-Citation-Index, 1976–1983', *Current Contents*, 16 (1987), 3–7. Liberal and feminist critics do not all advocate a critique of the Great Books; see Elizabeth Fox-Genovese, 'The Claims of a Common Culture: Gender, Race, Class and the Canon', *Salmagundi*, 72 (1986), 131–43; Richard Rorty, 'That Old-Time Philosophy', *New Republic*, 198 (4 Apr. 1988), 28–33.

[33]  Stanford University's reform of its Western culture course in 1988 and 1989 attempted an opening of this particular canonic discourse. Responses from various members of the university were strikingly public. See Mary Louise Pratt, 'Humanities for the Future: Reflections on the Western Culture Debate', *South Atlantic Quarterly*, 89 (1990), 7–25; Sidney Hook, 'Is Teaching Western Culture Racist or Sexist?: Letter from Stanford', *Encounter*, 73 (1989), 14–19. Documents relating to the affair by Sidney Hook and Bill King (chair, Black Students' Union, Stanford University) were published in *Partisan Review*, 55 (1988), 653–74. Writers on music also contributed to the debate: Herbert Lindenberger, 'On the Sacrality of Reading Lists: The Western Culture Debate at Stanford University', *Comparative Criticism*, 11 (Summer 1989), 4–11; William Mahrt, 'Course Focus on Classical Antiquity is Key to Intellectual Heritage', *Campus Report* (Stanford University), 24 Feb. 1988, 13–14. Responses from Europe are Christopher Hitchens, 'Whose Culture, Whose Civilisation?', *Times Literary Supplement*, 4431 (1988), 246, and Pierre Bouretz, 'Tempête sur un campus', *Esprit*, 2 (1989), 130–2.

[34]  The literature on the place of English in the National Curriculum is extensive. For two contrasting views see Martin Dodsworth, 'The Undermining of English: How the National Curriculum Threatens Literature Teaching', *Times Literary Supplement*, 4586 (1991), 11; Argi Bhattacharyya, 'Cultural Education in Britain: From the Newbolt Report to the National Curriculum', *Oxford Literary Review*, 13 (1991), 4–19.

[35]  Nicholas Temperley, review of Samuel Sebastian Wesley, *Anthems I*, ed. Peter Horton, Musica Britannica, 57 (London, 1990) and Maurice Greene, *Ode on St Cecilia's Day and Anthem: Hearken unto me, ye holy children*, ed.

Eliot, it hardly does justice to the wide range of commentary on the canon of literature in English and other modern languages that occupies some of sharpest scholarly minds in the Northern Hemisphere.[36]

The only definitions of 'canon' given in *The New Grove Dictionary of Music and Musicians* concern contrapuntal techniques, which are not what is at issue here.[37] Two other definitions take us in different directions. The term has been used in the last five years to describe the paradigms of musicological study, and this is the sense in which it is used in the recent collection of essays entitled *Disciplining Music*.[38] The conference session in which the idea behind that book was formulated was called 'Musicology and its Canons'.[39] Despite this emphasis on methodology and ideological orientation, many of the contributions drift into a different understanding of canon: the one at issue here. This was thoughtfully articulated by Joseph Kerman when he called the canon 'in other arts . . . an enduring exemplary collection of books, buildings, and paintings authorised in some way for contemplation, admiration, interpretation, and determination of value'.[40]

Although there are points with which one could take issue in Kerman's definition of canon in the other arts, as a working description which embodies a number of key concepts—value, exemplification, authority, and a sense of temporal continuity—it would be very useful. One has to say 'would be' because Kerman immediately goes on to say that in music we do not speak of canon but of repertory; and much of what he has to say in the same article consists of developing the distinction between canon and repertory.[41] He asserts that 'A canon is an idea; a repertory is a program of action', and goes on to suggest that 'Repertories are determined by performers, canons, by critics'.[42] This curious formulation assigns a more important role to the critic and a less important role to the performer than each seems to deserve. Even the example of Tovey and Sibelius shows how performance and criticism can be embodied in the same individual, and a move back a further century to consider the careers of

---

H. Diack Johnstone, *Musica Britannica*, 58 (London, 1991), *Journal of the Royal Musical Association*, 117 (1992), 304. The comment comes in the context of approval of a comment by Vincent Duckles that '[Englishmen] have never ceased to regard music as a realm of concrete experience, not a field for philosophical speculation ('Musicology', *Music in Britain: The Romantic Age 1800–1914*, ed. Nicholas Temperley, The Athlone History of Music in Britain, 5 (London, 1981), 483–502)'. Temperley continues: 'May it long remain so, Schenker and Barthes notwithstanding (*ibidem*).'

[36] Charles-Augustin Sainte-Beuve, 'Qu'est-ce qu'un classique', in *Causeries de Lundi* (16 vols., Paris, 1849–60), iii. 38–55; T. S. Eliot, 'What is a Classic?', Presidential address to the Virgil Society, 1944 (London, 1945); repr. in Frank Kermode (ed.), *Selected Prose of T. S. Eliot* (London, 1975; repr. 1987), 115–31 (page numbers refer to 1987 reprint).

[37] Alfred Mann and J. Kenneth Wilson, 'Canon (I)', in *New Grove*, iii. 689–93. The same is true of Julian Budden and Stanley Sadie, 'Canon', in *New Grove Dictionary of Opera*, i. 715.

[38] Katherine Bergeron and Philip V. Bohlman (eds.), *Disciplining Music: Musicology and its Canons* (Chicago, 1992).

[39] *AMS/CBMR/CMS, New Orleans, October 15–18 1987: Abstracts* (1987), 17–20.

[40] Joseph Kerman, 'A Few Canonic Variations', *Critical Inquiry*, 10 (1983), 107; repr. in Robert van Hallberg (ed.) *Canons* (Chicago, 1984); page numbers refer to the 1983 original.

[41] Ibid.                    [42] Ibid. 114.

Schumann and Berlioz suggests even more strongly that Kerman's distinction is open to challenge.[43] By contrast, his description of canon in what he calls 'the other arts' has much to recommend it. Both performative and critical impulses play a role in determining the canon in drama, art history (exhibitions), and literature (reading lists), as well as in music. Claiming that one discipline or field is in some way above the canonic restraints of its fellows is disingenuous, and may be seen as an attempt to fend off what might evolve into attacks on canonic works.

In this, Kerman has much in common with his slightly younger German contemporary, Dahlhaus, who also makes a bipartite distinction within the canon. But the latter distinguishes between a canon that is *chosen* and a canon that is *chosen from*. His claim is that 'It is this primary, pre-existent canon rather than the secondary, subjective one that represents a premise of music historiography'.[44] We might want to replace 'music historiography' with 'musical scholarship', since it is not just the writing of music history but any musicological endeavour that must take the canon as its premiss. Dahlhaus's distinction remains misleading, however. There can be no objection to the idea that individuals or institutions develop canons that are subsets of a larger one. However, Dahlhaus's intention is to make a much more significant—and doubtful—claim: that there is a difference between aesthetic standing and historical significance in the canon that is *chosen from*, and that this difference may be an indication of the value of individual works.[45] Coming to terms with Dahlhaus's approach to the canon is difficult. The sections on canon in his *Foundations of Music History* are shot through with contradictions, which suggests that parts were written at different times and for different purposes. More important, however, is that Dahlhaus never abandons the objectivist premiss that a musical work can have aesthetic standing that is independent of its historical circumstances.[46] It could convincingly be argued that this is related to Dahlhaus's defence of the Austro-German canon: a narrow segment of musical culture from Schütz to Schoenberg that not only conditions Dahlhaus's view of canon, but lies behind much of his resistance to reception theory.[47]

Both Kerman's and Dahlhaus's models of the canon are problematic; but both acknowledge, as least in passing, the existence of several interrelated canons: for Kerman, the idea of 'canon' and 'repertory', for Dahlhaus 'the canon *chosen*' and 'the canon *chosen from*'. Modern critical practice is to speak of a multiplicity of 'canonic discourses' that allow us to consider the interrelation of a number of

[43]  See Leon Plantinga, *Schumann as Critic*, Yale Studies in the History of Music, 4 (New Haven, 1967; repr. New York, 1976); Kerry Murphy, *Hector Berlioz and the Development of French Music Criticism*, Studies in Musicology, 97 (Ann Arbor, 1988).

[44]  Dahlhaus, *Foundations*, 93.

[45]  Ibid. 95.

[46]  Dahlhaus's objectivist stance is discussed further below, 405–6.

[47]  This point is made conclusively in James Hepokoski, 'The Dahlhaus Project and its Extra-Musicological Sources', *19th-Century Music*, 14 (1991), 221–46.

canons that may stand in a variety of relationships to each other: set–subset, set–interset, and so on.[48] This concept of canonic discourse immediately removes many of the repressive properties to which those whom Gerald Graff called 'Canonbusters' so strongly object.[49] In turn, this frees up the opportunities for constructive critique of canonic discourses; and if the term 'canon' is occasionally used in this chapter for the purpose of comprehensibility, it is always with this multivalent sense of canonic discourse in mind. Such a concept immediately neutralizes many of the objections to a critique of canon(ic discourses) raised both by Kerman and by Dahlhaus.

There are two principal critiques of canonic discourse: conservative and liberal. A conservative critic contemplates the canon, and views its contents as works that shape our culture, that have endured throughout history, and that have an appeal that transcends historical circumstances.[50] The conservative might happily speak of the *Kleinmeister*, and identify works that might have been popular in their time, but now—with the aid of our greater sensibilities and critical awareness—can be judged as being of less value than canonical works. A liberal critique accuses the canon of having an authoritarian and even coercive status, and 'Canonbusters' advocate either the inclusion of a wider range of material, in the process known as 'Opening up the Canon', or the establishment of alternative canons.[51] In Western European serious music and opera, this is today most clearly associated with works by women composers, and Marcia Citron's *Gender and the Musical Canon* is a recent case in point; but in literature this perceived hegemony is also challenged by both race and class.[52]

Both critiques of the canon are severely problematic. The conservative critique is the easier of the two to deal, with, and possibly the less contentious. Its fundamental claim—that canonic works exhibit values that are transcendental and objectively demonstrable—is open to challenge.[53] The recent literature on Beethoven's symphonies, for example, shows that the values identified by Hoffmann in the C minor symphony and those imputed by von Bülow to the 'Eroica' at opposite ends of the nineteenth century promote very different views of these canonic works.[54] Even the history of twentieth-century performance practice is enough to suggest that a symphony by Beethoven under the baton of Richard

---

[48] Jan Gorak, *The Making of the Modern Canon: Genesis and Crisis of a Literary Idea* (London, 1991), p. x.

[49] Ibid. 6.

[50] John Guillory, 'Canon', in Lentriccia and McLaughlin (eds.), *Critical Terms*, 236–7.

[51] See the essays in Leslie A. Fiedler and Houston A. Baker (eds.), *English Literature: Opening Up the Canon—Selected Papers from the English Institute, 1979* (Baltimore, 1981).

[52] Marcia J. Citron, *Gender and the Musical Canon* (Cambridge, 1993). The welcome discussion of reception (165–89) is marred, however, by an over-reliance on (and in some cases a lack of sympathy with) Holub, *Reception Theory*, and some curious emphases. Claiming that Hans-Georg Gadamer was a colleague of Jauss at Konstanz is strange in the extreme, and the chapter retreats from a serious engagement with questions of reception theory after the first two pages. It is difficult to understand how Patricia Howard can describe this as 'contain[ing] the clearest exposition of reception theory I have ever read' (review of Citron, *Gender, Musical Times*, 150 (1994), 36).

[53] Guillory, 'Canon', 237.

[54] Hans von Bülow is reported as having said, on 28 May 1892, that if Beethoven had known Bismarck, the 'Eroica' would have been dedicated to him (Sipe, 'Interpreting Beethoven', 232 n. 54).

Strauss develops a rather different meaning from one under the direction of Roger Norrington.[55] If we could agree on what qualities we value in a symphony by Beethoven today, we would have to give our consent to the view that these qualities are different from those we perceive in earlier authors and performers. These are difficult points to refute, although the stranglehold that the conservative critique of the canon has on all aspects of our musical culture results in a reluctance to acknowledge the fact.

The liberal critique of the canon is an attractive development within an academic or pedagogical context, and one that has resulted in the teaching of courses on women in music; a heightened awareness of the possibility of gender criticism has perhaps been an even more important consequence.[56] The great problem with the liberal critique of the canon is that it suffers, ironically, from the same pitfalls as the conservative critique that it seeks to supplant. If one asks that certain works should now be admitted to the canon on the basis that they are as good as those already included, and have only been excluded because they are by women, Caribbean authors, or for indeed any other reason, this is as much as to say that objective value may be identified not only in the works for which admission to the canon is sought, but also in its existing members. And this objective value is exactly what is so problematic with the conservative critique of the canon.

Literary critics who have addressed questions of canon reach the conclusion that neither the liberal nor the conservative critiques of the canon are satisfactory. Both John Guillory and Jan Gorak also agree that, although the canon has the effect of freezing responses to texts inside it, it is essential for the reproduction of culture from generation to generation.[57] The consequences of such a view are interesting, and bring us back to questions of reception. Guillory writes:

An individual's judgment that a work is great does nothing in itself to preserve that work, unless that judgment is made in a certain institutional context, a setting in which it is possible to insure the *reproduction* of the work, its continual reintroduction to generations of readers. The work of preservation has other more complex social contexts than the immediate responses of readers to texts.[58]

We might just pause for a moment on Guillory's use of the term 'institution'. In literary studies, it is assumed that the academy is the location of canon formation and preservation. In music, as has already been suggested, this is

---

[55] The two performances have been recorded: Richard Strauss, Berlin State Opera Orchestra (Koch 37115-2, 1928); Roger Norrington, London Classical Players (EMI CDC7 49656-2, 1989).

[56] One further development in the criticism of music in the last thirty years has had a limited impact on the opening-up of the canon: the historically informed performance of music. With regard to music before 1700 or perhaps 1750, the performance of 'early music' has automatically involved the representation of music previously outside the canon. But in those performances of music after 1750 that use period instruments and playing techniques, the approach to canon is no less narrow than that of traditional approaches to performance.

[57] Guillory, 'Canon', 237; Gorak, *Making of the Modern Canon*, 8.

[58] Guillory, 'Canon', 237; emphasis original.

much less so, and it may not be the case in literature as much as the denizens of the academy would like to think. Broadening the concept of institution to concert-giving organizations, opera-houses, journals, critics, and record-producers gives Guillory's statement a resonance that, for music, is very hard to ignore.

If these comments are given any sort of historical dimension, they suggest that we invoke a theory of reception to play an important part in the analysis of these canon-forming institutions. Indeed, Guillory calls for something very similar when he says:

> Let us try . . . to reconstruct a *historical* picture of how literary works are produced, dis-seminated, reproduced, reread, and retaught over successive generations and eras. . . . In order to understand the historical circumstances determining the constitution of the lit-erary canon, then, we must see its history as the history of both the production and the reception of texts. We must understand that the history of literature is not only a ques-tion of *what* we read but of *who* reads and *who* writes. . . . We must be able to ask and answer all of these questions in order to arrive at a historical understanding of the con-stitution of the canon.[59]

These comments echo those made by Klaus Kropfinger in 1973 in a musicolog-ical response to the implications of the early work of Jauss, and they are in turn quoted with approval by Krummacher, although—as he has already said—the relationship between reception and canon is too often unacknowledged.[60]

## Reception Theories, Canons, and Musical Value

In one of the more liberal moments of his discussion of canon and value-judgement, Dahlhaus admits the analysis of the nature of the canon as a viable study—although he immediately reinforces his objectivist claim that this would not affect the validity of what he calls the 'aesthetic' canon.[61] This sits awk-wardly alongside Jauss's view as presented just before the first of his seven theses in the 1967 paper.

The merit of a literary history based on an aesthetics of reception will depend upon the extent to which it can take an active part in the ongoing totalization of the past through

---

[59] Ibid. 238; emphasis original. Both Kerman and Dahlhaus reluctantly approach Guillory's position: 'But, if nine-teenth-century music is to be approached on the same basis [as an interpretation of Gregorian chant in the context of Frankish culture], that is, in terms of its own culture and ideology, the force exerted by the idea of the canon must be recognised and so must the practice of analysis which was developed to validate it' (Kerman, 'A Few Canonic Vari-ations', 117); 'For a historian to "receive" a predetermined canon—which in no way excludes the possibility of his criticising that canon—means first of all that *he reconstruct "value-relations" which have qualified works for inclusion in our imaginary museum*' (Dahlhaus, *Foundations*, 97; emphasis added).

[60] Klaus Kropfinger, 'Probleme der musikalischen Rezeptionsforschung', *Neue Zeitschrift für Musik*, 135 (1974), 741–6; Krummacher, 'Rezeptionsgeschichte', 159.

[61] 'Yet music historians must make aesthetic distinctions in order to determine just what does or does not belong to history in the strong sense' (Dahlhaus, *Foundations*, 97).

aesthetic experience. This demands on the one hand—in opposition to the objectivism of positivist literary history—a conscious attempt at the formation of a canon, which, on the other hand—in opposition to the classicism of the study of traditions—presupposes a critical revision if not destruction of the received literary canon. The criterion for the formation of such a canon and the ever necessary retelling of literary history is clearly set out by the aesthetics of reception. The step from the history of the reception of the individual work to the history of literature has to lead to seeing and represent-ing the historical sequence of works as they determine and clarify the coherence of literature, to the extent that it is meaningful for us, as the prehistory of its present experience.[62]

Kerman also approaches the relationship between reception and canon. At the end of his 1983 essay he apologizes, saying that his comments are 'coming to an end at a point where many readers . . . would like to see them begin: *How* are canons determined, *why* and on *what* authority?'[63] Kerman's concluding remarks are a claim that we can only answer these questions when we have built up a serious criticism of music, of the sort advocated in his *Musicology*.[64] Few would want to agree with this, probably none of the other contributors to the special issue of *Critical Inquiry* devoted to canons in which Kerman's essay was published. In considering specific ways in which theories of reception and the canonic discourses in music interact, Kerman's questions, and his refusal to answer, are a valuable point of departure.

Guillory, Kropfinger, Dahlhaus, and Kerman state or imply that a theory of reception could play an important part in addressing questions of canon, but do not suggest how this might happen. The hints they give may be developed by uniting agencies of reception (Guillory's 'historical circumstances') with what Barbara Herrnstein Smith has called 'contingencies of value'.[65] That is to say, characteristics of a work's reception overlap substantially those characteristics that may impart value to the work. In response to a hypothetical conservative critique of canon, she writes:

What is commonly referred to as 'the test of time' . . . is not, as the figure implies, an impersonal and impartial mechanism; for the cultural institutions through which it oper-ates (schools, libraries, theaters, museums, publishing and printing houses, editorial boards, prize-awarding commissions, state censors, and so forth) are, of course, all managed by *persons* (who, by definition, are those with cultural power and commonly other forms of power as well); and, since the texts that are selected and preserved by 'time' will always tend to be those which 'fit' . . . *their* characteristic needs, interests, resources,

---

[62] Jauss, 'Literary History as a Challenge to Literary Theory', 20. There are points in Jauss's formation of this view that the present chapter does not encompass: the idea of the *destruction* of the canon and the concept of a serial history of literature or music.

[63] Kerman, 'A Few Canonic Variations', 124; emphasis original.

[64] Kerman, *Musicology*, 113–54.

[65] The title of an article, 'Contingencies of Value', *Critical Inquiry*, 10 (1983–4), 1–35; and a book, *Contingencies of Value: Alternative Perspectives for Critical Theory* (Cambridge, Mass., 1988), in which the article is reprinted, 17–53.

and purposes, that testing mechanism has its own built-in partialities accumulated in and thus *intensified* by time.[66]

This list of cultural institutions is necessarily incomplete, and an inventory of those that might affect the value of a musical work would be very different. A list, similar in scope to that offered by Herrnstein Smith for literature, might add critics, concert series, foundations promoting composers' works, or poems and novels with narratives centred on musical works or performers, and might subtract others. An example taken merely at random, that of musical foundations and societies, illustrates how the relationship between reception, canon, and value might work.

Societies exist today to promote the work of a single composer or particular types of musical activity. Two may be considered here. The Britten–Pears Foundation at Aldeburgh is an important factor in the reception of Britten's works, a crucial element in the constitution of the canon and Britten's place within it. Promotion of the cause of a single composer is an attempt to enlarge the composer's position in the canon. This may be by means of performance or recording, or of such more routine bibliographical functions as the collection of a composer's working papers for the purposes of scholarship.[67] The Paul Sacher Stiftung in Basle goes one step further in acquiring the working papers of active composers; Stockhausen, Berio, Carter, Birtwistle, and Boulez are examples.[68] This philanthropic exercise has the same effect as that of the Britten–Pears Foundation, except that canonic pressures are enhanced by promoting the works of living composers.

If this understanding of reception theory and canonic discourses seems straightforward, the relationship has a darker side. Previous accounts of musical reception have exhibited a narrow view of canon. Composers whose works have been subject to this sort of enquiry—Beethoven, Mozart, Handel, Bach, and Wagner—are already assured of canonic status. In the light of the claims made

[66] Ibid. 51; emphasis original. Although she does not cite the work, in this passage Herrnstein-Smith is offering a critique of the essentially objective standpoint in Anthony Savile, *The Test of Time: An Essay in Philosophical Aesthetics* (Oxford, 1982). She does, however, cite Leonard B. Meyer, *Music, the Arts and Ideas: Patterns and Predictions in Twentieth-Century Culture* (Chicago, 1967), 22–41 ('Some Remarks on Value and Greatness in Music') as 'a naive and ambitious claim for empirical aesthetics'. It will become clear to anyone familiar with Herrnstein Smith's work that her book is a significant source-text for this chapter, and that, although direct quotations are acknowledged in the usual manner, her thinking informs large parts of the ideological structure of this study.

[67] The Britten–Pears Foundation acts as an umbrella organization for Britten Estate Ltd., the commercial arm of the foundation, the Aldeburgh Festival, various competitions, the Britten–Pears School for Advanced Musical Study, and the Britten–Pears Library, and provides various subventions and grants for contemporary music and music education. Many of these activities do far more than promote the music of Britten, but such promotion is central to the activity of the Foundation. I am grateful to Paul Banks (Britten–Pears Library) for a very useful discussion of the activities of the Britten–Pears Foundation.

[68] Boulez and Berio gave their names to individual collections in the mid-1980s (*The Paul Sacher Foundation* (Basle, 1986), 23 and 25). The most recent acquisitions of the two composers are Berio's *Brin, Canticum novum testamenti*, and *Epiphanies* and documentary material relating to Boulez's career (*Mitteilungen der Paul Sacher Stiftung*, 7 (1994), 4). I am grateful to Drue Ferguson for discussing the function of the Sacher Foundation with me, and drawing the relevant literature to my attention. See also Lewis Foreman, 'Reputations . . . Bought or Made', *Musical Times*, 121 (1980), 27. I am grateful to Stephen Banfield for drawing this article to my attention.

in this chapter about the value of a theory of reception to the understanding of canonic discourse, such a state of affairs is a paradox. This relationship is subject, as are all that involve canonic discourses, to the strictures of the conservative and liberal critiques of the canon. To date, the conservative critique of the relationship between reception and canonic discourse has had the upper hand (as the list of subjects given above demonstrates). One awaits explanations of the reception of the music of Vanhal, Auber, and Malipiero.

The relationship between canonic discourses and reception may be refined further by trying to protect the distinction between *Wirkung* and *Rezeption*, because this can be of theoretical value here. *Wirkung* focuses on the textual and musical aspects of the process, whereas *Rezeption* addresses the recipient of the text. The link between agencies of reception and contingencies of value can be enlarged by arguing for a tripartite link between agencies of reception, contingencies of value, and locations of effect (*Wirkung*). These three elements often share the same site; similarly, that site invites excavation in three ways. With reception, effect, and value combined as the basis for a consideration of canon, a second example will be considered.

On 10 April 1784, Mozart wrote to his father, giving a report of a concert that had taken place on 1 April that year.[69] He said:

I composed two grand concertos and then a quintet, which called forth the greatest applause: I myself consider it the best work I have ever composed.[70] It is written for one oboe, one clarinet, one horn, one bassoon and the pianoforte. How I wish you could have heard it! And how beautifully it was performed! Well, to tell the truth I was really worn out in the end after playing so much—and it is greatly to my credit that my listeners never got tired.[71]

We could try to neutralize the importance we attach to this very interesting assessment by saying that Mozart would continue to compose for seven and half years, and he might not have thought quite so highly of the Quintet for Piano and Wind, K.452, in, say, 1788. Nevertheless, such statements as these are sufficiently rare for us to probe just a little further. When Mozart gave this assessment to his father, he was setting the quintet alongside, but presumably above, the two piano concertos that he played in the same concert, K.450 and K.451, and also at least the first three of the quartets that would be dedicated to Haydn the following year, those in G major, D minor and E flat major.[72]

This letter from Mozart to his father embodies a value-judgement about the work. That judgement has not been shared by all those who have considered this

---

[69] The concert had originally been programmed for 21 Mar. 1784, and the work was entered into Mozart's *Verzeichnis* on 30 Mar.

[70] The original German is: 'Ich selbst halte es für das beste was ich noch in meinem Leben geschrieben habe' (Wilhelm Bauer and Otto Erich Deutsch (eds.), *Mozart: Briefe und Aufzeichnungen: Gesamtausgabe* (7 vols., Kassel, 1962–75), iii. 309).

[71] Emily Anderson (ed. and trans.), *The Letters of Mozart and his Family* (London, 1985), 873.

[72] Of the six quartets dedicated to Haydn that were published by Artaria as Op. 10 on 1 Sept. 1785, K.387, K.421, and K.428 were complete by summer 1783.

piece between 1784 and the present. In twentieth-century criticism, the quintet has fared rather badly. In Hans Keller's notorious contribution to the influential *Mozart Companion*, the work is not mentioned at all, and it appears in the book elsewhere only as a footnote to Donald Mitchell's discussion of the C minor Serenade in his account of the works for wind ensemble.[73] The work receives two mentions in such more restricted treatments as Stanley Sadie's essay in *The New Grove Dictionary of Music and Musicians*;[74] these refer to the problematic nature of the genre, and mention (albeit in a low-key way) Mozart's view of the work. Other standard texts treat the work similarly.[75]

The reception of the Quintet for Piano and Wind since 1945 is dominated by considerations of genre. This clearly related to performance; when we compare it with a piano concerto, we are comparing a work that survives today with no easy professional performance context (the quintet) with one whose generic status is being enlarged all the time by audiences, performers, and concert-giving institutions. This point was made as long ago as 1935 in the first edition of Eric Blom's Master Musicians volume on Mozart.[76] Considerations of genre also affect the critical literature: the generic organization of many scholarly texts means that such works are sidelined. Keller's contribution is therefore all the more extraordinary: in a chapter entitled 'The Chamber Music' that runs to forty-seven pages, one page only is devoted to the chamber music with wind instruments, and it does not include mention of the Quintet for Piano and Wind at all. Mozart's judgements of value on his work are sacrificed to Keller's organicist myopia.

The fate of K.452 in criticism and performance is counterbalanced by its favourable position in terms of recording. When set against the two piano concertos and three string quartets mentioned above, there are as many recordings of K.452 as K.451 in the current *Gramophone Classical Catalogue*, half as many again of K.428, and twice as many of K.453.[77]

For a wide range of reasons (only some of which have been discussed here), a work viewed by Mozart in 1784 as his finest is reduced to a mere also-ran in stature in musical criticism of the last fifty years. This conclusion may be enriched by considering the position faced by those who seek to interpret

---

[73] Hans Keller, 'The Chamber Music', in H. C. Robbins Landon and Donald Mitchell (eds.), *The Mozart Companion* (London, 1965; repr. 1977), 90–137 (*The Mozart Companion* was originally published in 1956); Donald Mitchell, 'The Serenades for Wind Band', ibid. 76 n.1.

[74] Stanley Sadie, 'Mozart, (3) (Johann Chrysostom) Wolfgang Amadeus Mozart', in *New Grove*, xii. 702 and 705–6. The references are unchanged in Stanley Sadie, *The New Grove Mozart* (London, 1982), 86 and 97–8.

[75] For a recent example, see Volkmar Braunbehrens, *Mozart in Wien* (Munich, 1986), trans. Timothy Bell as *Mozart in Vienna* (Oxford, 1991), 198 (page numbers refer to English trans.).

[76] 'Another endearing composition of the serenade type in [*sic*] the Quintet in E flat major for oboe, clarinet, horn, bassoon and piano (K.452), which suffers from neglect for the only reason that keeps the wind octet serenades from the public: the regrettably few opportunities wind players have to appear as chamber performers' (Eric Blom, *Mozart*, Master Musicians (London, 1935), 252). See also ibid. 129.

[77] The figures are as follows: K.451: 18; K.452: 19; K.453: 36; K.428: 27 (*The Gramophone Classical Catalogue* (1994), 462, 486, and 500).

Beethoven's Quintet for Piano and Wind Op. 16, composed in 1796, two years after the posthumous publication of Mozart's work. For Alfred Einstein, the relationship between Mozart's K.452 and Beethoven's Op. 16 was 'universally known'.[78] To question the Mozart that Beethoven knew is again to interrogate the issue of *Wirkung*, and is here a very productive enquiry. True, K.452 was published by Artaria as Op. 29 in February 1794; the edition ran to several issues; and André, Schott, and Götz all produced editions before 1800. But all these editions were of an arrangement for piano quartet (piano and strings). The first edition of the version for piano and wind instruments was not published until September 1800—by Gombert in Augsburg—four years after the composition of Beethoven's quintet.[79] Unless Beethoven had a manuscript copy of the original version, which is unlikely, why did he write his Op. 16? What is Op. 16 a reception of, if it is not of Mozart's piece? A piano quartet that he knew had originally been a quintet for piano and wind? The fact that was 'universally known' in 1945 appears much less clear in the wake of Gertraut Haberkamp's recent work on Mozart first editions.[80]

This example points up a variety of things. First, that among Mozart's works, the position the quintet holds has changed radically between 1784 and the present. However complex the position was in 1784—and the evidence comes from Mozart's pen only, not from the more widely articulated description of the culture of Francis II's Vienna—its critical position today is precarious in comparison with that of the piano concertos. Second, although critical writing on the work sets it to one side, recorded performances of the work seem to suggest that it is a work that might take a more central role in a canonic discourse associated with recorded rather than live performance. Finally, and perhaps most important, the example shows how views of canonic status are contingent on historical circumstance, which in turn demands systematic analysis. The value attached to a given work changes with time, and accounts for the position at the margins of certain canonic discourses of such a work as Mozart's Quintet for Piano and Wind. Reconstructing the horizon of expectations for the work and its recipients—even as sketchily as has been done here, with publication and

---

[78] Alfred Einstein, *Mozart: His Character, His Work*, trans. Arthur Mendel and Nathan Broder (London, 1945). 122.

[79] Gertraut Haberkamp, *Die Erstdrucke der Werke von Wolfgang Amadeus Mozart*, Musikbibliographisches Arbeiten, 10 (2 vols., Tützing, 1986), i. 219–22.

[80] Informal discussion of this matter with Mozart and Beethoven scholars leads to two conclusions: (1) that Einstein's view of the relationship between the two works is still widely held (although Haberkamp's work is almost a decade old); and (2) the important—even burning—question seems to be which of the works is better. In at least one instance this preoccupation has found its way into print: 'Although it [Beethoven's Quintet Op. 16] is scored for the same forces as Mozart's K.452, *a work which Beethoven must surely have known*, a comparison between the first movements of the two pieces serves mainly to highlight Mozart's extreme economy of material as opposed to Beethoven's over-extravagance [*sic*] (Nicholas Marston, 'Chamber Music with Wind', in Barry Cooper (ed.), *The Beethoven Compendium: A Guide to Beethoven's Life and Music* (London, 1991), 226; emphasis added). 'Economy' is one of Janet Levy's covert and casual values in writing about music (Janet M. Levy, 'Covert and Casual Values in Recent Writing about Music', *Journal of Musicology*, 5 (1987), 7–13. Her comments about the relationship of 'economy' to chamber music are important in the context of a critique of this quotation.

influence in the 1790s, recorded sound in the 1990s, and critical attitudes from the 1930s to the 1950s—demonstrates the merit of a theory of reception for the analysis of canon formation. The generic qualities that have determined this work's subsequent canonic position were both inscribed in the work at its creation and arise out of subsequent developments in musical culture.

Changes in the canonic status of a work, of a composer's output, or of a complete repertory can be associated very clearly with particular individuals or small groups. We will consider two examples. The first concerns the operas of Rossini. Until the late 1960s, two Rossini works formed part of what was—and still is—deviously called 'the repertory':[81] *Il barbiere di Siviglia* and *Guillaume Tell*.[82] Rossini's profile as a subject for scholarly enquiry was at that time negligible. This picture has changed radically, largely as a result of the intervention of Philip Gossett. Not only was a complete scholarly edition of the works of the composer planned, with Gossett as editor in chief, but performances all over Europe and North America were given as the result of both his entrepreneurial skills and his coaching of singers. This continues today, twenty-five years after his earliest endeavours: most recently, at the time of preparation of this chapter, a production of *Cenerentola* in Bologna. This aspect of the revival of interest in the works of Rossini needs to be stressed, because although Gossett is often credited with much of the project's success, it is often only on the grounds of his involvement with the complete edition of the composer's works.[83] But interventions in the performative elements of the tradition have been important in returning Rossini to something like canonic status.[84]

Such examples are rare; one is tempted to draw an analogy between opening up the canon to Rossini and T. S. Eliot's almost single-handed admission of the metaphysical poets to the canon of English literature in the middle of the century.[85] More often, such openings-up of the canon are the result of a series of events that may or may not be related. In the same way that the 1970s and 1980s were important points in the reception of Rossini's operas—and important contingencies of value—so too were the 1950s and 1960s for the music of Berlioz.

Throughout the first half of the twentieth century, there had been only a trickle of scholarly work on Berlioz, sparked off by the 1903 centenary that in

---

[81] See Kerman's evasive comments about canon and repertory quoted above (391–2).

[82] Philip Gossett, 'History and Works that have no History: Reviving Rossini's Neapolitan Operas', in Bergeron and Bohlman (eds.), *Disciplining Music*, 97.

[83] Citron, *Gender*, 27.

[84] Perhaps because the recording of opera is so often associated with performance, there is not the disparity between recorded and live performance in the promotion of Rossini's works as in, e.g., Mozart's Quintet for Piano and Wind.

[85] This example is often quoted in the literature on canon-formation in English literature. For the view that this was 'the most ambitious feat of cultural imperialism the century seems likely to produce' see Gabriel Pearson, 'Eliot: An American Use of Symbolism', in Graham Martin (ed.), *Eliot in Perspective: A Symposium* (London, 1970), 97–100. For the influence of Eliot on F. R. Leavis and *Scrutiny*, see Terry Eagleton, *Literary Theory: An Introduction* (Oxford, 1983), 38–43.

turn had set in motion the Breitkopf and Härtel collected works. It was the 1950s that saw Jacques Barzun's book *Berlioz and the Romantic Century*, the foundation of a Berlioz Society and its *Bulletin* in 1952, and the influential 1957 production of *Les Troyens* at Covent Garden.[86] Two powerful forces were at work in the admission of Berlioz into both scholarly and performing canonic discourses in the subsequent decade: the foundation of the *New Berlioz Edition* in 1965 and the beginning of Colin Davis's persuasive series of recordings of the composer's works.[87] Between 1960 and 1969, Davis recorded all the major works of the composer including *Béatrice et Benedict* and *Les Troyens*;[88] only *Benvenuto Cellini* was omitted. What is so striking about these endeavours is that they nearly all took place in the British Isles—which is even now a source of rancour in the Francophone world. A comparison between the status of Berlioz's music in 1945 and 1995 reveals a striking growth in many fields of musical activity: performance, recording, and scholarly action.[89]

There is an interesting, and less attractive, by-product of both the Rossini and the Berlioz projects that deserves attention. Put simply, many of those who promote a composer so avidly for inclusion in the canon are just as quick to decry those whose works have been left outside. It is rare to find documentary evidence of this, but such derision of those left outside often finds its way into less formal contexts. The author of the Master Musicians volume on Rossini, while a less significant player in the inclusion of the composer's works in the canon, is quick to point to the shortcomings of Rossini's contemporaries. Much of Richard Osborne's discussion of *L'italiana in Algeri* is built around an unfavourable comparison with Luigi Mosca's setting of the same libretto.[90] In an address to the Royal Musical Association in London in 1992, the same author offered an unscripted distinction between Rossini's *Il barbiere di Siviglia* and Morlacchi's work of the same name. The latter, he said, sounded like 'so much knitting'.[91] These are not straightforward, uncritical restatements of history: the versions by Mosca and Morlacchi were ultimately eclipsed by those of Rossini, but a dash to assign judgements of value is dangerous in an environment in which pro-

---

[86] Jacques Barzun, *Berlioz and the Romantic Century* (Boston, 1950); *The Berlioz Society Bulletin* was first published as a quarterly in 1952, and subsequently yearly from 1975; the significance of the 1957 *Les Troyens* production for scholarship in the 1960s is acknowledged in D. Kern Holoman, 'Troyens, Les', in *New Grove Dictionary of Opera*, iv. 828.

[87] Hugh MacDonald, 'The New Berlioz Edition', *Musical Times*, 106 (1965), 518.

[88] Colin Davis's Berlioz recordings from the 1960s include the following: *L'Enfance du Christ* (Oct. 1960); *Béatrice et Bénédict* (Apr. 1962); *Harold en Italie* (Oct. 1962); *Symphonie fantastique* (May 1963); Concert Overtures (Oct. 1965); *Roméo et Juliette* (Feb.–Mar. 1968); *Te Deum* (Jan. 1969); *Les Troyens* (Sept.–Oct. 1969); *Grande Messe des Morts* (Nov. 1969). For a complete list of the recordings of this period see Malcolm Walker, 'Discography', in Alan Blyth, *Colin Davis* (Shepperton, 1972), 61–3.

[89] Kerman ('A Few Canonic Variations', 115) lists Berlioz alongside Mussorgsky, Verdi, Rachmaninoff, and Sibelius as composers whose inclusion has changed the 'standard canon' between 1928 (the date of his example taken from Aldous Huxley's *Point Counter Point*) and 1983 (the date of Kerman's article).

[90] Richard Osborne, *Rossini*, Master Musicians (London, 1986), 159–61. The unfavourable comparison is based on the *duetto* 'Ai capricci della sorte' from Act I of both works.

[91] Osborne, 'Rossini and his Librettists', paper read at Royal Musical Association meeting, London, 15 Feb. 1992.

ductions and recordings, let alone accounts of the institutional and aesthetic background of the works, do not exist.[92] The historical circumstances that led to the exclusion of Morlacchi and Mosca from the canon—circumstances that extend from the beginning of the nineteenth century to the end of the twentieth—need serious consideration; their works do not deserve automatic condemnation.

Composers whose names begin with M seem to suffer badly at the hands of those eager to protect recent recruits to the canon. In the case of Berlioz, the victim is Meyerbeer. A surreptitious campaign to extract judgements on Meyerbeer from members of the editorial board of the *New Berlioz Edition* yeilded interesting results. Whereas Osborne's views on Rossini are at least based on an attempt to demonstrate value—or the lack of it—views on Meyerbeer tend to be visceral. One informant (an important figure in English musical circles from the 1960s to the 1980s) declared that he could not *stand* Meyerbeer, although he had only heard one unrepresentative work, and admitted that, although he owned a recording of *Le Prophète*, he had yet to listen to it.[93]

What is so interesting in these verbal documents of reception is that when individuals who seek to admit composers to the canon—and therefore subscribe to a liberal critique of the canon—have been successful, their critique moves subtly to the conservative: to close off canonic discourses to Meyerbeer, Mosca, and Morlacchi.[94] Why one might feel uneasy is that these adverse judgements of value are offered as scholarly comments, whether implicitly or explicitly, and so affect the ways in which historical research might subsequently be conducted. Does it matter, for example, that Rossini's *Il barbiere di Siviglia* was written for the public Teatro Argentino, whereas Morlacchi's work was written for the much embattled Italian court opera in Dresden? Does it matter, further, that Rossini was setting a new libretto by Sterbini, whereas Morlacchi was setting Petrosellini's libretto written for Paisiello in 1782? Does it matter, finally, that Rossini was writing for an Italian operatic culture, whereas Morlacchi was working in an environment much under threat from indigenous opera, his colleague at Dresden being Weber?[95] Answers to all three questions are of course yes, and it is worrisome that, although the now canonic Rossini and Berlioz are

---

[92] Osborne's comments were based on a comparison between the quintet 'Don Basilio! Cosa veggo!' from the Rossini work and the corresponding passage in Morlacchi, and treated the two passages as if they were based on the same libretto. Although both libretti at this point depend on Beaumarchais (*Le Barbier de Séville*, Act III, sc. xi), they are quite different; this makes a meaningful comparison—even in terms of style and technique, let alone a judgement of value—impossible.

[93] However interesting a historical account of the declining fortunes of Meyerbeer's works since *c.*1870, it is not appropriate here to discuss this subject.

[94] Such a procedure gives a focus to the essential conservative background to the liberal critique of the canon discussed above.

[95] The history of the relations between Weber and Morlacchi is a further illustration of differing perspectives on the subject. In January 1817, Weber and German opera must have felt quite clearly subordinate to Morlacchi and Italian opera; but, with hindsight of the most primitive sort, it is not difficult to see Morlacchi and Italian opera as in decline, in the face of works with German libretti and in a radically different style.

*bona fide* subjects for scholarly enquiry, those who work on Morlacchi and Meyer-beer may have to contend with hostile judgements of value from those who would have been in an identical position only thirty years ago.

Implicit in the foregoing discussion of liberal critics becoming conservative is the question of relativism. This was the point of disagreement, referred to earlier, between Krummacher and Dahlhaus in the early 1980s. The point at issue was that a theory of reception produces a wide range of documents that bear witness to the echo of a work across history, and therefore to a series of competing inter-pretations that affect our current view of their value and their place in a canonic discourse.[96] How are we to judge the value of one interpretation over that of another? If we consider again the example of Sibelius's Fifth Symphony, and arbitrate definitively between the composer and Tovey about the meaning of the Finale's second theme, many might agree that we should prefer the composer's view to that of Tovey. But why? In the English-speaking world at least, Sibelius's comments were not made known until 1993, and even in Finnish were not gen-erally known before 1965. For nearly sixty years, English musicians familiar with Tovey have had his image of Thor swinging his hammer at the back of their minds, and this clearly had value for conductors of the work, its audiences, critics, and scholars. Claiming that Sibelius's interpretation automatically has more value than Tovey's—just because it comes from the composer—is to privi-lege our *current* reception of the work over that of the period 1935–93. It is not merely to replace an 'incorrect' account by a critic by the composer's 'correct' interpretation.[97]

If there are problems with these sorts of evaluations, how have others attempted to come to terms with this question of relativism? Dahlhaus offered the idea of the kairos or *point de la perfection*: a time in a composition's history when its reception was more accurate, more sensitive, to the artistic nature of the work. His example, which he had been developing since the early 1970s, was the reception of Bruckner's symphonies in the 1920s.[98] Krummacher was rightly unhappy with this idea. His critique of Dahlhaus is well put:

But the suggestion does not only presuppose that it is known from the start where such a *Kairos* is to be found. It also presupposes trust in a hierarchy of values: one has to

---

[96] See the references provided in n. 14 above.

[97] It is striking that no reference to Tovey is made in Hepokoski, *Sibelius: Symphony No. 5*, not even in the index (107). The author declares that references to Tovey were omitted deliberately: 'Actually, I left out Tovey from my Sibelius 5th book on purpose. It was one of the early decisions. Basically, I was so tired of that old quotation that I didn't want to recycle it, even in refuting it. The idea was to eclipse it totally, to render it irrelevant. But it probably didn't work. It's too firmly ingrained into the reception tradition . . . the error, in all likelihood, will continue to persist' (electronic communication to the author, 24 May 1995). This is an extreme position to take in terms of the evaluation of competing interpretations, and could be seen as a once-removed example of privileging the composer over the context—preferring a just-recovered composer's view of a work to a critic's view of a work well embedded in a musical culture. It should be stressed, however, that the above comments represent no critique of the volume under discussion, but only of a general tendency of which the book is just one part.

[98] Dahlhaus, *Foundations*, 157; *idem*, 'Zur Wirkungsgeschichte musikalischer Werke', *Neue Zeitschrift für Musik*, 134 (1973), 215–16.

know right away which qualities of a work were received most appropriately at which time. Only then would one not have to be disadvantaged by divergent documents of reception.[99]

Krummacher's point of departure for this problem is to invite comparison of competing receptions of the work with analysis of the work itself, a position that assumes the objective status of a musical analysis, a position that it is difficult to accept at present. Both Krummacher and Dahlhaus cite Felix Vodicka's response to the question of relativism. Although such discussion is beyond the limits of this chapter, it may be said that Vodicka's views have been represented only partially, and that a consideration of his distinction between reception and concretization (borrowed from Ingarden) has been blurred by both Dahlhaus and Krummacher.[100]

The question of how to deal with competing interpretations that so troubled Dahlhaus may be answered by viewing the problem of relativism in the light of more recent thought on the subject, particularly the work of Nelson Goodman, Herrnstein Smith, and especially Paul Feyerabend.[101] Their starting-point—and this is enough to show how they differ from Dahlhaus in particular—is to draw a distinction between relativism and objectivism, and to show how an objectivist *must* distinguish between competing interpretations, whereas a relativist does not share the need to arbitrate.[102] In other words, why *should* a relativist case have to be argued *except* in the teeth of an objectivist onslaught that has as clear an ideological agenda as does a relativisit defence? Or, to return to Sibelius, why do we need to arbitrate between Tovey's and Sibelius's interpretations? The case has been put excellently by Herrnstein Smith in her book *Contingencies of Value*

[99] The German reads: 'Indes setz der Vorschlag nicht nur voraus, dass man von vornherein wisse, wo solch ein Kairos liege. Er bedingt auch das Zutrauen in eine Hierarchie von Werten: man muss vorab wissen, welche Qualitäten eines Werks in welcher Zeit am angemessensten rezipiert wurden. Nur dann müsste man sich auch durch divergierende Rezeptionszeugnisse nich irritierten lassen' (Krummacher, 'Rezeptionsgeschichte', 162).

[100] The two texts cited by both Dahlhaus and Krummacher are Felix Vodicka, 'Literárnich del: Problematika ohlasu Nerudova dila', *Slova a slovenost*, 7 (1941), 113–32; German trans. as 'Die Konkretisation des literarischen Werks—Zur Problematik der Rezeption von Nerudas Werk', in Warning (ed.), *Rezeptionsästhetik*, 84–112; English trans. by John Burbank as 'The Concretization of the Literary Work: Problems in the Reception of Neruda's Works', in Peter Steiner (ed.), *The Prague School: Selected Writings, 1929–1946*, University of Texas Slavic Series, 6 (Austin, Tex., 1982), 103–34; and *idem*, 'Dejiny ohlasu literárnich del', in Bohuslav Havránek and Jan Mukarovsky (eds.), *Cteni o jazyce a poesii* (Prague, 1942), 371–84; German trans. as 'Die Rezeptionsgeschichte literarischer Werks', in Warning (ed.), *Rezeptionsästhetik*, 71–83; English trans. by Paul L. Garvin as 'The History of the Echo of Literary Works', in *A Prague School Reader on Esthetics, Literary Structure, and Style* (Washington, DC, 1964), 71–81. Neither author does justice to Vodicka's appeal to literary history in these articles, in which reception is viewed as a quality inherent in history. Significantly, both articles appear in the influential collection of essays, *Rezeptionsästhetik*, ed. Rainer Warning; the popularity of this collection for works originally in German as well as translations from Czech lured both Krummacher and Dahlhaus into a mistaken view of the early work of Jauss (see above, n. 14).

[101] For Herrnstein Smith see above, n. 65. Influential on Herrnstein Smith, and therefore on this chapter, are Nelson Goodman, *Ways of Worldmaking* (Hassocks, 1978), and Paul Feyerabend, *Against Method: Outline of an Anarchistic Theory of Knowledge* (London, 1975); *idem*, 'The Spectre of Relativism', in *Science in a Free Society* (London, 1978), 79–86; *idem*, 'Notes on Relativism', in *Farewell to Reason* (London, 1987), 19–89.

[102] Herrnstein Smith's preference is to describe relativism and objectivism as 'cognitive tastes' (*Contingencies of Value*, 167).

and by Feyerabend in his critique of Popper and Putnam.[103] If one is wedded to an idea of a reception history of music that simply tracks the 'after-life' of musical works, there is contestable ground between a relativist and an objectivist. If, conversely, reception theory is taken as one of the premisses of a sophisticated history of music that takes its synchronic dimension seriously, it is difficult to identify any complaint that an objectivist might make.

The central claim of this chapter has been that locations of reception overlap substantially with contingencies of value, and therefore that a theory of reception is fundamental to a diagnosis of canonic discourse. This is a basis for a type of history that assimilates both synchronic and diachronic trajectories, and that fuses a traditional history of works, composers, and institutions with a fully worked-out history of music based on a theory of reception. The result would be a significant contribution to a history of music conditioned by, for example, cultural anthropology or *annaliste* thought.[104] This is a very different prospect from the arid concept of separate spheres of historical endeavour—one music history, one reception history—envisioned by Dahlhaus. Whatever type of historical narrative one is trying to write, whatever philosophy of history one adopts—and in this sense it does not matter whether the perspective is Whig, *annaliste*, or New Historicist—reception theory, and a critical account of canonic discourse, deserve a place centre stage in the theatre of music history.

---

[103]  Feyerabend, 'Notes on Relativism', 79–83.

[104]  Both these historiographical tendencies are the victims of a reluctance to engage with the practical implications they embody. For the cultural-anthropological view of history see Gary Tomlinson, 'The Web of Culture: A Context for Musicology', *19th-Century Music*, 7 (1984), 350–62, and the trenchant comments about its neglect in Philip V. Bohlman, 'On the Unremarkable in Music', *19th-Century Music*, 16 (1992), 207 n. 17. The *annaliste* school of historical thought has an even more tenuous grip on musicology; see Jane Fulcher, 'Current Perspectives on Culture and the Meaning of Cultural History in France Today', *Stanford French Review*, 9 (1985), 91–104, and William Weber, 'Mentalité, tradition et origines du canon musical en France et en Angleterre au xviii<sup>e</sup> siècle', *Annales: économies, sociétés, civilisations*, 44 (1989), 849–72. Although Fulcher's conclusion may not be entirely convincing, her explanation of *annalisme* is of great value, but should be read in conjunction with more sceptical views of the *troisième niveau* from the Anglo-American world (such as Robert Darnton's introduction to *The Great Cat Massacre and Other Episodes in French Cultural History* (New York, 1984) ). The publication of Weber's article in the journal *Annales: ESC* speaks for itself.

# 18

## *The Musical Text*

### Stanley Boorman

The principal subject of this chapter is that form of musical information which is written or printed, whether or not it is intended for use in performance. Given a number of developments during this century, questions can be asked as to whether a musical text need be written, whether a recording does not constitute a text, and indeed whether a performance, ephemeral though it is, may not also be a musical text. I shall return to these matters later in the chapter. But I propose to begin with a tacit assumption that the text being discussed is preserved on paper.

The written or printed musical text is an object to be mistrusted at every turn. It elicits blind trust exactly when belief should be suspended, and is subjected to questioning at many points where investigation is needless, even valueless. Two simple examples will illustrate this assertion.

The first is a case of opposites: modern editions of Beethoven's sonatas vary widely in the manner in which the editor treats the text. At one extreme are editions such as those of Artur Schnabel, full of the editor's own perceptions of the music, slurs, fingerings, added dynamics and staccato markings, comments on the tempi, and advice on how to articulate, accentuate, and comprehend much of the original melodic material. Such editions are valuable: they contain the musical understanding of (sometimes great) interpreters, and they encourage beginner and advanced musician alike to think about the content of the music.[1] Scholars, and many performers, know that these additions have no intrinsic validity as stemming from Beethoven, or even from a tradition of performance traceable back to the composer: their significance lies in the way they codify a performing view exemplified by the editor. Yet it is often difficult to determine exactly which annotations might have been in copies Beethoven authorized (in so far as that could imply specific approval),[2] and which have been added by the later editor.

---

[1] In selecting Schnabel's edition for comment, I am aware that I am doing it a disservice. It contains much wisdom, and is the product of a fine musical mind. I wish that the same could be said for many others among the most easily available editions.

[2] There is a brief but fundamental discussion of this issue in Alan Tyson, *The Authentic English Editions of Beethoven*, All Souls' Studies, 1 (London, 1963), 28–33.

At the other extreme are the so-called *Urtext* editions: here, the editor claims to have stripped away all later accretions to the musical text, to have avoided making additions, and to have made the simplest possible and most reliable decisions in case of doubt, always using the earliest or safest sources. Thus the editor asserts that it represents precisely the content as the composer would have wanted to see it—and (some even believe) would have wanted to hear it.

In both these cases, the user's trust is expected. If the first is perhaps a self-evident plea for faith on the part of the reader, the second is equally dangerous. It claims that every mark on the 'original' is to be trusted and interpreted, and that nothing else is needed. In this respect, the *Urtext* edition demands implicit trust, requiring an act of credulity. Worse, it also presumes a similar trust on the part of the editor, that everything in the 'original' source must be used and incorporated in some manner, that nothing was erroneous or the result of a casual loss of attention or interest.[3]

The trust that the average performer puts in the modern edition, or the average music student puts in the *Urtext*, the average scholar also puts in the autograph or the 'authorized' first edition—and that is equally dangerous. We cannot know what to trust, and what was a slightly misplaced slip of the pen, a casual mark which now looks suspiciously different from another one, a reading which the composer ignored in performance, or a blatant mistake, not caught by the composer, but which is now seen to present the great original moment of the work. At least the Schnabels of the editing world are prepared to say that the Beethovens, like Homer, nodded from time to time.

My second example concerns the many occasions on which scholars believe they can make minute distinctions where (perhaps) none existed for the composer, copyist, or printer. A classic series of instances involves alleged distinctions between the dot and the vertical dash as a mark for staccato. Of course, the two have had different meanings, at least since the mid-nineteenth century. But it is increasingly difficult to argue that a Haydn or a Schubert was invariably scrupulous about how he made the mark—even when not in a hurry.[4] There are other similar issues: the alignment of ends of hastily drawn slurs by some nineteenth-century composers has been the subject of careful enquiry;[5] the placing on the

---

[3] It hardly needs to be added that such a view also claims that the editor has not been faced with questions for which we have no answers at all—i.e. that the initial concept is in itself impossible of achievement.

[4] The best literature on this issue concerns the music of Mozart: see Hans Albrecht, *Die Bedeutung der Zeichen Keil, Strich und Punkt bei Mozart. Fünf Lösungen einer Preisfrage* (Kassel, 1957); Paul Mies, 'Die Artikulationszeichen Strich und Punkt bei Mozart', *Die Musikforschung*, 11 (1958), 428; and Robin Stowell, 'Leopold Mozart Revised: Articulation in Violin Playing during the Second Half of the Eighteenth Century', in R. Larry Todd and Peter Williams (eds.), *Perspectives on Mozart Performance* (Cambridge, 1991), 126–37, esp. 133–6.

[5] The general introduction to each volume of *The Works of Giuseppe Verdi* (under the general editorship of Philip Gossett) includes the following statement of the problem and its solution in the edition: 'There are occasions in which Verdi's slurs are ambiguous to the point of incomprehensibility, especially when a general legato is intended. In the few instances where it proves necessary, [the edition] adopts a system of double slurs: regular slurs showing precisely what is in the principal source, dotted slurs offering a possible interpretation.' In the edition of *Ernani* (Chicago, 1985), Claudio Gallico makes a series of pertinent observations about various levels of inconsistency: see pp. xxv–xxvi.

page of accidentals or the use of ligatures is a serious issue in interpreting early music;[6] scholars have trouble detecting differences in some composers' use of the two signs *sf* and *fz*; there are editions of sixteenth-century sacred music which try to follow exactly the text placement of the sources, even though theorists seem to have made it clear that other solutions were expected; we have trouble understanding how mensuration signs and early time signatures can differ in the way they do;[7] and so on.[8] Indeed, we impute to most composers at their desks, to most copyists and most printers, a sensitivity to nuance that is almost entirely a twentieth-century phenomenon. There is no reason to assume that earlier composers favoured such an approach to the notated text; nor is there any reason to believe that the performer felt bound by such nuances as appear in that text.

A key to how both did in fact view the musical text can be found by examining the functions of notation, and how it was used in performance.

## Notation and its Function

Obviously a text, as notated, is not actually the musical work: music exists as sound; it fills time rather than space; and it is normally perceived as sound-in-time (whether from an external source or within our own heads). Indeed, music is commonly thought not to exist except as sound, real or imagined, and the notated version is no more than a source of advice or instructions for re-creating the music.

Of course, to say that the composition does not fully exist when it is not being played or heard is not strictly analogous to raising the old philosophical chestnut about a tree falling unheard in the forest, for there is a sense in which the composition remains in existence, in the memories of the creator and earlier

---

[6] For *musica ficta*, the literature is vast: see e.g. the bibliography to the relevant article in the *New Grove*; for ligatures, see the article cited in n. 35 below.

[7] A major step forward in this complex area was taken in the recent book by Anna Maria Busse Berger, *Mensuration and Proportion Signs: Origins and Evolution* (Oxford, 1993), although Rob Wegman has pointed to a number of problems, and Ronald Woodley (in *John Tucke: A Case Study in Early Tudor Music Theory* (Oxford, 1993) ) has shown how idiosyncratic local traditions could be. Later practice is still not well understood in many instances, despite George Houle, *Meter in Music, 1600–1800* (Bloomington, Ind., 1987).

[8] In each of these cases, we have made real progress towards understanding the significance of the notations concerned, but have still not been able to grasp how often that significance was part of the copyist's apparatus. It will be apparent that I am sceptical of the value of many such investigations—and some additional reasons for my doubts will emerge shortly. I do believe that the investigations have to be made: because of the simplifying nature of musical texts, as well as their message-bearing function, we cannot always be sure that we know what is significant and what is incidental until such enquiries have been made. However, I also think that they are often the province of scholars, and not of performers or editors, who should be able to rely on the scholars' conclusions. Further, as will become apparent, I am sceptical of the extent to which most composers before the present century believed that every detail was binding on performers. The musical text, if it did not function as a blueprint to be followed in every detail lest the structure collapse, need not convey precision in detail.

listeners. But the text carries no more than the minimal necessary information for a new performance. It is not the composition itself.[9]

A necessary corollary of this is that every performance, and every hearing, is unique, for each one is a distinct, individual response to these instructions. How much it differs from the next is dependent on a number of factors. These include the levels of information carried by the notation, the conventions which composers applied to the notation and performers to the execution, the technical and musical abilities of the performers, the concentration of the listener, and the listener's previous memories or conceptions. These points have all been discussed elsewhere, perhaps most succinctly by John Cage, who writes: 'Composing's one thing, performing's another, listening's a third. What can they have to do with one another?'[10] There is no reason to assume that any listener will hear the piece as the composer heard it, and no reason to assume that any two performers will respond to the notation in the same way. Other recent writers have used a similar point of view to argue against trusting too much in the possibility of 'authentic performances' in the early music 'revival', and similar arguments are made about the analytical process.[11] Cage, however, was referring specifically to the notation of music, and its rendition in performance.

Given these factors, each performance will be different. In some cases, the performers will assume the right to transform the music in various relatively obvious ways—by displaying skill at ornamentation or embellishment, by adding parts, or by reinterpreting the rhythm or improvising accompaniments. On a lesser plane, most performers will decide to add rubato, to change the dynamics or pedalling or bowing, or to add a cadenza. In other cases, the level of change may consist in nothing more than conforming to current ideas about performance practice for the repertoire concerned. A musician of the 1890s played Beethoven very differently from one of the 1980s, and both differently again from a performer bent on resurrecting the 'original' style.[12] Yet all three worked from the notation, and all were working at the stricter end of the spectrum ranging from exact obedience to freedom-to-change.

Similarly, a listener brought up on the recordings of Toscanini has in the mind a different interpretation from that favoured by supporters of the later record-

[9] I stress the use of the word 'minimal'. Composers have very rarely written down things which they did not feel were essential—and the written text therefore comprises enough to reconstruct a good performance, and no more. I shall return to this.

[10] John Cage, 'Experimental Music: Doctrine', in *Silence* (Cambridge, Mass., 1966), 15.

[11] For a collection of views on the subject of early music see Nicholas Kenyon (ed.), *Authenticity and Early Music: A Symposium* (Oxford, 1988). On analysis see e.g. Peter Rabinowitz, 'Chord and Discourse: Listening through the Written Word', in Steven Paul Scher (ed.), *Music and Text: Critical Enquiries* (Cambridge, 1992), 38–56, and a series of recent articles in the journal *Musical Analysis*.

[12] I am not making a value-judgement: it is evidently true that no 'authentic' *hearing* can take place, even if an authentic performance were ever to become possible. For a straightforward presentation of some arguments regarding the merits of authentic performances, see Richard Taruskin, 'On Letting the Music Speak for Itself: Some Reflections on Musicology and Performance', *Journal of Musicology*, 1 (1982), 338–49. However, the argument that early performances takes us no nearer an understanding of what the composer intended is self-evidently fallacious. Whether it is a worthwhile exercise is a different matter.

ings by Klemperer. Both are valid; both are 'correct'; and both are deemed to be of the same piece of music. The same is true of readings that differ much more considerably, such as recordings of medieval monophony directed by Thomas Binkley or Sequentia or Russell Oberlin. It is evident, therefore, that there cannot be a strict correlation between the notation and the 'music', as performed and heard, whatever the repertoire.

From the early nineteenth century onward, composers have tried to impose a greater level of precision on the performer.[13] This can be seen at many levels in the score: the Mahlerian indication of which string violinists should use at certain moments, Schoenberg's use of signs to indicate the *Haupstimme* and the *Nebenstimme*, Webern's proliferation of indications of momentary accelerations or diminuendos, Boulez's attempt at indicating three different levels of pause (in *Le Marteau sans maître*), or Stockhausen's indications of the precise place on a drumhead or gong at which to strike. All these are signs that composers recognize the loose connection between notation and sound, and have been trying to tighten it.[14]

At the same time, and just as clearly revealing the composer's own view of his place in musical society, other composers are trying to loosen the connection. For them, the text allows a performer specific freedoms, sometimes circumscribed (as with most examples by Lutosławski) and conditioned by the composer's view of the sound-world to be created. In other cases, there is more freedom, even to the point where priority of conception seems to have passed from the composer to the performer.[15]

This willingness to incorporate the performer in the creative process is not new: from the emergence of notation, the musical text has allowed considerable flexiblity, and has even contained many elements which deliberately offered different levels of freedom. Some of these offered options were intended to be

---

[13] An early example would be Beethoven's use of the Maelzel metronome to indicate tempi. Perhaps the process began somewhat earlier, with regular crescendo and decrescendo markings, the demise of basso continuo, and the beginning of a serious composer–publisher relationship. But these are all only early signs of what becomes more serious with the impact of the German Romantic view of the status of the composer.

[14] It is interesting that, at the same time, we increasingly believe in the value of a composer's own performances and recordings. Even when (as in the case of Stravinsky) they vary from one to another, or (as in those of the surviving Dohnányi or Ravel recordings) the composer is not necessarily a convincing interpreter, we look to such performances to illumine some aspect of the composition that could not be committed to paper. At the same time, as other composers are allowing performers to return to their traditional freedoms, we should expect this viewpoint to become meaningless. But, in practice, the ensembles led by Stockhausen or Steve Reich, or the musicians close to Cage or Harry Partch, are presumed to give more authoritative performances. This seems to negate the attempt by these composers to achieve a looser relationship between text and performance. In practice, of course, it is more a reflection of the conservative view of audences than of the views of the musicians involved. The extreme result is the enshrining of performances of movements from Stockhausen's *Aus die sieben Tagen* or Cage's series of *Variations*.

[15] I am thinking here in particular of the repertoire of so-called intuitive pieces (among them pieces published in the West Coast journal *Source* or, again, Stockhausen's set entitled *Aus die sieben Tagen*). I do not think the same comment can be made about any works of Cage: even in those cases where he can have had no idea which sounds would occur—those involving radios, for example, or those in which the performer has to construct his music from imperfections in a sheet of paper—Cage has kept control of his basic conception, requiring the performer, and the subsequent sounds, to conform to his guide-lines.

completely at the performer's discretion. The notated 'text' of a classical concerto indicates the presence of a cadenza: the cadenza is inherently part of the concerto, as we understand it. Yet we cannot say much about its realization. All we can be sure of is that each performer did something different, allowing the audience to hear virtuosity or musicality or skill at counterpoint or one of several other possibilities. In this case, as in that of ornamented da capo repeats of arias, the details of the text remain constant (and are indicated as such in the notation), specifying a deliberately wide range of choices for the performer. It is the execution that changes.[16]

At the same time, there is also no direct correlation between the full text itself (as the composer conceived of it, and with all permissible freedoms) and the notated source (as the composer wrote it)—even though the only evidence for the text is usually that source. Some of this, again, is because no practical notation has been (or has been devised to be) comprehensive or precise. Each notation, and each source using it, assumes a series of understandings on the part of the reader. The most obvious examples are again the performance conventions that actually change the aural effect of the notation—double-dotting, portamenti in late nineteenth-century string playing, or canonic composition that is not written out. These were all implicit in the notation at the time of composition: thus, they did not need to be written down.[17]

This limited nature of musical notation is one of the key elements in the balance to be effected between a text and a performance. The limitations are traditionally seen as reflections of the two possible functions of notation: as 'prescriptive' or 'descriptive'. Descriptive notations record what has happened in a performance, attempting to give a full and detailed picture of the relevant elements. In all practical cases, they do not include every aspect of a performance, but emphasize some easily notated features, such as rhythm or pitch.[18] Prescriptive notations are assumed to lay out exactly what must be done by a

[16] Note again that it is not the musical text that has changed, but only its execution. The same holds true for aleatoric notations and for Cage's kits of instructions.

[17] A a result, research into each is complicated by the way in which the evidence we *do* have is not complete: for the example of string playing, see Robert Philip, '1900–1940', in Howard Mayer Brown and Stanley Sadie (eds.), *Performance Practice: Music after 1600* (London, 1989), 461–82 and the bibliography cited there. For double-dotting, as for *notes inégales*, the best simple statement of the situation is in the same volume, in David Fuller's chapter, 'The Performer as Composer' (117–46), though Fuller has to write (135) that 'No one any longer doubts the reality of the convention; what is questioned is the extent of its application'. While it might seem that canonic writing should raise the fewest problems, 'hidden polyphony' has been found in Machaut's *lais* (see Richard Hoppin, 'An Unrecognized Polyphonic Lai of Machaut', *Musica Disciplina*, 12 (1958), 93–104, and Margaret Hasselman and Thomas Walker, 'More Hidden Polyphony in a Machaut Manuscript', *Musica Disciplina*, 24 (1970, 7–16), while the correct solution of even so famous a piece as Baude Cordier's 'Tout par compas' is still not entirely clear (Ursula Günther, 'Fourteenth-century Music with Texts Revealing Performance Practice', in Stanley Boorman (ed.), *Studies in the Performance of Late Medieval Music* (Cambridge, 1983), 261–3).

[18] The most valuable area for such notations lies, of course, in the field of ethnomusicology, where transcriptions of actual performances yield much important information. These notations usually emphasize certain aspects of the music that can easily be portrayed graphically—showing e.g. exact microtonal pitch inflections. They are not designed to help the original performers to reconstruct the music, and are often useful only for analysis.

Perhaps the ultimate descriptive notation would be a full-scale spectrographic analysis on a time-chart. This would contain so much information, all of it on too detailed a scale, that it would be completely useless for reconstructing a musical work in its temporal space, even in the study.

performer: the sounds to be made or the actions to be taken. The presence of rhythmically notated pitches on a stave is a form of prescription, instructing the performer to use skill and technique to produce the sounds represented. Similarly, tablature notations for plucked-string or wind instruments indicate the positions for the fingers, and often little more; it is clear that such notations are limited in their content, and do not carry the full text of a composition.[19] But the same limitation applies to all prescriptive notations, which are restricted to those elements that can be described graphically or with few words and that are assumed to be essential to the work.

Neither range of notations can present the complete text of a work of music, not even as fully as a verbal notation presents a verbal text. This is so for three reasons: because practical notations are always imprecise; because notation does not carry those many elements of a composition that are understood (though in different manners) by all its readers; and because the source itself colours the way in which we look at the notation.

Pitch is an example. There are only two ranges of notation that give precise indications of pitch: one is that designed for re-creating an electronic composition (usually consisting of lists of wavelengths and wave forms); the other is similar in intention (though usually graphic in appearance), in that it is designed (often by ethnomusicologists) to indicate exactly the pitches of a previously recorded performance. Both of these are deliberately limited both in scope and in function, for neither is intended for the live performer.[20] In other notations, pitch is indicated according to conventional ideas—using, for example, only twelve different pitches for an octave.[21] Implicit in this simple, easy-to-read notation is the understanding that most performers (those not using fixed-pitch instruments) will always shade the written pitch, taking into account the key in use, the intonation of other performers, or the shaping of an individual line.

In the same ways, many other elements of notation give only vague instructions: dynamic, tempo, and staccato marks are among the more obvious examples. These variables operate at a specific, rather low, level, providing an approximate guide to the text as it will be interpreted by the performer.

More important, notation does not relate to text in those specific areas where conventional interpretations come into play. The continuing arguments over how to perform *notes inégales*, over-dotting, or bass notes beneath recitatives merely show the extent to which modern performers cannot reconstruct

---

[19] A parallel example would be dance notations that indicate the placement of the feet, while leaving everything else unnotated. For an example, see Caroso's *Nobiltà di Dame* (1600): even the much more complex Labanotation cannot convey all the subtleties of a balletic movement.

[20] It is worth noting that pieces using live electronics perforce cannot employ as precise a notation; e.g. in Stockhausen's *Mantra*, a graphic notation of pitch is employed, in which there is always some flexibility of interpretation.

[21] The notation may, in practice, precisely define a pitch, without knowing what that pitch actually is. Modern notation for keyboard—piano or organ—defines which key is to be struck: since the instrument cannot be retuned during performance, the notation does in a sense, therefore, define a pitch precisely.

performances from notations in the manner in which (we assume) the original readers did.[22]

These limits on the relationship between notation and the piece itself can be seen equally clearly when we consider those variant readings that frequently survive in different sources of the same piece. While there are cases in which the text itself is transformed, there are others in which changes in notation seem to be intended to provide the *same* text, for different readers. Once again, the most obvious example is a contemporary one: the habit whereby an *Opera omnia* is presumed to provide the one-and-only text for a composition is contingent on the present-day scholar being able to translate early notations into modern equivalents.

Finally, the nature of notation, and (even more importantly) the manner in which people look at it, is strongly influenced by the source and its technical and social context. From simplified notations for inexperienced singers (perhaps leading to more precise renderings) and alternative readings in nineteenth-century piano music,[23] to the change in choral music from single voice-parts to vocal scores, there are many examples of the manner in which the presentation of the musical text is a feature of its interpretation.

In other words, historically, a given notated version has never been used as if it represented the musical text precisely, but rather as providing a guide to its own interpretation, thereby offering a version of a text. To repeat, notations are imprecise; they conceal many well-understood elements; and they are influenced by the style of their presentation and the occasions for their use.

All forms of notation suffer from these drawbacks. As a result, they must omit much of the real text of a composition. They are unrelated to performance, and to the work, in very specific ways, omitting all aspects of interpretation and of extension (cadenzas, embellishment, improvised addition). Secondly, they are unrelated to performers' experience and tradition.[24] Finally, of course, it is the nature of all notations that they fix one version of a piece for each reader. They cannot take account of revision (in a Western view of composition) or of impro-visation and transformation (in any other).

---

[22] For the first two, see above, n. 17. In general, I am referring here to an aspect of the text which is being understood 'literally', i.e. without embellishment or other changes. Incidentally, as far as we can tell from the contemporary literature, eighteenth-century performers also did not have one consistent interpretation of the musical text. But that is not the point: each performer or group of performers had an understanding of the ranges of interpretation that were within normal conventional bounds.

[23] Stroke notation in late medieval English sources seems to have been devised for this purpose. The use of small notes in piano music works in both directions: in one, obvious simplifications of technical difficulties are inserted on smaller adjacent staves, as can be found in editions of Liszt's music; in a second, the opposite is true, in that the more complex or demanding version is itself marginalized in the same manner. There are two other printing practices which seem to be different, though they reflect very similar social situations: many editions from the first years of the century have to make allowance for the gradual spread of 'pianos with additional keys', providing versions of passages for those cottage pianos that did not extend so far in range; and Praetorius, in books such as his *Polyhymnia caduceatrix*, provided both simple versions of many melodies and possible decorated alternatives.

[24] This is equally true of an ethnomusicologist's or jazz scholar's descriptive score. By reporting on only one performance, this score is incapable of providing a vehicle for a further performance, in the same way that repeated playings of a recording do not constitute new performances or extensions of a performing tradition.

Because of these weaknesses, the two terms, 'descriptive' and 'prescriptive', are of little use when considering the relationship of notation to the composition itself (rather than to an individual performance), or the place that either holds in a view of the 'text'. Instead, we need a different concept, one that illumines the common elements of the two terms, as well as their limitations.

In practice, the function of many aspects of prescriptive notation is really to describe. The notation may indeed give instructions—'Play this pitch (as you understand it at this moment)', 'Detach these notes from each other', or 'Place your fingers here'.[25] But the intention is much more to describe the end result in some way which would make sense to the performer. This is true even while composers are trying to become more precise in more and more elements of their notation.[26] The notation alludes to the composition, and also to aspects of a performance. It specifies little or much, and leaves the rest to the performer. Given the performer's experience and training, the allusive aspects of notation will readily stimulate certain responses, and thereby extend the hold of the text over a performance. I have mentioned some examples— *musica ficta* is one, continuo figurings would be another—where it is self-evident that experience and training allow a performer to go beyond the precise meaning of the musical text, and interpret it with some probability of not erring too seriously.

This allusive view of notation, especially as it has developed for performers (rather than for scholars), is of much greater value. The notation may well contain prescriptive elements: but behind them there is another, more subtle world, present in the way these elements are spaced, in the other imprecise indications on the page, in the tradition which bred the notation itself. More centrally, the notation itself is allusive. It is not the piece of music: it is not even a complete guide to reconstructing that piece. Instead, it is an allusive guide, offering the performer hints alongside the instructions, and therefore depending on the musician's ability to understand these hints and allusions.

## Functions of the Musical Text

Why write down a musical composition? The obvious answer would seem to be to preserve it, for oneself, for others, even for posterity. None of these

[25] Tabulatures do not require separate consideration. They represent a special class of notation in which the basic instruction on the page is a technical one. That apart, they seem to fit into the same category as staff notations, with the proviso that they are normally even less capable of carrying a sophisticated level of performance information.

[26] It is equally true of those notations that seem to tell the performer less: the notation of Lutosławski's aleatoric sections gives clear instructions both for pitches and for the artistic effect (precisely through its imprecisions); Cardew's *Treatise* requires of the performer that he make some sense of its elegant form of notation. La Monte Young's *Composition 1960 No. 7* uses apparently vague words to convey clearly what would be impossibly vague and much harder to read if written in conventional notation: the complete score consists of two pitches, each with an open-ended tie to the right, and the instruction 'To be held for a long time'.

destinations need imply the intention of a performance: for centuries, luxury manuscripts of music were as much a royal or noble gift as luxury editions of Virgil or Dante. There is no reason to believe that they always, or perhaps even often, led to performance.[27] Similar points can be made about the presentation manuscript of Bach's Brandenburg Concertos or the gifts from Liszt and other virtuosi to admirers. But these examples are exceptional,[28] and most sources do presume some destination in performance.

If eventual performance was planned, yet the text had to be written down, we must assume that the piece could not be learned by ear, from some earlier performer or from the composer. With many contemporary scores, it would be virtually impossible to re-create a composition in this manner, but that has not always been true. Strophic forms, dance rhythms, contrapuntal rules simple enough that they could also be used to create improvised polyphony, and regular phrase lengths would all assist in memorizing. None the less, music writing has a history of well over a thousand years.

Recent theories argue that early music writing reflects very specific needs: to disseminate a group of (often liturgical) pieces widely and accurately, to preserve integrity in the notation and performance, and to preserve famous repertoires for others who have not heard them.[29] In each of these cases, purely verbal transmission was impractical, and the music could only be kept in the repertoire by means of a written source. Even if there could be some verbal transmission—for example, by a monk travelling with manuscript in hand to a distant centre—the need for a written copy of the music was clearly felt even at the earliest stages of notation, and rapidly became more obvious as styles became more complex. Indeed, the emergence of polyphony rendered written sources essential, and at

---

[27] We have tended to assume that presentation manuscripts were not normally used for performance, and that this was also true for non-musical manuscripts. Certainly, many of them are astonishingly clean, and quite a number carry serious errors in the music they contain, errors which would cause any performance from them to collapse in disaster. On the other hand, many manuscripts not intended as gifts are equally lavish: in musical terms, one could cite many in the Vatican collections and some for the Bavarian Court Chapel, all of which were probably used. Further, there is evidence that composers represented in donated manuscripts did become known in the new areas. The Flemish composers of the circle around Alamire begin to be found in German manuscripts, once presentation manuscripts were received in Munich and Jena; and contemporary chansons gained in popularity in Italy after the production of the first insular, lavish chansonniers: it is difficult to argue for cause and effect in either case, of course.

[28] This exceptional nature also extends to the content of such manuscripts: visual effect often takes precedence over usability or musical accuracy. Clearly, in discussing the role of a musical text, these sources can be left on one side.

[29] See the references to Levy's and Treitler's writings at the end of this chapter. See also Helmut Hucke, 'Toward a New Historical View of Gregorian Chant', *Journal of the American Musicological Society*, 33 (1980), 437–67. Implicit behind many of these arguments is a logical trap. On the one hand, notation was used so that pieces could be preserved accurately and precisely, whether or not an oral tradition coexisted with the written one; on the other, we accord to early performers a range of freedoms which reduce the need for accuracy in the transmitted score. This problem is enhanced by the pattern by which we assume authority existed in the written symbol, especially in the case of liturgical repertoires, and at the same time assert that there was no sense of unique authority residing in any one version of a composition. The two sets of positions are not entirely incompatible; but the problem does not seem to have been discussed very thoroughly.

the same time was (gradually) to force changes in the complexity of information carried by the notation.[30]

But a critical stage in the functioning of the written musical text was reached once sources started being sent (without accompanying performers) from one centre to a second too distant to have heard performances.[31] Singers at the new centre had no personal grasp of the conventions by which a performance could be created from the sparse notations. They had to build up their own conventional manner of creating the music, based no doubt on local or princely preferences as much as on hearsay.

The important question, therefore, is not, Why write down music?, but rather, If the musical text is to be used in this manner to re-create the piece, why is notation such an imprecise medium? How is it that one can write with confidence of the gaps in its information, to the extent of suggesting that it is merely 'allusive'?

In most cases, the deficiencies of the written text were not seen as defects, but rather as opportunities. This is self-evidently true for the original readers of a notation, for whom the apparent lacunae were effectively not noticeable, or even present.[32] Even now, in even the most carefully notated scores, imprecision in dynamics or marks of attack (for example) leaves room for the new performer to impose an individual view on the music. Much more do the lacks in earlier notations leave room for invention. Not surprisingly, performers expected and revelled in this freedom, and treatises were written to explain how it allowed room for them to display their prowess. The notation was intended to act as a stimulus.

The extent of this stimulus can range widely: the score could, at one end of the spectrum, be treated as a guide to an 'exact' re-creation of a work, based on a precise reading of the notation. This possibility represents a rigid view of the function of musical notation and of the document, and is historically a rare one, though currently conventional.[33]

At the other extreme, the text could be a stimulus to a flight of fancy—a jazz

---

[30] It does not follow that the new repertoires could only be learned from notation. Clearly, much music was still learned by rote, from a choirmaster, for example. But in performance, errors of pitch or rhythm could more easily bring a polyphonic composition to a disastrous collapse; and avoiding a repeat of such a collapse often required a more precise notation of just those two elements.

[31] That was not a single historical event, of course. It will have happened long before we have evidence of it, once people began to know of compositions or creators or performers only by hearsay. Much later, chapels wanted the works of Josquin or Isaac, even when no members had heard or taken part in performances with them. But, at the same time, their works were also being carried around by singers who had sung them and could convey some of the unnotated aspects of the tradition. The same pattern held true for nineteenth-century piano music and solo song, among other repertoires.

[32] I mean by this merely that any recurrent problem with notation would have been, and of course was, addressed by modifying the notation itself (in a process that has continued to the present). That so many elements of the music were left undeveloped in the notation surely implies that composers, copyists, and performers were not aware of a need to notate them, thereby constraining the performance.

[33] The development of this attitude followed by some decades the development of composers' concern for detail in their notation, and no doubt has a similar stimulus.

improvisation or a reconstruction of a *basse danse*. Here, the text is overtly seen as no more than an encouragement to the musician: in the case of jazz performances, the balance is recognized by the prominence given to the names of the musicians, in recordings or reviews.

There is a continuum between these extremes, ranging from the addition of dynamics and rubato or of simple layers of ornamentation (trills, cadenzas, etc.), through the addition of new material (extra voices or instruments, the presence of floridly embellished repeats), to the use of the text as a starting-point for creation (improvised variations, Lisztian fantasias, or the improvisations of the great French organists).

In all these cases but the first extreme, the notation is not performed *per se*; that is, it is not read strictly and restrictively. Perhaps even the first extreme is impossible—for there is no notation which is self-sufficient. But the point is clear, that all other performances extend the content of the notated text to a greater or lesser extent.

The relationship of the original musical text (the concept of the composer) to the notated text is the concern of the musicologist, rather than of the performer. The latter is expected to move forward from the notation, to produce a new musical text, reflecting both ability and musicality. The former is expected to understand the society that created the notated text and its sources, and the manner in which that society would have reacted to the notation. But for both, the musical text has to be read and understood, both its content and its 'defects'. Once that is done, the notations can be used to create a performance of a piece of music, in a way which reflects both the text and the time and place of the performer (or, equally validly, which tries to reflect something of the time and place of the composer).

## The Text in Transmission

Seen from the perspective of the present-day Western world, by far the most common way to perpetuate or disseminate a text is to copy a printed or written version. By using a notated exemplar, the modern scribe or printer feels confident that there is some reliability and authority in the new version. It can take its place in the lineage of sources which have preserved a work since its composition.

Of course, such a 'written transmission' is not fool-proof. Copyists make mistakes, typesetters misread their copy, and proof-readers often miss errors. In addition, there are always changes that are more subtle, and more significant. Most scribes make editorial changes, shifting accidentals, rationalizing dissonances, changing readings that they mistrust. By no means all of these changes are conscious or intentional. It has been shown, frequently for non-musical sources, that scribes also unwittingly change readings to conform to their own expectations. Banalization, the simplification of complex readings, is one example; but in many other cases, scribes will also make readings more subtle or more difficult to perform if that happens to fit some pattern that they have in their own ears.

At the other extreme is what is called 'oral transmission', which relies on a live performance of a composition or teaching by rote to create a new written or performed copy. Even allowing for the phenomenal feats of memory regularly achieved in orally oriented societies, this pattern just as frequently involves transformation of a composition.

The middle path is more frequent, involving dependence on both written and performing traditions. This so-called literate transmission implies an awareness of the oral patterns of performance, and of the ways in which they can be preserved and transmitted. At the same time, it assumes that the basic text is being passed down in writing (or in print). This basic text is not passed on without some impact from performing skills and preferences, which influence the scribe's editorial activities. Nor is it necessarily the source of the music for all performers, some of whom may in fact learn the music by ear from other performers or teachers, while others work from the written copies.

This is the pattern by which, for example, church congregations regularly learn hymns and other communal music, by which many big-band musicians read their scores, or by which budding opera singers learn the traditional ornamentation for nineteenth-century arias. In other words, such a manner of transmission is not limited to those unskilled in reading music, but is found wherever a lively performing tradition extends beyond the written notation. As such, it was presumably more common in earlier periods, if active performing conventions could be conveyed without notation.

When compositions are copied anew in such a society, the new copy will be derived from a blend of elements: one may be the musical text preserved in a previous copy; one will be the habits of performing that text, and another the similar habits in performing related texts; one will be the level of musical skill of the copyist, and another the requirements and abilities of the institution (church, collegium, professional orchestra, etc.) for which the copy is being made; and one will be the extent to which the copyist is accurate or careless.

If another copy is made from this one, the same factors come into play again. Thus, each new copy contains an amalgam of the decisions and lapses of the present scribe and those of each preceding scribe. The changes reflect, in each case, the particular situation faced by the scribe: they may sometimes cancel each other out, or they may (more usually) be cumulative, gradually removing the composition from the detailed presentation of the earliest sources.[34]

Relevant to the present discussion, there are two significant aspects of this

---

[34] It is this process that has justified the move towards so-called *Urtext* editions, which (whatever their other failings) seek to strip away the accretions of generations of editions.

pattern of transmission. One is that changes to some orally remembered elements frequently appear, almost as if at random, in written sources for many repertoires. Examples include the addition or removal of simple decoration (especially at cadences), precise indications of text underlay and repetitions of words in early music, or additions of slurs and pedalling patterns in later piano music. The extent of these additions must have varied from time to time, and (certainly) from scribe to scribe or from editor to editor; but individuals have their own tendencies—towards adding or removing decoration, towards adding performing guidance, towards misreading certain types of figuration, even towards 'improving' the voice-leading or the harmony.[35]

Such changes exist in the great majority of sources, not least in those prepared by the composer him or herself. However, it is not always easy to detect their presence, especially in early music, where we rarely have any solid ground on which to base our arguments. In the case of music after *c*.1800, we can usually see the evidence, for we will also have earlier editions or autographs for comparison. Thus, ornamented versions of Rossini arias can be compared with the extant simpler versions; and the gradual addition of detail in editions of Beethoven's piano sonatas is similarly easily detected. But it is only in the last century that we have looked for the changes, even in these more recent compositions.

A central part of the present discussion concerns the great extent to which change has historically been seen as acceptable, by both composer and later copyist and performer. Given this situation, the complexities of a literate transmission are only to be expected, and indeed welcomed. They allow us to see something of the range of possibilities that was thought to be acceptable in performing a piece. If we assume, as we must, that many composers changed details (great and small) each time they performed their own compositions (for they were acting as did contemporary performers of these works), then they must also themselves have expected (and perhaps also welcomed) the complexities of literate transmission. These complexities make difficult the search for an 'original' version of almost any composition—a search which (in many cases) is hardly a worthwhile exercise. For most music before the time of Bach, and for a fair proportion of later pieces, the composition will have been preserved in sources which are the result of a sequence of copyings and 'corruptions', changes which were acceptable—indeed, in some sense obligatory—in the minds of both composer and performer. The nature of the 'Ur-text', therefore, is hidden both behind the errors and omissions of multiple copyings and also behind those intentional or subconscious changes that reflect performing traditions and an oral memory of musical style and execution.

An attempt to study the transmission of almost any composition (or to recon-

---

[35] See Stanley Boorman, 'Notational Spelling and Scribal habit', in Ludwig Finscher (ed.), *Datierung und Filiation von Musikhandschriften der Josquin Zeit*, Quellenstudien zur Musik der Renaissance, 2 = Wolfenbütteler Forschungen, 26 (Wiesbaden, 1983), 65–109.

struct an *Urtext*), therefore, is not simply one of detecting the variants between sources, trying to decide which sources are related to each other, and then deciding which readings are later corruptions of an earlier pristine *Urtext*. That has been the traditional genealogical view adopted by many musicologists, and has yielded a number of insights. However, if each scribe is free to make changes within rather wide limits, the first task of the scholar must be to try to discover the musical and paleographical inclinations of that scribe and the extent to which he felt free to make change. This will give us some sense of what, in his source, reflects the earlier version of the musical text and what reflects the scribe's own understanding of it as it might have been performed in local circles.

The second result of this type of change is that, in many cases, individual performances function rather like sources in their own right. These performances influence the future copyist, giving rise to layers of decoration or changes of detail in the text as the performer read it, and revealing what works well or badly, and what seems inspired realization. Such a performer, in writing (and changing) the next copy, is using the performance as an intermediary 'text', deriving from it new readings and new traditions.[36] Jazz standards are changed by every performer, as are most other forms of popular music. When a band-leader has a new written copy prepared, he and his copyist take account of the performing tradition. The next generation of band-leaders will build on these copies, or on his recordings, to produce new versions, new texts. Without consideration of the (recorded) performances, we would be unable to understand how the original reached its most recent condition.

Each performance, in other words, is a 'text', conveying as much information to the next performer as would a written version, and influencing the direction in which that new performer will go.[37] He or she, however, with a different set of skills and inclinations, will add a different slant to the detail of the work, and start a new branch of the stemma.

## Authenticity

I argue that notation is merely 'allusive', carrying less information than the literal-minded might hope, while still offering additional guidance to the initiate. I also argue that the notated text as it survives is changed by the impact of each person who copied it, becoming less and less like the notation of the original. If, then, this newly notated text is to be used for performance—especially with the

---

[36] A plausible example of this sort of activity can be seen in the autograph copies of some of Mozart's piano concertos, where the piano part is occasionally subject to layers of change, usually written in at different times.

[37] A commendatory poem in Fletcher's play *The Faithful Shepherdess* refers to the first edition as 'This second publication', implying that the performance was the first. See the citation in Harold Love, *Scribal Publication in Seventeenth-Century England* (Oxford, 1993), 35.

traditional freedoms I have outlined—we need to question just what it actually represents.

This raises real problems. The presentation of a 'work' is presumed by most theorists to carry some authority. Walter Ong uses the word 'presence', and asserts that this presence is less strong in a written document than it is in the oral.[38] Although Ong is writing about verbal texts, his statement is clearly true for musical works, where the music comes to life, as we say, in performance; indeed, while one may have doubts about the application of the idea to some literary texts, which seem to be devised for presentation on paper and not necessarily validated by speech, there can be few such doubts where musical texts are concerned, even allowing for the evident rôle of analysis in clarifying many elements of, for example, serial music.

But Ong also argues that there is a further loss of 'presence' in the passage from manuscript to printed copies. At first glance, this might seem obvious: a composer's autograph has more authority, so we commonly believe, than a later printed edition, and this authority is manifest to the alert reader. For musicologists of Renaissance music, the manuscript (wherever prepared) has come to acquire more authority than the printed edition, for it is believed to have closer ties to a specific (and usually specifiable) place in contemporary society; and this leads to clearer evidence of the 'real' composition and of the performing tradition.[39] At the same time, however, scholars of nineteenth-century music have come to recognize that the holograph may not represent the composer's last thoughts, which instead may be better seen in a supervised first edition.

While there have been composers who seem to have written primarily with printed editions in mind, others seem to have planned to keep their material in manuscript.[40] Among the latter are Caccini (who claimed to publish *Le Nuove Musiche* because his music, circulating freely in manuscript, was being distorted), both Scarlattis (who produced repertoires that were not normally thought of as printable), and Bach. The reasons may be different in each case, but each presents a picture very different from that of Pleyel or (probably) Asola or the many chanson composers of the nineteenth century in France, all of

---

[38]  Walter Ong, *The Presence of the Word* (New Haven, 1967).

[39]  There is a grain of truth in this argument. A manuscript does carry very specific connotations for its places of origin and destination, extending to many aspects of its design and content. But it is not clear that these carry more authority, or that they are therefore closer to the readings or implications of the composer's holograph. Further, exactly the same considerations affected the decisions of the average printer's editor, with the exception (quite possibly an advantage) that the printed text had to carry the right messages for many more readers, in diverse situations.

[40]  I am not implying that these composers were not primarily writing for performance (although I think that, even as early as the sixteenth century, some composers were no longer writing for specific performances, and may not have had any performance in mind at all); but the planned manner of dissemination does seem to have had some impact on style and presentation. This is an issue discussed by Love (*Scribal Publication*), writing about seventeenth-century English literature. His arguments about how texts reflect this intended purpose and what this can tell us about the author's interests, have a number of applications to music.

whom seem to have written with the intention of having their latest production published and known through printed editions, rather than through manuscript copies.[41]

Given this range of intentions, it seems impossible to argue as a general position that there is additional 'presence' in musical manuscripts, as opposed to printed sources. In some cases, we can almost assume that the manuscript is further removed from 'presence'—and the oral original—than is the printed edition.

In addition, for the musical text, 'presence' need not be related to 'trustworthiness'. If the response of reader and performer to the text is as I have argued, neither regarded the details on the page as sacrosanct. These notations were there because the composer (or some intermediary) regarded them as essential indicators of some aspect of the execution, as stimuli, rather than as binding instructions.

Given the transmission pattern described above (in which performing conventions affect both the text and its execution) and an understanding of notation which uses its omissions as opportunities for musical expertise, the written text loses much of its 'authority', as we understand the term. The text represents an amalgam of decisions about only the essential components of a work. It is therefore rarely to be trusted as documentation of the composer's intentions.

It does, of course, stand for something. It is a depiction in symbols of what the latest (scribal or typesetting) copyist thought worth including in a kit for a performance. All the arguments about damage in transmission have to be weighed here. But, behind them all, errors as well as editing decisions, is the view that the copyist had of the work. In this sense, his activities are like those of Schnabel in my opening pages, but potentially much freer. The copyist did not have to regard any one specific symbol as essential; nor was he required to notate the optional or conventional. And the same is true for the composer and his source. A composer's view of his work, both its compulsory and optional elements, will be reflected in their presence or absence in his holograph, as too will be his view of the effect of each notational element on a potential performer.

The implications of this are that authenticity is at best a dubious concept. Not only specific readings, but also large-scale elements of a composition—even the composer's name attached to it—are suspect, the result of the last copyist's knowledge and preferences. If this scribe believed a piece to be by Haydn (or, equally seriously, if he wanted to add a worthy piece to the canon, for whatever reason), then the modern scholar is faced with an attribution, apparently as valid as many others.[42] If the scribe wished to play a symphony with only three other

---

[41] In the case of Asola, the composer was certainly filling a need by covering as completely as possible the liturgical repertoire of his Order.

[42] There is also the case of a composer—the names of Bach and Mozart spring to mind—copying someone else's work into a work-book, whence it acquires a new attribution.

string players, or with a wind band, or perhaps only for ten minutes, then a new version was created, and the decisions enshrined therein may survive today. Not infrequently, there are so few sources for major works, and those sources are far enough removed from the original place or time of conception, that we may be facing situations similar to these, but without any holograph source to act as a control. Even when we do have the composer's manuscripts, they do not necessarily carry the original musical text of a composition, as several cases in Bach's output attest.

We should therefore begin to question the concept of authenticity in sources, even as we have done for historical performance. Each source represents one unique situation: a composer, a scribe or printer with his or her own agenda, a performing requirement that might not be duplicated, and a series of conventional interpretations of the notation that are temporary and local. Such thinking has already been used to explain the extant scorings of Bach's cantatas and Haydn's symphonies, Handel's *Messiah* and Mozart's 'Haffner' serenade.

It allows us to assign to each source a different type of responsibility. Instead of carrying the burden of authority, representing the composer's best thoughts, it will carry the image of a specific interpretation of those thoughts, the interpretation of a given scribe, working in a given tradition, and writing to meet a given series of requirements.

## 'Text' as a Definer of 'Work'

In the light of these arguments, the notated text is no longer the definer of a musical composition as we understand it. Indeed, it is no more than a definer of a specific moment in the evolving history of the composition: it presents only those elements that a copyist, printer, or performer felt were important.

However, if this extant text remains the transmitter of a composition, and a guide for, and restraint on, the creative activities of the performer, at the same time as it gives licence, we need to ask which of its elements do define the composition. Later composers or scribes could add voices to, or recompose sections of, early Renaissance chansons; composers and performers could substitute arias and larger sections in operas; performers could rearrange the order of movements or embellish to the point where the original was completely lost to view. Yet the same composer's name was retained throughout the process. Soriano could add a second four-voiced choir to a mass by Palestrina, while the original composer's name was retained; and Chopin's First Piano Concerto could be radically rewritten by Tausig, among others, and still be ascribed to Chopin.[43] On

---

[43] Soriano's two-choir version of Palestrina's *Missa Papae Marcelli* (originally for six voices) was published in his first book of masses, in 1609; the same mass (with others) was reduced to a setting for four voices and continuo by Giovanni Francesco Anerio, and published in 1619. The addition of continuo was a fairly common practice in the

the other hand, a single phrase (of text and music) could be added to the beginning of a motet by Viardot, which thereafter carried the name of Josquin; and new contratenor parts to popular chansons often resulted in a new composer's name being attached to them.[44]

The addition to musical sources of composer's names (as opposed to those of the poets of the texts) is a relatively late phenomenon, first found at the end of the fourteenth century. Thereafter, the name became more significant, and (from the time of Dunstable) major composers' names acquired a particular cachet. The implication is that there was a 'work', with some set of attributes, which belonged to that composer, in the sense that he had created it. However, in the cases I have described, we can hardly be sure which elements of a composition were considered identifiers. Nor can we be sure which, if changed, remade the work, and thus changed the name of the composer.

The intrinsic feature of a musical work is therefore not easy to define—not solely from an aesthetic position, but simply from the evidence of the historical record. When does a work cross the line? And what might that tell us about the aesthetic criteria of a given time and place?

We can give vague, general answers to these questions, and for some repertoires the answers are easier than for others. For Mozart or Beethoven, the key centre, the melodic material, the formal structures, and some other elements are clearly fundamental; for Dufay, perhaps the modality, perhaps the underlying skeleton of thematic material, and perhaps the form (although this is subject to change, especially when the music is set to a *contrafactum*); for Gershwin, the skeleton of the melody, the underlying harmonic direction, and one or two significant intervals or figures in the melody. Such elements seem to be enough to require an improviser or arranger to acknowledge the composer's parentage. The other elements are apparently seen as optional, sounds that link together the key unalterable features.

This attitude must also have been that of many composers.[45] Josquin knew that each singer would use the notation to produce a different set of melodic features; Handel knew that each prima donna would add excessive decoration to his operatic arias; Machaut might expect additional voice-parts to be added to

---

early seventeenth century, and even this habit of rescoring was not very unusual, reflecting a long practice. The Soriano version has been recorded, by the William Byrd Choir with Gavin Turner.

Tausig's drastic rewriting of Chopin's concerto has also been recorded; it is paralleled by other examples, by Burmeister and Klindworth, e.g. The practice which it represents was typical of the period, and a brief discussion of the ethos behind it can be found in Harold Schonberg, *The Great Pianists* (London, 1965), 125–33.

[44] The setting of 'Dum complerentur' attributed to Viardot in a Vatican MS is elsewhere preserved with an added first phrase opening with the words 'Lectio actuum' and attributed to Josquin. Richard Sherr discusses the situation in his 'Notes on Two Roman Manuscripts of the Early Sixteenth Century', *Musical Quarterly*, 63 (1977), 48–73. Josquin was also involved in one of the many cases of the second phenomenon, when he added two canonic lower parts to Hayne van Ghizeghem's 'De tous bien plaine'. The version is preserved in *Odhecaton A* (but similar situations can be found in other chansonniers), and discussed in the modern editions.

[45] Again, we have to exempt much of the repertoire that follows the late eighteenth-century pronouncements on the importance of music among the other arts, and the direct link between composer and genius.

his works, and even some of his own rewritten. Given this common knowledge, composers would have recognized that certain elements of any composition were less significant than others. They had to write them down, of course, for a text is not viable in a fragmentary state. But that did not give those elements a canonical status.

The text, as it appears in sources, is not therefore a simple definer of the work: it is a version of the work, carrying elements believed to be essential to that composition, and other elements used to link these together. These other elements gave the copyist and performer wide discretion to change and embellish; but there is no reason to believe that every copyist could identify the essential elements correctly, or that every composer would have minded when the copyist erred.[46]

## Appendix: Further Reading

Atlas, Allan, *The Capella Giulia Chansonnier* (Brooklyn, NY, 1975).

Boorman, Stanley, 'Composition—Copying: Performance—Recreation: The Matrix of Stemmatic Problems for Early Music', in Renato Borghi and Pietro Zappala (eds.), *L'edizione critica tra testo musicale e testo letterario*, Studi e testi musicale, n.s. 3 (Lucca, 1995), 46–55.

Dearing, Vinton, *Principles and Practice of Textual Analysis* (Berkeley, 1974).

Feder, Georg, *Musikphilologie* (Darmstadt, 1987).

Greetham, David C., 'Textual and Literary Theory: Redrawing the Matrix', *Studies in Bibliography*, 42 (1989), 1–24.

—— *Textual Scholarship: An Introduction* (New York, 1992).

Hamm, Charles, 'Privileging the Moment of Reception: Music and Radio in South Africa', in Steven Paul Scher (ed.), *Music and Text: Critical Enquiries* (Cambridge, 1992), 21–37.

Ingarden, Roman, *The Work of Music and the Problem of its Identity*, trans. Adam Czerniawski (Berkeley, 1986).

Levy, Kenneth, 'On Gregorian Orality', *Journal of the American Musicological Society*, 43 (1990), 185–227.

Love, Harold, *Scribal Publication in Seventeenth-Century England* (Oxford, 1993).

Nattiez, Jean-Jacques, *Music and Discourse: Towards a Semiology of Music*, trans. Carolyn Abbate (Princeton, 1990).

Nettl, Bruno, 'Types of Tradition and Transmission', in R. Falck and T. Rice (eds.), *Cross-cultural Perspectives on Music* (Toronto, 1982), 3–19.

Oliphant, Dave, and Bradford, Robin (eds.), *New Directions in Textual Studies* (Austin, Tex., 1990).

---

[46] Outside musicology, there is an active discussion of these concepts of the text, often couched in polemical, fashionable language. A recent, balanced discussion of the basic approaches, with references to a wide range of literature, can be found in David C. Greetham, *Textual Scholarship: An Introduction*, ch. 8.

Some musicologists have recently argued, in line with developments in literary theory, that the text has no significance beyond what they, or you or I, can gain from it (see e.g. Lawrence Kramer, 'Haydn's Chaos, Schenker's Order: or, Hermeneutics and Musical Analysis: Can They Mix?', *19th-Century Music*, 16 (1992–3), 3–17). Their arguments are discussed elsewhere in this book. But it might surprise them to know that most musicians of the past felt similarly. The difference is that the historical performer interpreted the text in order to create a work of music, and thus to give pleasure to others.

Ong, Walter J., *Orality and Literacy: The Technologizing of the Word* (London, 1982).

Taruskin, Richard, *Text and Act: Essays on Music and Performance* (New York, 1995).

Treitler, Leo, 'Oral, Written and Literate Processes in the Transmission of Medieval Music', *Speculum*, 56 (1981), 471–91.

—— 'Reading and Singing: On the Genesis of Occidental Music Writing', *Early Music History*, 4 (1984), 135–208.

—— 'The "Unwritten" and "Written Transmission" of Medieval Chant and the Start-up of Musical Notation', *Journal of Musicology*, 10 (1992), 131–91.

# 19

# *Finding the Music in Musicology: Performance History and Musical Works*

## José A. Bowen

Fundamental questions are always the hardest, so perhaps it is not surprising if we avoid defining our terms before we begin. While it would seem essential to begin any study of musical works with the acknowledgement that they exist in a very different way from both performances (which are events) and scores (which are physical objects),[1] most of us assume that we and our audience know what we mean when we speak of a symphony or any other 'work'. After all, it doesn't help our credibility not to be able to define the very thing we are hoping to study. Still, I want to propose that the awareness of musical works as neither stable nor fixed phenomena does not have to be paralysing; rather, the fact that musical works change through both the creation and reception of performances presents us with a fundamentally new field of study.

In fact, it gives us too much to study: namely, all performances of all music, and it requires new tools and methodology. But then, musicology has been in a state of reinvention for some years now. In addition to offering a new, unexplored subdiscipline, the study of music *as* and *in* performance provides a context within which both the different branches of the 'new' musicology and the old and the new musicology can come together and talk about *music* once again. All this, however, is dependent on my contention that the history of performance is more than simply the history of performance practice.

I

Western music of the last two centuries is clearly more 'work-centred' than many other musics, and it comes as no surprise that ethnomusicologists and others who study more oral, 'event-centred' musical cultures have less trouble defining their terms.[2] For them, music is something that sounds. When there is

---

[1] Roman Ingarden's demonstration that musical works, scores, and performances are distinguishable and individual phenomena can be found in his *The Work of Music and the Problem of its Identity*, trans. Adam Czerniawski, ed. Jean G. Harrel (Berkeley, 1986), 9–23, 34–40.

[2] It would be interesting to write an event-centred history of Western music.

a musical work, a performance is an *example* of that musical work. Despite their predominance in Western music, scores are usually incidental to the production of music, and almost always post-date the musical creation. A score can be either a *sample* (a transcription of a single performance in all its particularity) or a *summary* (a unique, personal attempt to establish certain essential qualities for an idealized performance of the work). That is, a score can be a sample of only a single performance of a musical work or a summary of several actual or potential performances of the (presumably) same musical work. Similarly, in most of the 'pro-active' or 'prescriptive' scores of Western music, the score is an attempt to define the boundaries for future performances. In either case the score is a spatial representation of only *some* of the elements of the temporal phenomena we call music. Music is a sequence of sounds, each of which appears only in the present, and which, therefore, has no persistent physical existence. While the sound of a musical performance is fleeting, however, the musical work exists even when the performers are silent, and this continued existence is due to human memory. The ability to preserve a *sequence* of sounds and thereby generate music is unique to the remembering mind.[3]

Particular sequences of sounds (like musical works) are stored in the collective memory, which I call 'tradition'. Each performance, like every speech-act, is an attempt to mediate between the identity of the work (as remembered by tradition) and the innovation of the performer; musical performers are engaged in both communication of the work and individual expression. Each performance (and each score) attempts to include the qualities which the performer (composer or editor) considers essential to retain the identity of the musical work, along with additional interpretive or accidental qualities which are necessary to realize a work in sound.[4] If the listener's remembered version of the essential qualities differs from that of the performer, the listener may not categorize the performance as a performance of the musical work in question. This creates a problem, since the expectations of listeners can change rapidly. If Corelli were to reappear and perform his works in line with the most authentic expectations of eighteenth-century performers and listeners, changing the notes, he might today not even be recognized as playing the pieces he is said to have written.

The gap between performances and scores was wider in the eighteenth century than it usually is today. Since all performers were trained in composition (so much so that the distinction between performers and composers was

---

[3] Hegel captured this notion in his pithy remark that 'the notes re-echo in the depths of the soul' (G. W. F. Hegel, *Aesthetics: Lectures on Fine Art*, ed. H. G. Hotho (1835), trans. T. M. Know (Oxford, 1975), vol. 11, pt. III, sect. III, ch. II (Music), 3(a), p. 892). It is rather a paradox that music, to be music, must sound, but that, as only a series of sounds, it is not music. Music, in other words, is a perceived quality. Without the listener who remembers the last sound (which now no longer exists), there is only the sound of the present. A sound with no past or future is only a sound. For a sound to become music, it requires a past or a future which it can only acquire in the remembering listener. The distinction between sound and music is as much phenomenological as it is aesthetic.

[4] Stanley Boorman makes a similar point in the previous chapter.

*[handwritten marginal note:]* not necessarily — morton feldman, minimalism (in strict sense), etc.

often virtually non-existent), a 'composer' could assume that any 'performer' could 'realize' not only a figured bass, which was an explicit shorthand, but a melodic line, which was an implicit shorthand. 'Graced' editions with sample realizations of the melodic line (at least in the case of slow movements) were provided for less experienced performers. Example 19.1 compares the original 1700 edition with Etienne Roger's 1715 edition of Corelli's Opus 5 Sonatas 'with ornaments added to the adagios of this work, composed by Mr. A. Corelli, and as he

Ex. 19.1. *Corelli, Opus V Sonatas: the original 1700 edition and Etienne Roger's 1715 'graced' edition 'with ornaments added to the adagios of this work, composed by Mr. A. Corelli, and as he performs them'.*

performs them'.[5] The accuracy of the supposed transcription or the authenticity of the attribution to Corelli (now widely disputed) is immaterial if we recognize this notation as only a sample or example of how the work might have been performed. Like a realization of a figured bass in a modern edition, the graced edition serves both a pedagogical and a practical function: it allows a performance by the totally uninitiated to take place (albeit as a simple re-creation of an already specified performance), and it serves as a model for future performances. Only the complete novice is expected to reproduce Corelli's performance literally, and the results are likely to be about as convincing as the literal reproduction of a dialogue in a beginning language textbook: 'How are you?' 'I am fine. My hovercraft is full of eels.' For those with an understanding of the particular rules of syntax and style, the sample dialogue or ornaments become only one of many possible variations on the basic phrase. We are not meant to reproduce it literally, but to produce our own individual version.

While each performance attempts to mediate between tradition and innovation, it in turn becomes part of the remembered tradition. It is easy for an interpretive or accidental quality to become an essential quality of the work for later generations, especially since the advent of recording technology.[6] That is what happens when the novice imitates Corelli's sample ornamentation exactly. The boundary between interpretive and essential qualities can and does change, and the new boundary is then enforced by tradition. Tradition is, therefore, the history of remembered innovation, and it defines a set of normative assumptions or essential qualities about the work which can change over time. Each performance, therefore, looks both backward and forward in time. In other words, each performance is simultaneously both example and definition of the musical work.[7]

The absolute distinction we attempt to make between the technical and interpretive aspects (that is, between the essential and accidental qualities) of a performance is a false one. How we play the work determines what we think the work is, as well as the other way round. In certain musical styles (jazz, Italian opera, eighteenth-century adagios, and perhaps even early plainchant) the interpreter is free to add or delete notes. We need to hear enough pitches to be convinced of the identity of the work, but if we hear *only* the traditional pitches,

[5] The title of Roger's edition reads: *Sonata a violino solo e violone o cimbalo di Arcangelo Corelli da Fusignano, Opera Quinta Parte prima. Nouvelle Edition où l'on a joint les agrémens des Adagio de cet ouvrage, composez par M. A. Corelli, comme il les joue*; quoted from Marc Pincherle, *Corelli: His Life, his Work*, trans. Hubert E. M. Russell (New York, 1956), 111.

[6] Cultures, religions, and languages routinely change and create symbols in this way: one generation's innovations (or even accidents) become the next generation's tradition. An arbitrary location, colour, food, song, tempo, or note can accidentally become associated with a ritual, and eventually become an essential part. Singing 'Auld Lang Syne' was once simply someone's innovatory idea of a nice addition to a traditional New Year's Eve celebration.

[7] A more complete version of this theory of musical works can be found in my 'The History of Remembered Innovation: Tradition and its Role in the Relationship between Musical Works and their Performances'. *Journal of Musicology*, 10 (Spring 1993), 139–73.

the performance will be labelled 'derivative'.[8] Until recently, the same was true for most Western art-music; but recordings and a new performance aesthetic have limited a performer's freedom to change pitches in, for example, a Beethoven symphony. (It is worth remembering that conductors as recent as Toscanini and Furtwängler both made changes in notes quite frequently, and it was common in the nineteenth century.) While tradition may have established that the pitches in the score are now an essential quality for the performance of a Classical symphony, it remains unclear which of the other qualities (tempo, dynamics, timbre, instrumentation, orchestration, phrasing, and portamento, for example) are also essential and which are accidental. Various classifications have been made. Nelson Goodman argues, for example, that tempo is accidental (he calls it an 'auxiliary direction'), and that a performance at any tempo, however wretched, is still a performance of the work.[9] Composers, of course, define the essential elements on the basis of their own music's characteristics: Berlioz held that not only the orchestration, but the most minute details of instrumental timbre, were essential to the identity of his works. For Berlioz, the sound of a particular key of clarinet was an essential, not an incidental, part of the work; using standard B flat clarinets or valved horns (as is virtually universal practice today), he claimed, destroys the work.[10] (Is it possible, then, that a future generation will find Haitink and Harnoncourt as corrupt as Toscanini found Nikisch, and we now find Toscanini?)

While it might be easier to study the changing definition of the work by examining the pitch changes in the history of a jazz work or an opera aria, the interpretive qualities of a sonata or a symphony which we often call the nuances (and which may be more difficult to quantify) are just as real as those we have traditionally assumed are essential. While recent tradition has made pitch selection an interpretive choice in one genre (jazz, for example) but not another (classical symphony, for example), it is also clear that the difference between essential and accidental or interpretive qualities is defined, not given. If the sequence of pitches in a symphony is fixed, the way they are played is not. Unless we want to say that

---

[8] In Wittgenstein's terms, the set of performances which are said to belong to the same musical work are related by the concept of family resemblance (Wittgenstein, *Philosophical Investigations*, trans. G. E. M. Anscombe (Oxford, 1953), § 67). Like a family portrait, a set of performances of a musical work reveals a set of shared characteristics, but no one member of the group need have all of the characteristics, and any two members may have nothing in common (i.e. there is no one essential family trait). To be identified as belonging to this musical work, a performance must have 'some' of the characteristics, but obviously not every combination of characteristics will do. Wittgenstein's example is a war, which has winners and losers, but is not a member of the class of 'games'. Similarly, trills are an expected addition to eighteenth-century adagios, but not every combination will leave the musical work intact. Conversely, a performance with no trills might be a bad performance, but few would doubt that it was still a performance of the work. This 'blurred concept' (ibid. § 71) precisely describes the state of a musical work: a group of performances related to each other by various combinations of characteristics.

[9] Nelson Goodman, *Languages of Art*, 2nd edn. (Indianapolis, 1976), 185.

[10] Hector Berlioz, *A Treatise of Modern Instrumentation and Orchestration to which is appended The [sic] Chef d'orchestre*, trans. Mary Clarke (London, 1858); rev. edn. ed. Joseph Bennett (London, 1882), 256.

a musical work is a series of *pitches* (and not a series of *sounds*), we must ask if a symphony can change.[11]

Historically, the advent of the symphony signified a new ideal in the phenomenological status of music. In the eighteenth century, the composer was in charge of most performances, making the score a less important object, and music was, to a large extent, an *event*. In the nineteenth century, a new model of music as *work* evolved from Beethoven's 'finished' scores and the *letzter Hand* concept: the idea that an artist creates a final, fixed, immortal text.[12] As Carl Dahlhaus has pointed out, however, nineteenth-century musicians did not have a single aesthetic consciousness: composers like Rossini (from the opera-dominated South) continued to create unique musical events, while composers like Beethoven (from the symphonic-dominated North) began to create more permanent, fixed musical works, with composers like Liszt and Chopin usually somewhere in between.[13] Gradually, however, the idea of music as work (with the score as its inviolable sacred text) began to replace the idea of music as event (with the score as merely its blueprint).[14]

Musicology inherited both the aesthetic of music as work and the German symphonic repertoire to which it is best suited. Musicology has traditionally had difficulty with the 'music as event' genres (like jazz), and ethnomusicology has absorbed most of these genres.[15] Since ethnomusicologists have, in general, been less interested in Western art-music, Italian opera was long neglected by both. Rossini has recently made a come-back, but it is conspicuous that this has largely been driven by the new Rossini edition; the approach, in other words, is coloured by our (not his) desire for fixed texts. In musicology the first step is always to have a critical edition; our discomfort with the variable aspects of music largely explains why musicology has been reluctant to study performance events even as regards its central repertoire.

While performance practice has become an important subdiscipline for musicology, it has been treated as a study of something distinct from the individual

---

[11] In other words, if only the pitch relationships matter, then instrumentation does not; a transcription for kazoos leaves a symphony intact. If instrumentation does matter, then what about style? If we *need* to use violins to preserve the work, then what type of violins? What type of bow? What type of sound? If the sound of a work is important, then surely all works have changed. Even returning to the original instruments, in the original hall with the original audience and performers (if all this were possible), would still leave us in the dark about which qualities were essential and which were accidental.

[12] The title of the first edition of Goethe's complete works, e.g., is *Werke: Vollständige Ausgabe, letzter Hand* (Stuttgart, 1827–30). See also Lydia Goehr, *The Imaginary Museum of Musical Works: An Essay in the Philosphy of Music* (Oxford, 1992).

[13] Carl Dalhhaus, *Nineteenth-Century Music*, trans. J. Bradford Robinson (Berkeley, 1989), 9–10.

[14] See my *The Conductor and the Score: A History of the Relationship between Interpreter and Text from Beethoven to Wagner* (forthcoming).

[15] I would also venture that musicology has projected the concept of music as work backwards in time to genres and periods where it is largely inappropriate. Corelli, one imagines, would care more about the performing conditions, the unique style of the performer, the response of the audience, the sound of the instrument, and the overall impact of the performance than the critical edition upon which it was based. For performer-composers like Corelli and Rossini, the integrity of the performance was more important than the integrity of the work.

musical work, and few scholars have studied the changes in performance traditions for specific works. Those who have, have assumed that performance practice was a study separate from the study of the musical work itself.[16] What *I* am suggesting is that we study the performance tradition of a musical work not as a separate discipline, irrelevant to the immutable work, but as the history of the changing definition of the work itself. The study of the performance tradition of a musical work *is* the study of the musical work.

## II

In additional to *why*, however, it has been unclear *how* musicology could study performance tradition. The first answer is simply to listen. Amateurs and critics, more than academic musicologists, have long concentrated on their listening skills; but there are numerous scholars, record and concert reviewers, and knowledgeable devotees who know and study performers as well as works. Harold Schonberg, Joseph Horowitz, and Barry Millington, to name only three, bring together a depth of knowledge about both repertoire and performers in their work.[17] Robert Philip and David Breckbill also deserve recognition for the first studies of early twentieth-century performance style based on recordings.[18] These studies, and many more, are useful and informative, and they have taken a great stride from the subjective appraisal of quality (a typical, even essential, part of review writing) to a more scholarly interest in the analysis of the difference between styles. Future studies will build on their foundation.

Many of these studies, however, go no further than general observations. Critics especially have concentrated on identifying a few typical qualities of a performer's or a period style. Too often, statements about Toscanini and his fast tempos, for example, are simply repetitions of critical lore, and not the result of research. (Toscanini's performances at Bayreuth, for example, are some of the longest and slowest on record.[19]) But even the better studies, which are often

---

[16] Most of these scholars also want to prescribe a return to a particular, 'correct' interpretation thought to be somehow based on an earlier or original one. The current loyalty to the original performance practice of the piece (the new concept of 'authenticity') has replaced the previous loyalty to the composer's intentions (the old concept of 'fidelity'). Both claim to be loyal, one to what the composer wanted, the other to what he got. Authenticity is concerned with the external sound, while fidelity was more concerned with the internal spirit. The early history of this dichotomy is traced in my paper 'Mendelssohn, Berlioz and Wagner as Conductors: The Origins of the Ideal of "Fidelity to the Composer" ', *Performance Practice Review*, 6/1 (Spring 1993), 77–88.

[17] Harold C. Schonberg, *The Great Conductors* (New York, 1967); Joseph Horowitz, *Understanding Toscanini: How he Became an American Culture-God and Helped Create a New Audience for Old Music* (New York, 1987); Barry Millington and Stewart Spencer (eds.), *Wagner in Performance* (New Haven, 1992). All of the authors cited here have produced copiously, and these references represent only single examples from their large publication lists. A complete bibliography of performance analysis is forthcoming in the first issue of *Music in Performance* (Oxford).

[18] Robert Philip, *Early Recordings and Musical Style: Changing Tastes in Instrumental Performance 1900–1950* (Cambridge, 1992); David Breckbill, 'Wagner on Record: Re-evaluating Singing in the Early Years' in Millington and Spencer (eds.), *Wagner in Performance*, 153–67.

[19] Egon Voss, *Die Dirigenten der Bayreuther Festspiele* (Regensburg, 1976).

repertoire- or instrument-specific, have had difficulty getting past general observations. Robert Philip is right when he says that there is generally more portamento and more tempo fluctuation in early recordings; but there are, of course,
individual performers and performances which do not conform to these gener-
alities. We need to know when and why these devices were applied, and especially why they occur in some pieces but not others. In order to engage in more
specific analysis, we need to study the recorded repertory more comprehensively
and to develop new methodology for doing so.[20]

Although less well known to both musicologists and the general public, there
is also a large body of work on performance by music theorists, cognitive scientists, and psychologists. Eric Clarke, Manfred Clynes, Bruno Repp, Alf Gabrielsson, and many others have demonstrated that many variations in nuance
cannot only be measured, but also perceived.[21] Combining computers and MIDI
equipment with recent research in neurophysiology, these scholars are rapidly
constructing a coherent account of how the brain creates and perceives musical
expression. While it might seem anomalous to use machines to measure what
we might not otherwise hear, it is worth recalling that Czerny maintained that
'there is a certain way of playing melodious passages with greater tranquillity,
and yet not perceptibly slower, so that all appears to flow on in one and the
same time, and the difference would only be discovered by a reference to the beats
of the Metronome'.[22] It seems unavoidable—desirable in fact—that future research in this field will continue to seek measurable quantities in musical
performance. In fact, the short-term goal is to develop empirical methods which
will allow us to discover the objective correlates of what is a generally perceived
phenomenon.

While ostensibly interested in the same subject, these two approaches (the
critical/historical and the cognitive) are actually quite disparate in their methods
and objectives, and many musicologists will feel uncomfortable with both. On
the one hand, the general descriptive studies are (often unfairly) confused with
CD ratings, which usually seek only to justify or explain a particular response to

---

[20] Philip, e.g., concludes that the trend he has noticed to slower tempos is a general one (*Early Recordings*, 35). It
is not. Although Philip surveyed an enormous number of recordings (but usually only a few for each piece), he did
not listen to the complete recorded history for any work. For the limited number of pieces for which I have done this
(see Bowen, 'Tempo, Duration and Flexibility: Techniques in the Analysis of Performance', *Journal of Musicological
Research*, 16 (1996) 111–156), no such trend is apparent. Some pieces are speeding up, some are slowing down,
and most have a relatively stable spread of tempi throughout their recorded history. Looking at ten or even twenty
performances from the 80+-year history of recordings of Beethoven's Symphony No. 5 gives a very different picture
from looking at over 100.

[21] See e.g. Eric F. Clarke, 'Imitating and Evaluating Real and Transformed Musical Performances'. *Music Perception*, 10 (1993), 207–21; Manfred Clynes, *Music, Mind & Brain: The Neuropsychology of Music Perception* (New York,
1982); Bruno Repp, 'A Constraint on the Expressive Timing of a Melodic Gesture: Evidence from Performance and
Aesthetic Judgement', *Music Perception*, 10/2 (Winter 1992), 221–42; Alf Gabrielsson (ed.), *Action and Perception in
Rhythm and Meter*, Publication of the Swedish Academy of Music, 55 (Stockholm, 1987).

[22] Carl Czerny, *Über den richtigen Vortrag der sämtlichen Beethoven'schen Klavierwerke*, facs. ed. Paul Badura-Skoda
(Vienna, 1963), 87. English trans. quoted from *On the Proper Performance of all Beethoven's Works for the Piano*, facs.
ed. Paul Badura-Skoda (Vienna, 1970), 83.

a single recording; musicology (especially in America) has traditionally shunned this overtly 'subjective' criticism. On the other hand, we are often equally suspicious of scientific-looking 'data'. (Music psychologists and cognitive theorists have not helped with terms like 'microstructure' and 'cybernetics'.[23]) While the method of one seems to offer no evidence (only opinion), the other offers 'evidence' but not of an overtly musical nature. The aims also differ: reviewers are interested in making an aesthetic judgement, while cognitive research uses music as a means of gaining insight into perception and the human brain, and we rarely learn much about the musical works which appear as the manifest subjects of enquiry.

Given musicological suspicion of both subjective observation and objective numerical analysis, it is no wonder that this area has remained largely untravelled by musicologists; all available options appear to be blocked. Upon further inspection, however, this suspicion is perhaps neither such an unreasonable nor unrealistic position. While few would claim that a musical performance can be entirely reduced to numbers, we still want objective and quantifiable information which allows the perception that we are studying the most ineffable qualities of heard music. (We may dislike the idea that a musical performance could be reduced to its component acoustic parts, yet we feel perfectly comfortable reducing a musical composition to its component pitches.) With a growing number of scholars experimenting with a variety of methodologies, it should eventually be possible to combine the best features of these two approaches to music performance: to combine detailed empirical data with an analytical view of the entire interpretation.

There are, however, a number of practical steps which must precede this final stage. First, there needs to be an increase in the production and distribution of discographies. At the moment, the first stage for any project in the analysis of recorded music is a discography. While there are an increasing number of performer and institution discographies, there are still very few complete discographies for composers and individual works.[24] Where discographies do exist, they are often hard to find, and also vary in quality, format, completeness, and reliability. Discographies should include all recordings of a particular group, composer, work, performer, or institution and offer complete information for each recording (date, place, personnel, original matrix numbers, alternate takes, and company numbers for all issues in all formats); but this is often not the case.[25] Furthermore, since different scholars will want to search for different

---

[23] The latter is from the title of a recent symposium, 'Cybernetic Paradigms of Musical and Theatrical Performance', held as part of the annual meeting of the International Institute for Advanced Studies in Systems Research and Cybernetics, 16–20 Aug. 1995 in Baden-Baden, Germany.

[24] While it is possible (but not easy) to do a complete discography for a performer who has finished his or her career (although new reissues of old recordings will force updates), it is much harder to stay current with any work in the current repertoire. Since the publication of my discography of Thelonious Monk's 'Round Midnight', *Journal of Musicology*, 10 (Spring 1993), 169–73, there have been dozens of new recordings issued.

[25] For examples of excellent discographies, see those by Jerome Weber which have appeared in the Association for Recorded Sound Collections (ARSC) journal. What goes in a discography also varies with the given repertoire,

types of material, cross-references of various kinds are necessary: one should be able to find recordings with reference to each of the items of information in each entry.[26] This is hardly a trivial task to contemplate before beginning the real research.

Although CD reissues present problems of reliability (has the engineer chosen the right speed for playing early 78s, and is the information about the original recordings accurate or even included?), the collection and study of old recordings has never been easier.[27] There is more material in print now than at any other time in the history of recording, but this bonanza is usable only if there is sufficient discographical information to verify which recordings are which. Even given a complete discography, however, the task of securing reliable copies of all recordings is again hardly non-trivial. Most sound libraries collect specifically for breadth, not depth; many libraries might aim to have all the Handel operas available, but few would aim for all recordings of Brahms' First Symphony.

These problems are most pressing in the study of individual works, whereas for studies of specific artists and periods these initial stages are less problematic. (One can probably say something cogent about Karajan's conducting style without listening to every single one of his recordings.[28]) Similarly, studying an artist, style, or work which appears on only a few recordings makes completeness an achievable goal.[29] While a performance history of a single work involves an enormous amount of preliminary work, however, it also has enormous advantages.

First, having a relatively complete history in sound allows for the detailed tracking of changes in the performance tradition.[30] Only if all performances are considered can it be known for certain that a particular tradition originated with a specific performer. Second, a large selection of performances allows for the

and it is by no means clear that a single best format can be devised. See Michael H. Gray, 'Discography: Its Prospects and Problems', *Notes*, 35/3, (Mar. 1979), 578–92, and Martin Elste, 'Evaluating Discographies of Classical Music', paper presented at the IASA Conference, Vienna, 1988.

[26] Given that it is rare to find publishers willing to reproduce all the adequate indexes and the need for periodic updating, discographies might best be preserved on data bases. Further information is available from the Centre for the History and Analysis of Recorded Music (CHARM) at Georgetown University, Washington DC. See http://www.georgetown.edu/departments/AMT/music/bowen/CHARM.html.

[27] It is equally clear that with the ever-increasing number of previously unreleased live recordings, no discography or performance study will ever be complete.

[28] In an earlier study, I attempted to analyse a limited number of conductors' approaches to Mozart symphonies, and then to determine if the same traits manifested themselves in recordings of Beethoven. See José A. Bowen, 'A Computer-Assisted Study of Conducting', in Eleanor Selfridge-Field and Walter Hewlett (eds.), *Computing in Musicology* (Menlo Park, Calif., 1994).

[29] For his book *Early Jazz: Its Roots and Musical Development* (London, 1968) Gunther Schuller was able to listen to every single jazz recording made before about 1930. It is barely conceivable that he was able to do this for his next book, *The Swing Era: The Development of Jazz, 1930–1945* (London, 1989). But surely even he won't attempt this for his anticipated book on Bebop and Cool jazz.

[30] As has been noted, no performance history, even for a twentieth-century work, can ever be complete; there are always missing live performances. Live performances, however, are heard by a limited audience, and it is recorded performances which carry the greatest authority for most works. See my forthcoming 'Mahler, Authenticity and Authority'.

separation of period style from individual innovation. A researcher with only a few recordings from the 1950s, for example, will be unable to tell if the new performance traits observed reflect (1) the style of the individual conductors, (2) the style of the period or a national style, (3) the style of the orchestra, (4) an unusual recording session, or (5) a change in the performance tradition of the particular piece. This is particularly problematic in the case of the earliest recordings, where often only a single recording exists: the 1913 recording of Beethoven's Symphony No. 5 by Artur Nikisch is surely characteristic of his personal conducting style, as well as the style of the day and some specific traditions in the performance of Beethoven's Fifth. Sorting out the difference between period, geographic and national styles, work-specific performing tradition, and individual innovations becomes a great deal easier when there are multiple recordings for each geography, orchestra, conductor, period, hall, and performance condition.

Finally, more recordings equals more data, and hopefully more reliable conclusions. This is especially true for the generalizations about performance style which are so often made: 'Pieces slow down as they become more familiar', for instance—or, for that matter, 'Pieces speed up as they become more familiar'. Really large surveys, of course, are limited by human memory, a problem which computers don't share. While computers can't yet 'listen' to music, they can store a great deal of information about performances, and for statements about large-scale trends they are more accurate than human observation. The specific trade-off with numerical data is, in fact, that while we obviously lose something in the translation of musical observations to numbers, we gain the ability to handle large amounts of information. While there may be a suspicion that numerical data can only lead to generic conclusions, ironically, numerical data often lead to extremely tangible, specific conclusions.

Figure 19.1 presents four graphs from the recorded history of the first movement of Beethoven's Fifth Symphony.[31] The first (*a*) demonstrates that it now seems to take less time to perform this part of the movement than in previous years.[32] Not only is this not evidence that all pieces, or even all first movements, are speeding up; it is not even evidence that *this* movement is speeding up as a whole. While it is mathematically true that tempo and duration are inversely proportional, human performances always employ (whether intended or not) some degree of tempo fluctuation. Figure 19.1*b* demonstrates that the average initial tempo (taken after the opening fermatas) has been fairly constant over the eighty-year recorded history of the work.[33] The average closing tempo (Fig.

[31] Each dot represents a performance, and in all cases they are plotted by year. The line is a linear regression which is the computer's attempt to find a trend; 100 per cent accuracy would result if the line passed through all the dots. For more on this see my 'Tempo, Duration and Flexibility'.

[32] The changing practice of repeating the exposition has been factored out of this graph by considering only the time required to complete the initial performance of the exposition.

[33] There has been a slight increase of tempo, but not enough to be statistically siginificant (simply look at the data rather than at the line drawn), and certainly not enough to account for the magnitude of the duration change.

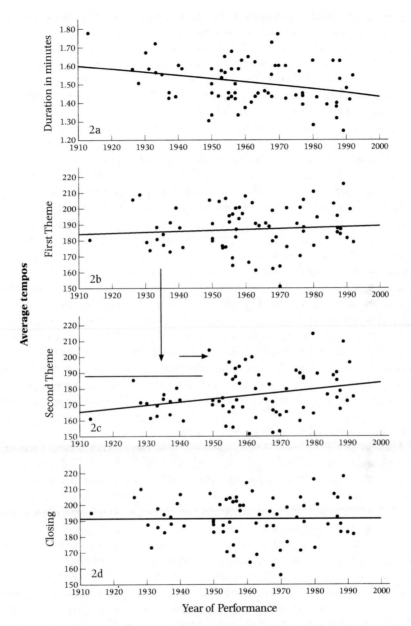

**Fig. 19.1.** Recordings of Beethoven, Symphony No. 5, first movement, exposition. *a.* Duration in minutes versus year of performance. *b.* Average initial tempo of the first theme versus year of performance. *c.* Average initial tempo of the second theme versus year of performance. *d.* Average initial tempo of the closing theme versus year of performance.

19.1*d*) is even more level, and has even fallen off slightly. The missing ten seconds or so have come from a dramatic increase in the speed of the second theme.[34] Figure 19.1*c* demonstrates that before the late 1940s, all the recorded performances followed the long nineteenth-century tradition of slowing down for the second theme.[35] After World War II, at least some conductors began to perform this material at a similar tempo to the opening material. While the tradition of slowing down for the second theme has by no means been entirely eliminated, a new tradition has gradually increased the average tempo, and so reduced the time needed to perform this section.

Traditional analysis often investigates the structure of a movement by the proportional weight given to themes and keys, and its typical unit of measure is the bar. While it is not clear that duration alone is the perceptual unit, this change in the performance tradition does affect the proportions of the movement. There is, therefore, no way to study *the* structure of a musical work; the structure of the music will vary depending on who is performing it, when, where, and for whom. We can, however, study the *changing* structure of the music in performance. What is crucial, then, is the recognition that musical works are inseparable from unique, individual performances. To say that musicology is interested in the objective musical work while criticism is interested in the subjective musical performance is to create a false dichotomy. Musicology's interest in musical works overlaps with criticism's interest in the individual performer and psychology's interest in how the human brain creates and perceives musical nuance. But musicology also brings an interest in history and in the analysis of works; the musicology of music in performance is the study not only of performance practice, perception, and reception, but of the individual *history* of each musical work.

In order to study the changing musical work, it is necessary to understand changes in performance practice, ideology, and expectations. While scores, reviews, memoirs, handbills, programmes, and music society records are familiar musicological territory, recordings need to be added as another important source of documentary evidence. Graphs and numerical data are neither necessary nor superfluous for the musicological study of music in performance; we don't need figures in order to make useful statements about performance history, but at the same time we shouldn't avoid statistical data when they can be gathered. The goal in the study of recordings is not to replace words, but to combine detailed description from careful listening with whatever quantification is possible and appropriate. The future will surely bring the ability to quantify more details about more recordings, but it is likely that a single musical 'sound example' will still be worth a thousand graphs.

Like late nineteenth-century musicology, the study of music in performance

---

[34] The average tempo for the second theme represents the average tempo of bars 59–93. The average tempo for the first theme was taken from bars 25–55, and for the closing section from bars 94–121.

[35] See José A. Bowen, *Rubato and the Second Subject: A Performance History* (forthcoming).

now needs catalogues of source material (discographies) and new tools to decode those source materials. In both cases (early manuscripts on the one hand, recordings on the other) the requirement is a technique for analysing the data in verifiable ways and new terminology to describe the resulting conclusions in prose. Guido Adler's charter of a search for compositional style also has its correlate in the search for performance style. The study of musical performances, however, involves an additional layer. First, there is the general style. While this breaks down into a host of period, geographic, and national styles, they all deal with general traits (like the slowing of the second theme or the use of portamento) which can be applied to a variety of pieces. Second, there are the traditions which become attached to specific works (substituting horns for bassoons in the recapitulation of the opening movement of Beethoven's Fifth Symphony, for example.) Finally, there is the individual innovation which happens within the parameters designated by the first two levels. The analysis of musical performance, then, begins with discography, involves the differentiation between style, tradition, and innovation, and seeks quantification when it is useful and possible.

## III

What should performers make of this research? On the surface, it would seem that modern musicians are deeply interested in performance practice; the early music movement has fostered a continued interest in earlier period performance styles. But our commitment to the importance of performing works using the performing conventions of their day is decidedly mixed.[36] As in the Corelli example above, we still have to choose between attempting to mimic the external aspects of the style (as is axiomatic to the recent study of contemporary theory and ornamentation guides), and trying to recreate the more internal aesthetic of variation, individual expression, and spontaneity. We do not, of course, have to choose one or the other, although it would seem logical that creative expression would flow from an understanding of period styles and conventions. Eighteenth-century specialists, however, tend to go only half-way, learning a great deal about the theories and techniques of the creative role of the performer, but refusing to actually adopt the most authentic role: that of composer/performer. Given the plethora of specialists who are skilled in both the theory and practice of earlier eras and our belief that performance style is essential to a musical work, there is remarkably little music-making which imitates both the external sound and the internal philosophy of earlier performers.

[36] For all our lip-service to the composer's intentions, when was the last time someone played a Mozart symphony with the forty violins, ten violas, six cellos, ten double basses, and double winds which he considered ideal! (See *The Letters of Mozart and his Family*, trans. and ed. Emily Anderson, 2nd edn. ed. A. Hyatt King and Monica Carolan (2 vols., London, 1966), ii. 724.)

Many performers claim that they do not listen to recordings while they are learning a new work; they want to take the information directly from the score. (A member of the National Sound Archive in London has, however, confided that some prominent artists come in more often than they would like it to be known—under assumed names.) This is a needless precaution, as most of us have been conditioned not only to the basic compositional conventions, but to the performance style of our parents' records long before we began to play an instrument. When we remember a favourite piece of music, we remember it in a familiar performance style, and very probably in a particular familiar version. (Long before I could read a score of Dvořák's Eighth Symphony, I was 'imprinted' with George Szell's recording of it. Today, when I 'read' the score, I still 'hear' his phrasing, dynamics, and even the rather inglorious sound of the Cleveland Orchestra string section.)

Not unlike speaking in our native language, the relization of a score in (imagined or real) sound is a rather transparent process to those who practise it frequently. Intellectually we realize that the process is highly conditioned and operates by the use of a large number of conventions; we recognize that to other people we speak with an accent. To our ears, however, our style of speech or performance seems natural, and it appears that it is everyone else who speaks with the accent. Early recordings, therefore, offer us a wide range of other accents.

At first, of course, we are confronted with a wide range of foreign-sounding performance practices; they sound quaint and mannered. Our imitation of them at this stage sounds artificial, and to native speakers is a cause for some hilarity. (Dick Van Dyck's cockney accent in the Disney film *Mary Poppins*, for example, is considered quite a hoot in Britain.) As with accents, some people adapt better than others. After years in a different country or region, accents do change, and the same can happen after immersion in a new performance style. The first realization when we begin to study earlier performance styles, and in some ways the most important, is that our pronunciation is neither natural nor absolute. We realize that many of the 'rules' which we take for granted—like 'Don't speed up when you get louder', or even 'A minim is twice as long as a crotchet'—are simply conventions which were drilled into us at an early age. (These conventions essentially define our home 'style', and they are invisible, like the rules of grammar, to the native speaker.) Not just Furtwängler, but Weingartner, Richard Strauss, and Toscanini too, all considered speeding up the music a little as it got louder a 'natural' part of music-making.[37] And at first hearing, tempo variations in early recordings can seem so extreme that minims really do sound like crotchets.

A special case is the piano-roll recording of Debussy's tenth prelude 'La Cathé-

---

[37] See José A. Bowen, 'Can a Symphony Change? Establishing Methodology for the Historical Study of Performance Styles', in *Der Bericht der Internationaler Kongreß der Gesellschaft für Musikforschung: Musik als Text* (Freiburg, in press).

drale engloutie' from the first book of Preludes (1909–10) made by Debussy himself.[38] In bar 7 of this performance, Debussy speeds up considerably at his direction *Doux et fluide*—so considerably that he seems to be playing minims at the speed he was playing crotchets. In bar 13, where the music returns to that of the opening, Debussy returns to his initial tempo. It happens a second time at bar 22. This time there is no expression mark, although Debussy's tempo doubling follows the fastest rhythmic section of the piece (marked *Augmentez progressivement (sans presser)*—'progressively louder without hurrying'). This too suggests that it was common in Debussy's day to get both faster and louder at the same time. Debussy returns to his initial tempo at the end of the piece, where the music is marked *Dans la sonorité du début*.

What are we to make of all this? There are two possible conclusions. One is that it seemed normal to Debussy that different performances would involve different tempo fluctuations: one *naturally* added them to a performance. On this account, hearing Debussy play the piano is not unlike hearing a poet read his work: the poet is not reading the poem with an accent because we must always hear the poem in that accent, but simply because that is how he speaks. From other performances we can confirm that this is simply the way Debussy plays. Yet even for Debussy, or any pianist from his era, these particular tempo changes seem extreme. Since Debussy is also the composer of the work, there is a second possibility: that he played it the way he wanted it, and simply wrote it down incorrectly. (Any pianist/composer understands the difficulty of correctly notating what he or she has played, and that of learning one's own scores from notation.) If this were the case, however, one would expect someone—any editor who heard the recording, for example—to have said something to Debussy, or at least to have corrected the score. For an editor of the period, however, it was natural for a performance to have tempo variations which were not written in the score; even in 1910 it was clearly recognized that a score is not a complete set of instructions, and a performer is not simply an executant. In recent editions, however, a footnote has been added: 'The direction $\downarrow = \downarrow$ should appear over the barline between mm. 6 and 7; it should be cancelled by the direction $\downarrow = \downarrow$ over the barline between mm. 12 and 13. (This faster tempo in mm. 7–12, and later in mm. 22–83, can be heard on Debussy's piano-roll recording of this prelude.)'[39] That the score must now be changed to match Debussy's performance is a symptom that, for the modern editor, a good score will allow only one rendition; that is the current 'natural' relationship between score and performance. Likewise, only a modern player would think of literally imitating the

---

[38] Debussy: Early Recordings by the Composer (Bellaphon CD 690-07-011).

[39] This is the footnote as it appears in the 1989 Dover edn. (which is a reprint of the 1964 Moscow edn. ed. K. S. Sorokin). The author of this footnote is unknown, but it is surely based upon the new complete edition (*Œuvres Complètes de Claude Debussy*, Sér. I, Vol. 5: *Preludes*, ed. Roy Howat with Claude Helffer (Paris, 1985)), where the minim = crotchet direction is added directly to the score. See also Roy Howat, *Debussy in Proportion: A Musical Analysis* (Cambridge, 1983) and Charles Burkhart, 'Debussy Plays *La Cathédrale engloutie* and Solves Metrical Mystery', *Piano Quarterly*, 65 (1968), 14–16.

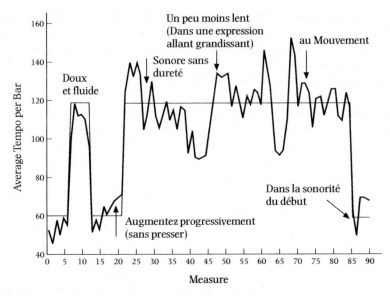

**Fig. 19.2.** Tempo map for the piano-roll performance of Debussy's 'La Cathérale engloutie' by Claude Debussy in 1913. The average tempo per bar is plotted for each measure. The straight lines gives the tempo relationships as suggested in the new edition.

nuances of another performance, which is what the new indications on the score suggest.

If we look more carefully at Debussy's performance of his own work, however, we can see that his performance is more subtle than simply twice as fast between bars 7–12 and 22–83. Figure 19.2 is a tempo map of this performance.[40] The straight lines indicate what we might expect from a performance which rigidly adhered to the performance instructions in the new editions. Debussy's performance is anything but rigid, and we can make three general observations about it. First, Debussy is not only generally flexible in his treatment of tempo, but he uses tempo to realize his emotive performance directions. Hence the doubling of speed at the direction *Doux et fluide* (tender and fluidly) and a gradual accelerando in response to *Peu à peu sortant de la brume* (gradually emerging from the haze) at bar 16. Second, Debussy does this even when he has warned other players not to do it! At bar 20, Debussy writes *Augmentez progressivement* (progressively louder) but then adds in parenthesis *sans presser* (without hurrying). This implies that the first direction without the parenthetical remark would produce rushing from some players, and, despite his own warning, Debussy

[40] Each beat in each bar was tracked three times, and the beats for each bar were averaged to produce a single average tempo per bar. All three trials were within ± two beats of each other at all points (i.e. an average tempo of 82 guarantees that the actual tempo is somewhere between 80 and 84).

makes a distinct accelerando both before and after his *sans presser* notation. Third, Debussy uses tempo to structure his performance; he makes a tempo change at every structural junction, and shapes virtually every phrase with tempo fluctuation.

If we are going to correct the score to follow his performance, we need to include many more directions. *Un peu moins lent* ('a little more slowly'), at bar 47, seems clear enough, but apparently Debussy also forgot to place a ritard (or *un peu lent*) in bar 42. (It is also unclear what *un peu moins lent* means in the context of his performance. This part is faster than the immediately preceding section, which has been slowing down, but not as fast as the initial tempo of the section.) *Peu à peu lent* should be added in bar 58 before the climax, followed by *rapprochant* in bar 66. Then there is a clear *più mosso* implied by Debussy's playing in the last four bars. But of course that still doesn't specify everything we can see in Figure 19.2. The real problem with re-marking the score to match the performance is not that it alters Debussy's sacred text (Debussy has already provided ample evidence that we should feel free to personalize our performance), but that there is simply no way to even begin to notate the complex nuances of Debussy's performance. While we can notate the broad strokes, there are essential characteristics of Debussy's interpretation that elude our grasp.

New technology, of course, gives us a way to capture and disseminate Debussy's performance; with piano rolls and CDs, the world no longer needs to rely on descriptions of performances. Similarly, Figure 19.2 demonstrates that graphs can be very useful in clarifying what is going on in a single performance. But while the graph does allow us to notate Debussy's nuances of tempo, it still leaves a riddle for the performer. What makes Debussy's performance unique is the way he changes the tempo in every phrase and in virtually every bar. (The graph indicates this nicely with all the up and down zigzags.) Debussy performs this piece in a rich nineteenth-century accent. The real problem is not how to notate this accent, but what to do about it. Here, scholars and performers have somewhat different goals and interests. If recordings by Beethoven were suddenly found, they would be of tremendous scholarly and general interest, but they would hardly signal the death of modern performances of Beethoven's music. It might be hard to compete for a while (although one would suppose that Karajan would still occur in larger letters than Beethoven), but performers would continue to make recordings and give concerts. It remains to be seen, in five or fifty years, if there is anyone secure enough not to play Debussy *à la Debussy*.[41]

What lessons, then, should performers learn from recordings by composers? The string portamenti in Elgar's own recordings, the tempo fluctuation in Debussy's, and the vibrato in Stravinsky's are all part of the external

---

[41] Ultimately the problem with performing Debussy *à la Debussy* is that it is utterly pointless. If the goal of a performance is to exactly mimic an *Urtext* recording, then why not simply play the *Urtext* recording and forget the concert? The point of live music is that it is always different.

performance tradition. According to current performance ideology, the goal is to replicate as nearly as possible the external sound of the original performance. If we think it important to perform Bach, Mozart, and Beethoven using period instruments played in the style of the day, then the same should apply to Elgar and Mahler. But for some reason, perhaps because we have to listen to Elgar's own performances and not simply a re-creation made in our own image, we feel more comfortable dismissing the performance style of the Elgar recordings *as* performance style and not including it in our modern re-creation. Surely we should be consistent; if performance style is crucial to the work, then it should be just as crucial for Elgar and Debussy as it is for Mozart—or, to put it the other way round, if it is not crucial for Elgar and Debussy, why should it be for Mozart?

Faced with a performance, a musician has a number of choices. First is a choice about the role of performance: is a performance meant to be a re-creation or a new independent creation? A performer can deliberately choose to recover old ground or to explore new territory. Performers in different styles and genres routinely make different choices. Jazz players, who need to create new sequences of pitches for each performance, tend to think of each performance as an opportunity for new expression. Classical musicians, by contrast, are taught an aesthetic of re-creation, which appears (but certainly isn't) more natural than the opposite approach. As Richard Taruskin has emphasized, for a performer interested in the new, the modern interest in early performance styles proves a boon, and certainly its popularity is a reflection of how both audiences and performers long for something different. Early recordings often present us with new (to us) ways of performing old pieces. This can make the performer's job a bit easier. More importantly, however, these studies of performance deepen our awareness that other styles exist and that our conventions of interpretation are merely that: conventions. Examination of older recordings demonstrates that there are other interpretive parameters, which have in most cases now been closed (like tempo fluctuation). Increasing the range of possibilities makes it easier to say something new, and performances are one of the ways in which we learn new things about old pieces. Debussy's piano roll, and the preceding analysis of it, demonstrate not an absolute standard for the modulation of tempo, but rather the amount of variation which is possible. We should use recordings to open parameters, not to close them.

The rediscovery of previous performance styles also makes the performer's job a bit harder. Previous performers simply played in the only style they knew, but tailored the individual expression to their own taste. Composers today still enjoy this mixed blessing. Performing (or for that matter composing) in an earlier style creates two sets of difficulties. First, the performer must choose a performance style, which will provide a palette of expressive devices—portamento in some eras, not in others. As was demonstrated above, this is not easily done. It takes time to acquire the right accent, especially when learning a foreign tongue. The second stage, however, is even more problematic. All too frequently modern players simply try to re-create a 'style' without engaging in the expressive conventions. It is not unlike the problems of acting in a dramatic play in a language you do not speak. You can learn to pronounce the words, but your performance will be wooden if you do not learn what they mean and also how they mean it; that is, you can learn a song text in Hungarian, and know what it means, but still not be able to 'speak' the meaning properly. A good accent is not sufficient. Even imitating all the nuances of a previous great performance is not enough. A direct imitation of the external sound is hollow, and misses the point. The reason for Corelli's ornaments or Debussy's tempo changes is that they personalize the performance; another performance in the same style would still be different. For music of all ages, the performance style is simply a guide to the expressive devices (that is, the space allocated for individual innovation) of the period. But without learning to speak the language, these expressive devices will be meaningless. This is equally true of Mozart and Mahler. We should not attempt to emulate the performance style without learning the conventions of expression.

## IV

There is plenty of scope, therefore, for music in performance as a subdiscipline. While the lack of discographies (roughly akin to catalogues of source material and manuscripts) presents a burden to any new field, the possibilities for future studies are enormous. (And the 'texts' for this field are by no means limited to audio recordings; the use of film or marked scores has hardly been explored.) While the aims of critics and cognitive theorists, as discussed above, should not necessarily be excluded, the goals of musicological enquiry fall between them in two broad categories.

The first is the study of style. Most studies to date fall into this category, and have attempted to identify and analyse a specific performance style. This may be repertoire-, genre-, or instrument-specific, and may deal with a single artist, an institution, a period, or a region. All these should include a historical dimension, because all individuals and groups change over time. Bruno Walter, for example, seems to have had a different style after World War II, especially when he conducted American orchestras; and any style analysis of Walter must take into account this stylistic change. One of the large issues here is the disentanglement of individual styles from schools, periods, and other factors. Does Furtwängler sound different in the studio than in concert? Are opera singers more affected by the production, the director, or the conductor? Do pianists play differently in their own countries, or in competitions? (All this, of course, has its parallel in the classical musicological study of compositional styles.) At a recent meeting of the American Musicological Society there was much discussion over whether or not the students of students of Chopin played with enough similarity to be considered a 'school'.[42] This is an excellent subject for both future research and further discussion of the problems addressed here.

The second is the study of traditions or performance histories of individual works. While the two studies are inextricably linked, this second study focuses on the oral histories which ultimately carry musical works to audiences. In addition to all the period, individual, regional, and institutional styles which stand between us and the score, each musical work seems to acquire its own personal history—a performance tradition. This is most readily apparent in Italian opera; while it is possible for any competent singer and pianist to read through a Schubert song (even one unknown to either or them) without having to stop, it is virtually impossible to do this for a Puccini aria. If, on the other hand, one knows a Puccini aria from performances and recordings, the printed score can often look rather foreign.[43] Unlike most instrumentalists, who attempt to learn a work directly from the score, singers have long recognized the importance of the accompanying oral tradition. No singer would dare go to an audition for *Il barbiere* or *Tosca* without knowing the performance traditions and the standard 'interpretations'; it is part of knowing the piece. These traditions occur in instrumental music as well, and they change. Understanding what and where they are will help us to understand not only the reception of works, but how our perception of works in turn changes future perceptions of them.

While there has been a great deal of interest in *Urtexts*, authentic performance styles, and the whole idea of returning to what composers heard, insufficient attention has been paid to the fact that audiences have always encountered works not through scores, but through performances. If we want to discover what lies at the core of a work, we cannot simply go to the score, for our own perception of the score is guided by current period style. We can reach an earlier conception or hearing of the work only by peeling away the outer layers of performing tradition: precisely, that is, by understanding the history of performance which has accumulated around each work. The aim is not to get back to the 'work itself', but to understand our own and previous generations' contributions to it. Ultimately, then, performance histories tell us a great deal more than simply the history of performance practice. Since our interaction with a musical work is always mediated by performance, understanding how the history of performance affects how we perceive the work is essential to our understanding of what the musical work *is*. Musical works change as they gather a body of performance and reception history around them (or, as Albert Einstein would have

---

[42] This discussion followed a paper delivered by Jeffrey Hollander entitled 'The Changing Interpretive Paradigm for the Chopin Berceuse, Op. 57: A Comparative Performance Study' at the 1994 annual meeting of the AMS in Minneapolis.

[43] Similarly, if one has learned to play Debussy's 'La Cathédrale engloutie' by ear, from Debussy's recording, or like George Gershwin by imitating the physical movements of a piano roll, the score would seem terribly lacking in its representation of the work as you know it. This is routinely the case with the sheet music of jazz and pop standards.

it, it may be we, not the works, that change, but we will never be able to tell the difference). If there is such a thing as the 'work itself', it is fully embodied and inseparable from its performance and reception.

All this analysis will also benefit performers and musical performance. It may help both to demonstrate where the interpretive levels of freedom are (and have been), and to free performers from the illusion that there is such a thing as a neutral (or natural) performance style. If all performance involves stylistic conventions, then an awareness of these conventions will allow performers to choose from a wider array of possibilities.[44] This new research will make performers aware of other levels of expression, and enable them to master not only new accents, but new languages.[45]

This research, in turn, should be guided by the needs and understanding of performers. Part of the researcher's job is to convey to performers what nuances are introduced and why. As in the introduction of many Eastern musics to the West, it is the *sounds* of a new musical style that make the initial impact; but later, as the inner workings of the music are better understood, the new musical *principles* also begin to have an effect. While the sounds of early recordings convey a different accent, they also convey a different system of expression. In order to fully understand another performance language, we need to understand both the stylistic possibilities and their meaning.

This means that the study of music in performance offers a common ground, where 'new' and 'traditional' musicology can meet. The recognition of musical works as changing traditions cuts both ways. For those who study individual performances, it means the realization that not all nuance is due to individual choice. Any study of music in performance needs to distinguish between the general *style* of the period, the specific *traditions* of the musical work, and the individual *innovations* of the performer. In other words, some of the nuances of performance are dependent upon what and when, not just who. Similarly, those who study works need to recognize that they also cannot afford to neglect the what, when, and who of performance. Any analysis of Beethoven's Fifth Symphony needs to consider that the proportions of the first movement have changed due to changes in performance practice. In this case, however, the change in performance practice is not specific to Beethoven or the Fifth Symphony; it is a general change in performance style, largely motivated by a new performance ideology. Both the specific performance practice of slowing down for the second theme and the general practice of using gradual tempo changes

---

[44] Surely we would all benefit if we could simply free performers from the illusion that there is a single correct performance style, and especially from the notion that it is universally applicable, as Roger Norrington seems intent on insisting. Note his recent attempt (9 Apr. 1995, Royal Festival Hall, London Philharmonic Orchestra) to 'cleanse' Mahler's Fourth Symphony.

[45] In many ways, then, this new form of analysis fulfils the traditional role of analysis, which is to articulate the moments in the piece where choices are required, to propose questions which the performer (not the analyst) must answer. It has always been the task of analysis to discover the moments of articulation in a piece of music, but not to prescribe what performance nuance should be used to mark these points.

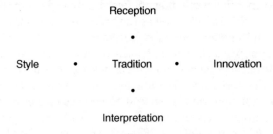

**Fig. 19.3.** The specific performance traditions of individual musical works provide an intersection between the elements of performance practice and the study of hermeneutics and reception: that is, between the what and the why of performance.

as an expressive or interpretive device have gone out of favour as a result of a new doctrine: that performances without tempo changes added by the interfering performer allow the work to 'speak for itself'.

It is also possible, however, for the individual traditions of a musical work to be altered. Here the performance traditions of the musical work form a nexus for the forces of both performance practice and meaning. In the history of performance practice, work-specific traditions stand between period style and individual innovation. In the history of hermeneutics they mediate between the reception of the work and its interpretation (see Fig. 19.3). In other words, the performance practice history intersects with the hermeneutic history.[46] Beethoven's Fifth Symphony, for example, was not always associated with a fateful or heroic military victory, and in what follows I shall demonstrate that this change in meaning is connected to a change in the performance tradition of the piece.

The hermeneutic history of this symphony is scattered among a variety of reviews, programme and liner notes, textbooks, scholarly writings, and music guides. Even a brief glance at these materials will demonstrate that by the second half of our century the fate and victory associations have become virtually universal: 'The music takes fate by the throat immediately, and by the last movement wrests from it a tremendous victory.'[47] Earlier interpretations, however, focused on neither fate nor heroism, but on love. For D'Indy it was love of country, and for Grove it was love of Theresa Brunswick.[48] For Berlioz the symphony expressed Beethoven's 'secret sorrows and his pent-up rage' over a lost

---

[46] Of course, not all changes in performance practice are tied to a hermenutic change. Some, like the tradition of slowing down the second theme in a sonata-allegro movement, have fallen away because of a change in the generic performance practice ideology. Other changes are the result of individual musical innovation: virtually all of Karajan's personal mannerisms were imitated by legions of younger conductors.

[47] Liner notes for Beethoven, Symphony No. 5, Solti, Chicago Symphony Orchestra (London LP: CS 6092, 1971).

[48] For Grove, the two themes of the first movement represented the 'fierce imperious composer' and the 'womanly, yielding, devoted girl' (Sir George Grove, *Beethoven and his Nine Symphonies* (London, 1898; repr. New York, 1962), 155–6).

love.[49] Hoffmann, on the other hand, heard only endless longing (*unendliche Sehnsucht*). True, he did hear 'a brilliant shaft of blinding sunlight penetrating the darkness of night' in the Finale, but he never mentions victory, and was careful to point out that the lasting impression is not even one of stability: 'The heart of every sensitive listener, however, is certain to be deeply stirred and held until the very last chord by one lasting emotion, that of nameless, haunted yearning.'[50] Then again, an anonymous critic in 1852 heard 'tears of joy and such emotions of pleasure, as may be supposed to have arisen in the breast of Columbus when he first observed the light that revealed the existence of the land he had so long and so ardently sought for'.[51] Even Schindler heard only 'a marvelous union of pathos, majesty, and grandeur'.[52]

In the twentieth century, however, hardly anyone can withstand the temptation to read the move from minor to major in the Finale as a victory. For some it remains a psychological victory: 'The blaze of sound coming out of a sort of "aural fog" symbolizes a psychological victory over the composer's deafness.'[53] For others it is artistic victory: 'Artistic victory is his, and he displays the dead body of his mortal enemy by bringing back the corpse of the bridge passage.'[54] Especially in the second half of the century, the symphony becomes 'a great moral drama. . . . He would fight destiny to victory, he resolved, and achieve reconciliation with the world . . . the struggle finally took finished form as the C minor symphony. . . . Beethoven's great symphony was thus a monument to an ordeal.'[55] Crucial to this ordeal is the victory over fate which is no longer 'the cold impersonal law of things indifferent to Man, but an active enemy'.[56] By the middle of the century, there is convergence of meaning, and it is declared to be universal:

[T]he Fifth is clearly patterned on a moral program capable of a single broad analysis. Each has termed the 'enemy' according to his own philosophical bent, from 'monster,' 'fiend,' 'forces of evil' to a malign Providence. All have viewed the contest as moving from abject despair and helplessness through prayerful truce to savage defiance and victory.[57]

---

[49] 'The first movement is devoted to the expression of the disorded sentiments which pervade a great soul when prey to despair' (Hector Berlioz, *A Travers Chant* (Paris, 1862; repr. edn.). *A Critical Study of Beethoven's Nine Symphonies*, trans. Edwin Evans (London, 1954), 63).

[50] E. T. A. Hoffmann, 'Review of Beethoven's Fifth Symphony', *Allgemeine Musikalische Zeitung*, 12 (4 and 11 July 1810), trans. Martyn Clarke in David Charlton (ed.), *E. T. A. Hoffmann's Musical Writings: Kreisleriana, The Poet and the Composer, Music Criticism* (Cambridge, 1989), 247.

[51] *The Musical World* (London), 17 Apr. 1852, p. 248.

[52] Anton Felix Schindler, *Beethoven as I Knew him*, ed. Donald W. MacArdle, trans. Constance S. Jolly (Chapel Hill, NC, 1966), 147.

[53] Antony Hopkins, *The Nine Symphonies of Beethoven* (Seattle, 1981), 152.

[54] Charles Burr, liner notes for Beethoven Symphony No. 5, Eugene Ormandy, Philadelphia Orchestra (Columbia LP: ML 5098, 1957).

[55] Louis Biancolli, quoted by Charles Burr, liner notes for Beethoven Symphony No. 5, Bruno Walter, Columbia Symphony Orchestra (Columbia LP: ML-5365, 1958).

[56] Robert Bagar and Louis Biancolli, *The Concert Companion: A Comprehensive Guide to Symphonic Music* (New York, 1947), 36.

[57] Ibid.

In the second movement, the second theme first occurs on the clarinets and bassoons at bar 23 in the tonic key of A flat. After a hushed diminished chord suddenly becomes a loud augmented sixth, the theme is heard again at bar 32 in C major on the trumpets and horns. For virtually every commentator, this second passage has some extra-musical meaning. At the very least, it reminds everyone of the Finale, where the brass will again emerge from a pianissimo harmonic fog and blast a fanfare in C major. Not surprisingly, nineteenth-century critics heard only a 'stately passage'[58] or 'broad masses of light'.[59] Grove heard 'martial' music;[60] but again, by the end of World War II, this music became 'triumphant'[61] or 'a sure victory sign'.[62] For Joseph Krips it indicated that 'we must not abandon hope'.[63] If the symphony has come to symbolize our victory over Hitler, then this passage is the 'call to action that presages the mood and key of the finale and psychologically brings hope and confidence in the eventual outcome of the struggle'.[64]

How does all this translate into performance? Despite Beethoven's complete lack of any marking to change the tempo, even the most rigid performance sectionalizes the piece with tempo changes. Everyone, for example, slows down for the cadence figures between the first and second themes (bars 7–22). Similarly, virtually everyone slows down as Beethoven modulates from the soft clarinets and bassoons in A flat to loud trumpets and horns in C. In nearly all performances before World War II and the V-for-victory interpretation, however, the C major version of the theme is faster than the A flat version. After the war the opposite trend became popular, with the C major version going slower. This can be demonstrated by calculating the difference in tempo between bars 23–6 (the first occurrence of the passage on clarinets and bassoons) and bars 32–6 (the second occurrence, this time with trumpets and horns in C major). In Figure 19.4, this value (positive if the performances gets faster in the second occurrence, negative if the performance gets slower in the second occurrence) is plotted against the year of recording.

[58] For Hoffmann it was simply the 'stately passage in C major' (*Musical Writings*, 245).

[59] Professor Thomson of Edinburgh characterizes the brass in C major as 'broad masses of light which burst at intervals from the brass instruments' (*Musical World* (London), 1 Apr. 1841, p. 195).

[60] Grove: 'very loud and martial' (*Beethoven*, 162). See also anonymous notes to Beethoven Symphony No. 5, Felix Weingartner, London Philharmonic Orchestra (Columbia 78: M 254, 1933): 'fanfare-like in outline'.

[61] 'A second subject is announced with a triumphal entry of trumpets and drums' (liner notes, Beethoven Symphony No. 5, Hans Swarowsky, Sinfonia of London (Liberty LP: SWL 15003, 1957)).

[62] 'The second theme begins ruminatively in A-flat but suddenly brightens to a triumphant C major, a sure victory sign' (Neville Cardus, liner notes for George Szell, Cleveland Orchestra (Epic LP: LC 3195, 1956)).

[63] Joseph Krips, liner notes, ed. Frederic V. Grunfeld, Beethoven Symphonies, Joseph Krips, London Symphony Orchestra (Murray Hill LP: S-2694, 1960). Also, 'the second of these themes, marked by rising triad figures, points forward to the victory theme of the finale' (Uwe Kraemer, trans. John Coombs, for a Special Gala Concert for Prisoners of Conscience, with the profits going to Amnesty International, Beethoven Symphony No. 5, live recording by Leonard Bernstein, Bavarian Radio Symphony Orchestra (DG LP: 2-DG2721153, 1977)).

[64] 'He contrasted it with another lyrical tune, at first in the same key of A flat but, after a moment's hesitation, suddenly blazing out in a C major call to action that presages the mood and key of the finale and psychologically brings hope and confidence in the eventual outcome of the struggle' (liner notes for Beethoven, Symphony No. 5, Solti, Chicago Symphony Orchestra (London LP: CS 6092, 1971)).

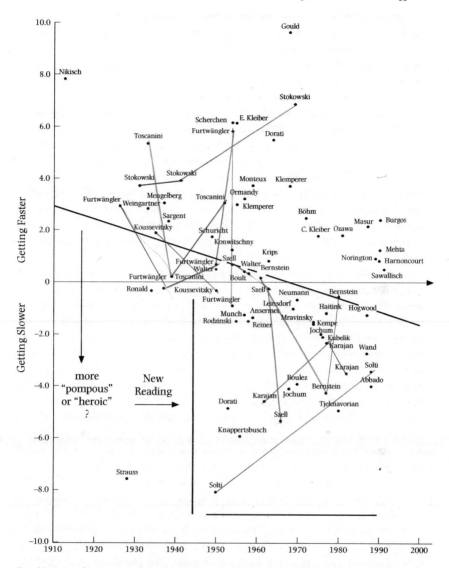

**Fig. 19.4.** Beethoven, Symphony No. 5, second movement. The difference between the average tempo in bars 23–6 (where the second theme occurs on clarinets and bassoons) and the average tempo in bars 32–6 (where the same theme occurs on trumpets and horns) is plotted against the year of the recording, and the conductor is labelled next to the dot which represents the performance. Dots on the centre line with the arrow represent performances which employ the same tempo for both passages. Dots above the line represent performances which get faster for the second passage, and those below represent performances which get slower. (The degree of increase or decrease is given in beats per minutes (i.e. tempo marks).)

In his book on performing the Beethoven symphonies, Weingartner warned 'against robbing the magnificent C major passages of their freshness by allowing the speed to slacken with the idea of producing a pompous effect'.[65] Before World War II, the passage was considered stately or bright, but there was no association with heroism or victory. With the exception of Strauss, whose problem is that he plays the first occurrence of the theme too fast, we can see from Figure 19.4 that everyone seems to agree with Weingartner; slowing the passage down to emphasize its martial character makes it 'pompous'. The dominant reading before the war, then, is to increase the speed slightly for the C major passage. After the war, with victory certain and the meaning of the symphony established as the triumph of man against a hostile enemy, a new reading and a new performance style emerge: the C major passage now slows down. The clarification of the 'meaning' of the symphony has brought about a change in the way we play the music. Either the dominant performance style has changed in response to a new interpretation, or what sounded 'pompous' before the war now sounds 'heroic'.

In 1970 Glenn Gould admitted that he avoided much of Beethoven's music because it was 'rather heroic in attitude and all rather triumphantly tonal'.[66] As it turns out, Gould's piano performance is at the most extreme 'unheroic' end of the spectrum. With regard to Beethoven, both Gould's attitude and performance practice belong to the first rather than the second half of our century. This seems to be the case for most of the conductors included here; that is, there seems to be a connection between what you think the piece means and how you play it. The study of performance traditions, therefore, provides a link between performance practice and hermeneutics.

Here, then, the new interests in cultural studies and performance practice intersect with the most traditional questions and repertoire of Western musicology. Investigating performance styles is a natural extension of the initial charter of examining compositional styles. Indeed, it provides an opportunity to integrate the analysis of compositions with an understanding of how they were performed and perceived. Discussions of how individual innovation is affected by period style, and of how styles and even works change, demonstrate how musicology can be both cultural and historical at the same time. In this context, for example, we see that authority has always been an issue in musicology. No one doubts that both the work and the myth surrounding Beethoven's Ninth Symphony cast an immense shadow over the compositional style of the nineteenth century; why should we doubt that Toscanini or Karajan cast an equally large shadow over the performance style of this one? In both cases the authority is

---

[65] Felix Weingartner, 'On the Performance of Beethoven's Symphonies', trans. Jessie Crosland, in *Weingartner on Music and Conducting* (New York, 1969), 132.

[66] Glenn Gould, 'Admit it Mr. Gould, You Do Have Doubts about Beethoven', *Globe & Mail Magazine* (Toronto), 6 June 1970, repr. in liner notes, Beethoven Piano Sonatas, Glenn Gould, piano, vol. 1 (Sony CD: SM3K 52638, 1994), 9.

dependent on market forces, visibility, and reputation, as well as intrinsically musical qualities. In both cases, influence (or what we might now want to call 'market penetration') can be gauged by sales (sheet music arrangements for one, records for the other, and performances for both) and by imitation from other artists. The study of performance histories offers insight into the study of authority and a mechanism by which musicology can analyse 'works' in a cultural context.

Methodologies are as varied as the repertoires studied, and they are likely to become even more widely divergent as further experiments are made. While some methodologies will prove more successful than others, it can only be to the good to have the widest possible range from which to choose. It will be especially interesting to compare studies of the same repertoire made by scholars using different methodologies.[67] A key issue will be the relationship between empirical data and descriptive analysis (in other words, between individual qualities and the whole interpretation). Methodologies will also be partially determined by aims. While the infusion of objective standards of verifiable evidence will be good for music criticism, the problem of creating criteria for evaluation could be equally good for musicology. If evaluation of performances is required, based perhaps on how well a performance exemplifies a particular analysis of the piece, then surely evaluation of analyses is also required. Music in performance simultaneously allows an injection of new materials and a chance to re-evaluate old ones. My argument, therefore, is not that musicology should abandon any of its current methodology or goals, but that it should now also bring to bear on its problems an understanding that music is heard, analysed, and even conceived in terms of individual, period, and geographic performance styles, of work-specific traditions, and individually innovative performances. Finally, the study of music in performance is not simply another new, alternative approach; rather, it offers a common ground where analysis, cultural studies, hermeneutics, and performance practice meet.

[67] I have tried in vain to discover a cognitive and critical study of the same work.

# 20

## Popular Music, Unpopular Musicology

### John Covach

### I

In June of 1956, singer/song-writer and prototypical rock guitarist and per-former Chuck Berry released a single entitled 'Roll Over Beethoven'.[1] A few years before this single became a hit on radios and juke-boxes across the country, a war of cultures had broken out in the United States, a phenomenon often referred to as the 'teen rebellion'; middle-class American youth were rejecting the culture of their parents, and insisting on creating a culture that addressed their own specific interests and needs. Films such as *The Wild One* (1953) and *Rebel without a Cause* (1955) featured youthful principal characters—played by Marlon Brando and James Dean, respectively—in open rebellion against white middle-class values.[2]

Music became one of the fields on which this battle was played out. The 1955 film *Blackboard Jungle* also worked the theme of disgruntled youth, but featured perhaps the *first* official 'rock and roll' song, 'Rock around the Clock' by Bill Haley and the Comets, played over the opening credits. The film also contains a pivotal scene in which tough (and poor) high-school students reject the music of their older (and more middle-class) teacher, a scene that ends with the students throw-ing the instructor's collectable 78 rpm records around the classroom as the teacher attempts in vain to catch them. Thus, when 'Roll Over Beethoven' was released, it was clear to Berry's listeners that he was playfully taunting high culture and the classical music that his audience would have perceived as going with it; the recurring lyric, 'roll over Beethoven, tell Tchaikovsky the news', makes the song's target abundantly clear.[3] Berry enthusiastically advocates rock and roll music and the dancing that goes with it, and he delights in the subver-

---

[1] Chuck Berry, 'Roll Over Beethoven', Chess no. 1653 (1956).

[2] For a fuller discussion of teenage rebellion and the perceived threat of juvenile delinquency, see Charlie Gillett, *The Sound of the City; The Rise of Rock and Roll*, 2nd edn. (New York, 1983), 15 ff.; and Ed Ward, Geoffrey Stokes, and Ken Tucker, *Rock of Ages: The Rolling Stone History of Rock & Roll* (Englewood Cliffs, NJ, 1986), 98–113.

[3] It is worth noting that before the success of 'Rock around the Clock' and its use in *Blackboard Jungle*, up-tempo, big-band jazz was used as the music of rebellion in *The Wild One* and *Rebel without a Cause*.

sive character of a musical style that would cause such an icon of high culture as Beethoven to turn in his grave.

A fuller interpretation of this Chuck Berry example would need to account for its many other aspects: the implied mind–body split between art-music and rock and roll (art-music being for cerebral contemplation, rock and roll for dancing and singing along); the racism prevalent in America in the 1950s (and the threat that white culture was being challenged either by black men or by white men singing and playing like black men); and the role played by the entertainment industry and its means of production and distribution of music, to name only a few. But this example is cited here merely to draw attention to a fundamental distinction that has tended, until recently at least, to be generally assumed in American culture: art-music in the Western tradition and popular music (especially popular music after 1955 or so) are radically different from one another in almost every possible way. Berry's lyrics celebrate that difference, and the instrumentation—including Berry's lead-guitar bursts that were to become so influential for the rock guitarists who followed him—and the twelve-bar blues progression upon which the song is based underscore the stylistic distance between Fifties rock and roll and nineteenth-century symphonic music.

More recently, another kind of culture war has been taking place in the United States. Since the mid- to late 1980s, curriculum committees and faculty senates on university and college campuses across the country have argued over what might be called the 'multicultural question': the extent to which curricula (especially undergraduate curricula) need to be redesigned to acknowledge that other cultures exist besides the Western tradition that has dominated academic study up to the present time. Great Books programmes, which overwhelmingly opt for the works of 'dead white (mostly European and American) men', have been a favourite negative example in arguments directed against such perceived cultural biases.[4] Advocates of curricular reform frequently argue for change on two fronts: first, non-Western cultures must be represented in the study of traditional subject areas such as literature and history; and second, other cultures *within* the Western one must be represented, and this includes the contributions of women and minorities, as well as folk and popular cultures.[5]

Music scholars, as Joseph Kerman has pointed out, tend to be a conservative group generally.[6] Thus, it has only been relatively recently that music departments at American colleges and universities have felt a certain pressure to

[4] Greater public attention was drawn to this issue during the summer of 1987, when Allan Bloom's *The Closing of the American Mind* (New York, 1987) became a national best-seller. For a collection of responses to Bloom's arguments, in what proved to be an extremely provocative book, see Robert L. Stone (ed.), *Essays on the Closing of the American Mind* (Chicago, 1989).

[5] This summary surely constitutes a simplification of the issues surrounding the ongoing multicultural debate. I will, however, forgo any further consideration of the merits of the many arguments on both sides of this highly charged issue. In the present discussion, I hope merely to establish a context for the impact which these issues have had on the study of music in American colleges and universities.

[6] Joseph Kerman, *Contemplating Music: Challenges to Musicology* (Cambridge, Mass., 1985), 37.

reconsider their course offerings in the light of the multicultural debates. The first part of the reform challenge—the study of non-Western musics—tends to be addressed by offering courses in ethnomusicology. And ethnomusicologists can often help out even in the second part of the challenge by offering courses in American folk-music (along with musicologists specializing in American music) and in African-American music and culture. Recent scholarship in feminist musicology has made it possible for musicologists who do not specialize in feminism to incorporate such perspectives in their teaching.[7]

The situation with regard to popular music presents far more of problem. It seems self-evident that musicology has tended to ignore popular music, and particularly rock and country and western music, despite the fact that popular music has at various times played an important role in the art-music tradition, especially in the twentieth century.[8] One reads often enough, for example, that jazz exerted a certain influence over composers such as Stravinsky, Milhaud, and Krenek; but musicologists almost never approach popular music styles as being interesting *in their own right*. This situation is especially curious with regard to twentieth-century art-music, a musical canon that enjoys—to put it mildly—a more limited audience than other styles of art-music. The decline of audience interest in 'post-*Pierrot*' art-music can sometimes drive musicologists specializing in twentieth-century music to despair, despite the fact that, as Susan McClary has pointed out, vital music is bursting out all around them in the form of popular music.[9]

But even if musicology has tended to deal with popular music in only a marginal way, popular music has received considerable attention from scholars outside the field of musicology. Even a cursory look through the bibliography provided by Richard Middleton in his 1990 book *Studying Popular Music*, a magisterial survey of work in this burgeoning field, should convince the most sceptical musicologist that popular music studies is a firmly established area of scholarly enquiry.[10] Despite the amount of careful work that has been done in popular-music studies, however, musicologists are not likely to find much information that could help in the preparation, say, of a unit on popular music in a twentieth-century music survey course. The reason for this is simple: popular-music studies have been dominated by cultural critics and sociologists, many of whom do not possess the specialized skills necessary to deal with the musical 'texts' in the ways that musicologists do. These scholars tend to be concerned

---

[7] While I suggest here that feminist musical scholarship is increasingly available for use in the classroom, the extent to which musicologists actually include feminist writings in their teaching is a separate consideration, beyond the scope of this chapter.

[8] That this restriction has been ideologically driven has been pointed out by Rose Rosengard Subotnik, 'The Role of Ideology in the Study of Western Music', *Journal of Musicology*, 2/1 (1983), 1–12; repr. in her *Developing Variations: Style and Ideology in Western Music* (Minneapolis, 1991), 3–14.

[9] Susan McClary, 'Terminal Prestige: The Case of Avant-Garde Music Composition', *Cultural Critique*, 12 (1989), 57–81.

[10] Richard Middleton, *Studying Popular Music* (Milton Keynes, 1990).

with the effect of musics on listeners, and on the ways in which musics can have various kinds of significance within cultures and subcultures; and they treat the music, in the words of John Shepherd, as a kind of 'inscrutable black box'.[11] Thus it is not so much that the musicologist will find this work uninteresting, but rather that he or she will find that it addresses what are often a completely different set of disciplinary issues.

The different way in which musicologists and sociologists approach music generally is often cast as a distinction between text and context: according to this formulation, the musicologist is primarily concerned with musical texts, while the sociologist is concerned principally with social, economic, and political contexts. While this distinction undoubtedly oversimplifies matters, it does capture a basic problem that exists between the fields of musicology and popular-music studies: musicologists tend to ignore popular-music scholarship (after all, it *is* more concerned with sociological issues); and popular-music scholars are only too glad that they do (after all, *their* methods of approaching music, mired as they are in the art-music tradition, can never really get at what is most important about popular music anyway).

Underlying the text–context issue is a basic attitude that takes us back to the consideration of Chuck Berry's 'Roll Over Beethoven' above. At the heart of this distinction is the tacitly accepted notion that art-music and popular music are fundamentally different, and both sides have been willing to abide by what they see as a basic musical and disciplinary separation. Yet it is not at all clear that this difference between Beethoven and Chuck Berry is as fundamental as it may appear; considering the fact that musicologists for the most part have been unwilling—until recently at least—to consider popular music in a careful manner, and considering that popular-music scholars often admit a lack of expertise in the study of art-music, it is surely premature to come to any conclusions about the underlying difference, or sameness, of the two types of music.

Recently there has been some movement toward the centre and away from these established disciplinary poles on the part of both musicologists and popular-music scholars. Susan McClary and Robert Walser, for example, have called on musicology to devote greater attention to rock music, and both Richard Middleton and John Shepherd have proposed grounds upon which musicology and popular-music studies could potentially come together. The arguments advanced by these authors make it clear that co-operation between the two disciplines is in the best interests of both. What is at stake, then, is not whether a closing of the current gap would be mutually beneficial; it is what the 'terms' of this disciplinary *détente* should be. This chapter will first survey the proposals made by McClary and Walser, Shepherd, and Middleton. All three proposals raise interesting, important issues, but, ultimately, are problematic in my view. I will

---

[11] John Shepherd, *Music as Social Text* (Cambridge, 1991), 206.

then sketch an approach to popular music that avoids the problems inherent in the other three proposals.

## II

In their 1988 essay, 'Start Making Sense! Musicology Wrestles with Rock', Susan McClary and Robert Walser explore the methodological, political, and ideological problems that arise when a scholar attempts to negotiate the space between conventional musicology and the study of popular music.[12] The essay takes its point of departure from a Bloom County comic strip, in which the characters, Opus and Hodge-Podge, read a review of their recent LP in *Time*. After making their way through a meaningless, but fairly typical-sounding interpretive sentence about their record, Opus asks, 'Yeah, but do we kick butt?' McClary and Walser then go on to argue that while musicologists tend to be able to describe how pieces of music work in a technical sense, they are ultimately unable to account for why and how music has the kind of effects it has on people: they cannot tell us if it 'kicks butt'.

McClary and Walser build their argument by first considering how difficult it is to capture music's effects in writing. While music of one's own culture seems to create its effects in an unmediated way, prose descriptions of how this occurs tend to result in either 'poetic or technical mystification'.[13] This discussion is followed by a survey of what the authors take to be the various dangers and obstacles that face the musicologist involved in the study of popular music (more on this below). They then move on to consider some of the pitfalls of pop musicology, which turn out to be over-reliance on song-lyric interpretation and attempts 'to control the music by means of a single totalizing method' (semiotics is used as an example).[14] The essay ends with a section entitled 'Fear of Music', in which the authors suggest why musicologists seem to avoid the issue of how music affects its listeners.

McClary and Walser argue vigorously that musicology must come to terms with popular music, and in the article they argue for rock; but their arguments could be extended to encompass other popular-music styles as well. They argue that one reason why musicology has avoided consideration of rock music is because any study of rock would necessarily have to confront an issue that musicology has been carefully avoiding all along: how music affects people, and how it affects them in *direct* ways.[15] They write as follows:

---

[12] Susan McClary and Robert Walser, 'Start Making Sense! Musicology Wrestles with Rock', in Simon Frith and Andrew Goodwin (eds.), *On Record: Rock, Pop, and the Written Word* (New York, 1990), 277–92. Though the essay appeared in 1990, the date 1988 appears after the title.

[13] Ibid. 280.

[14] Ibid. 286.

[15] This point is illustrated in what must rank as one of the most colourful analogies of the music-analytical process to date: 'In fact, musicologists sometimes approach music with the same attitude that gynecologists (quite rightly!)

We are not advocating shutting off the mind and playing air guitar as a substitute for rigorous scholarship (though if more musicologists had an irresistible urge to play air guitar instead of lunging immediately for their distancing techniques, we all—readers and musicologists alike—might be better for it). Rather we are suggesting that considerably more attention has to be paid to those aspects of music that trigger adulation in fans, even if (*especially* if) those are just the aspects that strike terror in the scholar's rational mind.[16]

If rock music is, then, a kind of potent stuff with regard to its unmediated effect on its listeners, the argument would seem to hinge on establishing precisely what kind of effects it elicits and from whom. In their survey of the kinds of dangers and obstacles the pop musicologist can encounter, McClary and Walser observe: 'Not only does traditional musicology refuse to acknowledge popular culture, but it also disdains the very questions that scholars of rock want to pursue: How are particular effects achieved in music? How does music produce social meaning? How do music and society interrelate?'[17] Here we get to the heart of the authors' concerns with the study of rock music: the kinds of effects that rock elicits in the listener—and, by extension, those with which musicology should be more concerned generally—are primarily socially constructed; this is clear from the example they use, which describes the reaction of rock fans in an arena-type concert. The authors, then, are eager to investigate how music's effects can be explained as a product of social context. Along these lines, they write:

What is important in music is, indeed, elusive. But this need not force us back to some mystified plea of 'ineffability'. What musicologists can contribute to the discussion of the politics of popular music is some way of explaining how the powerful moments in music are accomplished, without discrediting the impression that they are exciting, disturbing, or pleasurable. The focus should be on constructing models that serve as flexible backdrops, up against which the noise of the piece can reverberate. What do the norms signify? Whose are they? What is the piece's particular strategy of resistance or affirmation? What's the noise about?[18]

The notion that popular-music styles must be thought of in their social context, or that the most fundamental questions in popular music are social ones, plays on the tacitly accepted notion that art-music and popular music

approach female sexuality: gingerly. In both situations, a concerted effort is made to forget that some of the members of society regard the objects of their scrutiny as pleasurable. The staff historian takes the vital information (date of birth, height, weight) of the patient. Up into the stirrups goes the song. And the theorist, donning "objectivity" as a methodological rubber glove to protect against contamination, confronts the dreaded thing itself' (ibid. 287). This passage seems strongly influenced by a scene in David Lodge's novel, *Small World, An Academic Romance* (New York, 1984), in which American postmodern literary critic Morris Zapp delivers a paper entitled 'Textuality as Striptease' (28–32), a paper that shocks the provincial delegates at a conference in the small fictitious English city of Rummidge.

[16] McClary and Walser, 'Start Making Sense!', 287.
[17] Ibid. 280.
[18] Ibid. 289.

are—seemingly, at least—different at a basic level. After all, nobody doubts that rock music works its effects on its audiences in obvious ways; as the authors put it: 'the music plays, the body moves.'[19] This kind of effect has in fact become a familiar caricature since the 1950s, and the image of young people dancing in wild or strange ways to rock music is exactly what has always caused rock to be seen as a threat to 'decent' society in the eyes of some of rock's critics. By contrast, nobody expects dancing in the aisles at a symphony orchestra concert.

But McClary and Walser work a variation on the 'fundamental difference' theme that casts popular music as the model; they reject the notion that rock music can be studied in the same way that art-music is. In fact, this point is taken far too much for granted; it is asserted, rather than argued.[20] The authors suggest that methods that might be developed to study rock music and its effects on listeners could be used equally well in the study of art-music. The gap between musicology and popular-music studies is thus bridged not by folding popular music into the standard concerns of musicology, but rather by folding all music into what have to be seen in the end as sociological issues, or at least as issues that have tended to interest sociologists much more than musicologists. Thus the authors ultimately come to focus their argument less on the issue of incorporating rock music into the horizon of possible musics, which might be fruitful for musicological investigation, and much more on a call for a kind of disciplinary reorientation within the field of musicology itself. For them, musicology will 'start making sense' of music when it addresses how music can affect listeners in direct ways; that is, when it can tell us how music 'kicks butt'.

## III

John Shepherd has also addressed the current gap existing between musicology and popular-music studies. In his 1991 book, *Music as Social Text*, Shepherd calls for a bridging of this disciplinary gap, arguing in even stronger terms than McClary and Walser that musicology must become more sociologically oriented if it is to avoid condemning itself to 'an even more peripheral position in the academic world than it presently occupies'.[21]

---

[19] McClary and Walser, 'Start Making Sense!', 278.

[20] I pursue the question of whether music-analytical methods developed for the analysis of art-music can be applied effectively to popular music, and survey the arguments around this issue, in my 'We Won't Get Fooled Again: Rock Music and Music Theory', *In Theory Only*, 13/1–4 (September 1997), 119–41; also to appear in Anahid Kassabian, David Schwarz, and Lawrence Siegel (eds.), *Keeping Score: Music, Disciplinarity, Culture* (Charlottesville, Va., 1997), 75–89.

[21] Shepherd, *Music as Social Text*, 190. The following discussion is focused primarily on ch. 10 of this work, entitled 'Musicology and Popular Music Studies'. Although the book did not appear until 1991, portions of ch. 10 were published as early as 1985. For a more recent critique of musicology that takes up many of the same themes from the perspective of feminism, see Shepherd's 'Difference and Power in Music', in Ruth Solie (ed.), *Musicology and Difference: Gender and Sexuality in Music Scholarship* (Berkeley, 1993), 46–65; my thanks to Rosemary Killam for drawing my attention to this recent essay.

For Shepherd, an understanding of the sociological dimension of music—how a culture constructs meaning in and through music—serves as a foundation for the understanding of music generally. Toward the end of the book, for example, Shepherd reflects on the interaction of sociological and musicological concerns:

The arguments presented in the previous chapters clearly have implications for the disciplines of historical musicology and music theory as they have traditionally been practised in the Western world. At the very least, sociological dimensions add to the diachronic orientation of historical musicology a synchronic one. Over and above that, however, they bring to the understanding of music a sense of social grounding that historical musicologists . . . have tended to resist.[22]

So far, then, one gets the impression that sociological concerns complement the current interests of musicology; they offer a new, useful perspective that might be integrated into present concerns in the field. But just a few sentences later Shepherd writes:

there is a need to relate matters of context (historical musicology) to matters of text (music theory-music analysis). The way to do this is to provide a conceptual link in terms of the social ground of both the contextual and textual dimensions of musical processes. Nowhere have these issues been more sharply focused than in popular music studies. The proper interpellation [*sic*] of popular music studies into the curricula of university music departments . . . will point the way to an appropriate re-conceptualization of musicology as a discipline.[23]

Here, condensed into a few sentences, we come up against what Shepherd feels is at stake in negotiating the separation between musicology and popular-music studies. In the discussion that follows the lines cited above, Shepherd examines the division of labour that has tended to occur between musicologists and theorists: musicologists often act as historians, 'establishing facts on the basis of empirical evidence', whereas theorists tend to undertake technical analyses, working only from the context of the pitches and rhythms themselves.[24] Both tend to ignore the sociological aspects of the music, or at least think of them as secondary considerations, sometimes even priding themselves on the fact that art-music somehow transcends such concerns.[25] As noted in the introductory section above, this text–context division can also be seen to be operative in

[22] Shepherd, *Music as Social Text*, 189.

[23] Ibid.

[24] Ibid. 190. Shepherd also considers the field of ethnomusicology, a discipline devoted in principle to studying the relationships between music and society. He comes to the conclusion that ethnomusicologists have tended to deal almost exclusively with other cultures, and not with the popular music of Western society. This supports his general argument that musicology has not yet found a successful mode of accounting for popular music in its music-technical, music-historical, and sociological dimensions.

[25] For a critique of the notion of the autonomous artwork see Janet Wolff, 'The Ideology of Autonomous Art', foreword to Richard Leppert and Susan McClary (eds.), *Music and Society: The Politics of Composition, Performance and Reception* (Cambridge, 1987), 1–12.

popular-music studies, where the musicologically oriented have attempted to understand popular music primarily in terms of the music itself, while the more sociologically oriented have tended to understand popular music in terms of contextual processes that are 'extrinsic to the musical event, but which nevertheless imbue the event itself with meaning and significance for people'.[26]

For Shepherd, the common ground between music theory and musicology lies in the inherently social nature of music. Analysis can help reveal how the actual structural properties of music can reflect a society's image of itself; what is usually taken to be the untainted, absolute musical stuff itself turns out to be conditioned by social contexts.[27] According to this scheme, then, musicology takes the role of mapping out the musical territory itself in terms of repertory, including all styles on an even footing, and exploring the social bases of each.[28]

It is an understatement to note that this kind of scheme would require a fundamental change in the ways in which musicology and theory are currently practised. But if Shepherd's 're-conceptualization' were to occur, many of the problems that have tended to exist between the disciplines of musicology and popular-music studies would have a basis for resolution; for in this case musicologists could tell sociologists and cultural critics the kinds of things they need to know about music and have heretofore been unable to understand fully. Musicologists could provide technical, historical accounts of popular music—or even art-music—that feed into some of the broader concerns with which sociologists have tended occupy themselves. Like McClary and Walser, Shepherd believes that the study of popular music by musicologists calls for fundamental changes within the discipline itself; and like the argument of McClary and Walser, Shepherd's argument ends up focusing less on the study of popular music as a separate issue and more on a thoroughgoing critique of musicology, and to a lesser extent, music theory.

## IV

In his discussion of how musicology can reconceptualize itself, Shepherd depends on the work of Richard Middleton. In a chapter in his *Studying Popular Music* entitled ' "Change Gonna Come"? Popular Music and Musicology', Middleton provides a critique of the ways in which musicologists have studied popular music. He also offers his own proposal for how musicology can restructure itself to deal effectively with what he takes to be the most crucial concerns

---

[26] Shepherd, *Music as Social Text*, 196.

[27] For a sense of how such analytical work might be carried out in accordance with Shepherd's concerns, see chs. 6, 7, and 8 of his *Music as Social Text*, entitled respectively: 'Functional Tonality: A Basis for Musical Hegemony'; 'The Analysis of Popular Music: Class, Generation, and Ethnicity'; and 'Music and Male Hegemony'.

[28] Shepherd relies here on Richard Middleton's proposal for a 'critical musicology', which is discussed in greater depth below.

not only in the study of popular music, but also in the study of music generally. After discussing what he sees as the general problems with the application of the techniques of traditional musicology—which are mostly music-analytical techniques—to popular music, Middleton critiques what he regards as instances of problematic writing on popular music. He turns first to Alec Wilder's work on Tin Pan Alley and Broadway songs, then to Charles Hamm's writing on American popular song, and finally to Wilfrid Mellers's work on the music of both the Beatles and Bob Dylan.[29]

The general conclusion that Middleton comes to in his critical survey is that popular music simply cannot be studied in the same way as art-music; scholars applying traditional methods to popular music produce distorted readings. These readings emphasize harmony, melody, and form, but neglect what are often key components in popular music—components such as timbre, rhythmic structure and its subtle deviations, and expressive pitch deviations. While his critique focuses on how traditional musicological methods are inadequate to the challenge of understanding popular music on its own terms, Middleton is not willing to abandon the advanced techniques that musicologists and theorists have developed in accounting for musical structure and historical context. He writes:

it is not my intention to argue that musicology *cannot* understand popular music, or that students of popular music should abandon musicology. Nevertheless, it is true that the bundle of methods, assumptions, and ideologies which came to constitute 'mainstream musicology' in the later nineteenth and the twentieth centuries renders it a less than useful resource in many ways.[30]

Surveying what has been written about the gap separating musicology and popular-music studies, Middleton assesses the situation as follows:

There is a common tendency for the 'critique of musicology' to go too far. This is particularly true of the 'popular' versions which have become widespread in the popular music culture itself. Typically, these display either a retreat into sociology—the music interpreted solely in terms of the social categories into which the industry or the fans can be fitted—or an aggressive 'insiderism', which stresses that interpretation is 'intuitive', 'anti-academic', and intrinsic to the music culture itself. Underlying these attitudes is the assumption that popular music, especially recent genres, is *completely* different from 'academic' music, an antithesis; often this assumption is grounded in a naive revolutionism, which sees rock music as representing a decisive *break*. Now I, too, have been emphasizing the methodological implications of popular music's difference, but such totalizing views are misleading, resting on an inadequate historical knowledge or on an undialectical notion of the musical field. Between recent types of popular music and historical

---

[29] The books considered by Middleton are Alec Wilder, *American Popular Song: The Great Innovators 1900–1950*, ed. James T. Maher (New York, 1972); Charles Hamm, *Yesterdays: Popular Song in America* (New York, 1979); Wilfrid Mellers, *Twilight of the Gods: The Music of the Beatles* (New York, 1973); *idem*, *A Darker Shade of Pale: A Backdrop to the Music of Bob Dylan* (New York, 1985).

[30] Middleton, *Studying Popular Music*, 104.

traditions of popular, so-called folk, and even bourgeois music stretching back at least as far as the sixteenth century, there are innumerable links and parallels.[31]

Middleton is clearly concerned with a reformulation of musical scholarship and criticism that could accommodate both art-music and popular music; he conceives of an approach broad enough that the scholar can appreciate both similarities *and* differences among and between styles. The call is to develop analytical techniques that are suited to whatever music is being studied—techniques that do not force the music through an interpretive filter constructed especially for one broad style of music (Western art-music), but are rather designed to bring out what is most characteristic in the particular style under consideration. If seemingly disparate styles have musical features in common, this too must be acknowledged. The idea is, as Middleton explains, that:

a *critical* stance recognizes the need to 'walk round' the entire topography, holding this map in the mind so that there is ultimately a committed point of view which is nevertheless aware of a structure of mutually critical perspectives analogous to the structure of the musical practice itself. Methods applying to diverse musics a point of view deriving from one perspective, and methods which simply aggregate varying perspectives, are equally unsatisfactory. The musicologist has to recognize the existence and the interaction—within a society, within a history—of different musical problematics.[32]

Middleton's proposal, like those of Shepherd and McClary and Walser, calls for a fundamental change in the way that musicology is practised. Middleton stresses, however, that what musicology has accomplished in its study of art-music is valuable for the consideration of that music. He seems to suggest, in fact, that popular-music studies might in a certain sense model itself on traditional musicology; perhaps methods for analysing popular music could be developed that are as powerful for popular music as the traditional ones are for the study of art-music. But Middleton argues for more than simply a 'live and let live' kind of stance. He would like to see a unified field of 'critical musicology'—a field in which all musics are examined both in their specifically musical characteristics and in their specific social, cultural, and political contexts. Following Middleton's proposal, then, research that focuses primarily on musical issues, and which might not in so doing take much account of sociological issues, would be discouraged. The goal for Middleton, it seems, is for the scholar to be in a posi-

---

[31] Middleton, *Studying Popular Music*, 117. Middleton goes on to cite Peter van der Merwe's work, in his *Origins of the Popular Style: The Antecedents of Twentieth-Century Popular Music* (Oxford, 1989), as an example of how scholarship can uncover structural relationships between musical styles that would seem unlikely, when viewed only in terms of their respective social contexts, to share such features. Van der Merwe is careful to point out that his book 'is not a work of sociology', though he acknowledges that such work is extremely valuable (3). Two reviews of the book display the reactions that such a musicologically based study can elicit from popular-music scholars: Philip Tagg (*Popular Music*, 9/3 (1990), 375–80) begins his review by admitting that he was initially suspicious of the book, but that once he accepted its parameters and read it through, he found it extremely valuable; Robert Walser (*Journal of Musicological Research*, 12/1–2 (1992), 123–32), on the other hand, finds the lack of sociological perspective in the book unacceptable.

[32] Middleton, *Studying Popular Music*, 125.

tion to make what he considers to be *the* crucial connections between the way the music actually goes (texts, the domain of traditional musicology) and the social environment in which it is created, enjoyed, and consumed (social context, the domain of sociology). While Middleton acknowledges the accomplishments of musicology, he nevertheless proposes redirecting its disciplinary focus toward issues that many musicologists would consider to be sociological ones. For Middleton, it is not enough that musicologists begin to consider popular music carefully; the addition of popular music to the field of musicology should be part of a fundamental shift in our conception of the discipline.

## V

McClary and Walser, Shepherd, and Middleton each call for two kinds of change with regard to the disciplinary gap that currently exists between popular music and musicology. The first is that musicology must direct much more of its attention to popular musics within the Western tradition. In the arguments presented by the authors, though, the inclusion of popular music within the discipline requires a second kind of change: a basic reformulation of the fundamental intellectual concerns of the discipline. This basic reformulation in all three arguments requires that musicology consider the sociological dimensions of music as far more central to an understanding of music than they have been thus far. McClary and Walser envision musicology taking far more account of how music creates the kinds of effects it does on its listeners and within communities of listeners; Shepherd proposes that musicologists consider more carefully how cultures create musical meaning and even how music might play a role in creating cultures; and Middleton, perhaps taking the most conciliatory position with regard to traditional musicology, envisions a discipline broad and flexible enough in its methodologies to faithfully account for any kind of musical style, while viewing these styles as socially grounded.

To return, then, to the point from which this survey began, the question, ultimately, is not whether or not the gap between popular-music studies and musicology should be closed, but the terms of such a disciplinary interaction. In accord with the authors surveyed above, I would like to argue that this gap must be closed, and that musicology would benefit in a number of ways from including the careful consideration of both popular music and popular-music scholarship within its disciplinary horizon. But I reject the notion that a fundamental reformulation of musicology is required in order for the discipline to undertake research that will benefit itself and the field of popular-music studies generally. Thus, I accept the first kind of change outlined above, but find a number of problems with the second, more radical one.

In calling for, in Shepherd's words, a 'reconceptualization' of musicology, the authors are proposing something very much like what Thomas Kuhn termed a 'paradigm shift'.[33] Following Kuhn, there is no way of knowing at the present time whether or not the shift proposed by these authors will be taken up by the field of musicology in the future. This will depend on whether or not the musicological community finds the new models proposed by these authors more powerful than current ones in explaining and organizing the music with which its members are concerned. Popular-music scholars argue that when the repertory of music that is studied by musicologists is expanded to include popular music, their model will have more explanatory and organizational power than the current one.

But a crucial aspect of Kuhn's work parallels very closely some of the claims made by McClary and Walser, Shepherd, and Middleton. Each popular-music scholar claims that music's meaning—or its effects—are socially constructed. Kuhn's claim is that scientific and, extending Kuhn's claim, humanities disciplines are socially constructed as well. Thus, no matter how passionately the call for a reorientation in musicology is made, it will ultimately be the musicological community itself that will decide whether or not to adopt the new model proposed. Thought of in this way, it seems extremely unlikely that such a paradigm shift will occur. The musicological community is constituted not exclusively, but for the most part, by people who entered the field because they were interested primarily in music—and 'music' here is understood in the traditional, detached-from-social-concerns sense. Most have spent many years, in addition to undertaking musical studies and research, playing and even composing music. Popular-music scholars might argue that this kind of musical experience is meaningful precisely because it is socially grounded, and one must dig out the ways in which this kind of social reality can arise. The question, it seems to me, is not whether or not these kinds of sociological interpretations of musical experience are valuable—I believe they are—but rather, whether or not this should be the only kind of research that musicologists do, or even whether this should be *the* fundamental kind of question that *all* musicological work must ultimately address.

Extending their own argument, Shepherd and the other authors discussed above must admit that if an intellectual community constructs meaning in the music it studies in a manner that excludes or severely subordinates sociological concerns, such a community has a perfect right to do so; while such a disciplinary situation can be examined and explained sociologically, it does not necessarily follow that the resultant analysis will have any impact whatsoever on the community itself. Ironically, insisting on radical change within musicology on intellectual grounds that are not central to the discourse itself—which, in fact, are cast as contrary to a point of view held by most musicologists—seems to go

---

[33] Thomas S. Kuhn, *The Structure of Scientific Revolutions*, 2nd edn. (Chicago, 1970). Kuhn considers the ways in which paradigms arise, flourish, and perish only within the context of the history of science. But his characterization of the manner in which scientific communities are socially grounded can be very useful in understanding the ways in which humanities disciplines organize themselves.

against the very notion that communities decide for themselves which disciplinary issues are central. The argument is cast as a critique from *outside* the discipline, and the rhetoric is more prescriptive than suggestive.

As has been noted a number of times already, the argument that music is inherently social has arisen—in the initial stages at least—from the notion that popular music and art-music are fundamentally different. In pursuing sociological questions in music, popular music has been fertile ground for investigation. After all, this music is *popular*, and how or why communities of people are attracted to certain popular-music styles or performers is an issue open to systematic empirical investigation. One can interview fans and musicians, check record sales and radio air-play, analyse visual images associated with the music (album covers, concert posters, etc.), analyse clothing styles, observe behaviour at live performances, and so on. Needless to say, this kind of investigation has not been standard in researching art-music and the culture that surrounds it. But if these methods of investigating popular music and culture provide useful information, so the argument goes, then it is only natural that they could be utilized in the study of art-music and its culture as well. Thus, while the separation of the two general kinds of music provides a starting-point for the investigation of popular music, such study later returns to art-music to claim that it must operate in ways similar to its popular counterpart.

The basic premises of this argument can be questioned, however. The authority of the popular-music scholar claiming a social basis for the understanding of popular music has tended in the past to go unquestioned by musicologists. After all, musicologists are generally thought to know little about popular music—in fact, they may appear to pride themselves on this ignorance—and one clearly needs to know a fair amount of popular music in order to come to even the most preliminary scholarly conclusions about it. It seems, then, that it has been far easier for musicologists to allow the sociological interpretation of popular music to stand than to learn entirely new musical repertories in order to challenge it. But this image of the musicologist immersed in art-music but oblivious to popular music is no longer tenable.[34] Many musicologists and music theorists born after World War II came to music initially through popular music. Many played both art-music and popular music as children and as young adults; some did not come to the study of art-music until they had spent many years involved in popular music. In any case, it is difficult to imagine anybody growing up in the United States after 1955 who was not exposed to popular music, and to rock or country and western music especially. There are a number of young musicologists and theorists who know a lot of popular music, though most may never have made a systematic study of the repertory.

---

[34] In the discussion that follows, I am forced to depend on my own personal experience in speaking with numerous colleagues in musicology and music theory over the last decade or so.

Music scholars with a background in popular music need not accept the claim that popular music is inherently social in the thoroughgoing way that popular-music scholars have tended to portray it; they have their own experience of the repertory against which to measure such claims. One may acknowledge that the social dimension plays a certain role in popular music— in some popular music it may play a crucial role—and still argue that the principal significance of this music lies, for the musicologist, in the music itself— in the way it *sounds*. Writing as one who has spent many years playing and listening to popular music—and I do not want to rely too heavily on an 'insider' argument here—I have always been concerned with the way the music sounds, the way particular songs are situated within a single style and across various styles, and not so much with the kind of social or political statement that the music may have been making. In many years of playing in a wide variety of bands and performing situations, I found that most of the musicians with whom I worked shared this basic attitude. This is not to deny that others may have found that the same music makes social or political statements, or that there were social forces at work in my experience in unconscious ways; my claim is simply that this is not the principal manner in which its practitioners have tended to understand most popular music. I find that many of the claims made in popular-music scholarship, interesting and revealing though they sometimes are, never really capture the popular-music experience as I understand it. In short, I distrust the popular-music scholars' claims that this music is meaningful in ways that are principally socially constructed.

The problem lies in the assertion that there is a single way to view popular music: namely, as inherently and primarily social. I propose instead that popular music can also be considered as inherently *musical*, and only secondarily social. According to this model, the gap between the study of popular and art-music becomes far narrower for the musicologist than it is in the more sociologically oriented model. The study of popular music is an area of research that the musi-cologist can undertake without necessarily becoming a student of sociology; while an understanding of social context is crucial to the understanding of popular music, it need not be the central, fundamental consideration. At the same time, musicologists must take the warnings of popular-music scholars very seriously, and avoid casting popular music as if it were 'just like' art-music. The challenge then becomes the investigation of popular music along traditional musicological lines while maintaining a careful sensitivity to how popular music may differ from art-music in its specifically musical dimensions. I do not re-ject socially grounded interpretations of popular music; I am simply arguing that such interpretations are incomplete whenever they cannot account for the specifically musical aspects of the music. A musicological account of popular music can coexist with a sociological account; the two approaches are complementary.

# VI

For musicology, the problem of bridging the gap between popular-music studies and musicology can be addressed most profitably—in the initial stages at least—by exploring popular music *vis-à-vis* issues that already tend to occupy musicologists. There are a number of areas in the study of popular music that remain relatively unexplored in terms of the traditional concerns of musicology; in this section I will briefly sketch some of these areas.

One area that could benefit from musicological attention is the actual history of popular music itself. For instance, there is still a tremendous amount of work to be done simply in the historiography of rock.[35] Histories of rock music have tended to fall into one of two categories: those that are journalistic and targeted at a popular readership[36] and textbooks designed for undergraduate-level general-music courses.[37] In such writing, the repertory of rock music has tended to be divided up according to stylistic labels that are often derived from the way the music was marketed; labels such as 'British invasion' (or 'beat music'), 'folk rock', 'surf music', 'rockabilly', and 'classical rock' abound. But writers have tended to avoid thinking of these styles in terms of their specifically musical characteristics; or if they have done so, they have considered these musical aspects in only the most superficial ways. The development of specific artists has also tended not to be portrayed in musical terms; the Beatles, for instance, are often seen to progress from mop-top innocence to Sgt Pepper psychedelia without any substantial reference to the development of the technical features of their music-making (recording techniques and instrumentation aside).[38] The direct influence of earlier popular-music styles on later artists is also a potentially rich area of research that is often pursued in only the most superficial terms.[39]

[35] Since rock music is the area of popular music with which my own work is concerned, I will restrict my remarks to the situation as it stands in rock music scholarship.

[36] Two widely read books of this type are Ward *et al.*, *Rock of Ages*, and Greil Marcus, *Mystery Train: Images of America in Rock 'n' Roll Music*, 3rd rev. edn. (New York, 1990).

[37] See Charles T. Brown, *The Art of Rock and Roll*, 2nd edn. (Englewood Cliffs, NJ, 1987); Katherine Charlton, *Rock Music Styles: A History*, 2nd edn. (Madison, 1994); Joe Stuessy, *Rock and Roll: Its History and Stylistic Development*, 2nd edn. (Englewood Cliffs, NJ, 1994); and David P. Szatmary, *Rockin' in Time: A Social History of Rock and Roll*, 2nd edn. (Englewood Cliffs, NJ, 1991). A number of important studies of rock music do not fit neatly into either of the categories discussed here. Gillett's *Sound of the City* and *idem*, *Making Tracks: Atlantic Records and the Growth of a Multi-Billion-Dollar Industry* (New York, 1974) both consider popular music (mostly rock) in the context of its relationship with record companies. Both Simon Frith (*Sound Effects: Youth, Leisure, and the Politics of Rock 'n' Roll* (New York, 1981)) and Peter Wicke (*Rock Music: Culture, Aesthetics, and Sociology*, trans. Rachel Fogg (Cambridge, 1990)) approach rock music from a sociological perspective.

[38] Two recent studies that attempt to account for the development of a single artist or group in a music-technical manner are Walter Everett's 'Swallowed by a Song: Paul Simon's Crisis of Chromaticism' and Daniel Harrison's 'After Sundown: The Beach Boys' Experimental Music', both in John Covach and Graeme Boone (eds.), *Understanding Rock* (Oxford, 1997). Everett is also at work on a book that traces the Beatles' development from their earliest days to the demise of the group in 1970.

[39] Dave Headlam explores the ways in which American rhythm and blues was transformed in the British rock of the power trio Cream in his 'Blues Transformations in the Music of Cream', in Covach and Boone (eds.), *Understanding Rock*.

Taking up these issues in the historiography of popular music may lead musi-cologists into unfamiliar avenues of research. Though there are some good col-lections of popular-music recordings and other materials in university archives, one is still more likely, for example, to have to hunt down older recordings in used record shops.[40] Interviews with the artists themselves may appear in guitar or keyboard magazines, sandwiched between glossy ads for the latest guitars and amplification systems. The scholar may find it necessary to become familiar with recording techniques, or the machinations of record companies and radio stations. Tracing the history of any popular-music style demands that the musicologist be immersed in the popular culture from which the music arose, even when this constitutes a popular culture of the past. In the course of this kind of research, the musicologist is bound to depend, in part, on the work of popular-music scholars; and this dependence is bound to go a long way toward closing the gap between the two disciplines. The important aspect of the situation as portrayed here is that the musicologist come to this writing on his or her own terms; popular-music scholarship is used to create a complementary context to the specifically musical one *within* the overriding concerns of musical scholarship.

The study of popular music raises a number of issues that shed new light on topics that have traditionally interested musicologists. The issue of composi-tional process in popular music is largely unexplored. Many of the CD repack-agings of older recordings include 'bonus tracks' made up of alternative versions of important, influential songs. In rock music, for example, comparison of mul-tiple versions of a song can sometimes reveal the process through which the musicians came to the final version. This can suggest fresh perspectives on com-positional procedure.[41] The rapid, wide distribution of popular music radically speeds up historical and geographical components of style change and develop-ment, and this kind of change can be traced through a number of popular-music styles. These mechanisms of style change in popular music are bound to feed back into larger considerations of style change in music generally.

Popular music also challenges established notions associated with the study of art-music. Many popular-music songs, for example, are composed by two or more musicians; the Beatles' Lennon and McCartney are a well-known song-writing team. Add to this particular combination the roles played by band members George Harrison and Ringo Starr and producer George Martin in the arranging and recording process of Beatles music, and the single-composer model prevalent in art-music quickly breaks down. The role of the recording pro-

---

[40] Much older material has been re-released in CD format, but often repackaged in ways that do not preserve details of the original release. Mild casualties of repackaging can be the elimination of the original liner photos or song lyrics; more drastic repackagings combine tracks from different albums, or even include material that has been re-recorded to avoid licensing problems.

[41] Daniel Harrison explores this issue with regard to the music of the Beach Boys in a recent paper entitled '*Good Vibrations*: A Case Study of Compositional Process in Rock Music', presented at the annual conference of the Society for Music Theory, 4 Nov. 1993, in Montreal, Canada.

ducer is an especially interesting one in popular music, and has no direct parallel in art-music. For instance, Elvis Presley's music changed in important ways when he moved from Sun Studios in Memphis, where he was produced by Sam Phillips, to RCA's Nashville studios, where he was produced by Chet Atkins.[42] Thus the notion of a single artist controlling all aspects of a work's creation is no longer workable in much popular music, and needs to be replaced by a framework more faithful to the repertory. This kind of work is currently only in its most initial stages.

From even such a brief sketch as this, it is clear that the investigation of popular music by musicologists, in terms of the traditional issues of musicology, would benefit popular-music studies generally; but such investigation is also likely to suggest new angles on some of the traditional issues in musical scholarship, as well as new musicological issues altogether. I am not arguing that socially and culturally grounded readings of popular music somehow do not constitute *real* musicology. Recent work by Lawrence Kramer and Susan McClary, for example, interprets Western art-music from a socio-cultural perspective; but Kramer's hermeneutic readings of Beethoven, Wagner, and Liszt, and McClary's feminist interpretations of Monteverdi, Bach, and Brahms depend to a significant extent on the reader's knowledge of how the canon of Western art-music is organized.[43] While such approaches may challenge traditional musicological interpretations, they can at least assume that the reader is well acquainted with the traditional slicing up of the art-music canon. By contrast, the history—or histories—of popular music and its myriad styles has, for the most part, not yet been established in anything but the most preliminary sense. There is still plenty of 'traditional musicology' left to do in popular music; in fact, the work has hardly begun.

Ultimately, I am arguing that if popular music is going to be interesting to musicologists, it will be interesting because it engages issues that already exist in the current discourse, or because it raises issues that extend or are closely related to issues within the current discourse; this needs to occur before popular music can suggest new issues within the discourse. The proposals made by McClary and Walser, Shepherd, and Middleton not only ask musicologists to look at different music, but also tell them to care about different issues in all the music they study. This is too much to demand of the discipline, and this kind of radical change is therefore unlikely to occur. If musicologists are going to include popular music in their teaching and thinking about music generally, they will do so because popular music fits into the ways in which the discipline conceives of music in a universal sense. In the current climate of curricular reform,

---

[42] For an account of Sam Phillips and Sun Records, see Colin Escott with Martin Hawkins, *Good Rockin' Tonight: Sun Records and the Birth of Rock 'n' Roll* (New York, 1991).

[43] See Lawrence Kramer, *Music as Cultural Practice, 1800–1900* (Berkeley, 1990); Susan McClary, *Feminine Endings: Music, Gender, and Sexuality* (Minneapolis, 1991); idem, 'Narrative Agendas in "Absolute" Music: Identity and Difference in Brahms's Third Symphony', in Solie (ed.), *Musicology and Difference*, 326–44.

musicologists are increasingly called upon to teach popular music; but there are better reasons for including popular music in the teaching of music than those that arise through political and institutional pressures. The study of popular music opens up new repertories and introduces fresh perspectives on current issues in musicology; thus, it expands our understanding of the history of music and enriches our relationship to *music itself*.[44]

[44] I would like to thank Matthew Brown, Walter Everett, and Allen Forte for reading an earlier version of this chapter and offering many helpful comments and suggestions. The opinions expressed here are of course my own.

# 21

## *Gender, Musicology, and Feminism*

### Suzanne G. Cusick

### I. Gender and Musicology

#### Present at the Origin

My task here is to explain the relationship between gender and musicology, to explain the intellectual, musical, and political challenges that feminist scholarship poses to musicology, and to consider the reasons why feminist scholarship about music warrants the serious attention of all readers interested in 'rethinking music' as the twentieth century draws to a close.

I will begin by arguing that gender had been intrinsic to the practice of musicology in the United States, grounding my claim in a story of origins, the story of the founding in 1930 of the New York Musicological Society. This is the group that in 1934 dissolved itself so that it could be reconstituted on the same day as the American Musicological Society—the society whose corporate existence represents the institutionalization of musicology as a cultural practice in the United States.[1]

On 22 February 1930, the young American composer Ruth Crawford, lodging in the New York home of music patron Blanche Walton so that she could study dissonant counterpoint with musical polymath Charles Seeger, wrote thus in her diary:

The musicologists meet. It is decided that I may sit in the next room and hear [Joseph] Yasser about his new supra scale. Then when I come out for this purpose, I find someone has closed the doors. Blanche is irate, so am I. Men are selfish, says Blanche. You just have to accept the fact. Perhaps, I wonder, their selfishness is one reason why they accomplish more than women. . . . I walk past the closed door to my room, and when I pass I turn my head toward the closed door and quietly but forcibly say, 'Damn you,' then go on in

---

[1] See Claude Palisca's thorough and revealing history, 'American Scholarship in Western Music', in Frank Lloyd Harrison, Claude Palisca, and Mantle L. Hood (eds.), *Musicology*, The Princeton Studies: Humanistic Scholarship in America (Englewood Cliffs, NJ, 1963), 87–214. He describes the dissolution of the New York Musicological Society on 3 June 1934 and the immediate reconstitution of the group as the American Musicological Association on pp. 129–30.

my room and read Yasser's article. Later, my chair close to the door, I hear some of the discussion.[2]

Although she had not been told so at the time, the meeting from which Ruth Crawford was excluded was the meeting at which the New York Musicological Society was founded. Many years later, Charles Seeger, a principal organizer of both the New York society and the national one that succeeded it, and a foundational thinker about the nature of musicology in America, confessed to an interviewer that he had deliberately excluded Crawford 'to avoid the incipient criticism that musicology was "woman's work" '.[3]

This may strike many readers as a strange way of telling the story of one of the founding moments of American musicology. Yet my story demonstrates one prominent point of view from which a feminist musicologist might tell any story—the point of view of the woman excluded from the room.[4] And it demonstrates both the promise of telling stories from such a point of view and the strangeness of the story that logically results. For my story will seem entirely to miss the main point of the founding of the New York Musicological Society (just as Ruth Crawford missed it). Readers cannot expect to learn from my story what central principles were articulated to guide the disciplined study of music. Nor can they hope to learn who, besides Joseph Yasser and Charles Seeger, were present.[5] Yet my story, told from the point of view of a woman excluded from the room, needs no exegesis to reveal something of interest to women and to thinkers about musicology who are curious about the power relations and cultural politics implicitly embedded in our discipline. It reveals that to the founders of American musicology theirs was a kind of work that could be understood as gendered. Its gender, moreover, was unstable enough that musicology risked being mistaken for 'woman's work' unless biological women were excluded from perform-

---

[2] Matilda Gaume, *Ruth Crawford Seeger: Memoirs, Memories, Music* (Metuchen, NJ, 1986), 196. I am grateful to Ellie M. Hisama for leading me to this story, which is told in her essay 'The Question of Climax in Ruth Crawford's String Quartet, Mvt. 3', in Elizabeth West Marvin and Richard Hermann (eds.), *Concert Music, Rock and Jazz since 1945* (Rochester, forthcoming).

[3] The quoted passage is Hisama's paraphrase in 'Question of Climax', n. 7. Seeger's remarks appear in 'Reminiscences of an American Musicologist', interviewers Adelaide Tusler and Ann Briegled, Oral History Program, University of California at Los Angeles, 1972.

[4] At this point, I mean by the word 'feminist' a person interested in the experience and point of view of women. Other definitions of the word will emerge in the course of the chapter. Susan McClary's 'A Material Girl in Bluebeard's Castle', the preface to her collection of essays *Feminine Endings: Music, Gender and Sexuality* (Minneapolis, 1991), tells a story of musicology's exclusion of women from knowledge from a slightly different point of view— that of a woman admitted to the musicological room under the terms of a heterosexual contract, but who is none the less prevented from discovering the knowledge she seeks.

[5] According to Palisca ('American Scholarship', 129), the New York Musicological Society was founded by Henry Cowell, Otto Kinkeldey, Charles Seeger, Joseph Schillinger, and Joseph Yasser. On 3 June 1934, again in the home of Blanche Walton at 25 Washington Square North, Executive Committee Chair Charles Seeger called on the Society 'to dissolve in preparation for the foundation of the national association' (ibid. 130). The group then re-formed itself as the American Musicological Association. Present for that act were Seeger, Schillinger, Yasser, and six newcomers: George Dickinson, Carl Engel, Gustave Reese, Helen Heffrom Roberts, Harold Spivacke, and Oliver Strunk. Roberts's presence evidently did not represent a threat to the perceived gender of the new society's work, perhaps because she was an anthropologist who studied the musical cultures of various native American peoples. In any case, although she remained a member of the new society through the 1940s, Helen Roberts gave up her musical career in 1936, becoming (according to Barbara Krader in *New Grove*) a leading authority on gardening.

ing its practice. Like a man-child at the oedipal stage (when he enters the symbolic order by identifying with the phallic power of his father and separating himself from the limitless, engulfing love of his mother), the New York Musicological Society entered the cultural and corporate order—became an official and comprehensible voice in American intellectual life—by separating itself from the feminine.

This last, psychoanalytic reading of my story doubtless makes it seem even stranger to readers who long to know the story as it might be told from the point of view of the men inside the musicologists' room. For surely no gendering of musicology as practice or *persona* was effected by closing the door on Ruth Crawford. The issue, as one might imagine it from the point of view of the men in the room, was musicology's intellectual legitimacy, not its gender. Taking steps to ensure that the new discipline not seem to be 'woman's work' was but one piece in a strategy to 'establish the study of music in a position of give and take with the great studies of our day',[6] an effort that had engaged American musicologists since at least the 1880s.[7] Being perceived as 'woman's work' would threaten musicology's legitimacy and equality with 'the great studies' of the day, because it would automatically relegate musicology to a position in the intellectual world analogous to the position of women (and their work) in the 'real' world—a position of inferiority and relative powerlessness, characterized by emotionality, sensuality, and frivolity. Because music itself, the object of musicology's study, was already widely associated with the feminine in American culture, and consequently of embattled status, it was especially impo tant that musicology not seem associated in any way with music's feminine qualities. The gender of musicology itself, as a kind of work, was not really the issue. Like 'woman's work', like Ruth Crawford and Blanche Walton, gender was itself a marginal concern, incidental, a means to a larger, more important end. To the founders of the New York Musicological Society, gender was one metaphor among many to be manipulated so that a group of erudite men could legitimize their intellectual focus on music. The work of musicology was to be that of other academic disciplines; scientific, objective, and serious, it was to be clearly differentiated from its object of study. Existing on a plane above the distinctions of gender, like the other 'great studies of the day', musicology was to be universal.

## Gender and Musicology: Marginal or Central?

But was musicology universal, above the distinctions of gender? Can there be a universal that excludes the concept of gender? Or is the perceived marginality of

---

[6] Charles Seeger, 'On the Principles of Musicology', *Musical Quarterly*, 10 (1924), 250.

[7] On the early efforts to establish musicology as a legitimate discipline in the United States, see Palisca, 'American Scholarship', 122–49. Classic discipline-defining essays from before the establishment of the New York Musicological Society include Waldo S. Pratt, 'On Behalf of Musicology', *Musical Quarterly*, 1 (1915), 1–16; Seeger, 'Principles of Musicology'; and Carl Engel, 'View and Reviews', *Musical Quarterly*, 14 (1928), 297–306.

gender to musicology part of the problem that a feminist musicology must eventually address? I believe that the perceived marginality of gender to musicology has reinforced the discipline's historical marginalization of women's musical experiences.

Consider this statement, which I think to be one logical conclusion from the premiss that gender is marginal to musicology:

If gender is understood as only incidental to musical, intellectual or cultural practices, then the gender of a person embarking on a musical life of some kind would presumably also be only incidental—marginal—to her success or failure, to her choices of genre and form, to her negotiations with the cultural norms that govern biological and cultural (re)production.

If I had used the masculine pronoun 'he', most (pre-feminist) readers would have agreed with my claim that gender was marginal to the unfolding of a musical life. That is, readers would have seen it as self-evident that in the case of, say, Josquin des Prez, gender was marginal to *his* success or failure, marginal to *his* choices of genre and form, marginal to *his* negotiations with the cultural norms that govern biological and cultural reproduction. Concern for his biological reproduction would have seemed a little odd, for we usually imagine that the production of children makes no impact on a man's life progress. It might also seem odd for me to have associated Josquin's compositional work with cultural reproduction, perhaps because we assume that men are relatively uninvolved in biological reproduction.

Yet readers of this essay quite reasonably expect me to have been thinking of Ruth Crawford when I wrote my sentence about the marginality of gender to *her* musical life. Few readers would take the pronoun 'her' as a universal. And few would agree with the idea that gender is marginal to a woman's musical, biological, or cultural choices. For gender is, in our common-sense view of the world, always a concern for women.

If we think a bit about why this is our common sense about gender, we must admit it is thus because gender somehow marks a woman—as not a man, not the norm, not the universal. Of course gender matters, we infer, to the story of Ruth Crawford's musical life. Yet, we usually imagine that gender did not affect Josquin's musical life. We fail to see *his* gender as having empowered him to make certain kinds of choices unavailable to his sisters; just as, centuries later, *her* gender restricted the choices available to Ruth Crawford. We fail to see, that is, that gender affected them equally, but differently.

Once we do see that, we may begin to suppose that 'gender' somehow distributes social power differently among women and men, affecting them differently. If gender is an issue for all people, how can we imagine that gender is marginal to the scholarly study of any human activity? What interest is served by our persisting in the assumption that gender is marginal to our discipline—that it is mainly the concern of women, and mainly woman's work?

One logical consequence of assuming that gender is marginal to musicology is to make it nearly impossible for there to be a musicology that includes women's compositional work. For we will all agree on the basis of common sense that gender always affects women. Yet our view of musicology and musicological practice as universal, beyond gender, implies that gender is marginal to a person's musical life. Thus, the woman in 'the woman composer' must be discussed in terms of her gender, a thing that is marginal to the composer in 'the woman composer'. That is, we imagine that to tell the story of Ruth Crawford's musical life, we will need to tell two stories, while to tell the story of Josquin's musical life, we need tell only one. Her doubled story is not easily compared with his; her story does not easily fit into the usual life and works narrative.[8] One interest served, then, by the assumption that gender itself is a marginal concern to thinking about music is the systematic problematizing of women's musical experiences: when those experiences fail to fit the usual (universal) narrative, the marginalizing of women in musical life is reinforced. This marginalization of women in musical life, in turn, reinforces the marginalization of women in 'real' life. That is, the marginalizing of gender (and the resulting marginalizing of women, women's music-making, 'woman's work', and the musically 'feminine') within the intellectual microcosm that is musicology helps to sustain the gender system itself, with its intentional devaluing of practices that might be mistaken for 'woman's work'.

But what do I mean by 'the gender system'? What is gender, anyway? Is it really more of an issue for women than for men?

Our culture, like most, conflates gender with biological sex—that is, with people's reproductive capabilities. But in fact gender is a system of assigning social roles, power, and prestige that is sustained by a vast web of metaphors and cultural practices commonly associated with 'the masculine' or 'the feminine'.[9] When we refer to 'women' and 'men' in everyday speech, we imagine that we are distinguishing between people who can bear children and people who cannot, or between people who can beget children and people who cannot. But we know that what we imagine is only partially true: we know that many potential child-bearers routinely behave in non-reproductive matters as though they were 'men', and that many potential child-begetters routinely behave in non-reproductive matters as though they were 'women'. Furthermore, we know perfectly well that many potential reproducers of one kind or the other never

---

[8] Crawford herself was aware of the doubled nature of her life story, referring to herself in an early poem as 'the straddler'. Crawford's biographer, Judith Tick, has replicated this poignant image in two parallel essays that tell the same story for different audiences. In her unpublished paper 'The Straddler', written for the conference 'Gender and Music' at King's College, London, in July 1991, Tick writes empathetically about Crawford's conflicted opinion of her Sonata for Violin and Piano. Tick's published essay 'Ruth Crawford's Spiritual Concept: The Sound Ideals of an Early American Modernist', *Journal of the American Musicological Society*, 44 (1991), 221–61, adopts the objective, distanced tone that is virtually required of essays in American musicology's official journal.

[9] For an elaboration of this point, see Joan Wallach Scott, 'Gender: A Useful Category of Historical Analysis', in *Gender and the Politics of History* (New York, 1988), 28–50.

reproduce; many of those also take the liberty of behaving neither as 'women' nor as 'men'. That is, we know that gender behaviours often fail to match people's apparent reproductive capabilities (and most of us experience some anxiety when we perceive the discrepancies). Thus we know that gender is a set of behaviours we have come to associate with (or expect of) child-bearers or childbegetters. As philosopher Judith Butler puts it, gender is not a fixed identity.[10] Rather, it consists of a series of performances that, taken together, identify some people as having much more social power and prestige than others. In our culture, the socially powerful include among their privileges the right to claim themselves as the universal, and to identify other people as lacking the social power and prestige to make such a claim.

One important feature of the successful claimant's power is the ability to define themselves by opposition to whatever qualities they assert to be 'naturally' associated with the child-bearing bodies of 'women'. 'Women's' bodies serve as metaphors for all that the socially powerful claimants are not, or claim not to be. The result is that we who live in a gendered world—and that is all of us—constantly refer back to the bodily distinctions on which the power relations of gender are supposedly based, imagining that there is some necessary connection among social role, reproductive role, and prestige that can be deciphered. To the extent that we believe gender relations to be natural extensions of differences in reproductive capabilities, we can be called 'essentialists'—for we believe that 'masculine' and 'feminine' qualities are essential manifestations of 'male' and 'female' bodies.

But if we agree with Butler that gender is as gender does—that is, if we believe that the gender others perceive in us results from cultural practices that are intelligible as gendered, not from something inherent in our bodies—then we must acknowledge gender to be an unstable system for maintaining the power and prestige it assigns. One false move, and we could be mistaken for the wrong gender, either gaining or losing prestige accordingly. How, then, could gender ever be a matter of concern only to women? Surely the maintenance of a system that assigns power and prestige to 'men' would be most important to 'men'.[11] Surely, then, it would be 'men' who would be constantly concerned with the proper performance of masculinity, and with enforcing the proper performance of femininity as well.

Surely it was an anxiety about the proper performance of masculinity that induced Seeger to be so careful about musicology's possible association with 'woman's work'. Surely, that is, he too understood gender as performative. And surely he intended that the performance of musicology be recognizable as a performance of masculinity, so that musicology might acquire the cultural power and prestige assigned to masculinity. Surely, too, the door was closed to Ruth

---

[10] See Judith P. Butler, *Gender Trouble: Feminism and the Subversion of Identity* (London, 1990).

[11] It would seem equally logical that maintaining a belief in essentialism would also be of interest to those who benefit from the assignment of social power and prestige to 'men'.

Crawford to define the performance of masculinity by the exclusion not only of a woman's body, but also of metaphors and cultural practices that might have been perceived as performances of femininity. Thus he excluded Crawford's body from the room whose door metaphorically defined musicology's boundaries not because she was a potential bearer of children, but because her ways of participating in musical culture were associated in his mind with her potential ways of participating in biological reproduction. Surely, that is, he meant exactly what he told his 1972 interviewer: gender—masculinity as defined in opposition to a culturally recognizable femininity—was central to the practice and the identity he wanted to claim for musicology.

## 'Woman's Work' and Music: What Else was Excluded from the Room?

We have already seen that the presumed marginality of gender, and of women, to musicology had implications for musicology's ability to assimilate the stories of women's musical experiences to a narrative based on men's experiences. We have seen, too, that the consequent marginalizing of women's musical experiences within musicological discussion reinforces the marginalization of women in 'real' life, by reinforcing the distinction of gender. So we may conclude that the masculinity of musicology matters to people interested in women's musical experience, and to people interested in understanding the web of metaphors by which our ideas of 'gender' are constantly reinforced.

But does the possible gendering of musicology in 1930, at the origins, matter to the ways we think about music and musicology today? That is, does it matter to people who think of themselves primarily as musicians, rather than as gendered persons?

Earlier, I wrote that a reader could not expect to learn from my story—Ruth Crawford's story—of American musicology's founding what central principles had been articulated that day to guide the disciplined study of music. While that may be strictly true, I believe one can learn a great deal about musicology's implied self-definition by considering what kinds of musical practices, understood as somehow 'woman's work', were excluded from musicology when they were, as a feminist theorist might say, 'written on Ruth Crawford's body'. For the exclusion of Ruth Crawford—a woman and an active modernist composer—could not have been a more apt metaphor for other exclusions which America's first musicologists intended to make as a way of defining the new discipline.

### 1. *The erotic power of music*

It is easy to interpret the exclusion of a music-creating woman as a response to the centuries-old trope in European thinking about music that describes music's irresistible power as akin to the erotic power that women's bodies are supposed to have over men's. From Plato to Artusi to Hanslick, anxieties about music's power have been elaborated through metaphors of gender, sexual difference, and sexual allure.[12] The result has been a long tradition of metaphorically associating the control of music with the control of women. Seldom, however, have musical power and a woman's erotic power so conveniently met in one body as they did in the body of Ruth Crawford in 1930—a woman who conceived music that Charles Seeger admired, despite his oft-expressed doubts about women's ability to compose, and a woman with whom he would soon admit he was in love. For Seeger, if not for the other men in the room, Crawford's presence would have all too vividly resurrected the cultural similitude between musical and erotic power, distracting him from the main business at hand—achieving intellectual control over music's power by the accumulation of scientific knowledge about music. To exclude her was to exclude the erotic power both of women and of sounding music at a single stroke, to close the door of musicology on music, so that musicology might be practised from a space within which an active composer's quiet but forcible 'Damn you' could go unheard. Thus the musicologist's detachment from the object of his study was ensured. Safe from the possible intrusion of pleasurable sounds that might erode his objectivity, the musicologist could achieve control over his own pleasure and over music's power to give him pleasure, while claiming the right to speak for and about an art which he had constructed to have no voice of its own.[13]

## 2. The 'art of music': creating, making, and loving music

I believe it would be a mistake to consider Seeger's simultaneous exclusion of Crawford and the musically erotic as a personal matter. For the men who fostered the development of musicology in the United States made a clear distinction between 'the art of music' and 'the science of music', and they made it equally clear who ought to have the right to speak for and about whom. A dichotomy between 'the art' and 'the science' of music constituted the means by which Waldo S. Pratt had defined the new discipline in the prophetic initial essay of *The Musical Quarterly* entitled 'On Behalf of Musicology'.

Music, Pratt argued, was an extremely complex phenomenon, combining 'subjective experiences and objective things, facts, principles' in a 'disconcerting' way that invited 'scientific scrutiny' leading to a 'comprehensive science of

---

[12] See e.g. *The Republic of Plato*, trans. with introduction and notes by Francis M. Cornford (London, 1941), 398–400; on Artusi's use of gender metaphors, see my 'Gendering Modern Music: Thoughts on the Monteverdi–Artusi Controversy', *Journal of the American Musicological Society*, 46 (1993), 1–25; on Hanslick, see Fred Everett Maus, 'Hanslick's Animism', *Journal of Musicology*, 10 (1992), 273–92.

[13] See Seeger's ventriloquistic article about Crawford's compositional work in Henry Cowell (ed.), *American Composers on American Music* (New York, 1933), 119–24. The only woman composer whose work was discussed in the book, Crawford was one of seven composers who did not speak for herself; the others were Henry Brant, Colin McPhee, Carl Ruggles, Carlos Salzedo, Roger Sessions, and Edgar Varèse. Cowell's essay on Charles Seeger makes it clear that Seeger composed occasionally, but was too self-critical to allow his work to be known publicly.

music'. This 'science of music' was to be understood as quite different from 'the art of music', even though they might deal with the same materials. 'In the field of music', he wrote:

the artistic is the side of practical action, largely controlled by intuition, feeling, imagination; while the scientific is the side of logical or rational examination, descriptive, analytic, definitive, philosophical. The goal of the former is the actual creation of music. . . . The goal of the latter is the investigation of this artistic process in all its factors.[14]

'Intuition, feeling and imagination' were the very qualities which Arthur Elson had claimed to characterize 'woman's work in music' in his 1903 book of that title.[15] With Elson's ideas as a context for Pratt's remarks, it would be perfectly reasonable to imagine that women might practise 'the art' of composition as defined by Pratt. It would be equally logical, however, to understand from Pratt's comments that 'the science of music' would not generally be practised by those engaged in the creation of music—'the art' of composition. Rather, as Pratt's essay makes clear but a few sentences later, composers needed 'the science of music' in order to do their work.

Yet we may be sure that every powerful artist works with a large amount of implicit science at his command, and that all well-reasoned science tends to supply a broader and sounder basis for scientific procedure.[16]

Indeed, it was on the basis of just this premise that the woman composer Ruth Crawford was in New York to study composition—part of the 'the art of music'—with Charles Seeger, who was not a composer but a theorist of 'the science'.

Composition was not the only part of 'the art' of music that needed 'the science' for its improvement, however. In Pratt's vision, all 'music-making' needed to be guided by a 'discipline and training . . . which must be more scientific than artistic'.[17] The aim of such training would be to create composers who were more scientific than intuitive, and performers who would learn from the study of 'the science' of music 'to think music as the composer thought it'[18] (presumably after being taught to think that way by music scientists). Ultimately, Pratt concluded, there would be professors of musicology 'whose function would be to unfold the broad outlines of the science and to demonstrate . . . its practical utility on a large scale to hosts of musicians and music-lovers'.[19] The professors would form 'scientific' listeners who would learn to shun a love of music

---

[14] Pratt, 'On Behalf of Musicology', 4.

[15] Arthur Elson, *Woman's Work in Music* (Boston, 1903). For an earlier, less sympathetic discussion of the same subject, see also George Upton, *Women in Music* (Chicago, 1886).

[16] Pratt, 'On Behalf of Musicology', 5.

[17] Ibid. 13.

[18] Ibid. 14.

[19] Ibid. 16.

*[handwritten notes:]* loss of art presages state of modern music in 50s, 60s, and classical in general even today.

*=) music - musicality = musicology*

based only on 'intuition, feeling, and imagination', or on an urge to be practical 'music-makers', in favour of a more objectively-based musicality.[20]

Musical composition, music-making, and music-loving—the constituent elements of 'the art of music'—were thus all to be rendered scientific by the new discipline of musicology. Put another way, musical composition, music-making, and music-loving were all to be disciplined into rationality, controlled by reason rather than by the culturally feminine qualities of 'intuition, feeling, and imagination'. A hierarchy of musical thought over the various musical practices would thus be established: musicology would be at its apex, controlling through an objective approach to musical knowledge the subjective experience of music as creation, physical and social practice, emotional and sensual pleasure. Musicology would be as detached from 'intuition, feeling, and imagination', as detached from musical practice, as it was from the potentially seductive power of music. Musicology—the science of music which Seeger intended to claim as a performance of masculine identity—promised to rescue all American musical culture from the realm Elson had defined as 'woman's work in music'.

## Why does the Masculinizing of Musicology and the Feminizing of Much Musical Practice Matter?

The resulting masculine identity of institutional musicology in the United States has led to the establishment of implicitly gendered hierarchies within American musical life—especially academic musical life—that systematically devalue music performance and music education. The former has never become an institutionalized academic subject, and its practitioners are seldom if ever recognized as intellectuals. The latter has been marginalized to such an extent that most academic musicians view it as a non-subject, suitable for children and for practical musicians not bright enough to think analytically about music. Both areas have, in consequence, been treated in academic and intellectual circles as though they needed others to speak for them—and the others were the same people who claimed for themselves the right to speak for the implicitly feminine 'art' of music: musicologists. Musicology (and its institutional descendants, music theory and ethnomusicology) presumes to speak for performers, educators, composers, and for 'the music itself', while remaining serenely above the sweaty work of converting notes into sound or teaching the next generation how to cut their reeds, tighten their bows, or empty their spit valves. If I may put this thought another way, musicology remains serenely detached from what its founders characterized as the 'woman's work' of reproducing musical practice. Thus musicology achieves an autonomy from the kinds of musical work that are most

[20] On the importance of science to the legitimacy of professions in the United States, see Jerold S. Auerbach, *Unequal Justice: Lawyers and Social Change in Modern America* (New York, 1976); Burton J. Bledstein, *The Culture of Professionalism: The Middle Class and the Development of Higher Education in America* (New York, 1976); and Alfred D. Chandler, Jr., *The Visible Hand: The Managerial Revolution in American Business* (Cambridge, 1977).

socially enmeshed, most obviously based in part on the performance of human relationships—an autonomy that mirrors musicology's autonomy from the quasi-erotic power of musical sound.

## Autonomy, Masculinity, and the Music Itself

In its autonomy from the physical work of musical production and reproduction, the ideal knowing subject of musicology mirrors the desired condition of a middle-class person. More to the point, in its autonomy from all the ways in which musicality might be related to physicality, social connectedness, or sensual pleasure, musicology replicates the passage to maturity modern theories of human development have considered normal for males. Familiar to most of us from the writings of Freud and his followers, these theories assert that a successful passage to maturity requires a child to 'individuate' fully from the primal source of pleasure and fulfilment—the mother. This first individuation, if successful, is the model for adult relationships with other sources of pleasure and fulfilment: one learns to control one's needs for and responses to pleasure and fulfilment, and indeed with the world in general. One learns language so as to be able to control the sources of pleasure themselves, whether they be the bodies of beloveds or the sensually powerful sounds of music. Thus, the *persona* as well as the practice of musicology might be understood to be gendered masculine.[21]

In its autonomy from social embeddedness, musicology seems, too, to occupy an objective, god-like space strikingly similar to the space allotted to what musicology typically has proclaimed as the 'highest' form of music—absolute music, the free play of pure form in which the mind takes pleasure. Thus musicology, made in the image and likeness of modern 'man', matches and reinforces constantly the supremacy of a music that resembles in its autonomy the image and likeness of modern 'man'. Musicology and absolute music—music that is, like musicology, autonomous and free—thus meet as equals, reinforcing each other's prestige as defined in opposition to the culturally feminine.

In sum, the gendering of musicology's ideal subject and object as masculine, and the New York Musicological Society's self-fashioning in the image of middle-class man, has resulted in the growth of academic disciplines with increasing prestige based almost wholly on the valuing of speech about music over either the practice of music or the (re)production of it. It has had the effect, too, of preserving the autonomy of an entity frequently called 'the music itself' that is

---

[21] For an elaborate, persuasive argument that music theory is a discourse that defends its practitioners' masculinity by establishing objective control over the sensual power of music, see Fred Everett Maus, 'Masculine Discourse and Music Theory', *Perspectives of New Music*, 31 (1993), 264–93. Marion A. Guck's 'A Woman's (Theoretical) Work', *Perspectives of New Music*, 32 (1994), 28–43, may be read as a companion piece to Maus's essay, for it describes the same phenomonen from the perspective of a woman whose culturally feminine approaches to musical analysis have largely been received as eccentric.

understood to have qualities of the oracular, to speak of mysteries in a language of mystery that requires the interpretation of specialists.

## II. Feminism and Musicology

To rescue these people from the enormous condescension of posterity.

E. P. Thompson, *The Making of the English Working Class*

Since the 1970s, sparked by the women's movement that has since come to be called the 'second wave' of feminism, feminists who were also musicians or musicologists have asked two seemingly innocent questions about music: (1) where are the women in music, in music's history? and (2) what are the representations of women in music, in the music we love and continually re-canonize in our performances, our teaching, our speaking and writing about music? In effect, both questions represented symbolic efforts to rescue Ruth Crawford (and all she had represented) from her exile outside musicology's closed door.

Efforts to answer both questions have been strangely received and strangely stymied for nearly a generation. One wants to ask why these efforts were stymied, and why they have remained so threatening to traditional musicology. Were these unanswerable questions? Or were they questions that constituted a profound threat to our high culture's ideas of what 'music' is, and what sort of work 'musicologists' do? I will consider the implications of these feminist questions in reverse order.

The question of how women have been represented in the canonic works of what is called in the United States 'Western music history' would seem to be easy to answer. It is all too clear that many canonic works that overtly represent women also represent institutionalized misogyny. It is all too clear, too, that these works could be experienced by their listeners as forms of prescriptive culture—presenting public models of how the social and power relations known as gender ought to work themselves out.[22] Thus, at a musical level, the question of how women are represented threatens our ability to hear certain works with the innocent ear required for aesthetic hearing. At a political level, the question of how women or the norms of gender are represented in the music produced and valued at a particular time and place confronts us with the historically contingent, constantly changing nature of gender itself. That is, we are forced to recognize that ideas of gender have changed over time. Thus, we must recognize that our own daily gender performances are social constructions, as unnatural

---

[22] Examples of these sorts of arguments include Ruth Solie's superb 'Whose Life? The Gendered Self in Schumann's *Frauenliebe und Leben*', in Steven Scher (ed.), *Music and Text: Critical Inquiries* (Cambridge, 1992), 219–40; Catherine Clément's *Opera, or the Undoing of Women*, trans. Betsy Wing (Minneapolis, 1988); and Susan McClary, *Georges Bizet: Carmen*, Cambridge Opera Handbooks (Cambridge, 1992).

and arbitrary as those of any other epoch. This is a recognition that may be threatening.

But the question of the representation of 'women' has led to questions about representations of the 'feminine', questions that have invaded the sacrosanct territory of textless, 'absolute' music—music that does not overtly represent anything beyond what Hanslick called 'the free play of form'.[23] Asking the question of representation of this music poses a fundamental threat to the idea that music can be 'autonomous', somehow a kind of human utterance that is above—and free of—historically contingent ideas like the role of women at a given time and place, or the value placed on qualities commonly considered feminine. To threaten the idea of music as autonomous is to threaten the central definition of 'music' that has kept both 'music' and musicologists safe from music's sensual, quasi-erotic power. It is to change subtly the object of musicological study—and perhaps, in its denial of autonomy, to change the gender of that object.

The question Where are the women? also threatens the notion that music is an autonomous art, if only because it reminds one too sharply that human beings with extremely particular, socially constructed lives have composed it. Further, once it began to be answered in the 1970s, the question threatened to restore the idea that 'music' was a practice—a thing people did, a thing people paid others to do. For that was where the women turned out to have been in music's history, among the ranks of music-makers. As Bowers and Tick pointed out in their insufficiently praised preface to *Women Making Music*, women have been making music for centuries—even if they have not always composed it, or made it in circumstances that would reinforce the ideal of 'autonomy' that so nicely matched the early modernist ideal of masculinity.[24]

Both kinds of questions, then, threaten the intertwined control of women and of music's potentially erotic power that were intrinsic to the definition of 'musicology' as not 'women's work'. Thus both threaten to open the door and let all that Ruth Crawford was—to herself as well to the musicologists who excluded her—back into the musicological room.

But 'feminist musicology' can be understood to pose an even more fundamental threat to musicology: one can argue that 'feminist musicology' constitutes a challenge to the gender of (and thus the identity and legitimacy of) traditional musicology. One might argue further that this challenge to the gender of musicology's subject (as well as its object) accounts for the near-panic that greets feminist musicologies in some quarters.

---

[23] For feminist critiques of pieces of 'absolute music', see Susan McClary, 'Sexual Politics in Classical Music', in *Feminine Endings*, 53–79; idem, 'Narrative Agendas in "Absolute Music": Identity and Difference in Brahms' Third Symphony', in Ruth A. Solie (ed.), *Musicology and Difference: Gender and Sexuality in Music Scholarship* (Berkeley, 1993), 326–44; Marcia Citron, *Gender and the Musical Canon* (Cambridge, 1993); idem, 'Feminist Approaches to Musicology', in Susan C. Cook and Judy S. Tsou (eds.), *Cecilia Reclaimed: Feminist Perspectives on Gender and Music* (Urbana, Ill. 1994), 15–34.

[24] Jane Bowers and Judith Tick (eds.), *Women Making Music: The Western Art Tradition, 1150–1950* (Urbana, Ill., 1986).

## Re-gendering Musicology

Certainly it is clear that feminist musicologies differ deliberately from the most traditional musicology by making no pretence of objectivity, detachment, or autonomy. Rather, feminist musicologies are openly and avowedly political, their enquiries about music and musical practices motivated by one of two rescue plots. The feminist musicologies that ask, Where are the women? seek to rescue from obscurity the women and the women's musical work (compositional or otherwise) that have been marginalized in musicology's narratives. This attempted rescue is avowedly performed for the sake of giving musical women in our time an empowering awareness that they are part of a tradition. More broadly, however, the rescue of women and their musical work from marginality implicitly dismantles the means by which musicology could function as one of the cultural metaphors sustaining a gender system that marginalizes women and the so-called feminine. The feminist musicologies that ask, How have women and the feminine been represented? ultimately seek to rescue music itself from the disciplinary constraints that have sought to limit and control its power. This rescue is often described as a rescue of music's expressive, sensual, and erotic power, hence of the kinds of musical power traditionally linked to women's erotic power. It is a rescue performed for the sake of music, as well as for the sake of the women and men whose relationship to music (and, by analogy, to sensual pleasure) has been equally constrained.

The slightly different rescue plots that characterize these feminist musicologies share a vision of music as practice, as potentially mirroring or even teaching erotic practices, as a means by which people are inculturated, and taught behaviours that will eventually be markers of gender, ethnicity, and class, as a means by which people act out social relationships and relationships to the sensual.

Each kind of feminist musicology seeks to understand by the term 'music' much that Pratt and Seeger sought to understand by the ultimately dismissive term 'the art of music'—music as social practice rather than music as science. Feminist musicologies seek their knowledge from an implied subject position that is immersed in the experience of music as sensually powerful, socially constructed, and socially constructing: this subject is not detached from its object, but deliberately leaves itself vulnerable to its objects' various effects. Further, feminist musicologies are motivated by concerns that traditional musicology would consider 'extra-musical'. All feminist musicologies are necessarily concerned with relationships of power within the microcosm called 'music', because those relationships may be understood to reflect or reinforce gendered relationships of power in the 'real' world. All seek to change our collective understanding of how the musical world and the 'real' one interact by changing the power relations within and between these worlds. This explicit concern with musicology as an instrument of cultural power is what makes all feminist musicologies

'political'. By remaining thus intentionally and overtly enmeshed in an experience of music as power (so as to reconstruct the relationships of power expressed
or enacted), feminist musicologies again eschew the autonomy and detachment
prized by traditional musicology—symbolized by the closed door before which
Ruth Crawford quietly cursed.

Feminist musicologies' rejection of autonomy and objectivity, both as epistemological positions and as motivations, contribute to a regendering of the
persona of musicology. The preface to a recent American anthology of feminist
musicology, *Cecilia Reclaimed*, illustrates point by point the new persona for musicology implied by feminist scholarship.[25] Jointly authored by Susan Cook and
Judy Tsou, the anthology's editors, the preface describes feminist musicology's
intention to reclaim 'some kind of female identification with musical practice'.[26]
Aligning themselves with 'the art' rather than 'the science' of music, the authors
deepen the connection by affirming feminist musicology's roots in the understanding that history and culture shape the gender ideology of the present. Thus,
they argue, understanding female identification with musical practice necessarily participates in the larger project of feminism, which is to identify and dis-
mantle the power structures of patriarchy. Woman-identified, practice-identified,
part of a larger political project, feminist musicology is also affirmed to be interdisciplinary, open to insights and methodologies borrowed freely from other disciplines; to have been, throughout its history, closely tied to women's political
movements such as suffrage and 'second-wave' feminism; to be, like both the
preface itself and the anthology it introduces, multivocal, embracing diverse
interests and points of view so as to avoid the rigidities implied by the notion of
a 'party line'; and to be determined to concern itself with the gender implications of both 'woman's work' in music and 'men's work' (traditional objects of
musicological study).

Cook's and Tsou's preface describes the persona of feminist musicology, then,
as one that has not successfully individuated. It has porous boundaries, being
open to political and multidisciplinary influences; it remains connected to both
musical and social practices. This persona closely resembles the modernist
(Freudian) notion of the path female children take to maturity. Never able to fully
individuate from their mothers, because they recognize themselves as too similar,
females are believed to replicate their failure of individuation as adult 'women'
by being more concerned than (fully individuated, fully autonomous) 'men' with
maintaining the social fabric and by having porous ego boundaries that make
them move vulnerable to the personalities and desires of others.[27] Cook's and

---

[25] Cook and Tsou, *Cecilia Reclaimed*.   [26] Ibid. 1.

[27] For an overview of these ideas of female development, see Dorothy Dinnerstein, *The Mermaid and the Minotaur:
Sexual Arrangements and Human Malaise* (New York, 1976); Nancy Chodorow, *The Reproduction of Mothering* (Berkeley, 1978). The notion that female children grow to adulthood without considering themselves as separate from the
social fabric underlies Carol Gilligan's controversial argument that women's moral development proceeds along a
different line from men's. See her *In a Different Voice* (Cambridge, 1980). A good survey of various pscyhological and

Tsou's proposed persona for feminist musicology, then, closely resembles our culture's ideas of a 'woman'.

But if the persona of feminist musicology is partly constructed as a 'woman' (as the persona of traditional musicology was constructed as a 'man'), she is not a traditional 'woman'. Constantly interested in acting to effect social change, she is the opposite of the compliant, reactive, passive personality that Freud imagined to be the necessary consequence of 'woman' 's inadequate individuation. Further, she is constantly concerned with public issues of power, issues that our culture has traditionally considered to be 'man's work'. And she deliberately claims both 'woman's work' in music and 'man's work' for her field of study. Thus rejecting the dominant culture's intentional limiting of women's roles and proper areas of interest, she refuses to recognize the boundary between 'woman' and 'man' that the web of metaphors we call gender intends to enforce. She will instead behave as though the logical consequences of her lack of boundaries include interdisciplinarity, the right to speak with many voices, and the right to ignore all culturally imposed boundaries on her questions about music. In short, the persona articulated by Cook's and Tsou's preface can be understood to match our culture's ideas of a 'woman' who is also a 'feminist'.

Thus, an important part of the strategy whereby feminist musicologies seek to bring 'Ruth Crawford' into the musicological room is to remake both the object (musical practice) and the subject of musicology in the image and likeness of a reconstructed woman. This parallel re-gendering of both music and musicology is surely part of what many traditional musicologists have found so profoundly unsettling, leading one scholar who has shown some sympathy with feminist scholarship to ask in frustration, 'What are the rules of this game?'[28] The intellectual rules of the 'game' are not actually so inscrutable. But the practical rules require implicitly that players of a 'feminist musicology' perform a disquietingly blurred version of gender, one that is multivocal, multiply positioned, and deliberately in excess of the usual dividing line between 'masculinity' and 'femininity'.

One symptom of the extremely high discomfort which traditional musicologists feel at the prospect of such a 'game' gaining prominence within the discipline has been to limit discussion of feminist musicologies almost entirely to the ideas presented in one book proclaimed by its enemies as musical feminism's 'fundamental text', Susan McClary's 1991 collection of essays entitled *Feminine Endings*.[29]

---

psychoanalytic feminisms can be found in Jane Flax, *Thinking Fragments: Psychoanalysis, Feminism, and Postmodernism in the Contemporary West* (Berkeley, 1990).

[28] Leo Treitler asked this precise question in his essay 'Gender and Other Dualities of Music History', in Solie (ed.), *Musicology and Difference*, 43.

[29] The phrase 'fundamental text' is drawn from a column by Edward Rothstein, 'Did a Man or a Woman Write That?', *New York Times*, Section 2: Arts and Leisure, 17 July 1994.

## On the Use and Misuse of *Feminine Endings*

McClary's collection was not conceived to be a single fundamental text. Rather, it was meant to exemplify some ways in which a particular political, multivocal, boundary-refusing musicology—one feminist musicology among many—might construct arguments about the relationship between musical pieces and cultural ideas of gender and sexuality. Yet it is easy to understand why McClary's work would have seemed, at first, comprehensible to traditional musicologists in a way that more explicitly woman-centred musicology had not.

McClary is among those feminists whose explicit goal is to rescue music from the disciplinary constraints that would control its expressive and sensual power, the power so often likened to the emotional and erotic power attributed to women by heterosexual men. Because such an enterprise can be immediately understood to rescue, as well, both women and men from disciplinary practices that rigidly channel our relationships to sensual and bodily pleasures, McClary's feminist scholarship promises a kind of liberation for all of us. Thus it promises a space for feminist men with a clarity that some other feminist musicologies do not have. Further, McClary made strategic choices about her work that made it seem at first to operate from within musicology's mainstream—choices which ensured that her work would not be ignored as much feminist musicology has been.

First, she represented herself as largely working alone (a claim that was literally true in the mid-1980s, when these essays were written, but no longer true by the time of its publication). Thus she can easily be misread as having made her arguments from the autonomous, detached subject position of traditional musicology. Put another way, her work could be read as a performance of masculinity, albeit by a biological woman, and thus intelligible and non-threatening to other performers of musicological masculinity. Second, she chose to publish essays that investigated the representations of gender and sexuality in canonical works by men. Thus, she can be misread as intending no challenge to the mechanisms that have ensured that *all* canonical works are works by men. As we have seen, the mechanisms that sustain the marginality of women composers to musicology's narratives also sustain the marginality of women in 'real' life. Thus, McClary's apparent refusal to challenge the canon could seem like complicity with it—and thus could seem relatively unthreatening to those whose social power and prestige (in musicology and in life) depend on maintaining masculine hegemony. Third, she introduced her essays with a brilliant preface that subtly aligned feminism with American musicology's move toward criticism, and set it in opposition to the long American tradition of so-called positivist musicology. Thus McClary shrewdly invoked a dichotomy in American musicology that was gendered, but not yet recognized as such (positivist musicology being the direct descendant of Pratt's 'science', criticism being widely considered subjective and emotional, like 'the art'). The result was to draw many metaphorically feminized critics into sympathy with feminist scholarship.

Almost single-handedly, then, McClary's book moved feminist musicology to the centre of the discipline's attention, where it seems certain to remain for at least as long as the current legitimacy of critical studies lasts. Her success in moving issues of gender from musicology's margins to its centre is offset, however, by traditional musicology's continued focus on her anthology of essays as a fundamental text. If only because this focus has made McClary bear the brunt of a ferocious musical backlash, I believe that the phenomenon of equating her work with the whole of feminist musicology bears some examination.[30] As earlier in this essay, the questions I want to pose to this phenomenon are: what is the effect of it? and whose interests are served?

First it must be said that equating McClary's work with the whole of feminist musicology directly contradicts the explicit intention of her preface. There McClary was at great pains to articulate an extremely diverse range of questions which feminist musicologies might ask, a range far broader than the questions her own essays posed. Thus, to claim Feminine Endings as a fundamental text is to misread its author's intentions by wilfully detaching the individual essays' arguments from the whole in which they participate.[31]

Some of the uses of this strategy by those who feel threatened by feminist musicologies are fairly obvious. Boundaries are redrawn around the multivocal, out-of-bounds qualities of feminist musicology's reconstructed persona, restoring the autonomy and metaphorical masculinity of musicological practice. These boundaries have real as well as metaphorical consequences. First, they serve to silence other feminist voices that might pose even more radical challenges to musicological assumptions and methods. Second, these boundaries complement the silencing of other feminist voices with an apparent exalting of McClary as a musicologically 'exceptional woman', thus encouraging subtle barriers of envy within the community of feminist music scholars. Third, these boundaries isolate McClary's arguments from the specifically feminist intellectual context in which they were intended to resonate. This isolation serves to make her work a much easier target for those most discomfited by feminist musi-

---

[30] She must surely be one of the most misquoted musicologists in history. The misquotation that appears most often is the claim that in the essay 'Getting Down off the Beanstalk: The Presence of a Woman's Voice in Janike Vandervelde's Genesis II' she described the climax of Beethoven's Ninth Symphony as a rape. She did not, although she did describe it as 'one of the most horrifyingly violent episodes in the history of music' (Feminine Endings, 128). McClary surely suggests a narrative of violent sexual release in her remarks about the symphony, but she lets Adrienne Rich's poem 'The Ninth Symphony of Beethoven Understood at Last as a Sexual Message' provide the last eloquent words of her reading. Rich's poem need not be taken as describing a rape either, but rather as the explosive frustration of 'A man in terror of impotence/or infertility, not knowing the difference/a man trying to tell something/ . . . yelling at Joy from the tunnel of the ego'. For the entire Rich poem, see her Diving into the Wreck (New York, 1973), 205–6.

[31] McClary's intention to be heard as one feminist voice among many, and her commitment to furthering a multivocal feminist study of music can be inferred from her wide-ranging, generous review essay 'Reshaping a Discipline: Musicology and Feminism in the 1990s', Feminist Studies, 19 (1992), 398–423.

cologies, because it changes the terms on which her ideas are evaluated. Thus, her work is judged from the single 'objective' point of view of a musicology that supposes gender to be marginal to musical, cultural, and social practices, rather than from the doubled perspective we have already seen to be endemic to both a feminine and a feminist experience of the gendered world. Fourth, the isolation of McClary's work from its feminist context, coupled with the seemingly flattering move of proclaiming *Feminine Endings* as a fundamental text, allows those who are most unnerved by the questions and reconstructions of various feminist musicologies to conflate McClary's particular interests with the whole. They can thus seem to have dismissed all feminisms if they can succeed in dismissing McClary's 'fundamental' version. Finally, the conflation of McClary's work with the whole of musicological feminism discourages feminist scholars who may want to challenge her ideas from engaging in public debate about them, lest we seem to participate, however unwittingly, in the bashing of a colleague and comrade-in-arms.

There are other, more subtle effects wrought by an exclusive focus on McClary's work, effects that may be equally threatening to the musical and political promise of feminist musicologies, by reinscribing some of the very boundaries that McClary's work seeks to interrogate and transgress.

McClary's essays, in *Feminine Endings* and elsewhere, mainly focus on constructions of gender and sexuality in canonical works by men and on resistances to those constructions in non-canonical works by women. Both kinds of project are critical to an understanding of two larger questions all feminist musicologies ask: how does music teach us our gender and sexuality roles? How do actual women and men manipulate the metaphors by which gender is represented in a musical style to communicate their own positions, be those positions complicit or resisting? McClary's work in these areas has been ground-breaking, and is breath-taking in its refusal of such traditional intra-disciplinary boundaries as the conventional limiting of an essay's argument to one era or one genre.

But to conflate these two possible feminist approaches to music with the larger whole that considers gender as a constantly shifting system of power risks re-inscribing an identification of gender and sexual prescription with canonical works by men and of gender and sexual resistance with non-canonical works by women. Put another way, to conflate these two possible feminist approaches to music with the whole of feminist musicology risks reinscribing the assumption that 'men' are the makers of social rules, and that 'women' break social rules; the imaginary association of 'men' with order and 'women' with chaos is one of the metaphors by which Western culture has sustained gender's differential distribution of social power between the two. Thus, it is clear whose interests would be served by a widespread representation of McClary's particular essays as constituting the entire feminist enterprise.

The representation of McClary's particular interests as constituting the whole seems to have led many scholars to suppose that 'feminist musicology' might reasonably be limited to the practice which literary critic Elaine Showalter has dubbed 'feminist critique'—an examination of the ways in which gender is inscribed in canonical works.[32] Imitators of McClary's work, apparently ignorant of its political ramifications, engage in a 'feminist' critique that, unlike McClary's, sees no reason or need to challenge the canon. In a field where all the canonic works have been composed by men, a nearly exclusive focus of feminist critique on canonical works has the effect of limiting our understanding of gender to the point of view of those most likely to gain social power from enforcing gender norms. Feminist critiques of works by men are less likely to reveal instances of resistance to gender imperatives, or to reveal how people consigned to the social role 'woman' may have sought to renegotiate their social position through their manipulation of musical practices as metaphors. Yet the feminist critique of canonical works by men is vastly easier than feminist critique of works by women.

Indeed, any kind of critical evaluation of work by women is fraught with difficulties. Both the works and their creators remain unfamiliar to the general audience for musicological writing. Thus, more background than usual is required as an exordium to one's principal argument, and there will be fewer readers than usual with sufficient background to evaluate one's arguments critically. Arguments that seem to be gender-based must be very precisely worded so as to avoid the twin bogeys of essentialism and special pleading. And arguments that claim evidence of a woman composer's resistance to gendered conventions of style must simultaneously defend her presumed stylistic eccentricities against charges of amateurishness or simple ineptitude.

If developing a feminist critique of works by women remains difficult, privileging a feminist musicology that applies a feminist critique to a canon of works by men over other possibilities seems fraught with dangers to those whose purpose is to bring Ruth Crawford, and all she represented, back into musicology's room. As we have seen, such scholarship risks reinforcing the assumptions that 'men' make social rules and compose canonical music. Further, it risks reinforcing precisely the misogynist representations of gender it reveals by eroticizing them, or by subtly discouraging women from wanting to participate in classical music culture. Thus, an emphasis on studying images or constructions of gender in work by men may function as a new way of effecting the exclusion of women from the most prestigious arena of musical life. Talented women may increasingly turn to less prestigious musics—to popular music, church music, educational or functional music—or to no music at all.[33] Such scholarship may risk reinscribing an unnecessarily narrow view of gender as well. For in most

---

[32] Elaine Showalter, 'Feminist Criticism in the Wilderness', *Critical Inquiry*, 8 (1981), 179–205.

[33] Here one might remember the career path taken by Ruth Crawford shortly after her marriage to Charles Seeger: she gave up composing for nearly twenty years, expressing her musicality instead through the transcription and arrangement of American folk-music and the teaching of folk-music to America's children.

musicological writing on gender to date, 'gender' has been conflated with institutional heterosexuality.[34] This conflation risks reinscribing the assumption that the pleasurable or the erotic are normatively found in relationships between women and men. While this assumption is clearly not shared by some percentage of the musical population, including some percentage of the population of people who have composed music, its constant reassertion in culture has the effect of making heterosexuality all but compulsory—an effect that reinforces patriarchal social structures.[35] Finally, because it invites men into 'feminism', a feminist critique can quickly lead to musicologists simply being more open about their intention to tell stories only about other men and about masculinity, to the continued exclusion of stories about women and the experiences of culturally enforced femininity. That is, in our discipline more than in most, feminist critique of canonic works can serve to reinstate heterosexual men's control of the discourse, and to push aside the political goals of musicological feminism—understanding and improving the position of 'real' women and of 'the feminine' in the microcosm of texts, social practices, and relationships one might call 'music'.

## III. Gender, Musicology, and Feminism

### 'The Music Itself' as the Ultimate Feminist Issue

We have seen that the exclusive focus on one kind of feminist criticism as if it subsumed all possible feminist musicologies serves ends that contradict the political goals of feminism. It also serves to defend several of the most entrenched assumptions of musicology—particularly the central assumption that the principal object of musicological study is a vague entity called 'the music itself'.

What is 'the music itself', to which McClary herself, many of her imitators, and all her traditionalist detractors consistently refer as if to an unchallengeable authority? How has musicology been inextricably intertwined with the task of upholding the existence and authority of such an entity? What on earth might gender have to do with it?

The concept of 'the music itself' is a difficult one to trace. In conversational usage, the phrase seems to refer to an idea of music as aestheticized sound, for the most powerful rhetorical recourse to the authority of 'the music itself' is to musical sounds, as heard by a particular listener. Often enough, however, the actual reference is not to a direct, sensory experience of musical sound, but to

---

[34] Most of the exceptions—many of them essays showing a deep, subtle understanding of the relationships between gender and sexuality—can be found collected together in Philip Brett, Gary Thomas, and Elizabeth Woods (eds.), *Queering the Pitch: The New Gay and Lesbian Musicology* (New York, 1994).

[35] For an elaboration of this point, see Adrienne Rich's classic essay 'Compulsory Heterosexuality and Lesbian Existence', *Signs*, 5 (1980), 631–60.

the representation of that sound in a notated score. Thus, 'the music itself' is spoken of as if it were an entity that is always present for us to consult, that is independent of any particular performance or social setting, and that (ideally) communicates its meanings directly to listeners who are properly prepared to interpret them. No 'extra-musical' concern—such as a focus on the bodily acts that cause music to sound, or on bodily responses to sound other than those of the ear and mind, or on the interplay of aestheticized sound-patterns with the social, physical, and linguistic practices that surround and accompany performance and reception—is included in the definition. 'Musical' meaning is understood to be encoded in the patterns of sound that a well-prepared listener might interpret. Because the meanings are encoded in patterns that are independent of any performance, they are understood to be fixed: thus interpretation is confined to quite narrow limits. Those who call upon 'the music itself' as the ultimate arbiter of critical interpretations, then, confirm and reinscribe a definition of 'music' that limits 'music' to the communication in sound between an entity ('the music itself') with a fixed identity that has been detached from its socially grounded creator and that music's ideal listener. In practice, although not in conversational usage, the ideal listeners to 'the music itself' are the descendants of Pratt's 'professors of musicology', musicologists and music theorists—people with the special training required to interpret meanings that are encoded in patterns of sound.

Why should this view of music be challenged by feminist musicologies? In its ubiquity, independence, and power of direct communication, this is a 'music' that is godlike. Its definition by opposition to bodily performances, bodily responses, and the social and linguistic constructs that surround performance and reception imply that it is a music that transcends the always unpredictable, always subjective vagaries of the body. In this, too, it is a music that is free, and perhaps freeing for us to hear; it is a music that can bring us close to perceptions that are godlike. Is this not just what we would want 'music' to be?

Three reasons why we might not want to define 'music' so narrowly may occur to readers. First, the definition of music implied by the ideas adhering to 'the music itself' omits practical music-making. Part of what Pratt identified as 'the art', practical music-making, has also been shown by feminist music historians to have been a far more common expression of women's musicality, historically, than the composition of 'pieces' of 'music' has been. Thus, a cult of 'the music itself' would seem to risk perpetuating the omission of much of women's experience. Second, this is a definition of music that exalts one kind of relationship—that between 'the music itself' and its ideal listener—above all other musical relationships. The power relationship between these entities bears an uncomfortable resemblance to the characteristic power relationship of patriarchy, which exalts a male-dominated heterosexuality above all other human relationships. Third, the image of 'music' circumscribed by the phrase 'the music itself'—godlike, disembodied, and autonomous—bears a striking resemblance to cultural norms of masculinity.

   This last idea might best be explored by considering the close relation of the idea of 'the music itself' to the larger ideology that enshrines 'absolute music'—that is, music free of any verbal or dramatic association or explicit social function—as the most profoundly 'musical'. In current debates about music, women, and gender, absolute music is often claimed to be free from representations of gender, and thus invulnerable to feminist critique. Yet Marcia Citron has shown in several extremely perceptive, logical, and carefully historicized arguments that the very idea of absolute music is gendered.[36] God-like, proposed as the object of aesthetic worship, absolute music as Citron discerns it to have been described in nineteenth- and early twentieth-century aesthetic writings 'inscribes a male psychological profile of growth that stresses quest and transcendence . . . separateness, exploration, and adventure'.[37] If we take Citron's perception of the cultural masculinity of absolute music to be correct, two conclusions follow. First, we could conclude that the cult of such music, which is sustained by much musicology and music theory, is a cult inviting all of us to worship sonic images of the (god-like) masculine.[38] Second, we could conclude that absolute music's supposed transcendence of such narrow social concerns as gender (which renders it invulnerable to feminist critique) reflects precisely the conflation of the masculine with the universal that we considered earlier in this essay.[39] Either way, absolute music can be understood to be the music of patriarchy.

   The implication of Citron's scholarship, then, is to demolish our belief that an experience of 'the music itself' can be innocent, free of gender and free of politics. Instead, her critique ruthlessly (or joyously) reveals that 'the music itself'— the object of musicological study, principal substance of classical music culture, the music with which we as listeners have aesthetic experiences—has always been both a gendered and a political entity.

## The Ultimate Threat of Feminist Musicology

If 'the music itself' is understood to be a construct that results in our worshipping as 'absolute' an image of cultural masculinity, it would seem necessary that feminist musicologies refuse its authority, transgress and erase the boundaries that it draws in defining 'music', and legitimize all that was once excised as outside the boundaries of musicology, to be known only in so far as it could be dominated by 'scientific' knowledge. But before concluding this chapter with a rallying cry for such an enterprise, we would do well to consider the wider

---

[36] See esp. Marcia Citron, 'Gender, Professionalism and the Musical Canon', *Journal of Musicology*, 8 (1991), 533–43; *idem, Gender and the Musical Canon*; and *idem*, 'Feminist Approaches to Musicology'.

[37] Citron, 'Feminist Approaches to Musicology', 23.

[38] Indeed, this is the conclusion Fred Everett Maus infers from his reading of Hanslick's *On the Beautiful in Music*. See his 'Hanslick's Animism'.

[39] We might further infer a historical hypothesis about absolute music: that women have not typically been important or prolific composers of absolute music, but have instead focused mainly on vocal, dramatic, and functional genres. As we all know, this is no hypothesis, but a truism about women's compositional activity in the Western tradition.

political implications of dethroning 'the music itself'. For I believe that the prospect of such a dethroning constitutes a threat to one of the deepest, most cherished beliefs of Western capitalist democracies, the idea of the liberal individual.

How could that possibly be? To answer, I would like to consider power relations within the aesthetic experience of 'the music itself' as they have been reified in countless musicological and aesthetic writings since Hanslick. Briefly, I will describe these relations from the point of view of a middle-class listener, one with some awareness that musicological authority encourages aesthetic listening and promises to provide guidance to the meanings encountered in the aesthetic experience.

As the cult of absolute music encourages us to have it, the aesthetic experience is one in which we leave behind our concerns and anxieties in the real world and escape into the arcane one described by Hanslick as 'the free play of pure form'. There we can imagine ourselves to be angels, even gods; for 'the music itself' is a kind of ether in which we lose our selves. As we do so, we imaginatively lose our genders, our sexualities, our very bodies.

This loss of the listening self in the aesthetic experience of music is closely linked to the power claimed by those who would interpret 'the music itself' in language—musicologists and their institutional kin. For *they* do not lose themselves; they interpret for us the nature of the thing in which *we* lose *ourselves*—a thing the experience of which might be held to approximate that elusive desideratum denoted in French psychoanalytic and feminist theory by the word *jouissance*. There is tremendous pleasure—sensual, emotional, and intellectual—to be had from this kind of listening experience.

But what interest is served by a musicology that encourages us to lose ourselves in a substance and an experience called 'the music itself', so that the experience can be explained to us by experts who are beyond the loss of self? If, as Fred Maus has argued in 'Masculine Discourse in Music Theory', the loss of the self to an overwhelming music is an experience of being feminized,[40] or at least of being a 'bottom', then the experience of having it all explained to us by an authority who does not participate reinforces our sense of being 'bottoms'.[41] The authority who explains it all, however, re-enacts his ability to be a 'top'. Thus we who are 'bottoms' learn to experience both pleasure and knowledge as originating elsewhere. We learn to love a subordinated position, and we learn to confuse our subordination with an imaginary participation in godliness (through our identification with the entity called 'the music itself'). We who

---

[40]  Maus, 'Masculine Discourse and Music Theory', treats the issue of listening as gendered on pp. 272–3.

[41]  The concept of 'tops' and 'bottoms' has long been a commonplace in gay male culture in the United States, and is one of obvious importance to distinguishing power roles in sexual relations between people who seem to share gender and reproductive capabilities. For another application of 'tops' and 'bottoms' to musical experiences, see my 'On a Lesbian Relationship with Music: A Serious Effort Not to Think Straight', in Brett, Thomas, and Woods (eds.), *Queering the Pitch*, 67–83.

might, through our mastery of the 'science' of music, retain an identification with being a 'top' are encouraged to imagine ourselves as powerful, equal to the godlike 'music itself' in our ability to remain free of its power while understanding its messages; whatever our social position in 'real' life, that is, in the microcosm of music we can imagine ourselves to have godlike power. If either 'bottoms' or 'tops' were to remember their particular class, gender, or sexual roles in 'real' life during this experience, their imaginary participations in godliness would be disrupted.

Thus the feminist assertion that neither gender nor sexuality are absent from the experience of aesthetic listening is extremely threatening—to our ability to take pleasure in its illusions, and to the function of aesthetic listening for the achievement of social harmony. For the real threat of supposing that gender and sexuality may still be functioning in the aesthetic experience is the threat to the fantasy of a free-floating imagination. In a musical aesthetic experience we fantasize that by imaginative acts of identification with 'the music itself' we can shed the particularities of our gender, class, sexuality, and ethnicity and engage with the roles and identities of others—or with parts of them recombined. This fantasy is compelling, because it serves the same social and political ends as the fantasy of multiple identifications promised by the private reading of a novel. The real fantasy in both the musical aesthetic experience and the novelistic one is a fantasy of social mobility and social control: we experience the subject positions of others vicariously, but by retaining control over our vicarious experiences, we can imagine we control others' experiences as well. In the case of the musical fantasy, the combination of social mobility and social control is all the more salient for being acted out in paradoxical counterpoint with the fact of enforced physical immobility in the concert-hall. In a way, we are bottoms and tops at once, and this symbolic liberation from the rigidities of sexual and political roles can be exhilarating. Partly because this fantasy contradicts the physical reality of the audience, the ideology of listening that surrounds the repertoire usually called 'the music itself' strongly discourages physical engagement during listening. Even more, it discourages identification with the bodily work of performers. As each discouragement draws the listener's identification away from the physical, it directs it toward the imaginative mastery of all possible combinations embodied by 'the music itself'. Socially mobile, freed from physical work, seeming to encompass all possibilities in a unified whole, our imaginations' immersion in and identification with 'the music itself' provide us with a sonic experience of the middle-class self. It provides us, as well, with a sonic model of the middle-class's image of god—the liberal individual of classical political theory.

As Carol Pateman, among others, has shown, capitalist democracy is based on the theoretical existence of autonomous individuals free of social construction and social restrictions. These individuals control their own destinies by freely entering into social contracts with others like themselves, others whose circumstances and interests they can readily imagine because of their mental and imaginative freedom. The common belief that the 'liberal individual' is a universal category habitable by any human being underlies the political systems of Britain and the United States, as well as those of most other modern capitalist democracies. Cultural forms like novels and aesthetic listening to 'the music itself' reinforce that belief by encouraging fantasies of social and imaginative freedom in all people. Yet, as Pateman has demonstrated in *The Sexual Contract*, the category of 'liberal individual' is not legally or politically a universal one habitable by any human being. It is, rather, one more case of the masculine having been claimed as the universal—for the primary social contract defining the world of liberal individuals is quite clearly understood in classical political theory to be a man, a man whose first social contract is an agreement with other men about the exchange of women.[42] In practice, some would argue, he is a European man: he occupies a category not logically available to people who seem not to behave according to European ideas of rationality. In any case, social harmony requires that people who are implicitly not permitted to enter the category 'liberal individual' retain the illusion that they can. And anyone who can experience the 'free play of form' through an experience of aesthetic listening can imagine participating in European ideas of rationality, and so can imagine being eligible for inclusion in the category of individuals who can wield political and social power.

Thus, to the extent that aesthetic listening to 'the music itself' teaches us the mental and imaginative patterns of a liberal individual's life—social mobility, social control, freedom from both physical labour and social constraint—such listening helps to sustain our complicity with the illusion on which social harmony rests. Feminist challenges to the authority of 'the music itself' may be understood to complement feminist challenges to the social and political theory that conflates the masculine with the liberal individual, who is the ideal citizen. Feminist musicologies, therefore, may be as dangerous as feminist political theory. What is at stake in the debates about feminist musicologies, then, would be analogous to what is at stake in the most radical of feminist debates about the nature of the state: who will have power in a reconstructed world, how that power will flow, and how cultural forms may be used to create and sustain more equitable experiences of power and powerlessness. We are right to find feminist musicologies threatening.

## The Many Promises of Feminist Musicologies: Opening All the Doors

Do feminist musicologies promise only a critique of the past, one that challenges the traditional persona and practice of musicology, proposes that musicology be

---

[42]   Carol Pateman, *The Sexual Contract* (Stanford, Calif., 1988), 2.

performed as a cross-gendered practice, and threatens the very definitions of 'music' and musicality that help to uphold social order? What might be gained from opening musicology's metaphorical door to feminist musicologies, and thus to all that Ruth Crawford's exclusion shut safely away from our attention?

This is a question that can be answered from at least two points of view—just as the story with which I opened this chapter could be told from at least two points of view. From the point of view of women musicians, composers, students, musicologists, music theorists, ethnomusicologists, music educators, performers, music journalists, music editors, music-lovers, music listeners, music critics, music 'heads'—from the point of view of people who share with Ruth Crawford occupancy of the gender role designated in common speech by the word 'woman'—there is much to be gained. We gain a sense of who our ancestors have been, and thus a sense that the expression of our musicalities, too, can be legitimate. If Hildegard of Bingen or Sophie Drinker could find the social space in which to have a musical voice, then so can we. To the extent that 'woman's work' and the culturally 'feminine' might cease to be marginalized and devalued, but might be reinterpreted as important elements of a musical culture, we will be less inclined than previous generations to feel our choices of such work to constitute failures of musical achievement. If Ruth Crawford's choice to edit and arrange for educational use American folk-songs can be understood as something other than her failure to compose, then our choices to teach small children need not mean that we have chosen trivial work. Perhaps more importantly, to the extent that 'woman's work' and the culturally 'feminine' are revalued in the microcosm that is music, our status as 'women' in real life is likely to be subtly improved.

But what does 'musicology' stand to gain from opening the door to feminist musicologies? First, 'musicology' can only benefit from the new vision of that complex phenomenon 'music' that can be revealed by the simple act of changing point of view. By adopting the double, triple, or multiple vision that is endemic to a feminine, a feminist, or a gender-conscious experience of the world, we can see things about 'Western' musical culture heretofore invisible: the importance of convents and the social networks of religious women in the diffusion of repertoire in the sixteenth and seventeenth centuries, for instance; the relationship of the American 'opera queen' subculture to the careers of particular divas, to the programming choices of artistic directors, and to the general status of opera in American culture. Feminist musicologies lead us to new ways of thinking about the relationship of the canonic tradition to heretofore obscure musical practices, and to new ways of thinking about the ways in which ideas of social power and cultural prestige have been incorporated into that tradition through metaphors of gender. Further, feminist musicologies propose new and exciting questions about the gender implications of pedagogical and performance practices—suggesting in their questions that the rituals and bodily disciplines associated with music-making may be among the ways a culture teaches its participants gender and sexual roles. By legitimizing multiple perspectives on, and experiences of, music, feminist musicologies promise to provide us with ways to rejoice in the wide variety of phenomena that might be called 'music', the variety that Pratt found so 'disconcerting' that he sought to control it with 'science'. By seeking to reopen the door to all that Ruth Crawford represented, to herself and to the men who founded musicology, feminist musicologies promise to reopen our minds to alternative ways of thinking about 'music'. Further, they promise to liberate us from the intellectual restrictions imposed by an anachronistic, early modernist view of 'science', allowing us stunning new liberties in our interpretations of music and musical experiences. Among those liberties is the possibility that a subject may think deeply and profitably about music as an object without defining (or even redefining) the subject–object boundary. Feminist musicologies also promise to liberate us from participation in anachronistic power regimes that no longer suit our taste, our politics, or our emotional and aesthetic needs.

Finally, there are at least two ways in which opening the door to feminist musicologies can be understood to be in the interest of everyone who might read this chapter. First, feminist musicologies' liberation of the idea of musical pleasure—even when it veers over the boundary between the musical and the erotic—is in everyone's interest. Second, feminist musicologies' reconstruction of both the subject and the object of musicology promises a better resolution to the gender problem that Charles Seeger sought to solve by closing the door on Ruth Crawford.

Feminist musicologies provide a theoretical legitimacy for multivocal, interdisciplinary thinking. Further, they provide a theoretical legitimacy for reconnecting 'the music itself' with the fabric of human life. Thus, feminist musicologies provide an opening for us to rethink music as something that matters—and matters very much—to 'real' life. I believe that assuming music matters to 'real' life is preferable to exalting music as an escape from that life, because a music that is understood to have consequences in 'real' life is likely to gain status and prestige. Ironically, then, the feminist reconstruction of what we mean by 'music' promises to rescue music (and systematic thought about it) from the low status Charles Seeger feared. By raising the cultural status of the 'feminine', by showing that the 'feminine' matters to the rest of life, and that 'music' matters to the rest of life, feminist musicologies promise more fully to rescue 'music' from the low prestige it had at the beginning of our discipline and our century as the result of being considered 'woman's work'.[43]

---

[43] I acknowledge gratefully the contributions to this chapter's qustions and answers about feminist musicology of conversations with Marcia Citron, Susan Cook, Ellie Hisama, Susan McClary, Fred Everett Maus, and Elizabeth Wood. Some ideas were developed in discussion with the members of a graduate seminar entitled 'Feminist Criticism and Music' at the University of Virginia in the spring of 1994; I should like to thank Lisa Burrell, Leslie Hiers, Jennifer Hughes, Elizabeth King, and Sean D. Mays for their rigorous questioning of my premisses and politics, and Bridget Kelly Black, Francesca Katchini, Margaret McFadden, and Megan Emily Wadin for comments on the final draft.

# 22

# Musicology and/as Social Concern: Imagining the Relevant Musicologist

### Ralph P. Locke

## I. 'Social Concern' and 'Relevance'

How can a musicologist express her/his social concern? In what ways is her/his work socially relevant? And how might it become more so? Questions of this sort, often phrased in more or less these terms, have recently been raised by a variety of people in our field, as in the following two instances.

- A panel discussion at a California musicological meeting dealt with a practical problem of broad import: should the performer, scholar, or teacher who is 'socially concerned' (the organizers' own wording) alter or otherwise suppress the arguably anti-Semitic language found in certain medieval and Renaissance works?
- The electronic discussion list of the American Musicological Society has been carrying frequent messages from graduate students seeking some reassurance about the 'relevance' (the writers' usual term) of musical scholarship today. The students often wonder whether research, and sometimes even the teaching of music history, is becoming a pointless self-indulgence (and/or a profession with shrinking economic viability); after all, some of the very streams of music-making that these prospective scholars most prize and wish to elucidate—such as chamber music or the art song—hold an increasingly marginal place in post-industrial society. Some also wonder what music and musicology might do to help draw attention to, or even in some way alleviate, one or another of the many seemingly intractable national and world problems (e.g. social injustice in one's own country, 'ethnic cleansing' in Bosnia, war and famine in Eastern Africa, viral and parasitic diseases in South Asia).[1]

---

[1] The round table, 'Musical Bigotry from Busnois to Borodin: Offensive Texts and the Socially Concerned Performer/Listener', took place at the Northern California Chapter of the American Musicological Society (summary reported in Leta Miller, 'Subject: Musical Bigotry [da capo]', electronic posting on AMSLIST, the unofficial discussion list of the American Musicological Society [amslist@ucdavis.edu], 18 Oct. 1994). See also Lawrence Rosenwald, 'On Prejudice in Early Music', *Historical Performance: The Journal of Early Music America*, 5/2 (Fall 1992),

Musicology and a concern for social relevance and efficacy might at first seem an odd pairing, but only if one works on the operating assumption that musicology and music are more or less *irrelevant* to society, are indeed not *themselves* social phenomena. But, of course, many people do share this assumption to some degree; after all, it is one of the corner-stones of the idealist ideology that has long dominated aesthetic reflection in the West, especially among proponents and scholars of what sociologists call 'high culture'.[2] True, the doctrine of great ('high') art's autonomy from social currents has been repeatedly and insightfully dissected and challenged, with specific regard to music, by such critics (within and outside musicology) as Theodor W. Adorno, Carl Dahlhaus, Rose Rosengard Subotnik, John Shepherd, Janet Wolff, Edward Said, Susan McClary, and Philip Bohlman.[3] Much of this critique, argues Said, has gone unheeded; to a large extent, musicological and music-critical writing remain hobbled by an exaggerated attachment to 'reverence, scholarship, and the like'.[4]

Some have objected to Said's rather dismissive coupling of 'scholarship' and unthinking 'reverence', noting fairly that Said (who is by profession a literary and cultural critic) might profitably have informed himself about this or that musicological work rich in critical awareness and insight.[5] (Further examples will be noted at various points in the present chapter.) But most of us will instantly recognize, if with some discomfort, the warts-and-all truth in the portrait that Said draws of mainstream music scholarship. A good deal of our writing (most obviously in music theory and analysis, but also in historical musicology) continues to be nourished by—and to reinforce in turn—the belief that music, or at least Western art-music, is autonomous in significant ways (or, some would say, in nearly every way that matters) from the social milieu in which it is produced and consumed.[6]

69–71; the responses of four scholars and performers, published in the same issue of *Historical Performance* (73–83), and a heated retort from Clifford Bartlett: 'Censorship', *Leading Notes: Journal of the [British] National Early Music Association*, 6 (Autumn 1993), 13–15.

[2] Further on idealist (versus society-based) conceptions of music, see introduction (by Locke and Barr) to Ralph P. Locke and Cyrilla Barr (eds.), *Cultivating Music in America: Women Patrons and Activists since 1860* (Berkeley, forthcoming).

[3] Theodor W. Adorno, *Introduction to the Sociology of Music*, trans. E. B. Ashton (New York, 1976); Carl Dahlhaus, *Foundations of Music History*, trans. J. B. Robinson (Cambridge, 1983); Rose Rosengard Subotnik, *Developing Variations: Style and Ideology in Western Music* (Minneapolis, 1994); John Shepherd, *Music as Social Text* (Cambridge, 1991); Janet Wolff, 'Foreword: The Ideology of Autonomous Art', to Susan McClary and Richard Leppert (eds.), *Music and Society: The Politics of Composition, Performance and Reception* (Cambridge, 1987), 1–12; Edward Said, *Musical Elaborations* (New York, 1991); Susan McClary, 'Terminal Prestige: The Case of Avant-Garde Music Composition', *Cultural Critique*, 12 (1989), 57–81; idem, 'Narrative Agendas in "Absolute Music": Identity and Difference in Brahms's Third Symphony', in Ruth A. Solie (ed.), *Musicology and Difference: Gender and Sexuality in Music Scholarship* (Berkeley, 1993), 326–44; Philip Bohlman, 'Musicology as a Political Act', *Journal of Musicology*, 11 (1993), 411–36.

[4] Said, *Musical Elaborations*, 55 (amplified in pp. xiv–xvii).

[5] Reviews of Said, *Musical Elaborations*, by Nicholas Cook, *Music & Letters*, 73 (1992), 617–19, and Kofi Agawu, 'Wrong Notes', *Transition*, 55 (1992), 162–6. William Weber draws attention to other titles that (I suspect) Said would find intriguing, in 'Beyond Zeitgeist: Recent Work in Music History', *Journal of Modern History*, 66 (1994), 321–45.

[6] I do not wish to deny that there are aspects of music that can be profitably viewed as 'relatively' or 'provisionally' autonomous. (See Ch. 16 above.) It is indeed crucial to our larger task that we make space for more purely aesthetic

In these opening paragraphs, I have swiftly and intentionally narrowed the focus from music in general, as suggested in the chapter's title, to Western art-music in particular.[7] Such a focus helps by setting some limits to a dauntingly broad topic. In addition, the question of social concern or relevance has been explored less in Western art-music than in other types. For example, folk-music and non-Western art-music have long been subject to more systematic explorations of social context, and scholars in those fields are particularly eager to probe (rather than accept as innocent, uniformly beneficent, and unproblematic) the relationship between the scholar and the music, its makers, and its institutions, which he or she studies and then (re)presents to the public.[8] Much the same is true in regard to popular music; indeed, many popular-music scholars (especially those who come to the subject from sociology or American studies) treat *only* the social aspects of their material, eschewing more formal modes of musical analysis or even simple style description. Thus popular-music scholarship may well be in need of a very different sort of reminder (see John Covach's Chapter 20 above) than the one embodied here.

So, in the three central parts of this essay (sections II–IV), I not only focus primarily on Western art-music, but also further narrow the many-faceted question of the musicologist's 'social concern' to the following: How does our scholarly work carry out one or another social agenda, and how can we become more aware of our own agendas, and thereby sharpen the messages that we are (inevitably) doing our part to transmit and elaborate? I treat this question (or question-complex) in two different ways, focusing first (in section II) on various scholars' attempts to reveal the social messages that art-music has conveyed in Western societies in past centuries and conveys today.[9] Then I move (in sections III and IV) to the trickier issue of how music scholars themselves—ourselves— tend to express social values, including aesthetic ideologies, in published work and teaching, whether consciously or not. I might add here my belief that an increased willingness to make our assumptions explicit can strengthen musicological discourse in several ways: by making clear the underlying basis of certain differences of opinion that may currently seem inexplicable or confusing, by allowing individual scholars to make more nuanced or wider-ranging points, and, perhaps most importantly, by making our findings more easily

---

considerations in any discussions of the social meanings of music; I develop this argument myself in two writings: an article, 'Music Lovers, Patrons, and the "Sacralization" of Culture in America', *19th-Century Music*, 17 (1993–4), 149–73, and 18 (1994–5), 83–4; and a review of Joël-Marie Fauquet's book on French chamber-music concerts, in *Journal of the American Musicological Society*, 43 (1990), 505–13, and 45 (1992), 546.

[7] Also known as 'classical music', 'concert music', etc. All the available terms are in some way noxious or misleading.

[8] Timothy J. Cooley and Gregory F. Barz (eds.), *Shadows in the Field: New Perspectives for Fieldwork in Ethnomusicology* (New York, 1997). This book encourages new modalities of scholarly reflection, but also includes several warnings about how non-authoritarian scholarly writing—one current trend—can become self-indulgently confessional and no longer 'ethnographically relevant' (quotation from Cooley's introductory chapter, p. 17).

[9] Or, to some extent, still conveys: some of the original message gets lost or replaced, but some remains indelibly inscribed, at least for listeners familiar with the stylistic conventions of the music.

contestable, more obviously contingent. Clearly such considerations already begin to widen the focus, and, in the concluding discussion (section V), I widen it still further, by asking: What does a music scholar of whatever stripe (historical musicologist, theorist, ethnomusicologist, etc.)—and, more generally, a musician, a music-lover, a scholar, a teacher, a writer, a citizen, a resident on this planet—owe her or his fellow creatures?

I should add that, throughout, I take the term 'musicologist' to include not just the published scholar but also the journalist, the writer of programme notes, the classroom teacher, the radio broadcaster, and any others in a position to affect the wider discourse on music.

## II. Exploring the Social Work that Music Does

Musicology, it seems to me, might do well to reassert (or, in many cases, simply recognize and make explicit) its active social character. A first step in this process for many of us might be to resist consciously the blandishments of the autonomy doctrine. I say 'blandishments', because the doctrine flatters the practitioners of music: primarily composers and performers, but also, if to a lesser extent, musicologists. We bask in the reflected glory of the venerated master-work that we—in journal articles or concert reviews—examine, explain, or evaluate.

Some say that the problem is the near-exclusive emphasis, in much scholarship and certainly in many college and graduate school curricula, on Western art-music. There is truth to this: any teacher who wishes to render his or her teaching more overtly relevant to modern life must surely have wondered how to do so when teaching the Monteverdi Vespers of 1610, Haydn's Op. 33 string quartets, Mendelssohn's Piano Concerto in G minor, or Stravinsky's *Symphonies of Winds*. By contrast, a course on world music or the history of jazz or rock offers far more obvious opportunities for exposing students to questions currently recognized as being of wide cultural relevance. When Philip Bohlman wants to argue the possibility of musicology's becoming a progressive force in our society, he quite reasonably asks why musicologists don't devote more time to studying rap.[10] Indeed, it is precisely because such topics are so patently 'relevant'—because exploring them seems so natural a way for us to insert ourselves in today's cultural debate—that I will continue to leap-frog over them and deal with the more problematic case of those of us who persist in teaching and writing about Western art-music. (I will, though, return at a few spots to how folk- and popular music *impinge* on Western art-music.[11])

It has recently been argued that the problem is, if not Western art-music gen-

---

[10] Bohlman, 'Musicology as a Political Act', 411–14, 434–6.
[11] See passages at and in nn. 24, 47, 87, 96.

erally, then without doubt the 'canon': numerous writers have stressed that a scholarly focus on individual much-admired works and, more generally, on certain highly sophisticated (or, more to the point, highly prestigious) repertoires tends to serve as a barrier to social awareness, particularly as the works in question have been subjected primarily to certain canonical methodologies (e.g. style authentication) that tend to reify the musical object as 'the score', and thereby isolate it from its functional and performing contexts.[12] There is much truth in this, but for present purposes (and with Said's jibes in mind) I would prefer to argue the contrary. A focus on the masterpieces, the Western art-music repertoires most admired by critics and scholars over the past several centuries, is not inherently an impediment to social analysis. Quite the contrary: some of the clearest examples of social concern in musicological writings of the past several decades have consisted of attempts (such as even Said might applaud) to reveal the ways in which various elaborate, 'high-status' musical repertoires (e.g. concertos and polyphonic masses) were shaped by their contexts and functions.

Scholars of religious music, in particular, have often led the way: examples include Albert Dunning's study of the 'state motets' of Lassus and others (which also led to a stirring recorded anthology, conducted by Konrad Ruhland);[13] Patrick Macey's demonstration that certain works by Josquin and others echo Savonarola's millenarian challenges to ecclesiastical and secular authority;[14] the ongoing explorations of the role of music in the early Lutheran Church and the Counter-Reformation;[15] and the revelations by Alfred Dürr and others of J. S. Bach's attempt to create what to his mind was a worthy church music.[16]

Theatre music, too, has provided a profitable field for scholars interested in social context, from Claude Palisca on humanist thought in the earliest operas, to Ellen Rosand on seventeenth-century Venetian opera as glorification of the city-state, to Andrew Steptoe on the Mozart–da Ponte trilogy, to Julian Budden on Verdi's changing portrayal of the impact of the public sphere on the private, to Kim Kowalke and others on Kurt Weill, a composer whose richly resonant theatre work is gaining much attention in performance and criticism these

[12] Katherine Bergeron and Philip V. Bohlman (eds.), *Disciplining Music: Musicology and its Canons* (Chicago, 1992); Marcia J. Citron, *Gender and the Musical Canon* (Cambridge, 1993); see also Ch. 17 above.

[13] Albert Dunning, *Die Staatsmotette, 1480–1555* (Utrecht, 1970). *Staatsmotette der Renaissance*, Telefunken SAWT 9561–2, released 1971.

[14] Patrick Macey, 'Savonarola and the Sixteenth-Century Motet', *Journal of the American Musicological Society*, 36 (1983), 422–52; idem, 'The Lauda and the Cult of Savonarola', *Renaissance Quarterly*, 45 (1992), 439–83; idem, '*Infiamma il mio cor*: Savonarolan *Laude* by and for Dominican Nuns in Tuscany', in Craig A. Monson (ed.), *The Crannied Wall: Women, Religion and the Arts in Early Modern Europe* (Ann Arbor, 1992), 161–89.

[15] For a recent summary, see Iain Fenlon (ed.), *Music and Society: The Renaissance, from the 1470s to the End of the 16th Century* (Englewood Cliffs, NJ, 1989), 1–101, 263–85; and Curtis Price (ed.), *Music and Society: The Early Baroque Era, from the Late 16th Century to the 1660s* (Englewood Cliffs, NJ, 1993), 164–217.

[16] The findings of Dürr and others, especially as regards Bach's production of cantatas, are summarized by Gerhard Herz in his Norton Critical Score of J. S. Bach, Cantata no. 140, 'Wachet auf, ruft uns die Stimme' (New York, 1972).

days.[17] The art song and the solo piano piece, similarly, have proved to be rich in possibilities for social analysis.[18]

Many of the studies just mentioned engage methodologies that are analogous to, or even directly modelled upon, those in use in ethnomusicology and popular-music scholarship. Another similar trend within historical musicology is 'reception history', an umbrella term that can be taken to include issues of dissemination (including the history of music publishing) and performance and criticism as well: how works were (in various senses) 'interpreted' or 'made known' in their own day and in more recent times.[19] Particularly fascinating are studies of the functions of music at a particular time and place. William Weber, for example, reveals the process by which the canonical repertoires of church and concert music that we to some extent have inherited today were first formed in England in the eighteenth century, in part as a way of buttressing the political legitimacy of the monarchy and the Church of England, as well as of the growing merchant class.[20] Historians of various genres—for example, nineteenth-century Italian opera or, to pick a more obviously social, less canonical genre, French workers' choruses—draw attention to the ways in which the musical product provided a quiescent, often governmentally approved distraction for a social class that otherwise might have been politically volatile.[21] And Pamela Potter and others draw open a curtain that for decades has hidden from general sight the ways in which composers, performers, and scholars were co-opted by the Nazi propaganda machine. (Perhaps one might more justly say,

[17] Claude Palisca, *Humanism in Italian Renaissance Musical Thought* (New Haven, 1985) (other examples might include Gary Tomlinson, *Music in Renaissance Magic: Towards a Historiography of Others* (Chicago, 1993), and Barbara Russano Hanning, *Of Poetry and Music's Power: Humanism and the Creation of Opera* (Ann Arbor, 1980) ); Ellen Rosand, *Opera in Seventeenth-Century Venice: The Creation of a Genre* (Berkeley, 1991); Andrew Steptoe, *The Mozart–Da Ponte Operas: The Cultural and Musical Background to 'Le nozze di Figaro', 'Don Giovanni', and 'Così fan tutte'* (Oxford, 1988); Julian Budden, *The Operas of Verdi*, rev. edn. (3 vols., Oxford, 1991); Kim Kowalke (ed.), *A New Orpheus: Essays on Kurt Weill* (New Haven, 1986).

[18] Jürgen Thym, 'Cross Currents in Song: Five Distinctive Voices', in Rufus Hallmark (ed.), *German Lieder in the Nineteenth Century* (New York, 1996), 153–85; Susan Youens, 'Music, Verse, and "Prose Poetry": Debussy's *Trois Chansons de Bilitis*', *Journal of Musicological Research*, 7 (1986–8), 69–94; Ruth A. Solie, 'Whose Life? The Gendered Self in Schumann's *Frauenliebe* Songs', in Steven Paul Scher (ed.), *Music and Text: Critical Inquiries* (Cambridge, 1992), 210–40; Lawrence Kramer, 'The Schubert Lied: Romantic Form and Romantic Consciousness', in Walter Frisch (ed.), *Schubert: Critical and Analytical Studies* (Lincoln, Nebr., 1986), 200–36; Jeffrey Kallberg, 'Hearing Poland: Chopin and Nationalism', in R. Larry Todd (ed.), *Nineteenth-Century Piano Music* (New York, 1990), 221–57; James Parakilas, *Ballads without Words: Chopin and the Tradition of the Instrumental Ballade* (Portland, Ore., 1992); Jonathan Bellman, *The 'Style Hongrois' in the Music of Western Europe* (Boston, 1993); Charles Suttoni, 'Piano and Opera: A Study of the Piano Fantasies Written on Opera Themes in the Romantic Era' (Ph.D. diss., New York University, 1973).

[19] See the various studies in Hans Lenneberg (ed.), *The Dissemination of Music: Five Centuries of European Music Publishing* (New York, 1994). Also of crucial importance are the contributions of music periodicals, journalism, advertising, music teaching, and simplified arrangements for amateur performance.

[20] William Weber, *The Rise of Musical Classics in Eighteenth-Century England* (Oxford, 1992). This study receives a follow-up in a book that Weber published earlier: *Music and the Middle Class: The Social Structure of Concert Life in London, Paris and Vienna* (London, 1975).

[21] William Weaver cites numerous eyewitness accounts and memoirs testifying to the careful innocuousness of early nineteenth-century Italian opera, in his *The Golden Century of Italian Opera* (New York, 1980). On the Orphéon choruses in France, see Jane Fulcher, 'The Orphéon Societies: "Music for the Workers" in Second-Empire France', *International Review of the Aesthetics and Sociology of Music*, 10 (1979), 47–56.

in the case of prominent individuals such as Richard Strauss, that they *allowed themselves*, and along with them the whole prestige-bearing tradition of Austro-Germanic art-music, to be so co-opted.[22])

Thus far I have focused primarily on the more or less 'canonical' repertoire(s) of Western art-music, taken more or less as a whole, or as sets of repertoires and practices. Most often, though, scholars work on (and music-lovers want to read about) individual composers, their lives, and their works. And at this level, too, much has been revealed about the social context of music. Various recent 'composer-oriented' scholars have (in varying proportions) worked with the given composer's career choices, his or her letters, the opera librettos or song texts he or she chose or shaped or wrote, and of course the music itself; their studies have brought to light all sorts of things that previous generations would never have suspected (or have wanted to hear), such as Beethoven's delusions about his own aristocratic origins.[23] In the process, they have also made clear that our generation of musicians and music scholars is not the first to be aware of the larger world. Already in Mozart we find (very inconsistent) glimmerings of an awareness of political issues and foreign cultures unprecedented, or at least undocumented, in most earlier composers.[24] But with Schumann, Offenbach, Mahler, Ives, Janáček, and many other composers of the nineteenth and early twentieth centuries, a responsiveness to the workings of power in the larger society becomes quite palpable: in their writings, their life choices, and some of their most important works, one sees diverse reflections of various anxiety-producing issues of the day, such as diplomacy and war, industrialization and urbanization, the role of women in society, or the commercialization and commodification of bourgeois and mass culture.[25] Opera, in particular, tends, by its nature, to offer us an open window into the concerns of an age, including some concerns that are with us still. Saint-Saëns's *Samson et Dalila* and Borodin's *Prince Igor*, for example, convey complex, compelling, and sometimes contradictory messages about the relationship between European imperial powers and the

[22] Articles by Pamela Potter, Albrecht Riethmüller, and others, in a special issue of *Journal of Musicological Research*, 11/3 (1992), entitled *Musicology in the Third Reich*, ed. Hans Lenneberg; Michael P. Steinberg, *The Meaning of the Salzburg Festival: Austria as Theater and Ideology, 1890–1938* (Ithaca, NY, 1990); Bryan Gilliam, 'The Annexation of Anton Bruckner: Nazi Revisionism and the Politics of Appropriation', *Musical Quarterly*, 78 (1994), 584–609; Pamela M. Potter, 'Strauss and the National Socialists: The Debate and its Relevance', in Bryan Gilliam (ed.), *Richard Strauss: New Perspectives on the Composer and his Work* (Durham, NC, 1992), 93–113.

[23] Maynard Solomon, *Beethoven* (New York, 1977).

[24] See Georg Knepler, *Wolfgang Amadé Mozart*, trans. J. B. Robinson (Cambridge, 1994), esp. 28–34 and 288–304 (touching on the French Revolution); Maynard Solomon, *Mozart: A Life* (New York, 1995), esp. 320–35, 497 (anticlericalism, Masonry, possible Jacobinism); and Steptoe, *Mozart–Da Ponte Operas*. Mozart's attitudes toward Eastern Europe are pondered in Larry Wolff, *Inventing Eastern Europe: The Map of Civilization on the Mind of the Enlightenment* (Stanford, Calif., 1994), 106–15. Wolff leaves unexplored the possible implications of his study for Mozart's *music* and that of other eighteenth- and early nineteenth-century composers, such as the Polish-style sonatas of Telemann or the various Hungarian-style passages in Beethoven.

[25] See Georg Knepler's observations on Mahler's and Pfitzner's opposing attitudes toward the working class: *Geschichte als Weg zum Musikverständnis: Zur Theorie, Methode und Geschichte der Musikgeschichtsschreibung*, 2nd rev. edn. (Leipzig, 1982), 487–8; Robert P. Morgan, 'Ives and Mahler: Mutual Responses at the End of an Era', *19th-Century Music*, 2 (1978–9), 72–81.

more 'primitive' cultures over which they were, at that time, coming to exercise increasing authority.[26]

Indeed, it is worth noting—in part because it has been denied for so long—that numerous musicians of the past two centuries have been sensitive, well-informed, passionate observers of their society and the larger world. Some even professed deeply held social beliefs that scholars are now examining—though preferably with sharp theoretical tools, in that composers' statements are, no less than other human behaviours, highly contingent and sometimes self-conscious or self-deluding performances.

That evidence of musicians' social attitudes begins to proliferate in the last decades of the eighteenth century is not by chance: the liberating currents of the Enlightenment, followed by the destabilizing events of the French Revolution to which the Enlightenment (especially in its more critical, anticlerical phases) had helped give birth, stimulated wave upon wave of social theorizing throughout Europe and America. So we suddenly find composers and prominent performers—including Beethoven, Liszt, the opera-composer Halévy, the great tenor Adolphe Nourrit, and others—writing essays and letters that clearly indicate their feeling that, as public figures, they needed to take a stand on certain large social and political issues of the day. ('Génie oblige' was how Liszt put it in a spirited essay disapproving of Paganini's splendid isolation.[27]) Mendelssohn discusses heatedly how society might best develop a sense of 'striving and desire for advancement'; Berlioz attacks the stratified class structure of modern society (he argues specifically for 'the destruction of all kinds of privileges, . . . [which are] vermin in the creases of the social body'); and others sketch out—some in down-to-earth practical programmes, others in high-flown but empowering fantasies—entirely new social roles for the modern musician.[28] Even a composer such as Brahms, who has generally been thought of as untainted by socio-political concerns, can be shown to have shared a collection

---

[26] Or a half-open window, perhaps, since the scene is impossible for us to glimpse fully or interpret securely. Four explorations focusing on musical style are Thomas Bauman, *Wolfgang Amadeus Mozart: 'Die Entführung aus dem Serail'* (Cambridge, 1987), 62–77; Richard Taruskin, ' "Entoiling the Falconet": Russian Musical Orientalism in Context', *Cambridge Opera Journal*, 4 (1992), 253–80; Ralph P. Locke, 'Constructing the Oriental "Other": Saint-Saëns's *Samson et Dalila'*, *Cambridge Opera Journal*, 3 (1991), 261–302; *idem*, 'Reflections on Orientalism in Opera and Musical Theater', *Opera Quarterly*, 10 (1993–4), 46–64. Even more complex are the negotiations of Chopin, Grieg, and Bartók (city-dwellers all) with the (primarily rural) folk music of their *native* country.

[27] Franz Liszt, *Artiste et société*, ed. Rémy Stricker ([Paris], 1995), 258.

[28] Beethoven's proposal of a communal 'art depot' was apparently inspired by the writings of the proto-Communist Gracchus Babeuf (Maynard Solomon, 'Beethoven's "Magazin der Kunst" ', *19th-Century Music*, 8 (1983–4), 199–208). The remaining examples are discussed in ch. 9 of my *Music, Musicians, and the Saint-Simonians* (Chicago, 1986), 94–152. More generally, the Jacobins, the Saint-Simonians, the Young Germans (such as Heine and Börne), the leaders of the Risorgimento, the proponents of a democratic culture in America (such as Walt Whitman), and political ideologists of various stripes in the twentieth century assisted in various ways in this much-needed consciousness-raising, though certain of the social/political ends to which musicians applied their art may now seem repulsive to us, such as those of the Nazi regime. (I explore the risks of music's entering the public arena in my *Music, Musicians and the Saint-Simonians*, 226–34, and in my 'Musique engagée? The Experience of the Saint-Simonians at Ménilmontant', in Marc Honegger and Christian Meyer (eds.), *La Musique et le rite: sacré et profane*, Actes du xiii^e Congrès de la Société Internationale de Musicologie (Strasbourg, 1986), i. 145–55.)

of opinions and prejudices about larger issues which may arguably also be reflected in his music.[29]

Clearly, we must avoid the old habit of somehow finding admirable, of somehow defending, a given composer's response to (or reading of, or 'performed' stance toward) social reality, especially if that response is plainly bigoted in regard to one or another social category (such as race or gender). Wagner's belligerent anti-Semitism, for example, has too readily been whitewashed by certain scholars eager to erect a sanitary barrier between the master and certain of his unsavoury later admirers. This effort at denial, predictably, tends to give rise to exaggerated, under-documented accusations that, in turn, invite heated rejections, the whole creating an unhelpful cycle of polarized rhetoric. Meanwhile, barely touched by all the verbiage swirling around it, a real but complex phenomenon lies in wait of a complex (though not necessarily dispassionate) analysis.[30] Similarly questionable was the post-World War II (and in many ways still ongoing) attempt in American music-theory circles to reduce the writings of Heinrich Schenker and Alfred Lorenz to a set of purely technical observations, thereby ignoring the rhetoric of German cultural chauvinism in which their observations are couched and perhaps best understood.[31]

Inviting though all this work on the masters and the master-works is (and on the various institutional and ideological conditions acting upon them), musicology also needs at times to step back for a fuller view of the musical scene as it exists now or existed at a given time or place in history. That socially minded critics are feeling increasingly confident about moving in this direction—away from the gratifying individual masterpiece and the fascinating genius—can be seen in the recent, and the first even remotely comprehensive, social history of Western art-music: the eight-volume series edited by Stanley Sadie and published in the United Kingdom as *Man and Music* and in the United States as *Music and Society*.[32]

This series was all the more welcome in that it was for the most part written by musicologists. Until recently, the most captivating writings on the larger scale

[29] Margaret Notley, 'Brahms as Liberal: Genre, Style, and Politics in Late Nineteenth-Century Vienna', *19th-Century Music*, 17 (1993–4), 107–23.

[30] A recent, nuanced presentation is Marc A. Weiner, *Richard Wagner and the Anti-Semitic Imagination* (Lincoln, Nebr., 1995). Lawrence Dreyfus deals artfully with some standard oversimplified accusations in 'Hermann Levi's Shame and Parsifal's Guilt: A Critique of Essentialism in Biography and Criticism', *Cambridge Opera Journal*, 6 (1994), 125–45. On nationalism, ethnic chauvinism, anti-Semitism, and other related issues in opera (e.g. Wagner's *Meistersinger*), see James Parakilas, 'Political Representation and the Chorus in the Nineteenth-Century Opera', *19th-Century Music*, 16 (1992–3), 181–202; Arthur Groos, 'Constructing Nuremberg: Typological and Proleptic Communities in *Die Meistersinger*', *19th-Century Music*, 16 (1992–3), 18–34; and Patrick Carnegy, 'Stage History', in John Warrack (ed.), *Richard Wagner: 'Die Meistersinger von Nürnberg'* (Cambridge, 1994), 135–52.

[31] William Rothstein, 'The Americanization of Heinrich Schenker', in Hedi Siegel (ed.), *Schenker Studies* (New York, 1990), 192–203.

[32] Stanley Sadie (general ed.), *Music and Society* (8 vols., Englewood Cliffs, NJ, 1989–94), published in London as *Man and Music* (1989–93). Important predecessors were Henry Raynor, *Social History of Music from the Middle Ages to Beethoven* (London, 1972); idem, *Music and Society since 1815* (London, 1976); Wilfrid Mellers and Alec Harman, *Man and His Music: The Story of Musical Experience in the West* (London, 1962; also published in 4 vols.).

have tended to come from outsiders, including scholars from other fields (e.g. cultural historians) and performing musicians. (Three such books that jump to mind are Roger Shattuck's *The Banquet Years*, Paul Robinson's *Opera and Ideas*, and Arthur Loesser's *Men, Women, and Pianos*.[33]) Such writers often bring a welcome wide frame of reference to their musical topic and an appealing liveliness of style. But among musicologists, alas, liveliness is somewhat suspect, no doubt because we have noticed that it often—but surely not necessarily!—comes hand in hand with a lack of rigour or open-mindedness (as in much music journalism).

Wide-angle studies are particularly well suited to the non-musicologist author, because they can be carried out without much attention to technical details of musical style and structure. Almost by definition, though, much that is utterly crucial to our aesthetic experience of the music, and thereby to its social functioning (which is deeply dependent on those aesthetic aspects), gets sacrificed along the way. So the challenge remains: how to combine these two approaches—that is, how to find a way of incorporating astute remarks about musical matters, equivalent to the art historian's attention to details of line, colour, composition, and facture, within studies of music's involvement in various social projects; or (for those who work the opposite way) how to bring insights about society's effects on music into detailed discussions of individual repertoires and works.[34] I should add that this problem of integrating 'music' and 'society' remains much the same no matter whether we are speaking of scholarly articles or classroom teaching.

This necessarily thrusts the task back to scholars who possess a vocabulary of some precision for talking about music: namely, musicologists. There is a wide range of solutions here.[35] Studies of individual composers or of specific genres or 'streams' of music-making (such as those cited above on church music, opera, or—a more straightforward case—workers' choruses) tend to focus on such matters as the reasonably direct ramifications of a composer's social situation or the demands of the audience or commissioning agent. But even if we restrict ourselves for the moment to questions bearing on one or another composer, these ramifications vary widely, not least in the degree of assurance with which we can 'know' them.[36] Relatively objective, though still open to varying interpretation, are the raw facts of a composer's career—for example, Bach's frustrations with his superiors in Leipzig and theirs with him. More elusive, but no

---

[33] Roger Shattuck, *The Banquet Years: The Origins of the Avant-Garde in France, 1885 to World War I*, rev. edn. (New York, 1968); Paul A. Robinson, *Opera and Ideas: From Mozart to Strauss* (New York, 1985); Arthur Loesser, *Men, Women and Pianos: A Social History* (New York, 1954).

[34] Overviews of, and/or bibliographies on, music sociology are offered in *The New Grove Dictionary of Music and Musicians*, s.v. 'sociology'; Hans Lenneberg, 'Speculating about Sociology and Social History', *Journal of Musicology*, 6 (1988), 409–20; and Locke, 'Music Lovers', 150–1.

[35] Further on the possible ways of crossing the society/music gap, see my 'Music Patrons', 150–1, and my review of Fauquet (see n. 6).

[36] For a revealing comparison of different approaches to writing a composer's life, see Hans Lenneberg, *Witnesses and Scholars: Studies in Musical Biography* (New York, 1988).

less crucial, are such matters as the composer's choice of genres: why did Hummel write virtuoso concertos, whereas Mendelssohn (though also producing a few outstanding concertos) devoted particular effort to the oratorio? Why did the French song composer Loïsa Puget write dozens upon dozens of purely strophic *romances* but little else, whereas Schubert not only wrote songs of more varied kinds but also set to music one opera libretto after another, even though the resulting works were not getting accepted for performance?[37]

More mysterious still is the extent to which social concerns and ideas are encoded in the specifically musical features of a work. Much hard thinking is bound to go on in the future about the possible social implications of purely instrumental pieces: for example, a Baroque organ fugue or concerto grosso[38] or, in later periods, a Mozart string trio, a Chopin prelude, or a Scriabin sonata.[39] Then there is the whole problem of how much the title of a piece or its text (if a vocal work) or genre associations or style conventions might determine the way that the piece is heard. Charles Ford, for example, offers a more starkly ideological reading of the gender politics in Mozart's operas than does Wye J. Allanbrook.[40] Likewise, attitudes regarding how much to privilege the programme when interpreting programme music vary widely from one scholar to another.[41]

There is perhaps an opening here for empirical research on the current 'reception' of musical styles: if the ideological implications of a piece are determined not just by the composer's conscious or unconscious intention, but by the way the piece is *heard*, it could be enlightening to learn just how listeners at various times, places, and situations—listeners of different ages, social origins, and educational levels—hear and respond to specific pieces. One enterprising Israeli musicologist, for example, presented a number of 'mystery' pieces to a group of ninety-five Israeli listeners, then asked them which piece or pieces struck them as particularly 'Israeli' in character.[42] Similarly, we need to give increased

---

[37] A touching example of Puget's art is reprinted in Austin Caswell, 'Loïsa Puget and the French Chanson', in Peter Bloom (ed.), *Music in Paris in the Eighteen-Thirties* (Stuyvesant, NY, 1987), 97–116.

[38] Andrew Dell'Antonio, 'The Sensual Sonata: Construction of Desire in Early Baroque Music', *repercussions*, 1/2 (Fall 1992), 52–83; also Laurence Dreyfus, *Bach and the Patterns of Invention* (Cambridge, Mass., 1996).

[39] Mozart: Lawrence Kramer, 'The Musicology of the Future', *repercussions*, 1/1 (Spring 1992), 5–18. Chopin: Subotnik, *Developing Variations*, 112–65, and Lawrence Kramer, *Music as Cultural Practice, 1800–1900* (Berkeley, 1990), 72–101. Scriabin: Mitchell Morris, 'Alexander Skryabin, Decadent Style, and the Construction of Effeminacy', paper read at the conference on 'Feminist Theory and Music II: Continuing the Diaglogue', Eastman School of Music, 17–20 June 1993.

[40] Charles C. Ford, *Così? Sexual Politics in Mozart's Operas* (Manchester, 1991); Wye J. Allanbrook, *Rhythmic Gesture in Mozart: 'Le nozze di Figaro' and 'Don Giovanni'* (Chicago, 1984).

[41] e.g. Nicholas Temperley, 'The *Symphonie fantastique* and its Program', *Musical Quarterly*, 57 (1971), 593–608; R. Larry Todd, ' "Gerade das Lied wie es dasteht": On Text and Meaning in Mendelssohn's *Lieder ohne Worte*', in Nancy Kovaleff Baker and Barbara Russano Hanning (eds.), *Musical Humanism and its Legacy: Essays in Honor of Claude V. Palisca* (Stuyvesant, NY, 1992), 355–79; Carolyn Abbate, *Unsung Voices: Opera and Musical Narrative in the Nineteenth Century* (Princeton, 1991), 30–60 (on Dukas's *L'Apprenti Sorcier*). This problem of music and meaning is discussed elsewhere in the present volume, e.g. by Fred Maus and Scott Burnham in Chs. 8 and 9 respectively.

[42] The results were inconclusive but fascinating: pieces that were sensed as 'Jewish'-sounding (e.g. Schoenberg's String Quartet No. 4, mvt. 3) were sometimes perceived as more 'Israeli' than some pieces by Israeli composers; the

attention to the ways in which musical works are marketed, made part of an approved version of 'culture' (patriotic, middle-class, or whatever), as Meirion Hughes has shown with regard to Elgar.[43]

## III. Social Values in the Musicologist's Work

Just as science and medicine are ruled and modified by successive paradigms and structural assumptions,[44] so musicology, at any given moment in a given cultural setting, tends to act within a framework of given values. In the present section, I will review some of the major ones that recur in musicological writing—even in some of the best and most sophisticated. I do so briefly, and with apologies all around for much resulting oversimplification. My primary aim here is to open up these paradigms and methods to discussion, not to ridicule them or reject them as 'biased' (though I have not tried to hide my feelings about some of them). In fact, I consider it impossible to write meaningful history or criticism—as opposed to creating chronicles and other admittedly helpful repositories of data[45]—without adopting some reasonably coherent set of ideological, aesthetic, or music-historiographical assumptions.

Some of these value systems (paradigms, or whatever—I will use these terms rather interchangeably) are adopted more or less consciously, explicitly, and systematically (as in the writings of several generations of Soviet writers); others tend to be, as Janet Levy puts it, more 'covert' or 'casual', and perhaps more 'insidious' (her word), or at least more in need of being publicly exposed.[46] The distinction between these two categories of ideological assumptions—explicit versus inexplicit—is a crucial one for evaluating any given musicological text and the way that it was shaped by its anticipated reception. For present purposes, though, I would rather conflate the two categories, since it is the ideology itself that I wish to draw attention to, not the degree of the author's conscious intent in introducing it into the text (assuming that the 'covert' author is even aware of the ideological ocean in which he or she swims). And whereas the previous sections, for purely practical reasons, dealt almost exclusively with written

---

highest votes for 'Israeli'-ness went to a piece based on Arabic music by immigrant composer Alexander Uriyah Boskovitch. The report breaks down its findings by helpful categories (native-born versus immigrant, professional musicians versus non-professionals), and notes some of the factors that the listeners said helped them to define the nationality of a given piece (Jehoash Hirshberg, with David Sagiv, 'The "Israeli" in Israeli Music: The Audience Responds', *Israel Studies in Musicology*, 1 (1978), 159–73).

[43] Meirion Hughes, ' "The Duc d'Elgar": Making a Composer Gentleman', in Christopher Norris (ed.), *Music and the Politics of Culture* (London, 1989), 41–68.

[44] See Thomas S. Kuhn, *The Structure of Scientific Revolutions*, 2nd enlarged edn. (Chicago, 1970).

[45] Of course, most of these chronicles and catalogues are themselves shaped by the 'great man' doctrine, which is why it is so extraordinary and revealing when a first-rate scholar provides a research tool for a composer often now considered a lesser light (e.g. Herbert Schneider's forthcoming thematic catalogue of works by the nineteenth-century opera composer Auber).

[46] Janet M. Levy, 'Covert and Casual Values in Recent Writings about Music', *Journal of Musicology*, 5 (1987), 3–27.

research, here I will try, at least occasionally, to suggest specific implications for classroom teaching.

Perhaps the most notorious such framework or value system—in this case it is also a true 'grand narrative'—is the oft-told tale of the ever-increasing degree of organic unity in music, from Bach or Haydn via Wagner to Schoenberg and (as we used to be taught) Babbitt and Boulez.[47] Analogous versions of this tale of 'progress' seek and find evidence of an increasing complexity and sophistication in harmony, form, rhythm, or textural sonority (e.g. orchestration). Most such tales of progress deal with music of the past two or three centuries, leaving unmentioned the art of Gregorian chant or Josquin or Chambonnières. And even in the era of their purview, they omit much that might contradict their premiss: conservative composers in the twentieth century, such as Sibelius and Rachmaninov, and experimenters of genius in the nineteenth, such as the tonally subversive Albéniz or the rhythmically and orchestrationally inventive Glinka.[48] That all these are non-Germans is no accident. Often overlapping with these tales of progress is another familiar tale (or perhaps it might better be described as an often unspoken assumption): namely, that characteristically Germanic concerns or obsessions (including, most notably, the aforementioned concept of 'organic unity') deserve to be valorized beyond others, and ought to set the norms by which the others are evaluated. Thus, music and musical life in the countries of Scandinavia, Eastern Europe, southern Europe, and the Americas tend to be discussed briefly, if at all, in our historical and analytical studies, textbooks, and curricula; and, to the extent that they *are* discussed, they are often marginalized under the heading of 'nationalism' (as if the Austro-German tradition were the only truly 'universal' one). Even English and French musical traditions are often treated cursorily or ignorantly; Italy is often granted a special status as the source of naïvely tuneful tendencies and crude formal archetypes (such as the da capo aria, the concerto grosso, or the early overture and symphony) that Germanic types such as Handel, Bach, or Haydn will turn into true art.[49] Predictably, coverage is even skimpier, in books and courses on twentieth-century music, for music from various African and Asian countries, such as the work of Fela Sowande, Kevin Volans, or Toru Takemitsu.

[47] Christopher A. Williams, 'Of Canons and Context: Toward a Historiography of Twentieth-Century Music', *repercussions*, 2/1 (Spring 1993), 31–74. See also various contributions in Bergeron and Bohlman (eds.), *Disciplining Music*, as well as Ruth Solie, 'The Living Work: Organicism and Musical Analysis', *19th-Century Music*, 4 (1980–1), 147–56, and William Pastille, 'Heinrich Schenker: Anti-Organicist', *19th-Century Music*, 8 (1984–5), 28–36.

[48] For Albéniz, I am thinking of *Preludio* from *Cantos de España*, Op. 232 (1896), which lingers so insistently on the dominant that the piece can be heard as hanging irresolutely—as does much Spanish folk-music—between two keys: here, A minor and E major (with lowered second and seventh). The classic Glinka example is *Kamarinskaya* for orchestra (1848).

[49] French music of the Baroque often gets short-changed even more than Italian, perhaps because it contributed much less to the genres and styles of Handel and Bach. Similar problems exist regarding nineteenth-century Italian and Czech music: see, respectively, Philip Gossett, 'Carl Dahlhaus and the "Ideal Type" ', *19th-Century Music*, 13 (1989), 49–56, and Michael Beckerman, 'On Czechness in Music', *19th-Century Music*, 10 (1986–7), 61–73.

Several other ideological schemes have had similarly long and vigorous (or long and pernicious) careers within the musicological literature. The Romantic 'Great Man' doctrine, for example, saturates numerous standard biographies of composers, such as Lina Ramann's authorized multi-volume study of Liszt.[50] Closely related to this is the conservative canonizing that I mentioned in section II. Both of these are closely tied to the autonomy doctrine mentioned at the outset of the chapter.[51]

Yet another widely used interpretive scheme—again often intertwined with various of the preceding ones—is based on the category of the 'nation'. I will dub such approaches 'nationist', as opposed to strictly 'nationalist' ones. ('Nationalism' in this sense may be viewed as a subset of 'nationism'.) A writer (or teacher) adopting a nationist approach tends to begin by grouping composers by ethnic or national origin. Often he or she then goes on to evaluate or praise their work according to how much it matches certain features deemed characteristic of that nation. But instead he or she may try to link the composers in question into the canonizing system discussed earlier. Since that system tends to claim 'universal' merit for its heroes, a critic with a 'nationist' bent (whether or not the nation in question is actually the one to which the person belongs by birth) will often try to find a local candidate whose worthiness to be included in the larger story can then be argued: a Granados, an Ives, a Nielsen, a Skalkottas, a Pärt.[52] Another way that nationism works hand in hand with canonical thinking is when scholars try to prove the 'influence' of a local genre or minor composer on somebody or something that everyone in the international (classical-) music community can be expected to care about. An extreme case of this was the attempt by Luigi Torrefranca, early in our century, to claim for Giovanni Platti the laurel wreath of inventor of sonata form. Torrefranca can be made to look pretty silly, but he was doing nothing more than responding in kind to an equally self-serious (and equally silly?) debate between German and Austrian

---

[50] Lina Ramann, *Franz Liszt als Künstler und Mensch* (2 vols. in 3; Leipzig, 1880–94). Valuable for evaluating Ramann's sources and her treatment of same is the recent (belated) publication of Liszt's answers to her questionnaires: *Lisztiana: Erinnerungen an Franz Liszt in Tagebuchblättern, Briefen und Dokumenten aus den Jahren 1873–1886/87*, ed. Arthur Seidl, rev. Friedrich Schnapp (Mainz, 1983).

[51] It should also be stressed that such idealist concepts are not entirely devoid of their own version of 'social concern'. Quite the contrary, they are generally imbued with a kind of spiritual philanthropy: precisely because they view the art of music as not being tied to debilitating social conditions (some of which are seen as nearly irremediable), they value music as giving disadvantaged people one of their only means of access (besides religion and family life) to a higher plane of reality. See e.g. the efforts of people involved in 'music appreciation', such as Walter Damrosch, discussed in Joseph Horowitz, *Understanding Toscanini: How He Became an American Culture-God and Helped Create a New Audience for Old Music* (New York, 1987).

[52] The particular names that I have cited prompt me to note that a composer from a small or peripheral country will more easily seem includable in the canon if his or her work sounds distinctively 'national' or at least highly idiosyncratic. By contrast, composers of skilled and even moving music of a more cosmopolitan nature, such as, to pick some American examples, John Knowles Paine, Charles Tomlinson Griffes, and, to some extent, John Alden Carpenter or Walter Piston, may remain under-appreciated—compared to, say, Ives or Copland—because their music makes less show of its national origins. On the other hand, national traits can also relegate him or her to provincial status: see n. 63.

scholars: one centring on the relative priority of the Mannheim symphonists versus the Viennese.[53]

All the aforementioned approaches have a long pedigree. Some novel ones, of course, have arisen in the twentieth century, and some have even triumphed for a time. Marxist and other analyses based on class and other social categories have appeared in many different guises. In various countries, for example, critics and cultural officials have explicitly urged, even decreed, that music be exploited for the immediate social benefit of the 'working class' or other constituencies. Some of these programmes, such as the choral-singing movement in Hungary, are arguably admirable; others—or perhaps some of the same ones, depending on one's point of view—are scarily repressive. For decades, many Soviet and Soviet-bloc writers—journalists, textbook authors, but also respected academics—stirred up a powerful cocktail of national pride *and* working-class consciousness, with which they anointed ballets and concert works based on peasant tunes and the like. Similarly, prominent Chinese officials in the early 1970s attacked Beethoven's music as bourgeois and dangerously foreign, and permitted agitated squads of Red Guards to engage in such progressive actions as breaking pianists' wrists. Critics in both countries (and elsewhere, as in Nazi Germany) attacked jazz and rock as decadent and dangerous, much in the way that conservative cultural critics in America do today with gangsta rap.[54]

To be sure, Marxist analysis, so easy to castigate, has also offered lasting insights into musicians and their complex interaction with societal structures and reigning trends of thought. Ernst Hermann Meyer's classic book on early English chamber music still shows the strength of aligning a class analysis with judicious musical commentary (and careful sifting of the evidence), as does Georg Knepler's two-volume history of nineteenth-century music, not to speak of various perceptive essays and books of Adorno, Zofia Lissa, or, more recently, Janos Maróthy or Hanns-Werner Heister.[55] But class analysis can easily become

[53] Summary in William S. Newman, *The Sonata in the Classic Era*, 3rd edn. (New York, 1983), 326–8, 365–73, and for more on the Mannheim/Vienna debate, Eugene Wolf, *The Symphonies of Johann Stamitz: A Study in the Formation of the Classic Style* (Utrecht, 1981).

[54] Boris Schwarz, *Music and Musical Life in Soviet Russia, 1917–1981*, enlarged edn. (Bloomington, Ind., 1983); Bruno Nettl, *The Western Impact on World Music: Change, Adaptation, and Survival* (New York, 1985), 142–5 (on Chinese concertos). Recent reports of government censorship in Tehran remind us that there are yet other kinds of societies that find Western culture objectionable, not only plays and films (with their immodest exposure of the female body, their scenes of drinking, and so on) but also concerts of music by Mozart and Beethoven. In a poem recently published in a conservative newspaper, such music is condemned as élitist, catering to wealthy black-marketeers and ignoring the 'downtrodden'; see Robin Wright, 'Dateline Tehran: Testing the Limits of Cultural Freedom', *Civilization*, Mar.–Apr. 1995, pp. 12–14.

[55] Ernst Hermann Meyer, *Early English Chamber Music from the Middle Ages to Purcell*, 2nd edn. rev. Diana Poulton (London, 1982; orig. pub. 1946 as *English Chamber Music*); Georg Knepler, *Musikgeschichte des 19. Jahrhunderts* (2 vols., [East] Berlin, 1961); Theodor W. Adorno, *Introduction to the Sociology of Music* (New York, 1976); Zofia Lissa, *Aufsätze zur Musikästhetik: Eine Auswahl* ([East] Berlin, 1969); János Maróthy, *Music and the Bourgeois, Music and the Proletarian*, trans. Eva Rona (Budapest, 1974); Hanns-Werner Heister, *Das Konzert: Theorie einer Kulturform* (2 vols., Wilhelmshaven, 1983). Further discussion in Knepler's article 'Musikgeschichtsschreibung', forthcoming in the 2nd edn. of *Die Musik in Geschichte und Gegenwart*.

rather mechanical, especially when, having lost its Marxist core (and, in a sense, its original justification), it filters down into more mainstream musicological writings: the result is often a raw juxtaposition of social facts (including facts about musical life) with more purely musical observations, leaving entirely unexplained the relationship between the two. For example, the statement, often heard, that sonata form is some kind of musical response to the tensions and thrusts of late eighteenth-century European (capitalist) society is usually presented more as an impressive assertion than a closely argued thesis.[56] Fortunately, recent studies (including some noted earlier) have succeeded in restoring serious attention to issues of social class by combining concrete documentation with interpretive flexibility.[57]

Another factor has recently enriched music scholarship even more dramatically than social class: gender. Beginning *c.*1975, our attention has been insistently and helpfully drawn to the previously under-acknowledged ways in which women have shaped music history: as composers, teachers, and influential professional performers (notably opera singers), and as (collectively influential) amateur performers of and activists for musical culture in the home and the community.[58] Equally novel and enlightening (if somewhat riskier) are studies of how maleness and femaleness are constructed in opera, song, and oratorio.[59]

Most fascinating of all, perhaps, but necessarily also more controversial, are gender- and sexuality-conscious readings of symphonies and other instrumental works long described as 'abstract' or 'absolute'. Some such readings have been disparaged for assuming the very thesis that they are trying to establish (e.g. that chromaticism was a marker of the feminine in Classic and Romantic concert music and opera), or at least for jumping to such generalizations without first providing a sufficient evidentiary context.[60]

---

[56] See William Weber's trenchant critique, 'The Muddle of the Middle Class', *19th-Century Music*, 3 (1979–80), 175–85. Writings that suggestively invoke the rising middle and merchant class as a partial explanation of sonata form include Bence Szabolcsi, *Aufstieg der klassischen Musik von Vivaldi bis Mozart*, trans. Mirza von Schüching (Wiesbaden, 1970), and Charles Rosen, 'Social Function', in *Sonata Forms*, rev. edn. (New York, 1988), 8–15; the latter is quoted with cautious approval in Neal Zaslaw (ed.), *Music and Society: The Classical Era, from the 1740s to the End of the 18th Century* (New York, 1989), 1–14 (editor's introduction).

[57] Weber, *Music and the Middle Class*; Derek B. Scott, *The Singing Bourgeois: Songs of the Victorian Drawing Room and Parlour* (Milton Keynes, 1989); David Gramit, 'Schubert's Wanderers', *Journal of Musicological Research*, 14 (1994), 147–68 (based in part on Friedrich A. Kittler, *Discourse Networks, 1800/1900*, trans. Michael Melteer, with Chris Cullens (Stanford, Calif., 1990) ); Nancy B. Reich, 'Women as Musicians: A Question of Class', in Solie (ed.), *Musicology and Difference*, 125–46. Unusually intriguing but sometimes wildly speculative is Michel Faure, *Musique et société, du Second Empire aux années vingt: autour de Saint-Saëns, Fauré, Debussy et Ravel* (Paris, 1985).

[58] See Ch. 21 above. Two syntheses of current knowledge are Karin Pendle (ed.), *Women and Music: A History* (Bloomington, Ind., 1991), and Julie Anne Sadie and Rhian Samuel (eds.), *Norton/Grove Dictionary of Women Composers* (New York, 1995).

[59] See e.g. Allanbrook, *Musical Gesture*, Ford, *Cosi?*, and Solie, 'Whose Life?'; also several studies (e.g. by Terry Castle, Mitchell Morris, Mary Ann Smart, and myself) in Corinne E. Blackmer and Patricia Juliana Smith (eds.), *En travesti: Women, Gender Subversion, Opera* (New York, 1995).

[60] Particularly bold (and widely discussed) readings are in Susan McClary, *Feminine Endings: Music, Gender, and Sexuality* (Minneapolis, 1991), esp. 11–12, 53–79, 100–1, 104, 108–9. Ellen Rosand's review of a book by Cather-

In part, this (perceived?) circularity may be related to the underlying tension or contradiction in much feminist thinking and writing (including, I admit, some of my own work): however much we may position ourselves as gender egalitarians and may perhaps even work toward making the society in which we live more truly egalitarian, we often find ourselves 'cycling' back in our scholarly work to an emphasis on the unique experience of women or on certain widespread patterns in the roles or images that are assigned to women, whether in a given patriarchal society (such as our own still resistantly remains) or in all societies (inherently?). In particular, I would argue that the attempt to document and, within certain parameters, validate the distinctiveness of a 'woman's experience' or 'woman's sphere' remains an ongoing political necessity, for it helps counteract the tendency of a rigid egalitarianist discourse to leave intact the (usually unspoken) assumption that male experience and values are and should remain the universal norms.[61]

But more should be said about the accusation of circular or 'sloppy' thinking. I would warn about such easy dismissals of any kind of new or challenging work. Indeed, circular reasoning is rife in all branches of music scholarship, and may even be, to some extent, unavoidable, in that, as we have noted, any imaginable alternatives—a value-free objectivity, a totally rationalistic (deductive?) argumentation—prove to be chimerical. All scholars build on ideological and aesthetic premises, spoken or silent. What matters, to some extent, is how useful or persuasive or intuitively 'right' the particular set of premises proves to be when applied to the phenomenon in question. It is perhaps for this very reason that many of us find certain feminist approaches so fascinating and fruitful for musicology: an ideology that is itself torn in two or more directions—one that is 'multivocal' (as Suzanne Cusick puts in it Ch. 21 above)—is perhaps bound to be more flexible than a 'univocal' one, hence more responsive to the diverse and messy realities of musical art and its making and reception.

At the same time, though, we might want to be aware of a potential disadvantage of multivocality (in feminist or any other scholarly methodologies). An ideology that can make room for a phenomenon but also for its opposite may find it too easy to explain anything at all (and thus explain nothing). This is the case, for example, with post-structuralist approaches that set about demonstrating that texts (musical works, scholarly arguments) can subvert the very value

ine Clément objects to any easy equation of chromatic with female (*19th-Century Music*, 14 (1990–1), 75–83), as does Paula Higgins ('Women in Music, Feminist Criticism, and Guerrilla Musicology: Reflections on Recent Polemics', *19th-Century Music*, 17 (1993–4), 174–92). McClary herself seems, in more recent writings, no longer to be endorsing (if she ever entirely intended to endorse) the chromatic/feminine equivalence as some kind of general principle, even within Western art-music. See e.g. her 'Narrative Agendas in "Absolute Music"' (with reference to Brahms's Third Symphony, in which the 'feminine' second subject is utterly diatonic). Two further, nuanced appreciations of McClary's *Feminine Endings* are Mary Ann Smart's review (*Journal of Musicological Research*, 14 (1994), 77–84) and a broader overview by Andrea [Andrew] dell'Antonio, 'Il caso McClary: *Feminine Endings* e la musicologia femminista statunitense' (*Il saggiatore musicale*, 1 (1994), 209–18).

[61] See the introduction and chs. 1 and 10 in Locke and Barr, *Cultivating Music in America*. Further, see my 'Women in American Musical Life: Facts and Questions about Patronage', *repercussions*, 3/2 (Fall 1994), 81–95.

system that they outwardly support or (the reverse) reinforce a system that they overtly critique.[62] The danger is equally well exemplified by traditional criticism, which can praise a piece at one moment for powerfully fulfilling the requirements of its genre (e.g. for providing a satisfyingly passionate second-key theme in the relative major) and at another for its novelty in breaking with convention (e.g. recapitulating that theme in some key other than the tonic). When the game has rules like this, no great composer can ever misstep. And a minor composer may be blamed, rather than praised, for the very same features: following a rule becomes proof of textbookish thinking; breaking one, ineptness.[63]

A final ideological framework should be mentioned, though it has no recognized name. I propose two names: 'revisionist cultural critique' and 'inverted Whiggishness'. This viewpoint—revisionistically challenging the facile progressivism that still pervades much cultural discourse in the West—portrays the current socio-cultural situation as sliding downward toward depravity, rather than as edging ever closer to perfection (the classic attitude of 'Whig' and other progress-obsessed interpretations of history). Whatever one calls it, this framework consists of the attempt to find, in the past, situations that either contained the seeds of the problems of the modern world and modern musical life or that show healthy alternative solutions.

A few examples of recent writings on earlier American music may show how this works. When cultural historian Lawrence W. Levine's *Highbrow/Lowbrow* paints a picture of early nineteenth-century American culture as diverse and democratic, he is explicitly creating a counter-vision to the deep split between art and entertainment today. (I will return to his analysis in section IV.) When Paul DiMaggio similarly emphasizes the exclusivist impulse of critic John Sullivan Dwight and others who designed and built the American symphony orchestras, I would argue that he is (*not* explicitly, indeed perhaps quite inadvertently) reading back into the past the snobbery of mid-twentieth-century cultural élites.[64]

Such eager readings of the tea-leaves of yesteryear (whether conscious or not, and whether emphasizing the positive or the negative or both in some odd com-

[62] The arguments of such theorists as Jacques Derrida, Michel Foucault, Fredric Jameson, Richard Rorty, and Jean-François Lyotard regarding general concepts (or 'grand narratives') and their inherent self-undermining are compared and evaluated in John McGowan, *Postmodernism and its Critics* (Ithaca, NY, 1991), 89–210. The 'hegemony/subversion' model, in particular, makes room for stereotyped images and also for their inversion, dismantling, or creative reinterpretation (perhaps makes room too easily, as, arguably, in my own 'Constructing the Oriental "Other" ' and 'Reflections on Orientalism in Opera').

[63] A related dualism is the version of the 'nationist' paradigm used by Fauquet to condemn minor French composers of chamber music: they are epigones if they write like Haydn and provincial if they do something distinctively French. (See my review of his *Sociétés de musique de chambre*, cited in n. 6.)

[64] Lawrence W. Levine, *Highbrow/Lowbrow: The Emergence of Cultural Hierarchy in America* (Cambridge, Mass., 1988). Paul J. DiMaggio, 'Cultural Entrepreneurship in Nineteenth-Century Boston: The Creation of an Organizational Base for High Culture in America', and 'Cultural Entrepreneurship in Nineteenth-Century Boston, Part II: The Classification and Framing of American Art', *Media, Culture, and Society*, 4 (1982), 33–50, 303–22. DiMaggio, I contend, exaggerates certain of his points, through selective evidence and misleading paraphrase. See Locke, 'Music Patrons', 157–8, 168.

bination) can sometimes produce 'results' that then have to be painstakingly disproved. One glaring case occurred in the mid-1970s, when a musicologist and a theatre historian together produced a modern edition of Andrew Barton's early American ballad opera *The Disappointment* for performance at the Library of Congress. In press releases that received much play in the press, the two scholars stressed that one of the characters, Raccoon, was African-American (Jamaican, they added) yet was portrayed sympathetically, indeed with no negative (or, one might add, positive) comment on his race. ('His status in the play is one of equality with the other characters.') The editors were clearly delighted to promote, during the year of the American bicentennial (1976), an opera that, though written in a supposedly racist age, presumed, without even needing to preach the point, the modern concept of interracial tolerance.[65] Fortunately, all the publicity attendant on this production caused other researchers to parry with parallels from non-musical plays of the time, thereby demonstrating once and for all that Raccoon is in fact ethnically German and, incidentally, that wishful thinking offers a shaky basis for rewriting history.[66]

## IV. The Freedom and Responsibility of the Musicologist

Thus far I have narrowed the original topic considerably, focusing attention on specific ways in which musicologists have worked to reveal the social embeddedness of Western art-music and have in their own writings reflected and reinforced fairly concrete social (or social-aesthetic) ideologies, often without being aware of it themselves. (Among the most entrenched of these ideologies, as noted earlier, is the belief that musical scholarship, and music itself, are, or should try to be, free of contaminating ideology.) I would like now to inch my way back to the original broader focus of this chapter by touching briefly on the wide range of activities that we—musicologists of whatever type (not just those

---

[65] See Carolyn Rabson, 'Disappointment Revisited: Unweaving the Tangled Web', *American Music*, 1 (1983), 12–35, and 2 (1984), 1–28; citation from a widely disseminated early press release for the 1976 performances, as reprinted in the first part of Rabson's article, p. 19. The misunderstanding regarding Raccoon's group identity had been lovingly fostered by theatre historians since the 1930s. (One writer even argued, with astonishing *naïveté*, that the play proves that 'no color line was drawn in New York at this time'—quoted in Rabson, pt. 1, p. 18.) The evidence proffered by such scholars consisted primarily of the character's non-standard English and the name 'Raccoon'; the clear assumption (unsupported) is that the name must have been a neutral, or even affectionate, precursor of the pejorative term 'coon', familiar from nineteenth-century minstrel show lyrics and the songs later made famous by 'coon shouters' such as May Irwin (see H. Wiley Hitchcock and Stanley Sadie (eds.), *New Grove Dictionary of American Music* (London, 1986), s.v. 'coon song').

[66] Rabson, 'Disappointment Revisited', based in part on research of Irving Lowens and Patricia Virga. Rabson concludes, on the basis of Raccoon's particular dialect of English and his statement that he cannot speak High German, that he is Pennsylvania Dutch. The name may refer to a military regiment or to 'caps made of coonskin, used by backwoodsmen' (pt. 1, p. 25). Thanks to timely intervention by Rabson, the full and vocal scores of the 1976 version endorse her reading of Raccoon as German: Andrew Barton, *The Disappointment, or The Force of Credulity: 1767*, ed. Jerald C. Graue and Judith Layng, musical accompaniments by Samuel Adler (Madison, 1976). For many of the songs, though, Rabson's article provides more appropriate tunes (or an earlier or more 'authentic' source of the same tune) than those in the Graue–Layng edn.

dealing with western art-music)—engage in, whether or not in the musical sphere, and whether or not in our professional lives generally.

We would do well, first of all, to reflect on the choices that we make day by day in the work we do. It is easy to fall into a routine of one sort or another, and even to justify as highly principled what is really more an avoidance of an unpleasant or discouraging task. Take the famed conflict between teaching and research. It is a fact that doing *either* top-notch research *or* excellent, innovative teaching— much less *both*—can easily absorb a musicologist's entire time and energy (and this is not to mention the additional responsibilities that come with an academic position, such as curricular, search, and tenure committees, student advising, fund raising). Each of us makes choices all the time, which inevitably means giving less attention to some of our commitments than we might ideally like. But it is also easy for us to use our desire or obligation to do research as an excuse for not applying ourselves sufficiently to our teaching, or the opposite: to use our devotion to our students as an excuse for not getting around to writing up our research and sharing it with others in the field. (I've noticed that I make one or another of these excuses to myself at different points in the year.)

Rather than set research and teaching against each other, though, I would suggest that in each of these areas we need, at least periodically, to examine *what* we are doing, and *how* and *why*. A 1991 survey of German musicologists (in the *Neue Zeitschrift für Musik*) on the state of 'academic musical scholarship' brought the repeated call for a 'reflective discussion of method' such as has 'long ago recorded significant results in neighbouring disciplines'.[67] Several respondents went further, reporting that there *used* to be such discussions in some earlier, almost golden era: 'There are next to no larger methodological or conceptual controversies going on any more' in the field.[68]

As I write these lines, just a few years later, there surely can no longer be any doubt (perhaps even in Germany) that 'reflective discussions' and 'conceptual controversies' are indeed reinvigorating the field of musicology.[69] Many of us, at least in English-speaking countries, would personally date the wake-up call to our first encounters with the thinking of Carl Dahlhaus, or to Joseph Kerman's sometimes prickly proclamations, or to mind-opening articles by Ruth A. Solie, Leo Treitler, Janet Levy, or Rose Rosengard Subotnik, or to the constant stream of challenging essays from the pen of Edward T. Cone or Leonard B. Meyer.[70]

---

[67] Siegfried Mauser, cited in Lotte Thaler (ed.), 'Forum: Musikwissenschaft—quo vadis?', *Neue Zeitschrift für Musik*, 152/2 (2 Feb. 1991), 13–21 (citation from p. 19, echoed by Martin Zenck on p. 21).

[68] Ibid. 19 (Fritz Reckow). Peter Schleuning similarly sees progress in 'philological' research (Bach, Beethoven, early music) but 'substantial steps backward' in sociological and aesthetic areas of research (20). Hermann Danuser, too, emphasizes a moment of past glory for those who would broaden musicology's methodological reach: Dahlhaus's death tore 'an uncloseable hole' in the field (20).

[69] Evidence for this includes the present book and Philip Brett, Elizabeth Wood, and Gary C. Thomas (eds.), *Queering the Pitch: The New Gay and Lesbian Musicology* (New York, 1994); Bergeron and Bohlman (eds.), *Disciplining Music*; Solie (ed.), *Musicology and Difference*.

[70] Carl Dahlhaus, *Foundations of Music History*; Joseph Kerman, *Contemplating Music: Challenges to Musicology* (Cambridge, Mass., 1985), esp. 113–81; Solie, 'The Living Work'; Leo Treitler, *Music and the Historical Imagination*

We should resist, though, the urge to congratulate ourselves—as some literary critics have recently tended to do—on our new-found (or ongoing) willingness to question the concepts and methods upon which our own field has been based.[71] For, despite much recent progress in this area, social questions still remain. Furthermore, such progress does not receive universal endorsement. Indeed, people who object to feminist and other challenging new approaches—in musicology as in other fields—raise specific objections that often hinge, precisely, on social questions and that thereby gain a certain rhetorical advantage, the critic tarring the 'social' musicologist with the latter's own brush. Some complain that scholars are falling in line with academic 'fashion' (and thus sacrificing the responsibility to exercise considered judgement, to produce work that will be trustworthy and of lasting value);[72] some note pointedly that scholars who claim to be concerned with social ramifications of their art often seclude themselves from popular scrutiny by adopting an inscrutable jargon drawn from French Freudianism or whatever;[73] and, increasingly, one hears regret that musicologists and other who seek to demystify the *objets d'art* that Western society has long held up for admiration are denying the aesthetic aspects of those works and thus (most often unintentionally) weakening public interest in serious music generally.[74]

Such objections are often palpably unfair: they may at times bespeak a quickness to stigmatize and suppress what is sometimes called the 'New Musicology'. After all, new approaches, which I take as signs of vitality, cannot reasonably be expected to offer the secure, predictable results of less risky, more established (and often more declaredly limited) approaches.[75] Still, I would take the objections of the conservative critics seriously (they, too, are signs of health), only I

(Cambridge, Mass., 1989); Levy, 'Covert and Casual Values'; Subotnik, *Developing Variations*; Edward T. Cone, *Music, A View from Delft: Selected Essays*, ed. Robert P. Morgan (Chicago, 1989); Leonard B. Meyer, *Music, the Arts, and Ideas: Patterns and Predictions in Twentieth-Century Culture*, 2nd edn. (Chicago, 1994); idem, *Style and Music: Theory, History, and Ideology* (Philadelphia, 1989), 163–217 (on e.g. declining audience sophistication).

[71] Gerald Graff has been particularly active in defending recent literary criticism against charges that it is arcane and self-indulgent. I sense special pleading in his argument that such research is not at all a form of 'narcissistic specialization', but rather a trend toward 'new languages of generalization'. (Positivist minutiae, after all, are often far less arcane to the general reader than certain forms of philosophical speculation and theoretical generalization, e.g. Lacanian analysis.) To his credit, though, he goes on to argue that scholars have not tried hard enough to find ways to explain their work to outsiders: 'academic humanists need to take some responsibility for controlling the ways their ideas and projects are represented to a wider public.' Allowing others to do it for them, he adds, increases the risk of ignorant 'caricature' ('The Scholar in Society', in Joseph Gibaldi (ed.), *Introduction to Scholarship in Modern Languages and Literature*, 2nd edn. (New York, 1992), 343–62; citations from 353, 354).

[72] 'Modethemen' ('fashionable topics') is the objection that Thaler imagines (i.e. has heard?) people raising to various new seminars at German universities ('Forum', 13). 'Trendsville' is the put-down favoured by one American musicologist (reported in Ellen Rosand, 'The Musicology of the Present', *AMS Newsletter*, 25/1 (Feb. 1995), 8–10).

[73] David Bromwich, *Politics by Other Means: Higher Education and Group Thinking* (New Haven, 1992); Leon Botstein, review of Bergeron and Bohlman (eds.), *Disciplining Music*, *JAMS* 47 (1994), 340–7.

[74] Harold Bloom, *The Western Canon: The Books and School of the Ages* (New York, 1994), esp. 517–28. I argue similarly, though without bashing more commercial forms of culture, in 'Music Lovers', 169–73.

[75] I echo here the brief but trenchant comments of Robert W. Fink, editorial, *repercussions*, 1/1 (Spring 1992), 104–5, regarding a 'wary' (as he notes) discussion of papers at the 1991 American Musicological Society meeting (Edward Rothstein, 'The Politics of Sharps and Flats', *New York Times*, 17 Nov. 1991).

would pose them to the whole field and its practitioners. Scholarly work is predicated, as H. H. Eggebrecht noted in the longest single response to the aforementioned 1991 questionnaire, on 'seeking and finding, in *freedom* and *a sense of personal accountability* (*in Freiheit und Selbstverantwortung*), one's own conception of musicology'.[76] This pairing of conditions seems to me crucial and worthy of elaboration: freedom to explore new approaches must be balanced by concern for making our work as closely argued as we can, as 'responsible', and as persuasive to others—especially to those who might be sceptical or who do not share all our working assumptions. Rose Subotnik, who experienced in the 1970s and 1980s a good deal of institutional resistance to the Adorno-inspired questioning that she was bringing to bear on the field, has none the less stressed the importance of remaining as 'honest' as possible (her refreshing word) in our self-criticism and in our presentation of our arguments.[77]

Eggebrecht, elsewhere in his essay, makes a somewhat similar point, but his wording carries a very different charge. Musicologists, he urges, should be 'eager to learn the tools of musicology'—presumably including processes of argument and the interpretation of evidence—'and to use them cleanly and soundly' (*sauber und gediegen*).[78] I am surely not alone in finding the *sauber* redolent of concepts of Nordic racial purity. (The word *gediegen*, too, has troubling overtones: *gediegenes Gold*, for example, is unalloyed by baser metals.) But, even if we restrict our associative field to musicology proper, Eggebrecht's motto mistakenly implies that certain procedural norms are universally recognized by 'clean and sound' (i.e. responsible) scholars, and can be confidently invoked so as to weigh—and thus validate or invalidate—the work of newcomers. Subotnik is, to my mind, much *more* responsible than Eggebrecht, in that she goes on to balance her call for honesty (on the part of non-traditionalist scholars) with a warning to scholars in positions of power who would too quickly reject and suppress unfamiliar approaches: '[Accusations of irresponsibility and] incompetence ought not to be automatically accepted as the actual basis on which traditionalists deny the non-traditionalist a platform or professional footing, especially when there seems to be a pattern of ideological discrimination.'[79]

Whatever their differences, though, Subotnik and Eggebrecht stress one point in common: we should strive to do our chosen work as well, as reliably, as thoughtfully as we can. Such a principle is, of course, hardly new, being one of the ethical imperatives of various religions and world philosophies. (An early and oft-quoted instance: 'Whatsoever thy hand findeth to do, do it with all thy might'—Ecclesiastes 9: 10.)[80] It also forms a component of the identity of a 'pro-

---

[76] H. H. Eggebrecht's response, entitled 'Blickpunkt Musikwissenschaft', published in Thaler, 'Forum', 15–17; citation from p. 15, emphasis added.

[77] Subotnik, *Developing Variations*, 93.

[78] Eggebrecht, 'Blickpunkt Musikwissenschaft', 15.

[79] Subotnik, *Developing Variations*, 323 n.

[80] Similar injunctions may be found in (among others) Socrates, the songs of the Shakers, the preachings of the current Pope, and the wall plaques hand-made by the Roycrofters, a prominent Arts and Crafts collective in East

fessional', as embodied, for example, in the Hippocratic oath. When we take upon ourselves the mantle of learned authority, whether as teachers or writers, a sense of moral obligation and accountability should also come with it.

That obligation, though, is not a simple one (certainly not as simple as certain academic traditionalists—including, presumably, Eggebrecht—imply). For one thing, whose musical/educational needs are we obligated to serve? Shall we direct our energies entirely toward the students in our classrooms, plus the few specialists who may read our articles? In so doing, shall we hope that worthy scholarly insights will trickle down or outward to the general population, presumably through the efforts of others? Perhaps we should instead reach out ourselves to that public directly, through encyclopedia articles, feature pieces in newspapers and magazines, reviews (of concerts, recordings, and books), and the various electronic media (radio programmes, educational tape cassettes and videos, and now CD-ROM products).

Of course, to the extent that we do some of these things, we must also negotiate various pressures on us. Editors often want us to simplify, to engage in rhetorical overstatement (e.g. slash-and-burn language), in order to solicit and hold the reader's attention. We, for our own part, presumably share the aim of reaching out to the reader, and admit the need to simplify to a degree, but may not feel comfortable with the tactics proposed, feeling that they risk turning complex issues into consumable, unenlightening—and at times actively misleading—entertainment.[81]

Even in the more protected spheres in which most of us do most of our work—university classrooms and professional conferences and publications—our 'obligation' is not clear-cut. It is certainly not the old-fashioned obligation to tell the 'truth', as if we were witnesses in a court of law. No version of the truth is straightforward, objective, and unproblematic enough that we can simply recount it and walk away feeling unassailably virtuous. Explaining how a piece 'works', or how a genre 'developed', or how a Mozart opera 'reflects and also subverts' gender ideologies of its day: all these require us to *construct* an image of reality. But the twin principles of freedom and responsibility (accountability) hold that we be explicit about our methodological and ideological suppositions. This is one of Janet Levy's strongest arguments against the habitual use of metaphors of 'organic unity', 'rich complexity', 'contrapuntal density', 'concentrated expression', and so on: not that they are demonstrably 'untrue'

---

Aurora, New York, *c.*1905. One can appreciate the positive aspects of such mottoes without endorsing the quietist obedience to authority that they have often helped to enforce.

[81] A particular disappointment is the new classical magazine *TuTTi*, which focuses on (often spurious or inadequately contextualized) anecdotes about composers' (sex) lives. Some of my favourite positive examples of how to sail between the rocks of populism and accuracy/nuance are the articles in the *New Harvard Dictionary of Music*, the *New Yorker* columns of Andrew Porter and (now) Paul Griffiths, and certain feature pieces in the *New York Times* and elsewhere by Michael Beckerman, Will Crutchfield, Joseph Horowitz, K. Robert Schwarz, David Schiff, and Richard Taruskin. The CD-ROM products by Robert Winter (especially that for Dvořák's *New World Symphony*, marketed by Voyager) show what can be done in that realm by a combination of imagination and musical acuity.

(whatever that might mean) when applied to a given work of, say, Schubert, but that the value system to which they adhere is left totally unspoken, as if assumed, evident, and universally valid.[82]

Levy's argument, as she herself notes, really extends to the whole range of loaded metaphors that we often use unthinkingly to confer value on the music we study and, in the process, to assert the significance of our own observations. (Claiming to find the secret of a great work's beauty or meaning redounds, as I noted earlier, to the honour of the person making the claim.) But Levy's strongest point of all, to my mind, is that such covert infusions of aesthetic and social ideology cut off further enquiry, instead of encouraging it.[83] In other words, they replace open argument with closed dogma; for critical reflection they substitute self-satisfied labelling.

Levy's critique may be extended to other aspects of musicological work. Earlier in the chapter I noted (and supported) the growing call for more explorations of the social contexts of music-making. The call is of course already being responded to, partly within and partly outside the field. Philip Bohlman (a musicologist, in this case) gives a good example of how, I think, one should present a social analysis: in a brief but thought-provoking discussion of outdoor concerts in America, he frankly invokes images of music's complicity in various forms of Foucauldian 'order', 'policing', and cultural 'hegemony'. Social repression, he asserts, is at work in the ways that 'town bands and summer orchestras' transform and, in a sense, colonize public spaces by 'using music as a metaphor for the order of the park [which itself stands] as a context of [social] order'.[84] Many readers will wish to argue with this analysis: that they feel invited to do so is the result of Bohlman's having made overt the conceptual underpinnings of his argument.

Lawrence W. Levine (a cultural historian, as it happens), discusses this same phenomenon at much greater length, and reaches conclusions that, though not couched in Foucauldian language, would probably be happily endorsed by Bohlman. By contrast with Bohlman, though, Levine presents himself, quite misleadingly, as an unbiased recoverer of historical fact. This is not to say that his findings are entirely off base. Quite the contrary, much of what he asserts and demonstrates is convincing and important: for example, that America's concert and operatic life has moved from relatively democratic structures, such as the park bandstand in the mid-nineteenth century, to hierarchically organized ones, in which only certain élite repertories were/are permitted to be performed and, crucially, in which certain classes of people set the tone, ticket prices, and stan-

---

[82] Levy, 'Covert and Casual Values', 27. Another insightful remark of Levy's is that chamber music is often praised for being at once aristocratic and democratic, thus getting the music blessed by both ideological worlds (ibid. 14).

[83] Ibid. 25, 27.

[84] Bohlman, 'Musicology as a Political Act', 433.

dards of behaviour, thereby making people of lesser means feel less comfortable participating.[85] But, in the process of proving this point, Levine silently suppresses (or sometimes cavalierly dismisses) evidence of countervailing trends that led certain kinds of musicians and music-lovers to feel the need to create institutions of high culture in the first place. For instance, Levine reveals no awareness that the pot-pourri concerts of the mid-nineteenth-century bands often limited themselves to lighter or shorter works (Hérold and Suppé overtures rather than Beethoven or Schumann symphonies), and that the commercial opera companies of the same period were able to mount, at best, some rather ramshackle performances of a small number of 'hit-tune'-type operas, such as Donizetti's *Lucia di Lammermoor*. It was only the advent of the non-profit performing organization that enabled music-lovers of varied social backgrounds to hear well-rehearsed performances of major complex works, such as the Brahms Violin Concerto, Wagner's *Die Walküre*, or the Debussy String Quartet. If Levine had been franker about his attempts to rewrite American cultural history, readers would have been readier to interrogate his conclusions, instead of swallowing them whole, as many of them (and many reviewers) have done.[86]

It is hard to know what kind of mechanism might help us monitor such hidden agendas and distortions. Perhaps the existing ones are still the best: using book reviews, articles, and papers in professional forums to challenge and bring more nuance to other scholars' work. One way or another, though, we should be keeping our eyes open, and training our students to keep theirs open, to the hidden messages in work that presents itself as objective scholarship.[87] And this may mean reminding them of the silences in our own courses, and not only those intended for graduate students in musicology. On the simple level of repertoire studied, we might wish to point out (with short taped or 'live' examples, to briefly break this silence?) that the music we are studying in a course or unit on, say, 'Music in Paris, 1800–50' (e.g. by Méhul, Rossini, Berlioz, Meyerbeer, Auber, Chopin, Liszt) was only one rather thin stratum of a multi-layered musical culture that also included four-hand sight-readings of Haydn symphonies in the parlour, the sentimental but not unartful songs of Puget (mentioned earlier), the political songs of Béranger and various working-class poets, military and civic band music, quadrilles and waltzes for social dancing, and various contending

[85] Levine, *Highbrow/Lowbrow*, 85–168, 177–201.

[86] Further on Levine's use of evidence and rhetoric, see Locke, 'Music Patrons', 153–4 (including n. 16), 157–9, 168–9, 171–2; for reviews of his work, see 153 nn. 17–18, 155–6 (including n. 26), 158, and 167 n. 81.

[87] It is not impossible that this issue will be touched upon in the American Musicological Society's statement on ethics, currently being drafted, notably under the first of the eight headings currently projected, 'scholarly integrity'; the others are 'cultural diversity; peer review procedures; authorship and acknowledgement; responsibility to students and to colleagues in the work-place and scholarly community, and to the community-at-large; freedom of inquiry; and issues related to technological advances in information access and exchange' (*AMS Newsletter*, 24/2 (Aug. 1994), 5).

traditions of Catholic liturgical music, not to speak of numerous oral repertoires rooted in the countryside: lullabies, work songs, and so on.[88]

This same approach might apply to all sorts of other agendas—social, ideological, aesthetic—that give clarity and backbone, but also, inevitably, a certain 'slant', to our teaching. We teach more effectively, more truly, if we try to restrain a tendency to promote our own solutions to various questions about music and instead teach methods of examining such questions or, at the very least, are frank about what our premises are (as Levy argues that we should do in our scholarly writings). In so restraining—or declaring—ourselves, we help students to feel empowered to evaluate what they are hearing from us and so to arrive at answers of their own.


## V. The Music Scholar (Musician, Academic) and the World

This last concern, about the problem of social messages in our teaching, especially of undergraduate 'non-majors' (who are, in a sense, the 'outside world' in miniature), leads inevitably to the ultimate broad question: what of the possibilities of engaging with the larger world? Certain Left-leaning educators in the United States have, under the umbrella of the term 'cultural pedagogy', proposed that writers, scholars, and artists use their knowledge, critical sophistication, articulateness, and privileged social position to help reassert a non-élitist cultural policy for the country and a serious incorporation of cultural products and processes into the public schools and the media.[89] (Privilege is relative. In North America and Great Britain, and no doubt elsewhere as well, academics tend not to feel privileged, perhaps because we imagine that we could have been making more money—and had more direct impact on the outside world—in another line of work. Yet privileged many of us surely are, in comparison to the bulk of our country's citizens, never mind those of certain other countries.)

The phrase 'cultural pedagogy' is misleadingly innocuous: after all, educators of varied stripes have always aimed at achieving a successful cultural pedagogy,

---

[88] Some but not all of this is treated in Locke, 'Paris', and in Peter Bloom (ed.), *Music in Paris in the 1830s* (New York, 1987); Jean Mongrédien, *La Musique en France des lumières au romantisme* (Paris, 1986); and the collective work *La Musique en France à l'époque romantique: 1830–1870* (Paris, 1991). On workers' choruses, see Paul Gerbod, 'Vox Populi', in *La Musique en France*, 231–55, 313–14, as well as Fulcher, 'Orphéon Societies'. On the tradition of the literary and political song, see my 'The Music of the French Chanson, 1800–50', in Bloom (ed.), *Music in Paris*, 431–56. For more thoughts on ways to incorporate musical traditions beyond that of Western art-music, see Ch. 24 below.

[89] Unfortunately, David Trend, in his stimulating *Cultural Pedagogy: Art/Education/Politics* (New York, 1992), confuses the issue of who cultural workers are by including groups whose relationship to social issues is clearly more direct (and thus less mysterious, less problematic) than that of a composer, an oboist, or even a musicologist: e.g. lawyers, social workers, architects, doctors and nurses, theologians, and schoolteachers. Still, he deserves credit, to my mind, for trying to reassert a non-élitist cultural policy and for recognizing the mixed strengths and weaknesses of both private and public patronage for the arts. (See further on Trend and other proponents of 'cultural pedagogy' in Locke, 'Music Patrons', 163, 170.)

one that implants a love and understanding of some version of 'culture'.[90] The real question, then, is: What/whose culture? The attempt to defend or reinstall a conservative culture in the educational system—as in the writings of Allan Bloom or in recent British attempts at dismantling the relatively non-élitist National Curriculum—is equally an instance of social concern, with the significant difference that the cultural programme in question is quite different, as is, presumably, the social one. I say 'presumably', because it is unfair to assume that culturally conservative critics such as Bloom, who support static conceptions of 'great literature' and advertise their disgust with rock music, are *necessarily* conservatives in the political or social realm. Many people of liberal and Left-radical leanings are beginning to express similar (if not identical) concerns about certain aspects of popular culture that they find degraded and degrading. Feminists in the anti-pornography movement, for example, often express the hope that reducing the level of violence in films and rock music will lead to a reduced incidence of violence and sexual assault against women.[91]

'Whoa!' some may say. 'First the public-school curriculum, and now rape prevention? What does all this have to do with us?' Indeed, just what are the spheres of action in which music scholars might most productively lend a hand? Public musical life is clearly one such field. Some musicologists working from within a neo-Marxist tradition (e.g. Georg Knepler and Hanns-Werner Heister) stress that we should be doing what we can to encourage musical literacy and music-making among the general populace.[92] Ethnomusicologist Margaret Kartomi is particularly forceful on this point, arguing that the musical (and more broadly cultural) health of a society is indicated by the extent to which people make music instead of taking it in passively through the commercial mass media.[93]

For that matter, *which* society should receive our attention? The one to which we pay taxes? the one that we happen to study professionally? the world as a whole? Many musicologists feel themselves to be citizens of the world, perhaps more so than academics in certain other fields. (I imagine that this is related to the relative ease with which music crosses many, though hardly all, barriers of language and culture.) At the same time, we can often take action most effectively in arenas close to home. Some of us have over the years received petitions for world peace from fellow academics in such places as Japan or what was then East Germany, and I know that I am not alone in having hesitated to sign, since I was given no clear sense of how or by whom such documents might be used.

---

[90] By contrast, people who promote a non-Eurocentric curriculum are generally, and to their credit, frank about their aims, flying the 'multicultural' banner as they march into the public arena.

[91] Catherine A. MacKinnon, *Just Words* (Cambridge, Mass., 1993).

[92] Georg Knepler, 'Music Historiography in Eastern Europe', in Barry S. Brook, Edward O. D. Downes, and Sherman van Solkema (eds.), *Perspectives in Musicology* (New York, 1972), 22–48; Heister, *Das Konzert*, ii. 512, 538–40. Further on Heister's views see my 'Music Patrons', 171.

[93] Margaret J. Kartomi, editorial introduction to Kartomi and Stephen Blum (eds.), *Music-Cultures in Contact: Convergences and Collisions* (New York, 1994).

Most of us, I suspect, also declined to intervene when several musicologists sent a message through E-mail asking that we protest the Spanish government's decision to close musicology departments in the universities and to concentrate such activity in the conservatories instead. (I recall reasoning to myself: 'Maybe the decision is a sound, practical one, given limited resources'.)[94] Of course, the relative trivialness of this last issue compared to the grandiosity of the previous one—world peace—reveals something of the helplessness with which we face the world at large. Perhaps it is at the middle level—with issues bigger than musicology but smaller than ending war—that something of largish social significance can actually be accomplished. Alas, on those middle-level issues we have perhaps little knowledge and certainly little special influence. Should we join the fight anyway—as 'mere' laity, concerned citizens?

I would say yes: musicians (including music scholars), like any other individuals, have to learn to take an active role in the shaping of a juster society, rather than always quietly tending their/our own garden. It may be encouraging, as we face this problem of reaching beyond music to effect change in the larger world, to remember that we are not the first people in music to do so. As was hinted in section II, envisaging and working toward an active role *beyond* music became a real possibility for many prominent musicians in the nineteenth century— witness Giuseppe Verdi, who served in the national assembly of a newly united Italy in 1861–5 (though he attended irregularly). In our own century, Ignace Jan Paderewski served proudly as Prime Minister and Minister of Foreign Affairs of a newly independent Poland in 1919–21. (In both cases the popular pressure to get these musicians involved in directing the nation's fate was plainly a response to the nationalist thrust of some of their music.)[95] Using music to carry a message, or using one's own prominence or privileged position to try to influence society, became a more comprehensive possibility in the 1930s and 1940s, as seen especially in the Leftist political compositions of Hanns Eisler and Marc Blitzstein, but also in the overtly democratic or populist 'message' compositions of Kurt Weill ('Down in the Valley') and Aaron Copland ('A Lincoln Portrait') and of many composers living in Communist societies. Performers, too, have sometimes stepped forth to embody the hopes of their fellow citizens: one thinks of Myra Hess consoling her British listeners by playing daily lunch-time recitals during World War II (including some over the radio, during the bombing of London) or Marian Anderson singing on the steps of the Lincoln Memorial to 75,000 listeners in 1939 (after she had been denied the use

---

[94] Similarly, American academics offered little protest when tenured East German professors were replaced, with questionable legality, by West Germans during the recent reunification process. See Peter Marcuse, 'Purging the Professoriat: Fear and Loathing in the Former East German Academy', *Lingua franca*, 2/2 (Dec. 1991), 32–6. The final issues of the now defunct East German *Beiträge zur Musikwissenschaft*, notably 33/1 (1991), featured thoughtful statements by Knepler, Maróthy, and others.

[95] George W. Martin, *Verdi: His Music, Life, and Times* (New York, 1963), 298–320; Mary Jane Phillips-Matz, *Verdi: A Biography* (New York, 1993), 425–39. On Paderewski's nationalist opera *Manru*, see James Parakilas, 'The Soldier and the Exotic', *Opera Quarterly*, 10/2 (Winter 1994), 35–56, 10/3 (Spring 1994), 43–69, esp. 45–50.

of the Daughters of the American Revolution's Constitution Hall because of her African origin).

The options, the varieties of engagement, increase as we approach our own day, including such things as various musicians' creative responses to the AIDS crisis (such as the songs written for baritone William Parker in the early 1990s[96]), Michael Tippett's oratorio *A Child of Our Time*, Leonard Bernstein's outspoken involvement in a variety of political and social issues (not least the anti-war movement of the 1960s), and Vytautis Landsbergis's becoming Prime Minister of Lithuania (and thus no doubt the first musicologist to become a prominent actor in history-making events). The list goes on: feminist song-writer Holly Near, South African rock musician Johnny Clegg, and, to return to the 'classical music' scene, Kurt Masur, the distinguished East German conductor who, in a potentially incendiary situation, helped steer his country toward giving up, without violence and blood-letting, unworkable political and economic structures.

In most of these instances, the musician in question acts *as* a musician—that is, through her or his various musical activities. In a few, she or he addresses social and political issues more directly, though with a voice that carries far, thanks to the access to the mass media that comes with public eminence. These same two paths are open, if inevitably on a more modest scale, to other, less famed musicians and music scholars. As classroom teachers and writers, for example, we can help shape other people's views by doing such things as stressing music's social contexts (see Section II above), by drawing attention to the active roles of women in musical life, by exposing people to musics of other cultures, and by opening their eyes to the implications of the commercial musics that surround them in their daily lives.[97]

We should also not forget that we affect people at our place of employment and in other professional settings simply by the way in which we interact with them, as fellow human beings: the principles of honesty, accountability, tolerance, and simple civility and fairness noted earlier in regard to published research are that much more crucial (because more damaging if absent) in our daily encounters with other individuals, especially those over whom we exert some measure of power (untenured faculty, clerical staff, students, and of course

---

[96] A selection of the songs is now recorded (*The AIDS Quilt Songbook*, Harmonia Mundi CD 907602). One composer of AIDS-inspired music, Conrad Cummings, speaks of 'the eventual political ramification' of such artistic work: 'if some unexpected connection is made between a private emotion and a public topic, that will have an effect on a person's action. At the least, you are very definitely stirring the waters' (K. Robert Schwarz, 'Playing (and Singing) Politics', *New York Times*, Sunday, 23 May 1993, sect. H, p. 20).

[97] I would propose, for example, that music history teachers who remain committed primarily to teaching Western art-music none the less bring into the story relevant examples of folk, urban-popular, and non-Western musics— e.g. presenting an early twentieth-century recording of a Polish village band when discussing Chopin's mazurkas, or a Sidney Bechet cut when presenting Milhaud's *La Création du monde*. (One must of course use such comparisons with care: the folk-music recording, one must make clear, may differ greatly from what Chopin himself heard a century earlier; the Bechet is artful in itself rather than just interesting raw material for a 'real' composer, etc.)

the young scholars—from other institutions—whose manuscripts and grant applications we are asked to evaluate). The illusion that academics are powerless can easily become an excuse for neglecting the one sphere in which we *are* able to (indeed, are *paid* to) be influential, help nurture others, and serve as models of forthrightness (blended with tactfulness, in some magical proportion), open-mindedness (balanced by a certain intellectual passion that others may perceive as stubbornness), imagination, articulateness, common sense, and, sometimes, the courage to fly in the face of that same common sense.[98] Of course, such considerations form at best a behavioural ideal that none of us will ever attain in practice, given the various limitations noted earlier, such as the contending demands on our time. Still, this does not mean that the ideal should remain—as it so often seems now—an embarrassment never to be uttered in polite company.

Then there is the world outside music and the academy. Academics and intellectuals generally, as John McGowan points out in his *Postmodernism and its Critics*, often swing between overvaluing and undervaluing the power of thought to influence the world. On the one hand, he notes, we may sometimes fall into the trap of believing that we make a sufficient contribution, perhaps the highest of all, through the search for truth or through ever-increasing theoretical and critico-political sophistication.

> The fallacy of intellectual work's direct political efficacy takes two forms: the foundationalist (ultimately platonic) notion that apprehension of the true will guide all action and the critique[-based] dream that knowing that some social form is invalid will cause it to topple. Postmodernism has thoroughly attacked the [former] . . . but at times retains the critique's idealist assertion of thought's omnipotence.[99]

On the other hand, we may sometimes feel—perhaps upon waking from our flattering 'critique dream'—that nothing we do will have any measurable impact on what students and professors alike, in an anxiety-laden, supposedly humorous phrase, call 'the real world'.

The solution, McGowan concludes, is to engage in a 'pragmatic politics', a 'political action [that] takes place at local sites as a specific response to specific ongoing societal practices and arrangements'.[100] We musicologists, no less than other intellectuals, presumably bring more knowledge to bear on issues of current contention than do less well-educated citizens. Furthermore, we have skills that are far from widespread, including an ability to write persuasively and to analyse other people's evidence and arguments (helpful in exposing manipulative rhetoric). And, quite apart from the question of special knowledge or skills, we are as free as almost anyone in the world to speak up for causes in which we believe and to seek to persuade others to fight alongside us.

---

[98] This also means refusing to turn the teaching situation into the passing on of rigid doctrines, of whatever kind. (See the vivid anecdote about the high-school student in Leo Treitler, 'On Responsibility and Relevance in Humanistic Disciplines', *Daedalus*, 98 (1969), 844–52.)

[99] McGowan, *Postmodernism and its Critics*, 275.          [100] Ibid. 278.

In proposing that an individual musician or music scholar (and, I would add, each of the various larger musical communities and professional societies) take a stand on certain of the larger, pressing issues of our day, I realize that I am raising a topic that is rarely broached in our professional forums. The one notable exception (at the moment) is the fairly active discussion of how racism and sexism can be combated in the institutions in which we work and in our professional societies themselves. Another phenomenon that could certainly fall well within an academic's purview, as John McGowan points out, is the unfair or even exploitative employment practices at certain academic institutions—for example, the increasing reliance, these days, on part-time faculty in non-tenurable slots.[101] The real world, like charity, begins at home, and at work.

Certain music scholars have in the past distinguished themselves, in my view, on a somewhat broader front: namely, by taking a public stand against unjust American military actions (e.g. Vincent Duckles, during the Vietnam War, and Leo Treitler, during the Bush administration's publicity build-up to the Gulf War of 1991[102]). Various readers will have their own, perhaps very different models of principled behaviour and involvement in pressing social and political issues. These may well, for example, include people who work at what I described as 'middle-level problems': for protecting the environment, for better street lighting (so that people can walk safely at night), for sobriety behind the wheel, for universal health care or against drug abuse, for the prevention of spouse abuse and rape, and for better education in poor urban neighbourhoods. And to this very incomplete list I would add the ongoing need for us all to work against intolerance and religious, racial, and gender prejudice wherever we encounter them.

There is no one right answer to the question posed at the outset of this chapter, which might be rephrased: How can a musicologist make a difference in the world? There is no one path; nor are we all even standing at the same crossroads or heading in the same direction (nor, I would argue, should we be, except on large issues such as human rights and equality of opportunity). But I suggest that the isolation of which we sometimes complain might well be lessened by

---

[101] Ibid. 277.

[102] The anti-war and boldly internationalist activities of Vincent and Madeline Duckles are summarized by Joseph Kerman in a brief memoir printed in *Cum notis variorum*, 95 (Aug.–Sept. 1985), 8–9. (The couple brought a Vietnamese girl named Thuy to live with them for an extended time, so that her face, disfigured by a grenade, could undergo surgical repair.) Treitler wrote a forceful, memorable letter on Bush's militant foreign policy, published in the *New York Times* (Sunday, 27 Jan. 1991, Sect. 4, p. 16), and was one of many notable signatories to a petition published in the same paper. Treitler explores the Gulf War—and the whole problem of (political, musical, etc.) 'reality' and its varying representations—in his 'Postmodern Signs in Musical Studies', *Journal of Musicology*, 13 (1995), 3–17. At the same time, I do not intend to castigate as smug business-as-usual conservatives and careerists those who choose to focus their attention on more strictly professional matters. In this I echo Kermit Vanderbilt's assessment of the unfortunate polarization that occurred during the Vietnam War between some resurgent younger members of the Modern Language Association and older members (and officers), representatives of the Ivy establishment (*American Literature and the Academy: The Roots, Growth, and Maturity of a Profession* (Philadelphia, 1986), pp. xvi–xxii, and 552 n. 5).

raising that question and then trying to provide ourselves with answers to it—
or, if not answers, then small hints, gentle reminders—in the articles we write,
in the way we carry out our duties at our place of employment, in our activities
as members of the local, national, and international musical and musicological
communities, and in our varied initiatives as informed citizens and members of
the human race.[103]

---

[103] The present chapter has profited from readings by Jonathan Baldo, Philip V. Bohlman, Robert Fink, Robert Haskins, Ellen Koskoff, James Parakilas, and Jürgen Thym, although none of them should be held responsible for its contents. The author also wishes to thank Craig Harwood and Janet Wolff for helpful advice at crucial moments.

# 23

## The Impact and Ethics of Musical Scholarship

### Kay Kaufman Shelemay

If the discussion of music in context has become an increasingly important part of the musicological conversation in the late twentieth century, discourse about the broader implications of musicological research emphatically has not.[1] This chapter will deal with the potential impact of music scholarship outside academia and, in particular, upon its ostensible subjects. Though instances of such impact may be infrequent, I will suggest that they raise a host of important ethical and practical issues both during the research process and afterwards.

A concern with the implications of music scholarship presupposes a commitment to approach music in a broader cultural context. Indeed, the conviction that music has a long and deep relationship to other cultural arenas has driven ethnomusicological research for most of the twentieth century.[2] As historical musicologists have begun to enter into a more nuanced consideration of the relationship between music and society,[3] they have frequently found themselves on the same slippery ground that ethnomusicologists have long trod, raising admittedly important questions for which some answers are more convincing than others. Yet, if charting the relationship between music and context remains a challenging and not always fully realizable goal for scholarship, its theoretical frameworks and working methods have at least begun to be widely debated.[4] The broader impact of musicological scholarship, however, has not generally been a

---

[1] I use the term 'musicology' in the most general sense to incorporate historical, systematic, and ethnomusicological aspects of the field.

[2] While the search for homologies between music and extra-musical domains has been an increasingly prominent goal of more recent ethnomusicological enquiry, the successful outcome of such research is by no means assured. In some cases homologies appear to be present and quite well marked; a notable example is the striking correlation between musical cycles and calendrical cycles in Java (Judith Becker, 'Time and Tune in Java', in A. L. Becker and Aram A. Yengoyan (eds.), *The Imagination of Reality* (Norwood, NJ, 1979), 197–210). However, all too frequently, the search for homologies has moved simplistically between the musical surface and an aspect of social structure. The classical example of such an interpretative process is that of Alan Lomax's cantometrics, which analyses song in various social settings through a methodology that interrogates the social structure of music, travelling a circular path to arrive at the hypothesis with which it began (*Folk Song Style and Culture* (Washington, 1968). See Don Michael Randel, 'Crossing Over with Ruben Blades', *JAMS* 44 (1991), 319–20, for a similar critique).

[3] See Richard Leppert and Susan McClary, *Music and Society. The Politics of Composition, Performance and Reception* (Cambridge, 1987).

[4] See e.g. the essays in Ruth A. Solie (ed.), *Musicology and Difference. Gender and Sexuality in Music Scholarship* (Berkeley, 1993).

subject of discussion, perhaps because the discipline in general has constructed itself as operating strictly in the pursuit of knowledge, or simply because expectations for the impact of musicological findings are so low.

There does exist within ethnomusicology a lively sub-field in which the application of scholarly knowledge is of primary concern; this area is variously termed public sector, applied, active, or practice ethnomusicology.[5] Public sector ethnomusicologists work openly for the public interest in museums, community music organizations, and in federal, state, and local arts agencies. While public ethnomusicology (and similar initiatives in folklore) have sometimes been the targets of criticism, being accused of lacking primary research objectives and of having ostensible 'colonial' tendencies, their prominence in the United States has served to promulgate musical pluralism and to open a discourse on practice and agenda-driven activity.[6] The very presence of applied ethnomusicology and the issues it has raised for the field at large have at least begun to blur the 'mistaken dichotomies'[7] commonly thought to exist between what are often perceived as the distinct spheres of academic research and social action.

My subject here, however, is not the impact of musicological activity, such as public sector work, that is designed from its outset to have a practical outcome.[8] Rather, I want to focus on the possibility that musicological work which begins its life as a strictly academic pursuit may in the course of time have an impact outside the university. Such expectations for research are normative within most other disciplines: what self-respecting biologist, economist, or political scientist does not hope that his or her findings might in some way shape the workings of the world or, at the very least, the course of one or more disciplines? For example, a recent volume[9] argues that scholarly studies in and about Africa have shaped in a powerful way the history and methods of a variety of fields, ranging from history to economics. Beyond their academic impact, it is further proposed, findings of scholars in the humanities in particular have transformed the understanding of a broader public, ranging from illuminating the importance of literatures without writing[10] to opening eyes to the diverse nature of art.[11]

Certainly there are areas of musicological research already acknowledged to

---

[5] Jeff Todd Titon, 'Music, the Public Interest, and the Practice of Ethnomusicology', *Ethnomusicology*, 36 (1992), 315.

[6] An entire issue of the journal *Ethnomusicology*, 36/3 (1992), ed. Jeff Todd Titon, was devoted to the topic of 'Music and the Public Interest'.

[7] Barbara Kirshenblatt-Gimblett, 'Mistaken Dichotomies', *Journal of American Folklore*, 101 (400) (1988), 142–55.

[8] Nor is its focus what a recent article terms the 'politics' of musicological discourse, a wide-ranging critique of musicology's praxis and politics joined to a discussion of examples of music embedded within current political events (Philip V. Bohlman, 'Musicology as a Political Act', *Journal of Musicology*, 11 (1993), 411–36).

[9] Robert H. Bates, V. Y. Mudimbe, and Jean O'Barr (eds.), *Africa and the Disciplines* (Chicago, 1993).

[10] Christopher L. Miller, 'Literary Studies and African Literature: The Challenge of Intercultural Literacy', in Bates *et al.* (eds.), *Africa*, 213–31.

[11] Suzanne Preston Blier, 'Truth and Seeing: Magic, Custom, and Fetish in Art History', in Bates *et al.* (eds.), *Africa*, 139–66.

have helped shape the world outside musicology. Most notably, scholarly discourse on performance practice and the often disparaged production of critical editions[12] have, to quote Charles Seeger, 'prepared and tended the rails upon which the trains of music run'.[13] Recent debates revolving around gender, sexual orientation, and the musical style and output of a range of various composers have moved from the musicological literature to the media,[14] and begun to transform the manner in which a broader public perceives the music of Schubert, Tchaikovsky, Ives, and others.[15]

But dispersal of scholarly findings also carries with it substantial risks. The musicologist works within paradigms that reflect the fast-changing world of scholarly values, which are not necessarily congruent with those of the subjects of study, whether music-makers of earlier times or living 'informants'. Issues relative to the propriety of discussing the most intimate details of a late composer's life[16] are heightened further when the subject of the study can 'talk back', as current researchers of Australian aboriginal music are now discovering.[17] The sharp divisions still maintained within musical scholarship between synchronic and diachronic studies, as the subsequent discussion will make clear, constitute a further false divide, masking shared issues of scholarly concern, and impeding creative methodological moves that might truly enlighten. Indeed, it is the dialectic between the past and the present that holds the strongest possibilities for important insights. A nod to the 'trickiness of the past–present relation' is one way of acknowledging that our understanding of the present can inform our reinterpretations of the past, just as our findings about the past can have overwhelming consequences for the present.[18]

If we are to consider the broader impact of our findings, we must also raise the closely related question of how we conceptualize and present them. This issue, subsumed recently under the rubric of 'representation', is today widely discussed in anthropology as researchers have become sensitive to the manner in which their presentation of data may be regarded relative to the perspectives and positions of their ostensible subjects.[19] The concern with representation has tended to assume a binary, direct relationship between the researcher and the subject studied, on the one hand, and the manner in which one speaks for

---

[12] Joseph Kerman, *Contemplating Music* (Cambridge, Mass., 1985), 44.

[13] Charles Seeger, 'Music and Musicology in the New World 1946', in *Studies in Musicology 1935–1975* (Berkeley, 1977), 212.

[14] Edward Rothstein, 'Did a Man or a Woman Write That?', *New York Times*, 17 July 1994.

[15] Alex Ross, 'A Female Deer? Looking for Sex in the Sound of Music', *Lingua Franca*, 4/5 (July–Aug. 1994), 53–60.

[16] e.g. Maynard Solomon, 'Charles Ives: Some Questions of Veracity', *JAMS* 40 (1987), 443–70.

[17] Margaret Gummow, 'The Power of the Past in the Present: Singers and Songs from Northern New South Wales', *World of Music*, 36/1 (1994), 42–50.

[18] Leo Treitler, 'History and Music', *New Literary History*, 21 (1989–90), 307.

[19] James Clifford and George Marcus (eds.), *Writing Culture: The Poetics and Politics of Ethnography* (Berkeley, 1986); James Clifford, *The Predicament of Culture* (Cambridge, Mass., 1988); José E. Limon, 'Representation, Ethnicity, and the Precursory Ethnography: Notes of a Native Anthropologist', in Richard G. Fox (ed.), *Recapturing Anthropology: Working in the Present* (Santa Fe, N. Mex., 1991), 115–35.

another, on the other. Less consideration has been given to the very complicated challenge of representations that cross audiences and intersect different frames of reference.

Rather than discussing these issues in the general, theoretical terms in which they are so frequently treated, I would like to set forth a range of issues as they have arisen, and in fact continue to arise, within the life of a single (ethno)musicological research project. The anthropologist Leila Abu-Lughod, who has advocated a focus on 'ethnographies of the particular', argues that through grounded discussions of the particular and idiosyncratic we may be better able to identify issues that are amorphous on the level of 'culture' in its broader sense.[20] By setting forth a detailed case-study, she suggests, it is possible to address issues of ethics and impact, thus laying bare the humanistic aspects of our work.

In the fall of 1973, I began an ethnomusicological research project in Ethiopia, the first study of the liturgical music of the Beta Israel (Falasha), a people who were known to have perpetuated a heavily Judaicized religious tradition for centuries in the north-western Ethiopian highlands. The data relevant to this project are set forth in great detail in earlier publications,[21] and I will here provide only the bare minimum of information necessary to understand the broader conclusions of the study and its subsequent reception. I discuss the research process itself in a separate book.[22] I will observe only that there is little doubt that my ability to carry out this project and subsequent ethnomusicological work in revolutionary Ethiopia in the mid-1970s was due largely to the assumption that I here call into question: that music (and musical research) is removed from any practical reality, and that it holds no potential for, and poses no challenge to, our understanding of other domains of everyday life.

Discussions of the contexts of musical research tend to assume that a concern with context relates directly to the performance and transmission of the music itself. There are, however, broader forces at play that can shape scholarship's impact—in this case, the multiple, interacting political contexts that I will briefly summarize below. These contexts explain the heightened atmosphere surrounding the Beta Israel, who have, through the course of the twentieth century become a humanistic, religious, and political cause of special interest to outsiders in Europe, the United States, and Israel. My intent here is not to argue the hypothesis that emerged from music scholarship, but rather to discuss the multiple contexts into which the hypothesis has been received and has had continued impact for more than sixteen years. To achieve this, it is necessary to provide background on issues and events well beyond the world of music and music research.

---

[20] Lila Abu-Lughod, 'Writing Against Culture', in Fox (ed.), *Recapturing Anthropology*, 158.

[21] Most particularly see my 'Historical Ethnomusicology: Reconstructing Falasha Liturgical History', *Ethnomusicology*, 24 (1980), 233–58, and *Music, Ritual, and Falasha History*, 2nd printing (East Lansing, Mich. 1989).

[22] Kay Kaufman Shelemay, *A Song of Longing. An Ethiopian Journey* (Urbana, Ill., 1991).

## The Contexts of Beta Israel Research: An Overview

### The Changing Politics of Beta Israel Identity

While their history and ethnogenesis are sparsely documented in indigenous Ethiopian sources, the Beta Israel[23] past has for centuries been heavily mythologized by outsiders, who have speculated about their origin and generally characterized them as 'lost' Jews transmitting a biblical tradition. These mythologies were largely consolidated by the early twentieth century,[24] representing the Beta Israel as carriers of a Jewish practice of unclear origin that had somehow become established in Ethiopia before the country's adoption of Christianity in the fourth century.[25]

The Beta Israel image of themselves and their past derived from the broader Ethiopian Christian mythistory[26] of descent from King Solomon and the Queen of Sheba and their changing self-perception in the twentieth century have been shaped both by events within Ethiopia and the growing influence of many outsiders with whom they have come into contact.[27] This is ironic, since the Beta Israel themselves had no knowledge of or traditions about co-religionists outside Ethiopia until late nineteenth-century visitors informed them

[23] The traditional tribal name of the people in question, Beta Israel, literally translates as 'the house of Israel'. The Beta Israel have long been known in Ethiopia and in the scholarly literature as 'Falasha', a term possibly derived from a fifteenth-century imperial decree forbidding land ownership to non-Christians, or from the word 'falasyan', meaning 'monk'. Since the late 1970s, the term 'Falasha' has been considered increasingly pejorative by the Beta Israel and their supporters abroad; most of the community has since adopted the designation 'Ethiopian Jews'. Since my scholarship began in an era when the Beta Israel in Ethiopia called themselves 'Falasha' and which pre-dated the construction 'Ethiopian Jew' in a linguistic or ethnic sense, I always take care to define the various names in circulation. I generally use 'Beta Israel' when referring to aspects of traditional Ethiopian identity and cultural expression, 'Falasha' when discussing Ethiopian historical sources which themselves use that name, and 'Ethiopian Jews' when touching on aspects of late twentieth-century identity, particularly in Israel.

[24] While there exists a huge literature on the Falasha, their 'invention' in the twentieth century is largely due to the activities and writings of Jacques Faitlovitch, who visited Ethiopia in the first decade of the century and made popularizing the Falasha his life's work. See Steven Kaplan, 'The Invention of the Ethiopian Jews: Three Models', *Cahiers d'études africaines*, 132/33–4 (1993), 645–58; as well as Jacques Faitlovitch, *Notes d'un voyage chez les Falachas: Rapport présenté a M. le Baron de Rothschild* (Paris, 1905); Itzhak Grinfeld, 'Jacques Faitlovitch—"Father" of the Falashas', in Kay K. Shelemay (ed.), *The Jews of Ethiopia—A People in Transition* (Tel Aviv, 1986), 30–5; and Emanuela Trevisan Semi, 'The Education Activity of Jacques Faitlovitch in Ethiopia (1904–1924)', *Pe'amim*, 58 (1994), 86–94 (in Hebrew) for further details.

[25] This historical tradition draws on an Ethiopian legend that all of Ethiopia embraced Judaism before the Ethiopian court's fourth-century conversion to Christianity. Outsiders of the last century, themselves mainly of Jewish origin, extended the Ethiopian tradition by speculating on possible sources of Jewish influence, leading to multiple theories of external Jewish influence based largely on geographical proximity. See Steven Kaplan, *The Beta Israel (Falasha) in Ethiopia. From Earliest Times to the Twentieth Century* (New York, 1992), for a critical overview of these theories. The broader subject of the 'unique symbiosis' of Judaism and Christianity in Ethiopia (ibid. 156) has occupied numerous writers, and is far too complex to detail here. It is germane to note that the Ethiopian Christian Church itself maintained numerous Jewish traditions throughout its history, including Saturday Sabbath observance, circumcision of male infants, and dietary laws.

[26] After William H. McNeill, 'Mythistory, or Truth, Myth, History, and Historians', in *Mythistory and other Essays* (Chicago, 1986), 8–22.

[27] Ethiopian Jews in Israel have evidently rejected the Solomon and Sheba tradition within the last decade, dissociating themselves from shared origins with other Ethiopians. See Kaplan, 'Invention of Ethiopian Jews', 652–3.

that such a relationship existed.[28] The activities of Western Jews who sought to bring the Falasha 'up to date' during the first half of the twentieth century had a transformative impact on their religious practice and identity. Pro-Falasha organizations sponsored Beta Israel young people for Jewish studies in Europe and Palestine, many of whom then returned to Ethiopia in order to reshape Beta Israel custom and religious practice so that it would correspond more closely to modern Jewish models.

While Beta Israel identity shifted to a stance more closely aligned with that of Jews of the outside world, other Ethiopians continued to view them as one of the many distinctive religious minorities in a multi-ethnic empire, known for their skill at (low-status) crafts such as metalwork and pottery-making. Thus, when I entered the field in 1973, the Beta Israel had for some time been buffeted by several strong, and often contrary, currents: their own internal perceptions of themselves, their relationship to their Ethiopian compatriots, and the increasing contact with, and influence of, Jewish individuals and groups from abroad. Yet, as I began my ethnomusicological work, the political situation relating to the Beta Israel became even more complex.

## The Politics of Beta Israel Absorption into Israel

The movement to bring the Beta Israel into the broader world of Jewish practice eventually resulted in an active movement to ensure their recognition as Jews, and as a result, to enable their resettlement in Israel. This movement began in the 1950s, when a small group of Falasha young people were taken to Israel for education. Some returned to teach Hebrew and Jewish liturgy in Ethiopia, while others remained in Israel, providing the nucleus of a small Falasha community. During the 1960s and early 1970s, a modest number of Beta Israel individuals and families moved to Israel. Simultaneously, the long-simmering debate over the status of the Beta Israel as Jews broke out in Israeli religious circles, where many expressed substantial doubts about the Jewish origins of the community. The controversy culminated in 1973, when the Chief Sephardic Rabbi of Israel recognized the Falasha as descendants of the tribe of Dan, providing a legal basis for their immigration. Almost immediately, Western supporters mobilized, and an active campaign was mounted to help the Beta Israel emigrate.[29]

[28] The primary source was Semiticist Joseph Halévy, the first Jewish visitor, who arrived in Falasha villages in 1868; see Halévy, 'Travels in Abyssinia', trans. James Picciotto, in A. Lowy (ed.), *Miscellany of Hebrew Literature*, publication of the Society of Hebrew Literature, 2nd ser. (London, 1877), for discussion of his conversations with members of the Beta Israel community. Christian missionaries of the same period also stressed their own close relationship to Falasha religious practice, including one who claimed that he was a 'white Falasha' (Robert L. Hess, introduction to Henry A. Stern, *Wanderings among the Falashas in Abyssinia*, 2nd edn. (London, 1968), pp. xxii–xxiii). Protestant missions remained in Falasha areas at the time of my field-work, but had nowhere near the impact of Jewish groups interested in Falasha welfare. For further information, see Donald Crummey, *Priests and Politicians. Protestant and Catholic Missions in orthodox Ethiopia 1830–1868* (Oxford, 1972).

[29] It should be noted that Western pressure was exerted in two directions: on the Israeli government to sanction and support Beta Israel emigration, and on the Ethiopian government to permit members of this community to leave.

In the autumn of 1973, yet another variable entered the equation, the changing political situation in Ethiopia itself. Whereas former Emperor Haile Selassie I had earlier dismissed foreign requests for Falasha emigration, the Ethiopian revolution that began in 1974 foreclosed possibilities of negotiation on the subject. Unable to emigrate through legal channels, small groups of Ethiopian Jews left the country clandestinely, aided by individuals and organizations primarily from the United States.[30] As the political situation in Ethiopia worsened during the late 1970s, compounded by drought and famine, foreign support for Falasha emigration gained momentum. In the mid-1980s, thousands of the Beta Israel, along with other Ethiopians, fled to refugee camps in the Sudan, from which the Beta Israel were later flown to Israel in an operation known as 'Operation Moses'.[31] The final period of large-scale emigration took place during the last days of the Ethiopian socialist government in 1991, when most of the remaining Beta Israel community was airlifted to Israel as part of 'Operation Solomon'.[32]

## Implications of the Research

What does this tale of a century of cross-cultural contact, political upheaval, and transformation of identity have to do with research in ethnomusicology? Briefly, it provided a charged environment in which to carry out research, which both shaped and exacerbated its many political and ethical implications afterwards. Curiously, while by that time a great deal was known about Beta Israel literature and customs, the liturgy, transmitted as an oral tradition and completely sung, had never been investigated.[33] I had read much of the vast literature on the Beta Israel before entering the field and, implicitly accepting its premisses, assumed that I would be studying an ancient Jewish tradition somehow isolated in Ethiopia. During the initial months of my field-work in the north and subsequent residence in the Ethiopian capital through 1975, I continued on this

---

The support of so many in the American Jewish community in particular for the Beta Israel cause seems to derive from two notable aspects of their own recent history: a collective guilt that more was not done to rescue European Jews during the Holocaust and a strong commitment to the civil rights movement of the 1950s and 1960s, which became a site of some tension between Jews and Blacks who were early allies in that cause. Although one is here dealing with deep issues of motivation that probably cannot be fully documented and have no real place in the discussion, it seems likely that the deep, passionate commitment of so many to the Ethiopian Jewish cause arises at least in part out of a particularly American concern with both Jewish survival and racial equality.

[30] Some American activists came to Ethiopia posing as tourists, while actually working to facilitate Falasha emigration. On a number of occasions they crossed the bounds of legality, and came into direct confrontation with the Ethiopian authorities.

[31] Louis Rapoport, *Redemption Song: The Story of Operation Moses* (New York, 1985).

[32] Ruth Westheimer and Steven Kaplan, *Surviving Salvation: The Ethiopian Jewish Family in Transition* (New York, 1992).

[33] Wolf Leslau, a linguist who visited the Falasha in the late 1940s, published a recording with seven excerpts of Falasha liturgical prayers. Leslau, *Religious Music of the Falashas (Jews of Ethiopia)*, Ethnic Folkways FE 4442 (1950).

interpretative path, although I was at some moments aware of a lack of fit between the data I had gathered and the prevailing scholarly paradigms.

Only after five years of intensive analysis of the newly gathered musical and liturgical data[34] was I able to suggest a new interpretation of the Beta Israel liturgy and its musical content. These findings had major implications for under-standing the broader course of Ethiopian religious history and the unusual inter-action over time between forms of Christianity and Judaism in the country. Of more immediate interest to most readers, however, was the dramatically new perspective posed for the history of the Beta Israel themselves.

To briefly detail the findings, I was able to demonstrate that the Beta Israel did not transmit an old Jewish liturgy probably learned from an external Jewish source, but, rather, perpetuated a monastic office—one that had a remarkable resemblance to extant Ethiopian Christian worship, including the same musi-cal system, shared liturgical orders, and common prayer texts. Beyond the musical/liturgical evidence, I gathered oral traditions among surviving Beta Israel clergy and elders that their liturgy and its musical content had been received from Ethiopian Christian monks during a fifteenth-century schism in the Church, when monastic orders went into exile in outlying areas of the empire and founded new monasteries. Beta Israel oral traditions recalled names of influ-ential monks, the Ethiopian emperors during whose reigns they lived, and their particular contributions to Beta Israel religious practice and liturgy.[35] These new data from music, ritual, and oral history were further illuminated by findings of the early 1970s in Ethiopian historical studies.[36] Thus music is at the centre of a heavily contextualized study that moves from modern oral tradition in all its aspects back into historical sources and issues of greater time depth.

## Reception of the Study

The study has had varying impact on different sectors, and has evoked strikingly different responses.

### Among Other Researchers

By the early 1980s, the situation surrounding the Beta Israel was quite volatile, reflecting all the factors detailed above. The popular literature literally exploded,

---

[34] In fact, I came to the conclusions detailed here only after the completion of my doctoral dissertation, 'The Litur-gical Music of the Falasha of Ethiopia' (University of Michigan, 1977).

[35] Although mine was the first study to document the full dimensions of the impact of Beta Israel monks on modern Falasha liturgy and music, as well as their seminal role in formulating Beta Israel religious tradition at large, the presence of a monastic order among the Beta Israel since the fifteenth century was well known from prior research.

[36] Notably Sergew Hable Selassie's *Ancient and Medieval Ethiopian History to 1270* (Addis Ababa, 1972) and Tad-desse Tamrat's *Church and State in Ethiopia 1270–1527* (Oxford, 1972).

with stories in print and electronic media about the plight of the Beta Israel in Ethiopia and discussions of their prospects for emigration. As the number of Ethiopian Jews in Israel increased, a new contingent of Israeli researchers set to work, largely carrying out studies of an applied nature designed to diagnose problems and help the community in its adjustment.[37] As a result, by the 1980s there existed an unusually large group of people, ranging from scholars in Ethiopian and African studies to public sector researchers in Israel, who considered themselves knowledgeable about the Ethiopian Jews. It is during this period that my own new historical findings were first circulated, culminating in a situation described by historian Steven Kaplan. Concluding his own discussion of the crucial monastic period of the fourteenth and fifteenth centuries and its importance to our new understanding of Beta Israel religious history, Kaplan remarks that

For many readers the preceding section's description of the Beta Israel may come as a surprise. Outside of Ethiopianist circles, such opinions have had surprisingly little impact. Within academic circles, however, this view of the Beta Israel is gradually assuming a dominant position. Indeed, it is difficult to think of any field in which the gap separating scholarly and popular views is greater or has grown more so over the past two decades.[38]

## Among Political Activists

Although my work was greeted enthusiastically by many in Ethiopian studies and music scholarship, the activists who had worked for years to ensure recognition of the Beta Israel as Jews and to aid their eventual emigration to Israel did not welcome my findings. Their response is detailed elsewhere,[39] and need not be revisited here at length; but it has included an informal campaign to discourage Jewish organizations and institutions from inviting me to speak at community and educational events.[40] The only public attack against my work was a heavily orchestrated protest of my role as guest curator at an event held as part of the exhibition on the Ethiopian Jews in 1986 at the Jewish Museum in New York City. This included a demand that the museum remove *Music, Ritual, and Falasha History* from among the books about the Beta Israel on sale in the museum gift shop. Yet, throughout this period, there was no substantive written response to

---

[37] See e.g. Michael Ashkenazi and Alex Weingrod (eds.), *Ethiopian Jews and Israel* (New Brunswick, 1985). Ethnographic research on the Beta Israel in Ethiopia, and the large Ethiopianist literature on the subject, came to an end during the early years of the Ethiopian revolution. A late publication based on oral historical research carried out concurrently with mine in the mid-1970s is James Quirin, *The Evolution of the Ethiopian Jews. A History of the Beta Israel (Falasha) to 1920* (Philadelphia, 1992).

[38] Kaplan, 'Invention of Ethiopian Jews', 648.

[39] Shelemay, *Song of Longing*.

[40] My invitations to speak at Jewish communal events declined dramatically in the mid-1980s. That this was the result of an informal blacklist was confidentially confirmed by several individuals who invited me to speak at functions *despite* strong lobbying by activists against these invitations.

my research in the (numerous) publications of the organizations involved. Rather, they simply refused to mention new directions in scholarship, publicizing only approved writings in communications to their members.

## Among the Beta Israel

Until this point, my discussion has focused exclusively on the transformation of a people and their world by outsiders, and upon other outsiders' responses to new scholarly findings. That the response has primarily come from outsiders is perhaps predictable, since they have carried out virtually all the research to date on the Beta Israel.[41]

The reason why the Beta Israel have been silent is no doubt the distance of their lives and experience from the world of scholarly discourse and their engagement with much more pressing issues of survival and relocation. Other than conversations which I initiated with a few members the community, discussed below, I have received only one detailed Beta Israel response to my work. Remarkably, it made its way to me while I was in the process of drafting this chapter. Following a public lecture I presented on aspects of Beta Israel history and culture on 26 July 1994 in Washington, DC, I was approached by a man who introduced himself as a member of the Beta Israel community, and told me that he had read *Music, Ritual, and Falasha History*. Subsequently, he forwarded to me his written commentary on my findings, generally in agreement with my portrayal of the interactive nature of Judaism and Christianity in Ethiopia, but arguing that I did not give enough attention to evidence for the pre-Christian presence of Jewish traditions, or the subsequent hegemony of Christianity in the country, which masks the 'identity of the original seed'. At the end, he suggests 'that the permutation and combination of any probability equation should essentially include as many relevant variables as possible beyond musical liturgy, which is Christianized and Amharized, and beyond the views of some Falashas who have

---

[41] This is in contrast to other areas of Ethiopian studies, where Ethiopian scholars have made major contributions. In addition to the historians listed in n. 36, major contributions to the documentation and interpretation of Ethiopian literature have been made by Getatchew Haile in numerous publications (see, e.g. Getatchew Haile, *A Catalogue of Ethiopian Manuscripts Microfilmed for the Ethiopian Manuscript Microfilm Library, Addis Ababa, and for the Hill Monastic Manuscript Library, Collegeville*, vols. 4– (Collegeville, Minn., 1979– ); idem, 'Religious Controversies and the Growth of Ethiopic Literature in the Fourteenth and Fifteenth Centuries', *Oriens Christianus* (Wiesbaden), 4th ser. 65 (1981), 102–36.). The strong voice of indigenous Ethiopian scholars does not include many among the Beta Israel, the vast majority of whom lived in rural locales and were not literate. With the exception of the few dozen Beta Israel men schooled abroad over the course of the century, only the generation now coming of age in Israel has had opportunities for higher education. Individuals of Beta Israel descent who have made contributions to the literature about their people include Taamrat Emmanuel, a member of the Beta Israel community, whose notes on Falasha monks were published by the linguist Wolf Leslau ('Taamrat Emmanuel's Notes of Falasha Monks and Holy Places', in *Salo Wittmayer Baron Jubilee Volume*, English Section, vol. 2 (Jerusalem, 1974), 623–37) and Yona Bogale (1911–87), who was educated in Europe and Palestine under the sponsorship of Faitlovitch. After Bogale returned to Ethiopia, he became a government official and a representative of the Beta Israel. Most of his publications, such as the *Jewish Calendar*, 5734 (Addis Ababa, 1973), were generated by his commitment to introduce others in his community to Western Jewish practices; he also prepared a manuscript of a Hebrew–Amharic dictionary, envisioning it as a bridge through which his people could master the Hebrew language.

not had the luxury of access to academics and/or political power'.[42] Although I cannot here provide a detailed exposition of these and other specific points included in his commentary, I was both gratified and stimulated by his thoughtful feedback.[43]

## Ethics, Politics, and Representation

When in 1978 I finally arrived at an understanding of the import of the monastic component in Falasha tradition, I knew that my findings posed an ethical dilemma. On the one hand, I had carried out a classic 'emic'[44] study, basing my interpretations on data generated from within Beta Israel and broader Ethiopian society, including musical practice, oral testimony, and indigenous historical chronicles. On the other, my conclusions, however well supported by the data, had the potential to be used against the very people who had trusted me with their traditions.

Although the transformation of Beta Israel identity and the people's desire to emigrate emerged as a direct result of outside intervention and influences, by the period of my research in the 1970s, the Beta Israel had a very clear, firm commitment to a world-view as Ethiopian Jews. Thus ethics cut two ways. On the one hand, I had in fact conveyed the perspective of Beta Israel priests of their own religious history, as expressed through their memories and continued liturgical practice. On the other hand, these traditions were perpetuated in a modern social context in which they had lost all meaning, and could, if circulated, possibly threaten hard-won political gains and modern identity.

Colleagues with whom I discussed this dilemma were stumped at how to handle the situation.[45] I tried to discuss my findings with the few members of the Beta Israel community with whom I was still able to communicate at that time given the distance and disrupted communications during the Ethiopian revolution, hoping that their response might provide a solution. One such instance occurred when a leader of the Beta Israel community visited New York City in 1979; the second, during the summer of 1980, when I carried out field-work with two Beta Israel priests who were by then living in Israel. In both cases, we discussed the monks at length, and I was greeted with many additional oral

---

[42] Anon., written communication, 31 July 1994.

[43] For an earlier instance in the ethnomusicological literature in which a scholar details subject response, see Steven Feld, 'Dialogic Editing: Interpreting How Kaluli Read *Sound and Sentiment*', *Cultural Anthropology*, 2/2 (1987), 190–210.

[44] A study drawing on the native point of view, also referred to as an 'experience-near' approach. See Clifford Geertz, '"From the Native's Point of View": On the Nature of Anthropological Understanding', in *Local Knowledge. Further Essays in Interpretive Anthropology* (New York, 1983), 55–70, esp. 56–8.

[45] I raised this ethical dilemma tentatively in a scholarly lecture, published as 'Folk Memory and Jewish Identity: The Falasha Dilemma', in Nathaniel Stampfer (ed.), *The Solomon Goldman Lectures. Perspectives in Jewish Learning*, vol. 4 (Chicago, 1985), 43–53.

traditions about their impact on the community and its religious practice. On these points we had no disagreement. But all three men reiterated their belief that the Beta Israel had converted the monks to an existing Falasha religious practice, a perspective that seemed highly unlikely given what we now know about the tenacious monastic orders who went into exile from the Church precisely to preserve Judaic and biblical traditions then the subject of dispute.

Only after a considerable period of soul-searching was I able to decide on a course of action. Although I concluded that I could not conceal what I had discovered on account of the current political climate, I did have a responsibility to protect the community with which I had worked. I decided to publish my findings only in scholarly circles and to avoid unnecessary publicity that might unwittingly arouse controversy and perhaps damage the Beta Israel. Whenever I presented my findings, I would incorporate discussion of the Beta Israel response, as far as it was available, in my interpretation and articulate the ethical issues at stake. Finally, I stated clearly in all my publications that the data I had uncovered, and my resulting interpretations, related only to the past, not to contemporary politics.

This strategy largely succeeded. I was able to explore the implications of my findings within a receptive scholarly context, while contributing guardedly to an occasional public discussion or benefit on behalf of the Beta Israel. Now I am able to write more openly about these issues, in large part because the Beta Israel community have for some time been firmly established in Israel.[46]

## Conclusions

A recent issue of *The World of Music* (1994) contains multiple articles discussing issues of power and politics in Australian Aboriginal song research. This volume is one of the first in-depth explorations of issues of ethics and the impact of research emerging from a particular research site, and focuses on two main aspects of the research process: access, or permission to carry out research; and disposition and control of the research materials gathered. In the Australian case-studies, access and disposition have emerged over the course of the last several decades as the primary issues of ethical and political concern, as Aborigines have sought to exercise their own rights to control research in which they are subjects.

The issue at stake in the Ethiopian case-study discussed above are somewhat different from those that have arisen in Australia, and provide a useful illustration of the manner in which ethical considerations vary according to research

---

[46] *Song of Longing* is my first in-depth discussion. The reader should also be aware that new issues constantly arise, most recently, a public debate about the status of the Faras Mura, descendants of Falasha who converted to Christianity, and whether they should be allowed to emigrate to Israel (Steven Kaplan, ' "Falasha Christians": A Brief History', *Midstream*, 39 (1993), 20–1).

topic, site, and context. Permission for access through both governmental and local authorities was willingly given at the time of my Ethiopian field-work, and Ethiopian Jews in Israel continue to welcome researchers among them today. Likewise, the disposition of research materials has not become a source of conflict; my own recordings have been deposited in an archive for preservation and future use,[47] and Israeli researchers carrying out recording projects, for example, have done so under the sponsorship of the sound archives (Phonoteca) of the National and University Library in Jerusalem.[48] Rather, the contested area in the Ethiopian case is *interpretation* of the data, an issue raised to date mainly by supporters of the community desiring to shape the researcher's findings according to current political sensitivities. The Beta Israel community has not yet entered into this debate in any formal way, in contrast to the active role of Australian Aborigines in controlling research in their midst since the mid-1970s.[49] The Beta Israel silence, however, renders no less immediate the many ethical questions surrounding research about them which, in redefining scholarly perspectives of a people's history, potentially impinge upon the sensibilities of the community itself. As one Australian researcher has noted, the very act of visiting people to ask them about their past inevitably changes their perceptions of it.[50]

Ethics may be defined as 'standards of conduct and moral judgement',[51] conceptualized in the research field as a shared code guiding the behaviour of scholars while at the same time being sensitive to the values and beliefs of individuals and communities of various places and times who are the subjects of study. Indeed, it is at the juncture of scholarly values and local standards that most ethical dilemmas arise. If ethical awareness in music scholarship is in an 'embryonic state',[52] there is little doubt that such issues will proliferate as musical scholarship moves more deeply into issues of context and the manner in which music relates to broader worlds of meaning. Vexing questions of access, disposition, and interpretation will continue to arise. It is clear that solutions to ethical dilemmas must be local and contingent, sensitive to both the particular tradition and the individuals involved; such situations require constant vigilance by the

---

[47]  The Archives of Traditional Music at Indiana University, Bloomington.

[48]  Some recordings made in Jerusalem in 1986 have been put out on a compact disc entitled *Liturgies Juives D'Ethiopie*, Auvidis W260013 (1990). I have had one request for materials from a member of the Beta Israel community, the daughter of one of the priests with whom I worked in Ethiopia. While writing a biography of her late father for an M.A. thesis at the Hebrew University, she enquired if I had relevant biographical data and/or recordings. I sent her a lengthy interview in which her father details his life history and recordings of him performing the liturgy.

[49]  This process is detailed in Stephen A. Wild, 'Reflections on Field Research in Aboriginal Australia: Central Australia and Arnhem Land', *World of Music*, 36/1 (1994), 51–8. It seems important to note that problems are also inherent in community control of research, where carriers of the musical traditions may not be members of the official councils which extend formal permission for research. See Catherine J. Ellis, 'Introduction. Powerful Songs: Their Placement in Aboriginal Thought', *World of Music*, 36/1 (1994), 14–15.

[50]  Gummow, 'Power of the Past', 42.

[51]  *Webster's New Twentieth Century Dictionary*, unabridged, 2nd edn. (USA, 1978), 627.

[52]  Mark Slobin, 'Ethical Issues', in Helen Myers (ed.), *Ethnomusicology. An Introduction* (London, 1992), 331.

researcher and open discussion during the research process and afterwards. As we seek to redefine music scholarship, we need to anticipate the potential impact of our work on the individuals who, whether in the archive or in the field, have shared their music with us.

# 24

# What Do We Want to Teach When We Teach Music? One Apology, Two Short Trips, Three Ethical Dilemmas, and Eighty-two Questions

## Ellen Koskoff

All of us engaged in the transmission of musical culture today face a central problem: too many competing voices and not enough time or space to accommodate them all. The recent explosion of postmodernist critical theory from musicology, ethnomusicology, gay and lesbian studies, feminist, literary, and cultural criticism, and other disciplines previously thought to be only tangential to the study of music has exposed the hegemony of the dead, white, European, heterosexual, male musical canon; as a result, the canons of women, non-Western peoples, gays and lesbians (to name but a few) have finally been resurrected from their purgatory of otherness.

We now have a situation, as described by Nancy Fraser and Linda J. Nicholson, in which cultural criticism 'floats free of any universalist ground. No longer anchored philosophically, the very shape or character of social criticism changes; it becomes more pragmatic, ad hoc, contextual, and local.'[1] Postmodernism asserts that grand narratives of legitimation are no longer credible. Rather, we must now celebrate differences, multiple voices, conflicting perspectives, unorthodox readings. In postmodernist philosophy, according to Jane Flax, 'one deconstructs, that is, distances oneself from, and makes oneself skeptical about, beliefs concerning truth, knowledge, power, the self, and language that are often taken for granted within, and serve as legitimization for, western contemporary culture'.[2]

This long awaited, and much needed, democratizing movement in musicology, discussed admirably in such recent works as Ruth Solie's *Musicology and Difference: Gender and Sexuality in Music Scholarship* (1993) and Katherine Bergeron and Philip V. Bohlman's *Disciplining Music: Musicology and its Canons* (1992), has

---

[1] Nancy Fraser and Linda J. Nicholson, 'Social Criticism without Philosophy', in Nicholson (ed.), *Feminism/Postmodernism* (New York, 1990), 22.

[2] Jane Flax, *Thinking Fragments: Psychoanalysis, Feminism and Postmodernism in the Contemporary West* (Berkeley, 1990), 29.

done much to reveal the underlying power imbalances that are inherent within our musical systems and their transmission. But the consequence of hearing and valuing many different, and often conflicting voices, say the critics of these developments, is chaos. The canon as we once understood it is changing, being renegotiated, or disintegrating (depending on one's point of view) under the scrutiny of too many 'others', including a rebellious lot of postmodernists, with their individual readings, deconstructions, and non-centred non-theories. There is not enough time to hear all the voices, let alone absorb or teach them; no way to structure a curriculum that will be everything to everybody; no way to add any more to the canon without taking something (important, that we used to teach) out. Clearly, to simply add others and stir will not work any longer.

This chapter poses some questions that we might ask as we struggle for a new paradigm whereby to structure the learning, teaching, and experiencing of music within our colleges and universities. I will illustrate my ideas with examples drawn from the ethnomusicological literature, from my own research and field-work, and with small 'vignettes' taken from my many years of teaching both within a liberal arts programme and in a professional school of music. I do not pose a solution here, but try instead to examine some of the underlying assumptions about music and its teaching that are currently being called into question, and to offer some ideas that may help clarify the problems we now face.

## An Apology

I will state at the start that I have two fundamental goals in my professional life: first, I wish to pass on some of the sense of the overwhelming power and sheer beauty that I've experienced in music, especially in the music I love ('my music'); and second—a more political goal, to be sure—I wish to use my knowledge and experience of music to promote tolerance of difference—between races, ethnicities, classes, religions, sexualities, and genders. As an ethnomusicologist, I believe in the basic tenet of our field: just as all people are inherently equal, so are their musics. I do not mean equal in the sense that all musics (or people) are equally 'good', for that implies a value-judgement that I do not wish to make or am not always capable of making; but rather that all musics (and people) are equivalent in terms of the values, meanings, and integrity of their own contexts.

Lately, the discussion in many of the music disciplines has centred on the canon, specifically the Western art-music canon: how to expand it, rethink its boundaries, or deconstruct it altogether, and ultimately to ask if the concept of canon is still useful.[3] In the book she recently co-edited, *Disciplining Music*, Bergeron defines 'canon' as a set of works that embody [*sic*] value, as well as the rule

---

[3] As an ethnomusicologist who is Jewish, I have often been struck by the very word 'canon', and by the distinctly Christian bias inherent in the word as well as in the study and teaching of Western classical music. That so few Jewish composers or works have entered the canon seems no surprise, considering this framing.

by which such value is specifically measured and controlled within a discourse.[4] Old-style Western musicologists, say Bergeron and Bohlman, have for so long defined and been involved in the process of transmitting works that embody the values of Western art-music (in which they are heavily invested) that they do not often see themselves as part of the problem. Indeed, as Bohlman states, 'Quite simply, musicologists are engaged in making choices, usually at the behest of others, thereby establishing authority. . . . Creating canons and buttressing them is indeed a normative task for musicologists.'[5] And, later, in justifying the continual perpetuation of canons: 'The curricula of music departments depend on the scaffolding afforded by the essential repertoires and pedagogical pigeon-holes—which is to say, the canons necessary for graduation and degree-granting. Entrance into the field demands familiarity with a central set of canons' (201).

Let us distinguish, though, between the three different aspects of canon as defined above. First, a canon is a set of works; second, it is a set of values, which embodies basic philosophical and aesthetic principles of the people who make and experience the music; and third, canon, or more precisely *canonizing*, signifies the intricate socio-political process by which pieces of music composed or performed by musicians at certain historical and socio-cultural moments become ranked and codified by others, not necessarily of the same historical, social, or cultural moments (what Bergeron refers to above as the 'rule' by which such value is controlled within a discourse). Simply creating a canon is not a problem; nor is embodying it with one's own meaningful values. The problem comes with *canonization*—the institutionalization of certain works over others through the imposition of hierarchies of self-invested value upon other people and their musics.

Until recently, the focus on canon as a set of works (which dominated the work of previous generations of musicologists), rather than on a set of values (which marks the current generation's contribution), helped obscure the politics and power relations inherent in canonizing. Indeed, Bohlman cites the primary motivation for a split between the disciplines of musicology and ethnomusicology in the late 1950s as ethnomusicology's challenge to 'the very processes of canonization, which it believed hammered a wedge between our music and the other's' (135).

It is not simply hard-nosed Western musicologists, however, who are prone to create and perpetuate musical canons. All social, ethnic, religious, gender, age, and similar groups (even ethnomusicologists) create canons of a sort that fulfil the basic criteria defined above. It is only necessary to listen to any popular station on the radio for a while to understand the canon of rock. What would country and western music be without Hank Williams or Johnny Cash? Musical

---

[4] Katherine Bergeron, 'Prologue: Disciplining Music', in Bergeron and Philip V. Bohlman (eds.), *Disciplining Music: Musicology and its Canons* (Chicago, 1992). 16.

[5] Philip V. Bohlman, 'Epilogue: Musics and Canons', in Bergeron and Bohlman (eds.), *Disciplining Music*, 197–210, at 199; subsequent references to this item are given in the text.

comedy without Ethel Merman and *Annie, Get Your Gun?* How could we possibly teach a world music class without including the cultures of India, Indonesia, and Ghana? (Isn't that a sort of 'culture-canon'?) If we believe, as John Blacking did, that music is evidence for a 'Humanly Organized Sound' and a 'Soundly Organized Humanity',[6] then it is only 'natural' for all of us to express and value our unique social and historical humanness through our own music and not the music of others (however we may have constructed ourselves and others). Creating and perpetuating canons and their values is a way of defining ourselves musically and socially.

However, boundaries between groups and canons can be, and quite frequently are, permeable, malleable, and dynamic. This accounts for social and musical (ex)change between people and their groups (that is, 'reconfigurings' of selves and others). So when is it necessary to have boundaries, and when is it not? If we are inside, how do we know there is an outside? To gain a better handle on these questions, postmodernists say that it is helpful to move away from the centre toward the margin. That way, one can at least see a boundary and an outside. This new perspective can help make clear what the inside 'really' is. Soon, of course, the points of arrival on the margin or outside the margin become new insides (from their own point of view), interacting with others (who are also selves) in their orbit.

This inside/outside play is at the heart of much of the new thinking in postmodernist criticism. And constructing such categories has certainly been useful in that it has enabled us to understand that differences, in terms of value and meaning, truly do exist and are important. But is it now time to abandon these constructs altogether, and state once and for all that there is no inside or outside—there is only difference?

Let us take two short trips: the first to North India, where Daniel Neuman has examined a system of canon formation and transmission that will sound both familiar and 'exotic' to us; the second to Crown Heights, Brooklyn, where members of the Lubavitcher Hasidic court pass on their musical tradition in such a seemingly casual way as to belie their core belief in music as 'the pen of the soul'. Why is it necessary to take these trips? As they say, 'travel broadens'; maybe other societies have discovered ways to negotiate the ins and outs of their own musical systems that can be instructive to us.

## Two Short Trips

### North India

In the North Indian classical music system there are many important factors that define a musician as a master of the 'grand tradition': he must first know the

---

[6] John Blacking, *How Musical is Man?* (Seattle, 1973), titles of chs. 1 and 4 resp.

rules of *raga* (the scalar-melodic system, with its attendant emotional states, or *rasas*); he must master the intricate metric-rhythmic system, known as *tala*; he must know the history and written theory of Indian classical music from the earliest Vedic times (roughly 2000 BCE) to the present; and finally, he must be able to prove a musical lineage—that is, he must be able to establish a link between himself and at least one of many ancestral musical saints. This proof of a true musical pedigree is one of the most important features of the socio-musical culture of North India, and provides an intricate social structure by which musicians are taught, are evaluated in performance, and become masters themselves.

Essentially an oral tradition, North Indian classical music is passed on from master (*guru*) to disciple (*shishya*) through years of close musical and social interaction. The relationship between master and disciple has been described as that between father and son; and indeed, with other disciples ('brothers'), this system is viewed much as a family or brotherhood, often solidified through intermarriage between musical families.

In his book *The Life of Music in North India: The Organization of an Artistic Tradition* (1980), Neuman describes the *kalawant*, a hereditary vocal musician (Muslim) descended from a well-known musical ancestor, 'in whose pedigree there is no evidence of *sarangi* or *tabla* players'.[7] This purity must be provable for at least three generations. The lineage itself, referred to as a *khandan*, is most often patrilineal (descent is reckoned through the father), and the oldest living descendant of the original ancestral music-saint is considered the total authority over his family's musical style. Although patrilineal lineages are most revered, lineages can also be traced through a woman who marries into the family. Usually such women are members of prestigious *khandans* themselves, and many are accomplished, even virtuosic, players. To keep lineages pure, marriage between cousins is preferred, and families frequently exchange women with each other. Women, however, never reach the status of *guru*, or master.

The political and musical value of the pedigree is so great that the reputation of an entire family can rest on its purity. According to Neuman, pressure to conform to this scrutiny can result in serious violations. 'Pedigrees are sometimes consciously manipulated, although it is difficult to document such instances. I know of one ancestor who was dropped from a Kalawant pedigree because he associated with accompanists and singing girls, and there are other instances where individuals appear in a pedigree, only to be disputed by other musicians who claim they are artificial additions to bring (unjustified) honor to a family' (166).

A master representing a pure lineage can attract many disciples. The resulting group of hereditary musicians, their disciples, and a particular musical style

---

[7] Daniel M. Neuman, *The Life of Music in North India: The Organization of an Artistic Tradition* (Detroit, 1980), 95; subsequent references to this book are given in the text.

which they represent is known as a *gharana* (146). *Gharanas*, developed first in the late nineteenth century, frequently take their names from the ancestral home of their primary *khandan*. The oldest and most prestigious *gharana* is the Gwalior. It was founded by two brothers, Haddu and Hassu Khan, in the mid-nineteenth century, and most vocalists trace their lineage back to these men.

Instrumentalists face a slightly different socio-musical system. Considered of lower origins, instrumental music is not as prestigious or spiritual as vocal music, and instrumentalists, although often excellently trained, hold a slightly lower status in the overall musical hierarchy. All instrumentalists of hereditary musical families are known as *khandani* musicians (not *kalawant*, a title reserved for vocalists), and they trace their origins back to Tansen (sixteenth century), considered to be the founder of (the later-developed) instrumental genres.

Many present-day instrumentalists, not having pure hereditary lineages, have been 'adopted' into more prestigious instrumental families. An example is Ustad (Master) Alluadin Khan, the *guru* of the eminent sitarist Ravi Shankar (who called him Baba—Father); Alluadin Khan was adopted into the *gharana* of Ustad Wazir Khan, a direct descendant of Tansen. As recounted in Shankar's *My Music, My Life*, the process of adoption was not an easy one, and occurred only after Wazir Khan was convinced of Alluadin Khan's love and devotion to music. After many trials and false starts, Alluadin eventually won favour, and became Wazir's disciple, with one qualification: 'his master would never permit Baba to play the *been* [*sic*; *bin*] because it is traditionally restricted to the Beenkar *gharana*—his family—and he warned that if Baba were to play it Baba would never have an heir and his family would die out'.[8] Recent changes in the *gharana* system, such as the introduction of music schools similar to those in the West, have weakened it somewhat, but musicians agree that the master/disciple system still forms the core of musical and cultural transmission in India.

## Crown Heights, Brooklyn

Among Lubavitcher Hasidim, whose world-wide headquarters is located in the heart of Crown Heights, Brooklyn, the performance of music—specifically the paraliturgical songs known as *nigunim*—is considered a spiritual duty. *Nigunim* are so valued among this group that it is often said that their founder, Rabbi Schneur Zalman (1745–1813), proclaimed *nigun* to be 'the pen of the soul'.[9]

*Nigunim* are considered to be musical manifestations of two of the most important Hasidic principles: *simhah* (joy) and *hitlahavut* (enthusiasm). According to

---

[8] Ravi Shankar, *My Music, My Life* (London, 1969), 55.

[9] For a fuller discussion of Lubavitcher Hasidim and their music, see my article, 'Miriam Sings her Song: The Self and Other in Anthropological Discourse', in Ruth A. Solie (ed.), *Musicology and Difference: Gender and Sexuality in Music Scholarship* (Berkeley, 1993), 149–63.

Hasidic philosophy, these principles (really, emotional states) must be present in all thoughts and actions. Performance of *nigunim* is considered to be the most powerful and direct way to achieve communication with God (*devekuth*). *Nigunim* are frequently performed on such occasions as holidays and *farbrengen*, or gatherings. One of the most important contexts for performance is a Rebbe's *farbrengen*, one which unites the entire community in the presence of the Rebbe, or spiritual leader.

*Nigunim* are not considered by Lubavitchers to be a form of 'classical music' in the sense in which we normally use this term. That is, they are not usually written down when composed; they are not usually performed from notation; there is no real sense of compositional ownership of *nigunim*, although occasionally a story surrounds the composition of a *nigun* by a famous Rebbe; there is no 'music theory' of *nigun*, although every generation seems to generate new ones; and there is no formal system, such as a music school, *gharana*, or master teacher, that exists for their transmission.

*Nigunim* are frequently sung at the table following sabbath meals. In this way, they are casually passed on within the context of daily life from father to son.[10] Occasionally a newly composed *nigun* is introduced at a *farbrengen*, especially one near the time of the Rebbe's birthday, and is passed on quickly to the assembled crowd. In this way new songs become absorbed into the repertoire, and those responsible for their composition often become the Rebbe's musical assistants.

A total of 347 *nigunim* have been notated and preserved in three volumes published by the Lubavitcher publishing house, Kehot.[11] Although this number does not include many newer *nigunim* or others long forgotten, it is considered to be a core repertoire of songs that musically defines this group. Each volume includes notated transcriptions of the songs, the name of the composer, if known, or the name of the performer who brought the song into the repertoire (who may then become known as its composer), and a set of stories that tell of the miraculous properties of the *nigun* or its performance.

The first two volumes were compiled by the previous Rebbe, Joseph Isaac Schneersohn (1880–1950) shortly after his arrival in the United States, for the purpose of preserving what he and his followers perceived to be a dying tradition. The third volume, published more recently, includes *nigunim* remembered by newer immigrants who arrived after the 1940s. No one uses these scores for performance purposes. Indeed, most Lubavitchers cannot read Western notation, and even those that can, regard the notations as lifeless.

Originally, Rebbe Joseph Isaac Schneerson pulled together a committee of his close associates, one of whom could write music, to notate these tunes. This committee exists to this day as an arbiter of Lubavitcher musical decisions, such as

---

[10] Daughters also learn this repertoire, but the laws of Orthodox Judaism forbid adult men and women to pray or sing together, and men are more likely to sing publicly. (See ibid. for more on this.)

[11] Rabbi Samuel Zalmanoff (ed.), *Sefer Ha-Nigunim* (3 vols., New York, 1948, 1957, 1965).

which songs will be given to the Rebbe for his birthday (a competition is held every year), and which songs will be arranged for recording. It consists largely of lifetime Lubavitchers[12] who are related either to the Rebbe or to those in his inner circle. These men and young boys are chosen in part for their strong voices and fine musical memories, but more importantly for certain social and spiritual qualities that make them ideal transmitters of Lubavitcher musical culture: they are personally close to the Rebbe; they can trace their lineage back to the founder of the Lubavitchers, Rabbi Schneur Zalman; they are unquestionably knowledgeable about Torah, Talmud, and Hasidic religious philosophy; and they are able to sing in such a way as to communicate the essence of this philosophy through performance; and they are male. Although many men have served on this committee, the Rebbe himself is universally regarded as the best Lubavitcher musician.[13]

There are almost no 'professional musicians', as we understand this term, within Lubavitcher society; that is, there are no people specifically designated to perform or pass on the musical culture, and few who are financially rewarded simply for being musicians. Taking pride in any profession is avoided in Lubavitcher society, as one's 'profession' must always be to serve God. Nor is this the only bar to being a professional musician. Lubavitchers make a distinction between prayer, *nigun* (and other religious songs), and music. Prayer and religious songs, although composed of seemingly musical elements, are performed for a divine purpose; music is associated more with the surrounding and, by definition, contaminated culture, and carries with it the association of decadence and moral lassitude. Even Western classical music, although sometimes listened to and enjoyed by Lubavitchers, is regarded as existing within a 'neutral category', neither divine nor harmful, and not quite music.

Taken individually, both these musical cultures seem to 'make sense'; that is, each has a certain socio-musical logic that carries meaning for the people who 'live the culture'. It appears, though, that in creating their own canons, North Indians and Lubavitchers have no more (or less) understanding or tolerance for others' musics than we do. An Indian musician will not play with anyone who has had a tabla player in his family or has associated with a singing girl; in India a woman cannot become a *guru* at the head of a *gharana*; nor will a *guru* reveal the whole of his musical knowledge to a performer 'adopted' into his musical family. Among Lubavitchers, music itself is associated with the decadence of

---

[12] Although many American Lubavitchers were born into this Hasidic court, the majority came to it as adults. Known as *Ba'alei Teshuvah* (literally, Masters of Repentance), these 'converts' represent a large cross-section of the American Jewish population.

[13] This was brought home to me one Saturday evening when I attended a Rebbe's *farbrengen*. I commented to a friend who had taken me to this gathering that the Rebbe was getting pretty old and his voice was beginning to crack. It was difficult, I pointed out, for him even to hold the tune of the *nigun*. My friend glared at me, and announced that the Rebbe's performance was the best I would ever have the privilege to hear, simply because he was the Rebbe.

Western civilization; musical choices seem to be, at least in part, made by committee; and women can never become musical assistants to the Rebbe. North Indians and Lubavitchers cannot help us with our value-laden, inside/outside problems; they have too many of their own. Why, then, should we spend time learning about these systems? Simply because they are there?

There is an even worse problem: how can we even talk about these musical cultures meaningfully, analyse them, compare them, relate them to us, without abstracting certain categories of analysis? For example, if we want to show likeness, it is easy to see some similarities between these vastly different musical systems and our own. Musical lineage, for example, seems to be important to all three systems. In the West too, it does matter with whom we study and with whom our teacher studied, and so on back to a mythical musical ancestor. The familial/spiritual relationship between teacher and student is just as significant for us as for those in North India or Crown Heights. And certainly we can attest to the exclusion of women from various musical institutions and opportunities, not to mention the implication that women who perform publicly (i.e. 'singing girls') carry with them the vestiges of compromised reputations.

It is just as easy to show differences between our three musical cultures. What does it matter to us, for example, if an opera diva has a clarinet player in her family's musical closet? Or if a major conductor (male or female) associates with 'singing girls'? And don't Lubavitchers realize that prayer *is* music, or at least has musical properties? After all, we teach Catholic liturgy as music in our history surveys. Oh, those funny North Indians and Lubavitchers!

Now, in order to write those last two paragraphs, I made certain analytical choices. That is, I abstracted categories, such as 'musical lineage', 'student/teacher bonding', and 'gender', from my cultural descriptions above—which themselves are abstractions from real musical cultures as they are truly lived. But do these concepts really carry the same meaning in all the cultures we are discussing? What about even more basis concepts, such as 'music', 'musician', 'professional', 'canon'? For example, would North Indians or Lubavitchers truly feel comfortable with the concept of a 'professional musician'? Or would Lubavitchers ever use the word 'canon' with all its Christian nuances? Is there even an equivalent term in North India? Obviously, problems arise when we begin to analyse or compare, because we must separate certain features of the culture from the experience of living the culture, certain features and relationships between features that may tell us more about our own interests than those of the people we are discussing.

What, then, is our main goal in passing on our own, or anybody's, musical culture? To teach a body of musics that we value? To teach a body of values that we music? To inculturate our children to accept a power structure that creates hierarchies of value so that those canons can continue to be transmitted? To question or 'deconstruct' hierarchies of canons and their values?

## Three Ethical Dilemmas

### World Music Class

For a long time now, those of us who teach 'large subjects' such as world music have been faced with the same problem now confronting those used to teaching 'smaller subjects' (like Western classical music). One can't teach everything, so what to leave out? In the case of Western classical music, I suppose one could leave out, say, Smetana, or perhaps Busoni, at least the first time around. Or again, not *all* of the symphonies of Beethoven really need to be covered. Perhaps we could forget about the Second? But, in the case of the world, one feels a sort of moral tug when leaving out, say, Sri Lanka or Bulgaria (untold millions of living people). Unlike the colonialist catch-phrase of the New York City-based radio station, WNEW, which brags: 'Give us twenty minutes, and we'll give you the world,' I am trying to stress the complexities, the nuances of cultural systems, not serve them up like so many ethnic dishes.

'It's a survey,' people say. 'Just hit the highlights—only the major cultures.' What exactly is a major culture? One like ours with a classical music system? (India? Java?) One with a notation system? (China?) One with a grand oral tradition? (Ghana? Native America?) In our literate classical music culture, 'oral tradition' is often euphemistically described (and dismissed) as folk-music. Could a culture with an oral/folk musical tradition be considered major? What exactly is folk-music? Who are the folk? Could the folk be those people in the Beethoven class? Is this merely a scheduling problem?

It quickly becomes apparent to anyone faced with constructing a syllabus that any subject can be approached from the perspective of the large or the small. Perhaps the problem seems especially hopeless in the case of world music, because the underlying premiss of such a course is so grand at the start. Obviously, what to leave in or out must become a matter of individual or institutional choice. But how to establish standards? How to develop criteria for what and what not to teach? Must we determine if there really is something inherently better about the Fifth Symphony of Beethoven as opposed to the Second? Or if the music of Java is any more beautiful or worthy of study than that of Estonia? Or if some societies really are better able than others to produce great music (that is, some people and their musics *really are inherently better than others*)?

### Bali in Rochester

The Eastman School of Music recently purchased a Balinese gamelan *angklung*, an ensemble of thirty or so beautifully crafted instruments, that plays an essentially standard repertoire of Hindu-related temple music. Having never played this music myself, I hoped we could hire a teacher skilled in performing and teaching the *angklung* repertoire, preferably a Balinese. Much to my surprise, I discovered that a few Balinese musicians actually live within commuting distance of Rochester, so finding a teacher was not difficult. That teacher, in our first year, was I Wayan Suweca, one of the most well-known and respected contemporary Balinese musicians and composers, who just happened to be teaching in Montréal.

Suweca's status in Bali is similar to that of, say, Peter Serkin or Lorin Mazel in the West: a wonderful musician, composer, conductor, and teacher who inspires the best work. Our best work, of course, was only the simplest, baby pieces. Learning entire stretches of music without notation, keeping a steady pulse through the agony of a *koteken* (a section where the four scale tones interlock—what we call hocket), and simply learning to anticipate dynamic, sectional, and tempo changes by listening to the drummer, proved quite difficult, even for skilled Eastman School musicians.

In our struggle to learn this music, I often wondered what Wayan, as we came to call him, thought of us. How many adjustments did he have to make, especially socially, in order to teach us? For example, in Bali, men and women do not usually perform in a gamelan together. Occasionally, a woman will perform with her husband or a close family member, but mixed groups are considered inappropriate. 'When you sit across from a woman and your eyes meet while the music is playing, you never know what will happen,' Wayan would say, with a wink. Then there was the matter of us sitting on the floor, cross-legged in front of our instruments. Rehearsals often lasted hours, and we were not used to sitting in this position. Frequently we would have to open our legs and straddle the instruments—a position considered not only inelegant but indecent by the Balinese.

One of the most difficult adjustments we had to make was to Wayan's teaching style. He had lived in the West for many years, and had worked with most of the Balinese gamelans in the United States. He was used to our difficulties in learning this largely unfamiliar music orally/aurally, and had modified the seemingly 'laid back' teaching style of his own tradition to accommodate the Western student (for example, he broke the musical material into smaller chunks than is usual in Bali). Even so, most of the students facing that first year of gamelan had never had a teacher like Wayan, one who simply repeated and repeated without ever stopping to correct, criticize, or compare.

Many of them left the group within a few weeks, realizing the difficulty of adjusting to these differences. Some became uneasy, even hostile. 'How will we learn all of this by the time of the performance?' 'Why can't I write this down, just for myself?' 'Listen to her! She doesn't know her part!' 'I know I started late, but I spent a lot of time learning this music, so I'd better be able to play in the concert!' Many of them seemed to lose sight of what I called the 'gamelan spirit' in their unfamiliar state of being 'baby musicians' and in their competitive zeal to outdo each other.

Was I being naïve in holding on to a nostalgic, Margaret Mead-ish notion of Bali as a co-operative, non-competitive society?[14] Was I embarrassed by the cut-throat attitude of my students, an attitude they have been forced to develop in the openly competitive atmosphere of our Western music culture? I mouthed my standard (homey) phrases: 'When you learn your own part, help out someone else.' 'Don't worry about it—even if we don't get the whole piece, isn't the process of learning it the important thing?' 'What do you mean, "You'd *better be able* to play in the concert."  You should understand that it is a privilege merely to sit in the presence of this music, whether or not you ever play!' 'Get a life,' they said.

Wayan would sit and watch us with an amused smile. I would ask him, 'How can you stand this? You are a musician of high status in your own country, listening to us play like children. Here we are, men and women together, sitting awkwardly in front of our instruments, squabbling and clucking over who learns the quickest. You must be going crazy.' 'No,' he would say, 'the spirit of the gamelan is in the community. In Bali there is one kind of community, and here in America another, so this gamelan carries the spirit of America.' Just what was the spirit of America, I thought.

Ultimately, I wondered if all the adjustments were worth it to Wayan. Was he really teaching Balinese music if we were not really Balinese? Was learning Balinese music this way truly enriching to my students? Wasn't there also a down side to this? In addition to all the wonderful music we learned, didn't we also, if inadvertently, learn that it was OK for our (richer? superior?) culture to buy (for far less than we would have had to pay Peter Serkin or Lorin Maazel) the musicians and musics of another (poorer? less 'developed'?) culture so that we could hold up our heads in the current game of multiculturalism? Was I being too picky, too sensitive?

## Baroque Survey

After many years of teaching ethnomusicology courses, I was asked to teach the sophomore Baroque survey class for a professor on leave. In my earlier life as a student and performer (more than twenty years ago), I played the harpsichord, and at that time had considered Baroque keyboard music a possible speciality. I welcomed the chance to become reacquainted with the music I had loved since childhood.

The ethnomusicologist in me, however, rebelled somewhat against the 'narrowness' of the topic; so I built into my syllabus a few lectures called, 'What Else is Happening?' Every few weeks I would begin with something like, 'Well, it's

---

[14] See Uuni Wikan, *Managing Turbulent Hearts: A Balinese Formula for Living* (Chicago, 1990), for a full discussion of Balinese emotional life.

1680 in Italy—what's happening in India?', and we would spend a few minutes talking about the development of some other music systems of the world, growing and developing at roughly the same time as our 'Baroque'. I thought this was a good idea—it would give the students a chance to see a bigger picture.

Soon, some students began to complain. They said I was infecting Western music with 'creeping multiculturalism'. They argued that other cultures' musics were irrelevant for them to learn because they would only be tested on Western music when applying to graduate schools. Furthermore, they only performed Western music in concerts, and until there was a *sitar* major, they would stick to their own tradition. They had a point there. I was, after all, teaching in a Western school of music, and other people's musics, no matter how enlightening, were not really essential to its (or for that matter, any other American school of music's) primary mission. Was it time to chuck it all and go and live in Bali, like Colin McPhee?

But then I began to wonder about Italian Baroque culture, the one I was supposed to be making come alive to my survey students. What did I or my students really have in common with people living in Venice in 1680? Were we really connected through a genetic, social, or musical lineage to these people or their musics, any more than to contemporary North Indians or Lubavitchers? Certainly, we had been taught to think so (just as they had been taught to think an equivalent thing in North India and Crown Heights). We had been taught to regard Baroque music in Venice as 'our music', 'our heritage'.

Wait a minute! What heritage? Who is this 'our'? My grandfather Koskoff came here from Russia in the 1890s. He had been a fruit-buyer, whose musical tradition would probably have been more closely related to 'oral/folk'. When did classical music enter the picture? Of course, there *was* my Uncle Reuven, a composer of Jewish music, who had studied (so the story went) with Schnabel, who had studied with Czerny, who had studied with Beethoven. Was I, a musically talented youngster, inadvertently used by my family in their climb upward toward respectability? What would have happened if I had been left to develop musically without 'interference'? Where would I have gone? Maybe to the same place—maybe not.

Of course, there was the obvious fact that, no matter what, I loved this music. What difference did it make what my parents' motivations were? After all, I grew up playing and listening to classical music—my music. Bach really was part of my cultural heritage, even if only for one generation. And the music was so beautiful! Nothing I've heard anywhere else in the world has moved me as much as the fugue following the Toccata in Bach's E minor Partita (no. 6) or the opening theme of Brahms's Fourth Symphony, second movement. Why should I bother learning about and teaching other people's musics when I'd always have my own?

## Moving on to the Second Stage

Thanks to the postmodernists, and actually many others before them, we can no longer regard any process of canon formation or transmission as truly neutral. Those processes, we have lately come to realize, are fraught with political and ethical problems. And so, we must ask ourselves openly, do we really want to remain in the business of constructing musical lineages, teaching musical values, arbitrating musical standards? Some might say, yes. But what lineages? Whose values? What standards? Those same old white, male, Eurocentric, heterosexual ones? Some newer (more current and correct) ones that include the musics of women, people of colour, 'non-Western' peoples, gays and lesbians? A soon to be constructed set that includes EVERYBODY's values? Can we go that far and still retain a 'core'? What will become of 'our music' when everyone is a self and no one is an other (or vice versa)?

Perhaps we should stop looking at this from the perspective of canon, or even from that of multiple canons[15] with their boundaries and individual entities, and move more toward a new perspective of 'problem solving'. This is a two-stage process, the first of which we are in right now: becoming comfortable with moving effortlessly from centre to margin and back again—living with likeness and difference simultaneously, and perhaps livening up our journeys with friendly or not-so-friendly engagements between centres and margins, between insides and outsides.

Ultimately, however, in the second stage, we must give up insides and outsides as meaningful analytic categories. In our recent forays outside the Western art-music canon, through the study of other cultures (including the cultures of women, gays and lesbians, and so on) we have truly gained another perspective: an exhilarating super-view of all possible canons. And although we may individually, or even socially, be invested in the works, values, and meanings of 'our own music', our main responsibility as teachers is, I feel, to pass on our canon and our own canon's values *without canonizing*. Instead, we should be helping our students discover their own paths through the maze of all possible canons and values, past, present, and to come—with an underlying bedrock philosophy that all values, just like all people and all musics, have equivalent meaning to someone, somewhere.

I find that lately, in my quest for passing on musics that I love and promoting social tolerance, I am wanting to teach my students more than just the intricacies of the Indian *gharana* system, a dazzling *kotekan*, or even the magnificent operas of Monteverdi, although each of these is a privilege to teach and certainly worthy of being taught. What I want to be doing also is teaching them a new set of values that will enable them to know their own music well, but also to

---

[15]  Robert P. Morgan, 'Rethinking Musical Culture: Canonic Reformulations in a Post-Tonal Age', in Bergeron and Bohlman (eds.), *Disciplining Music*, 61.

become good musical citizens in a world where boundaries of all kinds will become more and more permeable, where identities will become more and more multiple, and where differences between people and their musics will become more and more fuzzy. In addition to implicitly passing on 'my music', 'my values', 'my politics', I want also to be teaching strategies for learning open-mindedness, fairness, and compassion for differences of all kinds. If we teach our students these values, then although it may matter a great deal what musics we as individuals or social groups love, give meaning to, and value, ultimately it will not really matter what musics we teach.[16]

---

[16] I would like to thank Robert Morris for reading an earlier draft of this chapter and for making some much-needed editorial and content suggestions.

# Index

Abdul Ghani, Muhammad Chaudrhi
   Muhammad 326
abstract expressionist painting 120
Abu-Lughod, Leila 534
Adler, Guido 38, 314 n. 11, 437
   *Vierteljahrsschrift für Musikwissenschaft*
   38, 288–310 *passim*
Adorno, Theodor W. 21, 47, 51, 74, 211,
   366, 500, 513, 520
adumbration 19
aesthetic:
   autonomy 51, 374
   listening 495–6
aesthetics 140, 280, 494
   idealist 40
   reception 44
African music, *see* music
Agawu, Kofi 58, 260
Albéniz, Isaac 511
Ali, Syed Wajid 326
Allanbrook, Wye J. 368, 509
American Musicological Society 471, 499
   Journal of 295–6
American concert and operatic life 522–3
Americans, Native 20–1, 31
analysis:
   class 513–14
   descriptive 451
   dialogic 64–5
   formal 213
   grammatical 58
   and history 56
   as interpretation 45
   language of 258, 261
   linguistic 58
   logical 58
   Marxist 513–14
   motivic 153
   music 58–9, 61, 64, 104, 140, 171–2,
      188, 196, 273–4, 369, 460
   performer's use of 223, 234–8
   poetic 213
   and poetic criticism 215
   poietic 42

practice of 197
of recorded music 432
reductionist 109
Schenkerian 82, 89, 103, 107–13,
   127–8, 136–7, 175, 198, 213, 257,
   261
semiotic 153
structuralist 102
technique 108–32, 462
Anderson, Marian 526
anthropology 291, 297, 308, 358–9
   representation discussed in 533–4
Aristotle 161–2
Arteaga, Estaban de 351
Artusi, Giovanni Maria 478
Asian classical music, *see* music
Asola, Giovanni Matteo 418
D'Astorga, Emanuele 348
Atkins, Chet 469
atonality 131
auditory stream segregation 167–8
Augustine, St. 24
Australian aboriginal song research 542
Australian aborigines 30
authenticity 32, 417–20

Babbitt, Milton 43, 191 n. 52, 275, 511
Bach, C. P. E. 342
Bach, J. S. 341, 418, 511
   attempt to create worthy church music
      503
   B minor mass 102
   Brandenburg Concertos 412
   E minor Partita no. 6: 557
   frustration with his superiors in Leipzig
      508
   manuscripts 420
   performance of using period
      instruments 442
   six-part Ricercare 130
Bakhtin, Mikhail 56–64 *passim*, 358
   critique of linguistics 58
Baker, Theodore 292, 296
Balinese gamelan, *see* gamelan

Barnard, John  338
Barry, Philips  21
Barthes, Roland  54, 56
Barton, Andrew  517
Barzun, Jacques  398
Baudrillard, Jean  121
Beatles, The  461, 467, 468
Bedford, Arthur  352
Beethoven, Ludwig van  197, 245, 263,
    343, 345, 348, 506
    attacks on by Chinese officials  513
    Bagatelles Op. 126  246
    Credo from *Missa Solemnis*  108–13
    'Eroica' Symphony  83, 198, 201, 212
    Fifth Symphony  187, 200–8, 211, 434,
        437, 445–50
    heroic style  214
    Ninth Symphony  82, 102, 129,
        208–12, 253, 370, 450
    music of  80, 132, 198–212, 340, 360,
        421, 429, 440
    performance of using period
        instruments  442
    quartets of  354
    Quartet Op. 131  185, 187–8
    Quintet for Piano and Wind Op. 16  396
    piano sonatas  316
    sonatas  403
    and Strauss's *Metamorphosen*  88
    symphonies  305, 346, 352, 389–90,
        554
    third *Leonore* overture  89
    Violin Concerto  264–9
Bekker, Paul  202, 206
Bellini, Vincenzo  349
Benjamin, Walter  379
Benveniste, Émile  144
Bent, Ian  39
Béranger, Pierre-Jean de  523
Bergeron, Katherine  337–9, 545–7
Berio, Luciano *Sinfonia*  128–32, 136
Berlioz, Hector  380, 388, 397, 399, 428,
    506
Bernstein, Leonard  240, 527
Berry, Chuck  452–3, 455
Berry, Wallace  239–40, 246–9, 251
Beta Israel  535–44
    absorption into Israel  536–7
    ethics, politics and representation  541–2

identity, changing politics of  535–6
interpretation of data provided by study
    on liturgical music  543
liturgy  537–8
reception of the study on liturgical
    music  538–41
study of liturgical music of  534–42
Bharucha, Jamshed  168
Bhatkhande, V. N.  326
Biget, Michèle  230
Binkley, Thomas  407
Blacking, John  140, 548
Blitzstein, Marc  526
Blom, Eric  395
Bloom, Allan  525
Bloom, Harold  89, 365, 381
    theory of poetic influence  56
    theory of poetic misprision  70–1
bluegrass  28
blues  28
Blume, Friedrich  293
Boas, Franz  300
Bohlman, Philip  252, 261, 500, 522
    discussion of canons  304, 337
    *Disciplining Music: Musicology and its
        Canons*  545, 547
    'Musicology as political act'  243, 502
Boilès, Charles  142
Boretz, Benjamin  171 n. 2, 191 n. 52,
    273, 275
Borodin, *Prince Igor*  505
Botstein, Leon  74
Boulez, Pierre  241, 407, 511
Bowers, Jane  483
Bowie, Andrew  39, 51
Brahms, Johannes  89–90, 340, 341, 343,
    506
    C minor quartet  89
    Fourth Symphony, second movement
        557
    *Haydn Variations*  165
    Intermezzo, Op. 118, No. 1  240
    Romance, Op. 118, No. 5  89–90
    string quartet, Op. 51, No. 1  64
    Third Symphony  90
    Violin Concerto  523
Brando, Marlon  452
Breckbill, David  430
Bregman, Albert S.  167

Brendel, Alfred 245
British Rationalist Press Association 326
Britten, Benjamin 393
Bruckner, Anton 102, 400
Budden, Julian 503
von Bülow, Hans 389
Bürger, Peter 51
Burney, Charles 290, 351
Busoni, Ferruccio 554
Butler, Judith 243, 476
Byrd, William 344, 348, 352
Byron, *Childe Harold's Pilgrimage* 224

Caccini, Giulio 418
cadence (in language) 58
Cage, John 143, 406
canonical thinking 512
canon 173–4, 304–7, 546, 553, 558
    authority bestowed on pieces in 350
    conservative critique of 389–90
    craft as an aspect of 341–3, 344, 349
    criticism as an aspect of 349–51
    definition of 547
    in ethnomusicology 304–7
    evolution of 341
    formation and transmission 548, 558
    and groups, boundaries between 548
    historical study of 349–50
    ideology as an aspect of 351–5
    liberal critique of 389–90
    meaning of term 338–9
    moral dimension in 354
    musical 373, 503, 547–8
    origins and development of 338
    pedagogical 339, 342
    performing 340, 342, 345
    repertory as an aspect of 343–9, 350,
        354
    of rock 548
    types of 339–41
    scholarly 339
    Western 558
capitalism 122
capitalist democracy 495–6
Carnatic music 21, 28
Carrington, John 142
Carter, Elliott 341
    *scrivo in vento* 91–9
cassette music 31

categories of knowledge 35
Central Sangeet Natak Akademi 324–5
Chailley, Jacques 340
Chaminade, Cécile 60–1
Chernoff, John 260
Cherubini, Luigi 346, 348
Chomsky, Noam 58, 140, 242
Chopin, Frederick 89, 420, 429, 444
    A minor prelude 81
    alleged influence on Debussy 68
    E major study 81
    First Piano Concerto 420
    Preludes Op. 28 68–70
    second prelude, Op. 28 77–81
Christensen, Thomas 74
Chrysander, Friedrich 290–1, 295
Citron, Marcia J. 337, 343, 389, 493
    discussion of Chaminade, Sonata Op. 21
        60–1
Clarke, Eric 166, 242, 431
Classical style 200, 212
Clegg, Johnny 527
Clifford, James, *Writing Culture* 358–9
Clynes, Manfred 431
Cohn, Richard 105–7, 173–4, 176–8
Coleman, Ornette 258
composers 407–8, 418–19
    attitude to musicologists 300
    identification of styles of 305
    identity of 22
    master 342
    nineteenth-century 218–19
    women 490
    writing with printed editions in mind
        418–19
composition 277–8, 420, 479–80
    transmission of compositions 415–16
concerto form 366–7
    cadenza in 408
Cone, Edward 97, 177, 183, 186, 518
connectionism 168
contextual awareness 219
contexts 50
    in music scholarship 543
    of musical research 534
contrapuntal technique 341
Cook, Nicholas 164–7, 211
    study of Beethoven's Ninth Symphony
        82

Cook, Susan  485–6
Cooke, Deryck  140
  *The Language of Music*  144, 154–6
Copland, Aaron  526
Corelli, Arcangelo  245, 341–2, 344, 425,
  437, 443
  Opus 5 sonatas  426
country-western  28
Crawford, Ruth  471–98 *passim*
criticism  254–5, 349–51, 436, 487–8
  cultural  545
  feminist  491
  formalist  378
  journalistic  381
  literary  59, 357, 380, 383
  music  195, 246–7, 350, 371, 381,
    395, 462
  poetic  198–9, 214, 215
  postmodernist  548
  reader-oriented  56
  rise of  40
  social  545
  traditional  516
Croce, Giovanni  39
Culler, Jonathan  60
cultures  289, 525
  American  453
  major, definition of  554
  popular  468
Cumming, Naomi  50
Cusick, Suzanne  243, 516
Czerny, Carl  431, 557

Dahlhaus, Carl  49, 73–4, 128–9, 145,
  222–3, 254–7, 351, 356, 378–402
  *passim*, 429, 500, 518
  *Fundamentals of Music History*  381
Davis, Colin  398
Dean, James  452
Debussy, Claude  68–70, 441, 443
  *Feux d'artifice*  69
  *La Mer*  102
  piano roll recording of *La Cathédrale
    engloutie*  438–41
  string quartet  523
deconstruction  60, 354–5
Delalande, Michael  345, 352
Deleuze, Gilles  134, 137
Dempster, Douglas  105–7, 173–4, 176–8

Derrida, Jacques  55–6
Deutsch, Diana  163
Dewey, John  179–81, 189–92
dialogic  56–7, 61
  *see also* analysis
Diamond, Beverly  317 n. 22
DiMaggio, Paul  516
discographies  432–3, 443
discontinuity  67
Dolphy, Eric  258–60
Donizetti, Gaetano  347, 523
Drinker, Sophie  497
Dubiel, Joseph  213
Duckles, Vincent  529
Dufay, Guillaume  421
Dunning, Albert  503
Dunsby, Jonathan  246, 253
Dürer, Albrecht  161
Durling, Robert M.  92
Dürr, Alfred  503
Dvořák, Antonín  438
Dwight, John Sullivan  516
Dylan, Bob  461

Eagleton, Terry  60, 270
Eco, Umberto  52–3
  *A Theory of Semiotics*  139
Eggebrecht, Hans Heinrich  520–1
Eigeldinger, Jean-Jacques  68–70
Einstein, Albert  444–5
Einstein, Alfred  363, 396
Eisler, Hanns  526
Elgar, Edward  441, 510
Eliot, T. S.  397
Ellis, A. J.  292
Elson, Arthur  479
embeddedness  19, 31
Engel, Carl  296
Enlightenment  39, 506
Eno, Brian  342
epistemology  42–6
Epstein, David  153
Epstein, Paul  125
Ermath, Elizabeth Deeds  65
Eskimo peoples  22
ethnomusicologists  424, 532
  areas of interest of  307
  and historians, distinction between
    306

ethnomusicology 287–310 *passim*,
  306–9, 316–18, 429, 454, 504,
  531–2, 537, 546
  *see also* canon
evolutionism 315
experience 179–81
expression, in musical performance
  218–19, 237, 243, 431

Fabian, Johannes 317 n. 23
Feld, Steven 306
Fellerer, Karl Gustav 293
feminism 490–8, 515
  *see also* criticism; musicology
Feroe, J. 163
Fétis, François 351
Feyerabend, Paul 401–2
Flathead Indians 20
Flax, Jane 545
Fletcher, Alice C. 300
Folio, Cynthia 258–9
Ford, Andrew 91, 93, 99
Ford, Charles 509
formalism 51–2, 54, 74, 100, 106–7,
  195–6, 199, 372, 376–7, 383
form 93
  Classical-style 206–7
  structural sense of 41
Forster, E. M. 204–7, 211, 214
Forte, Allen 43, 104–5
Foss, Lukas 129
Foucault, Michel 55, 58, 65–6, 68, 121,
  123, 131, 356
Fraser, Nancy 545
Freud, Sigmund 481, 485–6
fundamentalism 256–8
functionalism 315
Furtwängler, Wilhelm 428, 438, 443

Gabrielsson, Alf 431
Gadamer, Hans-Georg 195, 358
gamelan:
  Balinese 23
  Balinese *angklung* 554–5
  Javanese 30
  music 23, 29–31, 554–6
Gebrauch 315
Geertz, Clifford 358
Geiringer, Karl 90

gender:
  identity 243
  in music history 337
  in music scholarship 514–15
  readings of instrumental works 514
  *see also* musicology
Géricault, Théodore 80
Gershwin, George 421
Gestalt psychology 66
*gharana* 550, 552, 558
Gibbons, Orlando 348
Glinka, Mikhail 511
Gluck, Christoph Willibald 346, 347
Goehr, Lydia 43
Goethe, Johann Wolfgang von 82–8, 370
Göllerich, August 241
Goodman, Nelson 401, 428
Gorak, Jan 390
Gossett, Philip 397
Gould, Glenn 248, 450
Gounod, Charles 380
Grabócz, Márta 147, 225, 227, 229
Graff, Gerald 389
*grande ligne* 218, 225, 235–7
Gray, Cecil 385
Gregorian chant 360, 371, 511
Greenberg, Clement 120, 123, 128
Greek drama 193
Grieg, Edvard 307
Grout, Donald Jay 363
Grove, Sir George 203, 446, 448
Guattari, Felix 134, 137
Guillory, John 390–2
Gurney, Edmund 140
*guslar* 22

Haberkamp, Gertraut 396
Habermas, Jürgen 51
Halévy, Jacques 506
Haley, Bill 452
Hamm, Charles 461
Handel, Georg Friederich 342–52 *passim*,
  511
  *Messiah* 157–8, 420
  operatic arias 421
  word paintings 144
Hanslick, Eduard 49, 140, 243, 373, 478,
  483, 494
Harris, Roy 244

Harrison, George  468
Hasidic philosophy  551
Haslinger, Tobias  224
Hatten, Robert  58
Hausa, of Nigeria  31
Hawkins, John  290
Haydn, Joseph  340–9 *passim*, 394, 511
    Representation of Chaos  81
    symphonies  420, 523
    Symphony No. 83  240
Hegel, Georg Wilhelm Friedrich  196
Heister, Hanns-Werner  513, 525
Helfgott, David  245
Helmholtz, H.  167
Henrotte, Gayle A.  144
Hepokoski, James  384
Herder, Johann Gottfried  21, 25
hermeneutics  46, 100–1, 195, 197–8,
    213, 370
Herzog, George  300
Hess, Myra  526
Hildegard of Bingen  497
Hindu epics  30
hip-hop DJs  21
historical narrative  360
history  357, 359–65
    poetic  70–1
Hjelmslev, Louis  140
Hoffmann, E. T. A.  187, 200, 389, 447
Homeric epics  30
Horowitz, Joseph  430
Howat, Roy  68, 70
Howell, Tim  240, 249, 251–2
Hughes, Meirion  510
Hughes, William  225, 226
humanism  92, 319
Hummel, Johann  509
Hunt, Leigh  349

idealism  51
    *see also* aesthetics
improvisation  22, 70, 251
    eighteenth-century  236
    *see also* jazz
Indian Classical Music  22, 30, 305
    instrumentalists in  550
    North  31
    North, culture  550
    systems (North Indian)  548–9

Indian music studies  324–335
D'Indy, Vincent  446
Ingarden, Roman  44
integrity  184–5
intensity curve  234–7
International Folk Music Council  305
interpretation  219, 238, 375
    poetic  212, 214
Inuit, of Canada and Greenland  23
Iser, Wolfgang  381
Ishāq, Ibn, *Life of Muhammad*  26
Islam  27, 32
Ives, Charles  505, 533

Jackendoff, Ray  48, 58, 140, 166, 242–3
Jackson, Timothy L.  82–8
Jameson, Fredric  71, 120, 128–9
    *Postmodernism, or, the Cultural Logic of
        Late Capitalism*  121–3
Janáček, Leoš  505
Jander, Owen  200
Japanese music  29
Jauss, Hans Robert  381–3, 391
    aesthetics of reception  66
Javanese gamelan, *see* gamelan
jazz  63, 244, 301, 413–14, 502, 513
    improvisation  258–60
    musicians  259–60, 442
    standards  417
Johnson, Julian  363
Jommelli, Niccolò  344
Josquin des Prez  421, 474, 503, 511
Joyce, James  356

*kalawant*  549–50
Kalbeck, Max  40
Kallberg, Jeffrey  63, 70, 257, 348
Kaluli, of Papua New Guinea  23
Kant, Immanuel  35, 39, 49, 196, 211
Kaplan, Steven  539
Karajan, Herbert von  113–14, 240, 441,
    450
Karam Imam, Hakim Muhammad, *Mine of
    Music*  324–35
Kartomi, Margaret  525
Katchen, Julius  244
*kattajjait*  23
Keller, Hans  159, 395
Kellner, Hans  67

Kerman, Joseph  54, 173–4, 177, 187, 197, 253, 453, 518
  *Contemplating Music*  295, 297, 376
  discussion of canon  336–7, 349, 387–9, 394
Kermode, Frank  350
Khaldūn, Ibn  32–3
Khan, Haddu and Hassu  550
Khan, Ustad Alluadin  550
Khan, Ustad Wazir  550
*khandan*  549–50
*khandani*  550
*khayal*  329
Khusrau, Amir  329
Kielian-Gilbert, Marianne  80
Kinderman, William  211
Kinkeldey, Otto  293
Kirkpatrick, Ralph  248
Klemperer, Otto  407
Knepler, Georg  513, 525
Koch, Heinrich Christoph  48–9, 368
Koran  19, 27
Korsyn, Kevin  89–90
*koteken*  555, 558
Kowalke, Kim  503
Kramer, Lawrence  76–81, 89, 101, 158, 367–70, 469
  study of Haydn's 'Representation of Chaos'  81
  study of second Chopin Prelude, Op. 28  77–81
Krenek, Ernst  454
Kretzschmar, Hermann  82, 202, 206
Krips, Joseph  448
Kristeva, Julia  56
*kriti*  22, 28
Kropfinger, Klaus  391–2
Krumhansl, C  166–7
Krummacher, Friedhelm  382, 391, 400–1
Kuhn, Thomas  463–4
Kunst, Jaap  301–2

Lachmund, Carl von  221
Lambert, Constant  385
Landsbergis, Vytautis  527
Lang, Paul Henry  293
language, for music  258
Lassen, Eduard  241
Lassus, Roland de  348, 503

Leichtentritt, Hugo  49
Leitch, Vincent  68
Lennon, John  468
Lentriccia, Frank  380
Lerdahl, Fred  48, 58, 140, 166, 256, 257
  'Cognitive Constraints on Compositional Systems'  241–3, 252
Lester, Joel  245
Levine, Lawrence W.  516, 522–3
Lévi-Strauss, Claude  24
Levy, Janet  510, 518, 521, 524
Lewin, David  74, 176, 252–3, 257
  discussion of Brahms, String Quartet Op. 51, No. 1:  64
Lewontin, Richard  364, 365
Lidov, David  153–4
linear ascent  107–8
linguistics  58, 140
  structural  242–3, 251
Liszt, Franz  144, 219–38, 245, 342, 412, 429, 506
  *Album d'un voyageur*  219, 221, 224–6, 231
  *Années de Pèlerinage*  224–37
  Lina Ramann's study of  512
  transcription of Schubert's 'Der Wanderer'  226
  transformation of themes in Liszt's music  222, 225
  'Vallée d'Obermann'  223–38
literary criticism, *see* criticism
literary history  59
Loesser, Arthur  508
Lorenz, Alfred  507
Lubavitcher  550–3
  Hasidic court  548
  musical culture  552–3
Lully, Jean-Baptiste  342, 345
Lutosławski, Witold  407

*ma*  29
Maazel, Lorin  556
McCallum, Peter  59
McCartney, Paul  468
McClary, Susan  90, 366–9, 454–69 *passim*, 500
  *Feminine Endings*  486–91
Macey, Patrick  503
McGowan, John  528–9

Machaut, Guillaume de  421
McLaughlin, Thomas  380
McPhee, Colin  557
madrigals  92
Magritte, René, *L'Alphabet des révélations*
    121
Mahabhārāta  23
Mahler, Gustav  442, 443, 505
    Scherzo from Second Symphony  129
    symphonies  102, 182
    use of notation  407
Man, Paul de  61, 66, 174 n. 11
Mandieczewski, Eusebius  40
Manet, Edouard  80
mannerism  92
Manuel, Peter  31
*maqam*  329
Marcus, George, *Writing Culture*  358–9
Marenzio, Luca  348
Maróthy, Janos  513
Martin, George  468
Marx, Adolf Bernhard  41, 134–5, 195,
    200, 213, 374
Marxism  38, 383
    *see also* analysis
masterpiece, notion of  342
Masur, Kurt  527
Mattheson, Johann  220
Maus, Fred  247, 253, 257, 494
meaning, poetic  217–38 *passim*
Mellers, Wilfrid  461
Melville, Herman  137
Mendelssohn, Felix  506, 509
Mengelberg, Willem  250
Merriam, Alan  306, 309
Mersmann, Hans  41
Messiaen, Olivier, *Catalogue d'oiseaux*  23
Meyer, Leonard B.  167, 518
    'implication-realization' model  66, 126
    *Style and Music*  66
Meyer, Ernst Hermann  513
Meyerbeer, Giacomo  399
Middleton, Richard  454–5, 460–4, 469
Milhaud, Darius  454
Millington, Barry  430
minimalism  123–8, 132, 137, 241
Mississippi Delta style  28
Mitchell, Donald  395
Mitchell, W. J. T.  375

Mitchell, William  171
Mitter, Partha  335
modernism  29, 51, 52, 88, 92, 97, 98–9,
    121, 128–9, 135
Monelle, Raymond  46, 153
    *Linguistics and Semiotics in Music*
    139–40
Monk, Thelonius  258
Monson, Ingrid  63
Monteverdi, Claudio  558
    *Il Combattimento di Tancredi e Clorinda*
    92
    'Lamento di Arianna'  92
Morlacchi, Francesco  398–9
Mosca, Luigi  398–9
Mozart, Wolfgang Amadeus  166, 340–9
    *passim*, 366–9, 394–5, 421, 443,
    503, 505
    Adagio from Divertimento K.287:
    129–30
    *Don Giovanni*  380
    G minor symphony  155
    'Haffner' serenade  420
    K.453:  369
    operas  509, 521
    performance of using period
        instruments  440
    Quintet for piano and wind, K.452:
        394–6
music  136
    absolute  213, 483, 493–4
    aesthetic experience of  494–5, 508
    African  260, 305
    'ancient'  345
    art of  478–80, 484
    Asian  30
    avant-garde  241, 342
    Balinese, *see* gamelan
    Baroque  556–7
    beauty in  30–1
    canon, *see* canon
    classical  354, 365
    contemporary  298
    in context  531
    criticism, *see* criticism
    culture  553
    definition of  492–3
    and the emotions  154–6
    erotic power of  477–8

experiences of 269–70
as a feminist issue 491–3
folk 297–8, 501
function of 73–4
gamelan, *see* gamelan
German 21, 292
historians 55, 308, 336, 343, 371
historiography of 382
history 57, 65, 67–8, 350, 351, 360,
 362–6, 371, 377, 378, 499
Indian, *see* Indian classical music
Japanese 29
Javanese, *see* gamelan
and language 25, 73, 141–6, 194–5
as a language 48–9, 213
lineage 553, 558
meaning 140, 253, 464
modernist 121, 365
musical world 181–2
narrative content of 217–19, 223,
 234–8
in nature 23–4
non-Western 241, 296, 297–8
as an object 18–19, 34
orientalist writings on 319–20
organic unity in 511
origins of 307
perception 162–3
and poetry 221–2, 226
popular 241, 256–7, 297–8, 301, 354,
 463, 466, 501, 504
possessing theory 45
post-tonal 114
practice of 19, 483, 484
as a process 18–19, 21, 34
psychology 164
reception 245, 308, 357; *see also*
 reception history
religious 503
rock 456–8, 467, 502, 513, 525
scholarship 37, 290–1, 313–14, 322,
 462, 499–500, 524–30, 533, 543
as science 24–5
sign in 147
and society 508, 531
sources 421
specificity of 47
structure 102–3
study of 357

styles 509
surface of 176–8
text, *see* text
theatre 503
theorists 303, 373, 431
theory 41–6, 53, 103, 241–2, 252,
 271, 280, 282–3, 297, 371, 377,
 460, 500
in time 29–30
twentieth-century 454
Western 22, 244–5, 301–2, 308–9,
 311, 424, 425, 500–3, 505, 554
world 554
writing, early 412
*Music and Letters* 297–8
musical work 99, 142, 244–5, 308,
 357–8, 367, 374, 418, 421, 444
as changing traditions 445
interpretation of 377
Liszt's concept of 237
as object 53
Platonic 244
status of 41
musicological text, evaluation of 510
musicologists:
 Chinese 300
 feminist 60
 freedom and responsibility of 517–24
 German 300
 Indian 300
 historical 531
 knowledge of popular music 465
 Old-style Western 547
 organizations formed by 302
 and theorists 460
 Western 547
musicology 38, 100, 243, 261, 337, 382
 American 294, 296, 305
 canons in 304–6
 in China 298
 culture-specific 290
 definition of 292–4, 304
 East-European 36–7
 and ethomusicology 547
 and feminism 482–91, 515
 feminist 454, 482–98 *passim*
 field and discipline of 288–94
 and gender 471–82, 491–8
 German 36–7

musicology (*cont.*):
  in Great Britain  297
  historical  303, 307–8, 504
  in Hungary  298
  Indian  299
  interpretative  74–101 *passim*
  and its impact outside the university
    532
  masculine identity of  480
  New  37, 47, 99, 253, 358, 376
  as political act  243
  positivist  376, 487
  psycho-  298, 303
  social values in  510–17
  socio-  298, 303
  systematic  302, 305
  at universities  304
  works in  306
*musique concrète*  31

Narmour, Eugene  240–2, 245–6, 249,
    251, 256–7
  implications-realization models of
    126
narrative  67, 362–4
  *see also* music, narrative content of
National Curriculum (Britain)  525
nationism  512
Nattiez, Jean-Jacques  58, 140, 146–7,
    153, 159
Near, Holly  527
Neuman, Daniel  548–9
Neumeyer, David  84
Newcomb, Anthony  172, 182–3
*New Grove Dictionary of Music and
    Musicians*  303
New York Musicological Society  296,
    471–3, 481
Nicholson, Linda J.  545
Nietzche, Friedrich  205
*nigunim*  550–2
Nikisch, Artur  434
Norrington, Roger  250, 390
Norton series  306
Noske, Frits  147
notation  22, 417–19
  descriptive  408, 411
  East Asian plucked zither  28
  function of  405–11

  musical  28
  of pitch  409
  prescriptive  408–9, 411
  Western  28
Nottebohm, Gustav  40
Nourrit, Adolphe  506
novelistic discourse  61–2

Oberlin, Russell  407
objectivism  401
Offenbach, Jacques  307, 505
Ong, Walter  418
ontology:
  of artworks  43
  of music  103, 280
  plural  17, 33
opera  347, 354, 444, 505
organicism  39, 103
Ortega y Gasset, José  135
Osborne, Richard  398–9
otherness  312–13

Paderewski, Ignance Jan  526
Paganini, Niccolò  506
Palestrina, Giovanni Pierluigi da  341–2,
    348, 352, 420
Palisca, Claude  363, 503
Panofsky, Erwin  358
paradigms  257
  of representation  257–61
*pariahs*  21
Parker, William  527
Pärt, Arvo  129
Pastille, William  114
Pateman, Carol  495–6
Pederson, Sanna  374–5
Peirce, Charles Sanders  138–9, 146, 149,
    156, 159
performance  36, 406, 417
  conventions  408
  generative approach to  242
  hierarchical structure of  218, 223,
    235–7
  historical  217–23, 237–8
  literature of  252
  practice  429–30, 437–8
  rhetoric of nineteenth-century  220–1,
    237
  structurally informed  223, 249

style 434, 438, 442–5, 450
  tradition 430–1, 433–4, 444
performer 414, 437, 442, 445
  attitude to musicologists 300
Petrarch, 'Beato in sogno' 91–9
phenomenology 66
Philip, Robert 430–1
Philips, Sam 469
philosophy, postmodernist 545
Piaget, Jean 140
pitch changes in the history of a work
  428
Platti, Giovanni 512
Plato 478
Platonism 22
Pleyel, Ignace Joseph 418
pluralism 46, 74, 76, 88, 90
poetics 41–2, 100
  *see also* criticism; history; interpretation;
    meaning
polyphonic tradition 342, 352
positivism 54, 376–7
postmodernism 121–2, 128–9, 132, 369,
  545
  and analysis 51–4
  *see also* criticism; philosophy; theory
postmodernists 546, 558
post-structuralism 56, 65, 515
  *see also* theory
Potter, Pamela 504
Pratt, Waldo Selden 293, 478–9, 484,
  487, 492, 498
Presley, Elvis 469
Previn, André 240
process, *see* music
prolongation 113–20
Proust, Marcel 356
psychology 162–4
  *see also* music; Gestalt psychology
Puccini, Giacomo 444
Puget, Loïsa 509, 523
Purcell, Henry 342, 344

Rachmaninov, Sergey 245, 511
*raga* 325, 327–8, 549
Ramann, Lina 512
Rāmāyana 23
Rameau, Jean Philippe 58, 145, 155, 166,
  342, 349

Randel, Don Michael 304
Ranke, Leopold von 321
rap 502, 513
Ratz, Erwin 49
reader-oriented criticism, *see* criticism
recapitulation 203, 208
reception history 379, 504
  studies in 308
recording 31–2
reductionism 106–7
registral contrasts 279–81
Reich, Steve 121, 132
  *Piano Phase* 123–8
Reiss, Józef 51
relativism 46, 101, 400–1
Renaissance-Baroque thought 48
repertory, *see* canon
Repp, Bruno 431
representation 257, 533
research and teaching, conflict between
  518
Réti, Rudolph 153, 159
*Rezeption* 379–80, 383, 386, 394
rhetorics 280
Richault, Simon 224
Ricoeur, Paul 71
Riemann, Hugo 41, 49, 166, 381
Riethmüller, Albrecht 292
Riffaterre, Michael 56
Rink, John 247
Robinson, Paul 508
Rochberg, George 103, 128, 132
  *Music for the Magic Theatre* 128–32, 136
  'No Center' 130
  Third String Quartet 131
rock, *see* music
Romanticism 30, 81–2, 89, 193–4, 340
Rorty, Richard 174
Rosand, Ellen 503
Rosenwald, Lawrence 245, 247, 250,
  253
Rossini, Gioacchino 346–7, 349,
  398–400, 429
  arias 416
  *L'italiana in Algeri* 398
  operas 397
Rothstein, William 249
Rousseau, Jean-Jacques 290, 314
rubato 220–1, 251

Ruhland, Konrad  503
Ruwet, Nicolas  140, 147, 153, 159

Sadie, Stanley  395
    *Man and Music*  507
Sahai, Babu Ram  331
Said, Edward  323 n. 28, 500, 503
Saint-Saëns, Camille  505
Salzer, Felix, *Structural Hearing*  114–17
*Sangit Darpan*  331
*Sangit Sar*  331
*Sangīta*  24
*Sangita Ratnakara*  330
Sanskrit  24
Saussure, Ferdinand de  138–40, 144,
    156, 159
Savonarola  503
Scarlatti, Domenico  418
schematic structure  44
Schenker, Heinrich  40–1, 43, 45, 77–90
    *passim*, 103–37 *passim*, 145, 159,
    173 n. 7, 198–9, 241–6 *passim*,
    255–6, 260, 373, 381, 507
    analysis of *Concerto for Piano and Winds*
        (Stravinsky)  114
    analysis of *Eroica Symphony* (Beethoven)
        198
    analysis of second Chopin Prelude,
        Op. 28  77–81
    book on Beethoven's Ninth Symphony
        253
    discussion of third *Leonore* overture
        (Beethoven)  89
    *Free Composition*  114, 133, 135
    graphic notation  146
    reduction theory  104
    voice-leading graph  152
    *see also* analysis
Schering, Arnold  197–9
Schiff, David  93
Schiller, Friedrich von  209–10
Schleiermacher, Friedrich  195
Schmalfeldt, Janet  246
Schnabel, Artur  403, 419, 557
Schneersohn, Joseph Isaac  551
Schnittke, Alfred  131
    First Symphony  129
Schoenberg, Arnold  41, 48–9, 104–5,
    116, 129, 131, 214, 341, 511

*Pierrot Lunaire*  385
    use of dissonance  23
    use of notation  407
    *Verklärte Nacht*  224
    views on recording  31
    writing about Liszt  221–2
Schonberg, Harold  430
Schott, Bernhard  224
Schubert, Franz  343, 444, 509, 533
    *Der Wanderer*  226, 228–30, 233–4
    Ninth Symphony  181
Schumann, Robert  181, 342–3, 388, 505
    Second Symphony  172
    symphonies  182
score  251, 265, 425, 438, 444, 492
Scott, Sir Walter  356
Scruton, Roger  257
Second Viennese school  49
Seeger, Anthony  306
Seeger, Charles  293–4, 296, 306, 471–98
    *passim*, 533
semiotics  58, 104
    *see also* analysis; theory
Senancour, Pivert de  223–5, 237
Seneca, L. Annaeus  212
sentence  57
Serkin, Peter  556
Sessions, Roger  270
set theory  43, 45, 103
Shah, Wajid Ali  325, 332
Shakespeare  187 n. 45
Shankar, Ravi  550
Shattuck, Roger  508
Shepherd, John  314 n. 10, 455, 458–60,
    462–4, 469, 500
Showalter, Elaine  490
Sibelius, Jean  387, 401, 511
    Fifth Symphony  383–6, 400
sign functioning  139
signification, mode of in music  144
Sipe, Thomas  199
Smetana, Bedřich  554
Smith, Barbara Herrnstein  392, 401
social contexts, of music-making  522
societies  393
sociology  455, 459
Solie, Ruth A.  518, 545
sonata form  200, 207–8, 366–7, 512,
    514

Soriano, Francesco 420
sound 218–19, 237–8, 270–1
　recorded/authentic 31–2
　recordings 433–4
Soviet writers 513
Sowande, Fela 511
Stadlen, Peter 249–50
Starr, Ringo 468
Steiner, George 44, 51
Stendhal 349
Steptoe, Andrew 503
Stockhausen, Karlheinz 166, 407
Stokowski, Leopold 130
Straus, Joseph 116–17, 128, 365
Strauss, Richard 144, 389–90, 438, 445,
　505
　*Metamorphosen* 82–8
　*Der Rosenkavalier* 240
Stravinsky, Igor 121, 127, 441, 454
　*Concerto for piano and winds* 114
　neo-classical music of 114
　*Pulcinella* 130
　*Symphony in Three Movements* 113–20
　*The Rite of Spring* 104, 113–14, 120,
　　260
Street, Alan 46, 61, 174 n. 11
structural hearing 223
structural linguistics, *see* linguistics
structuralism 38, 46, 58, 195–6, 242–3
　*see also* theory
structure, of a musical work 436
*Stufen* 107
Stumpf, Carl 292
style, study of 443
Subotnik, Rose Rosengard 74, 77–81, 89,
　206, 500, 518, 520
　study of second Chopin Prelude from
　　Op. 28 77–81
Sufism 29
Suweca, I Wayan 555–6
Suyá, of Brazilian Amazon 21
symphonies 348–9, 373
Szell, George 438

Tagore, Sourindro Mohun 320 n. 31
Takemitsu, Toru 511
*tala* 549
Tarasti, Eero 147, 225–6, 229
Taruskin, Richard 90, 220, 442

Tausig, Carl 420
Tchaikovsky, Pyotr Ilyich 307, 533
teaching, social messages in 524
tempo 428, 440–1, 445–6
　fluctuating 220–1, 230–4, 236, 431,
　　439
　in performances of Beethoven's Fifth
　　Symphony 434–6, 448–50
Terhardt, E. 168
texts 318–23
text, musical 142–3
　as definer of 'work' 420–2
　functions of 411–14
　intermediary 417
　literate transmission of 415–16
　oral transmission of 415–16
　in transmission 414–17, 419
Thaler, Lotte 39
theoretical systems 254
theorists:
　Austro-German 42
　and performers 245
　*see also* music; musicologists
theory 261, 274, 276–8, 282–3
　of art 49
　critical 51, 298
　cultural 120–1
　Hegelian-Marxist 38
　modern 120–3
　music, *see* music
　postmodern 120–3, 545
　post-structuralist 216
　reductionist 106–7
　semiotic 50
　structuralist 38
Theweleit, Klaus 135
　*Male Fantasies* 133–4
Thompson, Oscar 293
Thoreau, Henry David 314
Tick, Judith 483
timing 219–20
Tippett, Michael 527
Todd, Neil 242
Tomlinson, Gary 174, 371, 375
tonality 131, 164–6, 366–7
tone poems 92
Tong, Jennifer 250
topos 156
Torrefranca, Luigi 512

Toscanini, Arturo  406, 428, 430, 438, 450
Tovey, Donald Francis  177, 185 n. 41, 187–8, 203–4, 207, 387
    writing on Sibelius's Fifth Symphony 383–6, 400–1
tradition  427–8
transcendentalism  372, 377
transcription  305–6
Travis, Roy  116
Treitler, Leo  253–5, 257, 518, 529
Tsou, Judy  485–6
Tylor, Edward B.  292

*Urlinie*  80, 84, 107–8, 112, 126
*Urtext*  420–1, 444
    editions  404
utterance  57

Verdi, Giuseppe  503, 526
Viardot  421
Vidyarthi, Govind  324
*vīnā*  21
da Vinci, Leonardo  161
Viotti, Giovanni Battista  345, 348
virtual pitch sensations  167–8
Vodicka, Felix  401
Vogler, Abbé  77
    *Handbuch zur Harmonielehre*  99
voice-leading  104, 123–8, 132
Volans, Kevin  511

Wagogo  24
Wagner, Richard  20–1, 144, 220, 254, 343, 507, 511
    *Die Walküre*  523
    *Parsifal*  102
    *The Ring*  20
Walker, Alan  153, 159

Waller Thomas 'Fats'  62
Walser, Robert  455–8, 460, 462–4, 469
Walter, Bruno  443
Walther, Johann Gottfried  290
Walton, Blanche  471
Wason, Robert  249
*wayang*  23, 30
Weber, Carl Maria von  346–8, 399
Weber, Gottfried  77
Weber, William  504
Webern, Anton  130
    Piano Variations  249
    use of notation  407
Webster, James  208
Weill, Kurt  503, 526
Weingartner, Felix  438, 450
Weitz, Morris  43
Wellmer, Albrecht  51
White, Hayden  362, 381
Wilder, Alec  461
Williams, Raymond  316 n. 19
Winter, Peter  349
*Wirkung*  379–80, 383–4, 386, 394, 396
Wittgenstein, Ludwig  45, 48, 428 n. 8
Wolf, Friedrich August  38
Wolff, Janet  500
Wolfe, Tom  99
Woodmansee, Martha  59
*The World of Music*  542
world music, *see* music
*Writing Culture* (Clifford/Marcus)  358–9

Yasser, Joseph  471–2

Zalman, Rabbi Schneur  550, 552
Zappa, Frank  342
*zikr*  29